| Period | Total labor force (includ- ing Armed Forces) | Civilian employment | | Unem- ploy- ment | Total labor force (includ- ing Armed Forces) | Civilian labor force | Total | tural | cul- tural | nt of r | Labor force partici- pation rate. |
|---|---|---|---|---|---|---|---|---|---|---|---|
| | | Total | Non- agri- cul- tural | | | | | | | | |
| | Thousands of persons 16 years of age and over | | | | | | | | | Percent | |
| 1969 | 84,240 | 77,902 | 74,296 | 2,832 | 84,240 | 80,734 | 77,902 | 3,606 | 74,296 | 2,832 | 3.5 | 61.1 |
| 1970 | 85,903 | 78,627 | 75,165 | 4,088 | 85,903 | 82,715 | 78,627 | 3,462 | 75,165 | 4,088 | 4.9 | 61.3 |
| 1971 | 86,929 | 79,120 | 75,732 | 4,993 | 86,929 | 84,113 | 79,120 | 3,387 | 75,732 | 4,993 | 5.9 | 61.0 |
| 1972 | 88,991 | 81,702 | 78,230 | 4,840 | 88,991 | 86,542 | 81,702 | 3,472 | 78,230 | 4,840 | 5.6 | 61.0 |
| 1973 | 91,040 | 84,409 | 80,957 | 4,304 | 91,040 | 88,714 | 84,409 | 3,452 | 80,957 | 4,304 | 4.9 | 61.4 |
| 1974 | 93,240 | 85,936 | 82,443 | 5,076 | 93,240 | 91,011 | 85,936 | 3,492 | 82,443 | 5,076 | 5.6 | 61.8 |

Source: Department of Labor, Bureau of Labor Statistics.

# NONAGRICULTURAL EMPLOYMENT

[Thousands of wage and salary workers; seasonally adjusted]

| Period | Total | Manufacturing (private) | | | Nonmanufacturing (private) | | | | | | | Government | |
|---|---|---|---|---|---|---|---|---|---|---|---|---|---|
| | | Total | Durable goods | Non- durable goods | Total | Mining | Con- tract con- struc- tion | Trans- porta- tion and public utilities | Whole- sale and retail trade | Finance, insur- ance, and real estate | Services | Federal | State and local |
| 1969 | 70,442 | 20,167 | 11,895 | 8,272 | 38,073 | 619 | 3,525 | 4,435 | 14,704 | 3,562 | 11,228 | 2,758 | 9,444 |
| 1970 | 70,920 | 19,349 | 11,195 | 8,154 | 39,010 | 623 | 3,536 | 4,504 | 15,040 | 3,687 | 11,621 | 2,731 | 9,830 |
| 1971 | 71,222 | 18,572 | 10,597 | 7,975 | 39,762 | 609 | 3,639 | 4,457 | 15,352 | 3,802 | 11,903 | 2,696 | 10,192 |
| 1972 | 73,714 | 19,090 | 11,006 | 8,084 | 41,284 | 625 | 3,831 | 4,517 | 15,975 | 3,943 | 12,392 | 2,684 | 10,656 |
| 1973 | 76,833 | 20,054 | 11,814 | 8,240 | 43,037 | 638 | 4,028 | 4,646 | 16,665 | 4,075 | 12,986 | 2,663 | 11,079 |
| 1974 | 78,334 | 20,016 | 11,837 | 8,179 | 44,034 | 672 | 3,985 | 4,699 | 17,011 | 4,161 | 13,506 | 2,724 | 11,560 |

Source: Department of Labor, Bureau of Labor Statistics.

# AVERAGE HOURLY AND WEEKLY EARNINGS — SELECTED INDUSTRIES

[For production workers or nonsupervisory employees]

| Period | Average hourly earnings — current dollars | | | | Average weekly earnings — current dollars | | | | Manufacturing industries | |
|---|---|---|---|---|---|---|---|---|---|---|
| | Total nonagri- cultural private | Manu- facturing | Contract construc- tion | Retail trade | Total nonagri- cultural private | Manu- facturing | Contract construc- tion | Retail trade | Adjusted hourly earnings, 1967 = 100 | Average weekly earnings, 1967 dollars |
| 1966 | $2.56 | $2.72 | $3.89 | $1.91 | $ 98.82 | $112.34 | $146.26 | $ 68.57 | 95.6 | $115.58 |
| 1967 | 2.68 | 2.83 | 4.11 | 2.01 | 101.84 | 114.90 | 154.95 | 70.95 | 100.0 | 114.90 |
| 1968 | 2.85 | 3.01 | 4.41 | 2.16 | 107.73 | 122.51 | 164.49 | 74.95 | 106.1 | 117.57 |
| 1969 | 3.04 | 3.19 | 4.79 | 2.30 | 114.61 | 129.51 | 181.54 | 78.66 | 112.4 | 117.95 |
| 1970 | 3.22 | 3.36 | 5.24 | 2.44 | 119.46 | 133.73 | 195.45 | 82.47 | 119.4 | 114.99 |
| 1971 | 3.44 | 3.57 | 5.69 | 2.57 | 127.28 | 142.44 | 211.67 | 86.61 | 127.3 | 117.43 |
| 1972 | 3.67 | 3.81 | 6.03 | 2.70 | 136.16 | 154.69 | 222.51 | 90.99 | 135.1 | 123.46 |
| 1973 | 3.92 | 4.07 | 6.38 | 2.87 | 145.43 | 165.65 | 236.06 | 95.57 | 143.6 | 124.46 |
| 1974 | 4.22 | 4.40 | 6.76 | 3.10 | 154.45 | 176.00 | 249.44 | 101.37 | 156.0 | 119.16 |

Source: Department of Labor, Bureau of Labor Statistics.

# Basic Economics

## FIFTH EDITION

THOMAS J. HAILSTONES

*Dean, College of Business Administration*
*Professor of Economics*
*Xavier University, Cincinnati*

H19

*Published by*
**SOUTH-WESTERN PUBLISHING CO.**

CINCINNATI    WEST CHICAGO, ILL.    DALLAS    PELHAM MANOR, N.Y.
PALO ALTO, CALIF.    BRIGHTON, ENGLAND

ISBN: 0-538-08190-2

Library of Congress Catalog Card Number: 75-37215

2 3 4 5 6 K 1 0 9 8 7

Printed in the United States of America

# PREFACE

Never before has so much interest and excitement been generated in the subject of economics. In the past few years we have experienced a war, full employment, inflation, an energy crisis, recession, an oil embargo, voluntary rationing, tax cuts and tax surcharges, price and wage controls, high interest rates, a money crunch, stagflation, massive layoffs, and a host of other economic forces that have affected our daily lives. The questions of why and how, the analysis of existing conditions, and the solutions to economic problems are discussed in schools, homes, offices, workshops, and the halls of Congress. To understand many of the social, political, military, and economic problems and issues of our society, it is necessary to know more about the nature and function of our economic system.

This textbook is designed for such a purpose. It is planned for a one-term course at the college level primarily for those students, such as pre-professional (engineering, medicine, law), liberal arts, agriculture, and others, who will take only one course in economics. It is also planned for a beginning course for economics majors and is likewise suitable for an adult evening or extension course in economics.

The intent of the book is to give the reader a basic understanding of the operation of our economic system; to explain the role of demand and supply in determining prices, to compare the merits of competition vs. monopoly, and to explain the use of antitrust regulations; to demonstrate the role of money and its effects on our economy; to present a measurement of production, employment, and income; to show the current methods of economic analyses and the development of economic policies that are used to stabilize the level of economic activity; and to relate international economics to our domestic economy. In short, the book endeavors to take the reader from scratch through a relatively high level of economic analysis in one semester.

*Basic Economics* deals with both micro- and macroeconomics. In terms of *microeconomics* it treats the pricing mechanism, the role of demand and supply, elasticities of demand, competitive vs. monopolistic pricing, and the need and purpose of antitrust regulation. From the viewpoint of *macroeconomics* the text deals with concepts of the economy as a whole, such as total production, total employment, total income, and the general price level, rather than with the problems of the individual or the firm. Thus, the reader will be able to see how various economic events or changes affect the total economy. A study of the text, furthermore, provides a better understanding of the measures and objectives of national economic policies.

This approach has been used successfully in a one-semester terminal course for nonbusiness and noneconomics undergraduate students, as an initial course for economics majors, and as a survey course for graduate students. Likewise, it has been used successfully in teaching economics to managment personnel in industrial education programs.

Numerous comments were received from professors and students who used the first four editions of *Basic Economics*. Many of these were suggestions for the incorporation of additional materials into the book. Although much has been added over the years, I have resisted enlarging the volume through careful pruning of some topics and effective consolidation and integration of others. A major change in this fifth edition, for example, is the addition of a chapter on pure competition and another on imperfect competition following the chapter on price determination. This was in response to numerous requests for a fuller section dealing with microeconomics.

Besides the debt of gratitude owed to all those who assisted with the first four editions, I wish to thank those who offered suggestions for the improvement of this fifth edition. In particular I appreciate the aid of Mrs. Marjorie Schmidt for her stenographic assistance.

Thomas J. Hailstones

# CONTENTS

Part **5** ECONOMIC ACTIVITY AND POLICIES

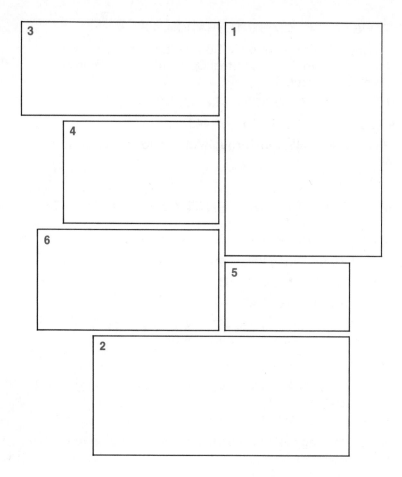

Each of the six photographs on the cover of this book is shown again at the beginning of the part to which it relates. The scenes shown in the photographs are: **1** The New York City skyline viewed from Brooklyn (photo by Holly Wemple, New York City Economic Development Administration). **2** Interior of a large shopping mall in central Ohio (courtesy of the Dayton Mall, Dayton, Ohio). **3** Modern downtown banking facilities adjacent to Fountain Square, Cincinnati (courtesy of The Fifth Third Bank, Cincinnati, Ohio). **4** Blaw-Knox steel processing line (courtesy of White Consolidated Industries, Inc.). **5** Ohio's first commercial nuclear power plant, the Davis-Besse Nuclear Power Station near Port Clinton, Ohio (courtesy of The Cleveland Electric Illuminating Company). **6** A water injection facility in the Pembina oil field in Alberta, Canada (courtesy of Ashland Oil, Inc.).

# Part 1

# The Economic System

# 1 THE NATURE AND SCOPE OF ECONOMICS

## ECONOMICS DEFINED

Every day it becomes more apparent that economics plays a major role in our lives. Our decisions on what profession to enter, where to work, and where to live are based in large part on economic considerations. If we own a business, economic factors dictate whether or not we earn a profit and continue to operate or fail and go into bankruptcy. Economics applies directly to the earning of our incomes and to the spending of our money. Aside from the direct application of economics to our lives, we are also affected indirectly. Economic policies help determine the level of production and employment in our nation, the amount of taxes we pay, how much we give in aid to developing nations, and how much of our resources we devote to preserving our natural environment. Economic measures influence the prices we pay, the purchasing power of our dollars, the availability of goods and services, and our standard of living.

Economics means many things to many people. To some it means thriftiness, but to others, the arranging of a large mortgage loan. To some it implies budgeting for household purchases or saving for an automobile, but to others it means the analysis of a multimillion dollar income statement. To the President of the United States it means the study of economic conditions of the nation, the presentation of a $350 billion federal budget, and the proposal of various economic measures that will maximize total production, employment, and income for the nation. The ubiquity of economics offers a challenge to the scholar in deciding where to begin the study of economics. As with any study, however, a logical place to begin is with a definition, since it serves as a good point of departure for explaining, examining, and analyzing the various aspects of the subject at hand. For our purpose, we shall use the following definition: *Economics* is a science that is concerned with the production, distribution, and consumption of goods and services.

2

## Economics Is a Science

We must keep in mind the fact that a *science* is an organized body of truth coordinated, arranged, and systematized with reference to general laws or principles. Frequently when a person thinks of science, one thinks of the physical sciences, such as physics, chemistry, and biology. There are, however, the nonphysical sciences, which include philosophy, mathematics, psychology, politics, and economics. Economics is considered to be a science because it is an organized body of truth coordinated, arranged, and systematized with reference to certain general laws and principles.

Unfortunately the laws and principles of this science, economics, are not so universal or ironclad as the laws of the physical sciences. For example, physics gives us the law of gravity. From this law we know that if we hold this book two feet above the desk and then release our grip, the book will fall to the desk with a bang. We could try this experiment for hours on end and we would get the same result each time. Never would the book remain freely suspended in air. The law of gravity is, therefore, a universal or ironclad law that will hold in all similar circumstances.

In economics we do have a few universal laws, such as the law of diminishing returns. According to this law, if all factors used in production are held constant except one, and if this factor is increased a unit at a time, the size of the increments of output resulting therefrom will eventually diminish. Likewise, the laws of supply and demand state in part that when demand increases and supply remains constant, the price of a commodity will increase. Many other laws in economics are general only — not universal, for they apply in most instances but not in every case. Take, for example, the law of consumption, which states that as the real income of a family or an individual increases, the percentage of income spent on consumption will decrease. This is generally true. Most of us, as our real income increases, will save a larger percentage of our income and, as a result, the percentage of our real income spent on consumption will decrease. Every tenth individual, however, might spend more than is earned regardless of how much that person's salary increases.

In the physical sciences we know what reaction to expect when we apply a certain stimulus to a given set of conditions. In economics, where we are dealing with individuals, the circumstances may never be exactly the same because of differences in personality, environment, I.Q., and other factors. Consequently, it is more difficult to develop hard and fast laws, and the study of economics becomes more difficult and complex than it would otherwise be.

## Economics Is Concerned with Production

In economics we define *production* as the creation or addition of utility. *Utility* is our term for usefulness. It is the ability of a good or service to satisfy a want. We are producing whenever we make a product or render a service that is useful. Of the several types of utility, the four most frequently recognized are: (1) form, (2) place, (3) time, and (4) possession. Form utility applies to products, which are tangible in nature, but not to services, which are intangible. The other three forms of utility apply to services as well as to products.

**Form Utility**   *Form utility* occurs when we improve or increase the usefulness of a commodity by changing its form or shape. Undoubtedly we would all agree that metal in the form of a late model Corvette is more useful than a heap of iron ore or a few steel ingots. Most of our factories add form utility in producing such items as furniture, toys, and plastics. Likewise, agriculture, in producing grains and livestock, creates form utility.

**Place Utility**   *Place utility* occurs when a good or service has more usefulness in one location than in another. The movement of the good to a more useful location creates place utility. For example, if a Texas millionaire buys that Corvette, he will pay a certain price f.o.b. Detroit. The car will be of little value to him, however, as long as it is in Detroit and he is in Houston. Consequently, he will pay an additional sum of money to have the car transported to Houston.

**Time Utility**   *Time utility* occurs when a commodity or service is more useful at one time than at another. Let us say that you are offered a position as the Southern California representative for a Midwestern firm. In addition to the education and the ability to do the job, assume that you must provide your own car to call on company customers. If you do not have a car, you might ask your prospective employer to wait a few years until you can save enough money to buy a car. You would probably be told, however, that the job must be filled immediately and that it would be out of the question to wait that long. In this situation the car is more useful to you now than later, for without it this job opportunity may be lost. Rather than let the opportunity pass, you may go to an automobile dealer, select a car, and pay for it on the installment plan. Suppose you buy a car in the low-price field, the price tag reads $3,200, and you arrange to pay for it over a two-year period. Assume a finance company lends you the money, and you agree to repay it at the rate of $155 a month over the next two years. In that case the car will cost a total of $3,720. Why are you and other people willing to pay an interest charge of $520, the difference between the price tag and your actual payments, for the car? The answer is simply that the finance company has created time utility for you.

The person, company, or financial institution lending you the money relinquishes that money for a period of time to make a product available to you now. The lender is entitled to some remuneration, usually in the form of interest, for the service in creating this time utility. Production in the form of time utility is a big business in our economy. In 1974, about $182 billion in installment and other consumer credit sales were registered, and family home mortgages were approximately $392 billion. Indeed, time utility is a potent force in our economy.

**Possession Utility**   *Possession utility* results when the ownership of a good or service is transferred from one person to another. For example, a set of carpenter tools on display in a hardware store window is of no value to the carpenter who may need them as long as they remain in that window. If he were able to obtain possession of them, however, he could use them to earn his living. In negotiating a transfer of the tools from the hands of the original owner or producer to the carpenter, a salesperson creates possession utility. That is true also of the transfer of the ownership of homes, food, clothing, and other items.

The many salespeople in our economy create possession utility in addition to place and time utility. Thus, there is a sound economic justification for the salaries and commissions they receive. In fact, the whole structure of marketing products and services in our economy is geared to the creation of place and time utility. In spite of the criticism some people have for the middleman, there is definitely a need for this person in the economy. He or she is entitled to a remuneration for the production of place, time, and possession utility just as the manufacturer is entitled to a profit for the creation of form utility.

### Economics Is Concerned with Distribution

At first glance many individuals may regard this part of our definition as referring to the physical distribution of goods and services from the producer to the consumer, or what is called "marketing distribution." If that were the case, however, our definition would be redundant since we have indicated that such distribution is part of production because it creates place, time, and possession utilities. But in our definition of *distribution* we are referring to the allocation of the total product among the factors of production. In monetary terms it can be considered as the distribution of money incomes among the factors of production.

**Factors of Production**   Before a person or business can engage in the production of goods or services, certain prerequisites or corequisites are necessary. These are: (a) labor, (b) land, (c) capital, and (d) entrepreneurship, known as the *factors of production*.

**Labor**   *Labor* refers to the time and the effort of human beings involved in the productive process. Labor includes both physical and mental application by individuals and groups — both executive and blue-collar workers. It includes the application of human effort for the production of services as well as the production of goods.

**Land**   As used in economics the term *land* is much broader than the concept of real estate. It includes not only real estate but all the resources of the land, sea and air. Such items as coal, oil, lumber, chemicals, water, coral, air, and rain are illustrations of this factor of production.

**Capital**   *Capital* includes those goods used to produce other goods. The goods produced may be consumed or used in production. Capital also includes goods that produce services. Such items as blast furnaces, punch presses, buildings, bulldozers, computers, trucks, airplanes, and the like are considered as capital. In a narrower sense the term "capital" is often applied to money. From an economic point of view this is correct insofar as money can be used to purchase the equipment, material, and labor necessary to produce other goods.

**Entrepreneurship**   *Entrepreneurship* is derived from a French word meaning an undertaking. The *entrepreneur* organizes the business enterprise and assumes the risk. This function is distinguished from that of the laborer, the landlord, and the capitalist. It is the entrepreneur, or enterpriser, who combines the other factors of production — land, labor, and capital — to produce the final product.

Today a renewed emphasis is being placed on the concept of the entrepreneur. Many universities and state industrial development departments are teaching special courses and conducting workshops in entrepreneurship. Both in America and abroad, particularly in developing countries, there is a growing need for the promotion of business and economic development by entrepreneurs, or in other words, by those who can put it all together.

**The Problem of Distribution**   In a self-sufficing barter economy, individuals produced for their own needs and, if there was any excess, they may have traded with their neighbors. Under this type of system, a man generally used his own labor or that of his family, his own land, his own tools, and his own entrepreneurship to produce the goods he needed. Using his own labor, land, and tools, and assuming the right of private property to exist, there was no question about the ownership of the goods he produced or about the share to which he was entitled.

In our modern, complex economy, the problem is more involved. An individual who wants to produce still must use the basic factors of production. In bringing together the factors of production, however, the entrepreneur may use the labor of one person, the land of another, and the capital of a third. By combining their activities, a product is produced

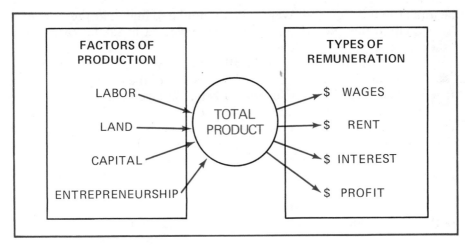

Figure 1-1    **FUNCTIONAL DISTRIBUTION**

that has a certain value. Now the big question arises: What shall be the share or remuneration of each of the factors for its contribution to the total product? In our economy remuneration for the factors of production — labor, land, capital, and entrepreneurship — is made in the form of wages, rent, interest, and profits, respectively, as shown in Figure 1-1.

The problem of distribution has plagued economists for nearly two centuries, and we still do not have a simple answer to it. Prior to the 1930s, most of our economists and textbooks devoted a considerable amount of time to this problem. Consequently, we have had a whole parade of theories about functional distribution.

**Theories of Distribution**    The theory of distribution is not a single, integrated theory. Instead, it is made up of numerous theories endeavoring to explain how the remuneration to one or more of the factors of production is determined.

Theories abound in the determination of wages, rent, interest, and profit. All add to the complexity of the issue. If one studies any economy other than that of capitalism, that person will find that the theory of distribution differs. Thus, in a way, the theory is a product of our economic environment.

**Allocation to Factors**    Although none of the theories can adequately explain how the remuneration to a particular factor of production is determined, each adds a modicum of understanding to the method or process of its determination. For example, profits may arise according to any one of several theories or a combination of several of the theories. Furthermore, in determining the remuneration to any one factor, the other factors cannot be ignored. Wages should not be so high that they leave an inadequate profit. Nor should wages be neglected in taking care of the other factors.

The problem of distribution or allocation is very much with us today. A labor union, for example, seeks a larger share of the total product when it requests a wage increase for its workers. Management may be seeking a larger profit and thus a greater share of the total product when it increases prices or reduces cost. Many of our current labor-management disputes arise from disagreement on this basic problem of allocation. The capitalist may demand a higher rate of interest for the use of his or her funds, or the landholder may raise the rent in an effort to increase his or her share of the total product.

Although it is impossible for every factor to increase its relative share of the total product, all can have a larger absolute return by contributing to an increase in the size of the total product. Thus, increases in productivity from various sources are the means of improving the return to all factors.

Today our national statistics reveal how much of our total production is being allocated to each of the factors of production. Later we will learn that approximately 75 percent of the national income goes for wages and salaries, about 3 percent for rental income, over 4 percent for interest, 8 percent for proprietors' income, and the remaining 10 percent for corporate profit. This is not to say, however, that this is what the allocation should be. To establish any criterion for this latter determination, it would be necessary to leave the realm of *positive economics*, dealings with what is, and delve into *normative economics*, what ought to be.

The attempts of the administration to impose the voluntary Presidential wage-price guideposts during the 1960s met with only limited success because, in large part, they froze the shares of the total product allocated to each of the factors of production. Labor unions particularly did not like this aspect of the wage-price guideposts. In this regard much objection, too, was voiced against the compulsory wage and price controls imposed in the early 1970s as a means of combating inflation.

### Economics Is Concerned with Consumption

*Consumption* refers to the use of a good or service. After getting up this morning, you may have had cereal or eggs for breakfast. If you drove to school or to work, your car consumed gasoline. It is not necessary to absorb a good completely in order to have consumption. A good may be consumed little by little, day by day, such as your automobile tires, your home, or the soles of your shoes. Consumption may be regarded as the most important function in economics in the sense that it is the ultimate end of economic activity. Without consumption there would be little need for production and distribution.

## Economics Is Concerned with Goods and Services

The last part of our definition deals with economic goods and services that satisfy wants. Economic goods may be in the form of wealth or income. Economic services are part of our income. This means little unless we elaborate on the meaning of an economic good and economic service.

**Characteristics of an Economic Good**   To be an *economic good*, an object must be: (a) material, (b) useful, (c) scarce, and (d) transferable. Let us look at these characteristics.

*Material*   To be an economic good, an object generally must be material. Thus, your books, pencils, automobiles, shoes, and thousands of other commodities are economic goods. Certain immaterial things, such as ideas, are productive and can satisfy wants in the same way that economic goods and services do. They are not generally classified as economic goods however, because they are immaterial.

*Useful*   To be an economic good, a commodity must have the ability to satisfy a want. Most commodities are useful. Examples of such commodities include typewriters, watches, homes, and thousands of other products. Since wheat is edible, it is an economic good. Ragweed, on the other hand, generally has no practical use and, if it does not, it cannot be classified as an economic good. Oddly enough, it is possible that a good may be useful in one circumstance and not in another. For example, garbage in one community is collected and sold for feed or is processed into fertilizer. Therefore, it is an economic good. In another community it may be an absolute nuisance and may have to be incinerated. In such a case it is not an economic good. Frequently a use will be found for a previously useless commodity, and it may change from a noneconomic to an economic good. In fact, many industrial by-products have made such transitions.

*Scarce*   Scarcity is an essential characteristic of an economic good because it is this element, along with the usefulness of the item, that determines the value or price. If a useful material object exists in such an abundance that anyone can readily obtain it without exerting much effort, it does not have an exchange or monetary value. Consequently, it is not an economic good. Such is the case of air, which is probably the most useful good in existence. However, who is going to pay for the air when all one must do is breathe it? You might object by saying that we pay for warm air in the wintertime and cool air in the summertime. That is true, but in such cases a particular type of air has become scarce and that is why we pay for it. In the winter we pay for fuel to heat our homes, offices, and factories or we buy an airline ticket to Florida to enjoy a few weeks in the warm sunshine. Other things being equal, the more scarce the good, the greater its value or price.

**Transferable**　If an object is material, useful, and scarce, but not transferable, it loses its value as an economic good. For example, the gold in seawater is not an economic good because the cost of extracting it is prohibitive. Certain minerals and metals known to be present in the Antarctic region are noneconomic because at the present time there is no way of extracting and transferring them to a place where they can be of use.

**Economic Services**　Usefulness, scarcity, and transferability may be obtained from a source other than a material good. For example, a doctor administers to the sick, a lawyer defends clients, an entertainer keeps the audience amused, and an instructor helps you to obtain an education. Such activities are classified as economic services. *Economic services*, then, are nonmaterial activities that are useful, scarce, and transferable. Services are rendered by the laundry, the auto repair shop, the hairdresser and hundreds of other businesses today. Presently, approximately 60 percent of our labor force is engaged in the production of services. It is estimated that by 1980, 7 out of every 10 workers will be employed in service occupations.

**Types of Goods**　In classifying goods in relation to one another, we can distinguish three principal types: economic goods, free goods, and public goods. As has been stated, an object that is material, useful, scarce, and transferable is classified as an economic good. A *free good* lacks the element of scarcity and, therefore, has no price. In this category we find air, sunshine, and, in some cases, water. A *public good* is an economic good to the supplier but a free good to the user. We often classify our public parks, our libraries, and the water from a public drinking fountain as public goods. In the final analysis, however, it might be said that since these goods are provided by tax money, which the user ultimately pays, they are economic goods. This same classification can also be applied to services.

Economic goods are also classified according to their use. *Consumer goods* are those that are directly utilized by the consuming public. Many items fit into this category. Examples include books, tires, shelter, food, and clothing. *Capital goods*, or producer goods, are those used to produce other goods, either consumer or capital goods. Buildings, machinery, and equipment are capital goods.

**Measurement of Wealth**　*Wealth* may be defined as things of value owned. Wealth, then, consists of a multitude of goods. Estimates of the total wealth of the United States range from $3 trillion on up. The differences in the various estimates arise from three sources: (1) differences in opinion as to what should be included in wealth, (2) the handling of intangibles, and (3) the valuation of the goods that constitute wealth.

As we have said, in general wealth is the sum total of our current economic goods. Some experts measure wealth by totaling the assets of the individuals and the firms of the economy. Others add to this the property and the assets of the federal, state and municipal governments. In counting resources, certain authorities want to include only those that have been extracted and are ready for use. Others want to include as wealth the total value of all resources whether extracted or still in their original state.

Many people think of money as wealth, but money, as such, is not wealth. It merely represents wealth or a command over goods and services. The more money the individual has, the greater the command over goods and services. Although money is not wealth, wealth can be measured in terms of money.

Concerning intangibles these questions arise: Should stocks, bonds, and mortgages be included in our count of wealth? The answer is no. To include the capital stock of a company as wealth, if the money obtained from the sale of the stock were used to purchase machinery and equipment that had been previously counted as part of our wealth, would result in double accounting. What about education and training? It would seem logical to include these factors in our wealth since they are used to produce other goods and services. Many economists would like to see these included in the valuation of our wealth.

A question often arises as to whether to use the original or the replacement cost of economic goods in determining their value. In the matter of intangibles, how do you measure the value of an engineering degree, the training of a doctor, the skill of a mechanic, or the knowledge of a school teacher? These problems multiply as the concept of wealth is analyzed, and it becomes exceedingly difficult to obtain agreement on the exact value of our wealth.

**Income**    Often there is confusion and misunderstanding between the concepts of wealth and income. Wealth is a stock concept; it is the total value of our economic goods at any given time. *Income*, on the other hand, is a flow concept; it is the total value of the goods and services produced over a period of time, usually a year. If we were to take a picture of the economy on the first day of a certain year, we might observe that the total wealth amounted to $3 trillion. Then, if we were to count the goods and services produced during that year, the total might be $1,400 billion. This would be our income. Does this mean that our total wealth at the end of the year has been increased by the total amount of production during that year? The answer is no, since all income or production is not counted as wealth. Most of our income is consumed as it is produced. Only that portion which is not consumed is added to our wealth. In recent years, for example, the addition to our wealth has been approximately \$100 billion annually. This consists of production in the form of machinery, equipment, and buildings that were not consumed or offset by depreciation during the year.

Although *real income* is the value of the goods and the services produced, we frequently think of income in terms of money. The *money income* is derived from the production of goods and services, since the owners of the factors of production are compensated in dollars for their productive contribution. Thus, the money incomes received are equivalent to the value of goods and services produced.

There is frequently a correlation between wealth and income. We use our wealth, that is, our buildings, machinery, equipment, and resources, to produce goods and services, or income. Usually the greater the wealth, the higher the income will be, for the more means we have at our disposal, the greater will be our productive capacity. The greater our production or income, the higher our standard of living. Consequently, it behooves a nation not to consume everything it produces but to channel a portion of its output into the form of machinery, equipment, and buildings in an effort to increase production and to improve the standard of living for the future.

Thus, we see that our definition or concept of economics is very broad. It encompasses all our business activity as well as many of our social activities. Furthermore, such special fields as production, finance, marketing, transportation, and labor are related to and are a part of the study of economics. Economics arises in connection with the individual, the family, the firm, the industry, and the nation as a whole. It is evident that economics pervades our entire society and affects our lives daily.

## ECONOMICS IS RELATED TO OTHER SCIENCES

As a science, economics is related to other sciences. Since some of its laws, such as the law of diminishing returns, are based on physical phenomena, economics is related to physics. Since it operates within a nation, it is related to the political structure of that nation and therefore to political science. Income determines the standard of living. A low standard leads to social problems. Thus, economics is related to sociology. Since it deals with human behavior, it shares this phase of its study with psychology. For example, the reasons why individuals spend or save are psychological as well as economical.

Economics is also related to philosophy. Economic acts are human acts, and human acts constitute a proper subject for ethics, a branch of philosophy. There should be no conflict between sound economic principles and moral principles, but occasionally someone advocates an economic doctrine that is in contradiction to a moral principle. In such a case the moral principle should take precedence over the economic principle. For example, an economist may advocate euthanasia as a solution to the problems of old age. Obviously this opinion is in conflict with moral principles.

Economics, especially at the advanced level, is closely related to mathematics. Economic theory and analysis today not only rely on the use of statistics, econometrics, calculus, linear programming, and other mathematical tools, but much progress has also been made through computer application to economic problems. In its relationships with both physical and nonphysical sciences and exact and non-exact sciences, economics is certainly related to logic, the science of correct thinking, just as any study should be. It is senseless to study any subject without adhering to the rules of logic, whether reasoning from a particular instance to a general principle (induction) or from a general principle to a particular application (deduction). A proper syllogism makes true conclusions easier to draw, especially when the premises can be substantiated.

### Prudential Judgment

But even in applying the rules of logic there may be many problems to which there is no one correct answer. Remember economics is not all black or all white. There may be many shades in between. Economists may disagree as to the best means of raising additional funds for a business, that is, whether it should be accomplished through the sale of additional stocks or through the sale of bonds. They may also disagree on whether a firm should raise prices or cut costs in an effort to increase profit, or they may argue that it is better to advertise through television than through newspapers.

In many cases there may be no way of determining who is right or wrong regarding some of the conclusions. Much depends upon the prudential judgment of the individual involved. Since prudence is an intellectual virtue by which one selects the best means for the end intended, a *prudential judgment* is based to a large extent upon the knowledge and the experience of the individual. Some economists may prefer to engage the government in deficit spending by borrowing more and increasing spending. Others may think that it is better to hold spending constant and to decrease taxes, which in turn would require the government to increase its borrowing to maintain the same level of spending. Both are aiming at the same end, that is, to increase deficit spending, but both are trying to accomplish it by slightly different means. It is often a matter of choice based upon individual prudential judgment as to which economic solution is to be preferred.

As a result of the influence of prudential judgments, we frequently find disagreement among economists. For example, every fall many forecasters predict the Gross National Product for the following year. These forecasts often differ to some extent. Each of the several forecasts is based on the judgment of the forecaster as to what assumptions should be incorporated into the respective forecast. As another example, a pre-summit economic conference of 28 economists from government, labor, business, and academia was held by President Ford in September, 1974, for the purpose of determining what should be done about the general state of the economy, and particularly what could be done to combat double-digit inflation. Recommendations were diverse. Some wanted to increase taxes, while others suggested tax reductions. Many recommended some leniency in our tight money policy, while others held fast that tightness of money should be retained. Some suggested an imposition of wage and price controls, but most were against the use of compulsory controls. Situations like this often cause confusion in the mind of the average citizen. But it is hoped that by the time you finish your study of economics you will be able to explain or reconcile such differences.

### Economy — Only a Part of Society

Frequently when we study economics, we mentally extract the economic system from its total environment and analyze it in isolation. We find out what makes it "tick," what its functions are, and how it can serve us. We study the individual parts, relate them to one another, integrate them, and analyze the economy as a whole. After we have done this, we should put the economy back into its original place in society and study its relationship to the rest of society. We frequently neglect to do this, however, or we tend to ignore or de-emphasize the other aspects of our society.

Although we may analyze the economy as an isolated unit, we must keep in mind it is a part of a larger unit, society. Consequently, after we have obtained our facts, established our principles, and drawn our conclusions, we must fit economics into its proper sphere and reevaluate our conclusions in relation to the cultural, social, political, and moral aspects of society. If we do not do this, we can be misled very easily. For example, economics may stress the improvement of our standard of living as a prime objective. To obtain such an economic objective at the expense of our political or moral welfare, however, could be highly dangerous.

## ECONOMIC THEORY VERSUS ECONOMIC POLICY

In the study of economics we need to distinguish between *economic theory*, which develops the rules and principles of economics and which serves as a guide for action under a given set of circumstances, and *economic policy*, which is that action taken under the same set of circumstances. It would be fine if our economic policy always followed our economic theory. Frequently, however, economic policy is modified by political, military, and social policy. For example, if economic theory dictates that we should maintain or increase taxes, we may find that during an election year the economic policy often yields to political policy and a tax cut is put into effect to woo the voters. Likewise, according to economic theory, international free trade is more beneficial than trade restriction. Political pressures by various groups, however, may lead us to an economic policy restricting foreign trade.

## ECONOMIC DECISION MAKING

Unlike some other sciences, economics cannot always be definitive or answer problems with certitude. Not only are economic policies often modified by political, social, and military policies, but many times there is no one answer or solution to a given problem or issue. There may be no right or wrong answer to a problem.

Furthermore, once a decision has been made to implement an economic measure, it cannot be undone. A physical scientist can experiment by applying a variable to a given set of constants to test and measure the reaction of the variable. The experiment can be repeated by duplicating the constants, applying another variable and measuring its effect. In this way the scientist can experiment until the variable, or solution, that has the most desirable effect on a given set of constants (conditions) is found. Unfortunately the economist, first of all, cannot keep all the constants, or economic factors, constant. The economist has very little, if any, control over them. Secondly, once the effects, or reaction, of a variable, have been measured, the constants (economic conditions) cannot be reconstructed exactly as they were prior to the application of the variable to test a new variable.

The economist, or policy maker, therefore, has to make a judgment in selecting the best variable (or means) to attain the desired objective. Full employment, for example, is a widely accepted objective for the economy. If the economy is not at full employment, as designated by point $A$ in Table 1-1, there are several approaches to attain this objective, as shown in Table 1-1. Although there may be widespread agreement on the objective, there will be a variety of opinions regarding the best means of attaining full employment, designated by point $B$ in Table 1-1. One group of economists may suggest raising economic activity and employment through the private sector of the economy. Another group of analysts, however, will stoutly maintain that it is better to work through the public sector of the economy. For those recommending the use of the private sector, some will propose that measures be taken to increase consumption. Others, however, will strongly advocate that it is better to increase investment to stimulate employment. Those touting investment may differ in their approach. Some will claim that the best way to stimulate investment is through the adoption of tax credits and/or accelerated depreciation. Others will vouch for increasing the money supply and/or lowering interest rates to increase investment.

Table 1-1    **ECONOMIC DECISION TREE**
Alternative Measures That Can Be Used To Increase
Economic Activity and Reduce Unemployment

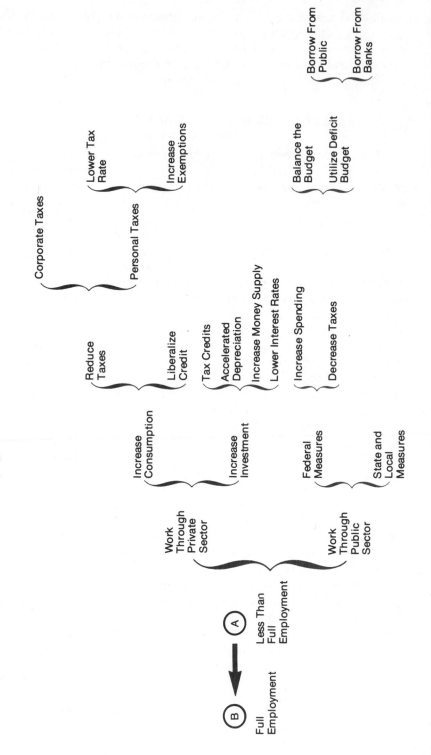

On the other hand, those wishing to work through the public sector may be split into two camps. Most will suggest working through the federal government. But a few may point out that state and local governments spend 50 percent more for goods and services than does the federal government, and therefore more can be accomplished by working at the state and local levels. If those suggesting expansion of federal government activity prevail, still another question has to be answered. Is it better for the federal government to increase government spending directly or to decrease taxes and let consumers and businesses do the spending? Once this decision is made, someone has to determine whether the federal government is going to operate with a balanced budget or a deficit budget. If the latter, one more question remains. Where is the government going to get the money — from the public or from the banks? Each of these sources of funds can have different effects on the economy.

You can see that to get from a position of nagging unemployment to full employment there are several alternatives. There is no one best way. There is also no certain way, since all factors cannot be controlled. In fact, it is possible to try several combinations of measures. Each approach can have differing effects on the total economy and can affect some sectors of the economy more than others. But right or wrong, someone, after taking into consideration all of the economic, political, social, and other factors involved, has to make a decision of what to do or not to do.

In effect, the policymaker can design a decision tree similar to the one shown in Table 1-1, which shows some of the alternatives that could be selected in an attempt to solve the problem of unemployment. Some attempt could even be made to quantify these measures by assigning probabilities to them, which in itself leads to still more decisions and prudential judgments.

## MICROECONOMICS AND MACROECONOMICS

The study of economics can be divided into two broad areas: microeconomics and macroeconomics. *Microeconomics* deals with the economic problems of the individual, the firm, and the industry. It endeavors to discover what motivates the individual to spend or to save. It treats the determination of price for the firm, the principle of supply and demand, the number employed by the firm, and other similar factors. *Macroeconomics* deals with the aggregates of economics. It includes in its subject matter total production, total employment, and the general price level. It analyzes the problems of the economy as a whole rather than those of the individual, the firm, or the industry. It suggests ways and means of obtaining a high level of employment. It formulates ideas on monetary and fiscal policy as a means of stabilizing the economy.

Fifty or sixty years ago economists dealt primarily with microeconomics. Since the 1930s, however, a great deal of emphasis has been placed on macroeconomics. Today we study both areas; but since in this book we are mainly interested in the explanation of our economic system in general, how it operates, the factors that affect output and employment, and the influences on our standard of living, we will concentrate primarily, though certainly not exclusively, on macroeconomics.

## SUMMARY

Economics is a science that is concerned with the production, distribution, and consumption of goods and services. It is a science because it is an organized body of truth coordinated, arranged, and systematized with reference to certain general laws and principles.

Production is a process that brings about the creation or addition of utility. Several types of utility exist, including form, place, time, and possession utility.

Distribution as used in economics generally refers to the allocation of the total product or income among the factors of production. The factors of production are labor, land, capital, and entrepreneurship. They are reimbursed in the form of wages, rent, interest, and profits, respectively, for their contribution toward the total product. Several theories exist that seek to explain distribution.

Consumption is the utilization of a good or a service. It is the ultimate end of all economic activity. Wealth is our total collection of economic goods. An economic good is one that is material, useful, scarce, and transferable. Any activity that is useful, scarce, and transferable, but that is not material is an economic service.

Goods can be classified as economic goods, free goods, and public goods. Economic goods may be divided into two groups, consumer goods and capital goods. Income is equivalent to the total goods and services produced over a given period.

Economics is related to other sciences, such as physics, psychology, sociology, political science, and philosophy. Logic, a branch of philosophy, is essential for the development of sound economic reasoning. Prudential judgments frequently enter into the determination of economic goals and principles, however.

There is a distinction between economic theory and economic policy. The first deals with the rules and principles to be used under a given set of economic conditions. The latter deals with what we actually do under such conditions. Differences between the two frequently occur, since economic policy is often modified by political, social, and military policy. Economic problems and issues often can be presented in the form of a decision tree showing alternatives and choices. After proper analysis a prudential judgment can be made regarding alternative solutions.

The study of economics is divided into two broad areas: microeconomics, dealing with the actions of the individual, the firm, and the industry; and macroeconomics, dealing with aggregates, such as total production, employment, and income.

Now that we are familiar with the nature and the scope of economics, we are ready to move on to an explanation of the economic system and the process of economizing.

## DISCUSSION QUESTIONS

1. Do you think that economics will ever develop into an exact science? Why or why not?
2. In what manner does production include more than the manufacture and fabrication of goods?
3. Is there any justification for the contention that there are only two factors of production — land and labor? Explain.
4. Can you cite recent instances that tend to show that the problem of distribution is a continuing problem in our economy?
5. Do you think we are moving toward a more service-oriented economy?
6. Can you name some commodities that were at one time free goods but are now economic goods?
7. How can the wealth of our nation be increased?
8. Do you think that an estimate of the value of education should be included in the measurement of our wealth? If so, how do you suggest that it be measured?
9. What is the relationship between economic theory and economic policy?
10. Explain why there are frequently different opinions or judgments among economists on matters of economic policy.

## SUGGESTED READINGS

American Enterprise Institute for Public Policy Research. "Dialogue on World Oil." *National Energy Study 4* (November, 1974).

Boulding, Kenneth E. *Economics as a Science*. New York: McGraw-Hill Book Company, Inc., 1970.

Cole, Charles L. *The Economic Fabric of Society*. New York: Harcourt Brace Jovanovich, Inc., 1969.

Du Pont de Nemours & Co., E. I. "Can the World Feed Itself?" *Context*, No. 4 (1974).

Eastburn, David P. "Economic Man vs. Social Man." *Business Review*, Federal Reserve Bank of Philadelphia (October, 1970).

Eyestowe, Robert. *Political Economy: Politics and Policy Analysis*. Chicago: Markham Publishing Company, 1972.

Galbraith, John Kenneth. *Economics and the Public Purpose*. Boston: Houghton Mifflin Company, 1973.

Greenspan, Alan. "The Challenge to Our System." Reprinted by American Enterprise Institute, No. 13 (1973).

Heilbroner, Robert L., and Arthur M. Ford. *Is Economics Relevant?* Pacific Palisades, Calif.: Goodyear Publishing Co., Inc., 1971.

"Income Distribution and Its Measurement." *Monthly Review*, Federal Reserve Bank of Richmond (August, 1971).

Marsh, Donald. *Grammar of Economics*. New York: Alfred A. Knopf, Inc., 1967. Chapters 1 and 2.

Marshall, Alfred. *Principles of Economics*. London: Collier Macmillan Publishers, 1961. Chapters 1 and 2.

Nickson, Jack W., Jr. *Economics and Social Choice*, 2d ed. New York: McGraw-Hill Book Company, Inc., 1974.

Parsons, S. A. *How to Find Out About Economics*. Elmsford, N.Y.: Pergamon Press, Inc., 1973.

Robbins, Lionel Charles. *The Nature and Significance of Economic Science*. London: Collier Macmillan Publishers, 1948.

Schultze, Charles L. "Is Economics Obsolete? No, Underemployed." *Saturday Review* (January 22, 1972).

Stans, Maurice H. *To 1990 – A Long Look Ahead*. Washington: U.S. Goverment Printing Office, 1970.

# 2 THE PROCESS OF ECONOMIZING

## WHAT IS ECONOMIZING?

Our material wants are nearly insatiable. No matter how much in the way of material goods and services we obtain, there is generally something else we would like to have. On the other hand, the means by which we obtain goods and services are usually limited. In other cases there may be a shortage of the goods and services themselves. *Economizing* is the process of applying scarce means in an endeavor to satisfy unlimited wants.

### Individuals Must Economize

Very few of us have all the means, or money, necessary to obtain all the goods and services we desire. Consequently, we buy first those things we need and then those we desire the most, and we do without the others. We consciously or unconsciously form a subjective scale of preference for goods and services and purchase accordingly.

In a family it frequently comes down to the point where Mom and Dad must decide whether to buy new bowling balls or new shoes for the children. Of course, in such a case the children would get the shoes (we hope!). Perhaps Mom and Dad are fortunate enough to have the pleasure of choosing between new bowling balls or new golf clubs. On a rare occasion they may find that all the bills are paid, the children are in good health, their clothes and shoes are in good condition, the house is in good repair, and the car is running smoothly. In such a case they might be able to consider buying the bowling balls and the golf clubs.

As an individual, you are forced to economize daily. Perhaps you have deliberated as to whether to buy a new car or to repair the old one. As a result of buying necessities, you frequently must give up such things as fine clothes, amusements, dates, and elaborate vacations. Even if you have a new car, mod clothes, and the like, upon contemplation you will realize that you had to give up other things to get these items. Thus, you are continually economizing when you apply scarce means, in this case money, to your unlimited wants.

## Nations Must Economize

We economize not only on an individual basis but also on a national scale. No country has all the means necessary to satisfy the wants of its people. It must use the available labor, land, and capital to produce the maximum amount of goods and services. The total output and standard of living of any nation are dependent upon the extent of and the use of the following: (1) population, (2) natural resources, (3) technological development, and (4) entrepreneurship, which are common terms for the factors of production when referring to them on a national scale.

**Population**    Generally the larger the population of a given nation, the greater is the total production of goods and services of that nation. Total output and the standard of living are influenced, however, by the composition and age structure of the population, the educational level of the population and the size of the labor force, the skill and the mobility of the labor force, and the industriousness and psychological attitude of the people.

**Natural Resources**    Since land, including natural resources, is an essential factor of production, it stands to reason that the greater the amount of such resources at the disposal of a nation the greater is that nation's productive potential. Natural resources consist of land space, raw materials, sources of power, and atmospheric conditions.

The topography of the land, for example, has a definite effect on its use. Mountainous or swampy lands are not conducive to residential or industrial development. The fertility of the soil affects the total output of crops. A nation with ample forests, coal, petroleum, iron ore, and other minerals is in a better position economically than a nation that lacks these resources. Rivers, lakes, and coastal waters are important not only as means of transporation and for the development of power, but also as possible sources of food and minerals. The land also gives us our sources of energy. Heat, water, steam, electric, and even nuclear power are derived or developed from the use of land, raw materials, and atmospheric conditions.

The Arabian oil embargo of 1973–1974, which resulted in fuel shortages, energy crises, and production shortfalls in many Western economies, manifests the heavy reliance of industrial nations on the resources of the land.

**Technological Development**    The degree of technological development has an important bearing on total production. People can produce more with the assistance of machinery, better technical processes, and the use of industrial power than they can with manual labor alone.

The continuous increase in the standard of living in most countries over the past decades has resulted from the use of better machinery and equipment. The development of better fuels to operate new and powerful machines, the discovery of new chemical mixtures that result in new products, the processing of minerals in new ways which make them less costly, the use of computers, and other developments all tend to enhance the output of goods and services and to improve their quality. Tremendous strides have been made in total production as a result of the development of electrical energy. Currently we are living in an era that will see even greater gains from the development of atomic energy and nuclear power. Furthermore, attempts are now being made to harness solar energy for industrial use.

**Entrepreneurship**    Although people have been able to make use of their labor, natural resources, and even capital equipment to produce goods and services, greater productivity can be obtained by a proper combination and direction of the use of these resources. Therefore, knowledge of how to utilize resources efficiently, and the production and allocation of goods and services among the people are important. Leaders with foresight and organizational ability are required. There also must be a proper framework or economic system within which they can work. In this regard, the nature and types of business enterprises, the monetary system, the capital structure of various industries, and the extent of government regulation have an influence upon the entrepreneurial activities within a nation and, therefore, upon the total production and standard of living.

### Economizing in the United States

In the United States we are blessed with an excellent combination of the four factors of production. First, we have a skilled, versatile, and mobile labor force of more than 90 million out of a total population of 212 million. Second, we have an abundant supply of natural resources. A study of economic geography will reveal that our resources are as good as, if not better than, those found in any other country of the world. Therefore, we have the raw materials from which we can produce an abundance of goods and services. Third, we have the highest degree of industrial technological development in the world. The average industrial worker has access to about $25,000 worth of machinery and equipment. In some industries, such as petroleum and electrical power, the investment per worker exceeds $100,000.

Consider for a minute the increases in productivity brought about by the use of farm machinery. A person tilling the soil with a hand shovel would be lucky to cover a quarter of an acre in one day. If he were to make a crude plow and have it drawn by horse as he guided it, he could work a few acres a day. With a modern tractor, however, he can easily plow ten or more acres a day. At harvest time one person with a combine can thresh 1,000 bushels of wheat per day.

The same is true for workers in other sectors of our economy. The painter with the spray gun can cover more area than a painter with the paint brush; the excavator with a bulldozer can move more dirt than a person with a wheelbarrow; the tailor can sew faster on a machine than by hand. Mechanization has increased cigarette production immeasurably, and assembly lines have boosted automobile production.

Today, machines and processes are also permitting us to make better use of brain power. For example, how long would it take you to do your math problems without log tables or a slide rule? A giant computer in use at one of our large jet aircraft manufacturers can complete in 10 minutes the calculations it would require a mathematician seven years to do on a desk calculator. Complex but routine calculation done by machinery frees the engineer to devote more time to new developments. The more machinery and equipment at the disposal of the worker, the greater is the productivity. Capital, as well as technological development, is truly responsible for much of our productivity.

In the United States we also have a high degree of entrepreneurial efficiency. We seem to have the technique and the ability for getting goods and services produced. We have developed a large body of managerial techniques, and we place considerable emphasis on the training of young people for positions in business. For example, nowhere else in the world can one find business schools at the university level to the extent that we have them in the United States. In recent years, however, a number of nations in Europe, Asia, and South America have been establishing graduate schools of business patterned after some of our outstanding American schools.

The United States today has the highest per capita output, as well as the highest total output, of goods and services among the major countries of the world. In 1974 we produced $1,397 billion worth of goods and services. This was nearly double the output of the Soviet Union, which was second in total production. On a per capita basis we produced over $6,000 for each person in the economy. Although the U.S. for decades has been the world leader in production and income, some nations are now beginning to approach our level on a per capita basis. Output per capita in Sweden, for example, is 92 percent of the U.S. level; Canada, 85 percent; West Germany, 80 percent; and France, 70 percent. On the other hand, U.S. output per capita is still double that of such major nations as Great Britain, the Soviet Union, Japan, and Italy.

The differences between absolute and per capita production of various countries are interesting. For instance, the Soviet Union does not rank nearly so high when its output is stated on a per capita basis. The same holds true for China and India. On the other hand, the output of Sweden, New Zealand, and Switzerland, although small in total, still provides a relatively high per capita income for the people of those nations. From another point of view, there is a wide difference in the level of per capita income between the developed and the poor or underdeveloped nations. In many cases production in the developed nations is 20 to 40 times greater than in the underdeveloped nations.

Our problems of economizing in America, choosing whether to use our resources to build highways or new homes, whether to buy a color TV set or to take a vacation, whether to go to college or to buy a car, are much more pleasant to deal with than the problem of economizing faced by many nations in which they must decide which crop will render the greatest yield from the land in order to feed the masses. But the United States and other industrial nations must start paying more attention to the process of economizing. With the accelerated depletion of world resources, the squeeze on energy, and the food shortages that have occurred throughout the world in recent years, there is a need to utilize resources and manpower more effectively to maximize output for the satisfaction of basic necessities and wants.

## Problem Nations

Unfortunately some areas of the world do not seem to have the proper ratio of population, resources, and technological development. In fact, we should consider ourselves very fortunate to live in a country that has all the necessary requisites for a large output and a high standard of living. It is something to be really thankful for when we consider that one half of the world population of 3.8 billion are living at the bare level of subsistence and go to bed hungry every night. Because of the lack of one or more of the essentials, productivity is insufficient to provide them with the basic requirements and necessities for a comfortable living.

**Nature and Scope of Problems**    Millions of people suffer from economic privation. Although mainland China, with its 800 million people, is said to have ample resources, it lacks the capital investment needed for the utilization of its resources, for the development of an adequate transportation system, and for the buildings, machinery, and equipment necessary to process the raw materials into finished products. What little is produced must be shared by an exceptionally large number of people. Thus, the per capita output or income is very small, amounting to approximately $200 per person. The countries of India and Pakistan are in a similar situation with their 667 million people, only moderate resources, and a shortage of capital.

Japan must economize very wisely to produce a sufficient amount to support 105 million people from the production of a land area that is about the size of Montana. Imagine what would happen if we were to crowd one half of the people of the United States into the state of Montana and tell them to feed and clothe themselves directly or indirectly from the resources of that area alone.

In spite of its large population that includes a skilled labor force, and its moderate degree of technological efficiency, Italy has a relatively low annual per capita income and output ($2,170). This is due in large part to its lack of resources. The situation in Italy is further aggravated by the fact that its technological development is not great enough to permit

Italian producers to import resources, to process them into finished goods, and then to sell the finished goods in competition with other industrial nations in foreign markets. Thus, the resources and the technological efficiency are inadequate to provide a comfortable level of living for many of the more than 54 million people of Italy.

Some areas are underdeveloped technologically, others lack natural resources, and some are plagued by a shortage of population. In colonial days the United States had an inadequate labor supply for proper development. Thus, various schemes were adopted to help populate the country with workers.

Even today there is a shortage of workers in Canada, Australia, New Zealand, and some other countries of the world. In these countries there is also a need for capital. In fact, the Gordon Commission Report on the future economic development of Canada issued several years ago stressed the need for increased population and recommended liberalization of the immigration laws. As the result of ample resources plus technological development, Canada and New Zealand rate high in per capita income among the nations of the world. Thus, population may cause trouble by being either excessive compared to the land area or by being too small.

**A Solution — Increased Productivity**   Frequently when a country finds itself lacking the population and/or natural resources necessary for a high level of output, it can overcome the deficiency with ingenuity and fortitude. Japan, for example, has been offsetting its lack of resources in the past few decades with an exceptionally high degree of industrial efficiency. This permits Japan to import raw materials, to process them into finished goods, and to sell them in the domestic and foreign markets at a profit.

A shortage of resources or labor may be overcome by discovery of new sources, the development of new and better techniques, and the use of better machinery which produces greater yields from existing sources. During World War II, for example, there was much discussion about the adequacy of our oil reserves. Consequently, large oil companies, aided by government tax allowances, accelerated oil exploration activities. Subsequently, new major pools of oil were discovered in such places as the Middle East, Latin America, many offshore sites in the U.S. and elsewhere, and more recently in Alaska and Mexico. In addition, the oil companies, along with government agencies, began to experiment after World War II with the production of shale oil. Early attempts to extract oil from shale were hindered because the costs were prohibitive. With improved mechanization and the use of atomic energy, however, the production of shale oil became more competitive with other sources of oil. Shale oil production was given a substantial boost as a result of the shortages and higher prices brought about by the Arabian oil embargo in 1973–1974. A similar development has also taken place in the experimentation of oil production from the tar sand fields of Canada, which today are contributing noticeably to our petroleum supplies.

Such examples of ways in which productivity has been increased can be multiplied thousands of times. Synthetic fibers for real fibers, plastics for metals, electric energy in place of water power, and other similar developments have increased productivity. In the future we will witness more extensive use of atomic and solar energy, commercial processing of seawater to extract its mineral contents, and new and better machines that will do things we now consider highly improbable. All such developments will ease the problem of economizing by obtaining more productivity from existing resources. People who have the ability to offset their shortages will improve their standard of living.

**Aid to Underdeveloped Nations**    Many nations, however, do not have the resources, the skilled labor force, or the technological ability to make offsetting changes for improvement in their standard of living. Furthermore, many of them are producing at the level of subsistence and are unable to devote resources to capital formation. Nations such as Nigeria, Uganda, Burma, Nepal, and Haiti have per capita output equivalent to less than 100 American dollars. Three dozen nations, approximately one third of the world's total countries, have annual per capita output of $300 or less as compared to annual per capita output of over $6,000 in the United States and outputs in excess of $2,000 per capita in most developed nations. These underdeveloped nations, many in which the rate of productivity is increasing at a slower rate than the population growth, need outside help. To alleviate hunger, poverty, and sickness, they need short-run aid in the form of food, clothing, and medical assistance. To solve their basic economic problem, however, they need long-run assistance in the form of technical assistance and the infusion of capital. It is for this reason that a blue-ribbon committee of the World Bank has suggested that each developed nation contribute an amount equivalent to seven-tenths of one percent of its GNP in the form of aid to underdeveloped nations.

## SPECIALIZATION AND EXCHANGE

Productivity determines income, and income determines our standard of living. Therefore, it behooves each individual or nation to increase its productivity. One way of achieving this goal is through the use of specialization and exchange.

### Nature of Specialization and Exchange

*Specialization* is the process by which an individual, a firm, a geographic area, or a nation limits the scope of its productive efforts instead of trying to produce everything that is needed by that unit in our economy. In this way the unit can become very proficient in production. *Exchange* is the process of trading the excess of specialized commodities over and above the needs of the individuals who produce them to others for goods required or desired by the specialists. We can produce more through such cooperation than we can individually.

As we have said, in our economy individuals, firms, geographic areas, and the nation as a whole specialize. Individuals usually concentrate on a particular occupation or profession. Most firms engage in the production of a limited number of items. Many parts of the country concentrate on the production of certain products, such as cotton in the South, cattle in the Southwest, and manufactures in the North and East. From an international point of view, Brazil is greatly dependent on coffee, Argentina on beef, Cuba on sugar, and England on industrial commodities.

An economy of specialization and exchange yields higher individual and total incomes than an economy characterized by self-sufficiency. Specialization gives an individual an opportunity to become more proficient in one particular field of endeavor. Therefore, the total production is greater than it would be if each person endeavored to produce all the goods and services that are needed and desired.

Consider what would happen if the members of your class were to pool their resources, then buy a plot of land and subdivide it, and each individual were to build a house. There no doubt would be some poorly constructed houses among the group because very few of us have the necessary ability, knowledge, or experience to build a good house. Even if each individual were able to complete a house, it would take a considerable period of time in which to do it. Think how much wiser it would be to check the class before starting. You might find among its members an architect, an electrician, a few carpenters, some bricklayers, a plumber, and other skilled laborers. You could let each person work in his or her specialized field, using the rest of the class members as helpers to do the unskilled labor. If the architect designed all the houses, the electricians wired them, and the carpenters, the bricklayers, the plumber, and others did their respective types of work on each house, the job of building all the houses could be completed much sooner and you would have better houses.

## Limits to Specialization and Exchange

Our American economy utilizes specialization and exchange to a high degree. This process has played an important role in raising our standard of living over the years. Very few of our people are self-sufficient even though they may not be specialized in one field. The degree of specialization and exchange is limited, however, by the size of the market. It is not profitable to engage in this process if the sale of the items produced is insufficient to provide the producer with a decent standard of living, or if one cannot produce enough to become any more efficient than others. Thus, we must look at the market. If it is adequate in size, then specialization and exchange have merit.

For example, a tremendous amount of specialization and exchange and a very fine *division of labor* (breakdown and simplification of jobs) exists in the automobile industry. A few decades ago, if you were to observe the workers on a motor assembly line, you could watch the engines pass by an individual worker's station at the rate of 5 or 6 per minute. During the few seconds the engine was passing through a given station, a person could do only a limited amount of work on it. Therefore, you might have seen one person do nothing but start by hand six hex nuts on the motor studs. The next person would tighten the nuts with a pneumatic wrench gun. The worker in the next station would insert cotter pins in the studs, and the following worker would simply bend them with a pair of pliers. As a result of this division of labor and specialization, each worker became very efficient in the job and more engines could be turned out each day than would be possible if each individual started from scratch and built a complete engine. Today these functions are still performed, but many of them are done by machines in the automation process. When a company produces hundreds of thousands of automobiles a year, the process of specialization and exchange is profitable. However, it would not be profitable if the total demand for autos amounted to only one or two thousand a year.

The size of the market is determined not only by the size of the population but also by the income or the purchasing power of the population. People cannot buy goods and services if they do not have the means to do so. The size of the market is also affected by the transportation system of the economy. The better and cheaper the system of transportation, the more people that can be reached.

## LAW OF COMPARATIVE ADVANTAGE

An individual, a firm, an area, or a country may develop naturally into an area of specialization, but frequently the principle of economizing must be applied to determine what should be the nature of a producer's specialization.

### Absolute Advantage

When a producer is endeavoring to specialize, it will pay the producer to engage in the type of activity in which he or she has an absolute advantage. Let us assume that a young woman can average $320 a week as a sales engineer. If she works an 8 hour day, 5 days a week, this amounts to $64 a day or $8 an hour. Suppose, however, that she must take time out, 2 hours a day, to type her reports. That means that she can engage in her professional work only 6 hours a day, or 30 hours a week. As a result, her earnings are reduced to $240 a week, or $48 a day. She would be much wiser to devote a full 8 hours a day to her sales engineering and to hire a stenographer, who probably could do a neater, more accurate, and faster typing job at less expense. If she were to pay the stenographer $3.00 an hour for typing 2 hours each day, her net earnings would be $58 a day ($64 minus a $6 payment to the stenographer) instead of the $48 she would make if she did her own typing. Thus, she would be better off to engage in her specialty and to let the stenographer do the typing, which is that person's specialty.

Similar situations occur when one section of a country is more proficient than another in the production of certain commodities. Texas can grow cotton better than Iowa. Thus, it specializes in cotton while Iowa concentrates in corn, and the two states exchange their products.

### Comparative Advantage

When each of two parties has an absolute advantage over the other in the production of a particular commodity or service, it is easy enough to decide the respective areas of specialization. But what happens when one party can produce two commodities or services more efficiently than a second party? Should the individual or the country with the absolute advantage produce both commodities for itself? Although one producer has the advantage in the production of either commodity, it is economically wise to specialize in the production of that commodity in which that producer has the greater comparative advantage, and let the other produce that commodity in which it has the lesser comparative disadvantage. This is the *principle of comparative advantage*.

Let us again consider the sales engineer. Suppose that, in addition to being a first-class sales engineer, she is more efficient in typing than anyone else whom she might hire. She might be able to type in one hour what it takes a regular typist two hours to do. Therefore, she reasons that instead of hiring a stenographer to do the work, she should do it herself. Is she right in doing her own typing as well as selling? This young woman may be an outstanding sales engineer and very proficient on the keyboard, but she missed out on economics somewhere along the line. If she does her own typing, she still must take time out, say one hour each day, from her selling to do so. This means that she would net $56 a day (7 hours times $8 an hour). But if she hired the typist, she could devote her full time to sales work. Her gross earnings would be $64 a day; and after she pays the stenographer $6 ($3 an hour for 2 hours) for typing services, she would have a net income of $58 per day. Thus, the sales engineer would be better off to specialize in that service in which she has the greater comparative advantage, sales engineering, and let the stenographer perform that service in which she has the lesser comparative disadvantage, typing.

### An Example of Comparative Advantage Among Nations

This same principle of comparative advantage applies to firms, areas, or nations. We shall consider an example from a national point of view.

Disregarding other factors (exchange rates, transportation charges, insurance payments, the law of diminishing returns, and national defense), let us compare two hypothetical countries. Suppose that each of the two countries has 5 units of production and that a productive unit is equal to a certain combination of labor, land, capital and entrepreneurship. Assume that each country devotes 3 units to the production of cotton and the remaining 2 units to the production of wheat. Assume further that Country X produces 30 bales of cotton and 60 bushels of wheat, while Country Y produces only 15 bales of cotton and 40 bushels of wheat. Country X would be more proficient than Country Y in the production of both cotton and wheat, as demonstrated in Table 2-1.

Table 2-1    **PRODUCTION OF COUNTRIES X AND Y BEFORE SPECIALIZATION**

| | Cotton | | Wheat | |
|---|---|---|---|---|
| Country | Productive Units Used | Bales | Productive Units Used | Bushels |
| X | 3 | 30 | 2 | 60 |
| Y | 3 | 15 | 2 | 40 |
| Total | 6 | 45 | 4 | 100 |

This table shows that 10 units of production are being utilized in a manner that yields a total of 45 bales of cotton and 100 bushels of wheat. Furthermore, Country X has an absolute advantage over Country Y in the production of both wheat and cotton.

Now the problem is to decide whether X should produce both cotton and wheat and let Y shift for itself, or whether X should specialize in just one of the commodities. If it were to apply the law of comparative advantage, X would produce the commodity in which it has the greater comparative advantage. According to our example, X should specialize in the production of cotton, for it has a 2 to 1 advantage in the production of this item over Country Y, while it has only a 3 to 2 advantage in the production of wheat. If Country X were to devote all its units of production to cotton, it would be able to produce 50 bales. If Country Y channeled its 3 productive units that had been used for cotton into wheat production, it could produce a total of 100 bushels of wheat. Thus, the new schedule of output can be seen in Table 2-2.

The two countries combined have gained a total of 5 bales of cotton. Now you may ask: Who gets what? That depends upon the exchange between the two countries, but it should work out favorably for both countries. In order to regain its former ratio of wheat to cotton, Country Y would demand 15 bales of cotton, the amount that it gave up in order to specialize, in exchange for 60 bushels of wheat. On the other hand, Country X could afford to give 20 bales of cotton, the amount it obtained

Table 2-2    **PRODUCTION OF COUNTRIES X AND Y AFTER SPECIALIZATION**

| Country | Cotton | | Wheat | |
|---------|------------------------|-------|------------------------|---------|
| | Productive Units Used | Bales | Productive Units Used | Bushels |
| X | 5 | 50 | 0 | — |
| Y | 0 | — | 5 | 100 |
| Total | 5 | 50 | 5 | 100 |

through specialization, in exchange for 60 bushels of wheat and still lose nothing compared to what it originally had. It is easy to engage in trade when one country needs only 15 bales of cotton and the other can afford to give as much as 20 bales of cotton for 60 bushels of wheat.

The exchange ratio of wheat to cotton will be set by haggling and bargaining between the two countries, and final settlements will depend upon many economic circumstances. If we assume that the countries are of equal economic strength, they might split the difference and set the exchange ratio at 17.5 bales of cotton for 60 bushels of wheat. Trading on this basis, assume that Country X exports 17.5 bales of cotton, reducing its total used domestically to 32.5 bales. This means that each country would have 2.5 more bales of cotton than it had when each country produced both wheat and cotton. In exchange for the cotton, Country Y would have to send to Country X 60 bushels of wheat. The amount of wheat remaining in Country Y would be 40 bushels, which would be the same amount it had under the first plan. Country X would have 60 bushels of wheat, the same amount it had before any specialization and exchange took place. The final position after the specialization and exchange would show a total gain of 5 bales of cotton, 2.5 for Country X and 2.5 for Country Y. Both would have the same amount of wheat as they formerly produced. This is depicted in Table 2-3. In this simple example both nations benefited by utilizing the principle of comparative advantage. In actual trade, however, many additional complex factors must be considered.

Table 2-3    **GAINS RESULTING FROM SPECIALIZATION**

| Country | Cotton (Bales) | Wheat (Bushels) |
|---------|----------------|-----------------|
| X[1] | 32.5 | 60 |
| Y | 17.5 | 40 |
| Total | 50.0 | 100 |

[1] X imports wheat from Y and exports cotton to Y.

## Comparative Advantage in Practice

Much can be gained by putting the principle of comparative advantage into practice. Individuals make use of it when they choose one occupation or profession in preference to another. Large firms increase their profits in this manner. For example, large automobile producers can make most of the parts that are necessary for the manufacture of cars. They buy most of the parts from independent suppliers, however, and devote most of their time, money, and effort to the actual assembly of the automobiles. Other companies build stores, sell them to a second party, and then rent them back. This permits them to use their money and time in their retail businesses instead of becoming part-time landlords.

A large portion of the sectional or regional trade within our nation is based on the law of comparative advantage. As a result we have a cotton belt, a wheat belt, a dairyland, a cattle area, steel-producing centers, textile-producing areas, and an automobile region. Since much of our international trade is based on this principle, we have similar areas of concentration throughout the world. For example, we see the concentration of coffee production in Brazil, sugar in Cuba, rubber in Malaya, tea in China, silk in Japan, ships in England, and automobiles in the United States.

## Limitations to Comparative Advantage

Although the use of specialization and exchange along with the principle of comparative advantage can increase productivity and enhance the standard of living, a region or nation must be careful not to overspecialize. An economy made up of specialists without anyone to direct its overall activity may not be able to accomplish its maximum potential. Furthermore, undue dependence upon one or a few products by a region or a nation can lead to difficulty if the demand for those products fluctuates or collapses. For example, Detroit is vulnerable to business recessions because of its heavy concentration of automobile production. When auto sales fall off to any considerable degree, widespread layoffs in Detroit occur. Likewise, the economy of Cuba is largely affected by the demand for sugar, just as the demand for coffee has a major influence on business activity in Brazil. It is economically wise to specialize, but it should not be overdone. Some diversification in production is beneficial.

Whether or not it is advantageous to specialize and to adhere to the principle of comparative advantage depends to a large degree on the demands of the market. There is no reason to produce goods and services if the people of the economy are not willing to buy them. Since consumption is the ultimate end of economic activity, we must channel our manpower, resources, and capital into the production of those commodities that are demanded by individuals in the economy.

Military consideration is another factor that limits the use of the principle of comparative advantage. Even though it may be more costly to produce certain goods domestically, it may be wiser in the long run to do so if those commodities are essential to military production. In the event that a war should occur, a country may be cut off from its source of supply. This occurred in World War II when the Japanese invasion of Southeast Asia cut off the United States from its rubber supply in Malaya. As a result, we encouraged and even subsidized the production of synthetic rubber in spite of its higher cost. Subsequent developments in the production of artificial rubber have made it comparable in price to natural rubber.

### SUMMARY

Economizing is a process of applying scarce means in an endeavor to satisfy virtually unlimited wants. Both individuals and nations must economize. Nations have the problem of making the best use of population, natural resources, technological development, and entrepreneurial functions to obtain maximum production.

Total production will be affected by the composition and age structure of the population, size of the labor force, the skill and the mobility of the labor force, and the industriousness and psychological attitude of the people. Productive ability also depends upon the natural resources of a nation, including the available land space, raw materials, sources of power, and atmospheric conditions. Technological development, whether it is in the form of better machinery and equipment, finer technological processes, or greater energy affects production. Even with ample population, resources, and technological efficiencies, a high degree of entrepreneurial skill is necessary to get the goods from the raw material stage to the market for the finished product.

Some nations, due to the presence of more or better factors of production, have a larger output and therefore larger income than other less fortunate nations. The United States leads the world in the production of goods and services and the level of income.

Total production can be enhanced by the use of specialization and exchange, but it has certain limits. Specialization and exchange operate in conjunction with the principle of comparative advantage. This principle states that a productive unit which has an absolute advantage over another in the production of two commodities should produce that commodity in which it has the greater comparative advantage, and the other producer should produce the commodity in which it has the lesser comparative disadvantage.

Whether the government be socialistic, communistic, or capitalistic, the basic function of any economic system is to provide the framework for economizing. There must be some way of deciding what and how much is to be produced, the manner in which it will be produced, and the means by which goods and services will be distributed to the people in the economy. Although it is interesting to compare the operations of different economic systems, we will concentrate on the American economy in which we live. In this regard we will endeavor to learn the motivation and method of production, distribution, and consumption of goods and services. Let us turn our attention in the next chapter to this problem.

## DISCUSSION QUESTIONS

1. Indicate to what extent you engage in the process of economizing in your everyday activities.
2. Is it true that an increase in population in a given nation will result in a decrease in the standard of living? Why or why not?
3. How will the development of nuclear energy or other new means of power affect the problem of economizing?
4. Should the nations with an abundance of resources share them in some way with nations that have inadequate resources for the attainment of a reasonable standard of living?
5. Cite any instances you can in which the development of machinery or a new process has made it possible to produce commodities whose former costs were too high to warrant large-scale production.
6. What do you think of the recommendation that the United States and other developed countries contribute an amount equivalent to $7/10$ of 1 percent of its GNP in the form of aid to underdeveloped nations?
7. The European Coal and Steel Community, established in 1952, provides for the sharing of resources by several nations of natural resources located within certain areas of Europe. What is the significance of such an operation in regard to the imbalance of resources throughout the world?
8. What do you think of the suggestion that the United States rent some of its unused farm lands to other nations and permit these nations' citizens to work the land and ship the commodities back home where there is a food shortage?
9. Indicate some ways in which you or your friends practice the law of comparative advantage.
10. Do you think a nation should try to become as economically independent as possible? Why or why not?

## SUGGESTED READINGS

Crocker, Thomas D., and A. J. Rogers III. *Environmental Economics*. Hinsdale, Ill.: The Dryden Press, 1971.

Enthoven, Alan C., and A. Myrick Freeman III (eds.). *Pollution, Resources and the Environment*. New York: W. W. Norton & Company, Inc., 1973.

Galbraith, John Kenneth. *The Affluent Society*, rev. ed. New York: The New American Library, 1970. Chapters 8–10.

Grossman, Gregory. *Economic Systems*. Englewood Cliffs, N.J.: Prentice-Hall, Inc., 1967.

Heilbroner, Robert L. *The Making of Economic Society*, 5th ed. Englewood Cliffs, N.J.: Prentice-Hall, Inc., 1975.

Kelso, Louis O., and Mortimer J. Adler. *Capitalist Manifesto*. New York: Random House, Inc., 1958.

Liles, Patrick R. "Who Are the Entrepreneurs?" *MSU Business Topics* (Winter, 1974).

"Making U.S. Technology More Competitive." *Business Week* (January, 1972).

McCracken, Paul W., *et al. The Energy Crisis*. Washington: American Enterprise Institute for Public Policy Research, 1974.

Root, Franklin R. *International Trade and Investment*, 3d ed. Cincinnati: South-Western Publishing Co., 1973.

Rostow, W. W. *Stages of Economic Growth*. New York: Cambridge University Press, 1960. Chapters 1 and 2.

Schramm, John C. *The Free Market and the Public Interest*. Wilton, Conn.: The Calvin K. Kazanjoam Foundation, Inc., 1964.

*Social Responsibilities of Business Corporations*. New York: Committee for Economic Development, 1971.

# 3 OUR ECONOMIC SYSTEM

## FREE ENTERPRISE CAPITALISM

Basic economic questions apply to any type of economic system. Decisions on what to produce, how much to produce, and what method to adopt in allocating goods and services are confronted by any society, but the questions are answered in different ways. We shall first consider fundamental principles and policies in terms of the American economy. Analysis of an economic environment with which you are already familiar will facilitate any later comparisons of other economic systems.

A *free enterprise capitalistic system*, or *market economy*, is distinguished from other types of economic systems by the fact that the decisions as to what and how much to produce, and the manner in which goods and services are to be allocated, are made primarily by the actions of individuals and firms in the economy. Both socialism and communism, on the other hand, advocate a considerable degree of government direction and control of the production and distribution functions of their economies.

Under our *capitalistic system*, capital goods are owned and used mainly by individuals and firms in the economy, rather than by governmental agencies. This capital may be in the form of machinery, equipment, and buildings, or it may be represented by money that can be used to purchase these capital goods. The institution of private property is essential to a capitalistic system. This implies more than the ownership of real estate. It means that individuals not only have the right to own, use, or sell machinery, equipment, and buildings, but that they also have the right to the ownership of the fruits of their productivity. Thus, when the farmer grows cotton on his land with the use of his labor and capital, the cotton becomes his property and he can dispose of it as he sees fit. In a similar fashion, a firm that produces shoes is entitled to the ownership of the shoes and can sell them if it desires. After compensating the owners of the other resources that have contributed to the production of the shoes, the firm is entitled to what is left of the total revenue. This residual return is called *profit*, and profit is the incentive for obtaining and using capital goods to produce goods and services that satisfy consumer needs.

37

### The Profit Incentive

Under the free enterprise system individuals may offer their services to someone else in exchange for a wage payment, let someone use their land in exchange for rent, or lend their money to another in exchange for an interest payment. On the other hand, instead of selling productive services to another, a person can combine several factors of production to produce goods and sell them at a profit. But to operate a business, one must produce goods or services that people want and must offer them at a price they are willing to pay. The farmer who grows cotton and sells it at a profit is benefiting not only himself but also the community by supplying a basic commodity that is needed or desired. Likewise, the shoe producer is satisfying people's wants for shoes in addition to making a profit. Since the cotton grower and shoe producer may use the labor, land, and capital of others, they provide jobs and income for other members of the community. Thus, in a model situation the producer, in the process of using property to make a profit, will increase the well-being of other people. To be successful, consumer demand must be satisfied. In some situations, however, the producer may suffer a loss or may exploit people by supplying them with an inferior product or by underpaying the factors of production that are utilized.

In the operation of our economic system, the ultimate use of our manpower and resources and the allocation of goods and services are determined primarily by consumer demand. Individuals express their demand in the prices they are willing to pay. Usually the stronger the demand, other things being equal, the higher the price that consumers will pay for a particular good or service. In an effort to make a profit, people in business cater to consumer demand. Through the prices we are willing to pay as consumers, businesses obtain the revenue necessary to purchase the manpower, resources, and capital goods necessary for producing the goods and services that are demanded. The opportunity to make profits serves as an incentive for businesses to produce these goods and services.

If the demand for a particular commodity is strong enough, it will be produced. Sometimes, however, there is such a large demand for total goods and services that we do not have sufficient manpower and capital to produce all of them. What, then, is produced? Once again, in a model system it is the consumers who decide. The firms and industries with the strongest demand for their products will have the revenues necessary to bid relatively scarce productive agents away from other uses. If consumer demand for a particular commodity is weak and the price offer is so low that it does not permit sufficient profit to the producer, few resources will be devoted to its production.

### The Role of Competition

Free enterprise capitalism, resting as it does on the institution of private property and on the profit incentive, relies upon *competition* to make the system function. Business firms compete for shares of the consumer's dollar. In the markets for productive resources they compete for scarce resources. In a command economy, production quotas are assigned to firms by a political leader or a planning committee. Similarly, resources are directed to employment in various industries. When allocation decisions are decentralized, however, competition serves to regulate the volume of output and the allocation of resources.

If competition is effective, the economy functions efficiently without an overseer. Through competition consumers are protected against the marketing of shoddy products and the charging of exorbitant prices. The prospect that rival firms will offer a better product at the same price or a comparable product at a lower price forces each firm to maintain quality and restrict price increases. Resource owners are protected against exploitation by the opportunity of alternative employments made available by competitive firms. The possibility open to the resource owner of selling resource services to the highest bidder prevents any one firm from keeping resources in its own employ at depressed prices. In this way effective competition regulates the power of business firms, preventing any one firm from dominating the market. Each firm is free to pursue its own profit without direct concern for the overall allocation of resources and products in the economy. Yet the impersonal force of competition assures the regulation of production and the flow of resources toward the most efficient firms that can afford to offer the highest prices for the factors of production.

Of course, competition is not always effective, and it is seldom perfect. Sometimes business firms may be able to exclude others from the industry and thereby exercise almost unlimited control over price, industry output, and employment conditions. When this happens, it is deemed the responsibility of government to restore competitive conditions. Rather than taking control of the industry or assuming ownership of the means of production, the central political authority is expected to impose legal sanctions against restraint of competition or abuses that are defended in the name of competition.

The guiding principle of competitive capitalism is that privately owned business firms should produce the goods and services wanted by consumers in the quantities they wish to consume. So that firms may satisfy consumer wants by pursuing the immediate goal of profit, competition is relied upon as a mechanism for regulating trade. Only where it is believed that competition cannot be made to work effectively — such as police and fire protection or public utilities — does the government operate to influence or control production. Otherwise the government is expected to create and enforce laws which assure that at least minimal conditions of competition will prevail.

## Price as a Rationing Mechanism

Although consumer demand is the primary determinant of what and how much is produced, the decisions are by no means made unilaterally by consumers. Supply also has an influence on the price of commodities and therefore on the determination of what and how much is to be produced. Because of a shortage in the supply of particular resources, consumers may have to pay a higher price than they desire to obtain a particular good or service. In such a case, they will have to pay the price or go without it. Thus, price serves as a rationing mechanism to decide who among the consumers will receive the particular good or service. It will be those who are willing and able to pay the highest price.

**Prices Allocate Factors of Production**  In determining what and how much to produce, our capitalistic system works in a democratic manner based upon dollar votes. Other things being equal, the use of resources and manpower is determined by the total number of dollars spent on particular goods and services. Thus, the more dollars an individual or group accumulates in some manner or other, the greater the potential influence for determining what is to be produced. Although this is a democratic process according to dollar votes, it is not necessarily democratic as to personal preferences. In fact, since those with the most dollars have the most votes, inequities may develop. If certain individuals or groups acquire an excessive number of dollars, it could be detrimental to the economy in general as well as to other individuals in particular. For example, large amounts of dollars hoarded rather than being spent or invested could lead to a decrease in business activity and result in unemployment and loss of income for workers and lower profits for business. Even when all dollars are spent, one can envision a situation in which an economy might be producing a great number of palatial homes, high-priced cars, and yachts, while the community is deprived of much needed low-cost housing. There might be much spending on entertainment and on frivolities in the economy in general while some families are short of basic necessities and modern conveniences.

**Prices Help Determine Incomes**  Individuals through consumer demand not only determine what and how much is produced in the economy, but they also determine, in part, the incomes paid to the various factors of production in the form of wages, rent, interest, and profits. Revenue from the sale of commodities provides businesses with the means by which they can obtain labor, land, and capital to produce the goods demanded. The payment of income to the owners of these factors or resources serves as their means to purchase a certain portion of the goods and services produced by the economy. Although many other things (such as the productivity of the factor of production, its supply, government regulations, the presence or absence of a labor union and other institutional forces) have a direct bearing on the payment of income to each of the various factors, the ultimate source of income payments to the factors of production is generally the revenue from consumer demand. In a model system each factor is remunerated according to its economic contribution toward the commodity or service being produced. In turn, its contribution is measured by the price that the firm was willing to pay for it, which in turn would be limited by consumer demand. Thus, our strong demand for automobiles is, in part, the reason why auto workers have historically been among the highest paid workers in the world. The income of a factor of production is affected, on the other hand, by its productivity and scarcity. If the supply of a particular type of skilled labor is limited, such workers will be able to command a higher compensation for their services than will unskilled workers.

## BUSINESS FIRMS

In our economic system the process by which we determine the allocation of our factors of production, the flow of income, and the final distribution of goods and services is facilitated by our business organization. Production for the purpose of satisfying consumer demand in our capitalistic economy usually is undertaken by privately owned enterprises. Some knowledge of the structure of our various types of business firms, therefore, is beneficial for a better understanding of the operation of our economic system.

There are more than 9 million business firms in the United States exclusive of our 2.8 million farms. Most of the firms have less than four employees. Less than $^1/_5$ of 1 percent are considered large firms employing more than 500 employees. The firms in the top 1 percent in size, however, provide approximately three fifths of all jobs in the United States.

There are more business enterprises in services, 34 percent, than in any other nonagricultural category, most of them single proprietorships. The second largest category, wholesalers and retailers, makes up about 31 percent of the firms. In the 6-year period, 1965–1971, the number of wholesale and retail establishments increased by 13 percent. A 12 percent increase came in services, such as TV repair, shoe repair, and cleaners. There was an 11 percent increase in contract construction firms, and finance enterprises showed a 16 percent increase. On the other hand, another of the large categories, manufacturing, had a negligible increase in the number of firms during the same 6-year period, while its total production increased substantially. This unusual phenomenon was caused by the fact that the average size of manufacturing firms increased during the period, partly as a result of mergers and consolidations.

In addition, during the 6-year period, 1965–1971, the total number of enterprises in the United States increased by more than 1,000,000. During that time over 2 million new firms came into existence, but around 1 million discontinued business. Furthermore, many others changed owners during the period.

Starting a business involves a risk, but the opportunity for profit induces hundreds of thousands of individuals annually to try to become successful entrepreneurs. More important than the success or failure of an individual business enterprise, however, is the freedom in our economic system that permits an individual to own property or the means of production, to set up a business, or to work at any job or profession for which he or she is qualified.

## Types of Business Firms

Not only are some business enterprises small and others large, but some are operated by one person while others are operated by several. Furthermore, many firms grow from small one-person operations into giant corporations. There are four basic types of business enterprises in the United States: (1) proprietorships, (2) partnerships, (3) corporations, and (4) cooperatives. Each has certain advantages and disadvantages.

**Single Proprietorships**　The *single proprietorship*, or one-person ownership, was the earliest form of business enterprise. It was used during the Middle Ages and became the predominant type of business in colonial America. It is still the predominant type of business organization in our economy today. At present there are 9.4 million individually owned businesses and farms. In a single proprietorship one individual owns and directs the business. This person risks individual property in the business. If the individual is successful, he or she receives all of the profit; but if the business fails, that person must suffer all the losses.

Ease of entry is one of the major advantages of the single proprietorship. Practically anyone who can accumulate a small amount of savings or can borrow some money can go into business. Another advantage is the flexibility of management in a single proprietorship. Decisions can be made by the proprietor without the necessity of obtaining the approval of a board of directors or of convincing other members of the firm.

One of the biggest disadvantages of the single proprietorship results from the lack of distinction between the business and the owner. If the owner fails, creditors, through court action, may take personal assets, such as the owner's house, automobile, and bonds, as well as the assets of the business, to satisfy the debts. Another disadvantage is the difficulty of raising sufficient funds for a large-scale type of operation. It is also difficult to obtain continuity of the business over an extended period of time, since the death of the owner automatically terminates the proprietorship. The business can, however, continue under a new proprietor.

**Partnerships**　A *partnership*, as defined by the Uniform Partnership Act, which has been adopted in forty states, "is an association of two or more persons to carry on as co-owners a business for profit." The partnership is usually found in small businesses that require a limited amount of capital which can be contributed by the partners. It is also found in professional practices, such as law, dentistry, and accounting, where legal liability for debts is at a minimum. There are at present slightly less than one million active partnerships in operation in our economy.

The partnership has an advantage over the single proprietorship in that it can usually raise more funds to operate the business, since it can obtain funds from the several partners. Another advantage is the diversity of management that it permits. Responsibility for various functions of the business can be divided among the different partners.

On the other hand, the partnership has most of the disadvantages of the single proprietorship, plus a few of its own. Its continuity is uncertain, since the withdrawal or death of a partner legally dissolves the partnership, although the business may be reorganized by the remaining or new partners. In many respects the action of any one partner can bind the partnership. Thus, poor decisions or unsound commitments made by any one partner bind them all. Furthermore, since a partnership, like a single proprietorship, is not a separate legal entity, the partners are legally responsible for the debts of the firm. This means that the personal assets of the partners may be seized if necessary to satisfy partnership debts. Furthermore, each partner is individually liable for all the debts of the partnership incurred while that partner is a member in the firm.

**Corporations**   In the Dartmouth College case in 1819, Chief Justice Marshall described a *corporation* as "an artificial being, invisible, intangible, and existing only in contemplation of law." Thus, a corporation is a separate legal entity apart from its owners. It is a "legal person" in itself. Contracts can be made in the name of the corporation, it can own real estate and other assets, and it can sue and be sued.

The corporation has several advantages over other forms of business enterprise. It has continuity of life since ownership in the form of shares of stock can be transferred without dissolving the corporation. Through the sale of stock it can raise large sums of money. Unlike a single proprietorship or a partnership, the corporate owners have *limited* liability. They can lose only what they have invested in the business. Furthermore, owners can pledge their stock as collateral for personal or business loans, whereas partners cannot pledge their interest in their business for such loans. Since the owners elect a board of directors, who in turn select the management personnel to operate the business, it is relatively easy to remove inefficient managers. Additional funds for expansion of the business can be obtained by issuing more stock or by floating bond issues.

Although a very attractive form of business enterprise, the corporation is not without its disadvantages. It is required to pay income taxes, and the stockholders must pay income taxes on the dividends they receive out of corporate income. No such double taxation exists on single proprietorship or partnership income. The state requires a fee for incorporating a business, and it often charges an annual franchise tax. A corporation can engage only in the business for which it is authorized. Before entering other types of businesses, it must have its charter amended by the state. Various reports must be filed annually in the state in which the business is incorporated, and in many cases in other states in which the corporation may be doing business.

One of the salient features of the corporate form of business enterprise is the fact that business ownership can be spread over a large segment of the population. Any individual can be a capitalist simply by purchasing a few shares of stock. Since most stocks sell for a price of less than $100, it is relatively easy for many persons to become stockholders. In fact, more than 30 million Americans own stock in the 1.7 million corporations in our economy.

**Cooperatives** A *cooperative* is a type of business enterprise owned primarily by the people who use it or buy from it. A cooperative may be incorporated and pay dividends to its stockholders. But unlike the corporation, each stockholder has only one vote in managerial affairs regardless of the amount of stock held by the individual. A major difference between a cooperative and other forms of business enterprise is that the net income, after payment of a nominal dividend to stockholders, is distributed among the customers of the cooperative on a pro rata basis according to their respective purchases from the cooperative.

Although the consumer cooperative has been in existence in the United States approximately 100 years, it has not achieved national significance. A major reason for its lack of acceptance or success in the United States is the fact that our large chain stores and discount stores, operating on a low-markup, large-volume basis, give us commodities at prices which are difficult for the cooperative to meet. Nevertheless, consumer cooperatives are of some significance in many European countries.

In the United States, marketing cooperatives are rather prevalent in agriculture. There are nearly 8,000 cooperatives that market farm commodities and provide farm supplies. Less than 10,000 consumer cooperatives exist in our economy, exclusive of our 23,253 credit unions.

### Business Integration and Combination

Frequently businesses are integrated or combined to provide more efficient operations, to lower costs of production, to offer wider varieties of goods and services, to obtain a larger share of the market, or sometimes just to obtain more power for the business.

One of the greatest eras of industrial combination occurred around the turn of the century. During that time and subsequently, numerous methods have been used for combining businesses. Among the most notable are the merger, the consolidation, the trust, and the holding company. In the past decade 13,000 mergers and acquisitions took place among business organizations.

### COMPETITION IN THE ECONOMY

In a market economy production and distribution are governed principally by a multitude of independent decisions made by individuals and business firms. Buying and selling are coordinated by the decisions of millions of different producers and consumers. Buyers manifest their demand for particular goods and services by their dollar votes. Some buyers with more dollars and a strong demand for particular commodities will outbid others to obtain the particular goods or services they desire.

Producers in a free market seek the business of individual buyers by underpricing other firms, by putting out a better product, or by giving better service. Competition among producers restricts one firm from charging an excessive price. Competition among consumers for products helps the company to receive a reasonable price for its product. Competition among firms often leads to more and better products for the consumers at lower and lower prices. Competition is responsible for new products, new techniques, and improved services. Thus, competition becomes the regulator of the free enterprise economic system.

Competition also implies freedom, that is, freedom in the choice of a position and freedom to enter or to go out of business. It provides the opportunity to make a profit, but it does not insure against losses. Under competition people are free to decide how they want to use their labor and whether they want to work for themselves or someone else. The right to choose the type of work they desire is limited only by their qualifications. Landowners are free to utilize their land or to rent it to others, and the capitalists are free to use their capital or to loan it to others in return for an interest rate. Entrepreneurs are free under a competitive system to combine the labor, land, and capital of others, provided they can remunerate the holders of these factors of production for their use.

In a free enterprise system workers compete against each other for jobs, and they frequently change jobs. Firms compete against each other. New firms continually come into existence, and old firms go out of business. New ideas, new products, and new services are continually appearing on the market, each competing for the consumer's dollar. In a free enterprise system, the consumer is sovereign. The consumer approves or disapproves of products by a decision to spend or not to spend and by a decision to buy this commodity or that commodity. Many institutional forces in our economy, however, hamper the smooth operation of our competitive system. But in total it provides us with trillions of economic goods and services.

### Competition and Monopoly

The degree of competition that exists in one economy compared to another varies greatly. Even within a particular economy, the degree of competition varies among different industries. Furthermore, not all markets fit the model of perfect, or free, competition used in our textbooks. Various qualifications, restrictions, hindrances, and regulations are imposed, voluntarily or involuntarily, on individuals and business firms in a market economy. Monopolies and oligopolies, as we shall see in subsequent chapters, exert pressure on prices and output; labor union activities modify the free operation of labor and wage markets; and the government regulates many industries directly or indirectly.

## Government Regulated Markets

Frequently a market for a good or service may be more orderly and may operate to the best interest of the consuming public if the firm that produces that good or renders that service is regulated to some degree by a governmental agency. Public utilities fall into this category. Experience has shown that it is better to grant one firm a monopoly to supply water, gas, electricity, telephone service, transportation, or other services for the community, rather than to permit free competition in these fields. In exchange for the *franchise* that gives a firm a monopoly to supply a particular type of service, the public service commission of the state or the community maintains regulatory powers over the monopoly to insure that it charges reasonable prices and provides adequate service.

Agricultural markets are regulated in large part by the Department of Agriculture. A firm cannot engage in interstate transportation without the approval and regulation of the Interstate Commerce Commission. Airlines are regulated for safety purposes. The sale of stocks and bonds is regulated to protect investors. The banking business is closely regulated for the interest of all concerned.

In a wartime economy the production of goods and services is regulated to insure an ample supply of military goods and services. War conditions may require the rationing of consumer goods. Prices and wages during wars, and at other times, may be regulated in the interest of the general public.

In addition to regulating certain markets, the government occasionally enters a business directly, such as the printing business and the making of rope for nautical purposes. At times the government enters a business indirectly as, for example, the production of electricity from our mulitpurpose water projects (such as TVA and Shasta and Hoover dams), which also provide flood control, irrigation, and improved navigation.

## Mixed Economy

Although the determination of what to produce, the amount to be produced, the prices to be charged, and the compensation to the factors of production is generally based upon the free decisions of individuals and firms, our economy is often referred to as a *mixed economy*. This stems from the fact that, even though the market economy is characterized by competition and freedom, the competition is not perfect and the freedom is not unqualified.

Some decisions regarding production, such as the building of roads and the erection of schools and municipal buildings, are made by federal, state, and local governments, while the use of labor in and outside of the armed services is determined in part by military authorities.

Regulated public utilities exist along with unregulated industries, monopolies stand side by side with highly competitive firms, giant corporations compete with small, single proprietorships, the government regulates some industries and not others, and government operations occasionally compete with private industry. Since we have many types of competition and the economy contains both free and regulated markets, it is appropriate to refer to it as a mixed economy.

## ROLE OF THE GOVERNMENT IN THE ECONOMY

The concept of a mixed economy brings into focus an important question: What should be the role of the government in the economy? Should it be active or passive? Should it regulate or not regulate? Should it engage directly in business? Should it encourage business activity or not? Historically the role of the government in our economy has been one of nonintervention. In the past few decades, however, there has been a tendency to move in the direction of increased government action.

### Economic Liberalism

Since economic liberalism was the prevailing economic philosophy in much of the 19th and the early part of the 20th century, our economy developed within its framework. With our capitalistic system, we became the strongest economic nation in the world, and our standard of living has risen to unbelievable heights. Economic liberalism implied freedom of action for the individual and the business enterprise. The major tenets of economic liberalism were free trade, self-interest, private property, laissez-faire, and competition.

According to this philosophy, individuals were free to seek their own occupations, were free to enter any business, and were free to act as they saw fit to improve their economic position. Economic society was held together by mutual exchanges that were founded upon the division of labor and which were prompted by self-interest. Self-interest was the motivating force of the economy. For example, to increase economic welfare, an individual might decide to produce goods and sell them for a profit. But, in so doing that individual automatically would benefit the community as well by supplying goods and providing employment. A laborer seeking to increase wages would do so by increasing productivity. This in turn would benefit the employer as well as the community in general. According to Adam Smith, often called the father of economics, the individual, in seeking his own gain, was led by an "invisible hand" to promote the welfare of his fellowmen and that of the whole community.

Under economic liberalism individuals were free to engage in the trade, the occupation, or the business they desired. Workers were free to move from one job to another, and there was freedom to enter into or exit from any industry. Workers were free to work or not to work, and businesses were free to produce or not produce, as well as to produce this commodity or that commodity.

Competition was the regulator of the economy under economic liberalism. Businesses were to compete with one another for consumer trade by developing new and better products and by selling existing products at cheaper prices. Free entry into the market assured ample competition, and prices were determined by the free forces of supply and demand. Competitive forces not only determined the prices of goods and services, but also wage rates.

Since self-interest was the motivating and driving force of the economy, because individuals, in promoting their own self-interest, would promote the welfare of the economy as a whole, and since competition was to serve as a regulator for the economy, a policy of *laissez-faire*, or nongovernment intervention, prevailed. This was a policy of government "hands off" in the economic activities of the individuals and businesses. From the economic point of view the government was merely to protect private property, to enforce contracts, and to act as an umpire in the case of economic disputes.

### Weakness of Economic Liberalism

In this system we can picture, on the one hand, each individual and firm seeking their own self-interest, competing one against the other for jobs, sales, and markets with the weak falling by the wayside. On the other hand, we can see the government standing by, relying on competition to regulate the economy, not interfering unless absolutely necessary. For various reasons this system was to enhance the welfare of all. Truly it was a philosophy of "rugged individualism."

In theory, economic liberalism was a sound philosophy and our economy prospered under it. It was not, however, without its weaknesses. The most pronounced weaknesses of economic liberalism were its extreme stress upon self-interest and its undue reliance on competition to regulate the economy and to promote the general welfare. Self-interest in many cases promoted greed, materialism, and the abuse of economic liberty; and competition proved to be an inadequate regulator to prevent or correct these abuses.

Economic liberalism left the door wide open for trouble. Certain individuals and firms began to interfere with the economic freedom of others. Under the aegis of economic liberalism and the guise of competition, large firms began to exploit small firms. Monopolies arose and business integrations became prevalent. Markets were controlled and consumers exploited. Competition beat wages down, and the market wage paid by the employer was often less than the just or living wage required by the dignity of human labor. In stressing the individual aspect of private property, the social aspect was often ignored. Thus, one person's private property was frequently used to the detriment of another's property.

### Government Intervention

As a result of these abuses, government intervention was and is necessary to remedy the inequities that developed under economic liberalism. Much of our railroad and subsequent interstate commerce regulation was designed to restrict the malpractices of carriers. The antitrust laws are necessary to prevent the restraint of competition by monopolies and large-scale business combinations. Labor laws are essential to protect the rights of laborers. Public utility regulation is necessary to prevent consumer exploitation, food and drug laws are designed to protect the health of our citizens, antipollution measures are enforced to preserve our environment, and safety regulations are enforced to protect workers.

In addition, government intervention in the form of socioeconomic legislation designed to promote the common good has been increasing. The Social Security Act, for example, provides aid to the needy aged, to widows, and to orphans. It further provides pensions and medical care for the aged and compensation for the unemployed. The minimum-wage laws protect our standard of living, and fair employment practices acts prevent discrimination in regard to job opportunities.

In other areas of the economy we have widespread regulation of agriculture, strict laws in banking, tariffs and quotas for foreign trade, and governmental approval is necessary for the sale of securities. We have government regulation of the airlines and government intervention in the coal mines. We also have government water-power projects, rural electrification projects, housing projects, and the war on poverty.

With increasing government intervention there is scarcely an area of importance in the economy today that is not affected by government legislation. There seems to be little doubt that the amount of government regulation, restriction, and intervention in our economy is substantial. Certainly we no longer have free enterprise to the extent advocated by 19th century economic liberalism. We have moved a long way from the laissez-faire aspect of the free enterprise system. Just how far we have moved is an interesting question.

Although most of the government intervention in our economy is necessary to correct abuses or to promote the general welfare, some of it might be considered unnecessary. Sometimes it is difficult to determine whether or not government action is needed. It is unfortunate that we cannot use a slide rule or computer to measure with exactness the degree of necessity, or lack thereof, of any particular piece of suggested government legislation. But we have no absolute measure of necessity. Whether the government should intervene in any particular case and to what extent frequently depends upon prudential judgment, and, as mentioned previously, prudential judgments of various individuals and groups differ widely.

### Subsidiary Role of Government

What, then, can we use as a criterion to determine the need for government action in any area of the economy? In the absence of anything better, we can use the well-regarded law of social philosophy based upon the concept that the community and the state are subsidiary to the individual. Since subsidiary comes from the Latin word *subsidium*, meaning to help or to assist, the *principle of subsidiarity* implies that each higher unit in the economy exists to give assistance to, or to benefit, lesser units. In the normal order of things individuals should do what they can for themselves. What they cannot do for themselves, they can cooperate with other people and do through the community. What the communities cannot do can be done by the state. According to the principle of subsidiarity, it is wrong for a higher economic unit to take unto itself a function that can be performed adequately by a lesser unit or by the individual.

The principle of subsidiarity helps to protect our free enterprise capitalistic system and to maintain some degree of laissez-faire. According to this principle, the federal government should encourage states, communities, subordinate groups, and individuals to handle all matters that they can handle adequately; higher economic or political units should intervene in the activities of the lower units only when necessary, and then in a subsidiary or helpful way and not in a manner that will destroy or absorb the lower unit. In short, it maintains that the higher unit be subsidiary or helpful to the lower unit or to the individual and no more.

In many cases it will easily be discernible whether government intervention violates this principle. For example, if the government were to decide which school you should attend, what subjects you should take, where you should work when you graduate, and what pay you should receive, it clearly would be a violation of the principle of subsidiarity. In most cases the main objective of working is to secure the income necessary to provide the goods and services necessary for your own livelihood and that of your family. In our present economic system the average individual is quite capable of earning a living through self-motivation and industry.

On the other hand, since the average individual is unable to protect life and property against invaders, rogues, thugs, vandals, fire, floods, etc., the maintenance of military, fire, and police protection by the states and communities does not violate the principle of subsidiarity. The use of broad-scale economic policies to stabilize the economy can be rendered effectively only by the federal government. The line of demarcation, however, sometimes becomes very nebulous. Take the concept of a federally guaranteed annual income for every American. Although experiments with it are already in process, arguments regarding its necessity are still being formulated. Legislation being prepared in Congress for enactment of a National Health Insurance Plan has elicited heated debate. President

Nixon's decision to impose direct wage-price restraints in 1971 was criticized by some and praised by others.

Today we are interested in preserving our environment to have clean air, pure water, and noise abatement. But we are having difficulty determining who should pay for it: consumers, businesses, or the government. Furthermore, it is being debated whether local, state, or federal regulation should take precedence in the enforcement of antipollution measures. In many actual cases the government is performing services or producing goods that can be obtained through private enterprise. Presently the federal government operates about 20,000 business enterprises.

In determining whether government intervention is necessary or not, much depends upon the prudential judgment of the individuals and the groups in the economy. Even though the principle of subsidiarity may be difficult to apply at times because of the inability to determine precisely whether a certain bit of suggested government action is necessary, or to determine whether or not a lower economic unit can perform a particular function adequately, the principle can be applied readily in many cases. Furthermore, it can serve as an excellent and consistent guide in helping to prevent indiscriminate and contrary decisions regarding government intervention.

## GOALS FOR THE AMERICAN ECONOMY

In recent years a number of goals for our economy have been established by various private and government agencies that analyze our economic system. These goals are not a set of hard and fast objectives that must be accomplished, but rather suggested goals or ends toward which the economy should strive. Dozens of goals have been suggested by various private and government organizations. The three primary domestic economic goals that stand above all others are: (1) full employment, (2) stable prices, and (3) economic growth.

### Full Employment

By full employment we mean a condition in which 96 percent of our civilian labor force is employed. This allows for 4 percent frictional unemployment. There are always workers quitting, getting fired, in transit from one part of the country to another, and those temporarily laid off. Furthermore, we have a number of persons who want to work but who have difficulty obtaining or holding a job because of physical or mental handicaps. Consequently, we can always expect some slack, or unemployment, in the labor force. For all practical purposes, we consider ourselves to be at full employment when unemployment is 4 percent or less. There has been much discussion in recent years, however, that this 4 percent figure should be changed to something in the vicinity of 4.5 percent due to the change in the structure of the labor force that has occurred over the past two decades. It is becoming increasingly evident that this 4.5

percent figure, or perhaps an even higher figure, will be more widely acknowledged and accepted as time marches on.

## Stable Prices

Stable prices are said to prevail when the Consumer Price Index, which measures changes in the cost of living, moves two percent or less in either direction during the period of a year. Changes of more than this amount have substantial effects on the purchasing power of families and on the value of the dollar.

## Economic Growth

The economy requires a healthy rate of economic growth. Total output must grow if we are to absorb the one and one-half million or more new workers who enter the labor force annually, plus the two million or more workers who are displaced each year as a result of technological development and automation. If we merely produce the same level of output each year instead of increasing it, we will have fewer jobs, growing unemployment, and a decline in the per capita income of the nation. In order to maintain, or increase, the existing standard of living, it is necessary to increase our gross national product continuously, unless, of course, workers are content to take the benefits of higher productivity in the form of shorter working hours instead of additional goods and services.

Experience indicates, for example, that with a real growth rate of 4 percent or less, the American economy suffers from nagging unemployment and limited gains in per capita output and income. Unemployment at the end of 1973, for example, was 4.3 million, or 4.9 percent of the labor force. But by the end of 1974, unemployment exceeded 6 million, or 7 percent of the civilian labor force. Why? Simply because the real output of goods and services, instead of growing, declined in 1974. Consequently, we failed to absorb all the new entrants into the labor force plus some of those who were displaced because of technological development and automation. Furthermore, a sizable number of workers withdrew from the labor force because they were unable to find work.

Full employment and substantial per capita gains, however, seem to occur when the economic growth rate exceeds 4 percent. The potential annual growth rate of the American economy is currently 4 to 5.5 percent, reflecting a 1.5 to 2 percent increase in available man-hours and a 2.5 to 3.5 persent rise in output per man-hour.

## Supplementary Goals

As our study progresses, we shall see more fully the meaning and importance of each of these goals and learn some of the difficulties that arise in our efforts to attain them, through national economic policies or otherwise. In addition, we will see how supplementary goals such as the elimination of poverty, a proper balance between private and social production, the rebuilding of our cities, the improvement of health care delivery, the preservation of our natural environment, and the improvement in the quality of life are taking on added importance.

## COMMAND ECONOMIES

In our capitalistic system, decision making is exercised primarily by individuals and business firms in the economy. It must be remembered, however, that there are other economic systems throughout the world. Not all people, including some in the United States, are sold on the advantages of capitalism. Many feel that its disadvantages, such as recurring recessions, the occurrence of unemployment and poverty, administered pricing by monopolies, the wasteful use of resources in some respects, and the unequal distribution of property and income, far exceed its advantages. As a consequence, in some nations the people prefer some form of economy other than capitalism. In other nations leaders prefer a more centralized type of economy because it is easier to exercise dictatorial control. Thus, in many parts of the world various forms of socialism, fascism, and communism exist. In contrast to exchange or market economies, these might be called *command economies*.

## SUMMARY

Our economy operates as a free enterprise capitalistic system. By capitalism we mean that capital, or producers' goods, is used for the production of additional goods and services. The right to private property is essential to the operation of this system.

Manpower and resources are utilized and allocated in this system by consumer demand. Since consumer demand is expressed in prices, businesses cater to consumer demand to make a profit. Consumers, through the prices they are willing to pay, provide the entrepreneurs with the means of obtaining the necessary manpower and resources to produce the desired goods and services. Profit serves as an incentive to get the goods and services produced and prices serve as a rationing mechanism in the distribution of these goods and services.

About nine million nonfarm business enterprises engage in production for the purpose of satisfying consumer demand in the United States. Some are large, but most of them are small firms, each employing only a few people. The relatively few large firms in the country, however, provide jobs for most of the workers. Four predominant types of business enterprises exist in the United States: the single proprietorship, the partnership, the corporation, and the cooperative. Each has certain advantages and disadvantages.

Competition is the regulator of the free enterprise system. Although competition is dominant in our economy, some of the markets are regulated for one reason or another, such as safety, economy, or protection. Occasionally the government enters a business directly or indirectly when it is essential for the good of the economy. Thus because of the complex mixture of competition, regulated and unregulated markets, and private and government-operated businesses, it is said that we have a mixed economy.

Our mixed economy developed within the framework of economic liberalism. The main tenets of this philosophy were free trade, self-interest, private property, laissez-faire, and competition. The undue stress on self-interest, however, led to abuses and inequities over the years, and competition proved to be an inadequate regulator. To correct these inequities, government legislation was required. In addition, much government intervention in the form of socioeconomic legislation has been enacted in the past few decades. As a result of this government intervention in the economy in the past 50 to 85 years, we have moved a considerable distance away from the laissez-faire aspect of economic liberalism.

Although most of our government intervention was and is necessary to prevent and remedy inequities in our economic system, and a good deal of it is in the form of socioeconomic measures designed to promote the common good, some of our government action may be considered as an infringement upon the economic freedom of both individuals and businesses.

Whether or not the government should intervene and to what extent it should intervene is a controversial question. In this regard the principle of subsidiarity serves as a good touchstone to determine the need for government intervention in any particular case.

In its operation, there are three generally accepted major or primary goals for our American economy: full employment, stable prices, and economic growth. These are supplemented by numerous minor goals, some of which are becoming more important, such as the preservation of our natural environment, the elimination of poverty, and the improvement in the quality of life.

From this chapter it can be seen that consumers, businesses, and the government all play an integral part in the operation of our economic system. With this in mind we can now move on to the next chapter to see how each of these sectors influences the general level of business activity.

## DISCUSSION QUESTIONS

1. In what way is the institution of private property essential to the operation of a free enterprise, capitalistic economy?
2. It is said that consumer demand influences the determination of individual income. Discuss how this can be so.
3. How does the price system serve as a rationing mechanism?
4. What is the role of profit in a capitalistic economic system?

5. Distinguish between "market economy" and command economy.
6. What are some of the advantages
   of the corporate form of business
   enterprise?
7. It is often said that laissez-faire
   and free trade are incompatible.
   Explain.
8. Explain a situation in which a high
   degree of competition may not be
   beneficial to consumers and to the

economy in general.
9. What has stimulated most of our
   government economic regulations
   in the United States?
10. Do you think that a federally
    operated national health insurance
    program for every American, fi-
    nanced through some form of in-
    come tax, would be a violation of
    the principle of subsidiarity? Ex-
    plain your opinion.

## SUGGESTED READINGS

American Institute for Economic Research. "Dr. McCracken on Price-Wage Controls." *Economic Education Bulletin* (January, 1972).

Blechman, Barry M., M. Gramlich, and Robert W. Hartman. *Setting National Priorities: The 1975 Budget.* Washington: The Brookings Institution, 1974.

Cassell, Frank H. "The Social Cost of Doing Business." *MSU Business Topics* (Autumn, 1964).

*Economic Report of the President.* Washington: U.S. Government Printing Office, 1972–1975.

Farmer, Richard N., and W. Dickerson Hogue. *Corporate Social Responsibility.* Chicago: Science Research Associates, Inc., 1973.

Feige, Edgar L., and Douglas K. Pearce. "The Wage-Price Control Experiment — Did It Work?" *Challenge* (July/August, 1973).

Ferguson, John M. *Landmarks of Economic Thought.* London: Longman Group Ltd., 1950. Chapters 10 and 17.

Friedman, Milton. *Capitalism and Freedom.* Chicago: University of Chicago Press, 1962.

Galbraith, John Kenneth. *The New Industrial State.* Boston: Houghton Mifflin Company, 1967.

Glos, Raymond E., Richard D. Steade, and James R. Lowry. *Business: Its Nature and Environment,* 8th ed. Cincinnati: South-Western Publishing Co., 1976.

*Goals for Americans.* The Report of the President's Commission on National Goals. Englewood Cliffs, N.J.: Prentice-Hall, Inc., 1960.

Gray, Alexander. *The Development of Economic Doctrine.* London: Longman Group Ltd., 1931. Chapters 3 to 10.

Griffen, Clare E. *The Free Society.* Washington: American Free Enterprise Institute, 1965.

Haberler, Gottfried. "Incomes Policies and Inflation." *Special Analysis.* Washington: American Enterprise Institute, 1971.

Hailstones, Thomas J., and Frank V. Mastrianna. *Contemporary Economic Problems and Issues,* 4th ed. Cincinnati: South-Western Publishing Co., 1976.

Hayek, Friedrich A. *Individualism and Economic Order.* Chicago: Henry Regnery Company, 1972.

Heilbroner, Robert L. *Between Capitalism and Socialism.* New York: Random House, Inc., 1970.

Heller, Walter W. *New Dimension of Political Economy*. Cambridge, Mass.: Harvard University Press, 1966.

Herendeen, James B. *The Economics of the Corporate Economy*. New York: The Dunellen Publishing Co., Inc., 1974.

"Inflation and the Budgetary Outlook." *The Brookings Bulletin*, Vol. 11, No. 2 (Spring, 1974).

Jacoby, Neil H. *Corporate Power and Social Responsibility*. New York: Macmillan Publishing Co., Inc., 1973.

Lecht, Leonard A. *Goals, Priorities & Dollars*. New York: The Free Press, 1966.

Lerner, Abba P. *Flation*. Baltimore: Penguin Books, Inc., 1973.

Okun, Arthur M. (ed.). *The Battle Against Unemployment*. New York: W. W. Norton and Company, Inc., 1972.

Ozaki, Robert S. *Inflation, Recession . . . and All That*. New York: Holt, Rinehart and Winston, Inc., 1972.

Solo, Robert A. *The Political Authority and the Market System*. Cincinnati: South-Western Publishing Co., 1974.

Tobin, James. *The New Economics One Decade Older*. Princeton, N.J.: Princeton University Press, 1974.

Wallich, Henry C. *The Cost of Freedom*. New York: Harper & Row, Publishers, 1960.

Weiss, H. L. "The Profit Ethic." Schenectady, N.Y.: General Electric Co. (May, 1974).

Wilcox, Clair. *Public Policies Toward Business*, 4th ed. Homewood, Ill,: Richard D. Irwin, Inc., 1971. Chapter 1.

# 4 THE CIRCULAR FLOW OF ECONOMIC ACTIVITY

## CIRCULAR FLOW DEMONSTRATED

In producing the goods and the services to satisfy consumer demands and to make profits, the various business firms in our economy must utilize the factors of production: land, labor, capital, and entrepreneurship. Since the first three of these factors are generally owned by someone other than the entrepreneur, the business firm must remunerate the owners of these factors for the services they render. The payments for the productive factors by the business firms naturally become income to the owners of these factors of production. This income in turn is used as purchasing power by which the owners of the factors of production can buy goods and services. Likewise, the profits of the entrepreneurs, or businesses, become purchasing power with which they can buy goods and services or secure additional factors of production.

The demand for goods and services by the income recipients leads to more production, which in turn brings about additional payments of income to the owners of the factors of production. This continuous operation of demand, production, income, and new demand sets up the *circular flow of economic activity* in our economy. Frequently it is referred to as the "wheel of fortune" because it is the mechanism by which we determine not only the use of our land, labor, capital, and entrepreneurship, but it is also the mechanism by which we determine the remuneration to the factors of production and by which we distribute income to various individuals and firms in our economy.

Since we will be referring repeatedly to this concept, let us demonstrate it graphically. At this point we will divide the economy into two segments: businesses and individuals. Government will be added at a later point. In our modern-day economy, most individuals work for business firms or are in business for themselves. Individuals offer their productive services to business in exchange for remuneration in the form of wages, rent, and interest, and the owners of the business receive a profit for their contribution.

These individuals use their incomes to buy the goods and the services produced by businesses. If all the goods and services produced are sold —

and they should be if people spend all the income they receive for the goods and services that are available — businesses will be induced to produce a second round of goods and services, and the process will start over again. Continuation of this process keeps our economy producing, paying incomes, spending, and allocating goods and services to the individuals according to their demands. This process is shown in Figure 4-1.

In this model it can be seen that all income finds its way into the hands of the individuals represented at the right in Figure 4-1. Since the profit of a business becomes income to its owner, these individuals include the owners of businesses as well as the owners of the other factors of production. The value of the goods produced is determined by the cost of production — payments for manpower, resources, and capital in the form of wages, rent, and interest, plus the profits for the entrepreneurs. We can say, therefore, that the total payment of income in the economy is equal to the value or cost (including profit) of the production. Individuals, including business owners who receive income in the form of profits, will have sufficient income to buy the goods and services produced by the economy.

### A Stable Economy

If all the income is spent, either on consumer or capital goods, businesses will move all the goods off the market and will be induced to produce the same amount again. But we know from our experience that individuals do not spend all the income they receive. Many people save some of their income. What happens to the circular flow in this case? This is an interesting situation because it is so prevalent in our economy. Unless there is additional spending from some source to make up for the amount of saving in the economy, saving may have an adverse effect on

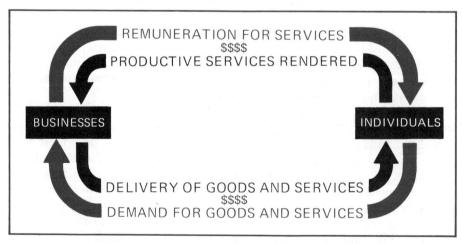

REMUNERATION FOR SERVICES
$$$$
PRODUCTIVE SERVICES RENDERED

BUSINESSES

INDIVIDUALS

DELIVERY OF GOODS AND SERVICES
$$$$
DEMAND FOR GOODS AND SERVICES

Figure 4-1　**CIRCULAR FLOW — SIMPLE MODEL**

the level of economic activity. Let us assume that businesses produce 100,000 units and distribute $100,000 income. If individuals spend the $100,000 to buy 100,000 units of consumer and capital goods, all production will be sold at an average price level of $1 per unit. However, if people spend only $80,000 on consumer goods and save $20,000, not all goods will be sold unless the savings are used directly to purchase capital goods or are borrowed by individuals other than savers to buy consumer or capital goods. Thus, we can maintain a given level of economic activity only if we have an amount of borrowing and/or nonconsumer spending in the economy equal to the amount of saving, as shown in Figure 4-2.

Since spending on capital goods is referred to as *investment* in current economic analysis, we can conclude by saying that as long as investment equals saving, we will have a stable flow of economic activity. In such a case total spending will equal total income. Since total spending is equal to total demand and income is equivalent to total production (supply), the demand for goods and services will equal the supply.

### A Contracting Economy

Any time that investment does not equal saving, there will be a disruption in the circular flow of economic activity. For example, suppose that out of the $100,000 received by individuals, $80,000 is spent on consumption, and of the $20,000 saved only $10,000 is invested directly by the savers or indirectly by the borrowers. In this case, after producing 100,000 units valued at $100,000, producers would see only $90,000 returning to buy the goods produced. This would result in a decrease in the level of economic activity because one of two things or a combination

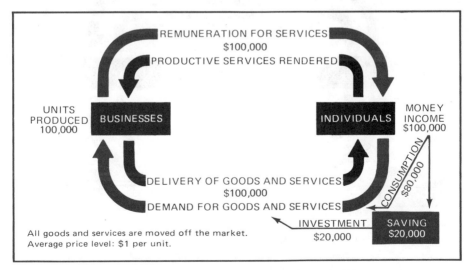

Figure 4-2   **CIRCULAR FLOW — STABLE ECONOMY (I=S)**

of both would happen: (1) an accumulation of unsold goods, or (2) a reduction in the prices of the goods.

**Inventory Accumulation**    If the price level is maintained at $1 per unit, the $90,000 that flows back will purchase only 90,000 units. This leaves 10,000 units unsold in inventories as shown in Figure 4-3. If the producers of 100,000 units sold only 90,000 units in one period, they might adjust their anticipated sales to 90,000 units for the subsequent period. Reduced production of 80,000 units plus an inventory stock of 10,000 units remaining from the previous period would yield the desired supply of 90,000 units. This move would cut back current production, and the producer would use less manpower and fewer productive resources. As a result, there would be less income paid out and spending would fall accordingly. The net result would be a decrease in economic activity in the subsequent period. In short, production, employment, and income would fall. This could lead to further declines in business activity resulting in more inventory accumulation.

**Drop in Prices**    Under certain circumstances, when $100,000 of income is paid out but only $90,000 returns to buy the goods produced, the market could be cleared; that is, all the goods could be sold by a reduction in the price level to 90 cents per unit. In that event $90,000 could buy 100,000 units. In fact, this is what frequently happens as competition forces prices down when total supply exceeds total demand. If prices begin to fall, however, certain high-cost producers may not be able to

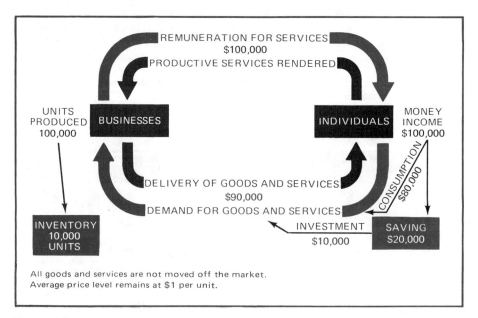

Figure 4-3  **CONTRACTING ECONOMY — INVENTORY ACCUMULATION (I<S)**

make a profit by selling at this lower price, and other producers will make less profit per unit. Consequently, the incentive to produce will be weakened, many firms will cut back production or go out of business, and total output in the subsequent period will be less. This means that fewer units of the factors of production will be utilized, less income will be received, and total demand will fall. (See Figure 4-4.)

Whenever investment, or borrowing, is less than saving, total spending will be less than total income and total demand will be less than total supply. This will lead to a decrease in production in subsequent periods because of inventory accumulation (goods not sold) or because of falling prices or a combination of both. As production is cut, incomes will fall, which will reduce employment and income. Hence, we will have a decrease in the level of economic activity, which might precipitate a business depression. Inventory depletion of more than $10 billion was largely responsible for the slowdown early in 1967, and was a contributing factor to the recessions of 1970 and 1974–1975.

### An Expanding Economy

If total investment were to exceed total saving, businesses and individuals would borrow more than they saved. This would cause spending to exceed total income and demand to exceed total production. Assume 100,000 units were produced and $100,000 was distributed in income. Assume also that individuals spent $80,000 on consumption and saved $20,000 that found its way directly or indirectly into investment. If businesses were to borrow an additional $10,000 from some source, such as a bank that can create money, for the purchase of machinery and

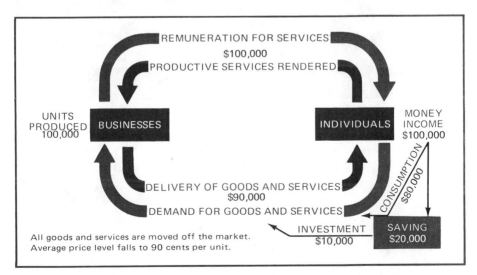

Figure 4-4    **CONTRACTING ECONOMY — PRICES DECLINE (I<S)**

equipment, total investment would be $30,000, which when added to the $80,000 in consumer spending would make total spending $110,000. Such action might cause an increase in the level of economic activity or an increase in the price level, depending on the circumstances. (See Figure 4-5.)

**More Goods and Services**　　Naturally businesspeople will endeavor to increase production to satisfy the additional demand for goods and services. If the economy is in a state of less than full employment, that is, if manpower, resources, capital, and capacity to increase production are available, additional goods and services will be forthcoming to satisfy the higher demand. Certainly if there is an additional $10,000 available to buy goods, some enterprising businesspeople are going to produce the goods demanded. When they do, total production will be increased to 110,000 units. In addition, the price level will remain at $1 per unit since the $110,000 in spending is exchanged for the 110,000 units produced. Businesses, which must pay for additional productive agents, will pay $110,000 instead of $100,000 as they did formerly and income will increase accordingly. This in turn will increase spending and bring about more production. As a result, the economy will be operating at a higher level of production and employment. Therefore, whenever investment exceeds saving, total spending will exceed total income, demand will be greater than supply, and there will be an increase in the level of economic activity, provided that we are at less than full employment. This increase in economic activity will be necessary to meet and to satisfy

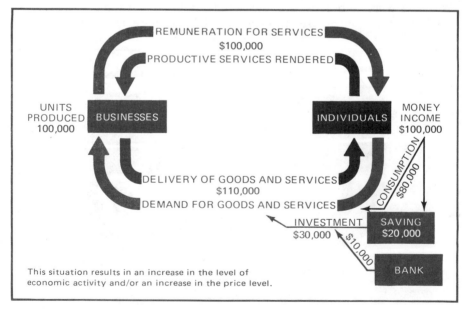

Figure 4-5　**EXPANDING ECONOMY — OUTPUT AND/OR PRICE RISE (I>S)**

demand. Much of the expansion of the 1960s and early 1970s resulted from such a situation.

**Higher Prices** If the same situation occurs in a period of full employment, the immediate result will be higher prices (inflation). Under full employment, businesspeople will be unable to obtain the necessary manpower, resources, capital, and capacity to produce additional goods. It is true that some businesspeople will endeavor to increase production to satisfy the demand for the additional 10,000 units, but the only way that they will be able to obtain the necessary factors of production in the short run to increase output will be to bid them away from other producers. This will force prices upward as entrepreneurs bid against each other for the relatively scarce factors of production. Furthermore, instead of having an increase in total production, the price level will rise to $1.10 per unit and the $110,000 of spending will be used to buy the 100,000 units of output as individuals bid against each other for the limited goods available. Although the composition of production (the amount of capital goods compared to consumer goods) may be changed, the total amount of production will not be changed, at least in the short-run period. If after a while productivity can be increased through more efficient use of manpower, better utilization of resources, and expanded capacity, the inflationary pressures will tend to be alleviated.

Thus, we can say that at any time investment is greater than saving, an increase in the level of economic activity will result, provided we are at less than full employment. If we are at full employment, however, this situation will merely cause prices to rise.

### Summary of Circular Flow Model

We can sum up the foregoing discussion regarding the relationship of investment (I) to saving (S) and its effect on the economy as follows:

Whenever I = S, the result will be *equilibrium* or a stable flow of economic activity. Prices will tend to remain stable.

I < S, the level of economic activity and/or prices will tend to decrease.

I > S, the level of economic activity will tend to increase if the economy is at less than full employment. However, if the economy is in a state of full employment, there will be no increase in the level of economic activity and prices will tend to rise.

## GOVERNMENT AND THE CIRCULAR FLOW

Prior to the last few decades the primary function and objective of federal financing was to raise sufficient funds through taxation to cover the cost of performing the necessary services expected of the federal government. Therefore, great emphasis was placed on balancing the budget, even though budget experts were not always able to balance the revenue and the expenditures. In recent decades, with the move away from laissez-faire, we have used government spending as a means of stabilizing the level of economic activity and at times we have purposely attempted to operate at a surplus or a deficit.

### A Balanced Budget

Since government spending can affect the circular flow of economic activity and the price level, a closer inspection is in order. Actually, if the government balances the budget, it will in effect spend the same amount as it collects in taxes. What individuals and businesses give up in spendable funds to pay taxes, and consequently reduce their total spending, will be spent by the government; and as a result, the total spending in the economy will remain the same. Thus, a balanced budget tends to have a neutral effect on the economy. For example, in our circular flow, if individuals, as shown in Figure 4-6, were taxed $10,000 out of their total incomes of $100,000, they would have only $90,000 for spending on consumption and investment. The adverse effect of the government tax on the economy, however, would be offset if the government in turn spent the $10,000 it received in taxes. Under such circumstances, total spending would remain at $100,000 and the total goods and services that were

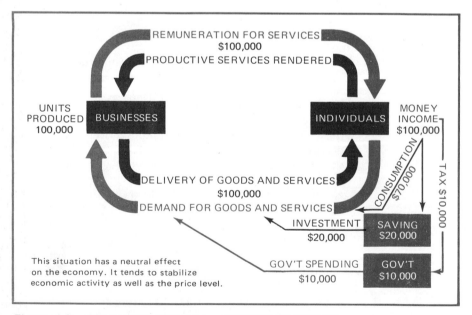

Figure 4-6   **BALANCED BUDGET — STABLE ECONOMY**

produced would be moved off the market. There might be a change, however, in the composition of the goods and services produced, insofar as government spending would be substituted for some of the private spending on consumption and investment.

### A Surplus Budget

If the government has a surplus budget, that is, if it spends less than it receives in taxes, this will tend to decrease the level of economic activity or cause a decline in prices. During a period when strong inflationary forces exist, a surplus budget is occasionally used as an anti-inflationary measure. Since the government spends less than it collects in taxes, this causes the total spending in the economy to decrease, which in turn will have a mollifying or deflationary effect on the economy. Assume in our circular flow that the government were to tax $10,000 but spend only $5,000. This would mean that total spending by consumers and investors would be reduced from $100,000 to $90,000 as a result of the tax payments. This would be offset, however, only to the extent of the $5,000 of government spending. In effect, total spending would be reduced to $95,000 for the economy as a whole. Consequently, spending would be less than income, demand would be less than supply, and there would be a decrease in the level of business activity or a decline in the price level. This is demonstrated in Figure 4-7.

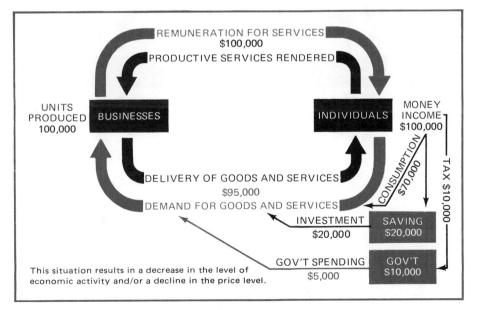

Figure 4-7   **SURPLUS BUDGET — CONTRACTING ECONOMY AND/OR DECLINING PRICE LEVEL**

## A Deficit Budget

If the government operates a deficit budget, that is, if the government spends more than it collects in taxes, this will tend to bring about an increase in economic activity or raise prices, depending upon the circumstances. Since the government spends more than it collects in taxes, the expansionary effects of government spending will more than offset the contracting effects on consumption and investment resulting from the taxation. Referring once again to our circular flow concept, if individuals receive $100,000 in income for producing 100,000 units of goods and services and the government taxes $10,000, total spending by consumers and investors will be reduced to $90,000. If the government spends not only the $10,000 it collects in taxes but also an additional $5,000, which we will assume it borrows from the banks, total spending will rise to $105,000, as shown in Figure 4-8. Since total spending will exceed total income, demand will exceed the supply of goods and services available. Consequently, a deficit budget will tend to increase the level of economic activity if we are at less than full employment. If the economy is at a state of full employment, however, it will merely cause a rise in the price level.

It must be realized that our examples were based on certain assumptions which may or may not be valid. For instance, it was assumed that

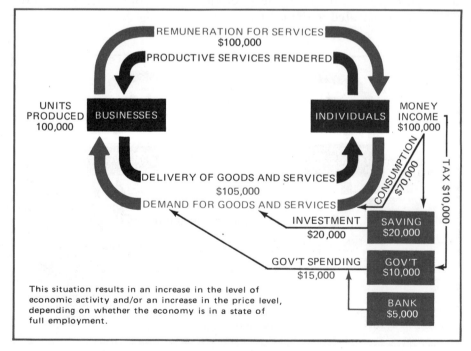

Figure 4-8    **DEFICIT BUDGET — EXPANDING ECONOMY AND/OR RISING PRICES**

individuals always pay taxes out of current incomes; we assumed that if individuals did not pay taxes, they would spend the money for consumption or investment; and we assumed further that the government borrows from the banks instead of from the individuals and business firms in the economy. We will see later that if these assumptions do not apply, our analysis will be modified. The reactions will be the same but less intense. However, we can sum up the effects of government spending on the circular flow of economic activity at this point as follows: A balanced budget tends to have a neutral effect on economic activity and the price level. A surplus budget tends to decrease the level of economic activity and/or the price level. A deficit budget, on the other hand, tends to increase the level of economic activity or the price level, depending on whether or not we are in a state of full employment.

## INFLATION

In our foregoing analysis we assumed that inflation occurred only in a fully employed economy. It may occur, however, in an economy of less than full employment.

### Definition and Types of Inflation

There are many definitions of inflation. In the simplest sense, *inflation* is merely a persistent increase in the price level. But inflation may be one of four types: (1) demand-pull inflation, (2) cost-push inflation, (3) structural inflation, or (4) social inflation.

**Demand-Pull Inflation**    The type of inflation that we have discussed thus far is known as *demand-pull inflation*. Sometimes this is referred to as *excess-demand inflation*, and it occurs when the total demand for goods and services exceeds the available supply of goods and services in the short run. This is much more likely to occur in a fully employed economy because of the difficulty of producing additional goods and services to satisfy the demand. Competitive bidding for the relatively scarce goods and services forces prices upward. The excess demand, or excess spending, may result from several causes. Consumers may dishoard past savings, consumer credit may be liberalized, commercial and bank credit may be extended, or the money supply may otherwise be increased. Generally when the money supply or other forms of purchasing power increase faster than the productivity of our economy, demand-pull inflation results.

**Cost-Push Inflation**    The second type of inflation is known as *cost-push inflation*. This may occur in a fully employed or an underemployed economy. Whether it starts with increased wages, higher material costs, or increased prices of consumer goods is difficult to say. If wages or material costs do increase for some reason, however, producers are likely to increase the prices of their finished goods and services to protect their profit margins. Rising prices in effect will decrease the purchasing power of wages. As a result wage earners, especially through their unions, may apply pressure for further wage increases. This in turn may lead to further increases in the price of materials and finished products, which in turn leads to further wage increases and develops into what we generally call the *wage-price spiral*.

Cost-push inflation has become more pronounced in the past few decades with the growth and strengthening of labor unions. It also has been aggravated by the use of administered pricing by large and powerful producers. *Administered pricing* is simply a situation in which a seller can exert an undue influence on the price charged for a product because of the absence of competition. Although usually referred to as cost-push, price-pull inflation, labor unions call it price-pull, cost-push inflation to de-emphasize the role of wages.

**Structural Inflation**   Another type of inflation that may occur with unemployment in the economy is *structural inflation*. This arises when there is a substantial shift in demand to the products of one industry away from other industries. It assumes that there is a certain amount of inflexibility and immobility among the factors of production, and specifically that wages and prices tend to have downward rigidity and upward flexibility due to administered pricing and labor union pressures. If there is a heavy shift in the demand to the products of Industry $X$ and away from the products of Industry $Y$, for example, it could push production in Industry $X$ to, or near, full capacity. Under such circumstances the increased demand could cause prices to rise in that industry as a result of demand-pull inflation. This will cause the general price level to rise, since it is assumed that prices in Industry $Y$ will not decline because of inflexibility. In addition, because of the immobility of labor and resources, Industry $X$ may have to pay higher wage and material costs as it endeavors to increase production. This whole situation is aggravated when the inflationary effects spill over into other industries. The increases in wages and prices in Industry $X$ may actually cause wages and prices to rise in Industry $Y$. The general increase in the price level could instigate wage increases and subsequently price increases in Industry $Y$. Although production and employment may be lessened as a result of demand shifts away from Industry $Y$, employers within Industry $Y$ may be forced to pay higher wages to offset the higher living costs in an effort to hold on to experienced and skilled workers. In effect, structural inflation, which can occur at full employment or with unemployment conditions, contains elements of both demand-pull and cost-push inflation.

**Social Inflation**   In recent years economists have observed the growing occurrence of a fourth type of inflation known as *social inflation*. It results from the increasing demand for more government services in the form of Social Security payments, improved unemployment benefits, the distribution of more welfare, wider health care coverage, better rent subsidies, and a host of other social services. Social inflation is also encouraged by the rising cost to private enterprise originating from greater fringe benefits, such as longer vacations, more paid holidays, shorter hours, better pensions, and broader hospital and insurance coverage for employees. Moreover, the cost of helping to preserve the natural environment through the use of expensive antipollution and depollution equipment, either by the government or by private enterprise, exerts increased pressure on the price level. Social inflation may occur at full employment, adding to demand-pull inflationary pressures, or at other times it may augment cost-push inflationary pressures.

One answer to each type of inflation is increased productivity. In demand-pull inflation, if productivity can be increased to provide the additional goods and services demanded, the inflationary pressure will be removed. On the other hand, the demand for goods and services can be decreased by reducing the money supply or by reducing spendable income. Cost-push and structural inflation can be modified if wage increases are kept in line with increases in productivity. If wage increases would accelerate in proportion to the increase in productivity, incomes would stay in balance with the amount of goods produced. Goods and services would be available when wage earners spent their higher incomes. Social inflation can be held in check, of course, by limiting government and private outlays for social services or by giving up spendable funds, through taxation and redirected expenditures, to cover their costs.

### Unemployment and Inflation

In recent decades we have had excellent examples of various economic situations. Changes in the relationship of investment to saving caused fluctuations of business activity and prices during the 1950s, when we saw the rise in prices during the Korean Conflict, the decrease of production and employment in 1954, the increased economic activity and price rises in 1955–1957, the recession of 1958, the slow recovery of activities in 1959, and the recession of 1960–1961. A major reason why we did not experience any substantial inflation in the 1958–1965 period, in spite of record-breaking production, employment, and income, was the fact that the economy was not operating at full employment of manpower or capacity, as observed in Table 4-1. But when we continued our high level of investment and federal deficits after reaching full employment in 1966, excess demand helped cause the price level to rise 2.9 percent during that year, after having increased only 1.3 percent annually during the previous eight years. Within a few years prices were rising 5 percent or more annually, in spite of the use of various measures to arrest the inflation.

Table 4-1    **PRODUCTION, CAPACITY, PRICES,**
**AND UNEMPLOYMENT, 1953–1974**

| Year | Production[1] (Billions) | Capacity[2] Utilized% | Price[3] Level | Percentage Changes[4] in CPI | Unemployment (Millions) | Unemployment as Percentage of Civilian Labor Force |
|------|------|------|------|------|------|------|
| 1953 | 413 | 90–95 | 80.1 | .6 | 1.8 | 2.9 |
| 1954 | 407 | 80–85 | 80.5 | −.5 | 3.5 | 5.5 |
| 1957 | 453 | 80–85 | 84.3 | 3.0 | 2.9 | 4.3 |
| 1958 | 447 | 75–80 | 86.6 | 1.8 | 4.6 | 6.8 |
| 1960 | 488 | 80–85 | 88.7 | 1.5 | 3.9 | 5.5 |
| 1961 | 497 | 75–80 | 89.6 | .7 | 4.7 | 6.7 |
| 1966 | 658 | 90–95 | 97.2 | 3.4 | 2.9 | 3.8 |
| 1967 | 675 | 85–90 | 100.0 | 3.0 | 3.0 | 3.8 |
| 1968 | 707 | 85–90 | 104.2 | 4.7 | 2.8 | 3.6 |
| 1969 | 726 | 85–90 | 109.8 | 6.1 | 2.8 | 3.5 |
| 1970 | 723 | 75–80 | 116.3 | 5.5 | 4.1 | 4.9 |
| 1971 | 746 | 75–80 | 121.3 | 3.4 | 5.0 | 5.9 |
| 1972 | 793 | 75–80 | 125.3 | 3.4 | 4.8 | 5.6 |
| 1973 | 839 | 80–85 | 133.1 | 8.8 | 4.3 | 4.9 |
| 1974 | 821 | 75–80 | 147.7 | 12.2 | 5.1 | 5.6 |

Source: *Economic Report of the President, 1975.*

[1]In 1958 constant dollars.
[2]Output as percentage of capacity.
[3]1967 = 100.
[4]Annual changes from December to December.

### Stagflation

With the slowdown in the economy and the decrease in demand associated with the recession of 1970, the price level continued to rise. By that time the demand-pull factors had been supplemented and eventually supplanted by pressures of cost-push, structural, and social inflation. Nevertheless, the decrease in investment in 1970 caused the real GNP to decline modestly and the rate of unemployment to rise from 3.5 percent to 4.9 percent. In fact, by the end of 1970 the unemployment rate had reached 6 percent. For the first time in recent history, we had the anomaly of recession and inflation simultaneously, which was labeled as *stagflation*.

A slow recovery from the recession failed to improve the unemployment or inflationary situation by mid-1971. The imposition in August, 1971, of a 90-day wage-price freeze, Phase I of President Nixon's anti-inflationary program, followed by Phase II controls, suppressed inflation but did not eliminate its causes. Controls helped hold the price level increases to 3.4 percent annually in both 1971 and 1972. With the removal of compulsory controls in January, 1973, however, and the adoption of Phase III voluntary controls, inflation resumed at a faster pace. The price level rose at an annual rate of nearly 9 percent in the five months after decontrol. Phase IV, which reimposed compulsory controls, was rather weak and ineffective and failed to halt the trend of rising prices. The price level, aggravated by fuel and energy shortages, food scarcities, world mineral shortages, and continued high demand, rose at a rate of 8.8 percent in 1973 and double-digit inflation of 12 to 13 percent prevailed through the first three quarters of 1974. By that time we were in the midst of the 1974 recession and unemployment had risen from 4.9 percent to 6.0 percent. By the end of 1974 the unemployment rate had risen to over 7 percent, and by early 1975 it was 8.9 percent and apparently still rising. This presented another case of stagflation.

Regardless of the causes, unemployment and inflation are major problems of the economy. Many business organizations, economic research bureaus, congressional investigation committees, and even Presidential commissions have spent considerable time and effort in the past decade seeking answers to the problems of unemployment and inflation, and particularly stagflation. Although we have many techniques for measuring and alleviating unemployment, complexities make it more difficult to measure the impact of inflation. Furthermore, it is more difficult to impose anti-inflationary measures, such as higher taxes, tighter money, and federal budget reductions, because they are politically and socially unpopular. Moreover, many of the measures designed to slow down inflation aggravate unemployment. On the other hand, measures designed to expand the economy and reduce unemployment often exert inflationary pressures on the price level.

## SUMMARY

Through the decisions of what and how much to produce that are made by millions of consumers and business firms, a circular flow of economic activity is generated in our economy. According to this pattern, as consumers express their demands, the entrepreneurs hire the factors of production to produce the desired goods and services. Incomes are spent either for consumer goods and services or are invested in capital goods. When any saving takes place in the economy, it disrupts the circular flow unless the saving is offset by an equivalent amount of borrowing and investment.

Whenever investment is equal to saving, total spending is equal to income, demand is equal to supply, and all the goods and services are moved off the market. This induces business to produce a like amount of goods and services in the subsequent period. Thus, whenever investment is equal to saving, equilibrium in the level of economic activity results and prices tend to remain stable. If investment is less than saving, however, a decrease in the level of economic activity and/or a decline in the price level results. On the other hand, if investment is greater than saving, an increase in the level of economic activity results if the economy is in a state of less than full employment. Otherwise it leads to higher prices.

Government spending also can have an influence on the level of economic activity and the price level. A balanced government budget tends to have a neutral effect on economic activity and prices, whereas a surplus budget can lead to a decrease in business activity and/or lower prices. On the other hand, a deficit budget can lead to an increase in the level of economic activity or higher prices, depending on the employment status in the economy.

Higher prices, or inflation, result from several causes. Demand-pull inflation arises when the total demand for goods and services is greater than the available supply of goods and services. It usually occurs during periods of full employment when we are unable to increase the output of goods and services in the short run. Cost-push inflation results when businesses increase their prices to offset an increase in the cost of labor and materials or for some other reason. Price increases lead to further increases in wages and materials, which bring about further increases in prices. Structural inflation is a combination of demand-pull and cost-push. Cost-push, structural, and social inflation may occur in an economy at full employment or less. In the past few decades the U.S. economy has experienced both unemployment and inflation due to a variety of causes.

Since prices play such an integral part in our economic system, both from a microeconomic and a macroeconomic point of view, in the next part we shall look behind the general scene to see how supply and demand determine prices, as well as how the various market structures affect prices and production.

## DISCUSSION QUESTIONS

1. Explain the relationship of investment to saving and the effect of that relationship on the circular flow of economic activity.
2. How can the accumulation of large inventories adversely affect the circular flow of economic activity?
3. Why does increased investment sometimes accelerate the circular flow of business activity and at other times merely affect prices?
4. Why is it necessary to consider the government sector of the economy as part of the circular flow?
5. What effect will a surplus budget have on the circular flow of economic activity?
6. Will a deficit budget always increase the level of business activity? Why or why not?
7. Do you think that government spending should be used to stabilize the level of production and employment? Explain.
8. Distinguish among the four types of inflation: demand-pull, cost-push, structural, and social.
9. What type of inflation is most likely to occur in a period of less than full employment? Why?
10. How does stagflation compound the difficulty of applying measures to stabilize the level of production and employment?

## SUGGESTED READINGS

The Suggested Readings for this chapter are included in Chapter 3, pages 55–56.

# Part 2

# The Market Mechanism and Competitive Structure

# 5 PRICE DETERMINATION: THE ROLE OF DEMAND AND SUPPLY

## THE MARKET MECHANISM

In a free enterprise system the forces of supply and demand are relied upon to determine prices. Consumers express their demand in the prices they are willing to pay for various products. Business firms seeking profit cater to consumer demand by offering goods and services at various prices. Consequently, a market is established in which the final price of a good or service is determined on the basis of costs to the producer and usefulness to the buyer.

Changes in either demand or supply bring about adjustments in the amount of goods and services sold, or price changes, or both. If consumers throughout the nation, for example, begin buying more lawn mowers, retail outlets will have to order inventory replacements and additional mowers from wholesalers. Manufacturers in turn begin to produce more mowers. Depending on the available supply and the cost of resources, these additional mowers may be supplied at the same or at a different price. At any rate, consumer demand is made known to the producers through the marketing structure. At other times, suppliers will endeavor to anticipate the demands of consumers and supply the goods before there is a strong reflection of demand. The system does not work perfectly; at times there are lags and leads in the market, gluts and shortages occur, and prices fluctuate. But considering the billions of items produced and sold each year, the system seems somehow to do an excellent job of satisfying consumer demand.

The demand for goods of all kinds — producer goods as well as consumer goods — can be traced to the demand for goods and services that directly satisfy human wants. For example, the demand or desire of individuals for shelter gives rise to a demand for brick and lumber which, in turn, gives rise to a demand for iron and steel with which to make tools and machines for the production of brick and lumber, and so on. Therefore, we may say that the demand for a commodity that grows out of the desire to satisfy the demand for some other commodity or service is *derived demand*.

### DEMAND

In studying the influence of demand on the price of any given commodity or service, we must recognize two levels of demand — individual, or personal demand and market demand. Market demand is merely the aggregate of personal demand.

### Individual Demand

Demand implies something more than need or desire. Of course, an individual must feel a need for the usefulness that a good can provide before considering ways and means of procuring the good. In addition, however, an individual must possess purchasing power if the need is to be satisfied. You may have a strong desire, for example, for a new model Corvette or Porsche; but unless you have the cash to pay for it, or the ability to buy on credit, your desire will have no influence on the market. Individual demand therefore implies a desire plus some purchasing power. It signifies the quantity of a good that an individual stands ready to buy at each price at a particular time.

The usefulness of a good to an individual at a particular time depends upon the number of units that the individual has recently consumed or that may be available for use when desired. If the number of units that have been consumed or that are available is large, the additional usefulness of an additional unit is likely to be lower than it otherwise would be. The price of a commodity will usually affect the quantity that an individual will buy at a given time. For example, a shopper may buy one pound of butter at the grocery at a given price, but would purchase less if the price were higher. On the other hand, the shopper may buy two pounds if the price is low enough. Again, merchants are aware of the relationship of the subjective prices of potential buyers — the prices that buyers will pay — to quantities that will be bought when they conduct sales at reduced prices and give quantity discounts.

### Market Demand

*Market demand* (or simply demand) consists of the total quantity of a good that would be bought in the aggregate by individuals and firms at each of several prices at a given time. *Demand*, therefore, is defined as a schedule of the total quantities that purchasers will buy at different prices at a given time. An accurate schedule of this kind for a specific commodity is difficult to construct in advance because it requires that we know just how many units people would actually buy at various prices. We do know, however, that at a given time people will usually buy more units of a good at a low price than they will at a high price. The reasons, of course, are the three simple and general facts that: (1) those who are willing to buy the commodity at a high price may purchase more of the product at a lower price; (2) some buyers in lower income groups may not be able to afford the product at a high price, but will buy the product at a lower price; and (3) some persons who could afford to purchase the product at a high price, but may not do so because they do not think that it is worth the price, will buy the product at a lower price. A lower price for an article, therefore, nearly always results in the sale of a larger amount of that product. Conversely, a higher price, other things remaining the same, usually tends to curtail the amount that can be sold. Thus, we are justified in concluding that the quantity of a good that people will buy tends to vary inversely with the price.

The expression "tends to vary inversely," as used here, does not imply that the variation in the amount sold is always proportionate to the change in price. Indeed, in many instances a decrease of 50 percent in the price of a good probably would not result in a 50 percent increase in the number of units sold; nor would an increase of 100 percent in the price likely result in a corresponding decrease in the amount that would be purchased. In some cases the change in the quantity sold might be more than proportional to the change in price; in others, it might be less.

### A Market Demand Schedule

Since the quantity of any good demanded ordinarily tends to vary inversely with its price, we can construct a hypothetical schedule of prices and quantities to illustrate this relationship. Let us assume on Tuesday at noon the buyers at the Winnipeg market would buy at different prices the amounts of No. 2 rye shown in the second column, $D$ (demand), in Table 5-1. Notice that larger amounts of rye would be bought at lower prices.

The relationship between price and the number of bushels that would be bought is represented graphically in Figure 5-1. The vertical line, $OY$,

Table 5-1   **DEMAND SCHEDULE FOR RYE**

| If the Price Is: | Thousands of Bushels of Rye That Will Be Bought | | |
|---|---|---|---|
| | $D$ | $D_1$ | $D_2$ |
| $1.50 | 2,000 | 3,000 | 1,000 |
| 1.45 | 2,300 | 3,400 | 1,300 |
| 1.40 | 2,800 | 4,300 | 1,610 |
| 1.35 | 3,500 | 4,800 | 2,100 |
| 1.30 | 4,200 | 5,600 | 2,700 |
| 1.25 | 5,100 | 6,625 | 3,425 |
| 1:20 | 6,075 | 7,650 | 4,400 |
| 1.15 | 7,250 | 9,000 | 5,410 |
| 1.10 | 8,500 | 10,400 | 6,700 |
| 1.05 | 10,000 | 12,000 | 8,000 |

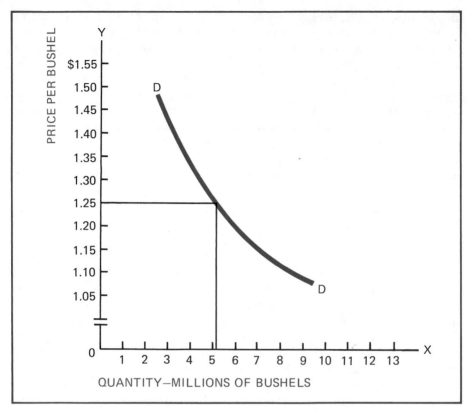

Figure 5-1    **DEMAND CURVE FOR RYE**

indicates at regular intervals the price per bushel, and the horizontal line, *OX*, shows the quantity in millions of bushels. We can locate points that lie at the intersection of a line drawn horizontally and to the right from each price shown on *OY* and a line drawn vertically and upward from each corresponding quantity indicated on *OX*. Thus, to locate the point for the demand for 5,100,000 bushels at $1.25 a bushel, a horizontal line to the right is drawn from that price and a vertical line upward is drawn from that quantity. The point of intersection of the two lines is thus determined by reference to the two coordinates, price and quantity.

When all the points have been located in this way, they suggest a curve that slopes downward to the right. If the price and the quantity changes were infinitely small and if they varied according to the proportions indicated in the schedules, the result in the graph would really be such a curve. For our purposes, therefore, we may construct a curve to indicate demand. This curve is merely a graphic way of representing how the quantity of rye that would be bought varies inversely with price.

The demand schedule may be represented by a curve or by a straight line. The curve may have a slight or a steep slope, it may be continuous or discontinuous, or it may be smooth or jagged, depending on the nature of the demand for the particular product and the ability to obtain sufficient information to plot the demand schedule. Consequently, there are all kinds and shapes of demand curves.

Although the normal or typical demand curve moves downward to the right, it is not uncommon to find a product for which the demand will move downward to the right over a given range of prices, but then eventually curve backward to the left. This would indicate, of course, that in certain price ranges less of the product would be purchased at lower prices. Prestige items are sometimes in this category. Mink coats, for example, are a status symbol to many people. As the price is lowered, more people will buy mink coats. But if the price became so low that almost anyone could afford to buy a mink coat, it would lose its prestige status and it is possible that few people would want to buy one.

### Changes in Demand

Remember that on a typical demand curve more will be sold at lower prices. Notice on the demand curve in Figure 5-1 that at a price of $1.25 a little over 5 million bushels of rye would be sold, but at a price of $1.20 more than 6 million bushels would be sold. Consequently, if a price of $1.20 were charged instead of $1.25, does this mean that there is an increase in demand? Absolutely not. Remember that we defined demand as a schedule of amounts that would be purchased at various prices at a given instant in time. Even though we altered the price from $1.25 to $1.20 and sold more, this is not a change in demand. Nothing has happened to the demand schedule. We simply moved to a lower price to take advantage of larger sales at lower prices. This is known as a movement along the demand curve, or sometimes referred to as a change in the quantity demanded, and should not be confused with a change in demand. To have a change in demand, or what is sometimes referred to as a shift in demand, a greater or lesser amount of the product would necessarily be purchased at given prices.

An increase in demand means that a greater quantity will be bought at the same price. Thus, in Table 5-1, $D_1$ is a schedule showing an increase in the amount that will be purchased at each of the prices as compared with that for $D$ in the second column. If the demand curve for $D_1$ is plotted, it will lie to the right of that of $D$, as shown in Figure 5-2. It indicates, for example, that at a price of $1.25, 6.6 million bushels will be sold.

A decrease in demand means that a smaller quantity will be bought at the same price. In Table 5-1, $D_2$ is a schedule showing a decrease in demand, as compared with that for $D$. The curve for $D_2$ would lie to the left of that for $D$, as shown in Figure 5-2. A change in demand may result from a number of different causes, such as a change in income, a change in population, new uses for a product, more advertising, and even a change in the prices of competing products.

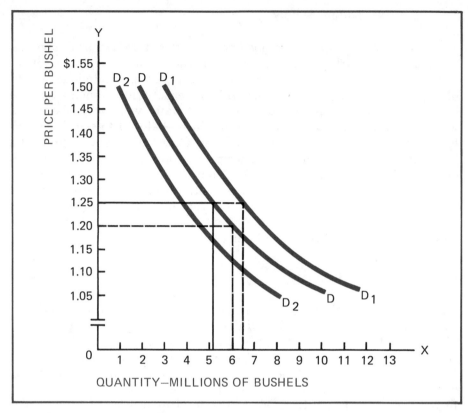

Figure 5-2    **DEMAND CURVES FOR RYE**

## Quantity Sold as a Function of Price

Although we usually think of the quantity of a good sold as dependent upon, or as a function of, price and express it as $q = f(p)$, it should be readily apparent now that many other factors besides price affect the quantity of a good sold. The quantity sold is also influenced by the level of disposable income, by the price of other goods (both complementary and substitute goods), by advertising promotion outlays, and by many other considerations. Thus, it is just as proper to write $q = f(DI)$, disposable income, or to combine all factors affecting quantity sold into one equation and express it as follows: $q = f(p, DI, p_x, a, \ldots)$ etc., where $p$ is the price of the product itself, $DI$ is the level of disposable income, $p_x$ is the price of other commodities, and $a$ is the advertising outlay.

## SUPPLY

As in the case of the demand for goods, there are also two aspects of the supply of goods: individual supply and market supply.

### Individual Supply

The *individual supply* of a good that is offered on a market signifies the quantities of the good that an individual stands ready to sell at various prices. To determine the total supply that any individual might offer to sell, it would be necessary to know exactly how much would be sold at each possible price. For example, if water were very scarce and you possessed a limited supply, you might be induced to sell a few gallons at a certain price. If the price offered were higher, you might sell a larger quantity; and at a still higher price, you might be willing to sell even more. But if your life depended upon retaining a minimum supply for your own use, you would not part with all of the remainder at any price. This example illustrates the point that individual supply, which is contributed to the total market supply, consists only of that portion of stock that an individual can be induced to sell at various prices.

### Market Supply

The *market supply* of a good consists of the total quantities of the good that sellers stand ready to sell at different prices at a given time. A schedule representing the market supply of a good would contain all the quantities of the good that all potential sellers would sell at various prices. As in the case of the demand for a good, it is essential to keep in mind that we are considering here the behavior of a great many individuals or firms. The market supply refers to the total quantities of a particular homogeneous product, one that is identical with all the sellers. Supply, like demand, is always specific. For example, it does little good to talk about the supply of automobiles in the market. To be meaningful as far as measurement is concerned, we must talk about the supply of Fords, Chevrolets, Plymouths, Cadillacs, Datsuns, and various other makes and models. It is obvious that the supply of and the demand for Cadillacs constitute a different market than the demand for Datsuns.

### A Market Supply Schedule

As in the case of demand, it is possible and convenient for purposes of analysis to construct a market supply schedule. Therefore, let us set up a hypothetical market supply schedule for No. 2 rye on the Winnipeg market at noon on Tuesday, as shown in the first and second columns of Table 5-2.

The same method used in plotting the demand curve for rye can be used to plot the supply curve, which is shown by S in Figure 5-3. A supply curve is a line indicating the number of units of a good or service that will be offered for sale at different prices. The supply curve rises from left to right because, as the price continues to rise, the intersections of lines drawn from prices and quantities climb higher and higher to the right.

Table 5-2   SUPPLY SCHEDULES FOR RYE

| If the Price Is: | Thousands of Bushels of Rye That Will Be Offered | | |
| | S | $S_1$ | $S_2$ |
| --- | --- | --- | --- |
| $1.50 | 10,000 | 11,050 | 8,950 |
| 1.45 | 9,600 | 10,800 | 8,400 |
| 1.40 | 9,200 | 10,400 | 7,800 |
| 1.35 | 8,475 | 9,800 | 7,200 |
| 1.30 | 7,800 | 9,050 | 6,250 |
| 1.25 | 6,850 | 8,400 | 5,250 |
| 1.20 | 5,900 | 7,250 | 4,250 |
| 1.15 | 4,800 | 6,400 | 3,000 |
| 1.10 | 3,600 | 5,250 | 1,600 |
| 1.05 | 2,000 | 4,000 | 0 |

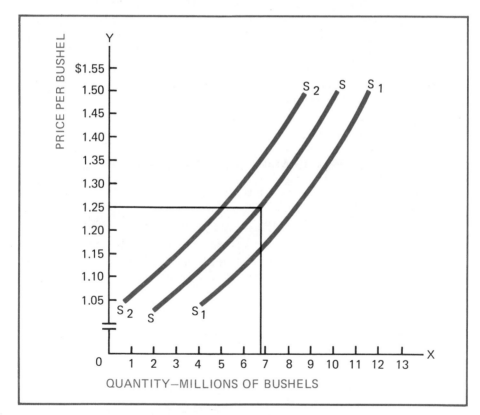

Figure 5-3   SUPPLY CURVES FOR RYE

An increase in supply means that a greater quantity will be offered at a given price. Thus, in Table 5-2, $S_1$, the third column, shows that at $1.50 more rye will be offered for sale than was indicated in the first schedule, $S$. And so for each price, a greater quantity will be offered for sale. A decrease in supply means that a smaller quantity will be offered for sale at a given price. If we plot the supply curve for $S_1$, the curve will lie below that for $S$; and the curve for $S_2$, showing a decrease in supply, will lie above that for $S$.

### Changes in Supply

Market supply is the obverse or counterpart of market demand. In the case of reproducible goods, the quantity demanded usually tends to vary inversely with price. The supply offered, on the other hand, ordinarily tends to vary directly with price; that is, a higher price usually — but not always — results in a greater amount offered for sale. But remember, just as with demand, when price changes, and a greater or lesser amount is offered for sale, that is not a change in supply. It is merely a movement or shift along the supply curve.

A change in supply means that a different quantity will be offered for sale at each price. An increase in supply means that a larger amount will be offered; a decrease in supply means that a smaller quantity will be offered at the same price, as shown in Table 5-2.

The total quantity that will be offered for sale is limited both by the quantity in existence at the time and by estimates of prospective sellers as to probable costs of producing future supplies of the good. In the long run, however, the supply of reproducible goods is conditioned by the availability of the factors of production and by the costs of production.

### HOW DEMAND AND SUPPLY DETERMINE PRICE

Now let us assume that at noon on Tuesday the demand for and the supply of rye on the Winnipeg market are as shown in the second columns of Tables 5-1 and 5-2. Table 5-3 reproduces these schedules.

Table 5-3   **DEMAND AND SUPPLY SCHEDULES FOR RYE**
(Thousands of Bushels That Will Be Bought and Sold)

| Price per Bushel | Demand | Supply |
|---|---|---|
| $1.50 | 2,000 | 10,000 |
| 1.45 | 2,300 | 9,600 |
| 1.40 | 2,800 | 9,200 |
| 1.35 | 3,500 | 8,475 |
| 1.30 | 4,200 | 7,800 |
| 1.25 | 5,100 | 6,850 |
| 1.20 | 6,075 | 5,900 |
| 1.15 | 7,250 | 4,800 |
| 1.10 | 8,500 | 3,600 |
| 1.05 | 10,000 | 2,000 |

At what price will rye sell on the commodity exchange? The price will be determined by the interaction of demand and supply and will be at the point where "demand and supply are equal." More precisely, the price will be determined where the quantity demanded equals the quantity supplied. Since the market is cleared, this price is known as the equilibrium price.

To show the interactive relationships of demand and supply, we can reconstruct the demand and supply curves for the schedules in Table 5-3, superimposing one on the other as in Figure 5-4 below. With reference to price and quantity, the curves intersect at a point that indicates a price of $1.21 and a quantity of 6 million bushels. What is the significance of this?

It simply means that at a price of $1.21, 6 million bushels will be bought and an equal amount will be offered for sale. According to our definition of competition, since no single transaction can affect the market price, any buyer who wants to buy rye at this price can buy as much as desired. Likewise, any seller can sell at the same price. No buyer whose subjective price is higher than $1.21 needs to pay more because at

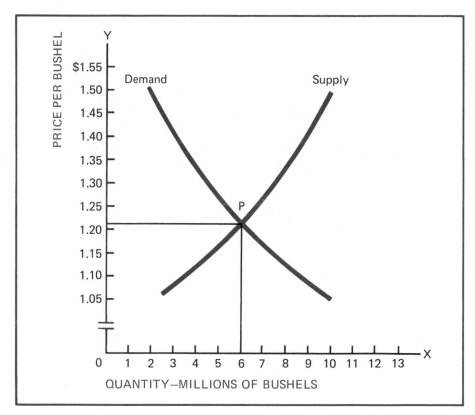

Figure 5-4    **DEMAND, SUPPLY, AND MARKET PRICE**

that price as much as is desired can be purchased. And no buyer unwilling to pay that much can buy.

On the other hand, sellers whose subjective prices are lower than $1.21 can sell at the higher price. And those who are unwilling to sell at that price will have to keep their rye because buyers can obtain all they want at that price. Therefore, the price of $1.21 is the equilibrium price and cannot change until there is a change in the relationships between demand and supply. This explains what we mean when we say that the forces of demand and supply are impersonal, and that under a condition of pure competition no one individual can influence the market price either by buying or refusing to buy, or by selling or refusing to sell.

Under these conditions of demand and supply, if the price were anything other than $1.21, the quantities consumers would be willing to buy and the amount of rye offered for sale would be out of balance. In such a situation forces of the market would come into play to adjust the price to $1.21, or the equilibrium level. At the price of $1.25, for instance, the quantity sellers would be willing to supply would exceed by approximately 2 million bushels the quantity demanded by buyers. Consequently, not all the rye would be sold. But notice that there are sellers who are willing to sell their rye at lower prices of $1.23, $1.22, etc. Rather than hold their rye, they will offer to sell at the lower prices. As the price is lowered, notice that certain buyers would not pay $1.25 for rye but will pay $1.24, $1.23, or less. Therefore, as the market conditions force the price of rye downward, the number of sellers decreases and the number of buyers increases until the amount of rye offered for sale and the quantity purchased come into balance at an equilibrium price of $1.21.

On the contrary, if a price of $1.15 exists in such a market, it cannot continue. At that price the quantity demanded exceeds the quantity supplied by more than 2 million bushels and some potential buyers would have to go without. But observe that some of the buyers are willing to pay more than $1.15 for a bushel of rye. Rather than go without they would offer higher prices of $1.17, $1.19, and upward. As they bid the price upward, a twofold action takes place in the market. The higher prices will deter some buyers from making purchases as well as induce more sellers to offer their product for sale. The resulting increase in the amount offered for sale and the decrease in the amount that will be purchased finally bring supply and demand into balance at the equilibrium price of $1.21. In a freely competitive market no other price can prevail. At any other price either a surplus or a shortage of the good will exist in the short run, as shown in Figure 5-5.

If someone wants to set the price at other than the market price established by the free forces of supply and demand, the market will have to be rigged or the forces of supply and demand changed. This is exactly what happens when the government sets a parity price for certain agricultural commodities that is higher than the market price, or establishes a ceiling price lower than the market price during a wartime period. Business firms charged with price fixing are often guilty of collusion with

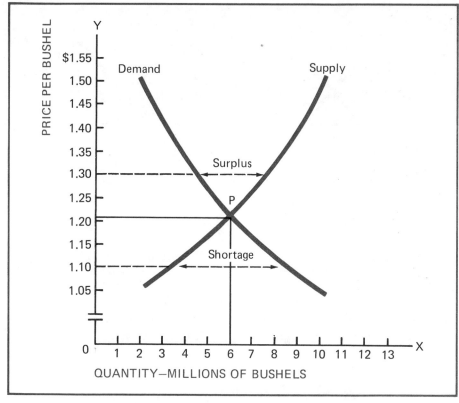

Figure 5-5   **SURPLUS, SHORTAGE, AND EQUILIBRIUM**

other firms in an effort to interfere with the free forces of demand and supply.

Under competitive conditions the number of possible relationships between demand and supply is practically infinite. For instance, demand may increase while supply remains constant, or vice versa. Again, demand may increase while supply decreases, or vice versa. Or both demand and supply may increase, but demand may increase more than supply.

In any case, however, we can rely on this simple principle: In any new relationship between demand and supply, an increase in demand relative to supply is sure to result in a higher price, and any decrease in demand relative to supply will result in a lower price. On the other hand, an increase in supply will lower the price, and a decrease in supply will raise the price, other things remaining unchanged, as can be seen in Figure 5-6. Based on these principles, it is easy to visualize why world oil prices skyrocketed in the early 1970s when the Arabian oil nations imposed a petroleum export embargo. The decreased supply of oil coupled with an increasing demand led to substantially higher world oil prices.

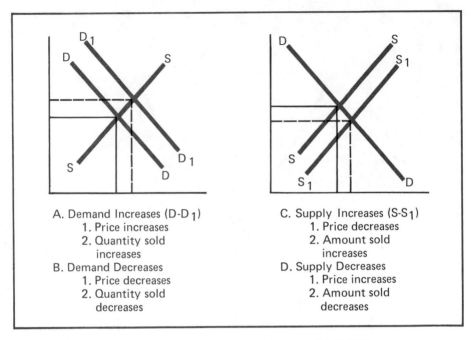

A. Demand Increases (D-D$_1$)
  1. Price increases
  2. Quantity sold
    increases
B. Demand Decreases
  1. Price decreases
  2. Quantity sold
    decreases

C. Supply Increases (S-S$_1$)
  1. Price decreases
  2. Amount sold
    increases
D. Supply Decreases
  1. Price increases
  2. Amount sold
    decreases

Figure 5-6    **ALTERNATE SUPPLY AND DEMAND POSITIONS**

## ELASTICITY OF DEMAND

Since demand is a schedule of amounts that will be purchased at various prices, the seller is often faced with a problem of determining at which price to offer goods for sale. It is true that a greater amount of sales can be made at lower prices. But will greater revenue from the larger sales offset the reduced revenue from the lower price? Since the change in sales is not always proportional to the change in price, this can present a real problem not only to sellers but also to buyers. Fortunately there is a way to measure the change in relationship between price and the amount sold. *Price elasticity of demand* is a measure of consumer responsiveness to a change in price. Whether a merchant will benefit by an increase or decrease in price will depend on the degree of price elasticity.

### Measuring Price Elasticity of Demand

Let us illustrate price elasticity of demand by constructing three demand curves and measuring their elasticities. In Figure 5-7, observe that for the demand schedule $D$, 1,600 units are sold at the price of $10; but if the sale price were only $8, the number of units sold would then be 2,000. Elasticity may be measured in either of two ways: (1) by the formula method, and (2) by the total revenue method.

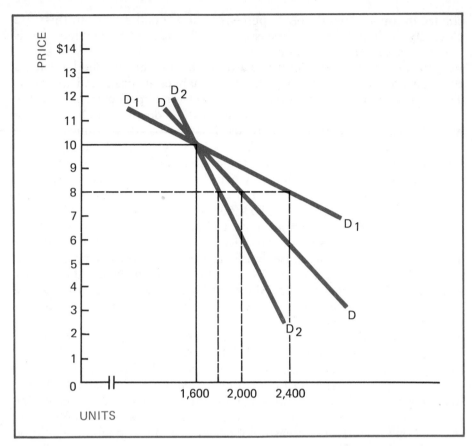

Figure 5-7   DEMAND CURVES SHOWING DIFFERENT ELASTICITIES

**Formula Method**   The formula simply measures the relative change in amount sold to the relative change in price and may be stated thus:

$$\text{Price Elasticity} = \frac{\%\ \text{change in quantity}}{\%\ \text{change in price}}$$

A few minor problems arise in applying the formula. The percentage changes can be computed by using the original price and quantity as bases. If this is done, however, the result will be a different measure of elasticity, depending on whether the price is being decreased or increased. If the price is decreased, notice that the $2 price change is a 20 percent change compared to the original price base of $10. If this 20 percent change is divided into the 25 percent change in quantity (400 ÷ 1,600 = .25), the measure of elasticity would be 1.25 (.25 ÷ .20 = 1.25). On the other hand, if the price has been moved from $8 up to $10 and the amount sold decreased from 2,000 units to 1,600 units, the percentage change in price would be 25 percent ($2 ÷ $8 = .25) and the relative change in amount would be 20 percent (400 ÷ 2,000 = .20). In this case elasticity of demand would measure .8 (.20 ÷ .25 = .8). Obviously this would lead to much confusion.

This difficulty of conflicting measurements can be avoided by using a constant base in calculating percentage changes in price and quantity. This can be done by always using the lower (or upper) extremity of the change as a base whether moving upward or downward. In the case above, if $8 and 1,600 units were used as the bases in computing the percentage changes, the measure of elasticity, whether lowering or raising prices, would be 1.0. Lowering the price from $10 to $8, for example, will result in a 25 percent change when the lower extremity is used as a base of the change ($2 ÷ $8 = .25). If the amount sold at the lower price, $8, is 2,000 units compared to the 1,600 units that would be sold at the higher price, $10, this also represents a 25 percent change (400 ÷ 1,600 = .25). This yields a measure of elasticity of 1.0 (.25 ÷ .25 = 1.0). Since the same price and quantity bases and the same absolute changes are involved when the price is raised from $8 to $10, the measure of elasticity is the same in either direction. Since the formula is designed to measure the effects of only small increments or decrements in price, any mathematical error will be minimal.

Another method often used is to calculate the percentage change by using an average base. Consequently, the percentage change will be identical whether moving up or down on the price axis. In the preceding example the absolute change in price of $2 would be divided by $9 (the average price between $10 and $8) and would be equal to 22 percent. The relative change in amount sold would likewise be 22 percent (400 ÷ 1,800 = .22). Consequently, the measure of price elasticity of demand would be 1.0 (.22 ÷ .22 = 1.0). This means that a given change in price will bring about a proportional change in the quantity sold. A 1 percent decrease in price results in a 1 percent increase in quantity sold. A 3 percent increase in price will result in a 3 percent decrease in quantity, and so forth. A coefficient of elasticity of 1.0 is known as *unit elasticity*, and is the point of demarcation between an elastic and an inelastic demand. Any value greater than 1.0 is known as an *elastic demand*, and anything less than 1.0 is referred to as an *inelastic demand*.

Now let us measure the elasticity for the demand schedule $D_1$ in Figure 5-7, page 87. Observe that when price is changed from $10 to $8, a 22 percent change when using the average price as a base of the change, the quantity demanded increased from 1,600 to 2,400 units, an increase of 40 percent (800 ÷ 2,000 = .40). In this case the measure of elasticity is 1.8 (.40 ÷ .22 = 1.8). This means that a 2 percent change in price, for example, will result in a 3.6 percent change in the quantity demand. In short, consumer demand is elastic and the quantity demanded will change in greater proportion than the change in price.

Demand schedule $D_2$ shows less consumer responsiveness to a change in price. Notice that a 22 percent decrease in price from $10 to $8 results in a mere 11 percent increase in quantity sold. This gives an elasticity of demand of .5, which indicates that the demand is inelastic and that a change in price will bring about a less than proportional change in the amount sold. A 1 percent change in price will result in a .5 percent change in the quantity sold. A 3 percent increase in price will result in a 1.5 percent decrease in sales.

**Total Revenue Method**    Of what importance is this information about elasticity, inelasticity, and measures of 1.8, .5, and 1.0? To the seller it is extremely important, since it indicates what is going to happen to total revenue received from the sale of products as prices increase or decrease. Likewise, it is important to the consumer. After all, total revenue received by sellers from the sale of the product is nothing other than total expenditures for the product by buyers. From a given consumer income, more spent on one commodity, of course, means that there will be less to spend on other commodities.

The total revenue method of measuring elasticity is less exacting, but it tells more directly what happens to total revenue. Furthermore, it shows more clearly the important significance of a coefficient of elasticity. The total revenue method of measuring price elasticity can be explained by remembering the following: (1) If price changes and total revenue remains constant, unit elasticity of demand exists. In such a case, for example, the decrease in revenue resulting from a lower price will be offset by the increase in revenue resulting from an increase in sales. This is so because if elasticity is 1.0, sales will increase in proportion to a price decrease. (2) If price changes and total revenue moves in the opposite direction from the price change, demand is elastic. In this case, the decrease in revenue from a decrease in price is more than offset by the increase in revenue from an increase in sales. This is so because when elasticity is more than 1.0, sales change in greater proportion than price changes. (3) If price changes and total revenue moves in the same direction as the price change, demand is inelastic. In this case, due to an elasticity of less than 1.0, the increased revenue from higher sales will be insufficient to make up for the loss of revenue due to a lower price.

The measure of elasticity can be applied to supply also. If a given percentage change in the price of a good results in a greater percentage change in the quantity supplied, the supply is elastic. If the percentage change in price results in a lesser percentage change in the quantity offered, the supply is inelastic. And if the percentage change in price results in a proportionate change in the quantity offered for sale, unit elasticity exists.

### Characteristics and Range of Price Elasticity

It is not easy to construct an empirical demand curve, let alone calculate the elasticity of demand for a product. In the first place, it may be difficult to gather sufficient statistical information to determine how much of a good consumers will buy at each of a series of prices. But it can be done and is being done more and more for firms by business economists and market analysts. Secondly, if a price change is made in an effort to observe the change in quantity demanded, the analyst must be certain that no other changes are taking place, such as an increase in income or greater advertising expenditures, that also will have an influence on the demand for the product.

The degree of price elasticity will depend on the nature of the product or service, such as whether it is a necessity or a luxury; whether it is a small or large budget expenditure for the buyer; whether it is a durable or perishable item; whether it is a complementary or substitute item; and the number of uses to which the item can be put, as summarized in Table 5-4.

The degree of elasticity may range from perfect elasticity, which indicates that an infinite amount of the product could be sold without a change in price (depicted as a straight horizontal line in Figure 5-8a), to perfect inelasticity of demand, which indicates that the same amount would be purchased regardless of price (represented by the straight vertical line in Figure 5-8b). Most goods and services, of course, have a price elasticity lying somewhere between the two extremes.

Table 5-4   **CHARACTERISTICS AFFECTING ELASTICITY**

| Tend Toward Elasticity | Tend Toward Inelasticity |
| --- | --- |
| Luxuries | Necessities |
| Large expenditures | Small expenditures |
| Durable goods | Perishable goods |
| Substitute goods | Complementary goods |
| Multiple uses | Limited uses |

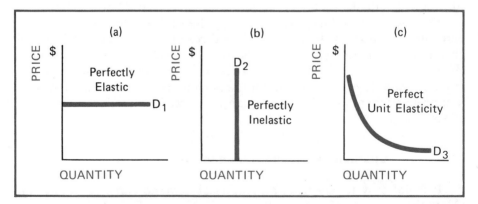

Figure 5-8   **THREE DEMAND CURVES SHOWING DIFFERENT ELASTICITIES**

Although we tend to say that the more horizontal the demand curve the more it tends to be elastic, this is not always true. Anytime you have a straight-line, slanted demand schedule, there will no doubt be certain areas of the schedule that are elastic, others that are inelastic, and at some spot it may measure unit elasticity. Related to this is the notion, which sometimes exists, that a 45° line represents unit elasticity. This would not be true on a conventional demand curve. Both of these errors can be clarified by referring to Figure 5-9. Notice on the demand line that a change in price from $9 to $8, a price change of less than 12 percent, brings about a change in quantity demanded from 10 to 20 units, an increase of 67 percent (using the midpoint as the base of the percentage change). At the lower end of the vertical axis a price change from $2 to $1, which represents a 67 percent change in price, results in an increase in quantity demanded from 80 to 90 units, or a quantity change of less than 12 percent. At one end of the scale we have a price elasticity of demand of more than 5.0 and a highly inelastic measure of less than .2 at the other end of the demand schedule. Observe further that, if price were changed from $5.50 to $4.50 and the quantity demanded moved from 45 units to 55 units, unit elasticity would prevail. Any change in price

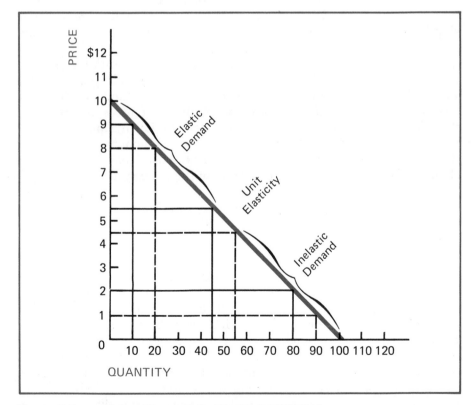

Figure 5-9    **DEMAND CURVE SHOWING DIFFERING
DEGREES OF ELASTICITY**

through the range of $10 to $5.50 is elastic, but any change in price between $4.50 and $1.00 is inelastic. In fact, on the given demand schedule the point of maximum revenue for the seller would be in the vicinity of $5, since a higher price would result in a decrease in revenue, as would a lower price. Obviously on a straight line demand curve it is possible for a product to be elastic at some price ranges and inelastic at others. For a demand schedule to possess unit elasticity throughout, it would have to be represented by a hyperbola as shown in Figure 5-8c, page 90. In such a situation, changes in price and quantity demanded are proportional throughout the curve.

The quantity demanded of a particular good or service is affected not only by its price but also by the price of other goods or services. A change in the price of commodity *A*, which may be a substitute or complementary product, can affect the sales of product *B*. This is usually referred to as *cross elasticity of demand*. In addition, the quantity demanded for a given good or service is affected by the level of income of potential buyers. As the level of income rises, the total demand for goods and services likewise will rise. But the demand for each good and service does not necessarily rise proportionally with a rise in income. The demand for some goods and/or services may rise in greater proportion than the increase in income and the demand for others less than proportionally. The relationship between changing income and changes in demand for a particular good or service is known as *income elasticity of demand*.

In previous chapters we learned that prices serve as rationing mechanisms in allocating final goods and services, that prices help allocate the various factors of production to their respective uses, and that prices in large part help determine incomes. The reliability of prices in performing these functions greatly depends on the extent to which competition prevails within the economy. The presence of monopoly, strong labor unions, government regulations, and other institutional factors, as we shall soon see, can modify the operation of the price system.

### SUMMARY

In a free enterprise system the forces of demand and supply are relied upon to determine prices. Individual demand signifies the quantities of a good that an individual stands ready to buy at different prices. Due to the operation of the principle of diminishing utility and to limitations of purchasing power, an individual will usually buy more units of a commodity or a service at a lower price than at a higher price. Market demand is the total quantity of a commodity that will be bought in the market at a given time. It may be represented by a schedule indicating the quantities of a commodity that would be purchased at different prices at a given time. An increase in demand implies that more of a commodity will be purchased at given prices; a decrease in demand means that fewer units will be purchased at given prices.

The supply of a good or service at a given time is the quantity that sellers will offer for sale at different prices. The term may refer to individual or market supply. Supply may be represented by a schedule of the quantities that will be offered at different prices at a given time. An increase in supply implies that more of a commodity will be made available at given prices; a decrease in supply means that fewer commodities will be made available at given prices. Under competitive conditions, price is fixed at that point where demand and supply are in equilibrium, and it cannot change unless there is a change in demand or supply or both.

Elasticity of demand refers to the ratio between the percentage change in price and the percentage change in the quantity of a good that will be purchased as a result of a change in price. There are various degrees of elasticity of demand. It is significant because of its relation to revenue. Price elasticity of demand may be measured by either the formula method or the total revenue method. An elasticity coefficient of 1.0 designates unit elasticity. Anything above 1.0 is said to be elastic, while any measure below 1.0 is inelastic. According to the total revenue method, if total revenue moves in the opposite direction from a price change, demand is said to be elastic. If it moves in the same direction, it is inelastic; and if total revenue remains constant, unit elasticity exists. Among the factors that affect price elasticity of demand are the nature of the product, its price in relation to total budget expenditures, the durability of the product, the availability of substitutes, and the number of uses. Elasticity of demand may range from one extreme to the other, from perfect elasticity at one extreme to perfect inelasticity at the other. It is also possible to calculate cross elasticity and income elasticity of demand. In many respects these are as important as price elasticity.

From this chapter we learned the importance of demand and supply in determining price and reiterated the role of the pricing mechanism. Since the efficiency of the pricing system in fulfilling its functions will depend in large part on the degree of competition that exists, we will now turn to the subject of competition within the economy.

## DISCUSSION QUESTIONS

1. Under most competitive conditions prices are determined by the impersonal forces of demand and supply in the market. Explain.
2. Define demand. What are the three basic elements in the definition?
3. Why does a normal demand curve slope downward to the right?
4. Distinguish between a movement along a demand curve and a change in demand.

5. Why does the supply curve slope upward to the right?
6. Explain why under competitive conditions market price cannot be higher or lower than that established by the free forces of demand and supply.
7. If both demand and supply increased, but demand increased more than supply, what would happen to price?

8. Define price elasticity of demand. If 46,000 units of a good could be sold at a price of $22, but 54,000 units could be sold at a price of $18, would the demand for the good be elastic or inelastic? What would be the elasticity coefficient?

9. Distinguish among perfect elasticity, perfect inelasticity, and unit elasticity of demand. In your answer indicate what type of demand curve represents each of these types of elasticity.

10. What other types of demand elasticity exist in addition to price elasticity of demand?

## SUGGESTED READINGS

Allen, C. L. *The Framework of Price Theory*. Belmont, Calif.: Wadsworth Publishing Company, Inc., 1967.

Friedman, Milton. *Capitalism and Freedom*. Chicago: University of Chicago Press, 1962.

Galbraith, John Kenneth. *The New Industrial State*. Boston: Houghton Mifflin Company, 1971.

Leftwich, Richard H. *The Price System and Resource Allocation*. New York: Holt, Rinehart & Winston, Inc., 1973.

Levenson, Albert M., and Babette S. Solon. *Essential Price Theory*. New York: Holt, Rinehart and Winston, Inc., 1971.

Liebhafsky, H. H. *The Nature of Price Theory*. Dallas: Business Publications, Inc., 1968.

Loucks, William N., and William G. Whitney. *Comparative Economic Systems*. New York: Harper & Row, Publishers, 1973.

Mansfield, Edwin. *Microeconomics*, 2d ed. New York: W. W. Norton & Company, Inc., 1975.

Neel, Richard E. *Readings in Price Theory*. Cincinnati: South-Western Publishing Co., 1973.

Schumpeter, Joseph A. *The Nature and Necessity of a Price System*. New York: Columbia University Press, 1934.

――――――――――, and James K. Kindahl. *The Behavior of Industrial Prices*. New York: National Bureau of Economic Research, 1970.

Watson, Donald S. *Price Theory and Its Uses*. Boston: Houghton Mifflin Company, 1972.

# 6 PURE COMPETITION: A MODEL

## PRODUCTION, COST, AND PROFIT

Under perfectly competitive conditions there is nothing the firm can do to control the revenue it receives per unit of output, for revenue per unit of output is nothing other than the product price determined by aggregate market forces of demand and supply. There is nothing the firm can do either regarding its cost per unit of input because cost per unit of input is the price of a factor of production determined by supply and demand in the factor or resource market. Nevertheless, the firm can alter its cost per unit of output. A decrease in cost per unit of output can be accomplished by using better production techniques, by obtaining more efficient use of labor, by spreading its fixed cost over a greater range of output, and by other methods. Since a firm's cost of production largely determines the supply of goods that it offers on the market and affects its profit position, a further insight into cost concepts is in order at this point.

## THE PRODUCTION FUNCTION

In providing a supply of goods or services, the quantity offered for sale will be affected by costs of production. Production cost, however, will in turn be affected by certain physical relationships between factor inputs and product output. The relationship between factor inputs and product output is called the *production function* of the firm. This production function exhibits certain properties that determine the way in which cost varies with output.

### Law of Diminishing Returns

The essential function of management in providing a supply of goods is to organize land, capital, and many types of labor so that the best combination of these factors of production will be used. There should not be too much of one factor and too little of another. The farmer, for example, realizes that a given amount of land requires a certain amount of labor and a specific number of machines. Likewise, the office manager knows that the most efficient operation of a certain number of machines requires a definite number of employees. In either case, if the factors engaged in production are not in the proper proportion, the unit cost will be higher than it otherwise would be and the farmer and the manager will not realize the maximum returns from their efforts.

In every instance where goods are being produced, there is an optimum proportion of the factors of production. This optimum or "best" proportion of the factors is determined in part by the *law of diminishing returns*, or the law of diminishing productivity as it is sometimes called.

To illustrate the law of diminishing returns and its effects on cost of production, let us assume that an entrepreneur owns a tool shop with four machines, adequate space, and an ample supply of raw material. If only one worker who attempts to operate all four machines is hired, the net result will be a limited amount of production, since it will be difficult for one worker to attend to all of the machines, keep the supply of raw material flowing smoothly, remove and package the finished product, maintain the premises, and do other jobs connected directly or indirectly with the operation of the machines. In fact, some of the machines may be idle a good part of the time. If a second laborer of equal ability were hired, the entrepreneur would find that total production would increase. It no doubt would more than double, since production would not only benefit from the physical labor of the second worker, but also the machines would be operating more of the time. Consequently, total output might rise from 10 units to 22 units.

A similar increase might take place when the entrepreneur hires a third worker if production rose to 36 units. In fact, if a fourth worker were hired, one person could attend each machine and production might rise still further to 52 units. In each case the increase in production per additional worker exceeds that of the previous worker. This increase in output per each additional worker is known as the marginal product of labor.

**Marginal Product**   The *marginal product* of any input is the increase in total output resulting from an additional unit of input. In this case our input is labor. But how long can this marginal product continue to increase? Provided all other factors — space, machines, materials — remain fixed, a point will soon be reached at which the fixed factors will become overtaxed or reach their maximum use compared to their underutilization in the early stages of production. Upon hiring a fifth worker, for example, the entrepreneur may find that production still rises. The fifth worker may run stock, package material, and do other jobs that permit the machine tenders to devote more time to their machines. But the increase in production may be less than it was with the addition of the fourth worker. Let us say production expands by 15 units instead of 16, as shown in Table 6-1.

Table 6-1   **INPUT, OUTPUT, MARGINAL PRODUCT, AND AVERAGE PRODUCT**

| Units of Input | Total Output | Marginal Product | Average Product |
|---|---|---|---|
| 1 | 10 | — | 10 |
| 2 | 22 | 12 | 11 |
| 3 | 36 | 14 | 12 |
| 4 | 52 | 16 | 13 |
| 5 | 67 | 15 | 13.4 |
| 6 | 78 | 11 | 13 |
| 7 | 84 | 6 | 12 |
| 8 | 88 | 4 | 11 |
| 9 | 90 | 2 | 10 |
| 10 | 90 | 0 | 9 |

If additional workers are hired, the marginal product will diminish further. As the hiring of additional workers continues, you can visualize a situation being reached in which the fixed factors are taxed to full capacity and there will be absolutely no increase in output. In fact, a stage might even be reached where workers begin getting in each other's way and a decrease in total production could result.

Although it is possible to have increasing marginal productivity, especially in the early stages of production, and even constant marginal productivity over a certain range of output, diminishing marginal productivity is more prevalent. Consequently, we hear much about the *law of diminishing marginal productivity*, or *diminishing returns*. This law may be stated as follows: As additional units of a factor of production are combined with fixed quantities of other factors, a point will be reached where the increase in output resulting from the use of an additional unit of the variable factor will not be as large as was the increase in output due to the addition of the preceding unit.

**Average Product**   In dealing with the cost of production, not only are we interested in the marginal product but also in the average product because it too affects the per unit cost. *Average product* can be defined simply as the output per unit of input. Thus, in Table 6-1, where 3 units of labor input are utilized and the resulting total production is 36 units, the average product is 12 units (36 ÷ 3 = 12). But observe, too, that the average product, like the marginal product, increases, reaches a maximum, and then declines. This follows from the fact that additions to the total product — marginal product — influence the average product. Any time the marginal product is greater, it pulls up the average product. When the marginal product is less than the average, it reduces the

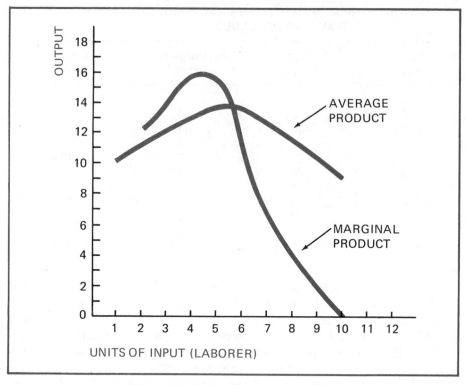

Figure 6-1    **RELATIONSHIP OF MARGINAL PRODUCT
TO AVERAGE PRODUCT**

average product. This relationship is shown in Figure 6-1. Notice that
even after the marginal curve reaches its peak and starts downward, the
average product curve continues upward until the two values are equal.

Remember that to pull the average product down, the marginal product must be less than the average product, not merely declining. Notice
in Table 6-1 and Figure 6-1 that marginal product with the addition of
the fifth unit of labor declined from 16 to 15 units, but the average product rose from 13 to 13.4 units. This is because the marginal product of 15,
although diminishing, is still larger than the average product of 13. But,
again, a point is actually reached where the average product, like the
marginal product, begins to decline.

### Returns to Scale

The law of diminishing returns applies when one or a few productive
agents in the input mix are varied and the remainder are held constant.
But what happens if all productive agents are varied proportionally?
Suppose, for example, that all factors in the input mix were doubled.

Would output double, increase by 50 percent, or perhaps even increase by 150 percent?

If output changes in a given proportion to the change in inputs, constant returns to scale exist. A doubling of all inputs, for example, will double output. On the other hand, when output increases in smaller proportion than the expansion of inputs, it is an indication of decreasing returns to scale. That is, if the entrepreneur were to double all inputs, then output would not double. In contrast, increasing returns to scale imply that a doubling of all inputs would more than double output.

## COSTS OF PRODUCTION

For all practical purposes the measure of production cost is money, and the amount of such production costs is figured in terms of payments for labor, capital, materials, and other items directly or indirectly related to production. In addition, in a capitalistic economy an imputed cost allowance is made for the services of the entrepreneur, since it is the opportunity for profit that induces the entrepreneur to assume the risks and to undertake the production. Once in operation, a certain minimum profit is essential if the entrepreneur is to continue efforts in producing a good or service. This amount of profit, therefore, is considered to be a cost of production.

### Alternative Uses and Opportunity Costs

Under a system of private enterprise, a factor of production is usually employed for the production of a specific good only if it is worth more when used for the production of that good than it would be if used to produce something else. For example, if there is competition for labor, the automobile manufacturer bids for the labor of mechanics by offering to pay at least as much for their labor as do other employers of mechanics. Other employers likewise compete for the labor of workers of all types.

The same principle operates to determine the cost of materials used by a producer. The automobile manufacturer and all other users of steel must pay a price for steel that is at least equal to the value of that material if used for some other purpose. Likewise, the cost of capital goods and borrowed funds in the form of bank loans is largely determined by the value of such goods or funds if devoted to some other use.

The amount of payment necessary to attract a given factor of production away from a similar or the next best opportunity for employment is referred to as *opportunity cost*. This cost exists whether payment is made in the form of cash expenditures or not. For example, suppose that you are a self-employed farmer and that you have a farm on which corn would be the most profitable crop to produce and wheat would be the next most profitable. If you decide to grow corn, the opportunity cost of producing a corn crop will be the value of your land and labor if they were used to produce a wheat crop.

### Explicit and Imputed Costs

Expenditures for production that result from agreements or contracts are *explicit costs*. Such costs are always recognized because they are stated in objective terms, usually in terms of money, and are a matter of record. Expenditures that are attributable to the use of one's own factor of production, such as the use of one's own land, are *implicit* or *imputed costs*. In normal accounting procedure imputed costs are often ignored. Nevertheless, in determining the true profit, imputed costs for the use of one's own land, labor, or capital must be recognized as a part of the real cost of production.

### Classifications of Costs

Now that we have seen how the physical factors of production can affect the supply of goods and the general cost of production, we can explain and analyze the various costs used by the economist to study business firms.

The costs of production in an individual plant may be classified broadly into fixed costs and variable costs. *Fixed costs* are those costs that remain constant as output varies. Unless the plant capacity is changed, the total amount of fixed cost in a firm does not vary with the volume of production. The aggregate of the items of fixed cost is frequently referred to as *overhead*. Such items include bond or mortgage interest incurred for the construction or purchase of plant and equipment, certain depreciation and obsolescence costs, property taxes, and insurance. In addition, a portion of salaries and wages paid for executive and supervisory services may properly be regarded as fixed expenses, for a minimum managerial staff must be maintained even when the business is operating at a limited capacity.

Although the total fixed costs remain constant, fixed costs per unit of production decrease with an increase in output. For example, if the total fixed cost in a given plant is $1,000,000 and 100,000 units are produced, the amount of fixed costs incurred in producing any one unit is $10. If production is increased to 1,000,000 units, the fixed costs per unit, or the average fixed cost, is $1.

*Average fixed cost* is calculated by dividing the total fixed cost by the number of units produced. As we have indicated, average fixed cost continues to decrease as it is spread over a larger number of units, but it never disappears entirely. Column 8 of Table 6-2, for example, shows

Table 6-2   **HYPOTHETICAL PRODUCTIVITY, COST, AND REVENUE**

| (1) Input | (2) Total Output | (3) MP | (4) AP | (5) TFC $ | (6) TVC $ | (7) TC $ | (8) AFC $ | (9) AVC $ | (10) ATC $ | (11) MC $ | (12) AR $ | (13) TR $ | (14) MR $ | (15) Profit $ |
|---|---|---|---|---|---|---|---|---|---|---|---|---|---|---|
| 1 | 10 | — | 10 | 50 | 10 | 60 | 5.00 | 1.00 | 6.00 | — | 2 | 20 | 2 | (−40) |
| 2 | 22 | 12 | 11 | 50 | 20 | 70 | 2.27 | .91 | 3.18 | .83 | 2 | 44 | 2 | (−26) |
| 3 | 36 | 14 | 12 | 50 | 30 | 80 | 1.39 | .83 | 2.22 | .71 | 2 | 72 | 2 | (− 8) |
| 4 | 52 | 16 | 13 | 50 | 40 | 90 | .96 | .77 | 1.73 | .63 | 2 | 104 | 2 | +14 |
| 5 | 67 | 15 | 13.4 | 50 | 50 | 100 | .75 | .75 | 1.49 | .67 | 2 | 134 | 2 | +34 |
| 6 | 78 | 11 | 13 | 50 | 60 | 110 | .64 | .77 | 1.41 | .91 | 2 | 156 | 2 | +46 |
| 7 | 84 | 6 | 12 | 50 | 70 | 120 | .60 | .83 | 1.43 | 1.67 | 2 | 168 | 2 | +48 |
| 8 | 88 | 4 | 11 | 50 | 80 | 130 | .57 | .91 | 1.48 | 2.50 | 2 | 176 | 2 | +46 |
| 9 | 90 | 2 | 10 | 50 | 90 | 140 | .56 | 1.00 | 1.56 | 5.00 | 2 | 180 | 2 | +40 |
| 10 | 90 | 0 | 9 | 50 | 100 | 150 | .56 | 1.11 | 1.67 | — | 2 | 180 | 2 | +30 |

what happens to a $50 total fixed cost when it is converted to average fixed cost.

*Variable costs* are costs of production other than fixed cost, such as labor and materials. *Average variable cost* is the unit variable cost, which is found by dividing the total variable cost by the number of units produced. Until the point or condition of diminishing returns from the use of the variable factors of production is reached, average variable cost decreases as production increases, if, of course, the prices of the variable factors do not increase. Soon after the law of diminishing returns begins to operate, however, average variable cost increases as the number of units produced increases.

**An Example**   In Table 6-2, for example, it can be seen that if the cost of a variable unit of input is $10, the total variable cost will increase by $10 each time an additional unit of input is added. Consequently, total variable cost increases from $10 to $100 as the units of input increase from 1 to 10. This total variable cost can be converted to an average variable cost by dividing the total output shown in column 2 into the total variable cost shown in column 6. Notice that the average variable cost starting out at $1 per unit of output drops to $.75 per unit in line 5 and rises thereafter, reaching $1.11 with the tenth unit of output on line 10. Notice also that the point of the lowest average variable cost corresponds with the point of diminishing average productivity, or the point of highest average product.

*Total cost* is the sum of total fixed and total variable costs at a particular level of production. *Average total cost* is found by dividing total cost by the number of units produced or by adding the average fixed and average variable costs. Total cost increases as production increases but not proportionately. Average total cost decreases, as a rule, until a certain number of units has been produced — depending on the intercost relationships and the point where diminishing returns begins to operate. Soon after the point of diminishing returns is reached, the average total cost increases as production increases. This is shown in column 10 of Table 6-2, which indicates that the lowest average total cost is on line 6 at $1.41.

An exceptionally important concept to the economist is incremental or marginal cost. *Marginal cost* is the increase (decrease) in the total cost resulting from the production of one more (less) unit of output. Marginal cost is influenced strongly by the law of diminishing productivity, and the shape of any marginal cost curve will depend on the shape of the marginal product curve. Column 3 of Table 6-2 shows the marginal product schedule. Column 11 of Table 6-2 shows the marginal cost for our hypothetical firm. Notice that the values of marginal cost decrease, reach a minimum, and then rise thereafter. Observe further that as the marginal product rises, the marginal cost declines. Then, when the marginal product starts to decrease, the marginal cost begins to increase. The point of lowest marginal cost, $.63 as shown on line 4, corresponds with the point of highest marginal product, also shown on line 4. This reveals the close, but inverse, relationship between marginal product and marginal cost.

In computing the marginal cost, remember that it refers to the increase in total cost per additional unit of output, not input. Since the increase in total cost shown in column 7 is the increase per unit of input, this incremental cost must be converted to incremental cost per unit of output (marginal cost). Since the second unit of input cost $10 more but resulted in an increase in total output of 12 units, the marginal cost, or increased cost per unit of output, will be equal to $.83, as shown on line 2 of column 11. Similarly, if the successive increments of total cost are divided by the respective marginal products, the marginal cost for each line will be found.

**The Example in Graphic Form**    The relationship of these cost values can be seen much more clearly, of course, if they are presented in graphic form, as shown in Figure 6-2. In this case the average fixed cost, *AFC*, will be represented by a curve continuously decreasing in value as total fixed costs are spread over a wider and wider range of output. The average variable cost, *AVC*, will be a curve decreasing, reaching a minimum, and then rising in value because of the presence of the law of diminishing marginal productivity. The average total cost, *ATC*, which is a combination of the *AFC* and the *AVC*, likewise will drop and then rise again. Notice that as both the *AFC* and *AVC* are falling the *ATC* will be falling. A point is reached at which the *AVC* starts to rise while the *AFC* is still declining. What happens to the *ATC* at this point will depend on the relative strength of the two curves.

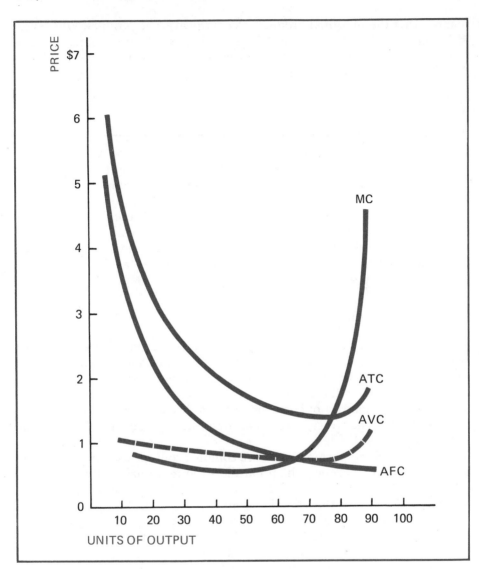

Figure 6-2  **RELATIONSHIP OF AVERAGE FIXED COST, AVERAGE VARIABLE COST, AVERAGE TOTAL COST, AND MARGINAL COST**

In Figure 6-2 notice that initially the downward pull of the *AFC* is stronger than the upward push of the *AVC* so that the *ATC* continues to drop for a while. But eventually the upward push of the *AVC* overcomes the downward pull of the *AFC*, and the *ATC* rises thereafter. Graphically, the marginal cost curve, *MC*, will decrease, reach a minimum, and then rise due to its close relationship with the marginal product curve. Anytime marginal cost is less than average variable cost or average total cost, it will effect a reduction in the *AVC* and/or *ATC*, in much the same manner that the marginal product affects the average product. Whenever *MC* is greater than the *AVC* or *ATC*, it will cause them to increase. Furthermore, by its very nature *MC* will cross, or intersect, the *AVC* and the *ATC* lines at their lowest points.

## REVENUE AND PROFIT

In the preceding chapter we saw that the demand schedule indicates the quantities of a commodity or service that will be purchased at various prices. It was pointed out, too, that under competitive conditions the price would be determined by the free forces of supply and demand. Although conditions are not always competitive and the forces of demand and supply are not always unencumbered, we will accept for the present the supposition that the market price becomes the price at which an individual firm can sell its product. This will permit us to look at some revenue concepts and relate them to the cost concepts to analyze the profit situation for an individual firm.

### Revenues

*Average revenue*, as used by the economist, is the price per unit sold. It is the market price from the viewpoint of the seller, and it may be computed by dividing the total revenue by the number of units sold. *Total revenue*, of course, is the amount of revenue or income received from the sale of a given quantity of goods or services. It can be calculated readily by multiplying the average revenue, or price, by the number of units sold.

An extremely important and more complex concept used by the economist is marginal revenue, which parallels the marginal cost concept explained earlier. *Marginal revenue* is the increase (decrease) in total revenue that results from the sale of one more (less) unit of output. This can be calculated by dividing the increase in total revenue resulting from the use of an additional unit of input by the increase in total product.

In our example in Table 6-2, the values of the marginal revenue and the average revenue are identical. This will not always be the case. Anytime you are dealing with other than perfectly competitive conditions, the values of the marginal revenue and the average revenue will differ. With a constant price, however, whenever the firm sells an additional unit at the market price of $2, it will add $2 to its total revenue, and the marginal revenue has to equal the average revenue, or price.

### Profit

Total profit is the difference between total revenue and total cost. Whether a firm makes a profit, and how much profit, depends on the relationship of its revenue to its costs. Even when a firm is not making a profit, the decision as to whether to continue to operate or shut down will depend, again, on its cost-revenue relationships. A firm can analyze its profit situation in many ways. For instance, it may compare its total revenue to its total cost by using a break-even chart, or it may engage in marginal analysis by dealing with marginal revenue and marginal cost concepts.

## Total Revenue Versus Total Cost

By comparing total revenue with total cost over a given range of output, a firm can determine at what levels it makes a profit and at what levels it suffers losses. Furthermore, by constructing a break-even chart,

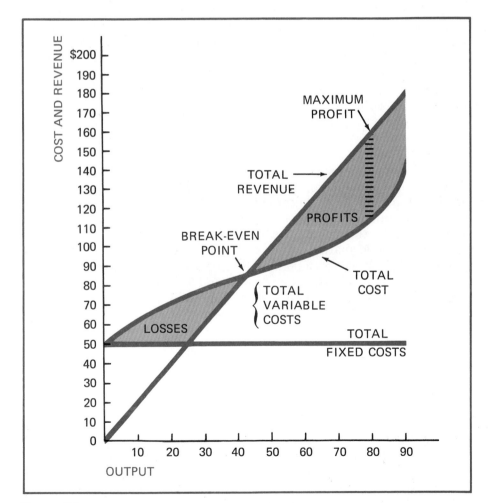

Figure 6-3    **BREAK-EVEN CHART**

it can determine at what point its losses cease and profits begin. This, of course, is known as the *break-even point*. It may be given in terms of the total output needed to break even, or it may be analyzed in terms of total inputs. Other firms construct their break-even charts in terms of capacity to indicate at what level they must operate their plant to avoid losses and make profits. Naturally a firm will endeavor not only to reach the break-even output or capacity but also to go beyond it as far as is profitable. It must avoid the pitfall, however, of pushing too far beyond, as it may encounter rapidly rising marginal costs at, or near, capacity levels. In such an event, total profits may actually decline in spite of higher output. The maximum profit position will be that level of output, or capacity, where there is the greatest gap between total revenue and total cost, as shown in Figure 6-3 on the preceding page.

Another advantage of a break-even chart is that cost can be broken down into total fixed cost and total variable cost. In fact, if desirable the variable cost can be segmented further into a variety of costs, including such items as direct and indirect manufacturing cost, material cost, labor cost, and selling costs.

Putting the values from our hypothetical firm into a break-even chart, as in Figure 6-3, shows the total fixed cost of $50 represented by a straight horizontal line. This indicates that the fixed costs remain constant at a given range of output. Total costs, which continually increase, are represented by a line moving upward to the right. The difference between total cost and total fixed cost represents the total variable cost. Since the price at which each unit sells is constant, the total revenue is shown by the line moving upward to the right at a constant slope. The break-even point is at 42 units of output. Although profits are made at all levels of production beyond this point, maximum profit is made when production is in the vicinity of 80 units.

The same information can be interpolated from Table 6-2, which indicates that the break-even point will come somewhere between the third and fourth units of input, or between 36 and 52 units of output. Likewise, the maximum profit position will be the seventh unit of input, which corresponds with production in the vicinity of 80 units.

### Marginal Revenue Versus Marginal Cost

It is only reasonable to assume that anytime a firm can add to its total profit by producing more or fewer units, it will act accordingly. Consequently, the firm's profit picture is often analyzed in terms of what happens to cost and revenue with the addition of one more unit of input or output. Whenever the production and sale of an additional, or marginal, unit adds more to revenue than it does to cost, profits are sure to increase, or losses diminish, whatever the case may be. If the production of one more unit adds more to cost than it does to revenue, the opposite is true. We have available two such concepts that tell us how much is added to revenue and how much is added to cost with each additional unit of output. To determine the point of maximum profit for the firm, all we have to do is observe their relationship.

Marginal revenue, *MR*, measures the increase in total revenue per additional unit of output, and marginal cost, *MC*, measures the increase in total cost per additional unit of output. Therefore, anytime *MR* is greater than *MC*, profits will rise or losses will diminish. On the other hand, if *MR* is less than *MC*, profits will decrease, or losses will increase. A firm will profit by increasing its production so long as its $MR > MC$. It will pay to reduce production whenever $MR < MC$.

In most cases marginal revenue is a constant or decreasing value, and the marginal cost is a continuously increasing value. Therefore, as a firm adds units of output, it eventually reaches a point at which $MR = MC$. This is its maximum profit position, since at any less level of production $MR > MC$ and at any greater level of production $MR < MC$. In our hypothetical firm, for example, it can be observed that the *MR* has a constant value of $2, while the *MC*, after reaching a low of $.63, continuously increases to more than $5 as production reaches 90 units. Comparing the *MR* in column 14 with the *MC* in column 11, it can be seen that, at all levels of production up to and including that associated with the seventh unit of input, *MR* exceeds *MC*. Therefore, the firm will continue to produce up to that point. It will not add the eighth unit of input, however, since the *MR* is less than the *MC* for the output that will be forthcoming. Consequently, the firm will maximize profits, according to the marginal analysis, at a level of output in the vicinity of 80 units. This, of course, corresponds with the maximum profit position indicated on the break-even chart illustrated in Figure 6-3.

### Minimizing Losses in the Short Run

Thus far we have been dealing with the pleasant situation of a firm making a profit, but what happens if the firm is suffering a loss? Suppose, for example, in our problem the average revenue received by the firm was only $1, as determined by the forces of the market. Assuming that the costs remained the same, our firm would not be able to make a profit at any level of production. It would, however, minimize its losses with 6 units of input, or 78 units of output. What then should the firm do — continue to operate or shut down? The answer will depend on the relationship of cost to revenue and on whether we are talking about the short-run or the long-run period.

In economics the *short run* is a period of time in which some factors of production are fixed. The *long run* is a period of time in which all factors of production, including machinery, buildings, and other capital items, are variable. In the short run, for example, it may be possible for a firm to increase its output within a given range by adding more workers, putting on another shift, buying more raw materials, and manipulating other variable factors without increasing the capacity of its fixed plant and equipment. If given enough time, however, it could increase its output greatly in the long run by adding to its capacity with the construction or purchase of new plant and equipment. Consequently, in the long run even the fixed factors become variable. The actual length of this period is rather nebulous and varies with different industries. Obviously the calendar time involved in the long run for the steel industry, which requires construction of huge mills, is much longer than the long-run period in the garment industry, where a firm can purchase additional machines, floor space, and loft capacity within a matter of a few weeks.

If a firm is operating at a loss in the short run, and we will assume it is minimizing its losses, the question still remains whether it should continue to operate or shut down. The answer will depend very much on the relationship of its fixed to its variable cost and the relationship of the variable cost to its total revenue.

Assume that a firm has a total fixed cost of $60,000 and a total variable cost of $40,000 for a total cost of $100,000. At the same time suppose its total revenue is $50,000. It is obvious that the firm is suffering a loss of $50,000. Nevertheless, it is better for it to continue to operate in the short run rather than shut down. Notice that by operating, the loss is only $50,000; but if it were to shut down, its loss would be greater. It is true that if it were to close down, its total cost would drop by the amount of its variable cost, $40,000; but keep in mind that its revenue would drop to zero. Furthermore, it would still have its fixed cost of $60,000 to pay, and its loss would be $60,000 instead of $50,000.

Therefore, it pays a firm to operate at a loss in the short run as long as it can recover its variable cost and make a contribution to overhead. If it cannot recover its variable cost, however, it is more profitable to shut down in the short run. One way of ascertaining quickly whether a firm is recovering its variable cost is to compare the average revenue with the average variable cost at the point of equilibrium, or the point of minimum losses. If the AR is equal to or greater than the AVC, it will pay the firm to continue its operation.

Whether under a loss condition the firm desires to continue operations in the long run will depend on a multitude of factors, such as the cost of new assets, its competition, the general outlook for its products, and the general status of the economy. But unless it can see some improvement in its profit picture, it would not be wise to pour additional capital into a nonprofitable enterprise.

## PURE PROFIT

From an economic point of view, profit is a residual of income over and above all economic costs, both explicit and implicit, that results from the operation of a business. Profits are dynamic in that they are constantly changing in amount. New business firms are established in the hope of making a profit and other businesses fail because of lack of profit. Starting a business involves a risk, but the opportunity for profit induces hundreds of thousands of individuals annually to try to become successful entrepreneurs.

Pure profit is a return to the entrepreneur from the operation of the business. It may be either large or small. It excludes any return from the use of the other factors of production utilized in the input mix. If the profit is too small or if the firm suffers a loss, it may go out of business. That amount of profit that is neither excessive nor minimal but is the amount necessary to induce the entrepreneur to stay in business is called *nominal profit*. It is measured by the opportunity cost of the services of the entrepreneur. Usually nominal profit is considered as an economic cost of doing business. When it is, the nominal profit position becomes a no-profit position as far as the business operation is concerned. Any amount over and above this can be called *pure profit*. Under conditions of pure competition, profit, in addition to being residual and dynamic, is a temporary phenomenon. The conditions of pure competition are such that anytime a pure profit exists, forces come into play to eliminate such pure profit. This is so because of the nature of pure competition, as we shall soon see.

Conversely, in a monopoly if a pure profit situation exists, the monopolist may be able by various means to effectively block the entry of new firms into the industry. Thus, profit becomes more than a temporary phenomenon. Furthermore, since the output of the monopoly becomes the total supply on the market, the monopolist can influence the market price by changing output. In this way the price can be set where it will yield the greatest profit. Under a condition of monopolistic or imperfect competition — which is usually the case — profits may be larger than they would be under pure competition.

## PURE COMPETITION

Many types of competition exist in the American economic system. Since there are over 8 million firms, exclusive of farms, doing business in hundreds of industries, it is possible to find various degrees of competition within each industry and numerous shades of competition between different markets. Market situations may range all the way from perfect or pure competition to pure monopoly. Although there are fundamental differences between types of competition, sometimes conditions in a firm or an industry will contain elements of more than one type. Furthermore, a firm may find itself in one type of competitive market in selling its products but in a different type of competitive market in buying its raw materials or hiring labor.

The basic types of market structure are pure competition, pure monopoly, monopolistic competition, and oligopoly. Among the distinguishing characteristics of different types of markets are the number of firms in an industry, the presence or absence of product differentiation, and the ability of any or all firms in an industry to influence the market price. Since pure competition affords a theoretical standard by which we measure the economic and social value of other forms of market structure, we shall first analyze the purely competitive industry.

## CHARACTERISTICS OF PURE COMPETITION

*Pure competition* is an ideal set of market conditions that assumes the following characteristics:[1]

1. *There are numerous sellers in the market, all selling an identical product.* This means there are no quality differences, no brand names, no advertising, nor anything else that would differentiate between the products of various sellers.
2. *All buyers and sellers are informed about markets and prices.* If one seller is putting a product on the market at a lower price than others, all buyers are aware of this. Furthermore, if one producer can offer a good on the market at a lower price than competitors because of certain cost advantages, other producers will soon learn why and how it can be done.
3. *There is free entry into and exit from the market.* It is a condition of a competitive market that anyone who desires to produce and sell goods in a particular market may do so, without any undue encumbrances. This, of course, would exclude the protection of patent rights, the absence of excessive capital requirements, the availability of the necessary factors of production, freedom from government regulations, and other conditions that may hinder or deter a person or firm from going into the production of a particular type of good or service. Pure competition also assumes that there is perfect mobility on the part of the factors of production.
4. *No individual seller or buyer can influence price. Price is determined by the aggregate actions of all buyers and sellers or by market supply and market demand.* To fulfill this condition, there must be enough sellers in the market so that each one's contribution to the total supply is infinitesimal. Consequently, whether a firm produces more or less has no appreciable effect on the total supply. Under such circumstances each seller must accept the market price as determined by aggregate demand and supply. The seller will not be able to obtain a greater price for his or her product because all products of that kind are identical. This does not preclude the possibility, however, that the market price could be changed by the

---

[1]Although the phrase "pure competition" is sometimes used interchangeably with the phrase "perfect competition," there is a degree of difference in the meanings of the two. *Perfect competition* implies that there is perfect information about markets and prices on the part of all buyers and sellers, perfect mobility of the various factors of production, and perfectly free entry into and exit from an industry. In short, perfect competition is more idealistic and a higher degree of competition.

actions of many, or all, firms. If an individual producer increased output by 50 or 100 percent, for example, the change in total supply would be so insignificant that it would not affect the market price. On the other hand, if each of a large number of producers increased output by 3, 5, or 10 percent, this could affect supply appreciably and result in a change in market price.

## PRICE AND PROFIT IN THE SHORT RUN

Under pure competition each producer faces a perfectly elastic demand curve; that is, the entire supply of a producer can be sold at the market-determined price. Profit will depend upon the difference between the average total cost of production and the selling price, multiplied by the number of units sold. Since producers are in business to make a profit, each producer will try to produce that number of units whose sale will yield the greatest profit.

Acting alone a producer can do little or nothing to change the market price. It will make no appreciable difference on price if a given producer sells much or nothing. This is not true, however, for the industry as a whole. If a great many or all producers increase or decrease production, the total market supply will be affected, which will result in a change in price, assuming that demand does not change.

A case in point is the production of wheat in America where there are more than one-half million producers. Whether Farmer Smith increases production from 100 to 1,000 or even to 10,000 bushels will have little, if any, effect on a market price of $3.50 per bushel when there is a total supply of more than 1.4 billion bushels on the U.S. market each year and 10.6 billion bushels on the world market. On the other hand, if each wheat farmer in America increased output by a mere 3 percent, it would increase the total U.S. wheat supply by more than 42 million bushels and no doubt would tend to lower the market price.

Under a condition of pure competition in an industry that is producing a standardized commodity, how many units of the commodity will each producer undertake to produce? This question cannot be answered exactly, but we can acquire an understanding of the factors that help to determine the amount that each one will produce.

Let us assume a period of time that is just long enough to allow each of the producers to adjust output to the most profitable level without enlarging or modernizing their plants. This is the short-run period. Under the assumed short-run conditions we shall see how each producer will attempt to set output where marginal cost becomes equal to marginal revenue. For the sake of simplicity, we assume that no new factories will be built in the industry and that existing plants will not be enlarged. But it is assumed that each firm is free to vary its volume of production from zero to its maximum existing capacity.

## Adjustment of Production to Price in the Short Run

Just how much will the single firm undertake to produce? In most real situations it would probably be impossible to say, for two reasons. First, it is not likely that the entrepreneur could predict exactly what the production cost would be at different levels of production. Second, the entrepreneur is likely to be satisfied with a "good" or "reasonable" amount of profit, which would cause the entrepreneur to refrain from attempting to squeeze out the very last possible cent of profit from the business.

Nevertheless, it is realistic to assume that, other things being equal, the producer is motivated by the desire to make as much profit as possible. This assumption does not deny the fact that the producer probably has values and interests other than those that relate to money. But for the purpose of economic analysis, it is necessary to give attention here only to those matters that affect the profit possibilities of a productive enterprise operating under conditions of pure competition.

Therefore, to arrive at a logical determination of the firm's output, we proceed on the assumption that the entrepreneur will undertake to produce that amount which will maximize the firm's profit or minimize its

Table 6-3  **COST AND REVENUE SCHEDULE**

| Number of Units of Output | Total Cost (TC) | Average Total Cost (ATC) | Marginal Cost (MC) | Average Revenue and Marginal Revenue (AR-MR) | Total Revenue (TR) | Total Gain or *Loss* (TG or *TL*) |
|---|---|---|---|---|---|---|
| 1 | $10.08 | $10.08 | | $1.80 | $ 1.80 | −$8.28 |
| 2 | 11.22 | 5.61 | $1.14 | 1.80 | 3.60 | − 7.62 |
| 3 | 12.12 | 4.04 | .90 | 1.80 | 5.40 | − 6.72 |
| 4 | 12.84 | 3.21 | .72 | 1.80 | 7.20 | − 5.64 |
| 5 | 13.44 | 2.69 | .60 | 1.80 | 9.00 | − 4.44 |
| 6 | 13.98 | 2.33 | .54 | 1.80 | 10.80 | − 3.18 |
| 7 | 14.52 | 2.07 | .54 | 1.80 | 12.60 | − 1.92 |
| 8 | 15.12 | 1.89 | .60 | 1.80 | 14.40 | − 0.72 |
| 9 | 15.84 | 1.76 | .72 | 1.80 | 16.20 | 0.36 |
| 10 | 16.74 | 1.67 | .90 | 1.80 | 18.00 | 1.26 |
| 11 | 17.88 | 1.63 | 1.14 | 1.80 | 19.80 | 1.92 |
| 12 | 19.32 | 1.61 | 1.44 | 1.80 | 21.60 | 2.28 |
| 13 | 21.12 | 1.62 | 1.80 | 1.80 | 23.40 | 2.28 |
| 14 | 23.34 | 1.67 | 2.22 | 1.80 | 25.20 | 1.86 |
| 15 | 26.04 | 1.74 | 2.70 | 1.80 | 27.00 | 0.96 |
| 16 | 29.28 | 1.83 | 3.24 | 1.80 | 28.80 | − 0.48 |
| 17 | 33.12 | 1.95 | 3.84 | 1.80 | 30.60 | − 2.52 |

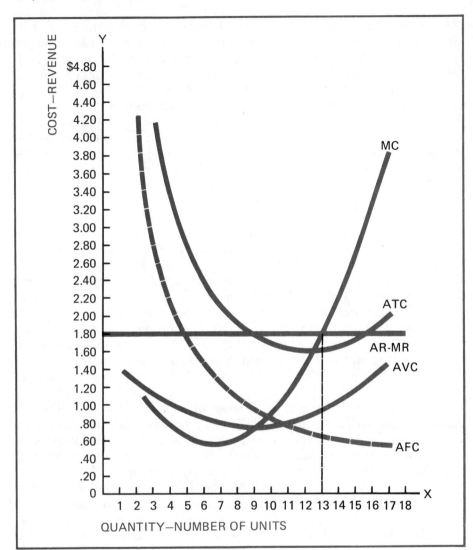

Figure 6-4    **COST AND REVENUE CURVES**

loss. What that volume of production will be depends upon the firm's cost and revenue relationships.

Let us assume that for a certain producer (1) total cost, (2) average total cost, (3) marginal cost, (4) average revenue and marginal revenue, and (5) total revenue are as shown in Table 6-3 and Figure 6-4. Remember that a firm will maximize its profits or minimize its losses at the point where marginal revenue equals marginal cost *(MR = MC)*.

A close inspection of Table 6-3 and Figure 6-4 reveals that at a price of $1.80 per unit the equilibrium output corresponds with the point of intersection between the marginal revenue curve and marginal cost curve at 13 units of output. The difference between average revenue (price) and average total cost at this point represents profit per unit. Profit per unit multiplied by the equilibrium output measures total profit.

The point of intersection of MR and MC is called the equilibrium point because, once the firm reaches that position, there is no incentive to move to any other level of output. If it is not operating at that point, the firm is motivated by the prospect of greater profit to either increase or decrease its output until the equilibrium position is attained. If MC is less than MR, an expansion of output will increase profit; if MC is greater than MR, a contraction of output will increase profit. When MC equals MR, total profit is at a maximum.

In this case if the price is $1.80 and if fewer than 9 units or more than 15 are produced, the producer will lose money, because it is only when 9 to 15 units are produced that average revenue (price) is above average total cost. Note that after producing 13 units, marginal cost rises above marginal revenue. Although some profit or net revenue could be realized by producing and selling 15 units, maximum profit cannot be increased by producing more than 13 units, the number for which marginal cost and marginal revenue are exactly equal. If marginal cost and marginal revenue did not coincide exactly for the production and sale of a whole unit, then it would be most profitable to produce that number of units indicated by the point that is nearest the whole number where they are equal.

Now suppose that the price, instead of $1.80, is $1.61, as shown in Figure 6-5. Note that at this price ATC, MC, $AR_1$, and $MR_1$ are practically equal at the point of intersection of the $MR_1$ and MC curves. What does this signify? It means that the most the producer can hope for is to "break even." By producing 12 units, average revenue will be just equal to average total cost. If any higher number of units is produced, average total cost and marginal cost will rise above marginal and average revenue and a loss will be incurred. If the producer stops short of producing 12 units, average total cost will be greater than average revenue and a loss will once again be incurred.

For another example, assume that the price ($AR_2$, $MR_2$) is $1.20 as shown in Figure 6-5. How many units will be produced? We can see that regardless of how many units are produced, the producer cannot hope to make a profit because, for any number of units, average total cost is above average revenue. The point at which the loss can be minimized is the production of 11 units, the number that is nearest the intersection of marginal cost and marginal revenue. The producer will not produce more than 11 units, however, because beyond that point marginal cost rises above marginal revenue.

In this case it will pay the firm to continue to operate in the short run rather than shut down. As mentioned earlier in the chapter, it will pay the firm to continue to operate in the short run rather than to shut down

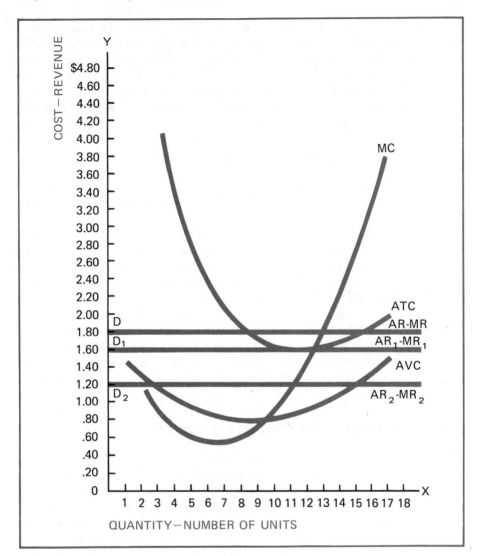

Figure 6-5    **COST AND REVENUE CURVES**

so long as it can recover its variable cost. Whether it can do so may be ascertained by comparing the *AVC* to the *AR* at the equilibrium level. If the *AR* is equal to the *AVC*, it will recover its variable cost. If *AR* > *AVC*, it will also recover a part of its fixed cost; or, as we stated earlier, it will make a contribution to overhead. How much of a contribution it will make can be observed from the graph. Although the fixed cost is not drawn on the chart, remember that since *ATC* = *AFC* + *AVC*, the *AFC* will be represented by the difference between the *ATC* and *AVC* curves at the point of equilibrium.

On the other hand, visualize a situation in which the market price may be only $.60 for the firm in question. Not only would the firm suffer a loss at any level of output, but even at the equilibrium level, or point of minimum loss, the AR would be less than the AVC. In this situation, the firm would not recover its variable cost and would find it less costly to shut down rather than operate in the short run. In such a case AR would be less than AVC at the equilibrium point.

### Short-Run Equilibrium Price

We may conclude, therefore, that competitive *short-run equilibrium price* is that price which results from the interaction of demand and supply over a short period of time.

What might be called "short-run equilibrium price" is not a stable price, for at the given market prices prevailing during the short-run period, *submarginal producers* — those whose total cost is greater than their revenue — could not break even. These producers would eventually improve their efficiency or disappear. If they disappeared, the supply would decrease, which would cause the price to rise. If they improved their efficiency, the supply would increase, which would cause market price to decline. Moreover, the presence of *supramarginal producers* — those who are making profits — would attract newcomers to the industry, which would result in an increase in the supply of the good and a decrease in the market price.

## PRICE AND PROFIT IN THE LONG RUN

Under conditions of pure competition economic profits are residual, dynamic, and ephemeral. Profit is residual insofar as it is revenue that remains after deducting both explicit and implicit costs, including a nominal profit as an imputed cost of the entrepreneur's service. Profits are dynamic insofar as they are constantly changing in amount and among firms. Under purely competitive conditions profits are ephemeral, or temporary, in that, if profits are being made, long-run forces will come into play that tend to reduce or eliminate economic or pure profit. On the other hand, if losses are generally being suffered, market forces tend to bring about adjustments that may cause profits to appear.

### Profit Differentiation Among Firms

It should be remembered that all firms under conditions of pure competition pay an identical price for input factors, and all sell their finished goods, or output, at a uniform market price. It is still possible, however, for profits among firms to differ. One of the main reasons for this difference is that, even though all firms have the same unit cost for inputs, some firms use their inputs more efficiently. In the short run some of them may be using better production techniques, they may be spreading their fixed cost over a larger range of output, and they may be using other measures to lower per unit cost of output. At any given market price, therefore, it is possible to have some firms making a profit, others breaking even, and still others suffering a loss. This is demonstrated in Figure 6-6.

A change in the market price, as it moves up or down, can affect the profit status of each firm. A change in the per unit cost of inputs, likewise, can affect the profit of each firm by altering its average cost curve. In the long run it is assumed that the submarginal firms will reorganize their productive factors to make a profit or else will drop out of business. Remember that pure competition assumes that all sellers are informed about markets, prices, and costs. Therefore, if one firm for some reason is able to produce at a lower cost, others will know how it can be done. In the long run adoption of similar production techniques will enable the others to adjust their factors to reduce costs.

### How Profits Disappear

Under conditions of pure competition, competitive forces tend to eliminate economic profit. This is due to the freedom of firms to enter into and exit from the industry. If a profit is being made by firms in the industry, outsiders can gather information on how to produce and share in the profits being made. Indeed, they have both the incentive and the freedom to do so.

It is true that no individual supplier can influence price under conditions of pure competition; but, if a number of new suppliers enter the

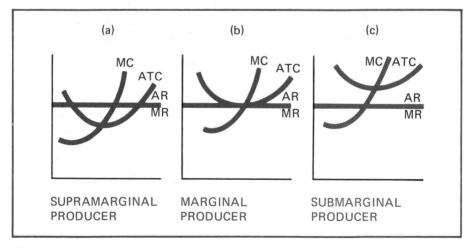

Figure 6-6   **PROFIT, BREAK-EVEN, AND LOSS POSITIONS**

market, the addition of their supplies to the total market supply could very well result in a decrease in market price. If profits still remain even at the lower price, firms would continue to enter the industry, continuously lowering prices until a point is reached at which the price will equal the average total cost and profit will be eliminated. On the other hand, if the price were below cost and firms in the industry were suffering losses, firms would drop out of the industry. In the long run the market supply would be reduced, causing price to rise and losses to disappear in the industry. This whole process can be demonstrated graphically, as in Figure 6-7.

Assume that the intersection of demand *(D)* and supply *(S)* in Figure 6-7a establishes a market price of $5 per unit. This then will be the average revenue *(AR)* for each of the firms in the industry, as shown in Figure 6-7b. Assuming that these cost and revenue relationships are typical for the industry, individual firms will be making profits. These profits, however, will induce new firms to enter the industry. As they enter, total supply on the market will increase, and market price will be lowered to $4, as shown by the intersection of $S_1$ and $D$. This in turn will lower the *AR* and *MR* curves for each of the firms in the industry, thereby reducing profits. Since profits still exist even at this price, firms will continue to enter the industry, increasing the market supply to $S_2$ and reducing the price to $3 per unit. At an average revenue and marginal revenue of $3, there will be no economic, or pure, profit for the firms in the industry. At this point there is no further incentive for additional firms to enter the industry. Not only are all the firms in equilibrium because they are

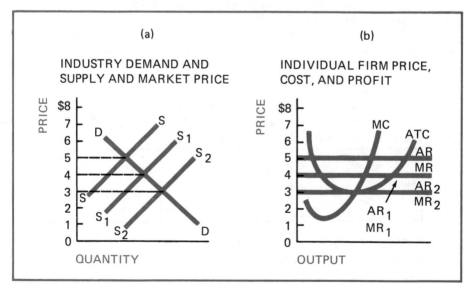

Figure 6-7    **LONG-RUN EQUILIBRIUM PRICE AND PROFIT**

operating at the point where $MR = MC$, but also equilibrium will exist in the industry because there is no incentive for firms to enter or leave the industry. There is no excess profit to attract new firms. On the other hand, since existing firms will be covering all explicit and imputed costs, including a nominal return to the entrepreneur, they will not necessarily be inclined to withdraw from the industry.

You can visualize what would happen if the initial market price were such that losses existed in the industry. As firms dropped out of the industry, the total supply on the market would decrease, raising the market price and the marginal and average revenue of the individual firms. This process would continue until the price was raised sufficiently to eliminate losses. At that point, no losses or no profit, there would be no further incentive for firms to leave the industry, and equilibrium would again be established.

Before leaving this topic, it should be remembered that we demonstrated the movement from a short-run profit position to a long-run, no-profit equilibrium by adjustments in the market price or average revenue. It is also possible, however, that the long-run profit squeeze may be accelerated by an upward pressure on the cost of inputs. Then the average total cost curve will shift upward. As new firms enter the industry, their combined demand for inputs may very well increase the total demand for raw material, labor, capital, and other inputs. This in turn could raise the market price of inputs and the average total cost curve for individual firms, causing a reduction in profits. Consequently, the competitive forces in the economy work from two angles — the downward pressure of prices and the upward pressure on cost — to eliminate economic profits in the long run.

### The Long-Run Cost Curve

Under pure competition, or highly competitive conditions, the consumer obtains a good or service in the long run at a price that equals cost. Another advantage of competition is the fact that price in the long run is equal to *minimum* average cost, that is, the lowest point on the average cost curve. As we mentioned previously, there are various types and kinds of firms under competitive conditions. Although the typical firm may be in equilibrium at a no-profit position, as shown in Figure 6-7, there may be other firms operating at a larger scale that are making a profit with the given market price. Pure competition assumes that all firms are informed about any cost advantages that may arise due to larger scale operations. Consequently, the no-profit firms, observing the larger scale operators making a profit, will be inclined to enlarge their operations to enhance their profits. As they move toward the larger scale of operations, of course, the total supply in the market will increase, forcing market price downward. If industry equilibrium comes into existence at the larger scale of operations and the firms reach a no-profit position, competition may very well lead some aggressive innovators to try operating on a still larger scale in the hope of reducing cost to make profits.

If the firm is successful and does make a profit at the larger scale of operations, existing producers will follow suit and others will enter the industry at this new, larger scale of operations. As they do so, the supply will increase once more, forcing the price down still further. Eventually a point of diminishing returns will be reached on the scale of operations. This will be known as the *optimum scale of operation*. At any larger scale there will be no further cost advantages arising from size. In fact, average total cost may increase due to inefficiencies arising from excessive bigness. By joining all the short-run average total cost curves, we can develop a long-run average total cost curve, as shown in Figure 6-8.

At any scale of operations up to the optimum scale, it is said that *economies of scale* exist because long-run *ATC* decreases as the size of the plant increases. Beyond the optimum scale, however, *diseconomies of scale* come into existence, causing the long-run *ATC* to bend upward.

### THE SOCIAL IMPACT OF PURE COMPETITION

Theoretically there are two virtues of industry-wide and economy-wide pure competition: (1) competition stimulates initiative and productive energy, and (2) competition results in minimum prices to consumers. Under an assumed condition of pure competition throughout the economy, efficiency in all divisions of production would be promoted and only the most efficient entrepreneurial undertaking would survive. The existence of high profits in any field of production would induce most of the producers to increase their outputs and encourage additional entrepreneurs to enter the field, with the result that the supplies of goods or services would increase and prices would decline. The demand for the

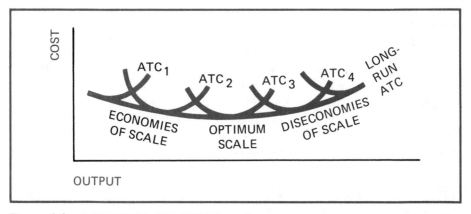

Figure 6-8  **LONG-RUN *ATC* CURVE**

factors of production would be competitive, which would enable the owners of each of the factors to obtain fair and reasonable prices for what they had to sell. Potential entrepreneurs would be encouraged to discover and to produce new types of goods and services that would be desired by consumers.

As a consequence of economy-wide competition, profits would either disappear or would be reduced to the minimum necessary to induce only the most efficient entrepreneurs to undertake the risks of production. At the same time, the prices of goods and services would be at the lowest possible level consistent with the practice of personal freedom by all individuals.

Pure competition would serve the consumer very well. It would result in greater production, the use of more resources and labor, lower prices, and less profits than would exist under noncompetitive conditions. However, competition is not without its disadvantages. It frequently results in an unnecessary duplication of plant and equipment; it often brings forth an endless and sometimes needless variety of models and fashions; and at other times it causes a waste of resources, especially in the extractive industries. Although competition benefits the economy as a whole, it can cause financial hardship for individual producers and displacement of workers as business firms are forced out of business by more efficient producers. It is also possible that in some industries, such as public utilities, many firms, each operating at a small scale, would not be able to provide a good or a service as cheaply as a few firms producing at a much larger scale.

## THE CONCEPT OF COMPETITIVE PRICE

The concept of competitive price assumes conditions that are not easily found in the everyday business world. Moreover, it may be argued that, if we assume conditions of pure competition in all areas of production with no change in demand or in the techniques of production, the result would be static economy.

That conditions of perfect or pure competition seldom, if ever, exist is readily admitted by economists. Nevertheless, the concepts of pure competition and normal competitive price serve as a model for comparing the social consequences of different forms of market structure. The abstract model of pure competition provides essential criteria for any serious analysis of pricing and profits under existing forms of imperfect competition. It is difficult to understand the disadvantages to consumers resulting from monopolistic pricing and restrictive practices unless one understands what the consumer would gain as a result of greater competition. It is difficult to understand the reason for antitrust laws that promote and protect competition until one understands what is being promoted and protected. Therefore, the study of pricing and profits under pure competition, instead of being a useless venture into the realm of mental gymnastics, provides a solid foundation for economic analysis in the world of reality.

## SUMMARY

In providing a supply of goods or services for the market, the cost of production is affected by physical factors such as the law of diminishing marginal productivity and returns to scale. The most widely recognized of these factors, the law of diminishing marginal productivity, means that as additional units of a factor of production are combined with a fixed quantity of other factors, a point will be reached where the output resulting from the use of an additional unit of the variable factor will not be as large as was the output due to the addition of the preceding unit.

In analyzing a firm's cost the economist considers not only the explicit cost but also the imputed cost of using one's own factors of production, such as labor or land, in the productive process. Imputed costs are generally measured in terms of alternative uses to which the factors of production could be applied. Costs may be classified as fixed or variable. Total cost is a combination of both. In addition to totals, cost may be broken down into unit cost, such as average fixed cost, average variable cost, average total cost, and marginal cost. The price received per unit of output, as determined by the forces of demand and supply in the market, is known as average revenue to the firm. Marginal revenue is the increase in total revenue that results from the sale of an additional unit of output.

A firm can analyze its profit position by means of a break-even chart on which is plotted total revenue, total cost, total fixed cost, and total variable cost. In addition to ascertaining the break-even point, a firm can also determine its maximum profit level on such a chart. The maximum profit position of a firm can also be determined by marginal analysis. A firm will maximize its profits or minimize its losses, whichever the case may be, by operating at the point where marginal revenue equals marginal cost. Even if a firm is suffering a loss, it will benefit the firm to continue operating in the short run so long as it is recovering its variable cost and is making a contribution to overhead.

There are several types of models of economic competition, ranging from pure competition at one extreme to pure monopoly at the other. Pure competition is an ideal set of market conditions in which there are numerous buyers and sellers of an identical type of product. These buyers and sellers are well informed about market conditions and prices. Although there is free entry into and exit from the market, no individual buyer or seller can influence the market price, which is determined by total supply and total demand. Under conditions of pure competition, each firm will operate at its maximum profit, or equilibrium, position as determined by the intersection of its marginal cost and marginal revenue curves. A firm that is suffering a loss may continue to operate, rather than shut down, in the short run so long as it is recovering its variable cost and making a contribution to overhead.

In the long run economic forces will come into play to reduce price and to eliminate economic or pure profit under conditions of pure competition. Consumers eventually will receive the product at a price that is equal to the cost of production. A long-run cost curve can be constructed from a series of short-run cost curves for firms at different scales of operations. Competitive forces arising from economies of scale in the long run will result in a lower price to consumers.

A knowledge of pricing and profits under idealistic conditions of pure competition serves as a basic foundation for analyzing the various forms of imperfect competition that exist in the economy today, as we shall see in our study of the next chapter.

## DISCUSSION QUESTIONS

1. What effect does the size of the marginal product have on the average product? Explain.
2. Explain why the average variable cost decreases, reaches a minimum, and then rises again, while the average fixed cost continues to decrease as output increases.
3. Is it true that whenever marginal cost is rising, the average variable cost and the average total cost must also rise? Why?
4. How is the maximum profit position determined on a break-even chart? What components are needed to construct a break-even chart?
5. Why is the point at which marginal revenue equals marginal cost the maximum profit position?

6. What is pure profit and how is it measured?
7. What characteristics or conditions must be present for pure competition to exist?
8. Explain why the individual seller in pure competition can have no effect on the market price.
9. By examining a marginal revenue and marginal cost graph, how can you ascertain the following: (a) whether the firm is making a profit or suffering a loss; (b) if the firm is suffering a loss, whether it should shut down or continue to operate in the short run?
10. Explain how profits disappear in the long run under conditions of pure competition.

## SUGGESTED READINGS

Boulding, Kenneth E. *Economic Analysis.* 2 vols. New York: Harper & Row, Publishers, 1966.

Brennan, Michael J. *Theory of Economic Statistics.* Englewood Cliffs, N.J.: Prentice-Hall, Inc., 1970.

Cohen, Kalman J., and Richard M. Cyert. *The Theory of the Firm.* Englewood Cliffs, N.J.: Prentice-Hall, Inc., 1965.

Cole, Charles L. *Microeconomics: A Contemporary Approach.* New York: Harcourt Brace Jovanovich, Inc., 1973.

Dooley, Peter C. *Elementary Price Theory*, 2d ed. New York: Appleton-Century-Crofts, 1973.

Ferguson, C. E., and S. Charles Maurice. *Economic Analysis*. Homewood, Ill.: Richard D. Irwin, Inc., 1974.

Gard, Gerald. *Introduction to Microeconomic Theory*. New York: The Ronald Press Company, 1968.

Hadar, Josef. *Elementary Theory of Microeconomic Behavior*. Reading, Mass.: Addison-Wesley Publishing Company, Inc., 1974.

Klein, John J. *Money and the Economy*, 3d rev. ed. New York: Harcourt Brace Jovanovich, Inc., 1974.

Lancaster, Kelvin. *Introduction to Modern Microeconomics*. Chicago: Rand McNally & Company, 1974.

Mansfield, Edwin. *Microeconomics*, 2d ed. New York: W. W. Norton & Company, Inc., 1975.

Marshall, Alfred. *Principles of Economics*. 2 vols. New York: Macmillan Publishing Co., Inc., 1961.

Nicholson, Walter. *Microeconomic Theory*. Hinsdale, Ill.: The Dryden Press, 1972.

Shapiro, Edward. *Understanding Money*. New York: Harcourt Brace Jovanovich, Inc., 1975.

Stigler, George J. *The Theory of Price*. New York: Macmillan Publishing Co. Inc., 1973.

Thompson, Arthur A., Jr. *Economics of the Firm: Theory and Practice*. Englewood Cliffs, N.J.: Prentice-Hall, Inc., 1973.

Watson, Donald S. *Price Theory and Its Uses*, 3d ed. Boston: Houghton Mifflin Company, 1972.

# 7 Imperfect Competition: The World of Reality

## MONOPOLY

At the other end of the competitive scale from pure competition is *pure monopoly*. This is a market condition in which there is only one producer or seller of a commodity. Furthermore, it assumes that there are no close substitutes for the particular good or service. This latter assumption, of course, makes it difficult for a pure monopoly to exist. It may be, for example, that Ford Motor Company has a monopoly on the production and sale of Ford cars. But so long as car buyers can turn to Plymouths, Chevrolets, Gremlins, and numerous other makes of autos, Ford truly does not have a pure monopoly power.

In many cases a landlord will have a monopoly on the location of a certain rental property. After all, the landlord is the only one who has that particular piece of property to rent. But since there may be several other choices of similar property near that location, it cannot be claimed that the landlord is a monopolist. Like pure competition, pure monopoly is more of an abstraction than a reality. There are very few, if any, markets in which there is a sole supplier; and in most cases there are numerous substitute products available.

### The Characteristics of Monopoly

The major characteristic of monopoly is the degree of control over price that can be exercised by the seller. In practically all markets demand and supply tend to set the market price. In pure competition the individual supplies of many sellers make up the aggregate or market supply. But with a monopoly the individual supply of the monopolist is identical with the market supply. On the other hand, since the monopolist is the only supplier, the total demand on the market becomes a demand for that supplier's product or service. Therefore, any time the monopolist increases or decreases supply, it will affect the market price. Instead of having to take the market price as given and adjust output to the most profitable position, as the case may be under pure competition, the monopolist can adjust output, within limits, to attain the most favorable market price. The monopolist does not have complete control over the market price, of course, because customers cannot be forced to buy at prices they are not willing to pay.

Because of the complexity of our markets today, it is rather difficult to determine who is and who is not a monopolist. A firm may produce a multitude of commodities, many of which are sold in the market in competition with identical or similar products. But among its products there may be one item for which there is no competition. Is this company then a monopolist or not? Furthermore, even a pure monopolist can claim to be in competition with other firms, not for the sale of a particular good or service, but for the acquisition of the consumer's dollars. Although there are a number of near monopolies in the American economy today, pure monopoly is nonexistent except for government-regulated public utilities. Industries that have at one time approached monopoly include aluminum prior to World War II, shoe machinery, nickel, and Pullman railroad cars.

### Sources of Monopoly

Monopolies may develop or come into existence from a number of sources. But the essence of obtaining and maintaining a monopoly is the erection of barriers to the entry of other firms into the industry. The stronger such barriers, the easier it is to protect a monopoly position. As we saw in the previous chapter, if a firm is enjoying a profitable operation, the normal reaction under competitive conditions is to induce additional firms into the market, which will result in a profit squeeze. But if a monopoly can effectively block the entry of new firms into the business or industry, it can continue to enjoy its monopoly profits.

**Economies of Scale**     In some industries it is uneconomical for firms to operate competitively. The "heavy industries," such as steel and heavy machinery, that require the centralized control of vast amounts of capital to achieve the economies of large-scale production, tend to be monopolistic. In such industries pure competition is not feasible, for if many firms were to supply the market, none could produce enough to take advantage of the low per unit cost associated with economies of scale. Even though most of the largest firms within these industries are not pure monopolies, they tend to have monopolistic characteristics.

**Natural Monopolies: Public Utilities**     Some industries by their very nature tend to foster monopoly and repel competition. For example, confusion, waste, and inconvenience would result if several gas companies were to compete for the trade of consumers in an urban area.

In addition to waste through duplication of assets, just think of what the condition of our streets would be if three or four gas companies were tearing up streets for the purpose of repairing gas lines. Traffic would be in a constant state of disruption. Visualize the unsightliness of three strings of telephone wires and poles of competing companies traversing the streets and lawns in a new residential subdivision. And what about the safety of passengers and pedestrians if buses from four different transit companies were to race each other from corner to corner to pick up passengers?

In such cases, where one or two firms can adequately supply all the service needed for a community, it is desirable to limit the number of firms within a given territory offering these services. Under these circumstances, it becomes imperative for the government to exercise its powers to regulate services and prices. This is done by granting a monopoly, or franchise, to one or a few firms subject to control by a public service commission.

**Control of Raw Materials**    Another effective barrier to entry is the ownership or control of essential raw materials. Here the right of private property can be exercised to prevent rivals from developing. Although it is difficult to gain complete control of raw materials, and in many cases there may be close substitutes for a particular raw material, this method of blocking competition was effective for years in the production of aluminum. The Aluminum Company of America retained its monopoly position for years through its control of nearly all sources of bauxite, the major ingredient of aluminum production. The International Nickel Company of Canada exercises near monopoly control through its control of nearly 90 percent of the known nickel reserves of the world. In Africa and elsewhere most of the diamond mines are owned by the DeBeers Company of South Africa, and a large portion of the world's molybdenum supplies are controlled by one company.

**Patents and Copyrights**    A patent gives the holder the exclusive right to use, to keep, or to sell an invention for a period of 17 years. In spite of safeguards against an undesirable amount of monopoly arising from the granting of such a temporary exclusive right, the control of patents is used as an important source of monopolistic power by some of the large corporations.

Possible procedures in using patents and the patent laws to stifle competition vary. The granting of patents for useless devices and processes increases the likelihood that inventors of worthwhile innovations will encounter lawsuits for infringement. By making slight changes or improvements in a patented device or process, the owner may file an amendment to a patent and thus prolong its life. Perhaps the most effective method for maintaining control that a patent gives a manufacturer is to scare away new rivals by threats of infringement suits.

Patent control and improvement has played an important role in the development of many of our well-known giant corporations of today, including International Business Machines, National Cash Register, General

Electric Company, Radio Corporation of America, AT&T, General Motors, Westinghouse, and many others. At the present time nearly two thirds of all new patents are obtained by corporations.

**Competitive Tactics**    A firm may eliminate its rivals or effectively block the entry of new firms into its field through the use of aggressive production and merchandising techniques. Sometimes unfair tactics are employed to drive out competition. Past years have seen the use of temporary selling below cost to weed out or bankrupt smaller competitors, the vilification of competitors' products, pirating of administrative personnel, applying undue pressure on suppliers or financial sources, and sometimes outright blackmail. Although many of these tactics have since been declared illegal by antitrust laws, there is still much aggressive competition taking place in our economy that makes it difficult for new firms to enter some industries.

### PURE MONOPOLY PRICE

In our attempt to understand how monopoly price is determined, it is important to keep in mind the definite and clear concept of what is implied by "pure monopoly." The concept of pure monopoly implies a situation where there is a single seller of a good for which there is no available close substitute. Whether the power of the monopolist is exercised to fix the highest possible price for what is sold depends largely upon whether the monopolist is deterred by fear of possible government regulation or potential competition, or by the desire to achieve or to maintain the goodwill of the public which affects the sales of the firm's product.

Pure monopoly occurs under one of two possible conditions: (1) the supply may consist of one unit of a unique good or it may consist of a limited number of *nonreproducible* units of a good for which there is no available close substitute; or (2) the supply may be *reproducible*. In this discussion we are primarily interested in the second condition, as most goods are reproducible.

### Determination of Monopoly Price

Within limits a monopolist can produce and maintain supply at virtually any level. Under such a condition the price will be uniform for all buyers and can be established by the seller at that point which will yield the greatest total profit. Where this point will be located depends upon the nature of the demand for the monopolist's product and the costs of production.

**The Monopolist's Demand Curve**    Under pure competition, demand for the output of a single firm can be represented by a straight horizontal

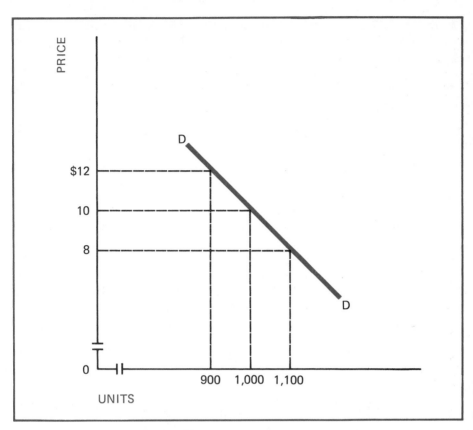

Figure 7-1    **THE MONOPOLIST'S DEMAND CURVE**

line. The individual producer is unable to influence the market price either by increasing or decreasing supply. The producer is able to sell any quantity offered at the current market price. The situation of the monopolist, however, is different. The monopolist is the only supplier of the good, and the demand curve for the monopolist's product slopes downward to the right *because it is the market demand curve of all buyers.* The less essential the product, the more elastic is demand. The more essential it is, the less elastic is demand. Hence, the first question to be considered by the monopolist is, "How many units of my good can I expect to sell at various prices?" The number of units to be produced will be determined by the answer.[1]

The monopolist's position is reflected in Figure 7-1. Since there is only one producer, the demand curve for the product of the individual firm is also the demand curve for the entire industry. *D* is the demand curve. The demand curve is also the average revenue curve for the firm.

[1]The student may find it helpful to review the discussion of elasticity of demand in Chapter 5.

In Figure 7-1 the total revenue at 1,100 units is $8,800, at 1,000 units it is $10,000, while at 900 units it is $10,800. Thus, the monopolist can obtain a higher price and a larger revenue by limiting supply. If sales were increased from 1,000 to 1,100, total revenue would decrease. Of course, if demand were elastic, it would be more profitable to increase output.

**The Monopolist's Cost Curves**    As in the case of most other producers, the monopolist's cost per unit usually decreases for a while as the number of units produced increases. If production is pushed to the point where marginal cost increases, however, before long the average total cost will also increase. The increase in the average total cost per unit does not manifest itself until after an increase in marginal cost has taken place because the increase is due to an increase in variable costs. The increase in variable costs must become great enough to offset the decrease in average fixed costs before there will be a rise in average total cost. How long the monopolist will continue to increase production after marginal cost begins to rise will depend upon the number of units that can be produced before the production of the next unit will result in a marginal cost greater than the corresponding marginal revenue.

**Relations Between the Monopolist's Cost and Revenue Curves**    Let us assume that the monopolist's cost and revenue situation is as shown in Table 7-1.

Inspection of this table reveals that the level of production at which profit is maximized is reached when 8 units are produced. Since marginal

Table 7-1   **COSTS AND REVENUES FOR A MONOPOLY**

| (1) Units of Output | (2) Average Total Cost | (3) Total Cost | (4) Marginal Cost | (5) Average Revenue | (6) Total Revenue | (7) Marginal Revenue | (8) Net Revenue or *Loss* |
|---|---|---|---|---|---|---|---|
| 1 | $20.00 | $ 20.00 | | $16.48 | $ 16.48 | | −$ 3.52 |
| | | | $14.72 | | | $15.00 | |
| 2 | 17.36 | 34.72 | | 15.74 | 31.48 | | − 3.24 |
| | | | 10.40 | | | 13.52 | |
| 3 | 15.04 | 45.12 | | 15.00 | 45.00 | | − 0.12 |
| | | | 7.04 | | | 12.04 | |
| 4 | 13.04 | 52.16 | | 14.26 | 57.04 | | 4.88 |
| | | | 4.64 | | | 10.56 | |
| 5 | 11.36 | 56.80 | | 13.52 | 67.60 | | 10.80 |
| | | | 3.20 | | | 9.08 | |
| 6 | 10.00 | 60.00 | | 12.78 | 76.68 | | 16.68 |
| | | | 2.72 | | | 7.60 | |
| 7 | 8.96 | 62.72 | | 12.04 | 84.28 | | 21.56 |
| | | | 3.20 | | | 6.12 | |
| 8 | 8.24 | 65.92 | | 11.30 | 90.40 | | 24.48 |
| | | | 4.64 | | | 4.64 | |
| 9 | 7.84 | 70.56 | | 10.56 | 95.04 | | 24.48 |
| | | | 7.04 | | | 3.16 | |
| 10 | 7.76 | 77.60 | | 9.82 | 98.20 | | 20.60 |
| | | | 10.40 | | | 1.68 | |
| 11 | 8.00 | 88.00 | | 9.08 | 99.88 | | 11.88 |
| | | | 14.72 | | | 0.20 | |
| 12 | 8.56 | 102.72 | | 8.34 | 100.08 | | − 2.64 |

cost and marginal revenue become the same for 9 units, the same amount of profit, $24.48, will be realized if 9 units are produced. But if more than 9 units are produced, profit will decrease because marginal cost rises and continues to rise above marginal revenue. If 12 units are produced, there will be a loss of $2.64.

Since average total cost is less at 10 units than at 9 units, and since at 10 units average revenue is still greater than average total cost, it might appear at first glance that it would be profitable to produce the larger number. This conclusion, however, is not justified because, after 9 units have been produced, the cost of producing another unit would be greater than the amount of revenue received from the sale of the additional unit (marginal cost, $7.04; marginal revenue, $3.16). Thus, it is the relationship between marginal cost and marginal revenue that is significant in determining the point at which the producer limits supply.

The relationships of the cost and revenue curves may be plotted as shown in Figure 7-2, page 132. $AR$, average revenue, is the monopolist's demand curve. This curve sloping downward to the right indicates that, as the selling price decreases, a larger number of units will be bought. $MR$, the marginal revenue curve, suggests that as the number of units sold increases, the amount of marginal revenue per unit decreases.

Because the monopolist is faced with a negatively sloped $AR$ curve (demand), marginal revenue will be less than the $AR$ curve, and the $MR$ curve will decline at a faster rate. Remember that in pure competition, where the seller has a horizontal or constant $AR$ curve, every time an additional unit is sold at the market price, let us say $5, that amount is added to the total revenue. Consequently, the $AR$ and the $MR$ curves are equal. The monopolist, however, faces a situation where to sell a larger quantity price must be lowered. For example, the monopolist may be able to sell 1 unit at $10 or 2 units at $9. Keep in mind that it is not a situation where 1 unit can be sold for $10 and 2 more at $9 each, because one of the two buyers who would pay $9 is the same one who is willing to pay $10. The monopolist's choice then is to sell 1 unit only at $10 or both of them at $9 each. If the latter is chosen, $AR$ will be $9 but $MR$ will be $8. This is so because total revenue from the sale of 1 unit is $10, while total revenue from the sale of 2 units is $18, an increase of $8. If, instead of selling 2 units at $9 each, 3 units were sold at $8 each, $AR$ would fall to $8 and $MR$ would drop to $6. This can be seen from Table 7-2, page 133.

In short, the $AR$ of the monopolist will decline because a lower price is received on the additional goods that are sold. The $MR$ will decline at a faster rate than the $AR$ because in selling a larger number of units the monopolist takes a lower price also on the units that could have been sold at a higher price had the monopolist selected to sell fewer units. Thus, if the monopolist decides to sell 2 units at $9 rather than 1 unit at $10, total revenue will increase by $9 from the sale of the second unit, as such, minus the $1 less that is taken on the sale of the original unit that

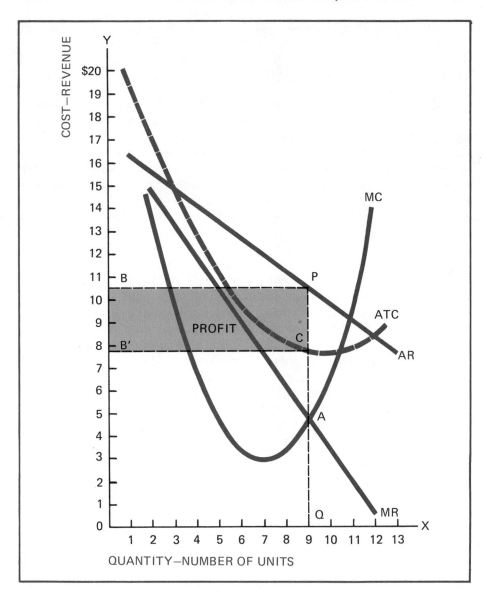

Figure 7-2   **COST AND REVENUE CURVES FOR A MONOPOLY**

could have sold for $10 had it been sold alone. Likewise, if the monopolist decides to sell 3 units at $8 instead of 2 units at $9, total revenue will increase by $8 from the sale of the third unit, as such, minus $1 less on each of the 2 previous units that could have been sold for $9 if only two units had been sold.

   *ATC*, the average total cost curve, shows the behavior of average total cost as an increased number of units is produced. *MC*, the marginal cost

Table 7-2    **MARGINAL REVENUE — COMPETITION VERSUS MONOPOLY**

| Pure Competition | | | | Monopoly | | | |
|---|---|---|---|---|---|---|---|
| Quantity Sold | Price | Total Revenue | Marginal Revenue | Quantity Sold | Price | Total Revenue | Marginal Revenue |
| 1 | $5 | $ 5 | — | 1 | $10 | $10 | — |
| 2 | 5 | 10 | $5 | 2 | 9 | 18 | $8 |
| 3 | 5 | 15 | 5 | 3 | 8 | 24 | 6 |
| 4 | 5 | 20 | 5 | 4 | 7 | 28 | 4 |

curve, indicates the decreasing or increasing amount of cost that is incurred as additional units are produced by the monopolist. The shapes of these curves are the same as those of a competitive firm and are traceable to the law of diminishing returns.

Under the conditions represented in Figure 7-2, at a production level of 9 units marginal cost and marginal revenue are exactly equal. Beyond point A it would become less profitable to produce an additional unit. Beyond that point the marginal revenues of additional units would be less than the marginal costs. Demand being what it is, the price at which 9 units would sell is $10.56. This is shown by the lines PB and PQ, which indicate price and quantity, respectively. The total revenue from the sale of 9 units, then, would be 9 times $10.56, or $95.04. In the figure the total receipts from the sale of 9 units are represented geometrically by the area OQPB.

The cost of producing 9 units is 9 times the average total cost of $7.84, or $70.56. The total cost is represented by the area OQCB', which is less than the area OQPB by the size of the area embraced within BPCB'; this area represents the net profit of $24.48 ($95.04 − $70.56).

It should not be difficult to visualize what would happen if additional firms were to enter this industry. The increase in supply and decrease in market price that would result would soon eliminate profits. But if the monopolist can effectively block entry of new firms, prices and profits can be maintained. Consequently, it is often said that monopoly results in a higher price, the use of fewer resources, and greater profit than would be the case under pure competition.

### Restraints on Monopoly Price

People often assume that monopoly implies an exorbitant price. There may be some justification for the belief that goods produced by a firm which is a monopoly, or virtually so, will be sold at a price that will exploit the public. It would be a mistake, however, to think that monopoly always means an exorbitant price. In the first place, the monopolist cannot charge more for a product than the consumers are willing to pay. In Figure 7-1 on page 129, it can be seen that all the monopolist desires to sell cannot be sold at a given price. For example, 1,000 units can be sold at $10 per unit, but notice that 1,100 or 1,200 units cannot be sold at that price. Consumers just will not buy that many. Furthermore, the monopolist cannot raise the price to $12 and still hope to sell as many units as were sold at $10. Just because a firm has a monopoly, it cannot arbitrarily set a price and sell all it wants to sell at that price. It is true that it can alter its supply to attain the best possible price for itself. But it still must price within the limits of consumer demand. It may very well be, however, that the price which is most profitable to the monopolist, and within the reach of a limited number of consumers, would deprive a large number of consumers from enjoying the product.

There are several major economic considerations which may deter the monopolist from selling the firm's goods at the highest possible price. These include such things as the monopolist's lack of specific knowledge concerning demand, elasticity, and unit production costs; a desire to discourage competition; a desire to maintain good customer relations; and a possible fear of governmental regulation.

## MONOPOLISTIC COMPETITION

Between pure competition and pure monopoly is a wide range of market conditions, which includes oligopoly and monopolistic competition. A market situation may border on pure competition at one extreme or monopoly at the other, or it may be somewhere in between. Oligopoly, which will be discussed later in the chapter, is a market condition with relatively few firms. *Monopolistic competition* is a market condition in which there is a relatively large number of firms supplying a similar but differentiated product, with each firm having a limited degree of control over price. Some idea of what is implied by monopolistic competition can be gathered from the term itself. It implies a blending of both monopoly and competitive characteristics. Monopoly indicates some degree of control over market supply or price. On the other hand competition of a purely competitive nature indicates that no individual supplier can influence price. Putting the two terms together indicates that there is some degree of control over price, but that it is limited.

The major characteristic of monopolistic competition is product differentiation. It is this product differentiation that permits the limited degree of control over price. The major difference between oligopoly and monopolistic competition is in the number of sellers. In oligopoly there must be few enough sellers that the actions of one on price and/or output noticeably affect the others. In monopolistic competition there must be a sufficiently large number of sellers that the actions of any one have no perceptible effect on the others. Some idea of the nature of monopolistic competition and its distinction with other forms of competition is apparent from the case of coffee. Assume that there were a large number of firms selling coffee of an identical quality, no brand names, no advertising claims, and all packaged in the same type of container. Assume further that a price of $1.10 per pound was established by the aggregate supply and demand on the market. Under such conditions of pure competition no seller could get more than the market price for his or her coffee. Why would a buyer purchase any one seller's coffee at a higher price when identical coffee for $1.10 per pound could be obtained from several other sellers? On the other hand, if there were only one seller, the market price could be changed by limiting or expanding the seller's supply on the market.

### Differentiated Products

More realistically, we have a relatively large number of coffee producers supplying a similar but differentiated product. It is different because some coffee is "good to the last drop," another is "mountain-grown," another is "decaffeinated," and one is "freeze-dried." There are many different blends with numerous tastes and packaged in a variety of containers. Although they may all be selling for about the same bulk line price as determined in the market by the aggregate demand and supply for coffee in general, it is the product differentiation, whether real or psychological, that permits an individual firm to have some degree of control over the price at which it will sell. On the other hand, it is the similarity among the coffees that limits this degree of control.

Consumers buy a particular brand of coffee because they like the taste, admire the package, or are swayed by an advertising jingle on TV. Consequently, if the maker of a particular brand, let us say Old Judge Coffee, decided to raise the price a little above the market level, all customers would not be lost, as would be the case under pure competition. We can assume that most of the Old Judge buyers would be willing to pay a few cents, 3, 5, or perhaps 10, more than the general market price because of the difference in Old Judge. But the seller cannot raise the price too much above the market price. When the price differential becomes too great, buyers may still feel that Old Judge is different, but not that different! When the price reaches a certain level, they will shift to other brands of coffee.

On the other hand, if Old Judge were to lower its price by a few cents from the average market price of $1.10, it would probably gain very few customers via the substitution effect. Homemakers buy certain brands because they feel there is something different about them. If their feeling is strong, they are not going to leave their particular brand favorite and shift to Old Judge for the sake of just a few cents. But if Old Judge reduces its price substantially, many of the homemakers may feel that the quality difference is not great enough to deter them from making a switch to the lower-priced Old Judge coffee. In such a case, a point may be reached at a lower price where the sales of Old Judge coffee would increase substantially, provided other coffee producers did not react by lowering their prices. Nevertheless, product differentiation gives the individual supplier a certain price range within which prices may be raised or lowered without substantially affecting either the supplier's sales or the sales of competitors. This is the monopolistic aspect of monopolistic competition. But if Old Judge raises its price too high compared to other brands, it will lose customers; and if it lowers its price sufficiently, it can draw customers away from other brands. This is the competitive aspect of monopolistic competition.

As a result, we will usually find products at a variety of prices within a general market price range in monopolistic competition. With a large number of sellers, there is less concern about competitors' reactions to a firm's reduction in price. But instead of strong price competition, the firms may stress product differentiation, use heavy advertising, and emphasize packaging to sell customers. With a large number of firms in the market, however, there is less likelihood of firms engaging in collusive practices to fix price or to limit output.

### Short-Run Price and Profit

The demand curve faced by the monopolistic competitor is not a horizontal, perfectly elastic demand curve characteristic of pure competition. Nor is the firm's demand curve identical with the market demand as is the case of monopoly. Even though there are a large number of firms, remember there may not be so many as there are in pure competition, and their products are differentiated. Consequently, the firm will be able to sell more or less by lowering or raising its price. But since this degree of control is limited by the fact that the firm's supply is a small portion of the total supply on the market, that it has many competitors, and that its product is still similar though differentiated, its demand or average revenue curve will slope downward to the right. Furthermore, it will tend to be more elastic than the demand curve for the total industry. Of course, the closer monopolistic competition approaches pure competition, the closer to horizontal will be the demand or average revenue curve of the individual firm. The more market conditions move in the direction toward oligopoly or monopoly, the less elastic the individual firm's demand curve will be and the closer it will approach the industry demand curve.

Again, keep in mind that when the demand, or average revenue, curve slopes downward to the right, the marginal revenue curve will move in the same direction but at a steeper slope. Typical short-run cost and revenue curves for a firm engaged in monopolistic competition are

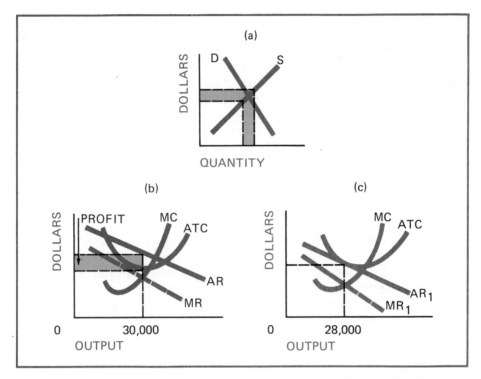

Figure 7-3   **POSSIBLE MONOPOLISTIC COMPETITION EQUILIBRIUM**

shown in Figure 7-3. Figure 7-3a depicts the general range of prices established in the industry around the intersection of total supply and demand. Figure 7-3b shows a monopolistic competitor making a profit.
Note that the price, although slightly higher than the average price established by supply and demand in the market, is still within the general
price range at which most producers will sell their products. Figure 7-3b
shows that with this price and the accompanying cost the firm will produce 30,000 units and enjoy profits as shown in the rectangle.

### Long-Run Equilibrium

If short-run profits are generally available in the industry, however,
they will be an invitation for new firms to enter. As these new firms enter
the market with their similar but differentiated products, the total supply on the market will increase. This, in turn, will decrease the market
price and lower the average revenue of each firm in the industry. So long
as there are no severe restrictions to entry, the process will continue until
supply and price are such that profits for the average firm will be eliminated, as shown in Figure 7-3c. Notice that at the point of equilibrium,
28,000 units of output, the firm will be making no economic or pure profit

in the long run. Furthermore, its total sales will have dropped somewhat as a result of competition in spite of the total increase of sales in the market. Thus, in the long run under conditions of monopolistic competition consumers will receive a differentiated product at a price that is equal to the average total cost of production for the firm. Of course, if firms in the industry had been suffering losses in the short run, the opposite reaction on price would have occurred. As firms dropped out of business, the total supply on the market would have decreased, forcing market price upward. Average revenues for the firms in the industry would have risen until losses were eliminated and equilibrium was established at a no-profit, no-loss position in the long run.

Notice, however, that even though the consumer receives the product at a price that equals the cost of production in the long run, this price is not as low as it would be under conditions of pure competition. Because of the slope of the average revenue curve, it cannot become tangential to the average total cost curve at the lowest point on the *ATC* curve as does the horizontal average revenue curve characteristic of pure competition. Hence, the equilibrium price under monopolistic competition must be higher than the price under pure competition, assuming identical costs.

## OLIGOPOLY

*Oligopoly* is a market condition in which relatively few firms produce identical or similar products. It might involve two or three firms or a dozen or more, depending on the nature of the industry. To be oligopolistic, however, there must be few enough firms that actions of any one on matters of price and output will have a noticeable effect on the others. The basic characteristics of oligopoly are: (1) the ability of individual firms to influence price, and (2) interdependence among firms in setting their pricing policies. If only three firms supply a particular good, any one of them could influence the market price by altering the amount it offers for sale. An increase in supply by any one firm would increase total supply and tend to depress the market price. If one firm cut its price, it would gain a larger share of the market at the expense of the other two firms. But the other firms might react by lowering their prices also. This retaliation would again affect all firms' market shares — and might wipe out the initial gain of the price-cutting firm. Whether or not the firms would gain from such price competition would depend on the elasticity of demand for the product.

An oligopolist may be reluctant to engage in price competition because of the possible reaction of competitors. Consequently, many forms of nonprice competition, of which product differentiation is very prevalent, are found among oligopolists. Oligopolistic conditions sometimes lead to collusive practices, such as price leadership, pooling, and other techniques designed to fix prices or limit quantity.

In addition to the aluminum, steel, and copper industries, oligopolies exist today in the manufacture of automobiles, farm equipment, chemicals, tires, oil, cigarettes, electric motors, tin cans, and tractors, among others. A number of oligopolies also exist in certain nonmanufacturing industries.

### Price Determination

Pricing under oligopoly is more difficult than it is under other market conditions. The firm may be faced with a determinate or indeterminate price situation; that is, it may or may not be able to determine what amount can be sold at various prices. What will happen to sales when an oligopolist changes price will depend in large part on the reaction of competitors. In fact, an oligopoly is often described as a market situation in which the number of sellers is so few that each must take into consideration the reaction of its rivals. This, of course, is a different situation from that of monopolistic competition, where the number of competitors is so large that an individual seller can ignore the reactions of its competitors. Fear of retaliation by competing firms can be a strong force limiting price competition under oligopolistic conditions.

Three reactions by rivals are possible when an oligopolist changes supply and/or price. First, competitors may choose to ignore the price change. In this event the demand and average revenue curve for the individual firm will be known with a reasonable degree of accuracy and may appear as $D$ shown in Figure 7-4, page 140. Secondly, a change in price by an oligopolist may be met by a similar change by rivals. If they do follow suit, the demand or average revenue of an oligopolist may appear as $D_1$ shown in Figure 7-4. Notice that the demand curve $D_1$ will tend to be less elastic, since the gain in sales resulting from lower prices will be lessened if competitors lower their prices also. On the other hand, the firm initiating a rise in price will not lose as many sales as it otherwise would if rivals increase their prices also. In short, the substitution effect resulting from the price change will be lessened if other firms follow suit regarding the price change.

A third, and more likely situation, may arise. Rivals may follow suit for a decrease in price but ignore a rise in price. If one firm were to reduce price, its increase in quantity sold might be less than anticipated as rivals cut prices also. This would tend to eliminate any substitution effect, or increase in sales at the expense of other firms. The price-cut initiator would experience some increase in sales, however, as total industry sales expand in response to the lower price charged by all firms. On the other hand, if a firm raised its price and its rivals did not, the decrease in sales might be greater than anticipated as a result of its loss of sales to rivals through the substitution effect. In this case the oligopolist's demand curve would be the same as that of $D$ for any price above

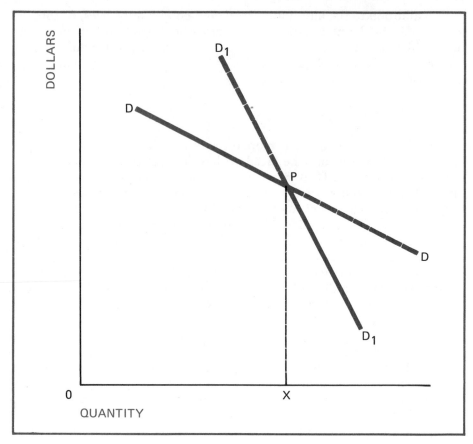

Figure 7-4    **POSSIBLE DEMAND CURVES FOR AN OLIGOPOLIST**

$P$, but identical with $D_1$ for any price below $P$. Such a demand curve would appear as $DPD_1$, as shown in Figure 7-4. This is referred to as a "kinked demand curve." Such a situation, of course, can lead to price stability, since the demand curve of the individual firm will tend to be inelastic if price moved downward and elastic when its price is moved upward. Under these circumstances, price $P$ may become the maximum revenue point for the firm, and $X$ becomes the equilibrium output. Thus, there would be little incentive for the firm to change its price or output.

### Price Rigidity

The tendency toward price rigidity in oligopoly contributes to non-price competition, often referred to as nonaggressive competition. As a result, great emphasis is placed on product differentiation, and there is tremendous stress on advertising as part of the competition among sellers. Sellers are constantly offering a great variety of styles, models, promotional deals, guarantees, and the like. But they seldom engage in price competition. Witness, for example, the pattern of competition in the production and sale of automobiles, soaps, cigarettes, toothpaste, tires, coffee, and transportation, where the emphasis is generally on nonprice competition. Sometimes oligopolists practice administered pricing. An *administered price* is a predetermined price set by the seller rather than a price determined solely by demand and supply in the marketplace.

The tendency of price stability associated with oligopoly, however, often leads to collusive practices. This occurs especially where there is a high degree of inelasticity for the product and relatively few firms in the industry. The highly inelastic demand, especially with a kinked demand curve, makes price competition unprofitable not only for the individual firm but also for the industry as a whole. The fewness of firms makes it easier for them to enter into an agreement, either tacit or formal, to limit output or to fix price. Court dockets in recent years have been replete with antitrust suits against such collusive practices in several industries.

## Pure Competition Versus Monopolistic Pricing

The weight of economic evidence indicates that a high degree of competition is beneficial for the consumer. As stated before, there is a tendency toward lower prices, the use of more resources, and less economic profits in the long run under competitive conditions. To the extent that competition exists in an industry, the amount of profit for each firm tends to decline to the point where average revenue is equal to average total cost. This means that the consumer will be able to purchase the good at a price equal to the lowest possible average total cost of production for a given scale of operation. Since the demand (the *AR* curve) for the output of a single firm under imperfect competition slopes downward to the right, the marginal revenue curve slopes downward also, but *below* the average revenue curve. Therefore, the two cost curves and the two revenue curves cannot coincide at the point where the average revenue and the average total cost curves coincide, as would be the case under pure competition.

In most cases of monopolistic competition there is a tendency, in the long run, for monopoly profits to decline and for cost-revenue relationships to become adjusted as shown in Figure 7-5. But even at the point of no economic profit, where average revenue equals average total cost, the price cannot correspond to the lowest point on the *ATC* curve. As a result of the less than perfectly elastic demand, or the downward sloping nature of the *AR* curve, the long-run equilibrium price will be higher under any form of imperfect competition than it will be under pure competition for identical cost conditions.

In Figure 7-5, *ATC* and *AR* coincide at *P*, and *MC* and *MR* intersect at *P'*. Thus, *OA* units would be produced, price being at *S*. If either fewer or more units were produced, a loss would result because, for any other quantity, average revenue is less than average total cost —*AR* lies below *ATC*.

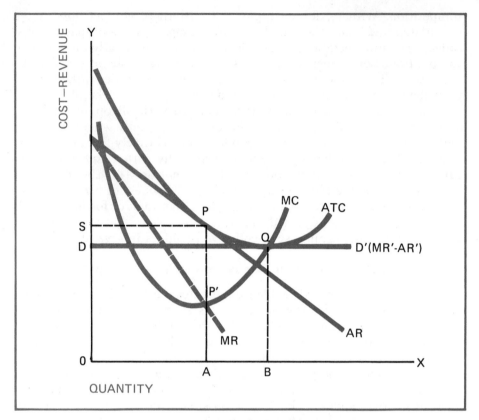

Figure 7-5 **POSSIBLE LONG-RUN MONOPOLISTIC PRICE**

Since there is a tendency for production to be adjusted to the point where marginal revenue and marginal cost are equal, the result of monopolistic competition in the long run might appear to be the same as that of pure competition. Such a conclusion, however, would be erroneous because, under monopolistic competition, the point of equality of marginal revenue and marginal cost does not coincide with that for average revenue and average total cost.

In Figure 7-5, *DD'* represents the straight-line curves for marginal revenue *MR'* and average revenue *AR'*, which coincide under pure competition (the demand to the individual seller being perfectly elastic). The point where marginal cost and marginal revenue are equal (point *Q*) is also the point at which average total cost and average revenue are equal. Thus, under a condition of pure competition the price would be at *D*, and *OB* units would be produced. Consequently, under pure competition (assuming that pure competition is feasible and possible), the price is lower and the supply greater than under monopolistic competition.

This assumes, however, that the scale of operation for the small firm in pure competition is the same as that for a larger firm in some form of

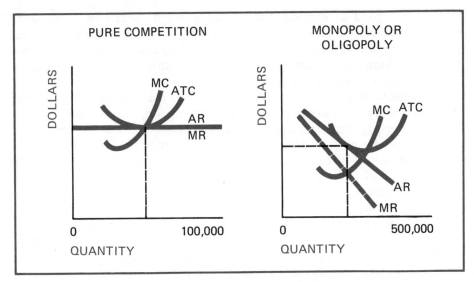

Figure 7-6    **POSSIBLE COMPETITIVE, MONOPOLISTIC,
AND OLIGOPOLISTIC EQUILIBRIUM**

imperfect competition, such as monopolistic competition, oligopoly, or monopoly. Although the scale of operation of firms in monopolistic competition may be similar to those in pure competition and therefore their cost curves nearly identical, oligopolies and monopolies generally operate at much larger scales of operation. With the resulting lower average total cost curve of the oligopoly or monopoly, it is possible to have an equilibrium price lower than that possible under purely competitive conditions. Nevertheless, the monopolist's or the oligopolist's price is not equal to the lowest point on either one's average total cost curve. This can be seen in Figure 7-6.

## COMPETITION AMONG BUYERS

Just as there can be different types of competition among sellers, there can be varying degrees of competition among buyers. Pure competition among buyers exists in cases where there are numerous buyers, who are well-informed about price and market conditions, purchasing a commodity under identical conditions, and where no individual buyer is large enough to change the total demand or influence the market price. The numerous shoppers in a given locality certainly form a purely competitive buyers' market for the products of the local grocery store. The Avon and the Fuller Brush sales representatives likewise have numerous household outlets for their products.

To distinguish a monopoly in selling from a monopoly in buying, we use the term *monopsony* to refer to a condition in which there is only one buyer for a good or service. Monopsonies can be found in local areas where there may be only one granary to service the local farmers. Sometimes a near monopsony will exist when a large-scale employer moves into a predominately rural area. Such an employer may be the only major buyer of labor in the area.

*Oligopsony* exists when a few buyers dominate the market. In the tobacco market, for example, there are numerous producers but relatively few buyers. It is quite possible for any of the four major tobacco firms to influence the market demand and consequently the market price by their decisions to buy more or less tobacco. A similar situation exists in the purchase of commercial jet aircraft and the buying of original automobile equipment, such as headlights, horns, steering wheels, and pistons, for which there is a limited parts market, or automobile aftermarket, compared to the original purchases made by Ford, GM, Chrysler, and American Motors. The author of a college textbook faces an oligopsonistic market in the publication of his or her manuscript, as do rookie professional baseball players in selling their athletic ability.

*Monopsonistic competition*, a condition in which there are many buyers but who offer differentiated conditions to sellers, is very prevalent in the American economy. In any large-sized community, for example, a large number of firms hire labor, offering a variety of working conditions and fringe benefits. Toy manufacturers deal with a monopsonistically competitive market in the distribution of their products.

## THE AMERICAN MARKET STRUCTURE

The variety and complexity of our markets certainly confirm the notion of a mixed economy, as referred to in Chapter 3. Not only is the economy in this sense mixed for the total economic system, it may be mixed for an individual firm. Quite often a firm dealing in a purely competitive market in buying its raw material, labor, and other units of input will have a monopoly or near monopoly in selling its finished product. At other times a *bilateral monopoly* may exist. This is a situation in which a monopsonist faces a monopolist. The monopsonist is the only buyer on one side of a market, and the monopolist is the only seller on the other. There are many times, too, when a multiproduct firm will sell some of its goods in a competitive market, others as an oligopolist, and perhaps have a monopoly in the sale of one product.

Of course, influence on supply or on price will depend on the nature of the market in which the seller is dealing. The type of market will also condition the seller's initiating actions as well as reactions to changes by others. Furthermore, as we have already seen, the type and degree of competition influences the price and output policies and the profit picture of individual firms and of industries in total.

Table 7-3   **CONCENTRATION IN 25 SELECTED INDUSTRIES, 1970**

| Industry | Percentage of Industry Shipments Accounted for by: | |
|---|---|---|
| | 4 Companies | 8 Companies |
| Telephone apparatus | 94 | 99 |
| Motor vehicles | 91 | 97 |
| Cigarettes | 84 | * |
| Tires and tubes | 72 | 89 |
| Soap and detergents | 70 | 79 |
| Aircraft | 65 | 87 |
| Photographic equipment | 75 | 86 |
| Aircraft engines | 65 | 87 |
| Blast furnaces and steel mills | 47 | 65 |
| Radio and television sets | 48 | 67 |
| Motors and generators | 50 | 62 |
| Farm machinery | 40 | 51 |
| Shipbuilding | 46 | 65 |
| Construction machinery | 42 | 53 |
| Malt liquors | 46 | 64 |
| Metal stampings | 40 | 46 |
| Toilet preparations | 39 | 52 |
| Petroleum refining | 33 | 57 |
| Refrigeration machinery | 31 | 48 |
| Shoes, except rubber | 28 | 36 |
| Bread and cake | 29 | 39 |
| Paints and allied products | 22 | 34 |
| Machinery tools | 24 | 37 |
| Book publishing | 21 | 35 |
| Women's dresses | 10 | 13 |

Source: *Statistical Abstract of the United States*, 1974, pp. 720–723.

*Withheld because data did not meet publication standards.

## Concentration Ratios

Although it is difficult to measure the degree of competition, monopoly, oligopoly, or monopolistic competition that exists on the seller's side of the market — or how much competition, monopsony, or oligopsony exists on the buyer's side — some indication of the concentration in production can be obtained from an inspection of Table 7-3 compiled from the Census of Manufactures. The *concentration ratio* is the percentage of total shipments in a given industry that is produced by the four leading firms in that industry. It is certain that imperfect competition (which includes monopoly, oligopoly, and monopolistic competition) exists in a substantial portion of the American markets for goods and services.

## Workable Competition

Economists for the past 35 years or more have been suggesting a concept referred to as *workable competition*. This implies that it is not necessary to have all the conditions of pure competition to serve the best interest of the consumer. It also implies that some forms of imperfect competition may be workable under suitable conditions. To have workable competition at least three basic conditions have been suggested: (1) there must be a reasonably large number of firms; (2) there must be no formal or tacit agreement regarding price and output; and (3) new firms should be able to enter without serious impediment or disadvantage. Others might add to this the fact that no firm should be large or powerful enough to coerce other firms. But even here, it is difficult to ascertain the exact meaning of workable competition. What is meant by a reasonably large number of firms? Is it 5, 10, or 25? Obviously it will depend on the type of industry. What is meant by "no serious impediment to entry"? Would an exceptionally large capital requirement qualify as a serious impediment?

It is easy to see that trying to decide on those industries in which workable competition does or does not exist depends largely upon the interpretation of the person making the judgment. Some economists, for example, would consider the automobile industry, with its relatively few major producers, an example of workable competition; but others would not. More would classify the steel industry as workable competition, but still some economists would disagree. Here again we face that perennial problem of implementing economic theory or knowledge. Nevertheless, many industries fitting the categories of oligopoly or monopolistic competition could readily qualify as cases of workable competition.

## HOW MUCH MONOPOLY IS TOLERABLE?

Capitalism suggests that prices should be determined by competition whenever possible. Most students of the subject "competition versus monopoly" feel that, as time has gone on, there has been a noticeable tendency for competition to diminish and be replaced by monopoly, oligopoly, or monopolistic competition.

We should not assume that pure competition has ever existed in the production and sale of most goods and services. For example, an antecedent of modern factories — the blacksmith shop — enjoyed a considerable degree of monopoly within its market area. Although not much capital was required to set up a blacksmith shop, that capital was not always easy to command; nor did everyone possess the requisite skill and brawn to be a blacksmith. Thus, while the number of productive establishments relative to the total population may have been greater than that of today, we should recognize that in earlier times the market areas were very much restricted because of the lack of easy and rapid transportation facilities.

Is monopolistic power increasing? Unfortunately we have no adequate measuring devices by which to judge the extent of monopolistic practices and conditions at present as compared with those in the past. For example, it is true that there are numerous giant industrial and business firms. At the same time, better means of communication and transportation have enlarged market areas. Nevertheless, the absolute size of some firms and the rate of increase in the number of business mergers since World War II give the impression that there are relatively fewer sellers now. This is the opinion of many economists. If this opinion is correct and the tendency continues, what does it portend for our economic order and for the economic and political welfare of the people?

Under pure competition price tends to equal production costs. At the same time, in the production of most articles the existence of a sufficient number of firms to provide the conditions necessary for competition is neither possible nor desirable. Moreover, where competition is keen and there are many small establishments, most of which are unable to make much profit, prices may be high because few, if any, of the establishments are of sufficient size to enable them to realize the economies of large-scale production. One large plant may be able to supply a greater variety and quantity of better articles at lower prices than a large number of small concerns that, in spite of real competition, are unable to reduce their costs. Would it be wise, for example, to have 100 or more firms of the more than 200 that entered the industry in the past 70 years still producing automobiles? Certainly if the industry had to support that many firms, producers would not be able to operate on the large scale that makes automobile prices today as relatively low as they are. It seems obvious, therefore, that it should not be an aim of public policy to eliminate large-scale production merely for the purpose of creating or maintaining the existence of a multiplicity of firms in an industry.

Nevertheless, the history of monopolies and oligopolies over the centuries seems to prove that when production is controlled by too few producers, the state must stand ready to insure consumer protection against any exploitative practices on the part of monopolists and oligopolists. As individuals in society have become more interdependent, therefore, and as the economies of large-scale production have grown more apparent and desirable — implying in many cases a decrease in the number of producers — the need for the adoption of a sound public policy for dealing with business and industry has become evident in our growing and complex economy.

## ANTITRUST LAWS

During the past century a series of antitrust laws have been enacted in the United States. The primary purpose of these laws has been to restrict unfair competitive practices by businesses, both large and small. A few of the more notable laws are explained here.

## Sherman Antitrust Act

The first two sections of the Sherman Antitrust Act of 1890 declare that: (1) "every contract, combination . . . or conspiracy in restraint of trade or commerce among the several states is hereby declared to be illegal"; and (2) "every person who shall monopolize, or . . . combine or conspire to monopolize any part of the trade or commerce among the several states . . . shall be deemed guilty of a misdemeanor. . . ." Section 7 provides for triple damages by making it possible for an injured party to "recover threefold the damages sustained by him and the costs of the suit" from a defendant who has been convicted of violating the law.

Although the statute condemns "every contract" intended to restrain trade by means of a monopoly, courts have generally held that the restraint must be "undue" and "unreasonable" before it is illegal. Of course, what is reasonable depends upon the judgment of the court. This "rule of reason" was emphatically enunciated by the United States Supreme Court in 1911 in the famous Standard Oil case.

In the case against the United States Steel Corporation by the government in 1920, the Court held that mere bigness was not a proof of violation. This principle was also invoked in the International Harvester case of 1927. Subsequent cases, however, have held otherwise, beginning particularly with the Alcoa case in 1945, in which Judge Learned Hand indicated that the concentration of economic power is undesirable even in the absence of unfair practices.

## Clayton Act

In spite of the Sherman Antitrust Act and of several convictions under the law, the tendency toward corporate combinations continued. In an attempt to "put teeth" into the Sherman Antitrust Act, the Clayton Act was passed in 1914. It prohibits: (1) price discriminations that would result in lessening competition or tend to create monopoly; (2) tying clauses in contracts whereby buyers of goods are required to agree not to use the product of a competitor of the seller; (3) the acquisition of the stock of one corporation for the purpose of lessening "competition between the corporation whose stock is so acquired and the corporation making the acquisition"; and (4) interlocking directorates.

The Clayton Act exempted labor organizations from the application of the Sherman Act — at least it seemed to. And it limited or restricted the issuance of labor injunctions for the purpose of breaking strikes. Consequently, the Act was often referred to as labor's *Magna Carta*, because it states that "the labor of human beings is not a commodity or article of commerce." Many labor leaders thought that under this law unions could not be considered as trusts or monopolies, hence subject to antitrust action. Unfortunately for their hopes, however, they were doomed to disappointment, for in 1921 in *Duplex Printing Press Company* v. *Deering*, the

Supreme Court held that the Sherman Act applied to unions under certain conditions.

Section 7 of the Clayton Act was amended in 1950 by the Anti-Merger Act, otherwise known as the Celler-Kefauver Amendment, so that now it is illegal for one corporation to acquire the assets, as well as the stock, of another company where the acquisition of such assets might: (1) "substantially lessen competition between them," (2) "restrain commerce," or (3) "tend to create a monopoly."

## Federal Trade Commission Act

The Federal Trade Commission Act of 1914 declares "that unfair methods of competition in commerce are hereby declared unlawful. The commission is hereby empowered and directed to prevent persons, partnerships, corporations, except banks, and common carriers subject to the acts which regulate commerce, from using unfair methods in commerce."

Originally the functions of the Commission were to investigate reports of violations of the Sherman Antitrust Act and other antitrust laws and to recommend needed legislation for the control of monopolies. The Wheeler-Lea Act of 1938 gave the Commission the power of initiative to restrain business practices that it considers detrimental to the public interest, including false advertising and the adulteration of manufactured products.

## Robinson-Patman Act

The Clayton Act was amended by passage in 1936 of the Robinson-Patman Act, which was primarily designed to prevent "unfair" competition in trade by the giving or the receipt of discounts or services when such act would amount to discrimination and result in a substantial reduction of competition. Unfortunately, however, it is often very difficult to apply the law to particular cases.

## The Public Uility Holding Company Act

The purposes of the Public Utility Holding Company Act of 1935, the provisions of which are administered by the Securities and Exchange Commission (SEC), are: (1) to eliminate the issuance of securities on the basis of fictitious asset values; (2) to eliminate and prevent an unnecessary "pyramiding" of holding companies in the public utility industry; (3) to limit powers of holding companies over their subsidiaries; and (4) to prevent the development or extension of holding companies that have little or no worthwhile relation to operating companies. The law contains what has been called a "death sentence clause," which requires the dissolution or simplification of holding company structures that are considered unjustifiably complex.

There have been several other acts passed to regulate businesses, and court interpretations of these various acts have been numerous. It should be kept in mind that these actions have been taken in an effort to protect, preserve, and promote competition in the U.S. economy.

## SUMMARY

Pure monopoly is a market condition in which there is one seller. The fact that the monopolist is the only producer and the fact that there are no close substitutes for the product give the monopolist the ability to set the price by altering the total supply. Monopolies may arise from a number of possible sources, such as economies of scale, the nature of the industry, control of raw materials, the granting of patents or copyrights, or the use of various types of competitive tactics.

A monopolist's ability to retain monopoly profits depends in large part on existing barriers to the entry of new firms into the industry. But monopolists do not always charge the maximum possible price because they may not know their true cost and revenue, they may desire to discourage competition, they may desire to promote better customer relations, or they may fear government regulation.

Monopolistic competition is a market condition in which a large number of firms produce similar, but differentiated, products. Product differentiation tends to give each firm a limited degree of control over the price of its product. Just as with pure competition and monopoly, the firm in monopolistic competition will maximize its profits, or minimize its losses, at the point where marginal cost equals marginal revenue. Pricing under monopolistic competition, however, is likely to be higher than it would be under conditions of pure competition.

Oligopoly is a market condition where there are relatively few firms producing identical or similar products. Because of the limited number of firms, each firm must consider the reaction of rivals in matters relating to output and price. A peculiar characteristic of oligopoly is the kinked demand curve, which exists when rivals follow one firm's drop in price but do not follow if it raises price. This and other conditions of oligopoly tend to result in price stability in an oligopolistic industry.

Competition among buyers also varies. In the buyers' market there exist pure competition, monopsony, monopsonistic competition, and oligopsony. The economy is made up of a complex mixture of many types and degrees of competition among both buyers and sellers. It is generally agreed that a large amount of competition is beneficial to the total economy. There are, however, some merits, as well as disadvantages, to other forms of competition in certain industries. Workable competition is described as a condition in which there is a reasonably large number of firms in an industry, there is no agreement among the firms regarding output or price, and new firms are free to enter the industry without serious impediment or disadvantage. Over the years a series of antitrust laws have been designed to promote competition and restrict unfair competitive practices.

In our economy all these market transactions are conducted with money, which serves as a medium of exchange. Therefore, it is important that we now turn to the roles of money and credit in our economy.

## DISCUSSION QUESTIONS

1. Explain how a monopoly can exercise control over price. Is this control absolute? Explain why or why not.

2. What is the economic justification for granting a monopoly franchise to a public utility?

3. What is the relationship between the average revenue curve for a monopolist and the demand for the product of that monopolist's particular industry?

4. Why do the average revenue curve and the marginal revenue curve of a monopolist diverge, whereas these curves are identical for a firm in pure competition?

5. How does product differentiation give a business firm engaged in monopolistic competition a certain

degree of control over price?

6. Is it possible for a monopoly or an oligopoly to make a profit and still have a lower price than a firm engaged in pure competition which is selling its product at a price that is equal to its cost of production? Explain.

7. Why does an oligopolist have to be concerned about the actions or reactions of rivals?

8. Explain the "kinked demand curve" characteristic of oligopoly. How does it tend to lead toward price stability?

9. What conditions are necessary for "workable competition" to exist?

10. Do you think we have too little competition in the American economy today? Why or why not?

## SUGGESTED READINGS

Adams, Walter. *The Structure of American Industry*. New York: Macmillan Publishing Co., Inc., 1971.

Bain, Joe S. *Industrial Organization*. New York: John Wiley & Sons, Inc., 1968.

Baumal, William J. *Economic Theory and Operations Analysis*, 3d ed. Englewood Cliffs, N.J.: Prentice-Hall, Inc., 1972.

Bilas, Richard A. *Microeconomic Theory*, 2d ed. New York: McGraw-Hill Book Company, Inc., 1971.

Blair, John M. *Economic Concentration: Structure, Behavior, and Public Policy*. New York: Harcourt Brace Jovanovich, Inc., 1972.

Boorman, John T., and Thomas M. Havrilsky. *Money Supply, Money Demand, and Macroeconomic Models*. Boston: Allyn and Bacon, Inc., 1972.

Clower, Robert W., and John F. Due. *Microeconomics*. Homewood, Ill.: Richard D. Irwin, Inc., 1972.

*Competition and the Motor Vehicle Industry*. A Study by General Motors Corporation, submitted to the U.S. Senate Subcommittee on Antitrust and Monopoly hearings, April 10, 1974.

Grayson, Henry. *Price Theory in a Changing Economy*. New York: Macmillan Publishing Co., Inc., 1965.

Holland, Thomas E. *Microeconomic Theory and Functions*. New York: Appleton-Century-Crofts, 1973.

Kogiku, K. C. *Microeconomic Models*. New York: Harper & Row, Publishers, 1971.

Lloyd, Cliff. *Microeconomic Analysis*. Homewood, Ill.: Richard D. Irwin, Inc., 1967.

Lyall, Katherine C. *Microeconomic Issues of the '70's: Exercises in Applied Price Theory*. New York: Harper & Row, Publishers, 1974.

Maxwell, W. David. *Price Theory and Applications in Business Administration*. Pacific Palisades, Calif.: Goodyear Publishing Company, Inc., 1970.

Needham, Douglas. *Economic Analysis and Industrial Structure*. New York: Holt, Rinehart and Winston, Inc., 1969.

Shows, E. Warren, and Robert H. Burton. *Microeconomics*. Lexington, Mass.: D. C. Heath & Company, 1972.

Stigum, Bernt P., and Marcia L. Stigum. *Microeconomics*. Reading, Mass.: Addison-Wesley Publishing Company, Inc., 1974.

Telser, Lester G. *Competition, Collusion, and Game Theory*. Chicago: Aldine Publishing Company, 1971.

Trescott, Paul B. *The Logic of the Price System*. New York: McGraw-Hill Book Company, Inc., 1970.

Watson, Donald S. *Price Theory in Action*. Boston: Houghton Mifflin Company, 1973.

# Part 3

# Money, Credit, and Banking

# 8 MONEY AND ECONOMIC ACTIVITY

## THE SUPPLY OF MONEY AND ECONOMIC ACTIVITY

Money may be regarded as the lubricant of the economic system. It not only facilitates trade and exchange, but the amount and flow of money also affects the circular flow of economic activity and the price level.

For many years economists held that money was passive and that it had no substantial effect on the economy. In analyzing the operation of the economy, they maintained that one must remove the veil of money to understand how the economy really operated. For this reason they frequently gave explanations of the economic system in terms of a barter economy. The classical economists endeavored to show the passive nature of money by the following type of explanation. Assuming full employment, they asked what would happen to the economy if everyone woke up some morning to find double the amount of money in their pockets, cash registers, and vaults. Since people could not buy any more goods and services because of the full-employment conditions, they held that the value of goods in terms of money would double but that the total real purchasing power of each individual would remain the same. Although this is a simplified version of their concept, classical economists truly underemphasized the role of money in the economy.

On the other hand, certain economists today reverse the situation, for they visualize money as a panacea for most of the ills of the economic system. Thus, they advocate manipulation of the money supply to remedy many undesirable economic situations.

What is the effect of money on the economy? From observation and analysis it is evident that changes in the volume of money can have a definite effect on the level of economic activity and on the price level, depending on the conditions existing in the economy. It is also quite true, however, that money cannot cure all or even most of the weaknesses of a particular economy. Changes in the money supply, however, can cause an acceleration or deceleration in the circular flow of economic activity.

### The Monetary Equation

One way that we can explain the effects of money on the economic system is in terms of its quantity. The *quantity theory of money* attempts to explain the relationship between the quantity of money and the price level. It assumes that any money received generally will be spent directly or indirectly to buy goods and services. This is known as the *transactions approach*.[1] The theory is expressed by a simple formula:

$$MV = PT$$

The various elements in the formula represent the following:

$M$ — is the total money supply. For our purpose this includes all types of money and credit.

$V$ — is the velocity of money or the number of times that the money supply turns over in a given period of time, such as a month. Velocity can be determined by dividing the money supply into the total spending in the economy.

$P$ — is the price level or the average price per transaction. We should keep in mind that $P$ has no practical value and that this formula is merely a tool of analysis to determine the relationship between the four elements $M$, $V$, $P$, and $T$, rather than a formula to determine the actual price level.

$T$ — is the total transactions in the economy. For our purpose we will consider it as the total physical units of goods and services produced and sold in the economy over a given period of time.[2]

The formula merely states that money times velocity, which equals the total spending in the economy, is equal to the average price times the total units produced and sold, which is equivalent to the purchase price. In short, it states that total spending in the economy is equal to the cost of goods and services produced and sold. The formula, $MV = PT$, then, is a simple truism.

**Stable Money Supply**    We can do more with the formula in a different form, especially if we isolate the element of price. This can be done by

---

[1]Another approach is known as the *cash balance approach*. It puts more emphasis on what individuals and firms do with their money — that is, spend it or save it — and the length of time they may hold on to their money. According to the cash balance approach $M = KTP$, or $P = \dfrac{M}{KT}$, where $M$ = the money supply, $T$ = total transaction, $P$ = the price level, and $K$ = that fraction of a year's transactions over which the community desires to hold cash. In this formula $K$ is the reciprocal of $V$ in the transaction formula.

[2]In the formula, $MV = PT$, it is possible to let $T$ represent either: (1) the sale of goods and services currently produced over a given period of time, or (2) the sale of goods and services whether currently or previously produced. Since the latter concept includes the resale of all commodities previously produced, such as used cars, old homes, and second-hand furniture, it is a much broader concept. The first concept is used here because the level of production and employment, and therefore the circular flow, is affected primarily by the sale of goods and services currently being produced rather than by the resale of old commodities.

simple conversion. It follows mathematically that if $MV = PT$, then the following formula is also true:

$$P = \frac{MV}{T}$$

With this formula in mind, let us assume for a very simple example that the total money supply in the economy is $5, that this amount of money is spent four times, and that four transactions take place. If $M =$ $5, $V = 4$, and $T = 4$, then $P = $5$, the average price per transaction. When these values are used in the formula, they appear as follows:

$$P = \frac{MV}{T}$$

$$P = \frac{\$5 \times 4}{4}$$

$$P = \frac{\$20}{4} = \$5$$

Other things remaining unchanged, if the money supply remains stable, there will thus be no change in either the level of economic activity or the price level. In short, the circular flow will remain stable.

**Increase in Money Supply**    Now let us see what effect a change in the money supply can have on the level of economic activity and the price level. Since the effect of a change in the money supply will depend to some degree on the status of employment, let us assume a full-employment economy. This implies full employment of resources and productive capacity as well as manpower. Under such conditions if we increase the money supply, for example from $5 to $10, higher prices will result. When we are at full employment, it is almost impossible to increase the total output of goods and services quickly, that is, in the short run. Therefore, the additional money available can be used by individuals and firms to bid against each other for existing goods and services. This situation will cause prices to rise, which means that inflation will result. In terms of our formula:

$$P = \frac{M \times V}{T} = \frac{\$10 \times 4}{4}$$

$$P = \frac{\$40}{4} = \$10$$

Since total spending will now increase to $40, provided that the velocity remains the same, and since our transactions cannot increase, the price level will rise to $10 per unit. An exception may result if individuals for some reason decide to save the additional money they receive rather than to spend it. In such a case the velocity would decrease. For example, if the money supply were increased to $10 but $5 of it were saved and not used, only $20 would be spent, as before. In calculating the formula under such conditions, the velocity would be equal to 2 ($20 ÷ $10 = 2) instead of 4. However, this is a rare occurrence. Usually an increase in the money supply in a full-employment period leads to higher prices, and rising prices usually induce people to spend their incomes faster to beat the price increases, which in turn increases $V$, the velocity. For this reason sizable increases in the money supply in a full-employment economy may lead to serious inflation.

If we make the same change under different circumstances, we will obtain different results. If we increase the money supply in an economy that is operating at less than full employment, it will likely lead to an increase in the level of economic activity instead of a rise in prices. For example, if the money supply were increased to $10, the additional money could be used to purchase additional goods and services that could be produced by the unemployed manpower, unused resources, and idle capacity existing in the economy. If production were increased in proportion to the increase in the money supply, the price level would remain stable. Thus, the formula would have new values ($M$ and $T$ would be doubled), but the same price level would result:

$$P = \frac{M \times V}{T} = \frac{\$10 \times 4}{8}$$

$$P = \frac{\$40}{8} = \$5$$

If we continued to increase the money supply, it might lead eventually to full employment, and any further increases in the money supply would again bring on higher prices. For example, if we push the money supply to $15 while $V$ and $T$ remain at 4 and 8 respectively, the price level will move up to $7.50 per unit, as shown below:

$$P = \frac{M \times V}{T} = \frac{\$15 \times 4}{8}$$

$$P = \frac{\$60}{8} = \$7.50$$

An increase in the velocity of money can have an effect similar to an increase in the money supply. In fact the two frequently go hand in hand to compound the effect on the price level. Individuals and firms could negate this influence of the increased money supply to increase prices and/or raise the level of economic activity if they were to enhance their savings when the money supply was increased.

**Decrease in Money Supply**    A decrease in the amount of money can bring about a reduction in the level of economic activity and/or a decline in the price level. For example, if we were to reduce the money supply to

$3 while $V$ remained at 4 and $T$ at 4, the price level would fall to $3, as can be seen from the formula:

$$P = \frac{M \times V}{T} = \frac{\$3 \times 4}{4}$$

$$P = \frac{\$12}{4} = \$3$$

This situation assumes, of course, that the goods would be sold at lower prices rather than permitted to pile up in inventories.

Such a movement in the price level could be offset easily by an increase in velocity. This will often occur in a full-employment economy when individuals are in a frame of mind to buy goods and services. They will increase velocity to compensate for a relative scarcity of money. Many times, however, a decrease in the money supply and in the velocity work hand in hand to aggravate a price decline, especially during a recessionary period.

**Changes in Money Supply and Velocity**    In general, we can say that an increase in the money supply will lead to an increase in the level of economic activity if we are in a state of less than full employment. This will mean more production, employment, and income to those in the economy. If we are at full employment, however, an increase in the money supply will merely lead to inflation. On the other hand, a decrease in the money supply will lead to a decrease in the level of economic activity and/or a decline in prices.

Similar effects can be brought about by variations in the velocity of money. If individuals spend their incomes faster or save a smaller portion of it, the turnover of the total money supply will be greater and total spending will be increased. This could lead to an increase in the level of economic activity and/or a price increase, depending upon the circumstances existing in the economy. A decrease in velocity, which results from spending at a slower rate or saving a larger portion of income, will lead to a decrease in production and/or a decline in prices. Thus, it would appear that the amount and flow of the money supply can affect business activity in the economy. This was demonstrated in the circular flow as we saw in Chapter 4.

As was stated previously, whenever investment is greater than saving, an increase in economic activity or a rise in prices follows. In the absence of a change in velocity, however, it requires an increase in the money supply to give businesspeople the means by which they can increase their investment. Such an increase of investment may come about from an increase in the amount of currency or through an increase in bank credit.

Likewise, it is frequently by means of an increase in the money supply generated by bank credit that deficit spending on the part of the government is financed. On the other hand, a decrease in investment or the accumulation of a government surplus could result in a diminution of bank credit, which would reduce the money supply.

From all indications there is some relationship between investment-saving decisions and the status of the government budget on the one hand, and changes in the money supply on the other. Furthermore, a change in any of these may affect the GNP and the price level. These relationships are shown in summary form in Table 8-1.

### Effect of Changes in Money Supply in the United States

Whatever the source of money, a definite correlation can be shown between the level of production, the price level, and the money supply. Table 8-2, page 160, shows the relationships that have existed for the past few decades.

In the early 1950s increased productivity resulting primarily from technological development and managerial efficiency tended to hold prices relatively stable. The price level then again increased during the mid-1950s. It was relatively stable, however, from 1958 to 1965, a period of "nagging unemployment." The price level increased about 1.3 percent annually and real production increased on an average of about 5 percent during that period. In the early 1960s increases in the money supply showed a closer relationship with the level of business activity than they did with the price level because the economy operated at less than full employment during most of the first half of the decade. During the 5-year period, 1960–1965, as shown in Table 8-2, the money supply increased 19 percent, the real GNP 27 percent, and the price level 6.5 percent, or 1.3 percent annually.

In the later half of the decade, when we reached full employment, however, the additional increases in the money supply helped contribute to the substantial rate of inflation that occurred in the economy. Between

Table 8-1    **RELATIONSHIPS OF INVESTMENT, SAVING, THE GOVERNMENT BUDGET, AND THE MONEY SUPPLY**

| Conditions Tending Toward a Stable Flow of Economic Activity and a Stable Price Level | Conditions Tending Toward a Decrease in the Level of Economic Activity and/or a Decline in the Price Level | Conditions Tending Toward an Increase in the Level of Economic Activity and/or an Increase in the Price Level |
|---|---|---|
| I = S | I < S | I > S |
| Balanced government budget | Surplus government budget | Deficit government budget |
| Stable money supply | Decrease in money supply | Increase in money supply |

Table 8-2   **MONEY SUPPLY, PRODUCTION, AND THE PRICE LEVEL 1952–1974**
(Selected Years)

| (1) | (2) | (3) | (4) | (5) |
|-----|-----|-----|-----|-----|
| | | Total | | Total |
| | Money | Production | Consumer[1] | Production[2] |
| | Supply | (Current | Price | (Constant |
| Year | (Billions) | Dollars) | Index | Dollars) |
| 1952 | 127 | 346 | 79.5 | 395 |
| 1956 | 137 | 419 | 81.4 | 446 |
| 1960 | 144 | 504 | 88.7 | 488 |
| 1965 | 171 | 685 | 94.5 | 618 |
| 1967 | 182 | 794 | 100.0 | 675 |
| 1969 | 209 | 930 | 109.8 | 726 |
| 1970 | 221 | 977 | 116.3 | 723 |
| 1971 | 235 | 1,055 | 121.3 | 746 |
| 1972 | 256 | 1,158 | 125.3 | 793 |
| 1973 | 271 | 1,295 | 133.1 | 839 |
| 1974 | 284 | 1,397 | 147.7 | 821 |

Source: *Federal Reserve Bulletin* and *Economic Indicators*, 1952–1974, and *Economic Report of the President*, 1975.

[1]1967 = 100.
[2]Current production deflated for price increase, 1958 dollars.

1965 and 1970 the money supply grew 29 percent, real production 17 percent, and the price level 23 percent, or 4.6 percent annually.

A slowdown occurred in the economy with the recession of 1970, wage and price controls existed for 17 months from 1971 through 1972, and the economy operated at less than full employment of manpower and capacity during much of the first half of the 1970s. In the four-year period, 1970–1974, the money supply increased 28 percent, the real GNP rose 13 percent, and the price level went up 29 percent, or 7.25 percent annually. This rise in prices occurred in spite of the fact that during the 17 months of wage and price controls, the price level increased at a rate of 3.4 percent annually. By 1974 the price level was rising at a rate of 12 to 13 percent annually. Much of this price increase, of course, was a combination of cost-push, structural, and social inflation, rather than demand-pull inflation. In addition, the energy crisis and crop shortages caused additional price increases which aggravated the inflationary spiral.

## MEASURING THE PRICE LEVEL

A change in the money supply can affect the level of economic activity and/or the price level. The level of economic activity is measured in terms of the gross national product and employment or unemployment, items that we shall discuss later. The price level is measured by a number of different price indexes. The most common and most widely used is the consumer price index.

### Price Indexes

Prices are constantly in a state of flux, moving up or down depending on the state of business conditions. Prices in general may be moving in the same direction. On the other hand, some may be rising, some may be declining, while others are remaining stable. It would be an almost impossible task to remember all these individual movements. Even if one could remember all the individual price changes, it would be of no great consequence. It is interesting to know that shoe prices are going up, that rents are coming down, and that potato prices are moving sideways; but such details may cause one to lose sight of what is happening to prices generally in the economy. It is convenient, therefore, to have some device by which to measure the general or average movement of all prices in the economy. For this reason, we construct price indexes.

Whether we observe the wholesale price index, the consumer price index, the spot market price index, or one of the numerous other price indexes calculated by various government agencies, it is worthwhile to know something about the makeup of such an index. A *price index* compares the average of a group of prices in one period of time with the average of the prices of the same group of commodities or services in another period. Prices are determined for a base period and the prices in all subsequent years are measured in relation to the base-period prices. The Bureau of Labor Statistics, which calculates the Consumer Price Index, uses the "Laspeyres' formula."[3]

**Consumer Price Index**    The Consumer Price Index (CPI) compares the price of a group of 400 basic commodities and services out of the more than 1,400 required by an average family of four in a moderate-sized industrial community. These items are weighted according to the percentage of total spending applied to each of several categories, such as food, rent, apparel, transportation, and medical care. A separate index is calculated for each of the categories as well as a composite for all commodities. Indexes are calculated for each of 37 metropolitan areas and for 17 nonmetropolitan urban areas as well as for the United States as a whole.

**Hypothetical Index**    In calculating these indexes it is essential to hold the items, the prices of which are to be measured, constant both in quantity and quality. Only in this way can an accurate price index be

---

[3]In its simplest form, the formula reads: $R_i = \dfrac{\Sigma q_0 p_i}{\Sigma q_0 p_0}$ where the $q_0$'s are the average quantities of each item used by families in the wage-earner group in the base period, the $p_0$'s are the prices for these items in the base period, and the $p_i$'s are the prices in the current period.

Table 8-3   **HYPOTHETICAL PRICE INDEX**

| (1) | (2) | (3) | (4) Price Index 1939 | (5) Price Index 1967 |
| --- | --- | --- | --- | --- |
| Year | Commodities | Price or Cost | Base Year | Base Year |
| 1939 | a b c d e | $200 | 100 | 42 |
| 1942 | a b c d e | 234 | 117 | 49 |
| 1948 | a b c d e | 344 | 172 | 72 |
| 1952 | a b c d e | 384 | 192 | 80 |
| 1956 | a b c d e | 388 | 194 | 81 |
| 1960 | a b c d e | 426 | 213 | 89 |
| 1965 | a b c d e | 454 | 227 | 95 |
| 1967 | a b c d e | 480 | 240 | 100 |
| 1970 | a b c d e | 560 | 280 | 116 |
| 1974 | a b c d e | 720 | 360 | 150 |

obtained. Table 8-3 includes a hypothetical set of figures that show the general principle by which an index is calculated.

Assume that it costs $200 per month to buy the five basic commodities represented by the letters $a$, $b$, $c$, $d$, and $e$ in 1939. The price index in the fourth column represents the comparison of the cost of the basic commodities in any year to their cost in the base year of 1939. The index for 1939 must be 100 since the cost of the commodities in 1939 was 100 percent of their cost in that year. By 1942, however, these same commodities cost $234. This meant that the price of these commodities, in general, increased 17 percent. Therefore, the index for 1942 was 117, that is, the prices were 117 percent of what they were in 1939 ($234 ÷ $200 = 1.17 = 117%). By 1948 the various commodities cost $344 and prices were 172 percent of what they were in 1939. In 1974 the price level reached 360, which meant that prices more than tripled in the period 1939–1974.

As you can see, the index gives us a means of comparing the prices at any time with the level that existed in the base year. The index for any given year can be obtained simply by dividing the cost in the given year by the cost in the base year. Any one year can also be compared with another simply by noting the change in the index.

**Changing Base Year**   For various reasons it is necessary to change the base year occasionally. This is necessary because our spending habits change over the years, new products enter the market, the proportions (weights) we spend on various categories change, and the comparison of current prices with prices in some earlier period may be meaningless to many individuals and businesspeople. Actually, the CPI was at one time based on the 1910–1914 period. In the late 1920s it was changed to a

1926 base. Later on it utilized a 1935–1939 base. Early in the 1950s it shifted to a 1947–1949 base. Then the Bureau of Labor Statistics shifted to a 1957–1959 base period, but now uses a 1967 base year.

A change in the base year does not change the actual prices but merely changes the year to which current prices are compared. For example, if the base year for the index in Table 8-3 were changed to 1967, the cost of buying the commodities in 1974 would still be the same, but the index would read 150 (720 ÷480) instead of 360 as it does when the index is based on 1939 prices.

The base year can be changed readily by dividing the series of data whose base is to be changed by the value of the data for the new base period. For example, the figures in the Hypothetical Price Index, 1967 base, as shown in Table 8-3, were calculated by dividing the 1967 figure of 480 into each of the other figures in column 3. Although this approximates the value of the current 1967 base-year figures, such a process should not be used as a permanent substitute. For a periodic revision of current index numbers, the construction of a new index is not that simple. With changes in the basic commodities and with changes in the weights of the various commodities, the absolute cost of buying the "market basket" of goods and services may be more or less than the absolute cost of buying the former package of goods and services.

**Components of CPI**   As mentioned earlier, the CPI market basket is made up of various components. These include such categories as all items, all commodities, durable goods, nondurable goods, food, apparel, all services, rent, transportation, and health and recreation. These in turn have subindexes. Since prices of some goods and services rise faster than others, it is essential to use appropriate geographic areas and item categories when utilizing the index for specific purposes. Figure 8-1, page 164, for example, gives some indication of how the prices of services have been rising faster than the prices of commodities. The surge in food prices can also be readily observed.

**Limitation of CPI**   The Consumer Price Index merely measures the relative change in the cost of living. It does not measure the actual cost of living. A higher index in one city may not necessarily indicate that prices are actually higher in that city than they are elsewhere. It may simply mean that the cost of living has increased more rapidly in one city than it has in other cities since the base period. For example, assume that the actual cost of living for a family in City A for 1967 was $6,000 and the cost of living in City B was $7,200. Both of these costs would represent 100 for the respective cities in the base period, 1967. If the actual cost of living in both cities increased by the same amount, say, $2,400, in some subsequent period such as 1975, the actual cost of living in City A would be $8,400 and that in City B would be $9,600. The cost-of-living index, or consumer price index, however, for City A would be 140, while that for

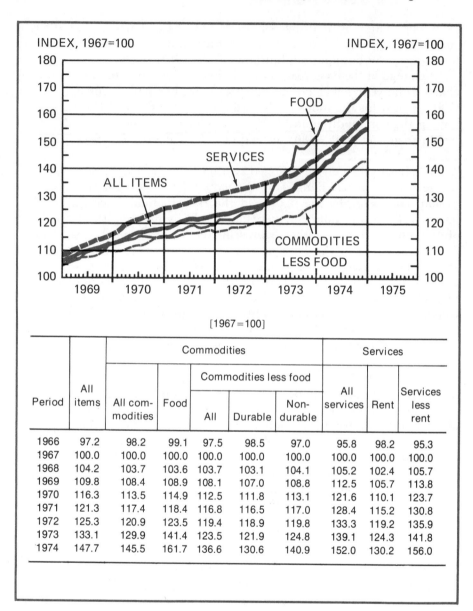

[1967=100]

| Period | All items | Commodities | | Commodities less food | | | Services | | |
|---|---|---|---|---|---|---|---|---|---|
| | | All commodities | Food | All | Durable | Non-durable | All services | Rent | Services less rent |
| 1966 | 97.2 | 98.2 | 99.1 | 97.5 | 98.5 | 97.0 | 95.8 | 98.2 | 95.3 |
| 1967 | 100.0 | 100.0 | 100.0 | 100.0 | 100.0 | 100.0 | 100.0 | 100.0 | 100.0 |
| 1968 | 104.2 | 103.7 | 103.6 | 103.7 | 103.1 | 104.1 | 105.2 | 102.4 | 105.7 |
| 1969 | 109.8 | 108.4 | 108.9 | 108.1 | 107.0 | 108.8 | 112.5 | 105.7 | 113.8 |
| 1970 | 116.3 | 113.5 | 114.9 | 112.5 | 111.8 | 113.1 | 121.6 | 110.1 | 123.7 |
| 1971 | 121.3 | 117.4 | 118.4 | 116.8 | 116.5 | 117.0 | 128.4 | 115.2 | 130.8 |
| 1972 | 125.3 | 120.9 | 123.5 | 119.4 | 118.9 | 119.8 | 133.3 | 119.2 | 135.9 |
| 1973 | 133.1 | 129.9 | 141.4 | 123.5 | 121.9 | 124.8 | 139.1 | 124.3 | 141.8 |
| 1974 | 147.7 | 145.5 | 161.7 | 136.6 | 130.6 | 140.9 | 152.0 | 130.2 | 156.0 |

Figure 8-1   **CONSUMER PRICE INDEX, 1966–1974**

City *B* would read 133.3. Thus, it is possible for a city with an actual lower cost of living to have a higher cost of living index number. The actual cost of living for a family in Dallas in 1972 was $10,422, while in San Francisco it was $12,324. The consumer price index in 1972 for Dallas, however, was 124.9, while that for San Francisco was 121.4 (1967 base year). Some idea of the actual cost of living can be obtained by checking the City Worker's Family Budget maintained by the Bureau of Labor Statistics for several major cities.[4]

Another limitation of the Consumer Price Index results from the fact that it is not a completely pure price index. The Bureau of Labor Statistics (BLS), which maintains the index, willingly admits that there may be certain elements of quality improvement reflected in the index. In measuring price changes each month over a period of time there may well be improvements in some of the standard items in the market basket. Ascertaining just how much a rise in the price of a commodity or service is due to a general rise in quality is difficult. Since the BLS does not have the time or resources to ferret out all such changes in quality, the CPI does reflect some value for increases in quality of goods and services contained in the market basket. Various studies indicate that the size of this upward bias in the index approximates one to two percentage points annually.

Finally, it should be remembered that the CPI endeavors to measure changes in the prices of consumer goods and services only. Since these account for only about two thirds of the total spending in the economy, the CPI does not give a full account of what is happening to prices. It does not take into consideration changes in the prices of machinery, equipment, buildings, raw materials, or even houses. A broader price measure is the "GNP implicit price deflator," which endeavors to take into account changes in the prices of all goods and services produced by our nation's economy.

### Value of Money

In addition to measuring changes in the price level, price indexes are also useful for determining the value of money. The value of money is based upon the amount of goods that a given amount of money will buy. If prices rise, a given amount of money will buy less and the value of money decreases. If prices fall, the value of money increases since a given amount of money will buy more. Today we usually talk in terms of changing price levels rather than in terms of changes in the value of money. You may have heard it said, however, that the value of the dollar is only 28 cents. Just what does this mean? It simply means that because of higher prices a dollar today will buy what 28 cents would have bought in the 1935–1939 period. Although the inherent value of the money is the same, its value relative to goods and services has changed.

The value of the dollar can be determined at any time by dividing the dollar by the price index and multiplying by 100. Thus, the value of the dollar in 1939, using the then current price index, was $1.00 ($1.00 ÷ 100 × 100 = $1.00). In 1942 the dollar was valued at 86 cents ($1.00 ÷ 117 × 100 = .86). In 1974 it was valued at 28 cents ($1.00 ÷ 360 × 100 = .28).

---

[4]See pages 241–242 of Chapter 12.

Table 8-4    **MONEY WAGE VERSUS REAL WAGE, 1939–1975**
Average Weekly Earnings in Manufacturing Industries (Selected Years)

| (1)<br><br><br><br><br>Year | (2)<br><br>Weekly<br>Money<br>Wage | (3)<br>Percentage<br>Increase in<br>Money Wage<br>over Base<br>Period (1939) | (4)<br><br><br>CPI<br>(1967 = 100) | (5)<br><br>Real<br>Wage<br>1967<br>Prices | (6)<br>Percentage<br>Increase in<br>Real Wage<br>over Base<br>Period (1939) |
|---|---|---|---|---|---|
| 1939 | $ 23.64 | — | 41.6 | $ 56.83 | — |
| 1945 | 44.20 | 87 | 53.9 | 82.00 | 44 |
| 1950 | 58.32 | 147 | 72.1 | 80.89 | 42 |
| 1960 | 89.72 | 280 | 88.7 | 101.15 | 78 |
| 1966 | 112.34 | 375 | 97.2 | 115.58 | 103 |
| 1967 | 114.90 | 386 | 100.0 | 114.90 | 102 |
| 1968 | 122.51 | 418 | 104.2 | 117.57 | 107 |
| 1969 | 129.51 | 448 | 109.8 | 117.95 | 108 |
| 1970 | 133.73 | 466 | 116.3 | 114.99 | 102 |
| 1971 | 142.04 | 501 | 121.3 | 117.10 | 106 |
| 1972 | 154.69 | 554 | 125.3 | 123.46 | 117 |
| 1973 | 165.24 | 599 | 133.1 | 124.15 | 118 |
| 1974 | 176.00 | 645 | 147.7 | 119.16 | 110 |
| 1975 (March) | 181.42 | 667 | 157.8 | 114.97 | 102 |

Source: *Economic Indicators* (April, 1975).

We should keep in mind, however, that the value of the dollar is only a relative comparison. There is nothing inviolable about this value. You can easily show that the dollar in 1974 was worth about 67 cents instead of 28 cents simply by using the base period of the current index, 1967 = 100 ($1.00 ÷ 150 × 100 = .67). In fact, you can always make the dollar equal to a dollar by using the current year as a base period.

### Real Income

Although the purchasing power of the dollar has declined since 1939, today we have many more dollars in income than we had in 1939. As a result, the total purchasing power of the average individual has increased noticeably in the past 35 to 40 years. It is true that total purchasing power would be even greater if the price level had remained constant; but if it had remained stable, money incomes might not have increased so rapidly. The increases in the money incomes brought about in part the increases in prices and a decline in the value of the dollar. Unfortunately prices frequently go up as incomes rise.

We can obtain some idea of the total increase in purchasing power for the average individual from Table 8-4. In this table, the money wage (column 2) represents the average weekly earnings in all manufacturing industries. Column 5 is the real wage, or the purchasing power of the money wage in constant 1967 dollars. Column 6 is the percentage increase of real wages over the base year, 1939. The *real wage* in column 5 is determined by dividing the money wage in column 2 by the consumer price index (1967 = 100) in column 4. For example, the real wage for 1970 is $114.99 ($133.73 ÷ 116.3 × 100 = $114.99). The money wage for 1974, $176.00, was divided by the price index of 147.7, which deflated the money wage to $119.16 in terms of 1967 dollars.

Some interesting observations can be made from Table 8-4. Notice that the money wage nearly doubled between 1939 and 1945, but because of price increases the real wage increased by only 44 percent. The effect of price increases on the purchasing power of money was even more pronounced during the 1945–1950 period. During that time money wages increased almost 33 percent, whereas the real wages actually decreased by $1.11, a drop of almost 2 percent. In effect, price increases obliterated the advantages of higher wages during that period.

The period 1950–1966 showed a sizable gain in real wages as the price level increased moderately. Weekly money wages nearly doubled, while the real wage increased by about 43 percent.

In 1967, however, price increases obliterated wage increases. The money wage rose $2.56 per week, but the worker's real wage declined by 68 cents. In another year, 1969, a $7.00 weekly rise in money wages netted an increase of only 38 cents in real wages. In 1970 real wages declined $2.96 in spite of a money wage increase of $4.22 per week. In 1974, the real wage fell $4.99, although money wages increased $10.76.

From 1939 to 1974, money wages increased more than 6½ times, $23.64 to $176.00 per week. In the meantime, real wages increased about 110 percent. Although the worker's real wage did not increase as rapidly as did the money wage, there was some gain in real income despite the increase in price level. In other words, the worker's money wage of $176.00 per week in 1974 bought more than double the amount of goods and services the money wage purchased back in 1939.

### Effects of Price Changes

The economy in general has profited by the fact that wages have increased more than have prices in the last few decades. Some individuals, however, have been hurt by rising prices. Price increases usually bring about a redistribution of income insofar as those with fixed incomes cannot buy as much when prices rise. This is one of the evils of inflation. Those whose incomes rise faster than prices actually can buy more goods and services than they could before the rise in wages and prices occurred.

Inflation benefits those whose incomes rise with increases in business activity and prices. For example, business profits, wages of industrial workers, and salespersons' commissions are very susceptible to change.

They change with increases or decreases in business activity and prices. It is to their advantage when prices are increasing. But since their incomes usually decrease faster than do prices, they are at a disadvantage when prices are decreasing. Others, such as civil service employees, some executives, school teachers, and pensioners whose incomes tend to remain fixed or relatively stable in spite of changes in business conditions and prices, are at a disadvantage in periods of rising prices. These individuals suffer from inflation, but gain during a period of deflation, provided they maintain their income and their jobs. It seems, then, that whenever prices move substantially in either direction, inequities will develop.

Changes in the price level also affect creditors and debtors, each in a different manner. Inflation is beneficial to debtors but detrimental to creditors. While deflation works a hardship on debtors, it enhances the value of the creditors' dollars. To illustrate, suppose you had borrowed $30,000 to build a home in 1961 with the stipulation that you repay the entire amount in one lump sum in 1976. In 1961, the creditor gave up $30,000, or the equivalent of a good three-bedroom home with an unfinished second floor. When repaid by you in 1976, however, the $30,000 that the creditor received would purchase only about two thirds of the same type of home, since the cost of such homes had risen to about $45,000. Thus, the money with which the creditor was repaid had less total purchasing power than that which he gave up in 1961. On the other hand, you would be making repayment with dollars that had two thirds the purchasing power of those that you borrowed. Increased incomes that accompanied rising prices would have made it easier for you to repay the loan. If prices had fallen, the situation would have been reversed. You would have been repaying with dollars of greater value than those that you initially borrowed.

### SUMMARY

Money has an influence on the level of economic activity and the price level. These effects can be explained by the use of the monetary equation which states that $MV = PT$, or $P = \dfrac{MV}{T}$. In short, an increase in the money supply in periods of less than full employment will tend to bring about an increase in the level of economic activity. During full-employment periods, however, increases in the money supply will lead to inflation. A decrease in the money supply will bring about a decrease in the level of economic activity and/or a decrease in prices.

Although the monetary formula, $MV = PT$, is merely a tool of analysis, the actual price level can be measured through a price index. The most common index is the Consumer Price Index calculated by the Department of Labor. It is currently maintained on a 1967 base year. The price index is useful for determining the value of the dollar and for determining the real income of the workers in the economy. It shows that, whereas the average weekly money wage in manufacturing increased over 6½ times in the past 35 years, the real wage, or purchasing power of the money wage, increased 108 percent.

Changing price levels bring about a redistribution of income. Those whose incomes increase faster than does the price level will experience an increase in real income. Individuals with stable incomes, however, will experience a decrease in purchasing power as the price level rises faster than do their money incomes. Changing price levels also affect creditors and debtors.

Since money can have a substantial influence on economic activity and the price level, let us look more closely at the nature and functions of money. For this we turn to Chapter 9.

## DISCUSSION QUESTIONS

1. Under what conditions will an increase in the money supply have more influence on the price level than it will on the level of economic activity?

2. Distinguish between velocity and transactions in the monetary formula.

3. Is it possible for changes in the money supply and changes in velocity to move in opposite directions? Explain why or why not.

4. Do you think the money supply should be increased a specific amount each year for the purpose of financing normal increases in business activity and stabilizing the level of economic activity?

5. The monetary formula serves as a tool of analysis rather than as a device for constructing a consumer price index. Explain.

6. It is said that the CPI is not a completely pure price index. Explain.

7. Assume the following: $M = \$2,000$, $V = 10$, and $T = 1,000$. Using the monetary formula, what will be the value of $P$? If the amount of money doubles, what will be the new price level?

8. In evaluating the cost of living for a particular city, can an individual rely on the consumer price index as a specific indication of how much it will cost to live in that particular city? Why or why not?

9. Distinguish between money wages and real wages. Are real wages today higher or lower than they were in 1970? Explain.

10. What is the level of the CPI today? What category of prices within the CPI has increased the most since 1974?

## SUGGESTED READINGS

"Behavior of the Money Aggregates and the Implications for Monetary Policy." *Monthly Review,* Federal Reserve Bank of Kansas City (September/October, 1974).

Bensen, Stanley M. *Introduction to Monetary Economics.* New York: Harper & Row, Publishers, 1975.

Bopp, Carl R. "Borrowing from Federal Reserve Banks: Some Basic Principles."
    *Business Review,* Federal Reserve Bank of Philadelphia (June, 1958).
Culbertson, John M. *Money and Banking.* New York: McGraw-Hill Book Com-
    pany, 1972.
"Federal Reserve U." *The Wall Street Journal,* July 20, 1972.
Horvitz, Paul M. *Monetary Policy and the Financial System,* 3d ed. Englewood
    Cliffs, N.J.: Prentice-Hall, Inc., 1974.
Kamerschen, David R., and Eugene S. Klise. *Money and Banking,* 6th ed. Cincin-
    nati: South-Western Publishing Co., 1976.
Kaminow, Ira. *The Myth of Fiscal Policy: The Monetarist View.* Federal Reserve
    Bank of Philadelphia, 1969.
Kreps, Clifton H., Jr., and O. S. Pugh. *Money, Banking, and Monetary Policy,* 2d ed.
    New York: The Ronald Press Company, 1967.
Ritter, Lawrence S., and William L. Silber. *Money,* 2d rev. ed. New York: Basic
    Books, Inc., Publishers, 1974.
"Slowing the Money Growth: The Key to Success in Curbing Inflation." *Review,*
    Federal Reserve Bank of St. Louis (October, 1971).
Weintraub, Robert E. *Introduction to Monetary Economics: Money, Banking and
    Economic Activity.* New York: The Ronald Press Company, 1970.

# 9 MONEY — ITS NATURE, FUNCTION, CREATION

## THE NATURE OF MONEY

Most of us use money every day. We see it, touch it, and spend it. But how many of us can define it adequately? Generally money is defined too narrowly. Some define it as the currency of a nation; others think in terms of legal tender. It is often referred to as the medium of exchange. Such definitions, however, automatically exclude the largest portion of our money supply — credit. In order that all segments of our money supply may be included, a broad definition is essential. Thus, we can say that *money* is anything that is commonly accepted in exchange for other goods and services.

### Types of Money

*Commodity money* is that type in which some commodity, such as wheat, tobacco, or stone, actually serves as money. Many commodities, such as stones, cotton, shells, beads, various crops, metal, and paper, have served as money in various countries of the world over the past several hundred years. In various periods of American history tobacco, corn, wampum, warehouse receipts, and bank notes, in addition to metal coin and paper currency, have served as money. In fact, many of these monies were given legal-tender status, which means that they were acceptable in payment of debts, both public and private.

There are two basic types of modern money, each of considerable importance: metallic money and paper money. *Metallic money* is a special type of commodity money in which some metal, such as gold, silver, or copper, is used. *Paper money* is in the form of bills and notes. Paper money may or may not be backed up by gold or silver. If it is, it may be convertible — that is, the issuing agent (government) agrees to convert it into gold or silver or into other forms of money — or it may be inconvertible. Although we have had various types of commodity money in the United States, all our currency today is in the form of bills (paper money) and coins.

Money may also be classified according to its inherent value as: (1) full-bodied money, (2) credit money, (3) representative money, and (4) demand deposits.

**Full-Bodied Money**    *Full-bodied money* is money in which the intrinsic value of the material content is equal to the monetary value (face value). For example, the inherent value of a $10 gold piece was equal to its monetary value of $10. Not only could you use the $10 gold Eagle to buy $10 worth of groceries, but also if it were melted, its gold content could be sold for $10 in cash in the gold market.

**Credit Money**    *Credit money* is money in which the intrinsic value of the material content is less than the monetary value. For decades a silver dollar would purchase a $1 admission ticket to the theater, but the actual value of the metal contained in the silver dollar only approximated 75 cents. Beginning in the 1960s, however, the value of the metal exceeded one dollar. Credit money may be made of either metal or paper, or it may be in the form of checking deposits. Frequently it is referred to as *token money*. Most coin money in the United States is token money. Sometimes money that is not backed 100 percent by reserves of coin or bullion is also referred to as credit money.

**Representative Money**    *Representative money* is money, usually paper, that serves in place of metallic money. It may be representative full-bodied or representative token money, depending on which kind of money it is representing. Gold certificates that circulated in the United States prior to 1933 were a good example of the former. The only type of representative token money that we have today is the silver certificate. For decades, instead of coining the silver, the government held it in the form of bullion and issued silver certificates that circulated in the economy. But even these are now being retired. One of the advantages of representative money is that it is more portable than metallic money. At one time anyone who visited Las Vegas or Reno soon became aware of this fact. In these resort towns many business establishments, whether motel, restaurant, gas station, drugstore, or gambling casino, would give silver dollars in change when you paid your bills. It was very cumbersome to carry large amounts of this kind of money around. Silver certificates were much more convenient.

The government also issues credit money in the form of bills or circulating promissory notes. Sometimes it is referred to as *fiat money*, which is money backed up by the promise of the government to redeem it or to exchange it for other types of money. United States notes, for example, are credit money. These were originally issued by the government during the 1860s when it was in need of money to finance the Civil War. Anticipating a short war, $150 million in United States notes, often called "greenbacks," was issued. However, with the prolongation of the war, there were two additional issues of $150 million each. Thus, a total of $450 million in United States notes was printed. Since they had no gold or silver backing, the value of the greenbacks fluctuated with the fortunes of the war. At times when the Union armies were doing well in the battlefield, the greenbacks were accepted at face value. When the tide turned, however, many persons, business organizations, and banks were reluctant to accept greenbacks for fear that the Union might be defeated and might be unable to redeem the notes. Other persons, because of the risk involved, would accept the greenbacks only at a reduced value. At one point during the war the value of the greenback fell to 35 cents. Some individuals made considerable capital gains by buying the United States notes at a low price during the war and then exchanging them for their full face value after the war.

The Confederacy also issued credit money. Unfortunately the issuing agents, both the Confederacy and the states in the Confederacy, were unable to redeem their money after the war because of the lack of funds. As a result, it became worthless.

Banks issue credit money in the form of notes and demand deposits. In fact, most of our currency is in the form of Federal Reserve notes, which are issued by the Federal Reserve Banks with the approval of the United States Treasury. At one time the gold reserve required for these notes was 25 percent. The other 75 percent of the backing was in the form of additional gold certificates, government securities, or note assets of the bank. Today there is no gold reserve requirement behind these notes.

**Demand Deposits**   The largest portion of our money supply, however, is in the form of *demand deposits* (bank checking deposits), which are, for the most part, credit money. For the time being it will suffice to say that checks written against these deposits serve as money. Since the monetary value of a check is greater than the intrinsic value of the paper on which it is written, it is, of course, credit money. We shall see later how demand deposits may arise even though the depositor (borrower) puts no money into the bank.

### Amounts of Money

Today all the money in the United States is credit money. The total amount in the economy is approximately $284 billion including the currency and coin held by banks. Of this, about one fourth, or $68 billion, is in the form of currency, that is, coins and bills. The remainder, $216 billion, is in the form of demand deposits.

Most of the total currency, $66 billion, or about 98 percent is in the form of Federal Reserve notes. These notes are issued by the twelve Federal Reserve Banks. Although gold backing is no longer required for these notes, many are still secured by some gold, with most of the remainder secured by government securities.

Silver certificates for decades were the second most important type of currency in the economy. At one time silver certificates made up about 5 percent of the total currency. These certificates were issued by the Treasury against silver it purchased in the market, and they were backed up by either silver dollars or silver bullion. In 1963, however, the Treasury started to replace silver certificates with Federal Reserve notes. The silver bullion released in the process was used for striking silver coins at the mints. Silver certificates now constitute a fraction of one percent of the money supply.

United States notes when originally issued were secured only by the promise of the government to pay. Today the very small number of these notes still outstanding are secured in part by gold bullion.

There is also a small quantity of other types of bills in circulation. This includes National Bank notes, which were issued by the various national banks and secured by government bonds deposited with the Comptroller of the Currency. In this category also are Federal Reserve Bank notes, which are like the National Bank notes except that they were issued by the Federal Reserve district banks. In addition, there are some Treasury notes of 1890 still outstanding. All three are now obligations of the United States Treasury and are secured 100 percent by other types of money. They are, however, in the process of being retired.

The remainder of the currency is composed of silver and minor coins, which include dollars, half dollars, quarters, dimes, nickels, and pennies.

This, then, is the currency that we use in the everyday transactions of the economy. It is the type of money used to buy groceries, pay rent, purchase clothing, cover medical expenses, pay taxes, and deposit in the bank.

The most commonly used measure of the money supply is $M_1$, which is composed of currency in circulation plus demand deposits in commercial banks. Since demand deposits are subject to immediate withdrawal, or use via check writing, they serve, in most cases, as readily as cash in the purchase of goods and services. A broader measure of money, $M_2$, is composed of $M_1$ plus savings deposits, time deposits, and time certificates other than negotiable certificates of deposit (CDs) of $100,000 or more. An even broader measure of money, $M_3$, consists of $M_2$ plus deposits of mutual savings banks and savings capital of savings and loan associations. These various classifications of the money supply are shown in Table 9-1.

## FUNCTIONS OF MONEY

As an essential ingredient for the proper operation of a complex economy such as ours, money performs four important functions: (1) a standard of value, (2) a medium of exchange, (3) a store of value, and (4) a standard of deferred payment. The first two are said to be the major functions and the last two are often called secondary functions.

Table 9-1   **TOTAL MONEY STOCK OF THE UNITED STATES, FEBRUARY, 1975**
(In Billions of Dollars)

|  | M₁ | M₂ | M₃ |
|---|---|---|---|
| Currency | $ 68.6 | | |
| Demand deposits | 215.1 | | |
| Total | $283.7 | $621.0 | $996.0 |

Source: *Federal Reserve Bulletin* (April, 1975).

### Standard of Value

Money serves as a standard of value or as a unit of account. This means that we can measure the value of all other commodities in terms of money. Without money it would be extremely difficult to compare the values of different commodities. How much would one horse be worth? We might say that it would be worth six pigs, twenty bushels of wheat, eight pairs of shoes, or one half of a cow. Without money we would have to compare the value of the horse in terms of each article or commodity for which we might trade it. With money as a standard of value, however, we can express the value of the horse in terms of money. Since the values of all other commodities are also expressed in terms of money, it is an easy matter to compare the value of the horse with other commodities by looking at their respective dollar values. If the horse is valued at $110, we know that it is equivalent in value to any other commodity or combination of commodities whose value is also equal to $110.

### Medium of Exchange

In a barter economy, the exchange of goods and services is extremely cumbersome. If a farmer has a lamb that she would like to trade for a pair of shoes, she must find someone who has a pair of shoes and wants to trade them for a lamb. Thus, she has a problem of double coincidence of wants. Frequently she will have to engage in multiple exchanges to obtain what she wants. She may be forced to exchange the lamb for two bushels of wheat, the wheat for a set of books, and the books for the shoes.

In a monetary economy, the individual can simply sell the lamb for cash and then spend the cash for the shoes. Thus, money serves as a medium of exchange. It is an economic catalyst. It initiates action between buyer and seller, and it is the means by which an individual exchanges labor directly for goods and services. Not only does it eliminate the need for a double coincidence of wants, but it also facilitates the exchange of goods and services.

### Store of Value

Money serves as a store of value insofar as we can convert excess goods into money and retain the money. It may be difficult to accumulate and to hold wealth in the form of commodities, for some commodities are too bulky to store, others are perishable, and for some the cost of storage may be prohibitive. Think how inconvenient it would be if the apple grower and the automobile producer had to store their wealth in the form of surplus commodities instead of money. If such persons convert these goods into money, however, they can easily store their wealth in this form. It is evident that if money is to be a good store of wealth, it must possess stability. People would be reluctant to store their wealth in the form of money if they knew the purchasing power of the money would decline substantially during the period in which the money was to be held.

When a nation has an unstable currency, its citizens may store their wealth in the form of some foreign currency or in gold or silver. If the value of money declines, perhaps they will be prompted to spend their wealth if it is in the form of money. Furthermore, if the price level of a nation is subject to severe fluctuations, its money will not serve as a good store of value.

### Standard of Deferred Payment

In our economy, a great many purchases are made for which we do not pay cash. Instead the buyer agrees to pay the purchase price over a period of time. Usually the buyer agrees to pay in cash and not commodities. Thus, money becomes a standard of deferred payment. If a family buys a home, it may take twenty years or more to pay for it. As the years go by and the payments are made, the creditor is trusting that the money received from the family will be usable and that its purchasing power will not decline to any serious extent. Thus, just as in the case of the store of value, it is important that money be stable.

Sound money must be able to perform all four functions. The American dollar has done well in this respect. Some monies do only a partial job. The currencies of Germany after World War I, and the currency of China at one time, although serving as a unit of account and as a medium of exchange, were not used as a store of value or as a standard of deferred payment to any great extent because of their great instability and rapid depreciation. In American colonial days, it was common to keep accounts in terms of British pounds, shillings, and pence, but French and Spanish money circulated as mediums of exchange along with the British money. All of them were serving as a store of value and as a standard of value. In some Latin American nations and in some other nations, where price levels have risen drastically in recent years, currency is experiencing difficulty in fulfilling its functions because of the serious inflation.

## CREATION OF CREDIT

In spite of the fact that demand deposits compose the largest part of our money supply, they are the most mystifying part of it. Demand deposits are credit money. There are two types of demand deposits. A *primary deposit* is one that arises when an individual puts money into his or her checking account. Such deposits are considered as part of the money supply. This is offset, however, by a decrease in currency outside banks that is counted as a part of the total money supply in the form of currency.

A *derivative deposit* arises, on the other hand, when a person borrows money from the bank. It is so-called because the deposit derives from the loan. Instead of giving the borrower cash, the bank may open a checking account for the individual. The checks written against this account serve as purchasing power. The bank honors the checks though the individual puts no cash into the bank. Thus, there has been an increase in the money supply to the extent of the demand deposits created. Because of the complexity of the monetary aspect of demand deposits, it will be explained gradually.

### Personal IOUs

Assume that Farmer Joe Jones needs $2,000 to buy foodstuffs, seed, and fertilizer, and to pay the help that he must hire to work his farm. Suppose that Joe requests his grocer to accept his IOU with the promise that he will pay when the crops are harvested. If the merchant does not know Joe or if she doubts his ability to repay the IOU, she will refuse the offer. Joe may encounter the same difficulty when he tries to buy seed and fertilizer from the supplier. When he attempts to hire workers, he may endeavor to pay them in IOUs, with the promise to redeem them when the crops are harvested. The workers, however, may protest that they will be unable to buy food, clothing, shelter, and family necessities with Joe's IOUs. What Joe is really trying to do is obtain credit, but because he is unknown, there may be uncertainties about his ability to repay. Since his personal IOUs are not negotiable, he will find it extremely difficult to operate on credit. But if Joe could get his IOUs accepted in exchange for groceries, feed, fertilizer, labor, and other necessary goods and services, his IOUs would be serving as a form of money.

### Bank Notes

Since in our example Joe is unable to use his own credit, let us assume that he goes to the only bank in the community to borrow funds. In discussing his problems with the bank official, he will be told that if he wants a loan, he will have to put up collateral. Assume that Joe has a farm and equipment valued at $5,000, which he pledges as collateral for a $2,000 loan. For safety purposes, collateral in excess of the amount borrowed is generally required. If the loan is for one year, Joe will be asked to sign a note payable to the bank stating that he will repay the $2,000 plus 6 percent interest ($120) at the end of the year.

If the bank gave Joe $2,000 in legal tender currency, he could easily buy the commodities needed. People would certainly accept the currency without question. If the bank would lend cash, however, its ability to make loans and thus to make profit in the form of interest income would be limited. Suppose that the bank had $100,000 in cash reserves. If it lent all the money at 6 percent, it would make only $6,000 a year in interest. It was this limitation that led banks to search for a more profitable method of lending money. They found it in the use of bank notes, which were common during the last century.

Instead of giving Joe currency from its cash reserves, the bank might give him its IOU in the form of a bank note. In such a case the bank would merely issue a note printed on fancy paper which would state that the bank will pay to the bearer, on or after a certain date, the particular sum of money stated thereon. Such notes, which would be exchangeable for United States currency, would be generally accepted as money by individuals and organizations in the community. Because the notes would be negotiable, they would be accepted in exchange for currency or commodities. Members of the community generally would be willing to accept a bank note whereas they probably would reject Joe's IOU. Furthermore, whether they realized it or not, those who accepted the notes would be protected by the fact that if Joe failed to pay his loan, the bank could sell his collateral to obtain the money to pay off the notes.

Since the notes would serve as money, any increase in the issuance of bank notes as a result of bank loans would increase the money supply. Furthermore, since the bank can easily print notes, it would not be limited in the amount of the loans that it could make. Instead of having $100,000 in cash to lend, the bank could lend $500,000, $1,000,000, or more in the form of bank notes. The more it would lend, the more it could make in interest charges. Thus, there would be a strong incentive for the banks to make loans. From the bank's point of view, it must be admitted that having $1,000,000 in loans of this kind at 6 percent, yielding $60,000 a year in interest, is more profitable than lending $100,000 in cash at 6 percent, which yields only $6,000 per year. In addition, the bank could hold its $100,000 in cash reserves. This process is demonstrated in Figure 9-1.

After the notes had been circulated for one year, the bearers could present them at the bank for redemption in Treasury currency. But who actually would pay the notes? The bank? Not quite. If the notes were to be redeemed on Wednesday, March 3, Joe would be scheduled to make repayment of his loan prior to this time, let us say on Monday, March 1. Thus, when Jones paid the $2,120 ($2,000 principal plus interest of $120), the bank simply would take the $2,000 and pay the note holders. The

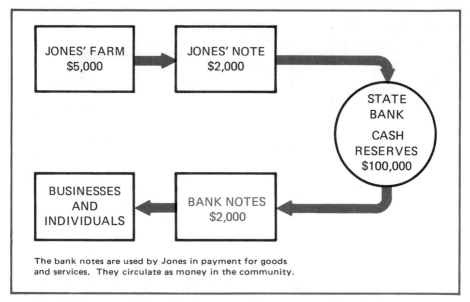

Figure 9-1    **LOAN MADE THROUGH PROCESS OF BANK NOTES**

remaining $120 would be income for the bank. This whole process could be accomplished without the bank's using one cent of its own money. It would merely be lending its credit or good name to the process.

Of course, if the notes were redeemable prior to the date that Joe was to repay his loan, the bank would have to use some of its reserve funds to pay the notes and would then return the money to the reserve fund when Joe paid his loan. Or, if some individual wanted to exchange the bank note for currency prior to its maturity date, the bank would pay from its own funds. However, the more that such practices occurred, the fewer notes the bank could issue.

### Demand Deposits

Although a bank should not let its note issues become excessive in relation to its cash reserves, the strong desire for profits lead some banks to ignore this safety measure. As a result of the overissue of bank notes during the last century, many states began to restrict the banks' ability to issue notes. The federal government also discouraged the issuing of notes by certain banks. Eventually, the bank note was supplanted by a new method of creating credit — the demand deposit, which is prevalent today.

If Joe were to come to the bank today to borrow $2,000, the bank, instead of giving him the loan in the form of bank notes or cash, would grant the loan by creating a derivative deposit for him. In this case Joe would put no money into the bank, but he would write checks against the

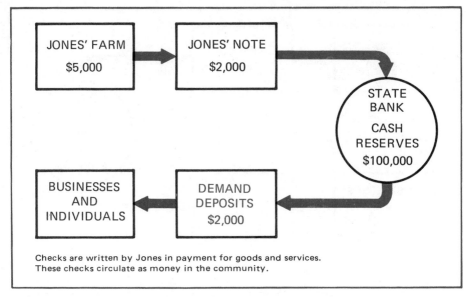

Figure 9-2    **LOAN MADE THROUGH PROCESS OF CREATING BANK CREDIT**

created demand deposit. These checks, which are drafts against the bank to pay the bearer a stipulated amount, serve as money and people usually accept them in good faith in exchange for goods and services. Thus, there is an increase in the money supply to the extent of the demand deposits created. By this process checks, of course, can be written against these deposits. Since the bank does not lend currency, it might seem that there is no limit to the amount of loans which it can make in the form of demand deposits. It will, however, need to keep sufficient cash on hand to provide for those who want to redeem the checks.

Assume again that Joe receives a loan for one year that is repayable on March 1, 1976. For simplicity, let us say that he dates all his checks on March 1, 1976. In this case, at the time of redemption, who actually pays the checks? Once again it will be Joe. When he repays his loan, the bank will have the means of redeeming the checks. Just as with the notes, the whole process can be accomplished without having the bank lend any of its cash reserve. It may lend only its credit or good name to the process. Usually, however, the bank will have to provide funds to redeem checks before Jones repays his loan. This process is demonstrated in Figure 9-2.

If everyone who received a check cashed it, and if the money were kept out of the bank permanently, the bank would need a reserve equal to the amount of checks written, or to the amount loaned in this case. If the bank had $100,000 in reserves to start with, it could lend only $100,000, because when checks equal to this amount were written and cashed, the reserve would become depleted. If the bank gave additional loans in the form of demand deposits, it could not honor the checks written against such loans.

In actual practice, however, this will not happen for three reasons: (1) Not all people cash checks immediately. Some of the checks may be endorsed and continue to circulate in the community before being cashed. (2) Some people, instead of cashing checks, will deposit them in the bank where they will be credited to the depositors' accounts. In this case no money leaves the bank. A bookkeeping entry merely transfers the cash from the account of the person who wrote the check to the account of the depositor of the check. There is no decrease in the cash reserve of the bank. (3) Even if someone cashes a check and takes the money out of the bank, the chances are very good that when the money is spent it will eventually come into the hands of another person who will deposit the cash in the bank. In such a case the decrease in cash reserves resulting from redemption of the check will be offset by the return of cash by the person making the deposit.

As a result of these three factors, the bank can keep less money on hand than the value of its checks outstanding. The possibility of all check holders coming to the bank to redeem their checks at the same time is very remote. Thus, the amount of checks that can be written and the extent of loans that can be made in the form of demand deposits is limited only by the bank's ability to take care of those who want to cash their checks immediately. Since banks are interested in making a profit, they are encouraged to make as many loans as is reasonably safe. However, because some banks in the past overextended loans in relation to reserves, they were caught short. To prevent such abuses of the credit system, the states and the bank regulators placed restrictions on the amount of loans that could be made by a bank. For example, banks are now generally required to keep 7 to 22 percent cash reserves behind demand deposits, depending on their size. The amount of this reserve requirement will limit a bank's ability to make loans.

If the bank is required to keep a 10 percent cash reserve behind its demand deposits (loans) and $100,000 is deposited in the bank, two alternatives are available to the bank for lending money:

1. The bank can hold $10,000 in cash as reserve against the $100,000 deposit and lend the remaining $90,000 to those who request loans. If it does this, its income will be limited to $5,400 ($90,000 × .06) if it charges 6 percent interest on the loans.
2. The bank can hold the entire $100,000 as cash reserves. In this case the $100,000 cash reserve can be used to back $1,000,000 in the form of demand deposits ($100,000 is 10 percent of $1,000,000).

Since the bank already has $100,000 on deposit as a result of the original primary deposit, it can extend its credit another $900,000 in the form of derivative demand deposits. If the bank followed this second alternative, its interest income on loans would be $54,000 ($900,000 × .06). The bank, however, would go to this extreme only if it were sure that it could retain its reserve intact. This is highly unlikely, but it could under the three conditions stated on page 181. For these conditions to prevail, however, there would have to be only one bank in the community and everyone would have to deal with this bank. All individuals who received checks written by the borrower would pass them on to others or deposit them with the one bank. Any cash received from the redemption of checks also would be redeposited in the bank.

The biggest difficulty involved in following the second alternative would be in maintaining proper reserves, $100,000, with $1,000,000 in demand deposits outstanding. If the bank in any one day had more checks drawn against it than it had new deposits, it would have a net withdrawal of funds from the bank. Technically, this is known as an *adverse clearing balance*. Such an event would decrease the bank's total reserves. Thus, unless the bank had excess reserves, that is, unless the bank had reserves over and above that which it is required to maintain, it might easily get into difficulty. In such a case any adverse clearing balance would leave the bank short of its required reserve. Banks, therefore, will follow the first alternative rather than the second. They will tend to hold $10,000 in reserve against the original primary deposit of $100,000 and to make loans to the extent of $90,000.

## Multiple Expansion of Bank Credit

Even if the bank holds $10,000 in cash reserves against the original deposit of $100,000 and lends $90,000 in cash, there will be an expansion of credit. This will come about because what an individual bank may fear to do — that is, hold the entire $100,000 in reserve and lend $900,000 in the form of the demand deposits, because of the possibility of an adverse clearing balance — the banking system as a whole can do through a multiple expansion of bank credit. This process can be shown in the following manner:

(1) If an individual bank were to extend credit to the full extent, the situation would appear as in Figure 9-3.

(2) The individual bank, however, will hold a 10 percent reserve against the original deposit and will lend the remainder in the form of cash or demand deposits, as shown in Figure 9-4. For simplicity's sake, cash loans are shown here, as well as later in the text, since loans in the form of demand deposits can be readily converted into cash or deposited, like cash, directly into other banks.

In this case the bank has less fear of adverse clearing balances because the loans were made in cash. There will be an increase in the money supply since there will exist $100,000 in demand deposits in addition to the continued circulation of $90,000 in cash as a result of the loan.

(3) Although the individual bank in the preceding situation increases the money supply to a limited degree, the cumulative action of all banks will increase the money supply nine times. This is brought about because the $90,000 in cash that is loaned will find its way into other banks.

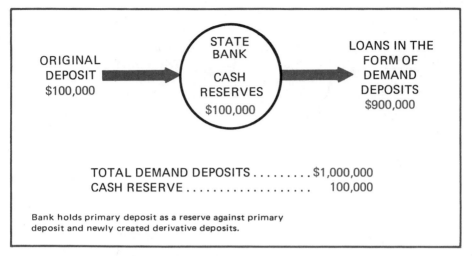

Figure 9-3    **MAXIMUM LOANS POSSIBLE BY AN INDIVIDUAL BANK**

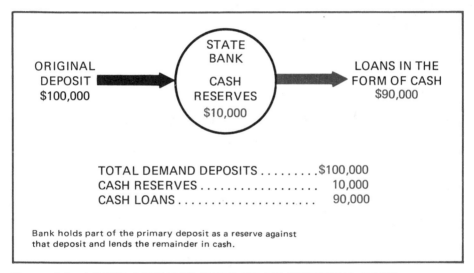

Figure 9-4    **LOANS ACTUALLY MADE BY AN INDIVIDUAL BANK**

These banks in turn will hold a portion of this money in reserve and will lend the remainder, which will eventually flow into other banks. For example, when the borrower of the $90,000 spends the money, it will come into the hands of others, and eventually the $90,000 will be deposited in other banks, which will hold $9,000 cash reserve against the $90,000 deposits. These banks in turn will have $81,000 to lend. This process can continue until the total loans outstanding will be equal to $900,000 and the original $100,000 will be held as reserves in various banks. At that time the banks can lend no more money. This process, known as the *multiple expansion of bank credit*, is demonstrated in Figure 9-5, page 184.

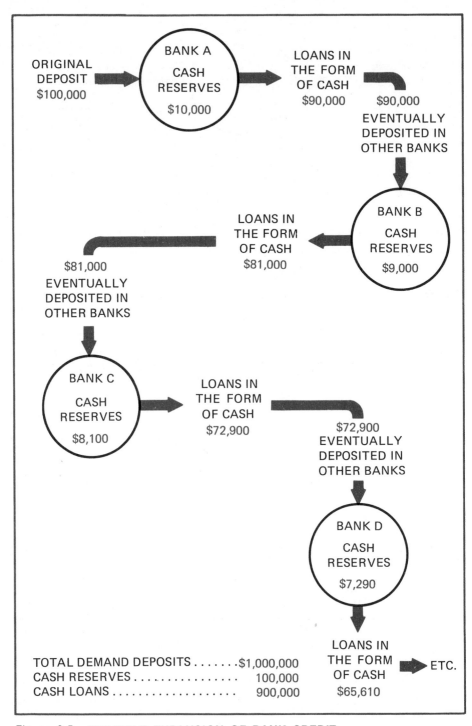

Figure 9-5   **MULTIPLE EXPANSION OF BANK CREDIT**

### Effect of Changes in Reserve Requirement

Another way of looking at this process is in tabular form as shown in Table 9-2. This table shows how $1,000 deposited in a bank (Bank A) can be expanded into $10,000 in demand deposits and loans of $9,000.

If there is a 10 percent reserve requirement, it is assumed that Bank A will hold $100 against the original deposit of $1,000. Thus, it will have $900 in cash that it can lend. People who borrow this money spend it and circulate it in the community until it finally ends up in other banks, as people make deposits there. If all of these deposits were made in Bank B, that bank would hold a $90 reserve against its deposits of $900 and lend the remaining $810. This process continues until all the money is tied up in reserves in various banks. At such time the total deposits will equal $10,000, the reserves $1,000, and the total loans outstanding $9,000.

It should be kept in mind that the expansion of credit which increases the money supply results when the banks make direct loans in the form of demand deposits or in the form of cash, which subsequently leads to demand deposits. Actually, depositors can write checks equivalent to $10,000, and these checks serve as money. Thus, in place of a mere $1,000 in cash, we now have $10,000 in checks buying goods and services.

Keep in mind also that just as we can observe the multiple expansion of bank credit whenever there is a net increase in deposits at the bank, we can also see a multiple contraction of bank credit whenever there is a net withdrawal of deposits.

If the banks were required to keep a larger amount of reserves, their ability to expand credit would be reduced. If we assume the reserve requirement to be 20 percent, which is closer to the national average, instead of the 10 percent used in our previous examples, the bank would

Table 9-2    **EXPANSION OF BANK CREDIT, 10% RESERVE REQUIREMENT**

| (1)<br>Bank | (2)<br>Deposit | (3)<br>Reserve | (4)<br>Loan |
|-------------|----------------|----------------|-------------|
| A | $ 1,000 | $ 100 | $ 900 |
| B | 900 | 90 | 810 |
| C | 810 | 81 | 729 |
| D | 729 | 73 | 656 |
| E | 656 | 66 | 590 |
| F | 590 | 59 | 531 |
| G | 531 | 53 | 478 |
| H | 478 | 48 | 430 |
| I | 430 | 43 | 387 |
| J | 387 | 39 | 348 |
| Etc. | Etc. | Etc. | Etc. |
|  | $10,000 | $1,000 | $9,000 |

need to hold twice as much in reserves. This would reduce the bank's ability to extend credit by approximately one half, as shown in Table 9-3.

On the other hand, if the reserve requirement were only 5 percent instead of 10 percent, the bank's ability to extend credit would more than double, going from $9,000 to $19,000.

Remembering our principle about the relationship of the money supply to the level of economic activity, we can relate this explanation of credit to the circular flow. If the reserve requirement on demand deposits can alter the bank's ability to extend credit, and if changes in the money supply can alter the circular flow, then it appears that we can influence the circular flow and encourage its acceleration or deceleration by changing the reserve requirement. This is exactly what happens in our economy. We use the reserve requirement along with several other monetary measures as tools to stabilize economic activity and the price level.

Table 9-3    **EXPANSION OF BANK CREDIT, 20% RESERVE REQUIREMENT**

| (1)<br>Bank | (2)<br>Deposit | (3)<br>Reserve | (4)<br>Loan |
|-------------|----------------|----------------|-------------|
| A    | $1,000  | $ 200   | $ 800   |
| B    | 800     | 160     | 640     |
| C    | 640     | 128     | 512     |
| D    | 512     | 102     | 410     |
| E    | 410     | 82      | 328     |
| Etc. | Etc.    | Etc.    | Etc.    |
|      | $5,000  | $1,000  | $4,000  |

## SUMMARY

Money is broadly defined as anything that is commonly accepted in exchange for other commodities. There are various types of money, such as commodity money, metallic money, and paper money. Furthermore, money may be full-bodied, it may be credit money, it may be representative money, or it may be in the form of demand deposits.

At present the U.S. money supply amounts to approximately $284 billion. Of this total amount only about one fourth, $68 billion, is in the form of currency. The remainder consists of demand deposits. Money has four basic functions: it serves as a standard of value, as a medium of exchange, as a store of value, and as a standard of deferred payment.

Money in the form of credit is created by commercial banks. It may come into existence through the issuance of bank notes, in which case the bank makes loans by giving the borrower bank notes instead of cash. Or it may come directly in the form of demand deposits or in the form of cash, which subsequently generates demand deposits. In either case, banks can lend more money than they actually have in cash.

To prevent the banks from overextending credit in the form of demand deposits, the banks are required to keep a certain amount of reserve behind their loans (demand deposits). This reserve requirement becomes a limiting factor to the amount of credit that may be issued by the bank. In general, the total amount of credit created through the establishment of demand deposits will be some multiple of the actual cash reserves of the banks.

Although an individual bank may not extend credit to the full extent permissible because of the fear of adverse clearing balances, the banking system as a whole is capable of extending credit to the full extent.

Changes in the reserve requirement can affect the supply of money that is made available by banks. Changes in the money supply can affect the level of economic activity and the price level. Therefore, changes in the reserve requirement can affect business activity and prices.

Since the reserve requirement and other monetary measures are used as tools to stabilize the economy, it might be beneficial to look at the framework in which they operate. Therefore, let us look at our banking system in the next chapter.

## DISCUSSION QUESTIONS

1. In a modern economy would it be possible for some commodity to serve as money? If so, how and under what circumstances?

2. What is the distinction between $M_1$, $M_2$, and $M_3$? Which do you think is the best measure of the money supply? Why?

3. What effect will a rapidly rising price level have on money in regard to its function as a store of value?

4. Explain how a derivative demand deposit increases the money supply whereas a primary demand deposit does not.

5. What would happen to the money supply if, as some have advocated, a 100 percent reserve requirement for demand deposits were established?

6. How do reserve requirements on bank deposits affect the bank's ability to create credit?

7. Why should credit in the form of bank notes and bank deposits be counted as part of the U.S. money supply?

8. Can you see any advantage to the demand deposit over the bank note as a means of extending credit?

9. In your opinion should banks be permitted to create credit? Why or why not?

10. Do you see any relationship between the multiple expansion of bank credit and the velocity of money?

## SUGGESTED READINGS

"A Time Series Analysis of Income and Several Definitions of Money." *Morgan Guaranty Survey*, Morgan Guaranty Trust Company of New York (April, 1971).

Gavett, Thomas W. "Quality and a Pure Price Index." *Monthly Labor Review* (March, 1967).

Leabo, Dick A. *Basic Statistics*. Homewood, Ill.: Richard D. Irwin, Inc., 1968.

*Money: Master or Servant?* Washington: Board of Governors of the Federal Reserve System, 1955.

"Money Stock." *Business Review*, Federal Reserve Bank of Dallas (September, 1972).

"New Economic Gauge (CPI) Will Affect Workers, Retirees, and Business." *Commerce Today* (December 27, 1971).

Rose, Peter S., and Lucy H. Hunt II. "Policy Variables, Unemployment and Price Level Changes." *Federal Reserve Bulletin*. Washington: U.S.Government Printing Office (January, 1972).

U.S. Department of Labor, Bureau of Labor Statistics, *Techniques of Preparing BLS Statistical Series*. Bulletin No. 993, Part I. Washington: U.S. Government Printing Office.

"The Wholesale and Consumer Price Indexes: What's the Connection?" *Monthly Review*, Federal Reserve Bank of Kansas City (June, 1973).

"Will the Real Money Supply Please Stand Up?" *Morgan Guaranty Survey*, Morgan Guaranty Trust Company of New York (April, 1971).

# 10 THE FEDERAL RESERVE AND THE MONEY SUPPLY

## EARLY HISTORY OF BANKING IN THE UNITED STATES

A few banks did exist during colonial and early post-colonial days, but the first attempt at centralized banking came with the chartering by the federal government of the First Bank of the United States in 1791 for a twenty-year period. The primary functions of the First Bank were to perform as a commercial bank for individuals and business, to act as a banker's bank, to serve as a fiscal agent for the federal government, and to endeavor to keep some order in the banking business by exercising certain restraints on state banks.

Opposition to the bank led to the defeat of the recharter movement. There followed for five years a period in which only state banks existed. In 1816, however, the Second Bank of the United States was chartered for a twenty-year period. Although it was designed to perform functions similar to those of the First Bank, it had a greater amount of capital stock and operated on a more widespread scale.

Despite its efficient operation, there was considerable opposition to the Second Bank. Some opponents disliked the idea of central authority, others objected to its strict regulations, some individuals disliked the fact that foreigners owned a certain amount of the stock of the bank, and still others thought the bank to be unconstitutional. Political difficulties between the bank officials and the Presidential administration were instrumental in the defeat of the Congressional bill that would have rechartered the bank in 1836.

Between 1836 and 1863 there was no central authority in the banking system. As a result, abusive banking practices became prevalent. Because of the existence of widespread malpractices, this period became known as the "wildcat banking period."

The National Banking Act of 1864 brought some order to the banking business by creating the National Banking System. Its stringent requirements and provisions for note security ended many unsound operations of the banks. The system, however, had several noticeable weaknesses, such as the perverse elasticity of the money supply, the gravitation of reserves toward the money centers, and the lack of assistance to the farm sector of the economy because real estate could not be used as collateral for loans. After several years of research and study, the National Banking

System was supplanted in 1913 by the Federal Reserve System with the passage of the Federal Reserve Banking Act.

## STRUCTURE OF THE FEDERAL RESERVE SYSTEM

The Federal Reserve System is a complex and intricate system composed of a Board of Governors, 12 Federal Reserve Banks, branch banks, member banks, a Federal Advisory Council, an Open Market Committee, and several minor organizations. It is a government instrumentality, yet it is not owned by the government. It is owned by the member banks, but its most important officials are appointed by the government. Each body within the Federal Reserve System has its individual function, but the functions of each are interrelated. Decentralization is an important characteristic of the Federal Reserve System.

### The Board of Governors of the Federal Reserve System

The Board of Governors consists of seven members who are appointed by the President of the United States with the consent of the United States Senate. Board membership is a full-time position and carries a salary of $40,000 a year. Each member is appointed for 14 years and is ineligible for reappointment. Appointments are staggered in such a manner that a new appointee is assigned every two years. Each member must be selected from a different Federal Reserve district. The President of the United States selects the Chairman and the Vice-Chairman of the Board.

The Board has numerous powers including the supervision of the Federal Reserve Banks. It must approve the Bank officers. It has the right to suspend or to remove officers of the Federal Reserve Banks, it must authorize Federal Reserve Bank loans between Reserve Banks, it reviews and determines discount rates established by the Reserve Banks, it establishes reserve requirements within legal limits, it regulates loans on securities, and at times it has regulated conditions of installment sales in addition to many other functions.

### Federal Advisory Council

To assist it, the Board of Governors may call upon the Federal Advisory Council. This is a committee of twelve members selected annually by the board of directors of each Federal Reserve Bank. They are individuals of prestige and banking acumen who meet at least four times a year with the Board of Governors. The FAC serves primarily in an advisory capacity to the Board of Governors. It confers with the Board on business conditions and other matters pertinent to the System.

In addition to the Federal Advisory Council, a number of other committees and conferences assist the Board of Governors on various problems. One of the most important of these is the Conference of Presidents of the Federal Reserve Banks, which meets occasionally of its own accord and meets with the Board of Governors at least three times a year.

## Federal Open Market Committee

The Federal Open Market Committee is also composed of twelve members, including the seven members of the Board of Governors. The other five members of the Committee are elected by the boards of directors of the various Federal Reserve Banks. Since there are twelve Banks but only five positions to be filled, the Banks are grouped into five units. Each unit elects one member for the Committee. The member selected must be either a President or a Vice-President of a Federal Reserve Bank. As we shall see later, the Federal Open Market Committee engages in the buying and selling of securities in the open market for the express purpose of influencing the flow of credit and money. Its actions also help in stabilizing the price level and the growth of economic activity.

## Federal Reserve Banks

The Federal Reserve System divides the United States into twelve geographic districts. Each district has a Federal Reserve Bank named after the city in which it is located, and each district is given a number starting from the East Coast and moving to the West Coast. The districts are organized on the basis of the concentration of financial activity, not on the basis of geographic area. As a result, the St. Louis district geographically is about one half the size of the Kansas City district, but it does as much financial business as the latter. Several of the districts have branch banks. The Federal Reserve Bank of Cleveland, District 4, has branches in Pittsburgh and Cincinnati, for example. See Figure 10-1, page 192, and Table 10-1 for a list of the districts, Banks, and branches.

Each Federal Reserve Bank is controlled by a board of directors consisting of nine members who are divided into three classes, with three

Table 10-1   **FEDERAL RESERVE DISTRICTS AND BANKS**

| District | Federal Reserve Bank | Branches |
|---|---|---|
| 1 | Boston | None |
| 2 | New York | Buffalo |
| 3 | Philadelphia | None |
| 4 | Cleveland | Cincinnati, Pittsburgh |
| 5 | Richmond | Baltimore, Charlotte |
| 6 | Altanta | Birmingham, Jacksonville, Nashville, New Orleans |
| 7 | Chicago | Detroit |
| 8 | St. Louis | Little Rock, Louisville, Memphis |
| 9 | Minneapolis | Helena |
| 10 | Kansas City | Denver, Oklahoma City, Omaha |
| 11 | Dallas | El Paso, Houston, San Antonio |
| 12 | San Francisco | Los Angeles, Portland, Salt Lake City, Seattle |

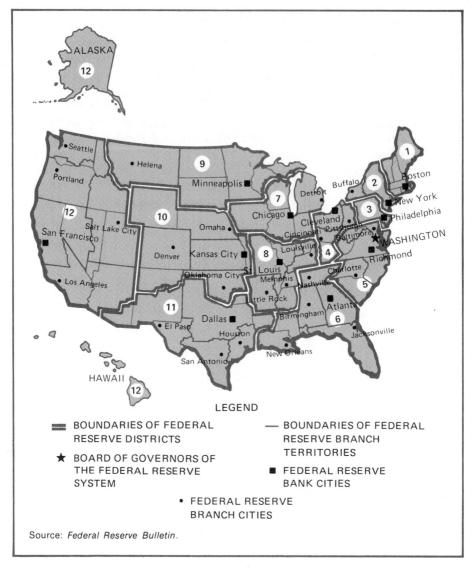

Figure 10-1  **THE FEDERAL RESERVE SYSTEM**

members in each class. Class A directors are bankers elected by the member banks to represent them on the board. Class B directors are elected in the same manner, but they cannot be bankers, for they are supposed to represent industry, commerce, and agriculture and should be engaged in such occupations at the time of their selection. Class C directors must not be officers, directors, employees, or stockholders of any bank. They are appointed by the Board of Governors of the System. One of the Class C directors is appointed by the Board of Governors as chairman of the board of directors of the Reserve Bank. The chairman serves also as a Federal Reserve agent. In this capacity the chairman is responsible for the issuance of Federal Reserve notes.

The public nature of the Federal Reserve System is attested to by the fact that nonbankers constitute a majority of the board of directors of each Federal Reserve Bank. The board of directors of each Federal Reserve Bank appoints a President and Vice-President who must be approved by the Board of Governors in Washington. These officers are responsible for the day-to-day operation of the Bank.

Federal Reserve Banks supervise member banks and conduct periodic examinations of the latter's operation. In the event that any member bank chronically engages in unsound banking practices, the Bank's board of directors has the authority to remove its officers and directors. Although such authority is seldom exercised, its presence helps to keep the member banks in line. The Federal Reserve Bank also has the power to set the maximum interest that may be paid by member banks on both savings and time deposits.

In addition to serving as central banks, or banker's banks, the Federal Reserve Banks also serve as fiscal agents for the federal government. They handle the detailed work of issuing and redeeming government bonds, they hold deposits and disburse funds for the Treasury, and they perform many other fiscal duties. They supply money for the business community in the form of Federal Reserve notes and regulate the member banks' ability to create money in the form of demand deposits.

## Federal Reserve Member Banks

There are approximately 14,384 commercial banks in the United States. Roughly 40 percent (5,767) belong to the Federal Reserve System, and they are known as *member banks*. About 4,690 of these are national banks. When the Federal Reserve System was established, each national bank was required to join or to forfeit its charter. Membership is also open to state banks that can qualify. Many of them cannot qualify because of the high minimum capital requirement. Some do not like the System's restrictions and regulations. Others are reluctant to join because as nonmembers they are permitted to use certain major facilities of the System anyway. Although less than one half of all commercial banks belong to the System, these banks do 75 to 80 percent of the total banking business in the United States.

Each member bank is required to buy stock of the Federal Reserve Bank of its district. The original stock subscription called for an amount equal to 6 percent of the member bank's own paid-up capital and surplus. The Federal Reserve Banking Act provided that stock would be sold to the public if the member banks did not buy sufficient amounts. It further provided that the federal government would buy stock if it was not all purchased by the banks and the public. To date, no stock has been sold to either the public or to the federal government. The member banks have purchased all the stock in the Federal Reserve Banks and have paid in over one half of their subscribed stock. As a result, we have a unique system in which the member banks completely own the Federal Reserve Banks, but most of the regulation or control of these Banks resides with the Board of Governors.

Although the member banks are operated for profit, the Federal Reserve Banks are operated strictly in the public interest. The Federal Reserve System pays a 6 percent dividend on its stock. Any profits over this amount are used to build up certain surpluses or are turned over to the United States Treasury. Member banks are required to maintain most of their legal reserves with the Federal Reserve Banks. In addition, member banks are subject to examinations and regulations by the Federal Reserve Banks. All member banks must insure their deposits with the Federal Deposit Insurance Corporation.

## FEDERAL RESERVE CONTROL OF THE MONEY SUPPLY

Through its control over bank credit, the Federal Reserve System can affect the money supply. Thus, its actions have an effect on the level of economic activity and /or the price level. The Federal Reserve has many instruments or measures through which it can control bank credit. Some of these are referred to as *general controls* because they affect the overall supply of money. Others are referred to as *selective controls* because they affect the use of money for specific purposes in our economy. Let us see exactly how these controls are utilized in an attempt to stabilize the flow of economic activity or the price level.

### GENERAL CONTROLS

In using its general controls, the Federal Reserve can influence the total amount and flow of credit and money; but these controls do little to encourage or restrict the use of money for specific purposes. There are occasions, however, when the Federal Reserve, by tightening credit as a hedge against inflation, for example, may cause a shortage of money for many specific uses in the economy. In fact, it may cause a shortage of money for some specific activity that the Federal Reserve has no desire to restrict. If offsetting measures are not available in such situations, the advantages of a generally tight money supply must be weighed against the adverse effects of a money shortage for specific uses.

#### Member Bank Reserve Requirements

In the discussion of bank credit in Chapter 9, we learned that a bank's ability to extend credit is affected by the amount of reserves it must hold for its demand deposits. We found that an increase in the reserve requirement would decrease the bank's ability to increase the money supply, and vice versa. Earlier in this chapter we learned that the member banks are required to keep most of their reserves in the Federal Reserve Banks. Now we can add the fact that the Board of Governors has the authority to determine, within limits, the amount of reserves which the member banks must hold against demand deposits. Such reserve requirements as designated by the Board are referred to as the *legal required reserve*. Any reserve over and above this amount that a bank may have is an *excess reserve*. Both are important to the determination of the money supply.

**Legal Reserve Requirements**   For purposes of setting reserve requirements, member banks are currently divided into two categories by the Federal Reserve: (1) reserve city banks, which are those having net demand deposits of more than $400 million (the city in which such a bank's home office is located is designated as a reserve city); and (2) other banks, which are any banks having net demand deposits of $400 million or less. These banks are designated as banks outside of reserve cities and as such are permitted to maintain lower reserves. At present the Board of Governors may alter the reserve requirement of the member banks between the minimum and the maximum amounts as shown in Table 10-2.

Although the Board may alter the reserve requirements, it must stay within the legal limits. There have been times, however, when special legislation of Congress gave the Board authority to go beyond the normal maximums, such as during the post-World War II period and the Korean Conflict.

**Effect of Lower Reserve Requirements**   The Board uses its power judiciously. During periods of low production, income, and employment, the Board may decrease the reserve requirements in the hope of increasing the money supply and bringing about an expansion of business activity. To show how this is accomplished, let us use a hypothetical example in which the banking system as a whole has no excess reserves on which to expand credit. Assuming a 10 percent reserve requirement, the situation at the beginning might appear as shown in Figure 10-2, page 196.

According to Figure 10-2, the banks are holding $100,000 cash reserves (10 percent) against total deposits of $1,000,000 ($100,000 in primary deposits and $900,000 in derivative deposits or loans). The banks in this situation cannot create any more credit. If the reserve requirement were decreased to 5 percent, however, the banks would have to hold only

Table 10-2   **RESERVE REQUIREMENTS FOR MEMBER BANKS**

|  | Demand Deposits | | Time Deposits |
|  | Reserve City Bank | Other Banks | All Banks |
| --- | --- | --- | --- |
| Minimum | 10% | 7% | 3% |
| Maximum | 22% | 14% | 10% |

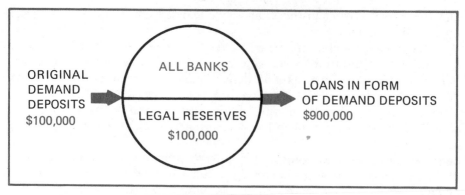

Figure 10-2   **10 PERCENT RESERVE REQUIREMENT**

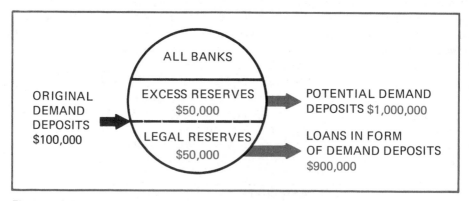

Figure 10-3   **5 PERCENT RESERVE REQUIREMENT**

$50,000 in legal reserves against the $1,000,000 in demand deposits. This would free $50,000 of the existing reserve. If it were left on deposit with the Federal Reserve Banks, it would become excess reserve. The banks could then extend another $1,000,000 in demand deposits. This is shown in Figure 10-3.

Thus, a decrease in the reserve requirement can increase the bank's ability to extend credit, and this in effect provides for an increase in the money supply. *Notice that reduction of the reserve requirement does not necessarily increase credit or the money supply, but merely the banks' ability to increase credit.* There will not be an increase in credit or in the money supply until businesspeople or others actually borrow the money in the form of demand deposits and begin issuing checks against these deposits. Frequently in a depression period, the Federal Reserve will lower the reserve requirement, but businesspeople will be reluctant to borrow and spend money because of the poor return on capital investment. There are situations, therefore, in which the lowering of the reserve requirement may not result in an increase in the money supply.

**Effect of Higher Reserve Requirements**   The Board of Governors can decrease the banks' ability to expand the money supply by raising the reserve requirement. Assume once again a situation such as we had in Figure 10-2, in which the banks were "loaned up to the hilt." If the Board of Governors increased the reserve requirements from 10 percent to 20 percent, the banks would actually be short of required reserves. In such a case they would have to increase their reserve or recall some of the loans outstanding. (See Figure 10-4.)

The action of the banks in recalling loans would reduce the demand deposits a total of $500,000. Thus, it would in effect decrease the money supply by $500,000. Actually the Board of Governors would not do this, for it would greatly disturb and disrupt business activity. It is more inclined to use its power to prevent undesirable conditions from developing. For example, it tries to ease the money supply by lowering reserve requirements when the economy enters a period of declining business activity in the hope that it will help arrest the downward action. On the other hand, the Board endeavors to tighten up on the money supply by raising reserve requirements and by using other methods when the economy begins to reach the full-employment, or the inflationary, stage of business activity, since it knows that further increases in the money supply through the extension of demand deposits will lead only to high prices. Let us demonstrate this point by setting up a new hypothetical case. Assume that there is a 10 percent reserve requirement and that the banks have excess reserves. The situation might appear as shown in Figure 10-5, page 198.

With $33,333 in excess reserves and a 10 percent reserve requirement, the banks can increase demand deposits by $333,333. If business activity is good, businesspeople will borrow and there will be an increase in the money supply. If the economy is at full employment, however, the increased money supply will merely lead to higher prices. Under these circumstances, the Board of Governors could absorb the excess reserves by

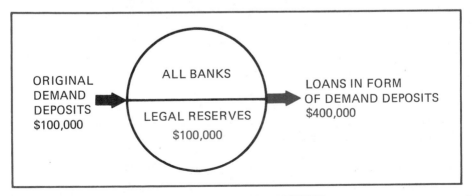

Figure 10-4   **20 PERCENT RESERVE REQUIREMENT**

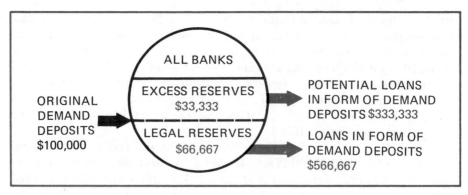

Figure 10-5  **10 PERCENT RESERVE REQUIREMENT**

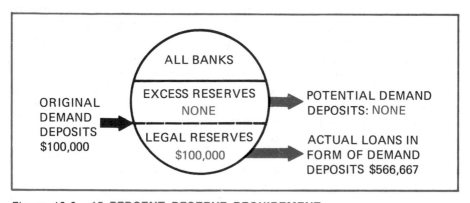

Figure 10-6  **15 PERCENT RESERVE REQUIREMENT**

increasing the reserve requirement. This would decrease the banks' abili-ty to extend credit and thus would act as a deterrent to inflation. In our case in Figure 10-5, if the Board increased the reserve requirement to 15 percent, the banks would need $100,000 in legal reserves against the $666,667 total deposits outstanding. The excess reserves of $33,333 would then become a part of the required reserve. The banks would have no excess reserves and would lose their ability to extend additional credit. After such a change the status of the banks' reserves in relation to de-mand deposits would be as shown in Figure 10-6.

Since the status of reserves in the individual banks will vary, some banks will be more affected than others by changes in the reserve re-quirements. For this reason, the Federal Reserve is somewhat cautious in the use of reserve requirements to control credit.

**Principle to Remember**  Regarding the Federal Reserve's control over the money supply through the use of reserve requirements, we may sum-marize by saying that an increase in the reserve requirements will decrease the banks' ability to extend credit. Conversely, a decrease in the reserve requirements will increase the banks' ability to extend credit.

### Discount Rate

The *discount rate*, which is sometimes referred to as the rediscount rate, is the interest rate at which the member banks may borrow funds from the Federal Reserve Banks. As you know, if you wish to borrow $100 at 8 percent from the bank for one year, you would have to sign a note payable to the bank (which becomes a note receivable for the bank). The bank would then discount your note for you. Instead of giving you the face value of the note, the bank would deduct the interest and pay you $92. However, you would repay the bank $100. The difference represents the interest, or discount.

A member bank may borrow from the Federal Reserve by rediscounting notes of its customers or by borrowing on its own promissory notes secured by its customers' notes, government securities, or by other satisfactory collateral. Borrowings by the first method are called *discounts*, and by the second method, *advances*. The latter is the more popular method. But in either case the discount rate governs the cost of borrowing. Federal Reserve Banks, however, are not obliged to discount member banks' eligible paper. Discount facilities are a privilege of the member bank rather than a right. Furthermore, credit through this process is extended primarily on a short-term basis to enable a member bank to adjust its reserve position when necessary because of such developments as a sudden withdrawal of deposits or an unusually large seasonal demand for credit.

**Discounting Process**    Assume a commercial bank in the United States has among its assets a considerable number of notes receivable that it discounted at 8 percent in exchange for loans in the form of cash and demand deposits. If a member bank is low on reserves, it may rediscount these notes, called commercial paper, at its Federal Reserve Bank, or member banks may borrow from the Federal Reserve Banks by using these notes or government securities as collateral. If the notes are used, this means that the bank can obtain money on the notes at any time instead of waiting until payments on the notes are due. However, if the Federal Reserve Bank were to charge the member bank 8 percent interest for borrowing funds, the member bank would have to pay interest to the Reserve Bank in an amount equal to that which it would secure on its notes receivable. In effect, it would make nothing on its own loans to individuals and businesses. Thus, when the discount rate is high compared to the commercial loan rate, the banks will be reluctant to use this rediscounting process to build up their reserves. If the discount rate is low, however, they will be more inclined to build up their reserves by discounting. Since reserves increase the banks' ability to extend credit, a decrease in the discount rate may increase the money supply.

This process can be demonstrated graphically, but to see how it operates we must look at an individual bank instead of all banks. Assume that an individual bank has no excess reserve, as indicated in Figure 10-7. Keep in mind that the individual bank does not necessarily lend demand deposits to some multiple of its reserve. It holds the proper fractional reserve against its primary deposits. The remainder becomes excess reserves that it can hold or lend. Thus, in our example the individual bank will hold $10,000 in legal reserve against the original $100,000 deposit and lend the remaining $90,000 in cash or demand deposits. As the $90,000 filters through the multiple expansion of bank credit, however, total demand deposits will be increased by some multiple of the original deposit.

According to the situation in Figure 10-7, the Acme National Bank will be unable to make further loans without excess reserves. The bank can build up its reserves through the discounting process. If the Acme Bank has made loans up to $90,000, it no doubt has among its assets $90,000 in notes receivable. Suppose that the bank is receiving 8 percent interest on these notes and that it can rediscount them at 6 percent. If the bank discounted $50,000 worth of the notes, it could still net 2 percent on them. This would mean an annual income of $1,000. However, when it receives the $50,000 cash (or, as usually happens, a $50,000 credit is made to its reserve account in the Reserve Bank), it can lend this cash or $50,000 in demand deposits and make 8 percent on these new loans. Thus, by discounting it will actually be making 10 percent on the $50,000, 2 percent net on the discounted notes plus 8 percent on the new notes. It will have interest income of $5,000 (2 percent on $50,000 in old loans plus 8 percent on the $50,000 in new loans) compared to $4,000 (8 percent of $50,000) if it had not discounted. In such circumstances it is

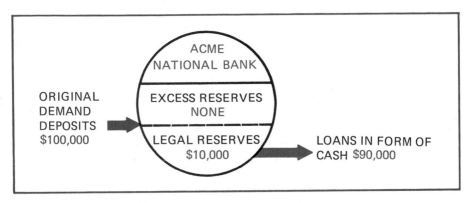

Figure 10-7    **10 PERCENT RESERVE REQUIREMENT**

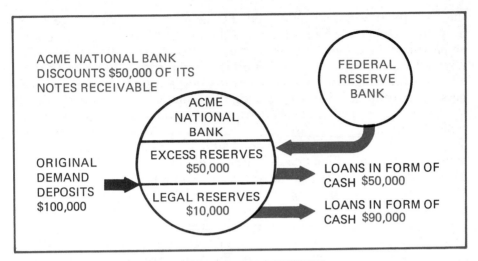

Figure 10-8    **10 PERCENT RESERVE REQUIREMENT**

profitable for the bank to discount its commercial paper, to build up its excess reserves, and to make additional loans. (See Figure 10-8.)

If the Federal Reserve Bank were to lower the discount rate, it would be even more profitable for the member bank to discount. On the other hand, if it raised the discount rate to 7 percent, it would be less profitable for the Acme Bank to discount. If it were raised to 8 percent, it would not profit the bank to engage in the discounting process. Thus, banks can be encouraged to expand or contract credit by changes in the discount rate. Just as with changes in the reserve requirements, however, changes in the discount rate do not automatically lead to changes in the money supply. Businesspeople and individuals must increase their loans to make changes in the money supply effective.

In this regard, changing the discount rate has a secondary effect. The commercial loan rate is influenced greatly by the bank discount rate. For example, the *prime loan rate*, that is, that rate at which the individuals and firms with the best collateral can borrow, is usually 1 to 1.5 percentage points above the discount rate. Thus, if the discount rate in Cleveland is 6 percent, the prime loan rate may be 7 to 7.5 percent. Usually when the discount rate is lowered, the commercial loan rates are lowered. This may encourage businesspeople to borrow. On the other hand, if the discount rate is raised, the commercial loan rates may be increased. This, in turn, may discourage businesspeople from borrowing. The Federal Reserve Banks are aware of this fact and use the discount rate accordingly. It should be remembered, however, that the funds will still be available but at a higher cost.

When business activity is falling, the Federal Reserve Banks lower the discount rate to encourage member banks to discount and increase

their ability to expand credit, and the member banks encourage businesspeople to borrow by lowering the commercial loan rate. During full-
employment inflationary periods, the Federal Reserve Banks raise the
discount rate to discourage discounting, which in turn has a restrictive
effect on the expansion of credit and discourages individuals and businesspeople from borrowing by raising the commercial loan rates.

Of course, the Federal Reserve uses its best judgment in the use of the
tools for control. The discount rate is changed by very moderate
amounts, usually one quarter or one half of a percentage point at a time
so that the change will not cause a serious disruption in business activity.
This action is primarily preventive rather than remedial. Sometimes, in
fact, changes in the discount rate lag behind changes in the commercial
loan rates. In such cases the Federal Reserve may raise or lower the discount rate to reduce the spread between the two rates.

The discount rate for each district is determined by the Federal Reserve Bank with the approval of the Board of Governors. Although the
Reserve Banks initiate changes in the discount rate, the Board of Governors still has authority "to review and determine" discount rates. The
discount rate often varies slightly for short periods between districts because of differences in the money markets. Usually when a district
changes its rate, most of the others follow suit, since factors of national
scope generally cause the change.

**Advances to Member Banks**　　Instead of discounting customers' notes,
however, member banks usually find it more convenient to borrow from
the Federal Reserve Bank by discounting their own promissory notes at
the Federal Reserve Bank, using government securities as collateral. This
method of borrowing, known as an *advance*, differs from the previous
method in form but not in substance. It is, however, a more popular
method of borrowing. Such loans increase the member banks' reserves
and enable them to expand credit. The members may request loans on
their own initiative. For example, if a member bank's reserve should fall
below the legal requirement, rather than attempt to recall loans to keep
its demand deposits in line with its reserves, the bank may borrow funds
from the Federal Reserve Bank to bring its reserves up to the legal reserve requirements. At other times when a bank is short of reserves, it
may borrow from the Federal Reserve Bank to build up its reserves for
credit expansion.

The Federal Reserve Banks may encourage member banks to borrow
by lending money freely and at lower interest rates during periods of
declining or slack business activity. At other times, especially during inflationary periods, the Federal Reserve Banks will discourage member-
bank borrowing to tighten credit and put pressure on them to increase
commercial loan rates. Whatever its objective, the Federal Reserve can
utilize the discount rate accordingly.

In addition to borrowing from the Reserve Bank, a commercial bank can adjust its reserve position by borrowing from other commercial banks that have surplus reserves. This interbank borrowing takes place in a fairly well-organized market, known as the *Federal Funds Market*.

**Principle to Remember**    It may be well to summarize our discussion on discount rates by reiterating that a decrease in the discount rate will generally encourage banks to extend credit and businesspeople to borrow, thus tending to increase the money supply, while an increase in the discount rate will discourage banks from expanding credit and businesspeople from borrowing, thus tending to limit increases in the money supply.

### Open-Market Operations

One of the most important instruments of monetary management consists of the Federal Reserve *open-market operations*. The Federal Open Market Committee (FOMC) has at its disposal the control over a portfolio consisting of government securities including bonds, bills, certificates, and notes. If the FOMC wants to encourage the expansion of credit, it can direct the Federal Reserve Banks to buy bonds from member banks and individuals. This increases member bank reserves and enables the banks to make more loans. All member banks hold government obligations, and the Federal Reserve can induce member banks to sell government bonds and other securities by offering a premium price for them.

**Purchase of Bonds**    When the Federal Reserve buys bonds, usually in slack business periods, it increases the excess reserves of the member banks and permits them to expand credit. Let us demonstrate this graphically. Suppose that member banks have no excess reserves and therefore cannot extend any additional credit, as depicted in Figure 10-9.

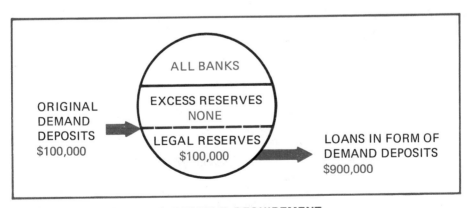

Figure 10-9  **10 PERCENT RESERVE REQUIREMENT**

Under such conditions, if the Federal Reserve buys $50,000 of government bonds from member banks, it puts the money directly into the banks or credits their reserve accounts. This increases excess reserves and expands the banks' ability to make loans by $500,000 through the multiple expansion of bank credit. This situation is shown in Figure 10-10.

Practically the same result can be accomplished by purchasing bonds from individuals and businesses since these sellers will usually deposit in banks the money received from the sale of bonds. These deposits in turn increase bank reserves and may result in a potential increase in the money supply. This process is shown in Figure 10-11.

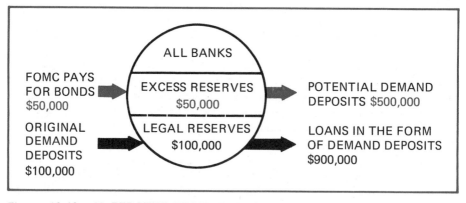

Figure 10-10   **10 PERCENT RESERVE REQUIREMENT**

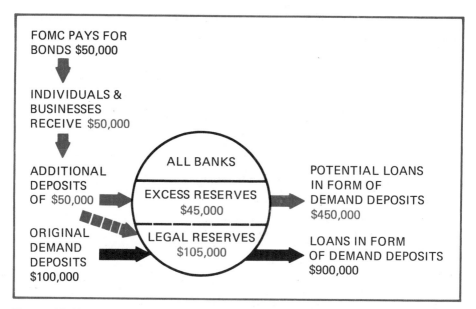

Figure 10-11   **10 PERCENT RESERVE REQUIREMENT**

In this case the potential expansion of credit is somewhat less than it is when the Federal Reserve buys government obligations directly from the member banks because the banks must hold $5,000 in required reserves against the new deposits of $50,000 made by the individuals and businesses that sold the bonds.

**Sale of Bonds**   During times of inflation or near inflation, the Federal Reserve may wish to absorb some of the excess reserves in existence. It can do so by selling government bonds to the member banks. The Federal Reserve can encourage the purchase of bonds and other government securities by offering them at a discount price. To buy bonds, member banks in all probability will have to give up some excess reserves, which in turn will decrease their ability to extend credit. If the Federal Reserve sells bonds to individuals or businesses, it is assumed that they will withdraw funds from member banks to pay for the bonds. This will reduce excess reserves and decrease the banks' ability to extend credit.

**Principle to Remember**   We must remember that the Federal Reserve's ability to affect the money supply through its open-market operation is restricted. Although the purchase of bonds from the banks will increase bank reserves, it does not mean that businesspeople will borrow. On the other hand, selling bonds will not prevent an expansion of credit unless a sufficient amount is sold to absorb all the excess reserves. The effectiveness of the Federal Reserve's endeavor to limit expansion of the money supply will depend on the status of excess reserves compared to the sale of bonds by the Federal Reserve.

Nevertheless, we can say in summary that the purchase of bonds in the open market by the Federal Reserve will increase the member banks' ability to expand credit, whereas the sale of bonds will decrease the member banks' ability to create credit. In this way, the supply and the cost of credit can be affected by the actions of the Federal Open Market Committee.

### Moral Suasion

*Moral suasion* is the term applied to a host of different measures that the Federal Reserve uses to influence the activities of member banks. In addition to altering reserve requirements and discount rates and engaging in open-market operations to liberalize and tighten credit, the Federal Reserve may employ various measures to encourage banks to act one way or another. It does this by sending to member banks letters in which it encourages or discourages the expansion of credit. At other times the Federal Reserve points out to businesspeople and bankers in public statements the status of the economic situation and endeavors to persuade businesses and banks to use or to restrain credit. Loan examiners may be directed to become more selective in making loans; or, during personal interviews, the Federal Reserve officers may warn against speculative loans or suggest that banks become more liberal with their loans. The Federal Reserve may ration credit and suspend the borrowing privileges of member banks if necessary. In general, moral suasion will affect the money supply only to the extent that banks and businesspeople are willing to cooperate.

## SELECTIVE CONTROLS

All the controls that have been mentioned thus far are general controls because they affect the money supply in total, regardless of the use to which the money may be put. If commercial loan rates are forced up through an increase in the discount rate, for example, people or businesses who desire to borrow for a multitude of different purposes are affected. The Federal Reserve, however, does have certain discretionary controls that affect the specific uses of money and credit in the economy.

For example, the Federal Reserve currently has the authority to set stock market margin requirements. This affects the amount of stock that may be purchased on credit. The higher the margin requirement the greater the down payment required to purchase shares of stock. This reduces the opportunity for speculation in the stock market, holds down the demand for stocks, and moderates the prices of stocks. At various times the Federal Reserve has had control also of the conditions or terms of installment sales. Such controls, which established the down payment and the length of time in which an installment loan had to be repaid, had the effect of limiting total demand. Credit controls of this nature have been used during war periods and at other times of full employment when the economy was suffering the pangs of inflation. Restrictions on mortgage credit for housing, when used at various times by the Federal Reserve, has had a similar anti-inflationary effect on the economy.

## POLICY OF FEDERAL RESERVE

The Federal Reserve is an independent organization and, as such, exercises a considerable amount of autonomy. Although the members of the Board of Governors are appointed by the President of the United States with the consent of the Senate, the Board is responsible only to Congress. As a result, it may or may not agree with the economic policies of a given administration. However, since both have the same objective, that is, to stabilize production, employment, income, and prices at high levels of business activity, their actions usually complement each other.

### The Late 1950s

The Federal Reserve keeps a close watch on production, employment, and prices. If it observes or foresees an adverse swing in either direction, up or down, it uses its monetary controls accordingly. For example, with the threatening inflation of 1955–1957, discount rates were raised seven times within a two-year period, increasing from 1¾ percent to 3½ percent. The stock market margin was raised from 60 to 70 percent, and the Federal Reserve began to sell bonds in the open market.

With the decline in the economy that took place in the late 1957 and 1958 period, the discount rates were lowered four times between October 31, 1957, and May 1, 1958, bringing them down from 3½ to 1¾ percent. During the same period the member bank reserve requirements were reduced by small decrements. Likewise, the stock market margin requirement was lowered from 70 to 50 percent. All during the recession, the Federal Open Market Committee was buying securities to increase bank reserves.

When the economy began recovery after its low ebb in the spring of 1958, the Federal Reserve ceased liberalizing the money supply and gradually shifted toward tighter money. In a series of changes the discount rates were pushed from 1¾ percent up to 4 percent by the fall of 1959. The Open Market Committee was busy selling bonds to absorb excess reserves and the Board of Governors began to warn against the dangers of renewed pressure on the price level. The net result was a general tightening of the money supply. But during the mild depression of 1960–1961 credit was again eased.

## The 1960s and Vietnam

After the 1960–1961 recession, the Federal Reserve continued its easy money measures, since the economy was still in a state of less than full employment. Its monetary policy, along with several administration fiscal measures, contributed to the six-year expansion in the economy from 1961 to 1967. As we approached full employment in late 1965, however, the Federal Reserve took steps to combat possible inflation resulting from record investment, high-level consumption, large government outlays for Great Society programs, and the escalation of the war in Vietnam. In December, 1965, it raised the discount rate from 4 to 4½ percent and engaged in open-market operations to tighten credit. Although some administration officials and others were critical of the Federal Reserve's action, the foresight of the Federal Reserve was instrumental in limiting the rise in the consumer price index in 1966.

Although the Federal Reserve backed off from its tight money measures during the mini-recession of early 1967, with the resurgence of inflation in mid-1967 it resumed measures to raise the cost and tighten the supply of money. It raised reserve requirements in 1968 and 1969. Through a series of moves it pushed the discount rate upward from 4 percent in 1967 to 6 percent in 1969. The stock market margin was also pushed up to 80 percent.

### The 1970s

By mid-1970, when unemployment reached 5.5 percent, the money supply was eased again, and by the end of 1971 the discount rate was down to 4.5 percent. Expansion of business activity and the resurgence of inflation after the removal of Phase II price and wage controls in January, 1973, led to a tighter monetary effort by the Fed through open-market operations. In a series of moves the discount rate within a year's time was moved to a record level of 8 percent and prime rates at commercial banks reached 12 percent. Furthermore, the reserve requirement at reserve city banks was raised one-half percent.

With the recession of 1974, however, the Fed liberalized the money supply through open-market operations, the prime rate receded from its peak of 12 percent to around 10 percent, reserve requirements were lowered, and a decline in the discount rate was expected in late 1974. The stock market margin was likewise lowered, this time to 50 percent. These trends continued into 1975, and by April the discount rate had fallen all the way to 6 percent and the prime rate was about 8 percent.

## RECOMMENDED CHANGES IN STRUCTURE AND POLICIES

Over the past 15 years several studies have been made of our financial and banking systems. These studies have recommended certain changes in the structure and policies of the Federal Reserve System. These recommendations include the following: that the discount rate be determined by the Board of Governors instead of by the Federal Reserve Banks; that open-market operations be vested in the Board; that the Board consist of five members only, eligible for reappointment after a ten-year term; that, although the autonomy of the Federal Reserve should be maintained, the term of office of the Chairman of the Board of Governors should be made coterminous with that of the President of the United States; that all insured commercial banks be required to join the System; that the reserve requirement for all classes of banks be identical; and that reserve-requirement limitations be set at 8 to 18 percent.

Congressman Wright Patman, past Chairman of the House Banking Committee and longtime critic of Federal Reserve autonomy, has suggested that the term of office of Board members be reduced from 14 to 4 years, that 12 members instead of 7 be appointed by the President, that the System be forced to obtain its operating funds from Congress, and that the Secretary of the Treasury be made Chairman of the Board of Governors as a means of curbing its independence.

On the matter of policy, an outstanding critic of the Fed has been Professor Milton Friedman of the University of Chicago. For years he has contended that the lag between implementation of certain monetary measures and their impact on the money supply and the level of economic activity is somewhat indeterminable and considerably longer than the Federal Reserve anticipates. In fact, it is suggested that the Fed aggravates fluctuations in economic activity and the price level because of this. For example, the Fed may implement measures to tighten the money supply to combat inflation, but the major impact of the tight money may not be felt until several months later when the economy may be sluggish or in a downturn and may actually be in need of monetary expansion.

To avoid this situation Professor Friedman and other monetarists recommend that the money supply be increased at a rate of 3 to 5 percent annually regardless of the condition of the economy. This they believe would do more to stabilize economic activity and the price level than the current policy of tampering with the money supply in an attempt to modify business and price fluctuations.

On still another matter, Arthur Burns, Chairman of the Federal Reserve Board of Governors, is concerned that the influence of the Fed on money matters and its ability to regulate the money supply is diminishing. He cites the fact that in the past 10 years a number of banks have left the Federal Reserve System. He indicates, moreover, that the majority of the newly chartered commercial banks are electing not to join the System. This can be emphasized by the fact that in 1960, 6,174, or 46 percent, of the commercial banks belonged to the System. Today 5,767, or 40 percent, of the commercial banks are members of the Federal Reserve System. Furthermore, the amount of commercial banking business done by member banks dropped from 83 percent of the total in 1960 to 77 percent in 1974.

Burns also points out that gaps and duplications exist in banking requirements and regulations. This occurs because the Federal Reserve System, the Comptroller of the Currency, the Federal Deposit Insurance Corporation, and the individual states all have regulatory authority over the banks. As a means of establishing more uniform and effective policies and measures, Burns has suggested that more of the authority to regulate and establish monetary requirements be centralized in one source. Burns, too, suggests that the Employment Act of 1946 be amended to include price stability as a major economic goal along with the present goals of maximum production, maximum employment, and maximum purchasing power.

## SUMMARY

The Federal Reserve System is a complex system composed of several bodies, organizations, and committees. The Board of Governors sets the overall policy for the System. Both the Federal Advisory Council and the Conference of Federal Reserve Bank Presidents meet occasionally with the Board. The 12 Federal Reserve Banks act as central banks, regulate member banks, and serve as fiscal agents for the federal government. The Federal Reserve Banks exercise a considerable amount of autonomy. Of the 14,384 commercial banks in the United States, approximately 40 percent belong to the Federal Reserve System. However, these banks carry on 75 to 80 percent of the total banking business in the nation. Consequently, the Federal Reserve through its policies and practices has a substantial influence on our banking system.

The Federal Reserve System has a certain amount of control over the nation's money supply, primarily through its ability to affect the volume and cost of bank credit. Some of its controls are general in that they affect the total potential money supply. Others are selective since they affect the use of credit for particular purposes.

The Federal Reserve can affect the ability of the banks to extend credit through its regulation of the reserve requirements. An increase in member bank reserve requirements decreases the banks' ability to extend credit, while a decrease in the reserve requirements has the opposite effect. A change in the discount rate also affects the amount of credit by influencing the borrowing of both the member banks and businesspeople. In general, an increase in the discount rate will discourage member banks from borrowing to increase their reserves. It also will discourage borrowing by businesspeople since an increase in the discount rate generally will force up the commercial loan rate.

The Federal Open Market Committee of the Federal Reserve can increase the member banks' reserves and therefore affect their ability to extend credit through the purchase of securities from the banks. When the Federal Open Market Committee sells securities to the member banks, it absorbs their excess reserves and therefore reduces their ability to extend credit. At other times, the Federal Reserve uses moral suasion to influence the credit policies of member banks. The member banks' ability to extend credit also will be affected by the ease with which they can borrow from Federal Reserve Banks.

The Federal Reserve has the authority to set stock market margin requirements which affect the amount of stock that may be purchased on credit. At various times the Federal Reserve has had control of installment sales. Restrictions on housing credit have also been utilized by the Fed at various times.

The general policy of the Federal Reserve has been to use its controls to help stabilize the level of economic activity and the price level. When the economy is moving at a pace that is too fast and inflation is likely to result, the Federal Reserve usually tightens the money supply to reduce the inflationary tendencies in the economy. On the other hand, the Federal Reserve lowers reserve requirements, reduces discount rates, engages in the purchase of securities from member banks and individuals, and uses moral suasion in an endeavor to offset declines in the economy. During the past 10 to 15 years a variety of recommendations have been made regarding changes in both the structure and the policies of the Federal Reserve System.

The current figures for most of these monetary controls can be found at any time in the *Federal Reserve Bulletin*. Why not make a check on the latest figures before we leave monetary controls and go on to our next subject — the measurement of the level of economic activity in terms of the national income.

## DISCUSSION QUESTIONS

1. Should all commercial banks be required to become members of the Federal Reserve System?
2. Do you agree with the policy of electing nonbankers to the board of directors of each Federal Reserve Bank? Why or why not?
3. It has been suggested that labor unions be given representation on the board of directors of each Federal Reserve Bank. Do you agree with this suggestion? Why or why not?
4. What are the merits of operating the Federal Reserve Banks on a nonprofit basis?
5. Since the federal government owns no stock in the Federal Reserve Banks, why should the government appoint the Federal Reserve Board of Governors?
6. Does the lowering of reserve requirements automatically increase the money supply? Why?
7. In what way can a change in the discount rate affect commercial loan rates?
8. What will be the effect of the purchase of bonds from individuals by the Federal Open Market Committee compared to the purchase of bonds from the banks insofar as the expansion of the money supply is concerned?
9. Do you think it is proper to permit the use of credit for stock market purchases? Why or why not?
10. In the past six months has the Federal Reserve been tightening or liberalizing the supply of money? If either, what measures have been used to bring about the change?

## SUGGESTED READINGS

Burns, Arthur F. "A Letter on Monetary Policy." *Review*, Federal Reserve Bank of St. Louis (November, 1973).

Eastburn, David P. *Money & Men & Policy*. Federal Reserve Bank of Philadelphia, 1970.

_____. "The Federal Reserve As a Living Institution: A Prescription for the Future." *Business Review*, Federal Reserve Bank of Philadelphia (March, 1970).

"The Case For and Against Indexation: An Attempt at Perspective." *Review*, Federal Reserve Bank of St. Louis (October, 1974).

"The Discount Window." *Monthly Review*, Federal Reserve Bank of Richmond (April, 1965).

*Federal Reserve System: Its Function and Purpose*. Washington: Board of Governors of Federal Reserve System, 1968. Chapters 3, 4, 5, 11, and 12.

Fishman, Leo. "The White House and the Fed." *Challenge* (July/August, 1966).

Klebaner, Benjamin. *Commercial Banking in the United States: A History*. Hinsdale, Ill.: The Dryden Press, 1974.

*Modern Money Mechanics*. Federal Reserve Bank of Chicago, 1968.

*Money and Credit: Their Influence on Jobs, Prices, and Growth*. Report of the Commission on Money and Credit. Englewood Cliffs, N.J.: Prentice-Hall, Inc., 1961.

*Monthly Review*, Federal Reserve Bank of New York (January/December, 1964). (Anniversary issue with series of historical articles on the Federal Reserve System)

Simon, William E. "Inflation, Controls, Energy, Taxes." *Department of the Treasury News*, US 161 (December 4, 1974).

"Two Critiques of Monetarism." *Review*, Federal Reserve Bank of St. Louis (January, 1972).

Yeager, Leland B. *Monetary Policy and Economic Performance, Special Analysis*. Washington: American Enterprise Institute, 1972.

# Production, Income, and Employment

# Part 4

# 11 GNP, NATIONAL INCOME, AND INPUT/OUTPUT

## THE GROSS NATIONAL PRODUCT

Instead of using hypothetical figures when discussing the circular flow of economic activity as we did in previous chapters, we can use actual dollar measurements. Fortunately in the United States the Department of Commerce keeps a running tab on the dollar value of the goods and services produced in our economy. This is broken down into various components, which makes it easier to analyze.

### Components of the Gross National Product

The dollar value of total production in the United States can be determined by adding the value of all the end products and services produced in a given period. In many cases, however, it is difficult to distinguish intermediate products (those used in the production of other products) from end products (those consumed directly). Should we count a tire as an end product, or should we count it as part of the value of an automobile? Is corn an end product, or is some of it included in the value of bacon when hogs are slaughtered? When we count the value of all the end products, we may count some items twice. For accuracy in calculating the total production, however, it is essential that we count goods and services only once.

The value of our total production can be obtained also by counting the value added to commodities and the value of services. This can be done in each instance by comparing the cost of materials to the market price of the finished product. The difference is the value added by the producer. It represents the amount that must be paid for wages, rent, and interest, and the profit the producer will receive on the product. Thus, the summation of the total value added to all the products by the various producers plus the value of the services rendered by others will equal the total production of the economy.

If we consider the processing of iron ore that goes into an automobile, we can demonstrate the idea of value added. If the iron ore and the other basic raw materials originally cost $200, they might be worth $400 after being processed into pig iron and other materials, $800 after being refined into steel ingots, etc., and so on down the line until they finally take the shape of the automobile at a value of $4,000. If we were to sum the value of the product at the end of each of these productive stages, the total value might be $12,000, as shown in column 2 of Table 11-1. Obviously there has been much double counting in the process. However, if we were to start out with the value of the basic commodities and add to it only the value added by each productive process, the total value added would be equal to the total price of the end product, as shown in column 3 of Table 11-1. Of course, the total value added will represent the total production that has taken place. Likewise, it will be equal to the total payments to the owners of the factors of production.

Our total production is not actually measured by the value-added method. It is measured from two principal points of view: as the summation of end products produced by the economy; and as the summation of costs incurred in producing those products.

**The Gross National Product**    Now that we have some idea of how total production is measured, we can consider the basic concept of production and its modifications. The basic concept is the *gross national product*, which by definition is the current market value of the total goods and services produced by our nation's economy over a given period of time. The GNP is stated on a yearly basis. The 1974 GNP was $1,396.7 billion.

In producing our total production each year we use up a certain amount of capital goods. Machinery, equipment, buildings, and tools

Table 11-1    **VALUE ADDED**

| (1)<br><br>Product | (2)<br>Current Value at<br>End of Each<br>Stage of Production | (3)<br>Value Added<br>by Each<br>Stage of Production |
|---|---|---|
| Iron ore & other<br>raw materials | $   200 | $  200 = Value of basic commodities |
| Pig iron & other<br>processed materials | 400 | 200 |
| Steel ingots, etc. | 800 | 400 Represents payments for: |
| Sheet steel, etc. | 1,400 | 600 Interest |
| Auto parts | 2,000 | 600 Wages Rent |
| Assembly | 3,200 | 1,200 Profit |
| Automobile delivered<br>at showroom | 4,000 | 800 |
| | $12,000 | $4,000 = True measure of production |

depreciate with use. Some become obsolete and lose their value. Thus, the GNP must be reduced by the amount of depreciation and obsolescence, generally called *capital consumption allowances*. Since capital consumption allowances totaled $119.5 billion in 1974, the *net national product*, or NNP, amounted to $1,277.2 billion. Capital consumption allowances generally are less than 10 percent of our total production.

**National Income**    The NNP can be reduced to another meaningful concept called the *national income*. The national income has a twofold definition. First, it is the total factor costs of the goods and the services produced by the nation's economy. In this sense it is equivalent to the amount that was paid (or cost) for the use of land, labor, capital, and entrepreneurship to obtain a given GNP. Second, the national income also represents the aggregate earnings arising from the production of the GNP. In this sense it is equivalent to the earnings or income of the owners of the factors of production, which were used in producing the GNP. Thus, the "total factor cost" and "aggregate earnings" are merely two sides of the same coin. The value of the national income can be obtained by adding all the earnings of labor and property in a given period. It can also be obtained by subtracting capital consumption allowances and indirect business taxes, such as sales taxes, from the GNP and making a few other minor allowances. After making such adjustments, in 1974 the value of the NI was $1,142.2 billion.

**Personal Income**    As far as individuals are concerned, the national income figure can be reduced to a more appropriate concept, personal income. By definition *personal income* is the current income received by persons from all sources. It includes transfer payments from government and business but excludes transfer payments among persons. A *transfer payment* occurs when a payment of money is made for which no current goods or services are produced. For example, an ex-serviceman attending college on the GI Bill may receive $220 per month. This is truly a part of his personal income, but he produces no current goods or services in exchange for the money. It is true that he may have earned it, but it is payment for service in a previous period. On the other hand, the factory worker and the government clerk receive income in exchange for their current production. Retired persons on business or government pensions are also receiving transfer payments.

Not only individuals but also nonprofit institutions are classified as "persons" for this purpose. Personal income is measured on a before-tax basis. It includes such things as wages, salaries, proprietor's income, rental income, interest, dividends, and transfer payments. The national income can be reduced to personal income by subtracting from national income corporate income taxes, plus the undistributed profits, because neither of these segments of corporate income is passed on to individuals. This will leave only corporate dividends to be counted as part of the personal income. Table 11-2 demonstrates this by subtracting all corporate income, along with an inventory valuation adjustment, and then adding corporate dividends to the total. In addition, we must subtract Social Security payments.

We must then add government and business transfer payments and make a few other minor adjustments. After doing this for 1974, we find that the personal income was $1,150.4 billion. It is easy to see that the biggest factor accounting for the difference between national income and personal income is corporation taxes when we consider that corporations paid $55.8 billion in taxes in 1974.

**Disposable Personal Income**    We are well aware that we do not have the opportunity to spend every dollar we earn. There is quite a gap between our earnings and our take-home pay. The main cause for this difference is the fact that we pay federal, and in some cases state and local, income taxes. What remains of personal income after these deductions have been made is known as *disposable personal income*. Since we can

Table 11-2    **RELATION OF GROSS NATIONAL PRODUCT, NATIONAL INCOME, PERSONAL INCOME, AND SAVINGS FOR 1974***
(Billions of Dollars)

| | | |
|---|---|---:|
| **Gross national product** | | $1,396.7 |
| **Less:** | Capital consumption allowances | 119.5 |
| | Indirect business tax and nontax liability | 126.9 |
| | Business transfer payments | 5.2 |
| | Statistical discrepancy | .0 |
| **Plus:** | Subsidies less current surplus of government enterprises | −2.9 |
| **Equals:** | **National income** | 1,142.2 |
| **Less:** | Corporate profits and inventory valuation adjustment | 105.4 |
| | Contributions for social insurance | 101.5 |
| | Wage accruals less disbursements | −.5 |
| **Plus:** | Government transfer payments | 134.6 |
| | Net interest paid by government and consumers | 42.3 |
| | Dividends | 32.7 |
| | Business transfer payments | 5.2 |
| **Equals:** | **Personal income** | 1,150.4 |
| **Less:** | Personal tax and nontax payments | 170.7 |
| **Equals:** | **Disposable personal income** | 979.7 |
| **Less:** | Personal outlays | 903.0 |
| | Personal consumption expenditures | 877.0 |
| | Consumer interest payments | 25.0 |
| | Personal transfer payments to foreigners | 1.0 |
| **Equals:** | **Personal saving** | 76.7 |

Source: *Federal Reserve Bulletin* (February, 1975).

*Department of Commerce estimates.

make the decision on whether or not to spend it and the direction in which it will be spent, this income is often called discretionary income. In 1974, income remaining to persons after deductions of personal tax and nontax payments to government, disposable personal income, was $979.7 billion. Of this total amount we as individuals spent $903.0 billion on personal outlays and saved $76.7 billion. These and other GNP figures for 1974 are shown in Table 11-2 on page 217.

### Allocation of the Gross National Product

The GNP, that is, the value of the total goods and services produced, is allocated to three major sectors of our economy: consumer, business, and government. Usually the largest bulk of goods and services is for the consumer. That part of total production in the form of machinery, equipment, buildings, inventories, etc., is known as *private investment*. In this category we have both domestic investment and net foreign exports, the latter representing the difference between exports from and imports to the United States. Government, the third sector, of course, must buy goods and services to perform its necessary functions. The allocation of the GNP to the three sectors (or four if you wish to count net exports separately) of the economy for 1974 is shown in Table 11-3.

Table 11-3    **GROSS NATIONAL PRODUCT OR EXPENDITURE FOR 1974***
(Billions of Dollars)

| | |
|---|---:|
| **Gross national product** | $1,396.7 |
| **Personal consumption expenditures** | 877.0 |
|     Durable goods | 127.8 |
|     Nondurable goods | 380.2 |
|     Services | 369.1 |
| **Gross private domestic investment** | 208.9 |
|     Fixed investment | 195.6 |
|         Nonresidential | 149.6 |
|             Structures | 52.2 |
|             Producers' durable equipment | 97.4 |
|         Residential structures | 46.0 |
|         Change in business inventories | 13.4 |
|             Nonfarm only | 11.0 |
| **Net exports of goods and services** | 2.0 |
|     Exports | 139.4 |
|     Imports | 137.5 |
| **Government purchases of goods and services** | 308.8 |
|     Federal | 116.4 |
|         National defense | 78.6 |
|         Other | 37.9 |
|     State and local | 192.4 |

Source: *Federal Reserve Bulletin* (February, 1975).

*Department of Commerce estimates.

It can be observed from Table 11-3 that approximately 63 percent of the total production of our nation was in the form of consumer goods and services. About 15 percent was in the form of private investment and the remaining 22 percent went to the government. It is interesting to observe also that $78.6 billion, or 68 percent of the federal government purchases, were used for national defense purposes. The federal government used $37.9 billion in goods and services, while state and local governments made $192.4 billion, or 62 percent, of total government purchases.

### Source of GNP

When the three sectors of the economy — consumer, business (including exports), and government — purchase goods and services, they must pay for them. These payments to the sellers of the goods and services are in turn used to compensate the factors involved in the production of the GNP. As was pointed out in our circular flow charts in Chapter 4, these factors are remunerated in the form of wages, rent, interest, and profit. Since these productive agents produce the goods and services, they are considered as the source of the GNP. Table 11-4 contains a breakdown of

Table 11-4    **NATIONAL INCOME BY DISTRIBUTIVE SHARES FOR 1974***
(Billions of Dollars)

| | |
|---|---:|
| **National income** | $1,142.2 |
| **Compensation of employees** | 856.1 |
| Wages and salaries | 751.1 |
| Commodity-producing industries | 270.9 |
| Distributive industries | 178.9 |
| Service industries | 142.6 |
| Government civilian | 158.8 |
| Supplements to wages and salaries | 105.0 |
| Employer contributions for social insurance | 53.6 |
| Other labor income | 51.4 |
| **Proprietors' income** | 93.0 |
| Business and professional | 61.2 |
| Farm | 31.8 |
| **Rental income of persons** | 26.5 |
| **Corporate profits and inventory valuation adjustment** | 105.4 |
| Profits before tax | 141.0 |
| Profits tax liability | 55.8 |
| Profits after tax | 85.2 |
| Dividends | 32.7 |
| Undistributed profits | 52.5 |
| Inventory valuation adjustment | −35.5 |
| **Net interest** | 61.6 |

Source: *Federal Reserve Bulletin* (February, 1975).

*Department of Commerce estimates.

the remuneration to the various factors of production. The allocation and distribution of the gross national product and the national income can be seen in Figure 11-1.

### Quarterly Reports on the GNP

To keep businesspeople and others informed and to have figures available as a guide for the implementation of national economic policies, the Department of Commerce publishes quarterly reports on the GNP and related figures. These quarterly reports are expressed in annual rates. This is accomplished in effect by adjusting the actual production in any given quarter for seasonal fluctuation and then multiplying the seasonally adjusted figure by 4 to convert it into an annual rate. For example, actual production for a given quarter may be $400 billion. The seasonally adjusted output may be $390 billion, which multiplied by 4 equals a seasonally adjusted quarterly total at an annual rate of $1,560 billion.

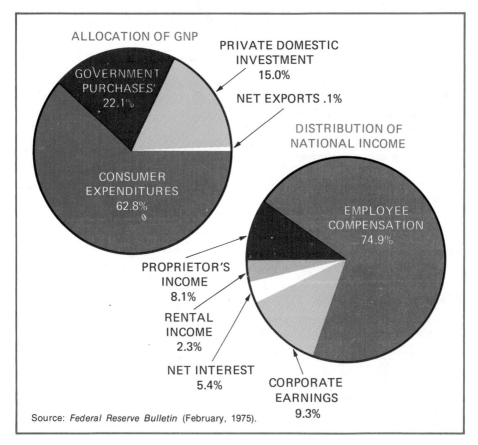

Source: *Federal Reserve Bulletin* (February, 1975).

Figure 11-1    **ALLOCATION OF GNP AND DISTRIBUTION OF NATIONAL INCOME, 1974**

The quarterly system makes it easier to analyze movements in the GNP. Any quarter can be compared against another or can be measured against the annual total. This permits easier scrutiny of fluctuations in the level of business activity. With this method it is easy to spot the high and low quarters of business fluctuations. Downswings and upswings in the economy can be recognized at an earlier date than they would be if the GNP were published on a yearly basis only. Observe the rate of change, for example, in Table 11-5.

Not only is the GNP given in quarterly figures, but also it is frequently revised. A preliminary estimate for a given year usually appears during February of the following year. A more accurate figure is released later in the spring and final revision is made available during the summer. For example, the GNP for 1973, first estimated at $1,288 billion, was revised upward to $1,295 billion. For this reason, various references may quote different figures for the GNP for any given period.

Frequently the various accounts of the GNP will not balance when checked against each other. This may be due to the fact that information for various tables is collected from different sources. These differences are usually adjusted by writing the differences off to a statistical discrepancy. In 1973, for example, the statistical discrepancy amounted to a minus $5.0 billion. This may seem like a huge amount — and it is — but it represents an error of less than ½ of 1 percent. You might note in Table 11-2 that the preliminary statistical discrepancy for 1974 was zero. In dealing with the GNP and related figures it should be remembered that the data are approximations rather than precise figures.

### GNP and the Circular Flow

The GNP is produced by numerous businesses and individuals, who in turn make payments to the various factors of production in the form of

Table 11-5    **GROSS NATIONAL PRODUCT, SEASONALLY ADJUSTED QUARTERLY TOTALS AT ANNUAL RATES, 1972–1974**

| Year | Quarter | GNP (Billions) | In 1958 Prices |
|------|---------|----------------|----------------|
| 1972 | III     | $1,169         | $798           |
|      | IV      | 1,205          | 814            |
| 1973 | I       | 1,249          | 833            |
|      | II      | 1,278          | 837            |
|      | III     | 1,309          | 841            |
|      | IV      | 1,344          | 846            |
| 1974 | I       | 1,359          | 831            |
|      | II      | 1,384          | 827            |
|      | III     | 1,416          | 823            |
|      | IV      | 1,428          | 804            |

Source: *Federal Reserve Bulletin* (February, 1975).

wages, rent, interest, and profits for their respective contributions to the GNP. Incomes received are used, in turn, to purchase goods and services. This sets up a circular flow of goods and services and money incomes such as that explained in Chapter 4 and demonstrated in Figure 11-2.

## GNP AS A MEASURE OF ECONOMIC PROGRESS

Since the GNP is a measure of the total production of goods and services, it is frequently used as a measure of economic progress. By comparing the GNP for various years, we can observe whether total output or income is increasing or decreasing. Since the GNP measures goods and services, as it changes our incomes change; and a change in income affects our standard of living. Consequently, many people like to measure the standard of living by the size of the GNP. However, whenever we use the GNP as a measure of economic progress or as a method of determining the level of the standard of living, we must keep certain modifications in mind.

### Price Level

We know that the GNP is the current market value of the total goods and services produced by our nation's economy. Actually the GNP can be increased merely by increasing the price of goods and services produced.

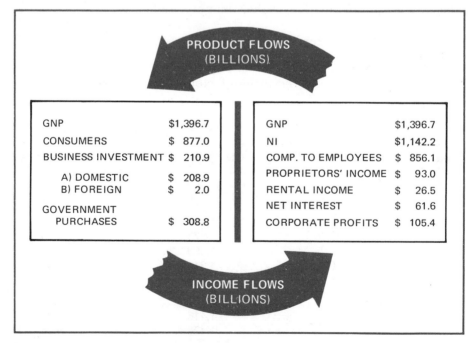

Figure 11-2    **NATIONAL CIRCULAR FLOW, 1974**

Therefore, comparing one year with another can be very misleading unless we make corrections for changes in the price level between the two years. In effect, we have to remove the element of price increases from the current GNP. This is true for all of the hundreds of thousands of commodities that constitute the GNP. Instead of adjusting each item individually, however, we adjust them all simultaneously by using the *implicit price deflators*. This is an index that takes into account not only the price changes but also some change in the quality of various products. Thus, by dividing the total GNP for any year by the value of the implicit price deflator for that particular year, we can adjust current GNP to a GNP in constant dollars, or as it is often called, *real GNP*, as Table 11-6 shows.

If we were to use the current GNP (column 2) as a measure of economic progress, we would be misled into believing that the GNP increased nearly fourfold between 1950 and 1974. If we look at the GNP in constant dollars, however, or the adjusted GNP (column 4), we can readily

Table 11-6    **GNP (1950–1974) CONVERTED TO CONSTANT DOLLARS (1958)**

| (1) | (2) Total Current GNP (Billions) | (3) Implicit Price Deflators 1958 = 100 | (4) Constant GNP, 1958 (Billions) |
|-----|------|------|------|
| Year |  |  |  |
| 1950 | 285 | 80 | 355 |
| 1953 | 365 | 88 | 413 |
| 1954 | 365 | 90 | 407 |
| 1955 | 398 | 91 | 438 |
| 1956 | 419 | 94 | 446 |
| 1957 | 441 | 97 | 453 |
| 1958 | 447 | 100 | 447 |
| 1959 | 484 | 102 | 476 |
| 1960 | 504 | 103 | 488 |
| 1961 | 520 | 105 | 497 |
| 1962 | 560 | 106 | 530 |
| 1963 | 591 | 107 | 551 |
| 1964 | 632 | 109 | 581 |
| 1965 | 685 | 111 | 618 |
| 1966 | 750 | 114 | 658 |
| 1967 | 794 | 118 | 675 |
| 1968 | 864 | 122 | 707 |
| 1969 | 930 | 128 | 726 |
| 1970 | 977 | 135 | 723 |
| 1971 | 1,056 | 142 | 745 |
| 1972 | 1,155 | 146 | 791 |
| 1973 | 1,295 | 154 | 839 |
| 1974 | 1,397 | 170 | 821 |

Source: *Economic Report of the President*, 1975.

observe that the physical output of goods and services increased by 131 percent during this period. The constant dollar GNP tells us what we want to know much better than the GNP in current dollars.

Looking at the GNP of 1974 as compared to that of 1973 in current dollars, we would be led to believe that production increased about 8 percent whereas it actually declined $18 billion in terms of constant dollars. Then, too, we might erroneously consider that production increased approximately 12 percent in 1973 by looking at the current figures. However, since 1973 was a period of high prices and the implicit price index increased 6 percent, we can get a true picture of increased production only by looking at the constant GNP. This reveals that there was a 5.9 percent increase in output and not a 12 percent increase as some might believe. The constant GNP shows better the declines in 1954 and 1958, and the recessions in the economy in 1970 and 1974.

### Population

Another modification that we should make before using the GNP as a measure of economic progress is the adjustment for population. It is true that the physical amount of goods and services produced in 1974 was about 2⅓ times as much as we produced in 1950. We must keep in mind, however, that more people produced this higher GNP. Thus, there also were more individuals sharing the goods and services we produced. It is necessary, then, to correct our constant, or real, GNP further to take into account the increase in population. This can be done simply by dividing the real GNP in any year by the total population in that year.

We can, however, obtain a better measure of the average amount of goods and services received per person by first reducing our GNP to disposable income, which is the spendable income or income after taxes. If we divide total disposable income by the total population, we will get per capita disposable income. This then can be adjusted for changes in the price level to give per capita disposable income in constant dollars, or the *real per capita disposable income*. Other things remaining the same, a comparison of the real per capita disposable income for any two years will give us a fair indication of what is happening to our standard of living. We must remember, however, that many people make less than, and others more than, the value of the per capita disposable income. At any rate, let us look at Table 11-7.

According to the table, the total disposable income indicated in column 2 more than quadrupled between 1950 and 1974. When we divide this total disposable income by the population, however, it shows that the per capita disposable income (column 4) rose a little more than twofold during the period. Finally, after adjusting the current per capita incomes for price changes, we see that the real per capita disposable income (column 5) did not quite double during the 24-year period. This is the best measure that we have of the standard of living or the measure of

Table 11-7    **TOTAL, CURRENT, AND CONSTANT DOLLAR (1958) PER CAPITA DISPOSABLE INCOME, 1950–1974**

| (1)<br>Year | (2)<br>Current Total<br>Disposable<br>Income<br>(Billions) | (3)<br>Current<br>Population<br>(Millions) | (4)<br>Current<br>Per Capita<br>Disposable<br>Income | (5)<br>Constant Dollars<br>Per Capita<br>Disposable Income<br>(1958 Dollars) |
|---|---|---|---|---|
| 1950 | $207 | $152 | $1,364 | $1,646 |
| 1955 | 275 | 165 | 1,666 | 1,795 |
| 1958 | 319 | 174 | 1,831 | 1,831 |
| 1960 | 350 | 181 | 1,937 | 1,883 |
| 1965 | 473 | 195 | 2,426 | 2,231 |
| 1970 | 692 | 205 | 3,376 | 2,610 |
| 1974 | 980 | 212 | 4,623 | 2,844 |

Source: *Economic Report of the President*, 1975.

economic progress in our economy. Although this is not perfect, it is closer to the truth to say that our standard of living has increased 73 percent since 1950 than it would be to say that it more than quadrupled. Even so, there are other reservations we should make in utilizing GNP figures as a yardstick for our level of living and our economic progress.

### Monetary Transactions

The GNP for the most part takes into account only goods and services for which there have been monetary transactions. If you buy a new desk, it is entered in the GNP, but if you make it yourself out of old lumber it does not become a part of the GNP. If you hire a commercial gardener to mow your lawn, the value of the service is entered in the GNP. If you mow your own lawn, however, it does not go into the GNP. There are many goods and services that, because they do not involve monetary transactions, never enter the GNP. Nevertheless, they are just as important to our standard of living as most of the items that are counted in the GNP. This is a substantial defect when we want to use the GNP as an indicator of our standard of living. For example, if we assume the current minimum wage value of $84 per week and apply a standard 40-hour week to common household chores done by members of the family, it would add over $150 billion annually to our gross national product.

### Type of Goods and Services Produced

We usually think that the more goods and services we produce, the higher will be our standard of living; but there are exceptions. Sometimes the nature of the goods and services is such that we cannot raise our level of living through their consumption. For example, as a nation we produced $864 billion in goods and services in 1968 during the height of the war in Vietnam. Out of that total output, however, $78 billion, or 9 percent, was in the form of military production. While it is true that tanks, guns, ships, bombers, grenades, and other weapons may protect our standard of living, they do not add to our enjoyment or standard of living as do food, new homes, autos, clothing, medical care, and numerous other consumer commodities and services.

Thus, in comparing the GNP of various years to get an indication of our change in living standards, we may be misled if we neglect to consider the type of goods and services produced in each of those years. Likewise, it is difficult to compare the standard of living in two different countries by comparing the respective value of their GNPs, for if one country is highly militarized while the other is not, it can make a substantial difference.

### Handling of Durable Goods

Except for houses, durable goods are added to GNP in the year they are produced. When we produce an automobile, a refrigerator, a set of golf clubs, a suit, or a bicycle, there is value added into the GNP for that commodity. Although we receive services from the commodity in subsequent years, national income accounting handles it as though it were consumed in the year in which it was produced. Normally, as our incomes increase during prosperity periods, we tend to produce more of these durable items; but we cannot get full utilization out of them in one year. This tends to exaggerate the value of our income. On the other hand, in depressions we have an inclination to decrease our production of durable goods, but we still get service out of the items we previously produced. This service is a form of real income. Since there is no accounting in the GNP for the length of service of durable goods bought in previous years, GNP frequently underestimates our standard of living, especially during periods of declining business activity.

### External or Social Costs

Another reservation that must be kept in mind when utilizing GNP data is the absence of social cost. When a firm produces goods and services, such internal factors as machine depreciation and obsolescence are considered as a cost of production. Consequently, in GNP accounting, these costs are subtracted from total production (GNP) to obtain net national product and national income. In addition to internal costs, however, external or social costs are involved in the production of goods and services. Effluence from a chemical plant into a stream or river, for example, may pollute the water, making it unsuitable for drinking, swimming, or even fishing. This in effect is a social cost to the community.

Smoke from a factory may pollute the surrounding air creating offensive odors or contributing to lung diseases. Aircraft noise from a jetport may create a sound hazard and decrease property values in the area. Since these external costs are not borne by the individual firm, they are not included in its total cost or the value added that enters the GNP. They are, however, real economic costs that must be borne by society in the form of deterioration of the environment. As the GNP increases in size, these external or social costs become larger and larger. Consequently, the net national product and the national income are overstated by several billions of dollars annually through the exclusion of these costs.

### Leisure

Lastly, the GNP makes no allowance for leisure time. Even if we wanted to take it into account, how would we value it? It means more to some people than it does to others. Nevertheless, it should be considered when using the GNP as a measure of economic progress. The increased output during the period of World War II, for example, came at the expense of a reduction in leisure. Certainly the fact that we can now produce more during an 8-hour day than we formerly did in a 10-hour day must be considered as a substantial improvement in our standard of living. This does not, however, show up anywhere in our GNP figures. Presently there is some movement toward a shorter workweek. If this comes, it will raise our economic standard of living, provided we maintain the same output of goods and services.

In summary, GNP figures are a fairly good indication of the total production of goods and services by our nation's economy. They can be used as a measure of economic progress or of the standard of living if we use them in the right way. Do not be like the politicians who boast that our total production of goods and services increased some fabulous amount during their party's administration, or like their opponents who charge that price increases obliterated all the advantages of higher incomes and wages. Get the facts straight and use them properly. This is important because we will see as we go along that the level of the GNP, along with the price level and the level of unemployment, will serve as a guide to the use of governmental action in an endeavor to stabilize the circular flow of economic activity.

### FLOW OF FUNDS

The GNP records transactions only of those goods and services that are currently produced. It does not measure the financial transactions of goods sold during the current period that were produced at a previous time. For example, suppose Ms. Smith purchased a new auto for $5,500 in March, 1976. When she bought it, there would be an entry in the GNP for $5,500. However, if she sold it through a used-car dealer for $4,300 in October, 1976, this later transaction would not be entered in the GNP. Only the profit or commission of the used-car dealer would enter the GNP as a payment for services rendered. Nevertheless, total monetary transactions as a result of the two sales totaled $9,800.

Furthermore, since the GNP measures only the value added by the producers, it eliminates double accounting. The financial transactions required to get a good produced, however, are much greater than the total value added. This frequently happens in intercorporate sales. For instance, in our example in Table 11-1, page 215, we eliminated double accounting by entering only the value added into the GNP. The value added was equal to the value of the end product, in this case, a car worth $4,000. To get the $4,000 car produced, financial transactions conducted primarily through intercorporate payments of $12,000 were necessary.

When one considers the resale of homes, automobiles, commercial property, and millions of other commodities that take place each year, it is easy to see why the GNP, although it does a good job of measuring current production, does not begin to measure the total financial transactions taking place within the economy in a given period. This is exemplified by the fact that in 1974 we had a GNP of $1,397 billion, but the total flow of funds for that year was probably four times as great.

The initial *flow-of-funds system of national accounts*, published in 1955 by the Federal Reserve, encompassed all transactions in the economy that occurred as a result of cash payments or extensions of credit. This system is broader than the GNP account, since the flow of funds arises from the transfer of existing assets as well as the sale and purchase of currently produced goods and services. It records the sale of old as well as new homes, and the purchase of used as well as new autos. It also includes purely financial transactions, such as a transfer of securities from one person to another.

One of the major contributions of the flow-of-funds system is that it records all monetary and credit flows into detailed statements of sources and uses for several major sectors and certain component groups of the economy, such as households, businesses, and commercial banks.

## NATIONAL WEALTH

Another concept of importance in the study of economics is that of wealth. Since wealth is composed of such things as machinery, equipment, buildings, land, and other economic goods, it is obvious that by applying labor and knowledge to the processing of this wealth we can produce additional goods and services, or income. Of course, the greater the base of wealth with which a nation has to work, the more goods and services it can produce and the higher will be its standard of living. Consequently, it behooves any nation to add continually to its stock of wealth as a means of improving its economic welfare. Although, as indicated in Chapter 1, there are various estimates of wealth, the one shown in Table

11-8, calculated by the National Bureau of Economic Research, indicates that total wealth exceeded $3.0 trillion in 1968. The largest portion of our wealth is in the form of buildings. Next in importance is land. See Table 11-9 for the delineation of the national wealth.

Our national wealth and our productive capacity have been increasing continuously, as seen in Table 11-8. In terms of constant dollars our real wealth has increased nearly sixfold since the beginning of this century. Since World War II it has been increasing at an annual average rate of 4 to 5 percent.

Table 11-8    **NATIONAL WEALTH IN CURRENT DOLLARS, 1900 to 1968**
(Billions of Dollars)

| Year | National Wealth | Year | National Wealth |
|---|---|---|---|
| 1900 | $ 88 | 1940 | $  424 |
| 1910 | 152 | 1950 | 1,055 |
| 1920 | 374 | 1960 | 1,851 |
| 1930 | 410 | 1968 | 3,079 |

Source: *Statistical Abstract of the United States*, 1974, and previous editions.

Table 11-9    **NATIONAL WEALTH OF THE UNITED STATES, 1968**
(Billions of Dollars)

| | | | |
|---|---|---|---|
| Total national wealth | | | $3,079 |
| Reproducible tangible assets | | | $2,364 |
| Structures | | $1,537 | |
| Residential (nonfarm) | $683 | | |
| Public nonresidential | 460 | | |
| Farm | 50 | | |
| Institutional | 55 | | |
| Other private nonresidential | 289 | | |
| Equipment | | 611 | |
| Producer durables | 377 | | |
| Consumer durables | 234 | | |
| Inventories | | 216 | |
| Private farm | 30 | | |
| Private nonfarm | 172 | | |
| Public | 14 | | |
| Land | | | 715 |
| Private | | 571 | |
| Farm | 153 | | |
| Nonfarm | 418 | | |
| Public | | 144 | |

Source: *Statistical Abstract of the United States*, 1974.

### INPUT-OUTPUT ANALYSIS

For years economists and forecasters have relied on gross national product and related data to interpret changes and developments in our economy. Through the GNP it is easy to trace the allocation of total production to the major sectors of the economy — consumer, private investment, and government. Through the related national income and personal income, one can see how much income was distributed in the form of wages, rent, interest, and profit.

In 1964, however, the Department of Commerce published an updated version of the input-output tables, which provided a more detailed breakdown and permitted a closer analysis of production in our complex economy.[1] The input-output analysis was not new, having been originated by Professor Wassily Leontief a few decades before. Until recently the necessary data for this type of analysis had been rather scarce. The Department of Commerce study, however, provided a major breakthrough in the utilization of this powerful tool of economic analysis. In 1969 the input-output tables were expanded and updated in 1963, and in 1974 the tables were updated once again, this time through 1967.[2]

The revised input-output studies divide the total economy into 85 basic industries and about 300 subgroups. Through the construction of matrix tables, much like the mileage grid on a highway map, the tables show the various inputs used by each industry in producing its final product. One table shows how the output of each industry is distributed to other industries or to final users. Consequently, one can trace the flow of output from one industry as it becomes input to another and finally ends up as consumer or producer goods.

Table 11-10 shows, for example, that for every dollar of output the automobile industry uses 7.1 cents worth of steel and 2.1 cents of rubber products. It spends less than 1 cent for glass, 5.7 cents for screws and bolts, and so forth. Included in the $1 value of its auto product is a value-added item of 30.6 cents, which includes compensation of employees, corporate profits, and a capital consumption allowance. These values are circled in the table for your inspection.

This means that for every $1 billion in auto sales the industry used $71 million in steel products. Further analysis shows us that to produce this $71 million worth of steel, the steel industry in turn spends $1.4 million for coal (.0203 × $1.00 × 71 million = $1.4 million), $3.35 million for iron ore, $1.8 million for electricity, and about $1 million for chemicals. It pays $39.0 million for value added. Thus, it is possible to determine the likely impact on 85 different industries that would result from a $1 or $2 billion increase in the demand for automobiles. Conversely, the

---

[1]Morris R. Goldman, Martin L. Marimont, and Beatrice N. Vaccara, "The Interindustry Structure of the United States, A Report on the 1958 Input-Output Study." *Survey of Current Business* (November, 1964).

[2]*Survey of Current Business* (February, 1974).

**Table 11-10  INTERINDUSTRY STRUCTURE OF THE UNITED STATES INPUT-OUTPUT DIRECT REQUIREMENTS PER DOLLAR OF GROSS OUTPUT, 1967**

For the composition of inputs to an industry, read the column for that industry.

| Industry No. — Inputs | 29 Drugs, cleaning, and toilet preparations | 30 Paints and allied products | 31 Petroleum refining and related industries | 32 Rubber and miscellaneous plastics products | 33 Leather tanning and industrial leather products | 34 Footwear and other leather products | 35 Glass and glass products | 36 Stone and clay products | 37 Primary iron and steel manufacturing | 38 Primary nonferrous metals manufacturing | 39 Metal containers | 58 Miscellaneous electrical machinery, equipment and supplies | 59 Motor vehicles and equipment | 60 Aircraft and parts | 61 Other transportation equipment | 62 Scientific and controlling instruments |
|---|---|---|---|---|---|---|---|---|---|---|---|---|---|---|---|---|
| 1 Livestock and livestock products | 0.00095 | 0.01994 | 0.00037 | 0.00070 | 0.01330 | 0.00009 | 0.00050 | 0.00088 | .0471 | 0.00022 | 0.00012 | 0.00217 | 0.00036 | 0.00010 | 0.00024 | 0.00137 |
| 2 Other agricultural products | .00014 | .00034 | | | | | | .00112 | .00180 | .05042 | | .00029 | | | | |
| 3 Forestry and fishery products | | | | | | | | | | | | | | | | |
| 4 Agricultural, forestry and fishery services | .00033 | .00007 | | .00052 | .00156 | | | .00507 | .02030 | .00058 | | | | | | |
| 5 Iron and ferroalloy ores mining | | | | | | | | | | | | | | | | |
| 6 Nonferrous metal ores mining | | | | | | | | | | | | | | | | |
| 7 Coal mining | .00026 | | .42840 | .00081 | | | | | | | | | | | | |
| 8 Crude petroleum and natural gas | .00098 | .00607 | .00234 | .00054 | | | | | | | | | | | | |
| 9 Stone and clay mining and quarrying | .00220 | | .00001 | .03734 | | | | | | | | | | | | |
| 10 Chemical and fertilizer mineral mining | .10871 | .00034 | .00010 | .16482 | | | | | | | | | | | | |
| 26 Printing and publishing | .00591 | .21047 | .02311 | .00121 | .00009 | .00071 | .01113 | .07227 | .00209 | .00018 | .04078 | .00006 | .00005 | .00022 | .00006 | .00042 |
| 27 Chemicals and selected chemical products | .05365 | .09463 | .00016 | .00164 | .05000 | .00132 | .00108 | .00377 | .00083 | .00013 | .00161 | .02312 | .00139 | .00064 | .00023 | .00006 |
| 28 Plastics and synthetic materials | .00428 | .01002 | .00056 | .04068 | .03596 | .00045 | .00021 | .00031 | .00045 | .00063 | | | .00056 | .00133 | .00273 | |
| 29 Drugs, cleaning and toilet preparations | .03121 | .00655 | .06787 | .00028 | .00275 | .00149 | .02302 | .01857 | .01236 | .00883 | .00075 | .00899 | .00350 | .00072 | .00365 | .00045 |
| 30 Paints and allied products | | .01565 | .00214 | .00181 | .00294 | .00012 | | .00524 | .00001 | .00741 | .00101 | .00022 | .00167 | .00409 | .00170 | .00016 |
| 31 Petroleum refining and related industries | .00001 | .00220 | (*) | | | | | .00041 | .00045 | | .00146 | | .00001 | .00384 | .01773 | |
| 32 Rubber and miscellaneous plastics products | .01535 | | | .00274 | .19935 | | | .00075 | .00366 | .00010 | | .00108 | .00807 | | | .00326 |
| 33 Leather tanning and industrial leather products | .00172 | .00003 | .00215 | .00468 | .00358 | .08686 | .00097 | .00944 | .00105 | .00052 | | .01894 | .00224 | | | .00407 |
| 34 Footwear and other leather products | .00005 | | .00031 | .00317 | .00165 | .18199 | .00508 | .01109 | .00003 | .00282 | | | .01538 | | | .00061 |
| 35 Glass and glass products | .00016 | .00343 | .00151 | .00144 | | | .06377 | .00027 | .00006 | | | .00035 | .00007 | .00005 | | .00066 |
| 36 Stone and clay products | .01561 | .00422 | .00326 | .00072 | .00101 | .02646 | .01673 | .00030 | .00355 | .00026 | | .00746 | | | | .00181 |
| 37 Primary iron and steel manufacturing | | .01050 | .00009 | | | .00021 | | .11165 | .18996 | (*) | .00298 | .02188 | .00067 | .00187 | .00292 | .01914 |
| 38 Primary nonferrous metal manufacturing | | .05788 | | | | | | .01133 | .02708 | .00004 | .36890 | .11107 | .12833 | .02056 | .00448 | .00087 |
| 39 Metal containers | | .00014 | (*) | | | | | .00233 | .00006 | .00190 | .04042 | | | .03329 | .11390 | .00200 |
| 40 Heating, plumbing and structural metal products | | | | | | | .00034 | .00112 | .00213 | .01627 | .00516 | .00223 | .00574 | .00034 | .03723 | .02681 |
| 41 Stampings, screw machine products and bolts | | | | | | | .00018 | .00097 | .00662 | .32214 | .00054 | .01174 | .00046 | .01800 | .03601 | .03324 |
| 42 Other fabricated metal products | .00362 | .00645 | .00059 | .00487 | .00248 | .00599 | .00074 | .00025 | .01435 | .00086 | .00393 | .02105 | .00145 | .00682 | .01960 | .00200 |
| 43 Engines and turbines | .01338 | | | .01480 | | .01413 | | .01036 | .00019 | .00031 | | | | .00017 | .03637 | .00155 |
| 44 Farm machinery and equipment | | | | | | | | .00083 | .00115 | .00213 | | | | | | .01823 |
| 45 Construction, mining and oil field machinery | .00412 | .00594 | .00091 | .00117 | | .00415 | .00345 | .00641 | .00300 | .00880 | | .00430 | .00182 | .00833 | .00335 | .02090 |
| 66 Communications; except radio and TV broadcasting | | | .01711 | .00011 | | | .00018 | .00520 | .02592 | .00027 | .00179 | .00692 | .00447 | .00491 | .00376 | .00126 |
| 67 Radio and TV broadcasting | | | .01121 | .00009 | | | .00074 | | | .00003 | | .03218 | .02116 | .02010 | .00588 | .00042 |
| 68 Electric, gas, water and sanitary services | .00406 | .00542 | .00927 | .00448 | .00853 | .00488 | .00345 | .03249 | .02943 | .02044 | .00742 | .00603 | .00261 | .00299 | .03953 | .00745 |
| 69 Wholesale and retail trade | .02934 | .03459 | .00101 | .01101 | .08247 | .00377 | .03565 | .02627 | .00572 | .03576 | .00972 | .00835 | .00264 | .01228 | .00389 | .00509 |
| 70 Finance and insurance | .00474 | .00453 | .00041 | .03183 | .00743 | .00608 | .03102 | .00812 | .00268 | .00555 | .00456 | .00061 | .00043 | .00001 | .00781 | .03655 |
| 81 Business travel, entertainment and gifts | .01344 | .01534 | .00042 | .00405 | .00229 | .00512 | .00521 | .00612 | .00060 | .00251 | .02605 | | .01485 | | .00061 | .00396 |
| 82 Office supplies | .00077 | .00130 | | .00868 | .00064 | .00153 | .00663 | .00091 | .02651 | .00036 | .00027 | | | | .00006 | .01659 |
| 83 Scrap, used and secondhand goods | .00001 | .01228 | | .00080 | | | .00095 | .00023 | | .04173 | | | | | | .00150 |
| V.A. Value added | .38401 | .32363 | .25541 | .44736 | .29566 | .43176 | .55479 | .45570 | .39047 | .27381 | .34874 | .41644 | .30630 | .43067 | .36985 | .42393 |
| T. Total | 1.00000 | 1.00000 | 1.00000 | 1.00000 | 1.00000 | 1.00000 | 1.00000 | 1.00000 | 1.00000 | 1.00000 | 1.00000 | 1.00000 | 1.00000 | 1.00000 | 1.00000 | 1.00000 |

Source: *Survey of Current Business* (February, 1974).

Table 11-11   INTERINDUSTRY TRANSACTIONS AT PRODUCERS' PRICES, 1967
(Millions of Dollars)

| Indus-try No. | For the distribution of output of an industry, read the row for that industry. / For the composition of inputs to an industry, read the column for that industry. | 11 New construction | 36 Stone and clay products | 37 Primary iron and steel manufacturing | 38 Primary nonferrous metals manufacturing | 39 Metal containers | 40 Heating, plumbing and structural metal products | 41 Stampings, screw machine products and bolts | 42 Other fabricated metal products | 43 Engines and turbines | 44 Farm machinery and equipment | 45 Construction, mining and oil field machinery | 58 Miscellaneous electrical machinery, equip-ment and supplies | 59 Motor vehicles and equipment | 60 Aircraft and parts | 61 Other transportation equipment | 62 Scientific and control-ling instruments | Total |
|---|---|---|---|---|---|---|---|---|---|---|---|---|---|---|---|---|---|---|
| 1 | Livestock and livestock products | 80 | | | | | | | | | | | | | | | | 30,638 |
| 2 | Other agricultural products | | | | | | | | | | | | | | | | | 28,540 |
| 3 | Forestry and fishery products | | | | | | | | | | | | | | | | 9 | 1,945 |
| 4 | Agricultural, forestry and fishery services | 161 | | | | | | | | | | | | | | | | 2,670 |
| 5 | Iron and ferroalloy ores mining | | 10 | 1,497 | 5 | | 1 | | 1 | | | | 7 | 16 | 2 | 2 | 3 | 1,744 |
| 6 | Nonferrous metal ores mining | | 12 | 57 | 1,052 | | 1 | 3 | 3 | 2 | 3 | 2 | 1 | 2 | 2 | 2 | 3 | 1,640 |
| 7 | Coal mining | | 56 | 644 | 12 | (*) | | | | | | | | | | | | 3,163 |
| 8 | Crude petroleum and natural gas | 670 | | | | | | | | | | | | 16 | 5 | | | 15,031 |
| 9 | Stone and clay mining and quarrying | | 797 | 66 | 4 | 137 | 1 | 2 | 2 | | 1 | 1 | (*) | 2 | 14 | 1 | 1 | 2,355 |
| 10 | Chemical and fertilizer mineral mining | 136 | 42 | 26 | 13 | 5 | 2 | 29 | 12 | 4 | 2 | | 73 | 61 | 29 | 2 | 20 | 1,027 |
| 26 | Printing and publishing | | 3 | | 184 | | 14 | 17 | 138 | 15 | 12 | 11 | 28 | 24 | | 21 | 25 | 22,118 |
| 27 | Chemicals and selected chemical products | | 205 | 392 | 155 | 3 | 9 | 4 | 69 | 8 | 11 | 20 | | 153 | 16 | 29 | 53 | 23,182 |
| 28 | Plastics and synthetic materials | | 58 | (*) | 11 | 5 | 102 | 21 | 44 | 1 | 130 | 98 | 1 | 73 | 90 | 13 | 4 | 8,424 |
| 29 | Drugs, cleaning and toilet preparations | | 5 | 14 | 48 | | 34 | 17 | 210 | | | (*) | 3 | 899 | 85 | 139 | 11 | 12,582 |
| 30 | Paints and allied products | | 8 | 116 | 59 | 91 | 26 | 59 | 19 | 33 | | | 59 | (*) | | | 119 | 2,914 |
| 31 | Petroleum refining and related industries | 456 | 104 | 113 | (*) | 3 | 56 | 2 | 57 | 4 | 11 | 42 | 23 | 353 | 1 | 23 | 5 | 26,975 |
| 32 | Rubber and miscellaneous plastics products | 1,400 | 123 | 33 | 1 | 5 | 38 | 4 | 872 | 15 | 655 | 951 | 69 | 98 | 41 | 35 | 12 | 13,809 |
| 33 | Leather tanning and industrial leather products | | (*) | 2 | 40 | 10 | 3,018 | 22 | | 8 | 82 | 58 | 348 | 3,103 | 452 | 890 | 166 | 1,090 |
| 34 | Footwear and other leather products | | 3 | 113 | 340 | 1,238 | 874 | 2,208 | 19 | 1 | | | | 673 | 732 | 291 | 206 | 4,240 |
| 35 | Glass and glass products | 163 | 1,231 | 6,017 | 6,723 | 136 | 298 | 524 | 57 | 384 | 13 | 40 | 37 | 29 | 8 | 281 | 12 | 3,801 |
| 36 | Stone and clay products | 6,177 | 1,125 | 859 | 18 | 2 | 278 | 22 | 90 | 195 | 105 | 54 | 66 | 2,498 | 396 | 53 | 10 | 11,026 |
| 37 | Primary iron and steel manufacturing | 2,155 | 126 | 68 | 45 | 50 | 339 | 176 | 210 | 43 | 72 | 72 | 14 | 1,239 | 353 | 153 | 113 | 31,723 |
| 38 | Primary nonferrous metal manufacturing | 7,796 | 11 | 210 | 184 | 13 | 29 | 116 | 442 | 283 | 294 | 129 | | 251 | 63 | 284 | 129 | 20,870 |
| 39 | Metal containers | 51 | 3 | 455 | 6 | 25 | 42 | 10 | 13 | 25 | 228 | 228 | 22 | 20 | 4 | 31 | 8 | 3,355 |
| 40 | Heating, plumbing and structural metal products | 1,531 | 114 | 6 | 1 | | 75 | 1 | 11 | 143 | 96 | 301 | 101 | 63 | 1 | 26 | 8 | 12,510 |
| 41 | Stampings, screw machine products and bolts | 91 | 9 | 33 | 44 | | 95 | 35 | 21 | 16 | 18 | 30 | 19 | 80 | 183 | 29 | 46 | 9,293 |
| 42 | Other fabricated metal products | 129 | (*) | 18 | 427 | | 409 | 82 | 58 | 19 | 24 | 40 | 26 | 195 | 108 | 46 | 32 | 12,519 |
| 43 | Engines and turbines | 294 | 71 | 95 | 746 | 33 | 84 | 179 | 121 | 129 | 173 | 201 | 1 | 926 | 442 | 309 | 226 | 3,825 |
| 44 | Farm machinery and equipment | 64 | 57 | 822 | 116 | 15 | 133 | 41 | 300 | 7 | 37 | 34 | | 114 | 66 | 30 | 25 | 4,826 |
| 45 | Construction, mining and oil field machinery | 6,503 | 358 | 934 | 52 | 87 | 11 | 33 | 83 | 34 | 30 | 34 | | 116 | 270 | 61 | 103 | 5,974 |
| 66 | Communications; except radio and TV broadcasting | 572 | 290 | 182 | 871 | | 32 | 4 | 83 | 3 | 4 | 5 | 14 | 212 | 21 | 5 | | 19,328 |
| 67 | Radio and TV broadcasting | 532 | 90 | 85 | | | | | 10 | 9 | 9 | 3 | | 30 | (*) | | | 3,183 |
| 68 | Electric, gas, water and sanitary services | 26 | 68 | 19 | | | 11 | | 16 | | | | | | | | | 37,321 |
| 69 | Wholesale and retail trade | | 10 | | | | | | | | | | | | | | | 163,365 |
| 70 | Finance and insurance | 29 | 3 | 841 | | | | | | | | | | | | | | 47,711 |
| 81 | Business travel, entertainment and gifts | | | | | | | | | | | | | | | | | 11,206 |
| 82 | Office supplies | | | | | | | | | | | | | | | | | 2,607 |
| 83 | Scrap, used and secondhand goods | | | | | | 32 | | | | | | 1 | | | | | 1,991 |
| I. | Intermediate inputs, total | 48,033 | 6,002 | 19,336 | 15,156 | 2,185 | 7,909 | 5,031 | 7,002 | 2,457 | 3,140 | 3,448 | 1,830 | 30,342 | 12,521 | 4,922 | 3,567 | 795,388 |
| V.A. | Value added | 31,856 | 5,025 | 12,387 | 5,715 | 1,170 | 4,601 | 4,262 | 5,517 | 1,368 | 1,686 | 2,526 | 1,306 | 13,398 | 9,472 | 2,889 | 2,625 | |

Source: *Survey of Current Business* (February, 1974).

adverse effect on other industries from an automobile strike or shutdown can be estimated in advance.

Table 11-11 shows how much of an industry's products goes to each of the other basic industries. For example, $3.1 billion, or about 10 percent of the steel industry's $31.7 billion output, is sold to the auto industry for its input. Nearly 5 percent, or $1.5 billion, of total steel output becomes input for new construction, and $3.1 billion is used by heating and plumbing industries. About 2.1 percent, or roughly $655 million of steel production, is used in the manufacture of farm equipment, and 3.9 percent is used by the metal container industry, as shown by the circled items in the table. From this table, for example, a firm in the steel industry may be able to determine whether or not it is keeping up with its industry in the sale of products to various other industries. Furthermore, it can be observed in the last column of this table that the value added, $795 billion, was equivalent to the GNP for that year (1967).

It is easy to visualize that input-output data can become very complex when one is trying to analyze the flow of inputs and outputs among 85 industries in the economy. Anytime the input-output relationship of one industry to another changes, the matrix, or set of tables, has to be modified. Thus, the use of computers is essential to keep track of perplexing changes. Although the Department of Commerce study updates the input-output tables to 1967 only, it plans further updating and frequent revision. Consequently, this new tool of analysis will permit economists, businesspeople, and government policymakers to interpret better the total effect of output changes at the industry and national levels. Furthermore, input-output data are compatible with the national income accounts so that the two can be used interchangeably in analysis.

## SUMMARY

The actual production and income of our economy can be measured in terms of dollars. The basic concept in this measurement is the gross national product, the current market value of the total goods and services produced in the nation's economy over a given period of time. The net national product is GNP minus capital consumption allowances. The national income is the aggregate income arising from the current production of goods and services. Personal income is the total income accruing to persons from all sources. The total personal income remaining after the payment of personal taxes is known as disposable personal income.

The GNP is distributed to three major sectors in our economy: consumers, private investors, and the government. These sectors must make payments for the goods and the services received. Such payments to the producers become the source of wages, rent, interest, and profits to the factors of production. In this way, the GNP affects incomes.

The GNP is frequently used as a measure of economic progress. When it is used for such a purpose, however, certain reservations must be kept in mind. For example, the GNP should be valued in constant dollars to obtain a true picture of the changes in the real output of goods and services. Account should also be taken of population changes by using the per capita disposable income for comparison. Other minor qualifications, such as the exclusion of nonmonetary transactions, the type of goods produced, the exaggerating effect of durable goods, the social cost of production, and the lack of a value for leisure, should also be considered.

A much broader concept, the flow of funds, measures the total monetary transactions that take place in the economy. It accounts for the monetary flows in several different but related sectors. It not only gives the sources from which each sector obtains funds, but also the uses to which it puts the funds.

National wealth is another important economic concept because it is a basis of our productive capacity. Current estimates place our wealth at more than $3 trillion. A recent addition to the tool kit of the economist are the input-output tables, which permit analyses of the flow of production from one industry to another and eventually to the final user.

A large income or flow of funds can be maintained only through the spending of our income groups. Furthermore, spending will be affected by the size of individual and family incomes. Therefore, we will next look at the distribution of income in the American economy.

## DISCUSSION QUESTIONS

1. How does the gross national product give rise to our total personal income?
2. Does the share of the national income that is in the form of corporate profit seem excessive? Why or why not?
3. Has the government's share of the GNP been increasing or decreasing in the past 10–15 years?
4. Why is it important to reduce the GNP and national income to constant dollar values when using them as measures of economic progress?
5. Should the performance of household chores and other nonmonetary services be included in the gross national product? Why?
6. In future years would you prefer to have a 25 percent increase in income or a 30-hour workweek? Is it possible to have both?
7. How much more does it cost American consumers to purchase goods and services whenever the price index rises one percent?
8. Do you think we should include in the GNP an adjustment for the social (external) costs of production? Why or why not?
9. How can the input-output tables be used to measure the impact on the total economy of a strike in a major industry, such as the steel or auto industry?
10. Is it true that as we produce more and more goods and services we deplete our wealth? Why or why not?

## SUGGESTED READINGS

The Suggested Readings for this chapter are included in Chapter 12, pages 247–248.

# 12 PERSONAL INCOME DISTRIBUTION

## INDIVIDUAL AND FAMILY INCOME

The fact that we have the highest total income and one of the highest per capita incomes in the world does not mean that America is the land of milk and honey for all of its citizens. Some individuals have sufficient income to provide for a high standard of living. Many others in America, however, live on limited incomes. In fact, a surprising number have no more than a subsistence level of living.

When we state that the per capita disposable personal income for the United States for 1974 was approximately $5,000, we should remember that this figure is obtained by taking the total disposable income for the nation and dividing it by the total population. This does not mean that every person in the economy is receiving a $5,000 income per year. Many are receiving less, and others are receiving more than the average figure.

### Income by Family Units

One of the best measures of income distribution is that of the U.S. Department of Commerce, which calculates income by family units. A *family unit* includes all persons living in the same dwelling who are related by blood, marriage, or adoption. Single-person families are also included as family units. The median family income (that amount below which one half of the families are receiving) in the United States in 1972 was $11,116 per year.

In Table 12-1 some further interesting facts are revealed. For example, 11.7 percent of the family units received less than $4,000 per year, and 7.2 percent received less than $3,000 per year. Such amounts cannot be considered as anything more than a subsistence income these days. However, over 70 percent of the families were earning more than $7,000 and 56 percent over $10,000 per year. Even then, many of the families in the higher income brackets were there as a result of having two or more members of the family at work. In 1972, for example, there were 20.9 million families in which both the husband and the wife were working. In these families the wife's earnings accounted for 26 percent of family

Table 12-1    **INCOME DISTRIBUTION BY FAMILIES BEFORE TAXES, 1972**

| Money Income Before Taxes | Percentage of Total Family Units | Cumulative Percentage of Total Family Units |
|---|---|---|
| Under    $  2,000 | 3.5 | 3.5 |
| $ 2,000–    2,999 | 3.7 | 7.2 |
| 3,000–    3,999 | 4.5 | 11.7 |
| 4,000–    4,999 | 4.9 | 16.6 |
| 5,000–    5,999 | 5.0 | 21.6 |
| 6,000–    6,999 | 5.2 | 26.8 |
| 7,000–    9,999 | 16.8 | 43.6 |
| 10,000– 14,999 | 26.1 | 69.7 |
| 15,000– 24,999 | 23.0 | 92.7 |
| 25,000 and over | 7.3 | 100.0 |
| All cases | 100.0 | |

Source: *Statistical Abstract of the United States*, 1974.

income. A family in the $25,000-or-over bracket can consider itself among the economic elite today.

It also can be shown from other sources that those in the lowest income brackets are receiving a relatively small percentage of the total income. For example, those earning less than $3,000 are receiving less than 5 percent of the total income although they comprise 13.2 percent of the family units. On the other hand, the 30 percent of the total family units in the income brackets $15,000 and over receive 50 percent of the total income.

Not only are there relatively few families in higher income brackets, but the numbers dwindle as the limits of the income brackets increase. Fortunately our income distribution has improved. Rather than a pyramid shape with a few families at the top and the majority of families at the bottom of the income scale, relatively few families are now at the lower and upper extremes and the bulk are in the middle income groups. This income distribution is shown in Table 12-1.

### Family Liquid Assets

Liquid assets are an important supplement to current income, especially during periods of family emergency when additional spending power is needed. Unfortunately, not only are many families receiving very limited incomes, but also a large number of them have very few, if any, financial assets. For example, about 42 percent of the families have liquid assets of less than $500, which include United States savings bonds, savings accounts, and checking accounts, but exclude currency. In fact, one out of every six families has no liquid assets. This is shown in Table 12-2.

Table 12-2   **LIQUID ASSETS OF SPENDING UNITS, 1971**

| Size of Holding of Financial Assets | Percentage of Spending Units | Cumulative Percentage of Spending Units |
|---|---|---|
| Zero | 16 | 16 |
| Less than $200 | 14 | 30 |
| $   200–$  499 | 12 | 42 |
| $   500–$1,999 | 24 | 66 |
| $ 2,000–$4,999 | 13 | 79 |
| $ 5,000–$9,999 | 9 | 88 |
| $10,000 and over | 12 | 100 |
| All cases | 100 | |
| Median holdings, $700 | | |

Source: *Statistical Abstract of the United States*, 1974.

### Income by Geographic Area

Income inequality exists not only within and between different occupations, but also among geographic areas in the United States. Some areas are known as conventionally high income areas, while others are known for their low incomes. These differences arise because of the locations of industries, differences in the cost of living, the accidental location of materials, the need for skilled labor in some areas, the presence or absence of labor unions, and numerous other factors. The highest personal income areas in the nation are the Far West, the Mideast, New England, and the Great Lakes. The highest income states are the District of Columbia, Connecticut, Illinois, Delaware, New York, Nevada, California, New Jersey, and Alaska. The lowest personal income areas are in the Southeast and in some of the western and southwestern states. The average per capita personal income for all the states is shown in Table 12-3. Notice that in about two thirds of the states the personal incomes are below the national per capita income of $5,434. State incomes range from a high of $7,479 per year in the District of Columbia to a low of $3,764 per year in Mississippi.

### Changing Income Distribution

Is income inequality bad for the economy? The answer is yes and no, depending on the degree of inequality. If it were such that it left most families without sufficient income to provide for the basic necessities of life, it would be detrimental to the welfare of society as well as disruptive to the operation of our economic system. On the other hand, a certain amount of income inequality is beneficial for the economic system. First of all, income serves a functional purpose since it is the means by which

Table 12-3    **PER CAPITA PERSONAL INCOME BY STATES AND REGIONS, 1974**

| | | | |
|---|---|---|---|
| **United States** | **$5,434** | **Southeast** | **$4,630** |
| | | Virginia | 5,265 |
| **New England** | **5,697** | West Virginia | 4,390 |
| Maine | 4,439 | Kentucky | 4,470 |
| New Hampshire | 5,143 | Tennessee | 4,484 |
| Vermont | 4,588 | North Carolina | 4,612 |
| Massachusetts | 5,731 | South Carolina | 4,258 |
| Rhode Island | 5,376 | Georgia | 4,662 |
| Connecticut | 6,471 | Florida | 5,235 |
| | | Alabama | 4,198 |
| **Mideast** | **6,045** | Mississippi | 3,764 |
| New York | 6,244 | Louisiana | 4,310 |
| New Jersey | 6,384 | Arkansas | 4,280 |
| Pennsylvania | 5,490 | | |
| Delaware | 6,227 | **Southwest** | **4,739** |
| Maryland | 5,881 | Oklahoma | 4,566 |
| District of Columbia | 7,479 | Texas | 4,790 |
| | | New Mexico | 4,137 |
| **Great Lakes** | **5,773** | Arizona | 4,989 |
| Michigan | 5,928 | | |
| Ohio | 5,549 | **Rocky Mountain** | **5,010** |
| Indiana | 5,263 | Montana | 4,776 |
| Illinois | 6,337 | Idaho | 4,934 |
| Wisconsin | 5,210 | Wyoming | 5,156 |
| | | Colorado | 5,343 |
| **Plains** | **5,206** | Utah | 4,453 |
| Minnesota | 5,450 | | |
| Iowa | 5,302 | **Far West** | **5,894** |
| Missouri | 5,056 | Washington | 5,651 |
| North Dakota | 5,547 | Oregon | 5,270 |
| South Dakota | 4,218 | Nevada | 6,073 |
| Nebraska | 4,877 | California | 5,997 |
| Kansas | 5,406 | Alaska | 7,023 |
| | | Hawaii | 5,882 |

Source: *Survey of Current Business* (April, 1975).

we remunerate individuals for their productive efforts. Since the productivity of some individuals is greater than that of others, one of the ways to recognize the differences is by the payment of a higher income to those who produce the most. If everyone received the same income regardless of productivity, much of the incentive in the economy would be destroyed. Would young people sacrifice to attend college or undertake the tedious task of learning a trade if they could not better their income? What would happen to risky business ventures which eventually enrich our standard of living if we were to remove the incentive of large profits as a reward for success?

Secondly, savings are essential to the development of capital formation, which is responsible for most of the increased productivity in our economy. Since savings are provided primarily by the higher income groups, the inequality of income in this respect helps to increase productivity in the economy. The higher the income, the greater the ability to save. Thus, high incomes that permit savings are beneficial. If we had perfect equality in the distribution of income, it would result in a minimum of personal savings and would hamper to some extent the economic growth of the economy.

An equal distribution of income does not imply a just or equitable distribution. It is true that we should have an equitable distribution of income; that is, income should be distributed according to some standard. Equity, however, means different things to different people, depending on their particular value judgment. For example, to some individuals the only equitable distribution would be an equal distribution of income. Others, however, would consider an equal distribution inequitable because the individuals who contribute the least to the economy would be rewarded as much as those who contribute the most.

The old saying that individuals should "contribute according to their ability and share according to needs" is advocated by some, especially those with little ability. This practice, too, would discourage incentive. Even though a policy of this type has been tried in some of the world's socialistic economies, it was soon recognized that differences in income were necessary to induce individuals into the more difficult and complex occupations in the economy.

In our capitalistic system we think of an equitable distribution as one in which income distribution is made according to the economic contribution of the individual. As a result, we are sure to have some inequality in the distribution of income. Our main task is not to eliminate income inequality. Rather, we should endeavor to keep the inequality from becoming too great. The best way to accomplish this is by raising the incomes of the lower income groups through higher productivity, rather than by taking income away from the higher income groups.

While it is true that we have inequality in the distribution of income, two important changes are taking place within the economy: (1) the average real income of the family is increasing, and (2) income inequality is diminishing to some extent. For example, the average disposable personal income per family in 1880 was $3,329 in terms of 1972 dollars. In 1972 the median family income was $11,116. Fortunately the lessening of income inequality is not coming at the expense of the higher income groups. Rather than decreasing the higher income groups, we are increasing the lower income groups. For example, in spite of our great increase in population, the number and percentage of family units receiving less than $3,000 in 1972 was less than the number of families in that constant dollar income classification in 1955. Likewise, the number and percentage of families in the income brackets above $10,000 increased substantially between 1955 and 1972. This movement is evident from an analysis of Figure 12-1. The shift toward middle and higher level incomes includes black and other minority families.

## FAMILY BUDGETS

Income is only one side of the economic picture for individuals and families. The other side is the cost of living. A high income means little if it is insufficient to provide the necessary goods and services to take care of a family. This brings up an interesting question: Just how much does it cost to provide the average family with the commodities required for a decent standard of living? Since costs vary in different parts of the country, since some families are larger than others, and since some families require more per member than others, estimates of the actual cost of providing family needs vary. A good estimate, however, is available from the recently revised Bureau of Labor Statistics (BLS) budgets.

### City Worker's Family Budget

The annual cost of an "intermediate" level of living for a four-person family in 1974 ranged from a high of $16,725 in the Boston area to a low

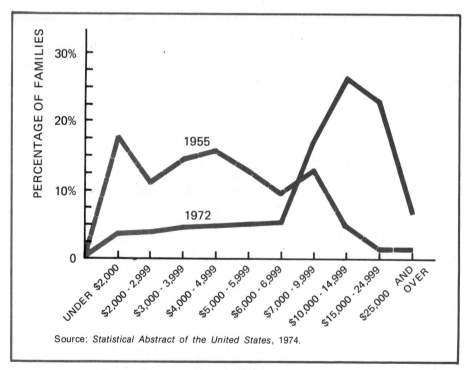

Source: *Statistical Abstract of the United States*, 1974.

Figure 12-1  **PERCENTAGE DISTRIBUTION OF MONEY INCOME OF ALL FAMILIES, BY INCOME LEVEL, 1955 AND 1972**

of $12,388 in Austin, Texas, according to the interpretation of the BLS estimates of the city worker's family budget in 38 metropolitan areas in the contiguous United States. Honolulu was higher still with a $17,019 budget figure, and Anchorage, Alaska, was the highest with a $19,092 budget. The average budget for the urban United States was $14,333. This *intermediate* budget was designed to determine how much it costs a four-person urban family to obtain the goods and services required to maintain a "modest but adequate" (not a minimum subsistence) level of living in various areas. The list of items included in the budget was developed for a family comprised of an employed 38-year-old husband, a wife not employed outside the home, and two children, an 8-year-old girl and a 13-year old boy. A *lower* budget for the urban United States, at a less adequate level of living, has been calculated by the BLS at $9,198, and a *higher* budget at $20,777.

The budgets, however, do not show how an "average family" actually spends, or is supposed to spend, its money. The budgets merely give the total cost of a representative list of goods and services considered essential by urban families to provide health, efficiency, the nurture of children, and some participation in social and community affairs. The budgets calculated by the BLS for 1974 are shown in Table 12-4. Of the $14,333 intermediate budget figure, about 76 percent is allocated to family consumption items. The remainder covers the cost of personal taxes, Social Security and disability deductions, and occupational expenses. Notice that 24.8 percent of family income is spent for food and 22.6 percent goes for housing. The budgets shown in Table 12-4 may be updated by adjusting them for the increase in prices since 1974. The urban U.S. intermediate budget for 1975, for example, would be more than $15,000 when adjusted upward because of rising prices.

When we compare the family personal income by income level and the city worker's family budget for recent years, it indicates that more than one half of the family units have insufficient incomes to maintain even the "modest but adequate" BLS budget. Even if we subtract from this group single people, who are included as family units in the income ladder, a substantial portion of the total families in the United States have incomes inadequate to provide a moderate level of living. However, many of these families have less than four members as described in the BLS budget.

### Retired Couples Budget

The recent census data show that over 20 million persons, or about 10 percent of the total population of the United States, are 65 years of age or older. Population projections indicate that the number of "senior citizens" will increase for a number of years to come. Since a large number of elderly individuals or couples will be living on reduced incomes provided through Social Security and other sources, living costs to these persons become very critical. Consequently, much interest has arisen in

Table 12-4    **ANNUAL COSTS OF AN INTERMEDIATE BUDGET FOR A
4-PERSON FAMILY,[1] 1974**
(In Dollars)

| | Budget Costs | | | | Personal |
| Area | Total Budget[2] | Food | Housing[3] | Trans-portation | Income Taxes |
|---|---|---|---|---|---|
| **Urban United States** | $14,333 | $3,548 | $3,236 | $1,171 | $2,010 |
| Metropolitan Areas[4] | 14,644 | 3,599 | 3,327 | 1,174 | 2,089 |
| Nonmetropolitan areas[5] | 12,945 | 3,321 | 2,828 | 1,158 | 1,653 |
| Boston, Mass. | 16,725 | 3,829 | 4,458 | 1,181 | 2,839 |
| Buffalo, N.Y. | 15,364 | 3,667 | 3,522 | 1,267 | 2,414 |
| Hartford, Conn. | 15,501 | 3,841 | 3,804 | 1,304 | 1,930 |
| Lancaster, Pa. | 14,130 | 3,715 | 2,964 | 1,167 | 2,045 |
| New York-Northeastern, N.J. | 16,648 | 4,099 | 4,072 | 1,085 | 2,757 |
| Philadelphia, Pa.-N.J. | 14,757 | 3,896 | 3,095 | 1,107 | 2,299 |
| Pittsburgh, Pa. | 13,876 | 3,669 | 2,853 | 1,130 | 1,995 |
| Portland, Maine | 14,697 | 3,768 | 3,420 | 1,219 | 1,908 |
| Cedar Rapids, Iowa | 14,092 | 3,151 | 3,198 | 1,197 | 2,143 |
| Champaign-Urbana, Ill. | 14,587 | 3,425 | 3,441 | 1,202 | 1,997 |
| Chicago, Ill.-Northwestern Ind. | 14,797 | 3,563 | 3,492 | 1,215 | 2,044 |
| Cincinnati, Ohio-Ky.-Ind. | 13,753 | 3,525 | 2,988 | 1,206 | 1,815 |
| Cleveland, Ohio | 14,617 | 3,463 | 3,488 | 1,203 | 1,933 |
| Dayton, Ohio | 13,391 | 3,519 | 2,825 | 1,154 | 1,619 |
| Detroit, Mich. | 14,390 | 3,594 | 3,251 | 1,162 | 1,919 |
| Green Bay, Wis. | 14,180 | 3,167 | 3,219 | 1,165 | 2,350 |
| Indianapolis, Ind. | 14,120 | 3,393 | 3,199 | 1,297 | 1,849 |
| Kansas City, Mo.-Kans. | 13,939 | 3,531 | 2,894 | 1,250 | 1,876 |
| Milwaukee, Wis. | 15,024 | 3,301 | 3,526 | 1,173 | 2,610 |
| Minneapolis-St. Paul, Minn. | 14,917 | 3,429 | 3,082 | 1,168 | 2,788 |
| St. Louis, Mo.-Ill. | 13,859 | 3,570 | 2,997 | 1,247 | 1,854 |
| Wichita, Kans. | 13,302 | 3,302 | 2,836 | 1,194 | 1,655 |
| Atlanta, Ga. | 13,098 | 3,444 | 2,615 | 1,165 | 1,589 |
| Austin, Tex. | 12,388 | 3,147 | 2,472 | 1,218 | 1,293 |
| Baltimore, Md. | 14,398 | 3,471 | 2,927 | 1,167 | 2,401 |
| Baton Rouge, La. | 12,928 | 3,464 | 2,627 | 1,171 | 1,468 |
| Dallas, Tex. | 12,917 | 3,200 | 2,732 | 1,226 | 1,373 |
| Durham, N.C. | 13,927 | 3,382 | 2,990 | 1,127 | 2,072 |
| Houston, Tex. | 12,872 | 3,403 | 2,605 | 1,195 | 1,373 |
| Nashville, Tenn. | 12,996 | 3,241 | 2,883 | 1,172 | 1,391 |
| Orlando, Fla. | 12,804 | 3,240 | 2,809 | 1,158 | 1,357 |
| Washington, D.C.-Md.-Va. | 15,035 | 3,671 | 3,354 | 1,211 | 2,425 |
| Bakersfield, Calif. | 13,000 | 3,235 | 2,674 | 1,192 | 1,544 |
| Denver, Colo. | 13,606 | 3,374 | 2,804 | 1,154 | 1,854 |
| Los Angeles-Long Beach, Calif. | 14,068 | 3,387 | 3,111 | 1,192 | 1,819 |
| San Diego, Calif. | 13,977 | 3,323 | 3,062 | 1,238 | 1,793 |
| San Francisco-Oakland, Calif. | 15,127 | 3,528 | 3,593 | 1,225 | 2,080 |

*(continued)*

Table 12-4    **ANNUAL COSTS OF AN INTERMEDIATE BUDGET FOR A
4-PERSON FAMILY, 1974** (continued)

| Area | Total Budget | Budget Costs | | | Personal Income Taxes |
| | | Food | Housing | Trans-portation | |
| --- | --- | --- | --- | --- | --- |
| Seattle-Everett, Wash. | 14,487 | 3,587 | 3,450 | 1,201 | 1,710 |
| Honolulu, Hawaii | 17,019 | 4,150 | 4,070 | 1,307 | 2,983 |
| Anchorage, Alaska | 19,092 | 4,118 | 5,033 | 1,373 | 3,331 |

Source: U.S. Department of Labor, Bureau of Labor Statistics, *NEWS* (April 9, 1975).

[1]The family consists of an employed husband, age 38, a wife not employed outside the home, an 8-year-old girl, and a 13-year-old boy.
[2]Total budget costs include personal income taxes, social security, other items and total consumption.
[3]Housing includes shelter, housefurnishings, and household operations.
[4]As defined in 1960–1961. For a detailed description of these and previous geographical boundaries, see the 1967 edition of *Standard Metropolitan Statistical Areas*, prepared by the Office of Management and Budget.
[5]Places with population of 2,500 to 50,000.

recent years regarding the cost of living for the elderly or retired couple. For this reason, the BLS computes a "retired couples budget" for the same cities for which it calculates the CWFB. The retired couples intermediate budget for 1974 was around $6,000. Generally the retired couples budget is about 40 to 45 percent of the 4-person CWFB for the various cities.

### Actual Family Spending

It can readily be seen from a comparison of family incomes and the typical family budgets that many families earn less than the budgets require for their particular standard of living. This no doubt explains in large part why each year millions of families spend more than they earn. The money required for spending above current income is obtained from past savings, liquidation of assets, and the use of consumer credit.

A sampling of average annual expenditures for current consumption indicates that the typical family spends 23.4 percent of its budget for food. Of this, 19.0 percent is for food prepared at home. Housing absorbs 24.6 percent of the budget, of which 13 percent is for shelter and the remainder for utilities, home furnishings, and equipment. Eight percent of the average family spending is for clothing and 7.5 percent is for personal and medical care combined. On transportation the family expends 9.5 percent of its budget. About 17 percent is used to pay personal taxes, while miscellaneous spending takes the remainder.

### THE NATURE AND EXTENT OF POVERTY

Before his death in 1963 President Kennedy became concerned about the number of families in our economy that were living on substandard incomes. As a result, he directed his Council of Economic Advisers to undertake a study of poverty in the United States. Although he did not live to see its fruition, the study served as a basis for designing the war-on-poverty program instituted by the passage of the Economic Opportunity Act in August, 1964. The findings of the Council of Economic Advisers is contained in large part in the 1964 *Economic Report of the President*.

### The Poverty Level

Realizing that the measurement of poverty is not simple, the *Report* defined poor to mean "those who are not now maintaining a decent standard of living," or those whose basic needs exceed their means to satisfy them. Since the needs of various families differ, and since there is no precise way of determining the number of families that have insufficient resources to meet their particular needs, the *Report* utilized what, by consensus, was thought to be a minimum acceptable standard of living for an American family. It considered the "low-cost" budget publicized by the Social Security Administration for a nonfarm family of 4 that cost $3,955 in 1962, "the economy-plan" of that budget, which was $3,165, and other studies. In the final analysis the *Report* established $3,000 (before taxes and expressed in 1962 prices) as the line of demarcation between poverty and nonpoverty.

This poverty level income was subsequently adjusted upward to account for price increases and changes in consumption patterns. Thus, the comparable poverty level income for 1972 was $4,150 annually for a 4-person family. As a result of continuing price increases, the poverty level income rose to $5,300 by 1975.

### Incidence of Poverty

The President's *Report* indicated that of the 47 million families in the United States in 1962, one fifth of these families, comprising more than 30 million persons, had money incomes below $3,000 per year. Of these, 5.4 million families, containing more than 17 million persons, had incomes below $2,000 per year. Furthermore, more than 1 million children were being raised in very large families, 6 or more children, with incomes of less than $2,000 annually. In addition to these families, 5 million "unrelated individuals," 45 percent of the total, had incomes below the $1,500 level. Thus, nearly one fifth of our total 186.6 million population in 1962 was poverty stricken.

Among other characteristics of the poor, the *Report* indicated a heavy concentration of poverty among nonwhites, the poorly educated, the elderly, rural dwellers, Southerners, and families headed by women. This is still the case today. But because of the seriousness of the poverty situation, Congress in August, 1964, passed the Economic Opportunity Act, frequently known as the antipoverty bill. This act provided funds to launch the war on poverty. Before the Office of Economic Opportunity (OEO), which was established under the auspices of the Economic Opportunity Act, was dismantled in the early 1970s, several billion dollars were spent on various programs designed to reduce or eliminate poverty.

### Progress Against Poverty

Since 1962 considerable progress has been shown in our "war on poverty." This progress has resulted not only from specific measures designed to reduce poverty, but, in large part, from the overall expansion of the economy during the decade. Data for 1972, for example, indicate that only 13.1 percent of all families were considered below the poverty level, as compared to 22 percent in that category in 1962. Furthermore, the total number of persons considered as living in poverty was reduced from more than 35 million to less than 25 million during that period, despite the fact that the United States population increased by 22.3 million in the interim.

## INCOME IN OTHER NATIONS

Data on personal income and poverty reveals that the process of economizing, as mentioned in Chapter 2, is a real, rather than hypothetical, problem with many families. Economizing occurs not so much because our incomes are low absolutely but because they are low relative to our desired high standard of living. What we bemoan as a low level of income in the United States is actually high when compared to incomes in other parts of the world. Comparative per capita income figures for the United States and other countries can be estimated from the data shown in Table 12-5, since income is closely related to production. The per capita

Table 12-5    **ESTIMATES OF PER CAPITA GROSS DOMESTIC PRODUCT FOR SELECTED COUNTRIES**
(United States Dollars)

| | | | |
|---|---|---|---|
| United States | $5,051 | Japan | $2,186 |
| Sweden | 4,438 | Italy | 1,876 |
| Canada | 4,301 | Ireland | 1,537 |
| Switzerland | 3,793 | Argentina | 1,261 |
| West Germany | 3,572 | Venezuela | 1,083 |
| Denmark | 3,491 | Mexico | 717 |
| Australia | 3,228 | Brazil | 449 |
| France | 3,192 | China (Taiwan) | 400* |
| Belgium | 2,989 | Vietnam | 186 |
| New Zealand | 2,543 | Nigeria | 125* |
| United Kingdom | 2,410 | India | 120* |

Source: *Yearbook of National Accounts Statistics, 1972* (New York: United Nations, 1974).
*Author's estimate.

income of the United States exceeds that of practically any other industrial nation in the world. Among leading industrial nations, our average per capita production or income is 14 percent greater than that of Sweden, the number two nation; about 50 percent greater than that of West Germany; and about one and one half times higher than the per capita income of Japan.

## SUMMARY

Although per capita income for the United States is the highest in the world, we have an unequal distribution of income and many families are receiving relatively low incomes. Whereas the median family income in 1972 was $11,116, over one fifth of the family units received incomes of less than $6,000 in that year. Almost 27 percent of the family units received less than $7,000.

Furthermore, the highest fifth in income rank was receiving 41 percent of total income, while the lowest fifth of the people received 5.4 percent of the total income. In addition, those in the lower income brackets own very few financial assets. About one sixth of the families in the United States have no financial assets at all, and another 26 percent have financial assets amounting to $500 or less. Fortunately the relative inequality in the distribution of our income has been decreasing over the past few decades.

Income also varies according to the geographic areas within the nation. The Far West, the Mideast, New England, and the Great Lakes are the highest personal income areas. The Southeast and the Southwest are the lowest personal income areas in the country.

The city worker's family budget, which required about $14,333 a year in 1974, calls for more spending than the actual income of many families. As a result, most families must continually economize. Fortunately our problem is not so much that of choosing between basic necessities, but that of determining which of the numerous additional goods and services desired should be purchased.

Although average incomes may be low by our standards, they are rather high compared to the rest of the world. The average income in the United States, for example, is 14 percent greater than that of the number two nation, Sweden. It is about 50 percent higher than that of West Germany and about 1½ times higher than that of Japan. Nevertheless, according to government standards, 13 percent of our American families are still classified as poor. Presently many programs costing several billion dollars are being conducted through numerous federal and state agencies in an effort to reduce or eliminate poverty in America.

Since the size of the GNP determines employment and income, and the distribution of income affects our standard of living, we shall next consider what determines the level of the gross national product.

## DISCUSSION QUESTIONS

1. *Equality* in the distribution of income may not be *equitable*. Explain this statement.
2. Does our current progressive income tax, which requires those in higher income brackets to pay a higher tax rate, tend to exaggerate or modify the unequal distribution of income in the economy? Explain your opinion.
3. It is possible to raise the income level of all families and individuals in the economy without substantially changing the distribution of total income. Explain.
4. Do you think that the incidence of poverty in the U.S. will ever drop below 5 percent? Why or why not?
5. What do you think of federal rent subsidies which permit families in the lower income brackets to live in higher income neighborhoods by having the federal government pay the rent differential?
6. Do you see any relationship between geographic distribution of income and migration of people within the United States?
7. In your opinion is the city worker's family budget too meager?
8. What do you think of the $5,300 family income level as a line of demarcation between poverty and nonpoverty? Should it be higher or lower?
9. It has frequently been proposed by various government agencies and other groups that the federal government, through some type of payment, should guarantee each American family an annual income of at least $5,000. Do you agree or disagree? Why?
10. What causes the great disparity of income among various nations throughout the world?

## SUGGESTED READINGS

"Annual Cost of City Workers Family Budget." *Monthly Labor Review* (April, 1974).

Berkwitt, George J. "Input-Output — Management's Newest Tool." *Dun's* (March, 1971).

Brackett, Jean. "Urban Family Budgets Updated to Autum 1972." *Monthly Labor Review* (August, 1973).

Cedney, Frances S. "Retired Couple's Budgets Updated to Autum 1972." *Monthly Labor Review* (October, 1973).

"Consumer Income and Spending." *Survey of Current Business* (December, 1974).

Denison, Edward F. "Welfare Measurement and the GNP." *Survey of Current Business* (January, 1971).

*Economic Report of the President*. Washington: U.S. Government Printing Office, 1970–1975.

Goldman, Morris R., Martin L. Marimont, and Beatrice N. Vaccara. "The Interindustry Structure of the United States, A Report on the 1958 Input-Output Study." *Survey of Current Business* (November, 1964).

Hailstones, Thomas J., and Frank V. Mastrianna. *Contemporary Economic Problems and Issues*, 4th ed. Cincinnati: South-Western Publishing Co., 1976. Chapter 4.

"Input-Output Analysis System Comes of Age." *Commerce Today* (November 2, 1970).

"Input-Output Structure of the U.S. Economy: 1967." *Survey of Current Business* (February, 1974).

*Manpower Report of the President*. Washington: U.S. Government Printing Office, 1970–1975.

Mayer, Lawrence A. "First Aid for Recession's Victims." *Fortune* (February, 1975).

"New Application of Input-Output." *Business Economics* (January, 1971).

Okun, Arthur M. "Should GNP Measure Social Welfare?" *Brookings Bulletin* (Summer, 1972).

Orr, Larry L., and Robinson G. Hollister. *Income Maintenance*. Chicago: Rand McNally & Co., 1971.

Radner, Daniel B., and John C. Henrichs. "Size and Distribution of Income in 1964, 1970, and 1971." *Survey of Current Business* (October, 1974).

Theobald, Robert. *The Guaranteed Income*. Garden City, N.Y.: Doubleday & Company, Inc., 1967.

U.S. Department of Commerce, *Survey of Current Business* (April, 1974).

"The U.S. Labor Force: Projection to 1985." *Monthly Labor Review* (May, 1970).

"Who Has the Wealth in America?" *Business Week* (August 5, 1972).

Will, Robert E., and Harold G. Vatter. *Poverty in Affluence*, 2d ed. New York: Harcourt Brace Jovanovich, Inc., 1970.

# 13 DETERMINANTS OF GNP AND ECONOMIC GROWTH

## GNP: PRODUCT AND INCOME FLOWS

In Chapter 11 we saw that the GNP is allocated to three major sectors of the economy — consumers, private investors, and the government. These three sectors, in turn, must pay accordingly for the goods and services they receive. These payments, made to the sellers of goods and services that make up the GNP, are distributed eventually to the owners of the factors of production who contributed the goods and services to produce the GNP. Thus, in exchange for the physical goods and services received by the three sectors, there arise monetary payments to the factors of production. As we learned in Chapter 1, each factor — land, labor, capital, and entrepreneurship — contributes toward the total product; and their owners are remunerated in the form of rent, wages, interest, and profits, respectively. In national income accounting the total product is represented by the GNP and the remuneration of the factors of production is in the form of wages and salaries, rental income, net interest, proprietor's income, and corporation profits. It is reasonable to assume then that the total demand for the three sectors determines the size of the GNP, and that the size of the GNP determines our income.

Table 13-1 on page 250 shows the GNP and the payments to the factors of production for 1974. According to the table, the total demand by consumers, private investors, and the government led to a GNP of $1,396.7 billion. When these sectors demand goods and services, they must make payment for them. This sets up a circular flow of economic activity — with the flow of goods and services to the three sectors according to their demand, and the flow of income payments to the factors according to their economic contribution. The greater the demand by consumers, private investors, and the government, the greater the income distribution to the factors of production. The less the demand, the smaller the income payments. It is primarily the demand by these three sectors that determines the total production, employment, and income in our economy.

Table 13-1   **NATIONAL PRODUCT AND INCOME ACCOUNT, 1974**
(Billions of Dollars)

| Product Flow | | Income Flow | |
|---|---|---|---|
| GNP | $1,396.7 | GNP | $1,396.7 |
| Consumer purchases | $ 877.0 | Capital consumption allow- | |
| Private investment | 210.9 | ances, indirect business | |
| Government purchases | 308.8 | taxes, etc. | $ 254.5 |
| | | National income | $1,142.2 |
| | | Compensation to | |
| | | employees | $ 856.1 |
| | | Proprietor's income | 93.0 |
| | | Rental income | 26.5 |
| | | Net interest | 61.6 |
| | | Corporate profit | 105.4 |

Source: *Federal Reserve Bulletin* (February, 1975).

## MULTIPLIER AND ACCELERATOR

If each of the sectors demanded the same quantity of goods and services in a current year as they did in the previous year, the same GNP and the same income would result for the current year. If any of the three sectors changed its demands, however, there might be a change in the level of economic activity and a change in the level of income. To be effective, a net change would have to take place. For example, if an increase of $10 billion dollars occurred in private investment while a decrease of $10 billion dollars in consumption took place, there would be no substantial change in total income. If investment increased by $10 billion, however, and both consumption and government remained the same, the net increase in spending would accelerate the level of economic activity.

### The Multiplier Effect

What would be the result of a net increase of $10 billion in private investment? Would it increase income by $10 billion? Actually it would increase the GNP and our total income not only by $10 billion, but also by some multiple of that amount. This comes about because of the *multiplier effect*. "Multiplier" is a sophisticated name for a very elementary principle. We all know that when one person spends money, it becomes income to the recipient. The recipient in turn may spend the money, and it becomes income to a third party, and so on. The total income resulting from the continual respending of a given amount of money will be larger than the actual amount of the money involved.

For example, suppose that $10 billion is spent by private investors; this may result in an increase of $10, $15, $20, $25, $30 billion, and so on,

as it is respent. The only limiting factor to the creation of income resulting from the respending of the original $10 billion will be a failure of
someone along the line to respend the money that is received. This would
be the case if a person were to save a portion of the money, to spend it
abroad, or to put it into a bank or an insurance policy where it was not
reinvested by the financial institution. In other words, any time that we
withdraw money from the circular flow, it will not be available to respend and create more income.

**Relationship to Consumption and Savings**    Savings of money constitutes the biggest leakage factor from the income stream. Thus, the multiplier will depend on the relationship of savings to income, or of consumption to income. For example, let's assume that people spend four fifths of
their income and save one fifth. The multiplier will be five, which means
that a net increase in investment of $10 billion would increase income by
$50 billion. This effect is demonstrated in Table 13-2.

According to this table, an increase in investment of $10 billion, when
originally spent, will become income of $10 billion to A. If A saves one
fifth, or $2 billion, and spends four fifths, or $8 billion, the $8 billion
respent by A becomes income to B. When B in turn spends four fifths of
the $8 billion income, it will create $6.4 billion income for C. This
process of receiving income and respending, which creates incomes for
others, will continue until the original amount of money is all held in
savings by the various individuals. At that time, no more income will be
created. Through this process the original investment of $10 billion
brings about an increase of $50 billion in income. Thus, the multiplier
has a value of five. The *multiplier*, then, is simply the relationship of a
change in income, brought about by respending, to a net change in investment (or consumption or government spending). The level of consumption, therefore, has a direct influence on the size of the multiplier.

Table 13-2    **MULTIPLIER EFFECT**
              (Billions of Dollars)

| (1)<br>Net Increase<br>in Investment | (2)<br>Increased<br>Income | (3)<br>Increased Spending<br>(Spend 4/5) | (4)<br>Increased Savings<br>(Save 1/5) |
|---|---|---|---|
| $10 | A  $10.0 | $ 8.0 | $ 2.0 |
|  | B    8.0 | 6.4 | 1.6 |
|  | C    6.4 | 5.1 | 1.3 |
| Multiplier | D    5.1 | 4.1 | 1.0 |
| effect | E    4.1 | 3.3 | .8 |
|  | F    3.3 | 2.6 | .7 |
|  | G    2.6 | 2.1 | .5 |
|  | Etc. | Etc. | Etc. |
|  | $50.0 | $40.0 | $10.0 |

*Higher Consumption*    The more people respend, or the less they
save, the greater will be the multiplier effect. For example, if individuals
and businesses were inclined to save only one tenth of everything they
received in income, the multiplier would be equal to 10. An increase of
$10 billion in investment would bring about a $100 billion increase in
income because the money would turn over more frequently before it was
all saved.

Compare Table 13-3 with Table 13-2. In this case the recipient of the
original investment, *A*, saves one tenth, or $1.0 billion, of the income of
$10 billion, and respends $9.0 billion. Thus, the amount of income created
by the respending is greater than it was in the previous example in which
only $8 billion was respent. The total effect of this stronger inclination to
respend, or *propensity to consume*, as it is usually called, will be a greater
increase in income. The total income of the economy, in this case, increased by $100 billion out of which income recipients spent $90 billion
and saved $10 billion.

*Lower Consumption*    The lower the propensity to spend, the less the
multiplier. If the income recipients were to spend only one half of everything they received, this would result in a multiplier of only two. In
Table 13-4 observe that a $10 billion increase in investment will increase
incomes by only $20 billion, of which people will spend one half and save
the other half.

**Calculation of Multiplier**    As we study the tables, it becomes evident
that the multiplier depends on the spending and saving habits of the individuals and businesses of the economy. In fact, the size of the multiplier
depends directly upon the propensity to consume, that is, the relationship
between income and consumption. To calculate the multiplier, the average
propensity to consume or the marginal propensity to consume may be

Table 13-3    **MULTIPLIER EFFECT**
(Billions of Dollars)

| (1)<br>Net Increase<br>in Investment | (2)<br>Increased<br>Income | (3)<br>Increased Spending<br>(Spend 9/10) | (4)<br>Increased Savings<br>(Save 1/10) |
|---|---|---|---|
| $10 | A  $ 10.0 | $ 9.0 | $ 1.0 |
|  | B     9.0 | 8.1 | .9 |
|  | C     8.1 | 7.3 | .8 |
| Multiplier | D     7.3 | 6.6 | .7 |
| effect | E     6.6 | 5.9 | .7 |
|  | F     5.9 | 5.3 | .6 |
|  | G     5.3 | 4.8 | .5 |
|  | Etc. | Etc. | Etc. |
|  | $100.0 | $90.0 | $10.0 |

Table 13-4   **MULTIPLIER EFFECT**
             (Billions of Dollars)

| (1) Net Increase in Investment | | (2) Increased Income | (3) Increased Spending (Spend 1/2) | (4) Increased Savings (Save 1/2) |
|---|---|---|---|---|
| $10 | A | $10.0 | $ 5.0 | $ 5.0 |
| | B | 5.0 | 2.5 | 2.5 |
| | C | 2.5 | 1.3 | 1.2 |
| Multiplier | D | 1.3 | .7 | .6 |
| effect | E | .7 | .4 | .3 |
| | F | .4 | .2 | .2 |
| | | Etc. | Etc. | Etc. |
| | | $20.0 | $10.0 | $10.0 |

used. The *average propensity to consume* is the percentage of total income spent on consumption out of any given level of income. Although the multiplier can be based on the average propensity to consume, it is more accurate to base it on the *marginal propensity to consume*. The marginal propensity to consume is simply the relationship between the last increment of income received by individuals and businesses and the amount of that income spent on consumption. Since the spending and saving habits of individuals and businesses change as incomes change, we can better tell what income recipients will do with their next increment of income by observing what they did with their previous increment.

The marginal propensity to consume will decrease as income increases. This stems from the fact that when people have low incomes, they must spend practically everything. Thus, ability to save is limited. While it is true that people spend more money on necessities, conveniences, and luxuries as their incomes increase, total spending is usually a smaller percentage of the new higher total income. As their incomes increase, the amount and the percentage of saving by individuals will increase since their ability to save increases. For example, take a young man recently out of college. Let us assume that he has a salary of $700 per month, of which he spends $630 and saves $70. When his salary increases to $800, he may spend $680 and save $120. He is spending more money, and he is also saving more; but the percentage of his total income that he is now spending on consumption has declined while his percentage of saving has increased. Notice this movement in Table 13-5, page 254.

Some individuals may continue to consume at a pace equivalent to their increase in income. In fact, there are always some who spend more than they earn no matter what their income. The general tendency in any economy, however, is for the marginal propensity to consume to decrease as real income increases, provided other things remain unchanged.

Table 13-5    INCOME, CONSUMPTION, AND SAVING OF A HYPOTHETICAL INDIVIDUAL

| (1) Monthly Income | (2) Amount Spent on Consumption | (3) Percentage of Income Consumed | (4) Amount Saved | (5) Percentage of Income Saved |
|---|---|---|---|---|
| $ 700 | $630 | 90 | $ 70 | 10 |
| 800 | 680 | 85 | 120 | 15 |
| 900 | 720 | 80 | 180 | 20 |
| 1,000 | 750 | 75 | 250 | 25 |

We can now state our formula for the multiplier in terms of the marginal propensity to consume as follows:

$$k = \frac{1}{1 - \dfrac{\Delta C}{\Delta Y}}$$

In this formula:     $k$ = multiplier
                       $\Delta C$ = the change in consumption
                       $\Delta Y$ = the change in income

When the marginal propensity to consume, $\dfrac{\Delta C}{\Delta Y}$, is subtracted from 1, we get the marginal propensity to save. Dividing the marginal propensity to save, $1 - \dfrac{\Delta C}{\Delta Y}$, into 1 gives us the multiplier, which is equal to the reciprocal of the marginal propensity to save. Thus, a rule of thumb for figuring the multiplier is simply to say that the multiplier is equal to the reciprocal of the marginal propensity to save.

In order to calculate the marginal propensity to consume (or save), we must observe two periods and compare the change in income to the change in consumption between the two periods.

Since we either spend (consume) or save our income, we can say at any time that income equals consumption plus saving. Thus, let us use the following example to work out the multiplier.

Let us assume that in Period I, $Y$ = $1,000 billion, $C$ = $800 billion, and $S$ = $200 billion. Thus,

$$Y \quad = \quad C \quad + \quad S$$
$$\$1,000 = \$800 + \$200$$

Out of the $1,000 billion income, people spend $800 billion and save $200 billion. Suppose that in Period II incomes increased to $1,200 billion and we spent $950 billion and saved $250 billion.

$$Y = C + S$$

Period I    $\$1{,}000 = \$800 + \$200$
Period II    $1{,}200 = 950 + 250$

The marginal propensity to consume will equal three fourths, since income was $200 billion higher in Period II, out of which we spent $150 billion and saved $50 billion. This is calculated as follows:

$$\frac{\Delta C}{\Delta Y} = \frac{150}{200} = \frac{3}{4}$$

Now if we put these figures into our formula, we find:

$$k = \frac{1}{1 - \dfrac{\Delta C}{\Delta Y}} \qquad k = \frac{1}{1 - \dfrac{150}{200}} \qquad k = \frac{1}{1/4} \qquad k = 4$$

The size of the multiplier based on the marginal propensity to consume is 4, or we can say that it is the reciprocal of the marginal propensity to save (1/4). Using the marginal propensity to consume gives us a good indication of what individuals and businesses will do with the next increment of income they receive.

Table 13-6 gives the value of the multiplier at various sizes of the marginal propensity to consume and save. It can be seen that the multiplier is related directly to the marginal propensity to consume and inversely to the marginal propensity to save.

Various estimates of the actual multiplier for the United States seem to place it somewhere between 2 and 3, depending on the level of employment and the degree of business activity. In determining the value of the multiplier, it is better to use the disposable personal income of an individual or a nation, for it gives the best reflection of what is done with increased incomes. The difficult part in calculating the multiplier is to

Table 13-6    **RELATION OF THE MULTIPLIER TO THE MARGINAL PROPENSITY TO CONSUME AND THE MARGINAL PROPENSITY TO SAVE**

| Marginal Propensity to Consume | Marginal Propensity to Save | Multiplier (k) |
|---|---|---|
| 9/10 | 1/10 | 10 |
| 5/6 | 1/6 | 6 |
| 4/5 | 1/5 | 5 |
| 3/4 | 1/4 | 4 |
| 2/3 | 1/3 | 3 |
| 1/2 | 1/2 | 2 |
| 1/3 | 2/3 | 1 1/2 |

hold all other factors constant. For example, we might show that $10 billion of increased investment was accompanied by an increase in disposable personal income of $30 billion for the nation. But part of the increase in disposable personal income could be due to a tax reduction or to a reduction of savings. Increased spending and consequently increased disposable personal income might result from such things as better products, more advertising, or a war scare. Thus, the change in income should be adjusted for such factors to determine a true multiplier.

### Accelerator

Granting that we have a multiplier and can estimate its size, we can see that an increase in investment (or consumption or government spending) will bring about an increase in income by some multiple of the original increase in investment. However, that is not all. As the increased income resulting from the multiplier effect is being respent, the demand for consumer goods and services will increase. This increased demand may lead businesspeople to increase their demand for machinery, equipment, and buildings to produce the additional goods and services being demanded. They will, in turn, increase their investment to obtain the capital equipment needed to increase production. The relationship between this secondary, or induced, investment brought about by the spending of the increased income resulting from the multiplier is known as the *accelerator effect*.

Following our example, we can assume that our original, or autonomous, investment of $10 billion will increase income by $50 billion, out of which people spend $40 billion and save $10 billion. When merchants see the additional $40 billion flowing over their counters, they will increase their orders of goods and services. This means that the producer will increase output. To do this, manufacturers and others may have to purchase new and modern equipment, buildings, and other items, which will result in an increased investment in capital goods. They might finance this investment with savings or by borrowing from the banks. At any rate, secondary or induced investment will take place. For purposes of simplification, let us say that this secondary investment amounts to $4 billion. This is shown in Table 13-7.

Some economists feel that because of the difficulty of distinguishing between original and secondary investment, it is impossible to measure the accelerator. They have a point. After all, on what basis are we going to make a distinction between the two? We could say that any investment which occurs in the first six months of the year is original and that which takes place in the last six months is induced. But what about the businesspeople who are induced to expand in April because of increased business activity in the first quarter of the year? Should it be called induced or original? Or what about the individual who, in the fall of one year, plans to expand in the fall of the next year? Is this induced investment? An arbitrary division between original and induced investment

Table 13-7   **RELATIONSHIP OF ORIGINAL AND SECONDARY INVESTMENT**
(Billions of Dollars)

| | Investment | Increased Income | Increased Spending 4/5 | Increased Saving 1/5 |
|---|---|---|---|---|
| Original, or autonomous, investment | $10 ——— Multiplier ——→ | $50 | $40 | $10 |
| | Accelerator | | | |
| Secondary, or induced, investment | $ 4 ◄ | | | |

would not give us a true measure of each. Nor could we ask each businessperson whether a particular investment was original or induced. But regardless of how we measure it or of our inability to measure it, we do know that the accelerator effect does exist.

### Interaction of Multiplier and Accelerator

Just as we have a multiplier effect on the original investment, we can have a similar multiplier effect on the secondary or induced investment. The original investment through the multiplier effect brings about increased income, which in turn brings about secondary investment. The multiplier effect on the secondary investment further increases income, which in turn leads to tertiary investment, which means more income, and so forth. Thus, the interaction of the multiplier and accelerator serve to augment each other and to boost income and investment. This can be depicted as shown in Table 13-8.

Table 13-8   **INTERACTION OF MULTIPLIER AND ACCELERATOR**
(Billions of Dollars)

| | Investment | Increased Income | Increased Spending 4/5 | Increased Saving 1/5 |
|---|---|---|---|---|
| Original investment | $10 ——— Multiplier ——→ | $50 | $40 | $10 |
| | Accelerator | | | |
| | 4 ◄——— Multiplier ——→ | 20 | 16 | 4 |
| Secondary investment | Accelerator | | | |
| | 2 ◄——— Multiplier ——→ | 10 | 8 | 2 |
| Totals | $16 | $80 | $64 | $16 |

If we measure the original investment, $10 billion, against the original increase in income of $50 billion, we get a multiplier of 5. Or if we measure the total investment, $16 billion, against the total increase in income, we get a multiplier of 5. This is known as the *simple multiplier*. However, if we measure the original investment, $10 billion, against the total income resulting from the interaction of the multiplier and accelerator, which is $80 billion, the multiplier is 8. This is what the British call the compound multiplier or, as we Americans with our superlatives like to call it, the *supermultiplier*. Since the multiplier effect is extremely difficult to measure because of the problems of distinguishing between the original and the secondary investment, we usually talk in terms of the simple multiplier. After all, we can get some idea of the simple multiplier by observing the change in disposable personal income and the change in investment in two successive national income periods. We can measure the total change in investment that occurs compared to the total change in income. The total effect that we obtain from investing $16 billion in our example leads to increased income of $80 billion. The net result is due partially to the multiplier and partially to the effect of the accelerator.

The possible cumulative effects of the multiplier and the accelerator are demonstrated in Figure 13-1. The dashed line shows the effect of the simple multiplier and the increase in economic activity with the spending of the original investment. Economic activity increases at a decreasing rate after the spending of the original investment takes place. The solid line shows what happens when respending brings about induced or secondary investment. Economic activity surges to a higher level before the rate of increase begins to decline. In effect, the cumulative action of the multiplier and the accelerator intensifies fluctuations in business activity. Although there is no certitude regarding the length of time that elapses between the spending on the original investment and the respending of it after it becomes income to others, most estimates place the time factor somewhere between 3 and 3½ months.

In Figure 13-1 the original increment of income A results from the original investment. In the second period, a portion of this money is spent creating additional income. The process continues through the third, fourth, and fifth periods, and so on. The effect of the original investment eventually will end, as shown by the dotted line. If secondary investment starts to take place in Period 2, however, this will further augment income in that and subsequent periods. By Period 3, tertiary investment takes place to augment income further in the third and subsequent periods. The net result is that income will reach a higher level with induced investment than it would with original investment only.

### Practical Effects of Multiplier

The effect of the multiplier on the economy is shown in the hypothetical situation in Table 13-9. From this table it can be seen that consumers

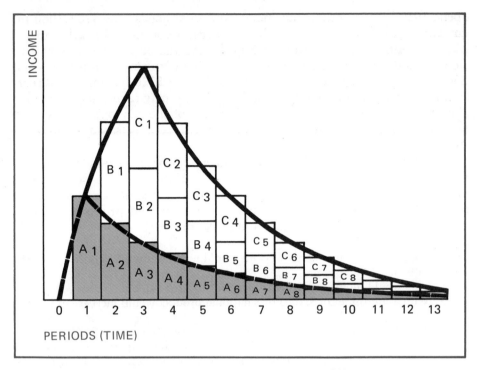

Figure 13-1   **MULTIPLIER AND ACCELERATOR ACTION**

Table 13-9   **GROSS NATIONAL PRODUCT, PRODUCT AND INCOME FLOW, PERIOD I**
(Billions of Dollars)

| Product Flow | | | Income Flow | | |
|---|---|---|---|---|---|
| Gross national product | | $1,500 | Gross national product | | $1,500 |
| | | | Minus: | | |
| Consumer purchases | | 950 | Capital consumption | | |
| Goods | $550 | | allowance | $130 | |
| Services | 400 | | Indirect business tax | 120 | |
| Private investment | | 250 | National income | | 1,250 |
| Construction | 120 | | Minus: | | |
| Plants and equipment | 100 | | Corporate taxes, | | |
| Inventories | 20 | | Social Security | | |
| Net exports | 10 | | payments, etc. | 75 | |
| Government purchases | | 300 | Undistributed profits | 50 | |
| Federal | 125 | | Personal income | | 1,125 |
| State & local | 175 | | Minus: | | |
| | | | Personal taxes | 105 | |
| | | | Disposable personal | | |
| | | | income | | 1,020 |
| | | | Consumer expenditures | 950 | |
| | | | Savings | 70 | |

spend $950 billion of their income on consumer goods. The $70 billion in consumer savings plus $130 billion in capital consumption allowances plus $50 billion in undistributed profits form the basis for the $250 billion private investment in the economy. The government purchases its $300 billion in goods and services by collecting $120 billion in indirect taxes, $75 billion in corporation and Social Security taxes, and $105 billion in personal income taxes. If each sector of the economy reacts in a similar fashion in a subsequent period, we will have the same output and income.

What would happen, however, if businesspeople increased their investment in plant and equipment by $15 billion in the subsequent period? Assuming a marginal propensity to consume of two thirds, and provided taxes, capital consumption allowances, and profits remained the same, the following changes would take place:

1. Spending on plant and equipment would increase from $15 billion to $115 billion.
2. This would increase private investment to $265 billion.
3. With a multiplier of 3, the gross national product would increase to $1,545 billion.
4. This money increase would increase the national income to $1,295 billion, personal income to $1,170 billion, and disposable personal income to $1,065 billion, assuming that taxes and other things remained constant.
5. Since the marginal propensity to consume is 2/3, people would spend $30 billion of their additional $45 billion increase in income and would save the remainder, $15 billion.
6. The additional spending of $30 billion on consumer products would increase consumer purchases on the product flow side to $980 billion and the $15 billion in additional savings would offset the original increase in investment.

After these changes take place, the hypothetical gross national product would appear as shown in Table 13-10.

From a more practical point of view, if we know the multiplier we can estimate the amount of investment that is needed to reach a particular level of gross national product. For example, with an average multiplier of 3, we know that a $500 billion investment is necessary to bring about a gross national product of $1,500 billion. Thus, if private investment were $200 billion and government purchases were $300 billion, which in effect means we have a total private plus government investment of $500 billion, the gross national product would be $1,500 billion. If we had a multiplier of 3, it would mean that the average propensity to consume would be two thirds. Therefore, people would spend $1,000 billion and save or pay in taxes $500 billion of their income. In 1973, for example, it took total investment, private investment plus government spending, of $490 billion to give us a GNP of $1,295 billion.

Table 13-10    **GROSS NATIONAL PRODUCT, PRODUCT AND INCOME FLOW, PERIOD II**
(Billions of Dollars)

| Product Flow | | | Income Flow | | |
|---|---|---|---|---|---|
| Gross national product | | $1,545 | Gross national product | | $1,545 |
| | | | Minus: | | |
| Consumer purchases | | 980 | Capital    consumption | | |
| Goods | $565 | | allowance | $130 | |
| Services | 415 | | Indirect business tax | 120 | |
| Private investment | | 265 | National income | | 1,295 |
| Construction | 120 | | Minus: | | |
| Plants and equipment | 115 | | Corporate taxes, | | |
| Inventories | 20 | | Social Security | | |
| Net exports | 10 | | payments, etc. | 75 | |
| Government purchases | | 300 | Undistributed profits | 50 | |
| Federal | 125 | | Personal income | | 1,170 |
| State & local | 175 | | Minus: | | |
| | | | Personal taxes | 105 | |
| | | | Disposable personal | | |
| | | | income | | 1,065 |
| | | | Consumer expenditures | 980 | |
| | | | Savings | 85 | |

## Production, Employment, and the Multiplier

The multiplier is also useful in deciding what additional investment may be necessary to reach a stage of full employment in a forthcoming period. We can determine what amount of GNP is necessary to maintain full employment in the following manner. If we multiply the number of people available for work by the average number of hours worked per person per year, and then by the average productivity per man-hour, we obtain the total current potential production, or GNP, of the economy. Thus, our formula for calculating the size of the GNP needed for full employment becomes:

Labor Force × Hours per Worker × Output per Man-Hour = Potential GNP

For example, if we assume the normally employed labor force in a given year to be 90 million, the average working hours per year per person to be 2,000, and the productivity per man-hour to be $7.95 per hour, we obtain the following:

$$90,000,000 \times 2,000 \times \$7.95 = \$1,431,000,000,000$$

Thus, our potential GNP is about $1,431 billion. If we produce anything less than this amount, we will not be fully employed. Some workers would be on short hours or without jobs. This is what happened in 1974, for example, when the size of the labor force was approximately 93 million and the GNP was approximately $1,400 billion. We operated at less than full capacity, and unemployment was nearly 1.5 million in excess of the 3.7 million which was tolerable.

It might be possible to avoid such unemployment, at least to a degree, if it could be anticipated. Therefore, forecasting the GNP has become a very useful technique of economic analysis. Some idea of the GNP can be obtained beforehand by studying various sources. For example, estimates of intended investment of businesspeople can be obtained through the Security and Exchange Commission and the Department of Commerce. Another excellent source is the McGraw-Hill Survey of Business Investment. Frequently it is possible to ascertain consumer attitudes from the Survey of Consumer Finances published by the University of Michigan. Estimates for government expenditures can be obtained by studying various proposed governmental budgets.

Suppose that by using various sources and methods it was estimated that the GNP for a forthcoming period would be $1,600 billion, as shown below:

|                          | Estimated GNP (Billions) |
|--------------------------|--------------------------|
| Consumer purchases       | $1,000                   |
| Private investment       | 260                      |
| Government               | 340                      |
| Gross national product   | $1,600                   |

If a gross national product of $1,648 billion is needed for full employment, it is obvious that we will have some degree of unemployment. If consumers, businesses, and the government follow through as indicated, total production will be 3 percent below that amount needed for full employment. This could mean excess unemployment of 2.5 to 3.0 million people, or total unemployment of more than 6.5 million or 7 percent of the labor force for the economy as a whole.

Faced with such a situation, the logical thing to do would be to increase spending by any or all three sectors. But how much additional spending is necessary? The answer depends in large part on the size of the multiplier. The gap between the estimated and the potential full-employment GNP is $48 billion. It is not necessary, however, to increase initial spending by this amount. If the multiplier were 3, an original increase of $16 billion in investment, for instance, would increase the GNP to $1,648, an increase of $48 billion. Out of the $48 billion of higher income, people would spend $32 billion on consumer goods (assuming a marginal propensity to consume of two thirds). This would in effect give us sufficient output to maintain full employment since the GNP would then be as shown at the top of the next page.

|                          | Estimated GNP (Billions) | Increased Investment (Billions) | Final GNP (Billions) |
|--------------------------|:---:|:---:|:---:|
| Consumer purchases       | $1,000 |         | $1,032 |
| Private investment       | 260    | +$16    | 276    |
| Government               | 340    |         | 340    |
| Gross national product   | $1,600 |         | $1,648 |

Actually when it is observed that the estimated GNP may be less than that needed for a high level of employment, the administration and agencies of the federal government may take steps to encourage consumption and private investment. They can use indirect governmental measures to bolster the level of economic activity. If consumers and businesses are conservative and do not respond to the stimulus, the government, as a last resort, can use more direct measures, including deficit spending, in an effort to raise the level of economic activity.

## ESTIMATING FUTURE GROWTH OF THE ECONOMY

It is important from the viewpoint of macroeconomic analysis to know what may happen to the economy in the future. Will we have sufficient savings and credit to finance expansion? Will we have the resources to expand at the same rate in the future as we have in the past? These and many other questions are of interest from an economic, social, political, and military point of view. On the other hand, the future of our economy is important from a microeconomic point of view. A firm should have some idea of what our total income will be in 5, 10, or 15 years from now so that it may plan properly. There are several methods of obtaining a reasonable estimate of our GNP for the future. But these are all estimates and do not purport to measure precisely the rate of growth or the level of economic activity for any particular year in the future.

A number of growth projections, based on an annual real growth rate of 4 percent, indicate that the GNP will be in excess of $2 trillion by 1985 in terms of 1975 constant dollars. If a modest 3 percent annual inflationary factor is injected into the forecasts, it means that the current dollar GNP in 1985 will be in the vicinity of $3 trillion. That, of course, is a tremendous quantity of goods and services to produce, distribute, and finance.

By 1985 the U.S. population is projected to be in the vicinity of 235 million, compared to 214 million in 1975. Some geographic areas will grow at faster rates than others and there will be some change in the age structure of the population. The labor force will grow to more than 100 million and the length of the workweek will decline. Per capita production in current dollars will be in the neighborhood of $13,000 annually, and average family income will be well in excess of $18,000 annually. It is anticipated that the distribution of income will show an increase in the percentage of families in the middle and upper income groups and the decline in the incidence of poverty will continue. Of course, for a number of reasons not all industries will grow at the same rate.

One factor common to most of these forecasts is that they are based for the most part on population increases anticipated in the future. The rate of population increase, however, could continue its shift downward, as it has been doing in recent years, or it could reverse itself. Thus, the projection of the GNP would have to be scaled downward or upward accordingly.

### SUMMARY

The level of economic activity is determined by the total demand of the three basic sectors in our economy: consumer, private investment, and government. If a net change in the total demand by these three sectors occurs, it will cause a change in the level of economic activity.

If an initial increment in demand by any of the sectors takes place, it will increase the size of the GNP not only by the amount of the initial increment but also by some multiple thereof. This multiplier effect is measured by the relationship between the original increase in investment (consumption or government) and the increase in income that results from it. The size of the multiplier varies directly with the marginal propensity to consume and inversely with the marginal propensity to save.

In calculating the multiplier, based on the marginal propensity to consume, the formula is $k = \dfrac{1}{1 - \dfrac{\Delta C}{\Delta Y}}$. The multiplier is usually considered to be somewhere between 2 and 3 for our economy.

The increased income resulting from the multiplier effect causes a greater demand for goods and services. This respending in turn may induce secondary investment in the economy. This phenomenon is referred to as the accelerator effect. Just as there is a multiplier effect on the original, or autonomous, investment (consumption or government spending), so too can there be a multiplier effect on the secondary investment. This in turn will increase incomes still further and perhaps bring about tertiary investment. The relationship between the original investment and the total increase of income resulting from the interaction of the multiplier and accelerator is known as the supermultiplier. Period analysis is used in an endeavor to plot the combined effects of the multiplier and the accelerator.

The multiplier is useful for calculating the additional amount of investment or government spending that may be required to bring the economy from a state of low economic activity and employment up to a state of higher employment. It can also be used to determine the total amount of investment and government spending that is needed in the economy to maintain a given level of economic activity.

Methods exist to estimate the level of economic activity for future dates, essentially in terms of the GNP. The usual procedure is to determine the size of the labor force for a given future date, to determine the total man-hours that will be worked for the given year, and then to multiply the total number of man-hours to be worked by the projected productivity per man-hour. Such calculations, however, give only rough estimates since a number of assumptions must be made and the assumptions are subject to change.

Now that we have had an introduction to the determinants of GNP, an even more detailed analysis of our national income and expenditures will be made in the next chapter.

## DISCUSSION QUESTIONS

1. The size of the multiplier is determined by the marginal propensity to consume. Explain.
2. What are the similarities and differences between the multiplier and the velocity of money? (Refer to Chapter 8 for a review of the velocity of money.)
3. Is the marginal or the average propensity to consume a better basis on which to calculate the multiplier? Why?
4. If a tax reduction is proposed to stimulate the economy, what effect will the multiplier have on the size of the tax reduction?
5. What makes it so difficult to measure the accelerator effect?
6. It is said that the supermultiplier

actually contains some measure of the accelerator. Explain.
7. On the basis of the relationship of private investment plus government spending to GNP last year, what is the approximate size of the multiplier for the U.S. economy?
8. What reservations must be kept in mind when using GNP estimates of the future?
9. Do you think that the assumption of a reduced workweek in the future is realistic? What economic forces do you see working toward a reduced workweek?
10. Of what practical use is a prediction of the gross national product for a future period to a business firm today?

## SUGGESTED READINGS

*A Look at Business in 1990.* A Summary on the White House Conference on the Industrial World Ahead. Washington: U.S. Government Printing Office, November, 1972.

"A Look at the Great Economy of 1985." *Business Week* (December 18, 1971).

*The American Economy: Prospects for Growth to 1985.* New York: McGraw-Hill Book Company, Inc., 1972.

"The Debate Over Gauging the GNP Gap." *Business Week* (June 9, 1973).

Ehrlich, Paul L., and Anne H. Ehrlich. *Population, Resources, and Environment*. San Francisco: W. H. Freeman and Company, 1972.

Hailstones, Thomas J., and Frank V. Mastrianna. *Contemporary Economic Problems and Issues*, 4th ed. Cincinnati: South-Western Publishing Co., 1976.

"How to Fight Inflation and Recession." *Business Week* (December 7, 1974).

Jones, Sidney L. "Are Economists Answering the Right Questions?" *Business Economics* (January, 1975).

Samuelson, Paul A. "Interaction Between the Multiplier Analysis and the Principle of Acceleration." *Review of Economic Statistics* (May, 1939).

Siegel, Barry N. *Aggregate Economics and Public Policy*. Homewood, Ill.: Richard D. Irwin, Inc., 1974.

Surkin, Alan. *Education, Unemployment and Economic Growth*. Lexington, Mass.: D. C. Heath & Company, 1974.

"The Theory Behind the Tax Cut." *The Morgan Guaranty Survey* (January, 1964).

Tobin, James. "The World Economy in Retreat: The United States." *First Chicago Report*, First National Bank of Chicago (May, 1975).

U.S. Department of the Treasury. "Economic Growth: The Key to Jobs and Opportunity." *Treasury Papers* (August, 1975).

"White House Conferees Seek Answers to 1990 Business Problem." *Commerce Today* (February 7, 1972).

# 14 INCOME-EXPENDITURE ANALYSIS

## INTRODUCTION

John Maynard Keynes, a British economist, was primarily responsible for the initiation and early development of the income-expenditure analysis of the economy. Subsequently many others improved and expanded the original Keynesian presentation, and it has developed into an excellent tool of economic analysis. Modern monetary, fiscal, and psychological policies are difficult to understand without a knowledge of the principles of the income-expenditure analysis. Although the principles have been widely accepted, controversy still arises concerning economic policies based on these principles. But keep in mind that it is possible to accept the Keynesian tools of analysis without agreeing with the economic policies of Keynes, other leading economists, or political figures. It is possible, for example, to accept the income-expenditure analysis of why we have unemployment without agreeing with the President's Council of Economic Advisers in regard to what we should do about it.

## INCOME-EXPENDITURE ANALYSIS AND CLASSICAL TRADITION

Since the development of the income-expenditure analysis involved a breaking away from classical tradition, it might be wise to begin with a brief description of some major classical doctrines. The principles, precepts, and doctrines of this school of economics are not listed or enumerated in any one place. They were developed over a period of more than a century by various economists as they gradually accepted certain basic assumptions and principles to be the foundation of economic analysis. Thus, a complete understanding of the classical tradition requires a good background in the history of economic thought. Nevertheless, the basic principles and assumptions that were in dispute can be summarized here.

### Full Employment

Of greatest importance is the classical assumption that the only point at which the economy can be in equilibrium is that of full employment. It is contended that if the economy is not at full employment, the situation is merely a temporary deviation from full employment. According to the classical theory, the economy operates on a basis of free trade and laissez-faire. Competition, the regulator of the economy, is an important factor in maintaining or moving the economy toward the full-employment stage. It is assumed, for example, that competition will force prices downward to insure that all goods are moved off the market. Competition likewise will insure that all savings are invested, since it will force the interest rate down until it becomes profitable for businesses to borrow and to invest all available funds. It is explained that, because of thoroughgoing competition, unemployment for extended periods of time is improbable if not impossible. If laborers are unemployed for any reason, it is assumed that those unemployed will compete for jobs against each other and against those still employed by offering to work for a lower wage. As a result of this competition, according to the classical theory, wages will be forced down. As wage rates decline, it becomes profitable for the entrepreneurs to hire more workers.

Thus, the normal tendency of the economy, according to the classical tradition, is to move toward full employment. If the economy is at less than full employment, the deviation is only temporary. Such a temporary deviation may be caused by several factors but primarily by monopolistic restrictions, labor union interference, and government intervention in the economy.

## Income Equals Expenditures

Since the classicalists hold that the primary purpose of money is its use as a medium of exchange, they maintain that all income will be spent. People will use money primarily for purchasing power. Accordingly, they will buy the current goods and services they need. What they do not spend on current consumption, they will spend to build up their inventories of consumer goods or invest in capital goods. If anything is saved, it will be borrowed by others and spent in various ways, especially for capital goods investment. Thus, any decrease in consumption will be offset by an increase in investment. Fluctuations in the interest rate will insure that all of the savings will be borrowed.

## Supply Creates Demand

The classical theory holds that production which creates supply also creates an equivalent amount of monetary purchasing power (demand), and it is assumed that all the income will be spent. Thus, supply and demand will always be equal. If supply creates its own demand and the goods can be moved off the market, then, according to the classical presentation, there should be no reason why the economy should not move right up to, and maintain equilibrium at, the full-employment position.

The income-expenditure analysis holds that purchasing power does not automatically become demand for goods and services. In short, people may have the purchasing power, or potential demand, and not effectuate it. After producing goods and exchanging them for money, individuals may decide to hold on to the money instead of spending it. In such a case, the total demand for goods and services may be less than the supply, and goods produced may not be moved off the market. Thus, there will be no incentive to increase production or to move to a higher level of employment.

According to the income-expenditure analysis, a problem arises in a monetary economy when individuals substitute a demand for money in place of a demand for goods and services, and this demand for money (saving) is not offset by borrowing and investing. As goods are produced, they create supply, which also creates purchasing power; but some of the purchasing power may be held in idle balances. As a result, the total supply will be greater than the effective demand for goods and services. It is only when investment sufficient to offset savings takes place that the economy will maintain equilibrium.

Before leaving this exposition on classical economics, it should be emphasized that there is much more to the classical doctrine than the few principles and assumptions mentioned. In fact, the bulk of our present microeconomic theory developed from classical theory. The advocates of the income-expenditure analysis are not desirous of overthrowing the entire classical tradition. Economic theory would be in a sad state without it. Both the classical doctrine and Keynesian economics have a place in current economic analysis.

### EFFECTIVE DEMAND

The income-expenditure analysis can be described as a theory of output, employment, and income. In seeking an explanation of what determines the actual level of employment at any given time, the theory is centered around effective demand. *Effective demand* is defined as the actual demand for goods and services by both consumers and businesspeople. It is demand backed up by purchasing power. This effective demand is measured by the spending of current income. Total output and, therefore, total employment and income are determined by effective demand. The income, derived from the output of goods and services, in turn will be instrumental in determining the total effective demand. If spending of current income for consumer and capital goods is high, effective demand will again be high. Thus, a continued high rate of spending will assure a strong effective demand, which in turn will assure a high level of production, employment, and income. This action, in effect, gives us the circular flow of economic activity previously described in Chapter 4.

According to the income-expenditure theory, as employment increases, income will increase. This will cause consumption to increase. It is a fundamental principle, however, that as the real income of the economy increases, consumption will increase but by less than the increase in income. In short, it holds that the marginal propensity to consume declines as the real income of the individuals and the economy as a whole increases. This is an integral and exceptionally important point of current economic analysis.

Although the absolute amount of consumption increases with higher income, consumption decreases relative to income. Therefore, as the economy expands, there is an increasing difference between the amount of production, which is equivalent to income, and the amount of consumption. Investment, which is expected to absorb this difference, is not always forthcoming. Therefore, there may be less total effective demand than is necessary to clear from the market all the goods the economy is capable of producing. In such a case, production, employment, and income will be cut back.

Since it is assumed that supply will be forthcoming in response to demand, provided the economy has the means of producing the desired amount of goods and services demanded, it is obvious that the heart of the income-expenditure theory centers around the concept of effective demand. Difficulty arises, however, when the effective demand is less than total output or income. This means that some of the goods produced will not be moved off the market. Since the cause of unemployment is inadequate effective demand, the theory concentrates its efforts in large part on the analysis of effective demand and its three important basic components of consumption, investment, and government spending.

Of great significance is the fact that consumption is generally less than total output, and as a result, investment is necessary to absorb the difference between what is produced and what is consumed. Furthermore, as output increases, the marginal propensity to consume declines. This means that the higher the output, the greater the gap between output and consumption. Thus, the higher the output and employment, the greater the amount of investment required to maintain a given level of employment. Lastly, the theory contends that because of the relative stability of the consumption function, effective demand will fluctuate primarily according to changes in investment.

The relationship between income and output on the one hand and the consumption function on the other is an important key to the income-expenditure analysis. It is this relationship that determines the amount of investment needed for any given level of employment. Furthermore, because of the nature of the consumption function, a larger amount of investment is required to increase output, income, and employment. In the income-expenditure analysis, the third element of effective demand, government spending, is considered as a means of raising the total effective demand when the first two basic elements, consumption and investment, are inadequate to maintain a satisfactory level of production and employment for the economy.

### Equilibrium Level

The economy reaches equilibrium at a point where total investment is equal to the difference between total output (or income) and total consumption. In Figure 14-1, since output equals income, the value of each is shown on the income-output line moving upward to the right at a 45° angle. Line *CC'* is the consumption function representing the propensity to consume at various levels of income and employment. As income increases, consumption will increase but not so much as income. Therefore, consumption can be represented by a line moving in the same direction as income, upward to the right, but at less of an angle.

At very low levels of income, consumption may actually exceed income. This can result if people use credit in addition to their regular incomes to buy goods and services. It may also occur as a result of inventory depletion, since it is possible to sell more than is currently being produced by supplying out of inventory. In most instances, however, consumption will be less than income. This difference between income and consumption represents saving, as shown in Figure 14-1. Therefore, it is necessary to have sufficient investment to fill the gap between output and

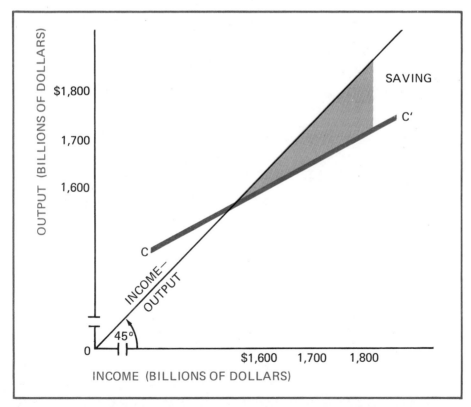

Figure 14-1  **INCOME-OUTPUT AND THE CONSUMPTION FUNCTION**

consumption (saving) if all the goods and services are going to be moved off the market. Since there will be a larger gap between output and consumption at the higher levels, at any given time it will require an increasing amount of investment to maintain equilibrium and to move all the goods off the market at higher levels of output. This requirement can be seen in Figure 14-1.

The level of economic activity, then, will be determined by the amount of investment. Output will adjust itself to the point where investment just fills the gap, no more and no less, between output and consumption. At this point, total effective demand will equal total output and all the goods and services will be moved off the market. At any lower level with this given investment total effective demand will be greater than output, as illustrated by point a in Figure 14-2. Thus, if the economy were at a lower level, such as point a, economic activity would rise until the equilibrium position, such as point b, was reached. At point b in Figure 14-2 it can be observed that total effective demand, composed of consumption and investment, equals total output. At any higher level, such as point c in Figure 14-2, with the given investment, total effective demand will be less than output. Thus, if the economy were operating at a

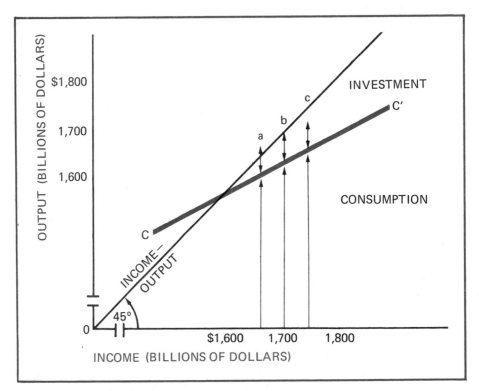

Figure 14-2  **EFFECTIVE DEMAND GREATER THAN, EQUAL TO, AND LESS THAN TOTAL OUTPUT**

higher level, all the goods produced would not be moved off the market. This would bring about a decrease in economic activity until it reached the equilibrium point, where investment is just sufficient to fill the gap between output and consumption.

### Relationship of Investment to Savings

In analyzing Figure 14-2, it should be kept in mind that the difference between the income line and the consumption line represents savings. In this way we can relate investment to savings and see their relationship to the level of economic activity as pointed out in Chapter 4. At point a in Figure 14-2, for example, it can be seen that the actual amount of investment is more than that necessary to fill the gap between output and consumption. Therefore, investment is greater than savings. This means that the total effective demand, made up of both consumption and investment, is greater than output. As a result, there will be an increase in business activity as businesses increase production to satisfy the demand. As the economy moves upward, income increases, the marginal propensity to save increases, and the gap between output and consumption widens. The economy comes into equilibrium at point b where investment will fill the gap between output and consumption. At this point, investment is equal to savings. Therefore, total effective demand is equal to total production. All goods produced will be cleared from the market, and the economy will be in equilibrium.

With this given amount of investment and consumption, there is no incentive to move to a higher level of output because it would not be profitable to do so. For example, if the economy did move up to point c without a change in investment, it would soon fall back to point b. In Figure 14-2 it can be noted that at point c investment is insufficient to fill the gap between total output and consumption. Therefore, investment is less than savings. This means that total effective demand is less than total output and all production will not be moved off the market. As a result, businesses will curtail their activities. This will bring about a decline in output, employment, and income. As income decreases, the marginal propensity to save decreases and the gap between output and consumption becomes less and less, until point b is reached at which investment is just sufficient to fill the gap between output and consumption. Here once again investment will equal savings, total spending will equal total income, total effective demand will equal total output, and the economy will be in equilibrium.

Thus, with any given amount of investment there is only one point of equilibrium. If the economy is at any other level of economic activity, forces come into play to accelerate or decelerate the level of business activity until it comes to its equilibrium point. The direction in which the economy moves will depend on the relationship of investment to savings. Whenever investment is greater than savings, there will be an increase in the level of business activity if we are at less than full employment. If investment is less than savings, there will be a decrease in the level of economic activity. When investment is equal to savings, there will be a stable flow of economic activity and the economy will be in equilibrium.

### The Problem of Unemployment

In Figure 14-2, page 272, point *b* is the equilibrium level for the economy. Here total output is $1,700 billion, which gives a total income of $1,700 billion. Total consumption is $1,600 billion and savings equal $100 billion. However, the amount of spending on investment, $100 billion, offsets the savings. Therefore, total spending equals total income, and total effective demand equals total output. The economy is at an equilibrium point from which there is no incentive to move. This is fine if the economy is at a position of high-level employment. But, an important problem arises if the economy is in balance at an undesirably low level of employment. For example, suppose that a GNP of $1,750 billion were necessary for full employment. The economy would be stuck at a level of $1,700 billion output and with no automatic adjusters, according to the income-expenditure theory, to move it up to a level of $1,750 billion.

**Increased Investment**    The income-expenditure approach does not deny the possibility of increasing the level of employment through increased spending on consumption. Since consumption spending is dependent primarily on income, however, it is thought improbable that the propensity to consume out of any given level of income would change sufficiently to raise the level of business activity. This is an essential part of the income-expenditure analysis.

Since consumption is not likely to increase, increased investment will be necessary to move the economy to a higher level of employment and income. This is shown in Figure 14-3, where it can be seen that a greater amount of investment is necessary to maintain the economy at point *c* than is required at point *b*. Out of their higher income, people will spend more; therefore, the absolute amount of consumption will increase. However, since consumption increases but not as much as income or, to put it another way, the marginal propensity to consume declines as income increases, there will be a larger gap between income and consumption at the higher level that must be filled with investment. According to the income-expenditure theory, increased consumption from increased income will be helpful in moving the economy toward a higher level; but higher income and consumption therefrom can only result if something else initiates the increase in output and income.

**Greater Consumption**    An increase in the propensity to consume out of given levels of income, however, will be helpful in moving the economy

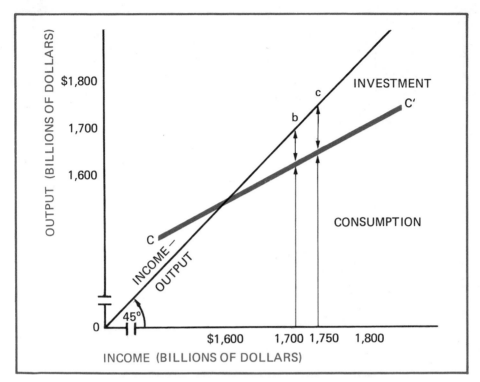

Figure 14-3    **HIGHER INVESTMENT RESULTS IN A HIGHER LEVEL
OF OUTPUT AND INCOME**

toward a higher level of employment because it will decrease the gap
between output and consumption. This means that less investment will
be required to maintain any given level of economic activity and it will
make it easier to reach and maintain a full-employment economy. In fact,
if the propensity to consume were raised to 100 percent, there never
would be any problem about maintaining full employment because the
effective demand for consumer goods would always be equal to total output. There would be nothing to stop the economy from moving right up
to and staying at full employment. No investment would be necessary.

Although it is improbable, in the short run at least, that the propensity to consume would increase sufficiently to move the economy substantially toward full employment, it might increase sufficiently to help
reduce the amount of investment necessary to obtain a higher level of
employment. This is shown in Figure 14-4 on page 276. The same investment that gives equilibrium at point *b* could result in equilibrium at
point *c* if the propensity to consume were to increase sufficiently.

The amount of investment shown at point *b* fills the gap between
output and consumption, as measured on the line *CC'*. Whereas this
amount of investment is insufficient to fill the gap between output and
consumption at point *c*, as measured by line *CC'*, it will fill the gap

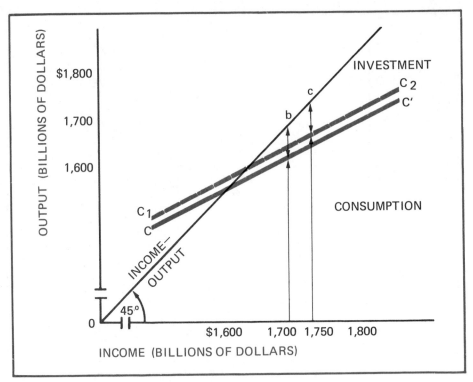

Figure 14-4   **HIGHER CONSUMPTION RESULTS IN A HIGHER LEVEL OF OUTPUT AND INCOME**

between output and consumption at point $c$, as measured on the new consumption line $C_1C_2$. In this case, the higher level of consumption makes it possible to obtain a higher level of output, income, and employment without increasing investment.

The increased effective demand necessary to move to a higher level of employment need not come from one source; that is, either investment or consumption alone. It could very well, and often does, come from a combination of the two forces. In fact, it would be easier to attain a higher level of employment if investment and consumption increased simultaneously. On the other hand, it is possible to have the advantages of an increase in one factor offset by a decrease in the other. This, however, is improbable. If investment increases, income will increase, and in turn consumption should increase. If consumption increases, effective demand will increase, which in turn will cause firms generally to increase rather than curtail investment. Likewise, they generally will move downward together.

If the economy were in equilibrium at less than full employment and it were desirable to move to a higher level of employment, every attempt should be made to increase the level of economic activity. According to the income-expenditure theory, the economy will not move automatically to a high level, or full-employment position, as the classicalists maintained. According to the classical approach, employers and employees merely had to wait for the competitive factors to make the adjustments necessary to move the economy to a full-employment position. In the absence of monopolistic restraints, labor union interference, and government intervention, it was only a matter of time before the economy would be back in equilibrium at full employment. According to the income-expenditure approach, however, the competitive system is not as free as the classicalists anticipated, and laissez-faire not as prevalent as they assumed. Therefore, there may be no automatic adjustment to the full-employment level. Rather than let the economy hover in a lull of unemployment and uncertainty, the income-expenditure analysis suggests that the economy can be stimulated to move to a better position by the use of various measures designed to increase the level of investment and consumption.

**Government Spending**    Rather than permit the economy to drift in a sea of chronic unemployment, many advocates of the income-expenditure analysis, and particularly Keynes, suggest that government intervention be used to bolster the economy when the necessary effective demand for a high level of employment is not forthcoming from consumption and private investment. Thus, whenever consumption and private investment are insufficient or fail to respond to measures designed to raise them to give us a satisfactory level of employment, the income-expenditure analysis points out that government spending may be used as a means of bolstering the economy. To reach any given level of output and employment, government spending can be used to absorb the difference between production and total effective demand. This means that the total effective demand of private enterprises can be supplemented by the effective demand of government. Therefore, in the economy we have three forces making up the total effective demand, with the third force — government spending — acting as a stabilizer of the economy.

The use of government spending in this way is revealed in Figure 14-5 on page 278. It shows that the normal equilibrium position is at point *b* where output is equal to $1,700 billion. If the economy were to move up to the full-employment level, point *c*, without increasing either investment or consumption, it could not stay at that level because the total effective demand, composed of consumption and private investment, would be less than total output. Investment would be less than savings, spending less than income, and effective demand less than output; therefore, the economy would slide back to equilibrium with unemployment, point *b*. However, if government spending were injected to fill the gap between total output and total effective demand resulting from consumption and private investment at point *c*, the total investment, including government spending, would equal savings. As a result, total spending

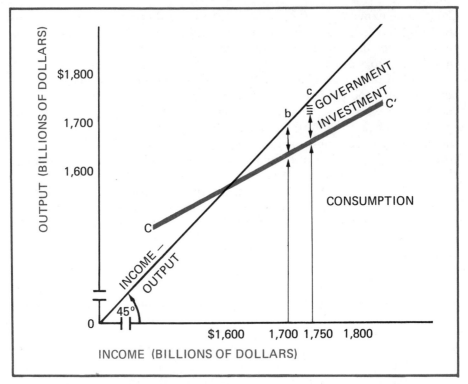

Figure 14-5    **GOVERNMENT SPENDING RESULTS IN A HIGHER LEVEL OF OUTPUT AND INCOME**

would equal total income and total effective demand, including government, would equal output. In such a case, all the goods and the services produced would be moved off the market and there would be equilibrium at the higher level of output, income, and employment.

It was originally thought that government spending would increase business activity and encourage consumption and private investment to such an extent that the stimulus of government spending could be removed. This process is known as *pump priming*. It implies that all it takes is a bit of government spending to increase and maintain the flow of goods and services at a higher level.

Although the economy may respond to the stimulus of government spending, there is no assurance that income and consumption will continue at their higher levels when the government spending is removed. As a result, government spending may need to be used for a considerable period of time before the economy makes the proper adjustment to continue at a higher level of consumption and private investment without the assistance of government spending. This sustained process of government spending is part of what is called *compensatory spending*. It implies that government spending must be sufficient to make up, or compensate, for the lack of adequate consumption and investment during periods of unemployment.

In either case, when using government spending to bolster the economy, caution must be exercised in the matter of securing the funds that the government spends. The government must raise the funds in such a manner that it does not result in a reduction of consumption or private investment. Government spending should be in a direction and a manner that would in no way compete with or discourage consumption and private investment. Furthermore, all other efforts to raise effective demand should be exhausted before resorting to government spending. According to the income-expenditure approach, government spending can be used as a strong tool for stabilizing the economy, increasing spending as needed, and also decreasing it when feasible. It suggests the use of government spending to offset undesirable fluctuations in the level of investment. This, of course, is contrary to the classical tradition of laissez-faire.

In general, then, the income-expenditure analysis disagrees with the classical viewpoint that the normal equilibrium position for the economy is that of full employment. The income-expenditure theory holds that it is just as easy to have equilibrium in the economy at less than full employment. Proponents of the income-expenditure analysis usually advocate adopting means to bolster the economy when it is at less than full employment, whereas the classicalists would rely on the automatic adjusters supposedly inherent in the free enterprise, laissez-faire economy to make any corrections needed in the level of business activity.

### Income-Expenditure Analysis and Business Fluctuations

Relating the income-output analysis to business cycles, it can be observed that as output, income, and employment fluctuate with changes in investment, the level of economic activity will fluctuate between two extremes. It will not fall below the point where the consumption function is equal to output (at least not for long) because below that point the effective demand for consumption alone exceeds the total output. Since effective demand is greater than output, entrepreneurs will be induced to increase production and employment to satisfy the excessive demand at this point. Sometimes it is difficult to realize that we can consume more than we produce. This can occur, however, when we supply goods out of inventory to such an extent that we have a net decrease in inventory at the same time that we are consuming all of our current production. This occurred in the 1974–1975 recession when businesspeople were trying to deplete their inventories. Another way we can consume more than we produce is through failure to replace our worn-out machinery and equipment. This results in a net disinvestment in the economy.

At the other extreme, the real level of economic activity cannot move upward beyond the full-employment stage. Increased consumption, investment, or government spending at this stage can lead only to higher

prices. There may be an increase in the monetary value of the total output brought about by the inflation in the economy, but there will be very
little if any increase in the absolute output of goods and services. Therefore, the economy fluctuates between point *x*, the point where consumption is equal to output, and point *c*, full employment, as shown in Figure
14-6. It does not necessarily fluctuate from one extreme to another. It
may move back and forth between various intermediary points. Fluctuations are caused primarily by variations in investment, but they may also
result from changes in consumption. Government spending may be used
to offset undesirable fluctuations in investment that result in a low level
of employment.

### The Inflationary Problem

If investment, consumption, or government spending continues to increase once the economy has reached the full-employment level, inflation
will set in. In such an event, measures should be used to discourage further consumption and investment, since such a situation will lead to still
higher prices as investors and consumers bid for the use of the limited

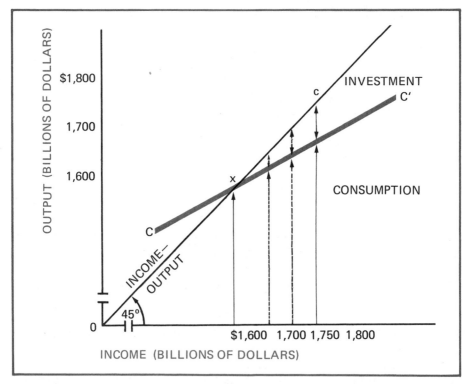

Figure 14-6    **LEVEL OF ECONOMIC ACTIVITY FLUCTUATES BETWEEN *X* AND
C ACCORDING TO AMOUNT OF INVESTMENT**

manpower, resources, and productive capacity. To combat these inflationary tendencies, government spending can be decreased, taxes increased, interest rates pushed upward, and credit restrained. Strong inflationary tendencies seldom occur in the absence of large government
outlays. Therefore, the first order of anti-inflationary policy would seem
to be that of reducing government spending. The large government outlay, however, often occurs during wartime or emergency periods. Under
such circumstances it would be rather unwise to win the battle against
inflation by reducing government spending but to lose the fight against
the enemy because of the lack of war materials. Thus, during wartime
and emergency periods when larger government outlays for armaments
are necessary, inflation has to be combated by reducing consumption and
private investment on nonwar commodities. Devices to accomplish this
include such programs as controlled material plans, wage and price controls, rationing, taxation, and credit restraints.

This situation is demonstrated in Figure 14-7, where it can be seen
that because of government spending the total effective demand at point
$c$ is greater than total output. Normally there would be an increase in

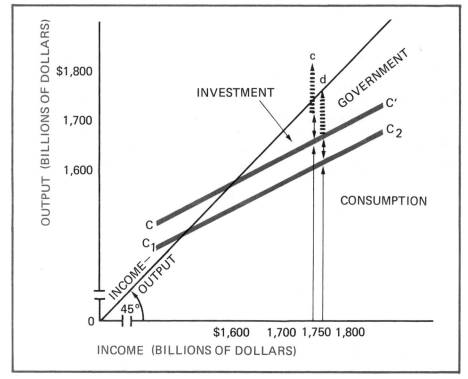

Figure 14-7    **REDUCTION OF INVESTMENT AND CONSUMPTION NECESSARY
TO ALLOW FOR INCREASE IN GOVERNMENT SPENDING IN A
FULL-EMPLOYMENT ECONOMY**

output in response to this demand but, because of the full-employment status of the economy, it is extremely difficult to increase output. As a result of competitive bidding, prices move upward. The problem, then, is to reduce either consumption or private investment, or both, to allow a sufficient gap between total effective demand for consumption plus private investment and output to permit the necessary amount of government spending without having total effective demand, including government, exceed total production. This could be accomplished if consumption were reduced to line $C_1 C_2$ and investment reduced as designated at point $d$ in Figure 14-7.

In Figure 14-7, point $d$ is set a little apart from point $c$ for clarity. Actually, it should be superimposed on point $c$.

## INCOME-EXPENDITURE ANALYSIS RESTATED

In the income-expenditure analysis, as output increases, income increases. As income increases, consumption increases. Consumption, however, increases at a lesser rate. Since the marginal propensity to save increases as income increases, a larger and larger amount of investment is needed to fill the gap between income and spending for consumption if all the goods produced are to be moved off the market. The economy, of course, comes into equilibrium at a point where investment is equal to saving. At such a position spending on investment will make up for the difference between consumption and output. This means that total spending will equal total income, effective demand will equal output, and all the goods will be moved off the market.

From another point of view, employment will fluctuate with investment. It may fluctuate between a low level of economic activity and the full-employment level, depending on the amount of investment. Thus, investment becomes the important determinant of output, income, and employment. Since the consumption function is relatively stable in the short run, the level of employment cannot be increased without an increase in investment. The higher the level of consumption, however, the less the investment required to obtain any given level of employment. If the economy becomes stabilized at any undesirable level of employment because of inadequate investment, the adoption of monetary, fiscal, and other measures designed to encourage consumption and investment to raise the level of income and output are recommended. If the attempt to raise the level of effective demand through consumption and private investment is unsuccessful, the use of government spending can be utilized to supplement the inadequate investment and consumption to bring the economy to a higher level of employment.

### Purpose of Theory

The ultimate purpose of the income-expenditure theory is to explain what determines the level of employment — whether full employment, widespread unemployment, or some level in between — and to show the cause of unemployment. It seeks a practical explanation to the operation of the economic system, in the hope of discovering those variables that cause changes in the level of economic activity. Once the variables are found, pressure can then be applied on them to move the economy to a more favorable position. To solve the problem of unemployment, the theory seeks those variables that could be managed or controlled within the sphere of the capitalistic system. Although many of the advocates of the income-expenditure analysis are not averse to using government action whenever effective demand is such that it fails to support a high level of employment, it should be emphasized that other measures should be utilized before resorting to government intervention to bolster the economy.

### Marginal Efficiency of Capital and Rate of Interest

According to the income-expenditure analysis, output, employment, and income depend on effective demand, which is determined by the amount of consumption and investment. Consumption is determined by the size of income and the propensity to consume out of the given level of income. If the propensity to consume remains stable, total effective demand and, therefore, total output and employment will be determined by the amount of investment. An increase in investment will increase employment, and employment will probably not increase except through increased investment.

Investment is dependent upon the *marginal efficiency of capital* (MEC) and the rate of interest (RI). The marginal efficiency of capital is the expected rate of return on investment, or in other words, the expected profit from a given investment. If the marginal efficiency of capital is high compared to the rate of interest, businesspeople will borrow and invest. If it is low compared to the rate of interest, however, they will not be inclined to invest and may even disinvest. The marginal efficiency of capital, according to the income-expenditure analysis, is the active factor in determining whether businesspeople are going to borrow and invest. The rate of interest is a passive factor. Businesspeople do not borrow just because the interest rate is low; they borrow and invest because of profit expectations. A sizable and favorable gap between the marginal efficiency of capital and the interest rate will bring about an increase in the level of economic activity. Since the marginal efficiency of capital is based on profit expectation, it is to some degree psychological and dependent on the attitude and outlook of the business community. It will be based on anticipated sales and prices. The marginal efficiency of capital will be determined by the expectation of profits compared to the replacement cost of capital assets. In short, it is a measure of the net rate of return on investment. The marginal efficiency of capital can be enhanced by an increase in productivity, sales, or prices, or by a decrease in the costs of production. By its very nature, the marginal efficiency of capital is dynamic and subject to sharp fluctuation arising primarily out of changes in prices and sales. Thus, it can easily account for variations of investment.

Furthermore, it is the relationship between the marginal efficiency of capital and the rate of interest that causes expansion, equilibrium, or contraction in the economy. Whenever the marginal efficiency of capital is greater than the rate of interest, it will bring about expansion in business activity. As expansion proceeds, however, the marginal efficiency of capital eventually declines when sales begin to slacken and the price level stabilizes or begins to decline. In the process of expansion, the increased demand for money and the pressure on bank reserves tend to force the rate of interest upward. The decline in the marginal efficiency of capital and the rise in the rate of interest finally bring the two into balance. At this point, there is no further incentive for businesspeople to borrow and invest. This point may or may not correspond with the point of full employment. If it does not correspond to full employment, or a high level of employment at least, monetary measures can be used in an attempt to keep the rate of interest below the marginal efficiency of capital until a high level of employment is reached.

On the other hand, if the marginal efficiency of capital should become less than the rate of interest, contraction would commence in the level of economic activity. There would be no point in businesspeople borrowing to invest in replacement or new productive facilities only to lose money. As a result, there will be a decrease of investment in the economy and consequently a decrease in effective demand. In turn, production, employment, and income will further decline. In fact, according to the income-expenditure theory, depression is a period in which the rate of interest exceeds the marginal efficiency of capital. As the contraction proceeds, the rate of interest will begin to decline and eventually the marginal efficiency of capital will pick up after the economy has experienced a depression. When they come into balance again, the economy will be in equilibrium.

Thus, whenever MEC>RI, forces come into play to bring about an increase in the level of economic activity. As the expansion takes place, forces will bring them into balance. Whenever MEC=RI, there will be a stable flow of economic activity. But whenever MEC<RI, forces will contract the level of economic activity. As the contraction takes place, forces will bring them into balance again. In this process, the marginal efficiency of capital is the more important and active factor. It is easier to make artificial adjustments in the rate of interest, however, than it is in the marginal efficiency of capital when it is desired to bolster the economy through governmental policies.

### Determinants of the Rate of Interest

Because of the possibility of manipulating the interest rate to improve the level of employment or as a means of combating inflation, it is important to know its determinants. According to the income-expenditure analysis, the rate of interest is dependent upon the strength of *liquidity preference* compared to the quantity of money in the economy. Liquidity preference is the desire to hold assets in the form of cash. In short, firms and individuals often desire to hold money for the sake of holding money. Liquidity preference may be desired for any one of three reasons: (1) the transactions motive, (2) the precautionary motive, and (3) the speculative motive.

**Transactions Motive**   Money is saved to carry out future monetary transactions. Many people, for example, save to accumulate sufficient funds for a down payment on a home or an automobile; firms save to buy machinery and equipment. Even those who are paid once a month, like college professors, save for future transactions.

**Precautionary Motive**   Individuals and firms save for the proverbial rainy day. Individuals like to save to have funds for emergencies, in case they become unemployed, and for their old age. Firms likewise desire to have reserves for various contingencies that may arise. This motive is very substantial when one considers the effects of Social Security funds, OASDHI and unemployment compensation funds, industrial pension funds, guaranteed annual wage funds, private insurance policies, and the like.

**Speculative Motive**   Individuals and firms hold money to take advantage of movements in the price level. Individuals and firms will postpone purchases if they think that the price level, or the price of the particular commodities or services they intend to buy, is going to decline in the immediate or near future. Investors will not purchase stocks or bonds if they expect prices to go down or the interest rate to rise. This type of liquidity preference is important in relation to the rate of interest. When it is anticipated that business activity is going to be good, the demand for money for speculative purposes will be great and the interest rate will rise. When the demand for speculative funds decreases, the interest rate will fall. The speculative motive is more dynamic and subject to sharper changes than either the transactions or precautionary motives and has a substantial effect on the rate of interest.

The liquidity preference will vary with individuals and firms. In general, however, it will fall with a rise in prices and increase when prices are declining. The stronger the liquidity preference, the more one has to pay to induce those with the funds to part with their liquidity. Therefore, the rate of interest will vary directly with liquidity preference.

The other factor affecting the rate of interest is the amount of money existing in the economy. The greater the amount of money compared to liquidity preference, the lower the interest rate. To look at it another way, if individuals and firms desire to hold a certain amount of liquid funds and the money supply is increased, it will automatically reduce the relative liquidity preference and lower the rate of interest. If the quantity of money is decreased, the relative liquidity preference will increase and the rate of interest will rise.

## EVALUATIONS OF THE INCOME-EXPENDITURE ANALYSIS

There are many criticisms of the income-expenditure analysis. Some of them are major, but most of them are minor insofar as they affect its use as a tool of economic analysis. Although we will evaluate only a few of the important criticisms here, a close inspection of the income-expenditure analysis and its related criticisms and shortcomings would prove fruitful.

### Socialistic

It is often claimed that policies based upon the income-expenditure approach tend to be socialistic or that they will lead to government domination of the economy. These opponents claim that as income increases, the gap between output and consumption becomes larger. Since investment may be insufficient to fill the gap between consumption and output, government spending will be used to make up for the inability of private investment to fill this gap. As the economy expands, according to the critics, it will be more difficult for private investment to fill the larger and larger gap. They conclude, therefore, that increasing amounts of government spending will be required, and that a point will be reached eventually at which government spending will become an unduly large part of the total spending in the economy. They envision something similar to that shown in Figure 14-8.

This figure shows a full-employment economy at the $1,800 billion level (point $a$). At this point only a moderate amount of government spending is used to maintain full employment. As the ability of the economy to produce increases to point $b$ or $c$, it shows a larger amount of government spending required to maintain full employment. There are three major faults with this criticism: (1) It does not allow for a higher amount of investment to maintain the higher level of economic activity. In fact, as shown, the absolute amount of investment has remained stable, which means the ratio of investment to output has decreased. (2) It does not allow for any long-run change in the propensity to consume. (3) It does not allow for an increase in population. If the expansion in the economy results from an increase in population, there probably will not be a decline in the propensity to consume as shown in Figure 14-8. In the long run it is quite feasible that the consumption function for the economy will increase. Furthermore, the absolute amount of investment no doubt will have to increase to support a higher level of economic activity. Therefore, consumption and investment may change, as indicated in Figure 14-9 on page 288.

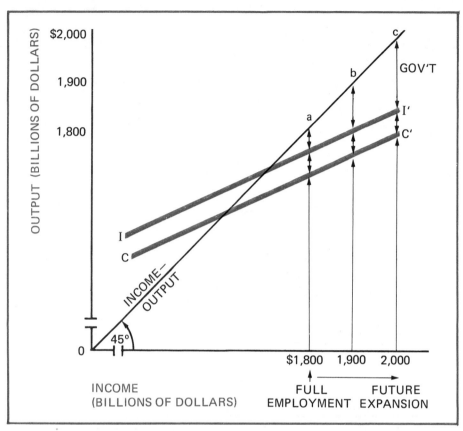

Figure 14-8    **GOVERNMENT SPENDING BECOMING AN EVER LARGER PART OF TOTAL SPENDING**

Here it can be seen that a long-run increase in consumption from $CC'$ to $C_1C_2$ and the increase in total investment will make it possible to maintain a higher level of employment without a substantial increase in government spending. For example, in Figure 14-9 no government spending would be required to stabilize the economy at point $a$. In addition, less government spending would be required in Figure 14-9 than in Figure 14-8 at points $b$ and $c$.

Many people consider the income-expenditure analysis socialistic in character. It might be noted, however, that Keynes, its leading proponent, was endeavoring to find a substitute for socialism or communism. He thought it would be better to improve the free enterprise, capitalistic system than it would be to substitute some collective form of economy. One of the vulnerable aspects of capitalism is its recurring periods of unemployment. If these became frequent, serious, and prolonged, people would be encouraged to look for a change in the economic system as a possible remedy. Keynes implied that it would be better to use the

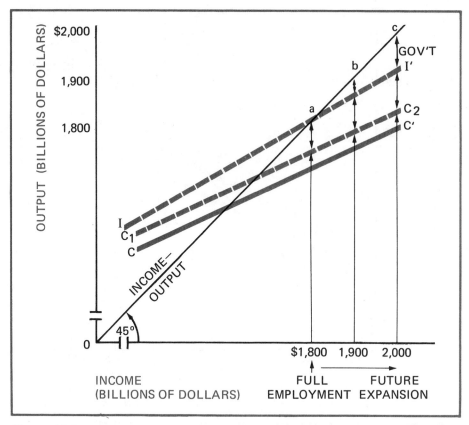

Figure 14-9   **CHANGING LEVELS OF CONSUMPTION AND INVESTMENT LEAD TO LESSER INCREASES IN GOVERNMENT SPENDING**

means available, including government intervention, to raise the level of employment rather than change the form of the economy.

Although it is rather evident that the income-expenditure analysis is not socialistic in nature and that most of its advocates are interested in preserving the free enterprise, capitalistic system, it cannot be denied that income-expenditure economics is a move away from the concept of laissez-faire and toward government intervention. Government action is often suggested when necessary to alleviate unemployment. Whereas the rugged individualist may feel that such government intervention is an infringement upon economic freedom, collectivists suggest government intervention to a much greater degree and of a different nature. We should avoid either of these extremes. What is needed are measures that can operate within the structure of the free enterprise system to promote a high level of employment.

Certain income-expenditure analysts are criticized for their lack of faith in the ability of the private economy to maintain a high level of employment. But a decade of the most serious depression known to the world in the 1930s made pessimists out of some of the sturdiest of capitalistic supporters. More recently the reoccurrence of recessions in the 1970s has dampened the enthusiasm of some regarding the attainment of our goals of full employment and price stability. On the other hand, the fact that free enterprise capitalism has proven in the past that it can establish records of prosperity and employment without large-scale deficit spending should not render the income-expenditure analysis invalid. The fact that an economist is incorrect in an opinion about the future does not invalidate the basic principles of economics, any more than the fact that a meteorologist is wrong in a weather forecast invalidates the laws of physics. Even when the economy is enjoying high levels of prosperity and employment, the income-expenditure analysis can still be used to show that a high level of consumption and investment makes it unnecessary for deficit spending by the government during such periods. Furthermore, the income-expenditure analysis can be applied to the study of inflation.

### Premature Use of Government Intervention

Many proponents of the income-expenditure analysis might be validly critized for their haste in suggesting the use of deficit spending. It seems that more attention might be given to the encouragement of consumption and private investment before resorting to deficit spending. More emphasis might be given to business research, the development of new products, cost-reduction measures, more advertising, improved methods of distribution, new forms of energy, and probably many unexplored measures that could encourage consumption and investment. Furthermore, greater stress could be placed on the use of indirect measures to raise the level of employment.

The impact of various measures, such as tax reductions, public works spending, worker retraining programs, the extension and increase of unemployment compensation, poverty programs, regional economic development, deficit budgets, and other expansionary measures as a means of reducing nagging unemployment and stimulating economic growth is still subject to analysis and evaluation.

### What About Today's Problems?

According to the income-expenditure analysis the primary determinant of economic activity is effective demand. Fluctuations in effective demand, for whatever reason, cause production and employment to increase or decrease and prices to rise or fall. Having been developed in an era of abundance of labor and resources, the income-expenditure analysis assumed that supply would always be forthcoming in response to an increase in effective demand. Today, however, production, employment, and prices are being affected increasingly by shortages of materials,

energy crises, international financial manipulations, and a general depletion of the world's natural resources. Consequently, it can no longer be
assumed that effective demand is the sole, or even in some cases the primary, determinant of economic activity.

Today the defense budget is a larger and more permanent portion of
total effective demand. As a result, military spending, as well as other
more general government spending, has to be reckoned with in analyzing
the determinants of economic activity.

On still another score, the income-expenditure analysis gives the
tools to analyze the economy in terms of recession, depression, and full
employment. It explains demand-pull inflation, but it does not explain
cost-push, structural, or social inflation. Moreover, it does not give us an
effective remedy for the stagflation, or the combination of stagnation and
inflation, associated with the 1970s. For analyses or answers to these current problems, we often have to look elsewhere.

### SUMMARY

The relationship of the various elements of the income-expenditure
theory can be summarized as follows:

1. Output, income, and employment depend on effective demand.
2. Effective demand is made up of consumption, investment, and government spending.
3. Consumption depends on the size of income and the propensity to
   consume.
4. The propensity to consume is relatively stable; therefore, assuming government spending to have a neutral effect, changes in employment will
   result primarily from changes in investment.
5. Investment is determined by the marginal efficiency of capital compared
   to the rate of interest.
6. The marginal efficiency of capital is dependent upon profit expectation
   compared to the cost of capital assets.
7. The rate of interest depends upon liquidity preference compared to the
   quantity of money.
8. Liquidity preference depends on the strength of the transactions, precautionary, and speculative motives for saving.
9. In the absence of sufficient consumption and investment, government
   spending can be used to influence the level of output, income, and
   employment.

The relationships are outlined schematically on page 291. From this
outline, one can easily determine what general effect a change in any of
the various factors of the economy will have on the level of economic
activity. For example, other things remaining the same, an increase in
the size of income will result in higher consumption, increase the effective demand, and thereby increase the level of economic activity. A decrease in the propensity to consume, on the other hand, will result in

## Table 14-1  OUTLINE OF THE INCOME-EXPENDITURE ANALYSIS

| | | | Characteristics |
|---|---|---|---|
| CONSUMPTION | Propensity to consume | Average propensity to consume | Basic national income where C=Y. |
| | | Marginal propensity to consume | As income increases, consumption increases but by less than income. |
| | Size of income | | An increase in investment (or gov't) causes a multiple increase in income. |
| INVESTMENT | Rate of interest | Liquidity preference { Transactions, precautionary, & speculative motives | Quantity of money can be controlled by monetary authority. |
| | | Quantity of money | |
| | Marginal efficiency of capital | Profit expectations | Profits unstable influenced by stock market, business confidence, etc. |
| | | Cost of assets | MEC fluctuates in short run. Affects business cycles. |
| GOVERNMENT | State & local | Regular spending { Balanced, surplus, or deficit budget | Effect of government spending depends on type of budget and source of revenue. |
| | Federal | Emergency spending { Tax, borrow, or print money | |

Effective Demand → PRODUCTION EMPLOYMENT INCOME PRICES

Source: Adapted from *The Economics of John Maynard Keynes* by Dudley Dillard, by permission of Prentice-Hall, Inc., Englewood Cliffs, New Jersey.

decreased employment if not offset by other changes. An increase in the quantity of money will reduce the rate of interest; this, in turn, will increase investment. An increase in effective demand will result and, therefore, a boost in output, employment, and income. A reduction in prices will lower profit expectations. This reduces the marginal efficiency of capital, which in turn reduces investment and brings about a decrease in production and employment.

Not only is the outline an aid in analyzing the effects of changes in the various forces in the economy, but it is also useful for the purpose of determining the appropriate measures necessary to improve the level of economic activity, to combat inflation, or even to handle the problems of stagflation. For example, if the economy is in equilibrium at less than full employment, it can be visualized easily that a higher investment will result from lowering the interest rate, and that a lower interest rate can be obtained by increasing the quantity of money. Thus, a liberalization of the money supply can be helpful in raising the level of employment. On the other hand, a decrease in the money supply can be effective in combating inflation. Employment may also be increased with higher consumption. Therefore, measures designed to increase the propensity to consume, such as tax reductions, liberal consumer credit, and improved products will tend to increase the level of production and employment.

This outline can be used as a means of analyzing the effect of governmental monetary, fiscal, and psychological policies on the level of economic activity. Furthermore, it points up the importance of the three strategic variables: the propensity to consume, the marginal efficiency of capital, and the rate of interest. As a result of its many advantages, it would seem worthwhile to keep this outline in mind as a handy reference for analyzing the effect of various factors on the general level of economic activity.

The income-expenditure analysis has been criticized because many of the policies developed therefrom require government action. Although some economists suggest heavy government intervention, many of our policymakers have been against any undue government interference in the economy.

The income-expenditure analysis has also been criticized because it is said that in the long run it will require a larger and larger amount of government spending. This argument, however, neglects the need for increased investment in an expanding economy, it does not allow for a long-range increase in the propensity to consume, and it does not take into consideration an increase in the population.

Moreover, the income-expenditure analysis, having been developed in the 1930s, does not provide the framework to analyze and answer many of the current issues and problems of today's economy.

Now that we have a grasp of the fundamental principles of the income-expenditure analysis, we can better understand the expansionary and anti-inflationary measures and policies suggested in subsequent chapters. In the interim, we now turn to the issue of full employment.

## DISCUSSION QUESTIONS

1. What is your opinion of the classical assumption of full employment as the normal equilibrium level for the economy?

2. Explain what is meant by the statement, "supply creates its own demand."

3. What does the income-expenditure analysis say is the cause of business cycles?

4. Empirical data that have been gathered for recent years indicate that with rising income the marginal propensity to consume may not decline as much as Keynes and others assumed. If this is true, what happens to the validity of the income-expenditure approach as a tool of analysis?

5. How is it possible to have the consumption function relatively stable but still have different amounts of consumption and different propensities to consume along the consumption function line?

6. Why does a high level of consumption make it easier to maintain a high level of employment?

7. Why is the consumption function not necessarily stable in the long run? What factors may cause it to change?

8. Do you agree that government spending should be used to bolster the level of business activity whenever consumption and investment are insufficient to provide a high level of employment? Why or why not?

9. Whenever investment is greater than savings and the economy expands, exactly what is it that causes investment and savings to come into balance?

10. What measures has the government taken in recent years to manipulate the various factors of the income-expenditure analysis to bolster the U.S. level of economic activity?

## SUGGESTED READINGS

Ackley, Gardner. *Macroeconomic Theory*. New York: Macmillan Publishing Co., Inc., 1961.

"Can Capitalism Survive?" *Time* (July 14, 1975).

Chandler, Lester V. *America's Greatest Depression, 1929–1941*. New York: Harper & Row Publishers, 1970.

Dillard, Dudley. *The Economics of John Maynard Keynes*. New York: Prentice-Hall, Inc., 1948.

Francis, Darryl R. *Public Policy for a Free Economy*. St. Louis: Washington University Center for the Study of American Business, June, 1975.

Galbraith, John Kenneth. *Economics and Public Purpose*. Boston: Houghton Mifflin Company, 1974.

Hansen, Alvin. *A Guide to Keynes*. New York: McGraw-Hill Book Company, Inc., 1953.

Hazlitt, Henry. *The Critics of Keynesian Economics*. Princeton, N.J.: D. Van Nostrand Company, 1960.

Hicks, John. *The Crisis in Keynesian Economics*. New York: Basic Books, Inc., Publishers, 1975.

Hitch, Charles J., and Roland N. McKean. *The Economics of Defense in the Nuclear Age*. Cambridge, Mass.: Harvard University Press, copyright 1960, by The Rand Corporation.

Keynes, John Maynard. *The General Theory of Employment, Interest, and Money*. London: Collier MacMillan Publishers, 1951.

Klein, Lawrence R. *The Keynesian Revolution*. New York: Macmillan Publishing Co., Inc., 1966.

Kurihara, Kenneth K. *Introduction to Keynesian Dynamics*. New York: Columbia University Press, 1956.

———————. *National Income and Economic Growth*. Chicago: Rand McNally & Company, 1961.

Leijonhufvud, Axel. *On Keynesian Economics and the Economics of Keynes*. New York: Oxford University Press, 1968.

Lekachman, Robert. *The Age of Keynes*. New York: Random House, Inc., 1966.

Marshall, Natalie. *Keynes: Updated or Outdated?* Lexington, Mass.: D. C. Heath & Company, 1970.

"The New Economic Braintrusters in Congress." *Business Week* (May 5, 1975).

"New Keynesians Have a New Prescription." *Business Week* (May 12, 1975).

Nickson, Jack W., Jr. *Economics and Social Choice*, 2d ed. New York: McGraw-Hill Book Company, Inc., 1974.

"Recession Is Capitalism As Usual." *The New York Times Magazine* (April 27, 1975).

Tobin, James. *The New Economics – One Decade Older*. Princeton, New Jersey: Princeton University Press, 1974.

# 15 THE MEANING OF FULL EMPLOYMENT

## THE LABOR FORCE

A definite relationship exists between the level of employment and the size of the GNP. When the real GNP decreases, unemployment usually increases. In fact, as we shall see, unemployment may develop even when the GNP remains constant or increases moderately over any extended period of time. Unemployment is detrimental to the economy because it decreases incomes. This in turn reduces consumer spending, which further decreases demand and eventually the GNP.

Previously in referring to full employment we were considering full employment of manpower, resources, and productive capacity. In this chapter, however, we are concerned primarily with employed and unemployed manpower. In this sense, unemployment causes individual hardship to the workers and their families. From Table 15-1, page 296, it can be seen that we have had periods of full employment and periods of widespread unemployment. As the years pass, the size of the population will increase and the labor force will grow. This will make the problem of maintaining full employment more complex.

Customarily, between 40 and 45 percent of our total population are members of the labor force. This seems to be the norm for industrial nations throughout the world. However, the labor force is limited by definition. Many individuals who work just as much as do those in the labor force are excluded because of the nature of their work or because they receive no remuneration for it.

### Size and Composition of the Labor Force

To understand the problem of maintaining full employment, let us look more closely at our labor force and our population. In 1974 we had a total population of 212.2 million. Of this total, 150.8 million were in the category of noninstitutional population, that is, all persons 16 years of age or older, including members of the armed forces but excluding persons in institutions.

Table 15-1    **POPULATION, TOTAL LABOR FORCE, AND UNEMPLOYMENT, 1930–1974**
(Millions of Dollars)

| (1) Year | (2) Total Population | (3) Total Labor Force | (4) Unemployment |
|---|---|---|---|
| 1930 | 123.1 | 50.1 | 4.3 |
| 1935 | 127.3 | 53.1 | 10.6 |
| 1940 | 132.6 | 56.2 | 8.1 |
| 1945 | 140.5 | 65.3 | 1.0 |
| 1950 | 152.3 | 63.9 | 3.3 |
| 1955 | 165.9 | 68.1 | 2.9 |
| 1960 | 180.7 | 72.1 | 3.8 |
| 1965 | 194.6 | 77.2 | 3.4 |
| 1970 | 204.8 | 85.9 | 4.1 |
| 1974 | 212.2 | 93.2 | 5.1 |

Source: *Statistical Abstract of the United States*, 1974, and *Employment and Earnings* (January, 1975).

**Total Labor Force**    In 1974, of the noninstitutional population, 93.2 million were in the total labor force. The *total labor force* is made up of all those in the noninstitutional population who are working or are seeking work. Thus, it includes the unemployed as well as the employed. Furthermore, it includes proprietors, the self-employed, and members of the armed forces. However, the labor force excludes all persons engaged in incidental unpaid family work (less than 15 hours) and all persons engaged exclusively in housework in their home or attending school. Thus, students as such are not members of the labor force. If they work or look for work during the summer vacation period, however, they become members of the labor force. Likewise, when they graduate, they generally become members of the labor force.

**Civilian Labor Force**    If we subtract the number of persons in the armed forces from the total labor force, the remainder is the civilian labor force. By definition the *civilian labor force* consists of "all persons in the total labor force except members of the armed services." Since 2.2 million persons were in the armed services in 1974, the civilian labor force was 91.0 million, and of this total, 5.1 million, or 5.6 percent were unemployed. The *unemployed labor force* includes all persons in the labor force seeking work, including those who are currently engaged in emergency relief work. A breakdown of the population and the labor force is shown in Table 15-2.

The *employed civilian labor force* is the difference between the civilian labor force and the unemployed. Technically, it includes all employed workers, including persons who did not work at all during the census week because of illness, bad weather, vacation, or labor disputes, but

Table 15-2    **POPULATION AND LABOR FORCE, 1974**

|  | | Millions |
| --- | --- | --- |
| Total population | | 212.2 |
| Noninstitutional population | | 150.8 |
| Total labor force | | 93.2 |
| Armed forces | | 2.2 |
| Total civilian labor force | | 91.0 |
| Unemployed labor force | | 5.1 |
| Employed civilian labor force | | 85.9 |
| Agricultural employment | | 3.5 |
| Nonagricultural employment | | 82.4 |
| Persons not in the labor force | | 57.6 |
|     Keeping house | 35.2 | |
|     In school | 9.1 | |
|     Unable to work | 2.9 | |
|     Others | 10.4 | |

Source: *Statistical Abstract of the United States*, 1974, and *Employment and Earnings* (January, 1975).

who had a job or business. It includes part-time as well as full-time employment. In 1974 the number of employed was 85.9 million, and of this total 3.5 million were engaged in agricultural work while 82.4 million were in nonagricultural employment.

There were 57.6 million persons in the noninstitutional population who were not in the total labor force. It is interesting to keep in mind that 35.2 million of this group were keeping house. Although the housekeeper often puts in a harder day than the breadwinner of the house, the housekeeper is not included in the labor force. Another 9.1 million of those not in the labor force were in school: high school, college, or elsewhere. Nearly 3 million people were unable to work. The remainder, 10.4 million, was composed of those who are retired, individuals who do not want to work, and those who do not have to work.

**Source of Employment**    The bulk of the labor force is engaged in nonagricultural employment. The largest portion, 19.2 million, is engaged in manufacturing. The second largest category, which is trade, has 17.6 million, and government employment is third with 14.8 million workers. A breakdown of the nonagricultural employment is shown in Table 15-3 on page 298.

### Trends in the Labor Force

Our labor force has definite characteristics, but these same characteristics change as time progresses. Some of the most pronounced trends that have been developing in the labor force in recent decades are included in the following sections.

Table 15-3    **EMPLOYMENT IN NONAGRICULTURAL ESTABLISHMENTS BY INDUSTRY DIVISION, 1974**

| Industry Division | Millions |
|---|---|
| Nonagricultural employment[1] | 78.5 |
| Manufacturing | 19.2 |
| Mining | .7 |
| Contract construction | 3.7 |
| Transportation, communication, and public utilities | 4.7 |
| Trade — wholesale and retail | 17.6 |
| Finance, insurance, and real estate | 4.2 |
| Services | 13.7 |
| Government — federal, state, and local | 14.8 |

Source: *Employment and Earnings* (January, 1975).

[1]Excludes proprietors, the self-employed, and domestic servants. The total derived from this is not comparable with estimates of nonagricultural employment of the civilian labor force reported in Table 15-2, which includes proprietors, the self-employed, and domestic servants; which counts persons as employed when they are not at work because of industrial disputes; and which is based on an enumeration of population, whereas the estimates in this table are based on reports from employing establishments.

**Teenage Employment**    The percentage of teenage employment has decreased. At present more than 50 percent of the persons in the 18–19 age group are in school compared with 35 percent in 1950. Some of the decline in teenage employment is the result of federal and state legislation that restricts the use of child labor. The larger influences, however, are probably compulsory school regulations and the increased educational facilities in the United States today. Since more teenagers are in school, there is less chance that they will also be part of the labor force. In the early 1970s, however, there was some decline in the percentage of 18–19 year old teenagers attending school. This was in part due to the elimination of the military draft with its student deferment, the movement of more youngsters into technical trades, and the desire of an increasing number of young people to sit out a year or two between high school graduation and college entrance. Nevertheless, it is projected that the labor force participation rate of males aged 18–19 will decrease from its present rate of 71.4 percent to 65.1 percent in the next decade.

**Older Workers**    The percentage of older male workers in the labor force has decreased. This has been the result of the introduction of federal old-age and survivor's insurance and the advent of industrial pensions. In 1974 only 22 percent of the men 65 years of age or over were in the labor force compared with 58 percent in 1930 and 60 percent in 1920. It is anticipated that by 1985 less than one fifth of those men over 65 years of age will be in the labor force.

**Female Workers**    The number and percentage of women in the labor force have increased. The increased amount of clerical and retail sales work, the increased need for stenographers, and the development of light manufacturing (those occupations in which women historically have been employed) have increased the demand for female labor throughout the United States. In addition, the opening to women of many other occupations as a result of equal employment opportunity laws has increased and will continue to increase the demand for women at the managerial and professional levels. Currently, nearly 40 percent of the employed civilian labor force is composed of women. It is also interesting to note that more than one half (63 percent) of these are married women. Thus, it appears that the old saying that "the woman's place is in the home" belongs to a past era. From another point of view, 46.3 percent of the noninstitutional female population in our economy are members of the labor force.

Table 15-4 shows the number and the percentage of women in the labor force in the past few decades.

Table 15-4   **EMPLOYMENT OF WOMEN IN THE CIVILIAN LABOR FORCE, 1930–1974**

| (1)<br>Year | (2)<br>Total Civilian Employment (Millions) | (3)<br>Female Employment (Millions) | (4)<br>Female Employment As Percentage of Total |
|---|---|---|---|
| 1930 | 45.5 | 10.7 | 23.5 |
| 1940 | 47.5 | 12.0 | 25.3 |
| 1950 | 58.9 | 17.3 | 29.2 |
| 1955 | 62.2 | 19.6 | 31.5 |
| 1960 | 65.8 | 21.9 | 33.0 |
| 1965 | 71.1 | 24.7 | 34.7 |
| 1970 | 78.6 | 29.7 | 37.8 |
| 1974 (Dec.) | 85.2 | 33.8 | 39.7 |

Source: *Statistical Abstract of the United States*, 1974, and *Employment and Earnings* (January, 1975).

**Skilled and Unskilled Workers**   The percentage of unskilled laborers in the labor force has decreased. With increased use of complex machinery and equipment, it has become necessary for more workers to learn how to operate such machinery and equipment. As a result, we have had an increase in the percentage of semiskilled workers while the percentage of skilled workers in the labor force has remained relatively constant. We have also had substantial increases in the percentage of professional and technical workers, which includes primarily skilled and semiskilled workers, as well as an increase in the percentage of clerical workers.

**Service-Oriented Jobs**   Another pronounced trend in the labor force is the growing number and percentage of service-oriented jobs. Today about 43 percent of our total output is in the form of services as compared to goods. The demand for workers in goods-producing industries, such as manufacturing, construction, and mining, is declining, while the demand for workers in service-producing industries is growing in both absolute and relative terms. Today only 30 percent of nonagricultural workers are engaged in the production of goods as compared to 41 percent in 1950. On the other hand, the percentage of workers in service industries has risen from 59 percent to 69 percent during the same period. This trend can be observed in Table 15-5. Notice the rising trend of workers in service-producing industries, particularly in government and regular services. The latter category includes workers in services such as hotel and tourist trade, laundries, advertising agencies, motion pictures, the medical and legal professions, and certain educational services.

Table 15-5    **PERCENTAGE OF NONAGRICULTURAL EMPLOYEES IN GOODS-PRODUCING AND SERVICE-PRODUCING INDUSTRIES, 1940–1974**

| Industry | 1940 | 1950 | 1960 | 1970 | November, 1974 |
|---|---|---|---|---|---|
| Goods-producing | | | | | |
| Manufacturing | 34 | 34 | 31 | 27 | 25 |
| Construction and mining | 7 | 7 | 7 | 6 | 5 |
| Total | 41 | 41 | 38 | 33 | 30 |
| Service-producing | | | | | |
| Transportation and public utilities | 9 | 9 | 7 | 6 | 6 |
| Wholesale and retail trade | 21 | 21 | 21 | 21 | 22 |
| Finance, insurance, and real estate | 5 | 4 | 5 | 5 | 5 |
| Services | 11 | 12 | 14 | 16 | 17 |
| Government | 13 | 13 | 15 | 18 | 19 |
| Total | 59 | 59 | 62 | 66 | 69 |

Source: *Employment and Earnings* (December, 1974).

**Agricultural Employment**    There has been a definite move away from agricultural occupations. Aggregate labor force data show that in 1930 we had 10.3 million workers in agriculture. By 1940 there were 9.5 million; by 1950, only 7.2 million; and by 1960, 5.5 million. For 1974, as shown in Table 15-2 on page 297, the figure was 3.5 million. As a result of increased productivity, we produce more and more agricultural commodities with fewer and fewer farmers as the years go by.

Table 15-6    **TOTAL UNION MEMBERSHIP IN THE UNITED STATES, 1935–1972**

| Year | Union Membership (Thousands) | Percentage of Total Civilian Labor Force | Percentage of Nonagricultural Employment |
|------|------|------|------|
| 1935 | 3,728 | 6.7 | 13.4 |
| 1940 | 8,944 | 16.7 | 23.5 |
| 1945 | 14,796 | 27.5 | 33.5 |
| 1950 | 15,000 | 24.2 | 29.0 |
| 1955 | 17,749 | 27.3 | 31.8 |
| 1960 | 18,117 | 26.0 | 30.0 |
| 1965 | 18,519 | 24.8 | 27.7 |
| 1970 | 20,752 | 25.1 | 27.7 |
| 1972 | 20,894 | 24.2 | 26.7 |

Source: *Statistical Abstract of the United States*, 1974.

**Organized Workers**    Figures indicate that there was a substantial increase in the number and the percentage of organized workers in the labor force between 1935 and 1955. In the past several years, however, labor union membership has remained fairly stable at about one fourth of the total labor force, as shown in Table 15-6. This stabilizing effect has resulted in large part because the labor force has not been growing as fast in those types of occupations and skills in which workers traditionally have been organized, such as the unskilled, semiskilled, and craft occupations. A considerable amount and proportion of the increase in the labor force has been in professional, technical, sales, clerical, and other white-collar occupations not traditionally organized by labor unions.

**Size of the Labor Force**    The size of the labor force has been increasing continually. This increase in the labor force has come primarily as a result of the increase in population. We have been adding over 1.5 million persons per year to our labor force during the present decade. The average annual increment in the 1960s was approximately 1,380,000 per year. The continuous growth in the labor force is shown in Table 15-7 on page 302.

Even greater growth for the labor force is predicted for the next several years. Projections indicate that in the decade of the seventies the labor force will grow by 18.3 percent compared to 18 percent for the decade of the sixties.[1] By 1980, the civilian labor force is expected to reach the 100 million level. During the 1970s the number of workers in the 25–31 age group will increase by a dramatic 49 percent, while there will be a decline in the percentage of 16–24 year old workers. During the sixties the increase in the percentage of youth 16–19 in the labor force

---

[1]These and other projections are contained in U.S. Department of Labor, *U.S. Manpower in the 1970's* (Washington: U.S. Government Printing Office, 1970).

grew by 43 percent. In the 1970s it will grow by only 11 percent. This should help reduce unemployment among the youth of the nation, which, at an average rate of 12 percent in the 1960s, was 3 to 5 times more than the adult unemployment rate in the sixties. But there will continue to be a rapid increase, 43 percent, in the number of young blacks entering the labor force during the decade. Unemployment rates among black teenagers are usually double what they are among white teenagers.

Table 15-7   **LABOR FORCE AS A PERCENTAGE OF TOTAL POPULATION, 1930–1974**

| (1) Year | (2) Total Population (Millions) | (3) Total Labor Force (Millions) | (4) Total Labor Force Participation | (5) Total Civilian Labor Force | (6) Civilian Labor Force Participation |
|---|---|---|---|---|---|
| 1930 | 123 | 50 | 40.8% | 49 | 40.0% |
| 1935 | 127 | 53 | 41.7 | 52 | 40.9 |
| 1940 | 132 | 56 | 42.5 | 55 | 41.6 |
| 1945 | 140 | 65 | 46.5 | 54 | 38.6 |
| 1950 | 152 | 64 | 42.1 | 63 | 41.5 |
| 1955 | 166 | 68 | 41.0 | 65 | 39.2 |
| 1960 | 181 | 72 | 39.9 | 70 | 38.6 |
| 1965 | 195 | 77 | 39.6 | 74 | 38.0 |
| 1970 | 205 | 86 | 42.0 | 83 | 40.5 |
| 1974 | 212 | 93 | 43.9 | 91 | 42.9 |

Source: *Statistical Abstract of the United States*, 1959 and 1974, and *Employment and Earnings* (January, 1975).

As shown in Figure 15-1, there will be substantial increases in the number of white collar and service workers in the decade. Note the 50 percent increase in professional and technical workers and the 45 percent rise in service workers. On the other hand, blue collar workers will grow at a much slower rate, and the number of farm workers will decline.

**Labor Force Participation**   Although the labor force has grown in size, the labor force participation rate has remained relatively stable. The *labor force participation rate* is the percentage of the total population in the labor force. The participation rate can also be calculated as a percentage of the noninstitutional population. In either case, labor force participation shows remarkable stability. Since 1910, the percentage of noninstitutional population in the labor force has been between 52 and 60. The labor force participation rate compared to total population also has been very stable.

From Table 15-7 it can be observed that, with the exception of World War II, the total labor force participation rate has been between 39.6 and

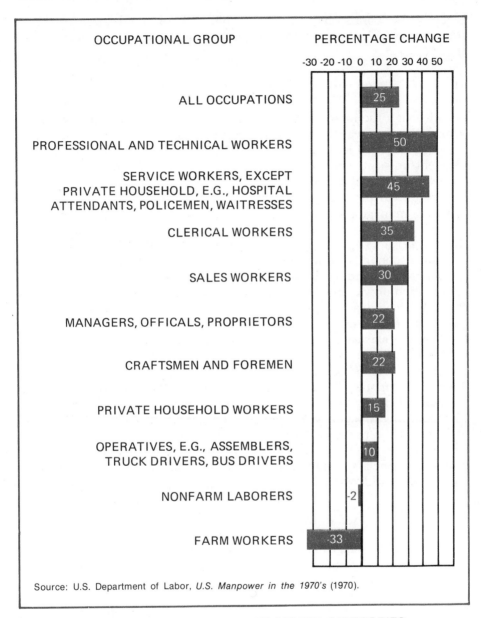

Figure 15-1    **LABOR FORCE GROWTH BY SELECT CATEGORIES, 1968–1980**

43.9 percent of the total population. The fact that it did increase to 46.5 percent during World War II reveals that the rate of participation had some elasticity. This proved to be beneficial to the war effort. Had it not been for this elasticity, which accounted for 10 million more persons coming into the labor force, war production would have been hampered severely. As can also be seen from Table 15-7, the total labor force participation rate has been somewhat higher in the 1970s as compared to the 1960s.

## EMPLOYMENT ACT OF 1946

Although the increase in the labor force helped to fill the gap during World War II, it was thought that trouble would arise after the war when veterans returned looking for jobs. It was thought that many of the wartime entrants into the labor force would hesitate to leave and this would cause a surplus labor force as the veterans returned, especially with the decline of war production. Many women, however, left the factories and offices to manage their homes. Youngsters reluctantly returned to school and oldsters went back to their fishing. Nevertheless, the civilian labor force did rise by 6.5 million within two years after World War II.

Some economists and government officials anticipated that we might have between 6 and 8 million unemployed in 1946, mainly because of the termination of wartime industries. However, the economy made a quick transition from wartime to peacetime production. In spite of the fact that government defense spending decreased more than $50 billion from 1945 to 1946, the slack was taken up by large consumer spending, expanded business investments, and strong foreign demand for our products. As a result, the GNP fell only moderately in 1946. Unemployment averaged 2.3 million for the year and never exceeded 4 million in any one month.

Nevertheless, the fear that widespread depression and chronic unemployment might occur with the cessation of war production led, in part at least, to the passage of the Employment Act of 1946. With the long depression of the 1930s still in mind, many individuals, organizations, and public officials supported the Act, which was introduced shortly after the end of World War II.

### Purpose of the Act

The original suggestion, known as the Full Employment Bill, would have made the government directly responsible for maintaining full employment, and it called for a planned federal budget designed to take up any employment slack in the economy. However, this proposal was not enacted. The Employment Act that was passed merely declared that it was the government's policy to use measures at its disposal to promote maximum employment, production, and purchasing power. Section Two of the Act reads as follows:

> The Congress hereby declares that it is the continuing policy and responsibility of the Federal Government to use all practicable means consistent with its needs and obligations and other essential considerations of national

policy, with assistance and cooperation of industry, agriculture, labor and State and local governments, to coordinate and utilize all its plans, functions, and resources for the purpose of creating and maintaining, in a manner calculated to foster and promote free competitive enterprise and the general welfare, conditions under which there will be afforded useful employment opportunities, including self-employment, for those able, willing, and seeking work, and to promote maximum employment, production, and purchasing power.

## Council of Economic Advisers

The Employment Act set up a Council of Economic Advisers (CEA) appointed by the President with the advice and consent of the Senate. Each appointee must be a person who is exceptionally qualified to analyze and interpret economic developments and to appraise programs and activities of the government in the light of the provisions and objectives of the Act. The Council reports to the President on current and foreseeable trends. He in turn makes recommendations for a program to promote a high level of employment.

Specifically, it is the function of the Council "to develop and recommend to the President national economic policies to foster and promote free competitive enterprise, to avoid economic fluctuations or to diminish the effects thereof, and to maintain employment, production, and purchasing power." The Council has the further function of analyzing existing programs and activities of the federal government for the purpose of determining whether they are consistent with the express purpose of the Act of maintaining maximum employment.

The Act also requires the President to transmit to Congress an annual *Economic Report* within sixty days after the beginning of each regular Congressional session. The President customarily delivers this report in January of each year.

## Joint Committee on the Economic Report

The *Economic Report* and all supplementary reports, when transmitted to Congress, are referred to the Joint Committee on the Economic Report. This Committee is composed of seven members of the Senate appointed by the President of the Senate and seven members of the House of Representatives appointed by the Speaker of the House. The functions of the Joint Committee are: (1) to make a continuing study on matters relating to the *Economic Report;* (2) to study means of coordinating programs to further the policy of the Employment Act; and (3) to file a report with the Senate and the House containing its findings and recommendations with respect to each of the main recommendations made by the President in his *Economic Report*.

## Meaning of Full Employment

The Act says nothing about a guarantee of jobs, but it does oblige the government to take steps to maintain a high level of employment. Nowhere in the Act, however, does it define or state what is meant by maximum or full employment. The 1953 *Economic Report of the President*, however, did state specifically that "Under the Employment Act, full employment means more than jobs. It means full utilization of our natural resources, our technology and science, our farms and factories, our business brains, and our trade skills."

It is expected that we will have some unemployment in the economy at all times because of job terminations by employees, discharges, relocation, and other causes. Included in this group are a number of people who are chronically unemployed because of certain mental, physical, or psychological handicaps. Over the past several years a number of organizations, committees, and government agencies studying the problem of unemployment have come to the conclusion that the amount of this so-called *frictional unemployment* should be about 4 percent of the total civilian labor force. Thus, in 1946 full employment would have been construed to be a condition in which 2 million or less in the labor force were unemployed. Today, however, with a civilian labor force exceeding 90 million, normal frictional unemployment can be expected to be in the vicinity of over 3.6 million. This 4 percent unemployment, or 96 percent employment figure, is cited frequently as a major goal for our economy.

The 4 percent unemployment figure has to be observed with certain reservations, however. Even when unemployment is higher than our national goal, some categories of workers will still be experiencing lower unemployment rates than the national average. Notice in Table 15-8 that in November, 1974, when total unemployment was 6.5 percent, unemployment among white workers and among married men was 5.8 percent and 3.3 percent, respectively. On the other hand, when we reach the full employment level we should not become complacent. At that level there are still sore spots of unemployment in the economy. In January, 1966, for example, when the economy was in a state of full employment with unemployment averaging 4.0 percent, unemployment among females was slightly higher at 5.0 percent. Notice also the much higher rates of unemployment among nonwhite workers, 7.2 percent; male teenagers, 12 percent; and nonwhite teenagers, 24.7 percent.

In the early 1970s it was suggested by various authorities that perhaps our full employment standard of 96 percent employment and 4 percent unemployment was outmoded. It was proposed that the structure of the labor force was changing and that a new unemployment figure might be more appropriate as a measure of full employment. There are currently in the labor force larger numbers of youngsters, women, and minority workers than existed in the late 1950s when we came to accept the 4

Table 15-8   **UNEMPLOYMENT RATES FOR VARIOUS CATEGORIES OF WORKERS IN THE LABOR FORCE**
(November, 1974, and January, 1966)

|  | Unemployment Rates | |
|---|---|---|
| Category | 1974 | 1966 |
| Married men | 3.3% | 2.0% |
| Males | 5.7 | 3.4 |
| White workers | 5.8 | 3.5 |
| Total labor force | 6.5 | 4.0 |
| Females | 7.8 | 5.0 |
| Nonwhite workers | 11.7 | 7.2 |
| Male teenagers (16–19) | 17.4 | 12.0 |
| Nonwhite teenagers | 37.4 | 24.7 |

Source: *Employment and Earnings* (December, 1974, and February, 1966).

percent figure. These groups usually have higher rates of unemployment than the labor force as a whole. Consequently, it is argued that if more weight were given to these categories in establishing a normal unemployment figure today, it would be a figure in excess of 4 percent, perhaps 4.5 to 5 percent. A 4.6 percent figure, for example, was suggested in the 1974 *Economic Report of the President*.

Not only is it desirable to hold unemployment to a minimum, but it also is economical to reduce underemployment. What is the difference between unemployment and underemployment? *Unemployment* refers to the number of workers not employed, whereas underemployment refers to the utilization of the workers. *Underemployment* occurs when a worker is employed but is not working to full capacity. It is possible for the economy to be in a state of full employment and yet be underemployed. Such would be the case if large numbers of workers were on jobs that did not require their full skill or productivity. For example, situations are found in which engineers are doing clerical work, artists are painting signs, mechanics are sweeping floors, or skilled secretaries are doing filing work. Annually many individuals are trained for skilled jobs but fail to find job openings. Often college graduates with tremendous potential never reach their full productive capacity. Although much has been done to prevent and eliminate unemployment, very little has been done on a nationwide scale to reduce underemployment. Underemployment can occur also when workers for some reason or another, such as the occurrence of a recession, do not work a full workweek.

### Administering the Act

Since the original implementation of the Act, the government has had several challenges in maintaining full employment as a result of slowdowns or recessions in the economy. The first recession came in 1949, the second in 1953–1954, the third in 1958, and the fourth in 1960–61. Then, too, there was the problem of "nagging unemployment" in otherwise prosperous years from 1961 to 1965, as well as the fifth and sixth economic recessions that occurred in 1970 and 1974–1975. Particularly vexing was the high unemployment rate, in excess of 9.0 percent, in the early months of 1975, which continued to be accompanied by double-digit inflation.

In the first two recession periods, unemployment approached the 6 percent mark. In 1958 it exceeded 7 percent. In each case the use of monetary, fiscal, and psychological measures by the federal government helped to send the economy back toward a high level of employment. In all instances, organized labor urged the government to take more drastic action to alleviate what the unions considered critical unemployment. On the other hand, many business organizations and a few labor leaders felt that the degree of unemployment was not too severe.

In the 1960–1961 recession unemployment again exceeded 5 million or 7 percent of the labor force. In fact, in the seven-year period 1958–1965 unemployment averaged nearly 6 percent of the labor force and was below 5 percent in only three months during that time. The problem of maintaining full employment in the early 1960s was aggravated by record annual additions to the labor force and the occurrence of a high rate of job displacement resulting from rapid technological advancements. Consequently, President Kennedy in his 1962 and 1963 *Economic Reports* called for strong measures to move the economy back toward maximum employment. Subsequently several bills were passed in Congress, such as the Area Redevelopment Act, the Manpower Development and Training Act, the Emergency Public Works Act, the Economic Opportunity Act, the Appalachian Regional Development Act, and a tax credit bill to stimulate new investment. A record income tax reduction of $11 billion, $5 billion in excise tax cuts, and deficit federal budgets of more than $10 billion annually were also used during this time as a means of attaining maximum production, employment, and income under the Employment Act of 1946.

Another challenging period arose in the recession of 1970 when the economy was characterized by unemployment between 5 and 6 percent with inflation of more than 5 percent annually. Caution had to be exercised so that measures designed to expand employment would add only minimal inflationary pressures to the economy. A similar situation developed with the recession of 1974–1975 when unemployment reached 9.0 percent, and was moving higher at this writing, and the economy was still experiencing double-digit annual inflation.

Although in recent years there has been growing agreement as to the meaning of full employment, considerable disagreement still arises over the degree of government action that should be taken to prevent either moderate or widespread unemployment from developing. Should government action, including deficit spending, be used to maintain employment for all those in the labor force, including the suburban farmers who are working in the cities on industrial jobs, students who are working after school, the sons and daughters who are living at home, and the 21 million married women with husbands present who are holding down jobs?

These are difficult questions. The Employment Act does not give us the answers. Some supporters of the Act would like the role of the government to be spelled out more definitely. They would like to see concrete procedures set up by the Act for automatic action whenever unemployment reaches a certain level as specified by the Council of Economic Advisers. It has also been recommended by several noted economists, including a former chairman of the CEA, that the Act should be amended to include stabilization of the price level as a specific part of its policy.

The President each year in his *Economic Report* gives a review of economic developments of the past year, the economic outlook for the forthcoming year, and an outline of the measures he would like to see adopted to obtain or maintain the objectives of maximum production, employment, and income. The President's message is then followed by a more detailed analysis of the current economic situation by the Council of Economic Advisers.

In its first three decades of operation, the Council of Economic Advisers has proved to be a worthwhile and successful organization. It has performed its task well and has greatly enlightened members of Congress, administrators, businesspeople, and many others on economic matters involved in the operation of the economy. The Employment Act of 1946 plays an important role in the operation of our economy. Both parties, Democrat and Republican, continually support the main objectives of the Act.

## UNEMPLOYMENT RATES IN THE UNITED STATES AND ELSEWHERE

Before concluding our chapter on employment, it may be enlightening to compare unemployment rates in the United States with those elsewhere in the world. The faster economic growth rates of several other nations, such as West Germany, Japan, and France, often have been compared to the slower rate of economic growth in the United States. Likewise, critics have called attention to the fact that unemployment in many other countries is lower than it is in the United States. Studies in the early 1960s revealed that after making adjustments for differences in counting procedures among the various nations, unemployment rates in the United States were still considerably higher. Recent figures for the early 1970s indicate that this is still true, as shown in Table 15-9.

Table 15-9    **INTERNATIONAL COMPARISONS OF UNEMPLOYMENT RATES FOR SELECTED YEARS**
(Adjusted to United States Definition)

| Country | 1960 | 1967 | 1970 | 1973 |
|---|---|---|---|---|
| United States | 5.5% | 3.8% | 4.9% | 4.9% |
| Canada | 7.0 | 4.1 | 5.9 | 5.6 |
| France | 2.2 | 3.0 | 2.2 | 3.1 |
| West Germany | 0.7 | 1.0 | 0.6 | 1.1 |
| Great Britain | 2.4 | 3.1 | 3.9 | 4.1 |
| Italy | 4.3 | 3.8 | 3.5 | 3.8 |
| Japan | 1.4 | 1.4 | 1.1 | 1.3 |
| Sweden | — | 2.2 | 1.5 | 2.5 |
| Australia | — | 1.4 | 1.4 | 2.1 |

Source: *Statistical Abstract of the United States*, 1970 and 1974.

## SUMMARY

In 1974, the total population amounted to 212 million persons. Of this total, 151 million were in the noninstitutional population; that is, those over 16 years of age and not confined to any type of institution. Thus, we had a potential work force of 151 million. Since many of these people were managing homes, were in school, or were not seeking work, there were only 93.2 million in the total labor force. The total labor force is composed of all those who are working or seeking work, including the armed services. After subtracting the number of persons in the armed forces, 2.2 million, a civilian labor force of 91.0 million was left in the economy in 1974. Employment averaged 85.9 million and unemployment 5.1 million.

The labor force has certain characteristics, but some of these have been changing in the past few decades. The following trends in the labor force are observable: (1) a decrease in teenage employment; (2) a decrease in the number of older workers; (3) an increase in the number of women in the labor force; (4) a decrease in the percentage of unskilled workers; (5) an increase in the number and percentage of service-oriented jobs in the economy; (6) a move away from agricultural employment; (7) a fairly stable percentage of the labor force engaged in organized labor activities over the past few decades; (8) an overall increase in the size of the labor force; and (9) a relatively stable labor force participation rate, between 39.6 and 43.9 percent of the total population for the past several decades.

Although we continuously strive for full employment, the exact concept of full employment is sometimes nebulous. Most economists seem to agree that if 4 percent or less of the labor force is unemployed, the economy for all practical purposes is in a state of full employment. There is, however, a movement to raise to 4.5 percent or more the unemployment figure that would be consistent with full employment.

The Employment Act of 1946 declared it to be a policy of the federal government to use the means at its disposal to create conditions favorable to a high level of production, employment, and income. To implement the objectives of the Act, the Council of Economic Advisers (CEA) was created. It is the function of the Council to study the economy in light of the objectives of the Employment Act and make reports and recommendations to the President, who is required to transmit to Congress an annual *Economic Report*.

The annual report and all supplementary reports are referred to the Joint Committee on the Economic Report, composed of 14 members of Congress. It is the function of the Joint Committee to continue study on matters relating to the *Economic Report of the President*, and to file its own report to Congress concerning the merits of the *Economic Report*.

It is hoped that by the time you have finished this book, you will be able to analyze the economy well enough to anticipate the recommendations that will be made in the *Economic Report* each January. However, for a proper understanding of the stabilization measures designed to prevent widespread unemployment on the one hand and inflation on the other, which are often suggested in the *Economic Report*, it is necessary to know more about business fluctuations and what causes them. This is the subject matter of the next chapter.

### DISCUSSION QUESTIONS

1. Why are homemakers not included as members of the labor force? Do you think they should be?

2. Do you think that everyone who is seeking work should be classified as an unemployed member of the labor force? Explain.

3. Do you think there should be a nationwide compulsory retirement age to make more opportunities available for young people coming into the labor force?

4. Do you think that unemployed wives, whose husbands are still working, should be counted as unemployed as far as our national employment figures are concerned?

5. Technological development and automation displace more than 2 million workers annually. Does this mean that they all become unemployed? Explain.

6. Do you think the Council of Economic Advisers could function better if it were responsible to Congress, or to an independent agency, rather than being part of the President's administration? Why or why not?

7. In calculating unemployment, do you think an adjustment should be made in the unemployment figure to reflect the element of underemployment (less than full workweek)

for the labor force as a whole? Why or why not?

8. Should price stabilization be made a specific objective of the Employment Act? Why or why not?

9. Do you agree with those who would make a 4.6 percent unemployment rate consistent with the concept of full employment? Why or why not?

10. It has been suggested that we consider the economy to be at full employment so long as job vacancies are equal to or greater than unemployment. Do you agree? Why or why not?

## SUGGESTED READINGS

"At Last, a National Manpower Policy." *Business Week* (August 7, 1971).

Chandler, Lester V. *America's Greatest Depression, 1929–1941*. New York: Harper & Row, Publishers, 1970.

*Economic Report of the President*. Washington: U.S. Government Printing Office, 1970–1975.

Hailstones, Thomas J., and Frank V. Mastrianna. *Contemporary Economic Problems and Issues*, 4th ed. Cincinnati: South-Western Publishing Co., 1976.

"High Employment Without Inflation." *Review*, Federal Reserve Bank of St. Louis (September, 1971).

"Jobs for All: Any Time Soon?" *U.S. News and World Report* (August 2, 1971).

*Manpower Report of the President*. Washington: U.S. Government Printing Office, 1974 and 1975.

Moore, Geoffrey H. *How Full Is Full Employment?* Washington: American Enterprise Institute for Public Policy, Study No. 14 (July, 1973).

Okun, Arthur. "Three Pitfalls for Presidential Advisers." *Monthly Labor Review* (March, 1974).

Paul, Robert J. "Training the 'Hard Core' Unemployed." *Marquette Business Review* (Winter, 1974).

Rosenthal, Neal, and Hall Dillon. "Occupational Outlook for the Mid-1980's." *Occupational Outlook Quarterly* (Winter, 1974).

Schrank, Robert. "Work in America: What Do Workers Really Want?" *Industrial Relations* (May, 1974).

Stein, Herbert. "Internal and External Functions of the CEA (Council of Economic Advisers)." *Monthly Labor Review* (March, 1974).

"Unemployment Rate Gives Only Part of the Picture." *Business Review*, Federal Reserve Bank of Dallas (January, 1975).

U.S. Department of Labor. *The U.S. Labor Force: Projections to 1990*. Special Labor Force Report 156. Washington: U.S. Government Printing Office, 1973.

U.S. Department of Labor. *U.S. Manpower in the 1970's*. Washington: U.S. Government Printing Office, 1970.

# 16 BUSINESS CYCLES

## ACTUAL VERSUS POTENTIAL OUTPUT

One of the striking features of our national income is its dynamism. It does not grow at a steady rate. Sometimes it expands rapidly. At other times it shows only a modest increase or decrease. In spite of its growth in recent years, it has in the past declined at a rate that was disastrous to the welfare of the country. Fluctuations have been characteristic of the national economy since the early days of our nation.

Why does the economy not continuously produce income at full capacity, with jobs for all who want to work? What is implied by balance, or equilibrium, in the national income, especially with full employment? What are the characteristic features of the so-called business cycle? Can these fluctuations be eliminated by the concerted action of business and government?

Most of us would agree that it would be great to have a national income as large as possible, one that continued to grow as the population increased, without serious fluctuations or adverse side effects, and with jobs for all. As stated by the late President Johnson in one of his last *Economic Reports:*

> We seek a free and growing economy which offers productive employment to all who are willing and able to work, generates steady and rapid growth in productivity — the ultimate source of higher living standards — while providing the new skills and jobs needed for displaced workers, and permits every American to produce and to earn to the full measure of his basic capacities.

The importance of maximizing income and output is best realized when the losses from depression or even operations at less than full capacity in the prosperous periods are considered. Production losses were staggering during the Great Depression of the thirties; but even in the relative prosperity of the past few decades, much has been lost in the way of production and employment through minor depressions or recessions and the failure of the economy to maintain operations at full capacity. Figure 16-1 on page 314 shows not only a sizable drop in production during the recessions of 1954, 1958, 1960–1961, 1970, and 1974, but substantial underproduction during the 10-year period, 1955–1965, and then again during 1969–1973. In fact, a rough estimate places the loss of

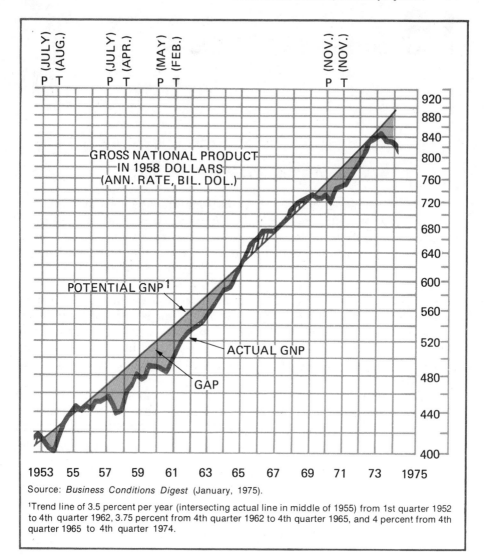

Source: *Business Conditions Digest* (January, 1975).

[1]Trend line of 3.5 percent per year (intersecting actual line in middle of 1955) from 1st quarter 1952 to 4th quarter 1962, 3.75 percent from 4th quarter 1962 to 4th quarter 1965, and 4 percent from 4th quarter 1965 to 4th quarter 1974.

Figure 16-1　**ACTUAL AND POTENTIAL GROSS NATIONAL PRODUCT**

production during the 1969–1973 period, as a result of our failure to maintain maximum operations, in the vicinity of $150 billion. It has been estimated that the loss from the recession in 1974–1975 alone will approximate more than $200 billion.

## THE BUSINESS CYCLE

National income is subject to various types of disturbance, but the most pronounced is the business cycle. What is called a *business cycle* may be considered a process of cumulative change over a time span longer than a year. During the cycle all parts of the economy display marked changes in activity as they move through periods usually called prosperity, recession, depression, and recovery. Production, prices, incomes, and employment activities all show characteristic changes during the cycle; in fact, there is no part of the economy that is not affected in some way. Extensive studies have shown that these cyclical fluctuations are found in economies throughout the world. Because of the pervasive character of business cycles and their persistence during many years, it has been assumed that they inevitably accompany all complex modern economies, although they appear most clearly in those economies where free markets and private enterprise prevail.

## Types and Length of Cycles

A study of past economic data reveals that there have been many and varied business fluctuations in our economy. Some cycles have been long, others short. Some have been severe while others have been mild. An analysis of the historical data reveals that business fluctuations may be classified as (1) minor cycles or (2) major cycles.

*Minor cycles* are those of relatively mild intensity in which the fluctuations are noticeable but not severe. They are shorter but more numerous than major cycles. Evidence seems to indicate that minor cycles occur every three to four years. In fact, some specific measurements show the average length of the minor cycle in the United States to be 47.6 months, with 26.2 months spent in the expansion stage of the cycle and 21.4 months in the contraction phase of the cycle. Since the end of World War II, we have experienced six minor downswings in the economy, in 1949, 1953–1954, 1958, 1960–1961, 1970, and 1974–1975. The 1974–1975 recession was the deepest and most prolonged downswing since the Great Depression of the 1930s.

*Major cycles* are those which show a wide fluctuation in business activity. They are usually characterized by serious depressions. This means widespread unemployment, lower income, and low profits or losses in many cases. Business cycle data indicate that major cycles occur about every ten years. Since World War II, however, we have experienced no major cycle. This may be due to our use of modern monetary, fiscal, and other measures and our built-in economic stimulus in the form of large-scale defense outlays.

Other types of cycles or fluctuations, such as long-wave building cycles, commodity price fluctuations, and stock market price fluctuations, have been revealed by research and economic analysis. In fact, cycles have a certain degree of ubiquity in the study of all aspects of economic activity.

### Phases and Measurement of the Cycle

Today business cycles are considered to have four distinct phases: prosperity, recession, depression, and recovery. *Prosperity* exists whenever there is an overall high level of economic activity. A *recession* occurs whenever there is a noticeable drop in the level of business activity. *Depression* is the period in which the level of business activity has dropped as far as it is going to drop in a particular cycle. *Recovery* occurs when the level of business activity begins to rise.

The duration or intensity of any of the four phases has little to do with their definition; that is, a business cycle consists of a series of changes that includes all four phases whether the trough is as deep as we experienced in the 1930s or as slight as we experienced in 1961 or 1970. The four phases of the business cycle are shown in Figure 16-2.

It has become customary, however, for much of the public and even business analysts to refer to a mild depression as a business recession. The practice of referring to a mild depression as a recession has been somewhat authenticated by the National Bureau of Economic Research in recent years. In answer to whether a recession took place in the economy in the early part of 1967, it defined a recession as a period in which the real GNP declines in two consecutive quarters. Subsequently, in the spring of 1971 the NBER labeled 1970 as a recession year. This in effect changed the conventional meaning of recession. However, it left us without a specific definition of a depression. Consequently, there was much discussion in 1974 and 1975 as to whether the economy, which declined

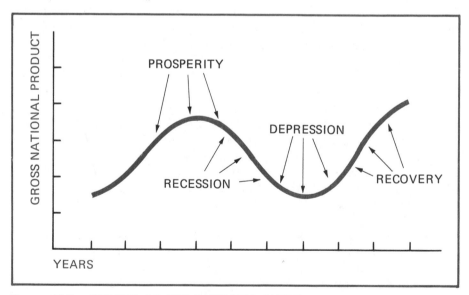

Figure 16-2   **PHASES OF THE BUSINESS CYCLE**

in each quarter of 1974 and in the first quarter of 1975, was experiencing a recession or suffering a depression. Since production and employment were down considerably, some individuals began referring to the period as one of depression.

In the absence of a quantitative definition of depression, one business cycle analyst suggested that a depression occurs when we have double-digit unemployment. Given this definition, 1974–1975 came close to being a depression period.

Although we have more or less definite measurements of the length of the total cycle and even the length of the expansion and contraction periods of the average cycle, it is difficult to obtain a conclusive measurement of the average length of each of the four phases of the cycle. The main difficulty to such a measurement stems from the fact that there is no agreement as to exactly when we leave one phase and go into another.

It is a bit easier to measure the amplitude of a business fluctuation. In measuring the business cycle, however, it is necessary to make allowances for any forces affecting business fluctuations other than those that are inherent in the business cycle. The level of business activity at any time is affected by four forces or types of economic change: (1) the trend, (2) seasonal, (3) irregular, and (4) cyclical.

The *trend* is the directional movement of the economy over an extended period of time such as 30 to 50 years. It represents the long-run average change (growth or decline) in the economy. *Seasonal variations* are recurring fluctuations in business activity during a given period, usually one year. The cause of this fluctuation may be natural or artificial. We produce more farm commodities, for example, in the summer than we do in the winter because of a natural cause, the weather. On the other hand, department store sales increase substantially during November and December due to our custom of giving Christmas presents.

*Irregular* or *random fluctuations* in business activity result from some unexpected or unusual event. Such factors as a serious flood, plague, pestilence, or drought can affect the economy as a whole or certain areas in the economy. *Cyclical fluctuations* are changes in the level of business activity that come about regardless of the trend, seasonal, or irregular forces. Business cycles may occur because of inherent forces in the economy. They may be influenced, however, to a considerable degree by external forces, such as wars, changes in the monetary system, and changes in population.

The intensity of the cycle may be determined by measuring the movement of the seasonally adjusted business activity above and below the trend line. If the actual business data are corrected for seasonal fluctuations and for any possible irregular forces, the actual data can then be compared to the trend line simply by measuring the difference between the actual data and the trend line values. In Figure 16-3 on page 318, for example, the seasonally adjusted business activity is shown by the

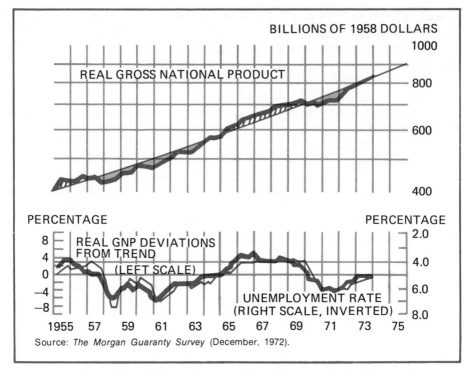

BILLIONS OF 1958 DOLLARS

Figure 16-3    **MEASUREMENT OF BUSINESS ACTIVITY, 1955–1973**

fluctuating line. The trend, which is the average level of business activity over a period of time, is shown by the straight line. The magnitude of the cycle at any point is measured by the difference between the value of the actual data and the trend line value. The value can be calculated also in percentage terms, as shown along with the rate of unemployment in the lower half of the figure.

### Pattern of the Cycle

Although some business cycles are short and others long, some fluctuations intense and others mild, and although there are considerable differences among economists as to the exact causes of the fluctuations, a definite pattern of the cycle appears to exist. Once a downturn has started there is a cumulative action among several elements in the economy that tends to augment the downswing. During this downswing, however, forces eventually come into play to arrest the depression and to start an upward movement. Once this upward motion begins, reactions of individuals and businesses will be such that the upswing will be augmented. During prosperity, however, a force will build up that eventually will effect a downturn.

The elements or forces operating to bring about business cycles are of two kinds — internal and external. The internal forces, or *endogenous forces*, are those elements within the very sphere of business activity itself. They include such items as production, income, demand, credit, and inventories. The external, or *exogenous forces*, are those elements usually considered as being outside the normal scope of business activity. They include such elements as population growth, wars, basic changes in the nation's currency, floods, drought, and other catastrophes that have a pronounced effect on business activity. We will first analyze the endogenous forces.

To see how the relationships among the various elements change and to see how these changes bring about oscillation of business activity, let us look at each phase of the cycle. We shall start with the depression phase and then move on to the others.

## DEPRESSION

In addition to an adverse economic effect, depression may have serious social and political consequences. There is naturally more public concern about a serious depression than there is about a mild depression, but unemployed individuals and bankrupt firms are involved regardless of whether the depression is serious or mild.

### Production, Employment, and Income

During a depression, production, employment, and income are at a low ebb compared with their respective status during prosperity. If income is low, the demand for consumer goods will be low; and a low demand in a period of ample supply generally will force prices down. Cost, too, will be relatively low because unemployed manpower, resources, and capacity will be bidding against each other for jobs, sales, and rent, respectively. Because sales are off and prices generally are down, profits will be low during a depression. This means low investments, for businesspeople do not invest in new ventures or add to existing capacity unless they anticipate profits.

### Inventories and Borrowing

Although in the early phases of a depression inventories may be rather high because of a previous inventory build-up, they will dwindle to a low position as businesses supply goods out of inventory and cut orders from producers. Since production will be at a low level, businesses will have little need for borrowing for capital expansion. With the decline in commerical loans, bank reserves should be relatively high. Thus, we have a situation in which the banks have the ability to expand credit, but businesses are reluctant to borrow because profit expectations are dim. In addition, many firms that would like to borrow for refinancing will be poor risks; and the banks will not be too anxious to accommodate them, since banks tend to become more selective during depressions. In total, business loans will fall off substantially. This will tend to make excess reserves relatively high; and with the excess reserve high and demand for loans low, the normal reaction will be to force interest rates down.

### Liquidity Preference and Saving

During the contraction phase of the cycle when prices are declining, the value of money rises. Individuals and businesses, if possible, will have a tendency to convert their idle assets into money. Therefore, we have a strong liquidity preference during depressions.

As incomes are lowered, on the other hand, the average worker will generally be required to spend a larger portion, if not all, of his or her income to provide the basic necessities and conveniences of life. Thus, our propensity to consume will increase while our propensity to save will decrease accordingly. Keep in mind, however, that although we are spending a larger percentage of our income, the total amount of spending on consumption will be lower than it was during the previous prosperity period.

### Replacement of Durables

When we are not producing at full capacity, there is less effort to replace worn-out machinery and equipment. Instead of replacing depreciated machinery, a firm can merely use other machinery that has not been in use. Only when it is really necessary, or when production starts picking up, will the average firm replace its machinery and equipment as quickly as they depreciate. Although some individuals and firms claim that a depression is the ideal time to replace their machinery and equipment because of the low prices, relatively few firms follow this policy. The lack of capital funds, the uncertainty of the future, and the fear of obsolescence discourage firms from following such a policy. Thus, the tendency of firms not to replace their worn machinery and equipment during a depression brings about sizable reductions in the production of such items.

Consumers, too, will have a tendency to repair and to patch up their durable goods instead of replacing them. People will be inclined to get a new set of tires and a tune-up and to keep the old car instead of trading it in for a new one. We are more inclined to get our shoes resoled rather than buy new ones. We patch our worn overcoats, darn our socks, repair our appliances, put off buying a new home, and, in general, postpone our purchases of durable goods and other items that we can do without during a depression period.

### Psychological Forces

All this, of course, has a tendency to keep the demand for capital goods and durable consumer goods low. Total production will be low and will result in idle capacity throughout the economy. With production, employment, income, prices, and profits low, a pessimistic attitude will undoubtedly prevail. Businesspeople will not invest under such conditions, and their reluctance to invest will have a deflationary or contracting effect on the economy. Only when the businessperson thinks that conditions are going to improve will investments be made. Thus, this pessimistic outlook will have an adverse effect on the economy. Likewise, the consumer will decrease spending. When employment slackens and workers are no longer receiving overtime pay, when some fellow workers are put on a short workweek, or when layoffs begin to appear in the plant, people will be more cautious in regard to spending money and will cut down on installment buying. Thus, the actions of businesses and individuals during a depression have a tendency to hold down the total demand for goods and services and make the climb to prosperity a little more difficult.

## RECOVERY

Although corrective and expanding forces may be at work, their effect may be a bit slow as far as the unemployed individual and the unprofitable firm are concerned. Nevertheless, recovery always comes sooner or later. When it does, it may lead to a high level of business activity or something less than full employment.

### Starters

What leads us from the road of depression to that of prosperity? It may be some exogenous force such as population increase, war, or the use of monetary or fiscal policy. Even without such external factors, however, the relationship of certain of the basic elements of the business cycle may shift eventually to a more favorable position and initiate an upward movement in the economy. Five changes that frequently occur may start the recovery.

**Cost-Price Relationship**    After a depression has existed for a period of time, a better cost-price relationship will develop. Statistical evidence shows that costs generally lag behind prices in their movements during the cycle. On a downturn, prices fall first and at a more rapid rate than costs. They also reach their low point before costs do. It is quite possible for prices to reach their minimum point while costs are still dropping. Eventually costs will dip lower than prices, and it will again become profitable for businesses to produce certain goods that may not have been yielding a profit. Prices frequently begin to rise sooner and faster than costs. Thus, on the upward swing of the cycle the margin between price and cost is widened, resulting in increased profits and additional investments.

In a free competitive economy, during a depression unemployed workers will bid against each other for jobs; firms with decreasing profits will compete against each other for sales; and landholders will compete against each other for rents. The total effect will reduce the costs of products and will gradually bring costs sufficiently below prices so that firms will find it profitable to operate. Firms will also be looking for new techniques and cost-saving devices to meet costs and make profits. Thus, after we have been in a depression for some period of time a more favorable price-cost relationship develops which tends to increase productivity.

**Inventory Changes**    A second factor that tends to spur production is the method of handling inventories. After we remain in a depression for a period of time, inventories become depleted. Sales demand will be filled out of inventories for several months, and companies will finally come to the point where inventories will get so low that they will have to be replaced. When inventories stabilize at lower levels, all current sales will have to be satisfied indirectly by ordering goods from the producer. This may result in production increases sufficient to stimulate the economy.

**Interest Rates**    The accumulation of excess reserves and the downward pressure on interest rates may encourage some borrowing by businesses. A businessperson who can make an 8 percent return by investing money in machinery, equipment, and buildings necessary to produce goods or services may defer doing so if it is necessary to pay 6 percent interest on the money borrowed for investing. However, if the interest rate were to fall to 5 percent, 4 percent, or even less, the businessperson might be encouraged to invest either the business' or borrowed money. Such investment would increase production and employment.

**Replacement Demand**    Another stimulant to production may come in the capital goods area. Although firms and individuals have a tendency to postpone replacement of capital goods and durable consumer goods during a depression, they cannot do so forever. The old machinery can take only a certain amount of repair. Likewise, equipment wears out. Furthermore, improvements in new machinery that increase productivity may make it more economical for a businessperson to replace old machinery. So it is also with the consumer. The old shoes can be resoled only so often before the uppers start falling apart. The family car may reach such a condition that it needs more than new tires. It may be more economical to get a new car than to make major repairs. Spending by businesses and individuals for replacement of capital goods and durable consumer goods will increase demand in those areas. This will lead to increased production and will give a boost to the economy.

**Psychological Outlook**    The general outlook may change. While it is true that businesspeople and consumers tend to be pessimistic during a depression, most individuals realize that depressions do not last forever. Thus, after being in a period of low business activity for a number of months, people will begin to look for an upturn. In fact, many individuals may decide to spend on the presumption that an upswing is just around the corner. Businesspeople also figure that they should get ready for better things, or they may figure that it is about time to look at the long-run view of the economy. In either case, a decision to invest in anticipation of future improvements may occur. Such action could start or help start the economy upward.

### Incipient Stage of Recovery

A favorable change in any of these five areas — cost-price relationship, inventories, interest rates, replacement of capital assets and durable consumer goods, and the psychological outlook — may lead to an increase in employment. Sometimes the increase will be insufficient to bring the economy out of the depression. In fact, we may have a short spurt in business activity only to be followed by a slackening. The pickup may be substantial, however, especially if there is a concerted move of several of the forces.

### Production, Employment, and Income

Regardless of what causes it, the force that leads us out of depression is the increase in production. If production increases, employment and income will naturally increase. With higher incomes, people will increase their demand. Prices will remain fairly constant during the early part of the recovery since the increase in demand will be met by an increase in the supply of goods and services. However, when demand increases sufficiently, prices will begin to rise. Cost, too, will remain relatively low, especially during the early part of the recovery, since competitive bidding for idle materials and manpower will be limited because of their abundance. Profits will increase as sales increase. Larger inventories will be held in the expectation of higher sales. Increased profits will bring about increased investment, which in turn will lead to greater demand for bank loans, and excess reserves theoretically will decrease. Higher bank deposits, however, often forestall the decrease of excess reserves until late in the recovery period or well into the prosperity period. As a result, interest rates will rise slowly.

As incomes increase, people will spend more and there will be a weakening of liquidity preferences. People will be inclined to spend their increased incomes because they were probably forced to do without many things during the depression period. Idle capacity will tend to diminish as output increases, and if the economy picks up to any extent, the general outlook will become more favorable. If businesspeople are optimistic and think that business conditions are going to improve, they will be inclined to invest in machinery, equipment, buildings, and materials. As they do this, production, employment, income, and demand will increase. Likewise, consumers will increase their spending. In fact, with a rosy outlook they will probably go into debt to obtain the goods and services they desire. Thus, the economy will get an added boost and the recovery will be on its way.

## PROSPERITY

Prosperity generally has favorable social and political consequences as well as a good economic effect on society, especially if it is high-level prosperity with full employment. Prosperity, however, is not all milk and honey. Certain ill effects, such as inflation, shortages of goods, and reckless spending, may develop.

### Cost-Price Relationship

As production, employment, and incomes begin to rise, the interactions of the endogenous forces are such that they work congruously to augment the upswing. Although prices, for example, remain steady in the early part of the recovery, they will rise if the upswing continues. With increased production the economy eventually reaches the "bottleneck" stage, a period in which some goods are relatively scarce and marginal, higher cost facilities are pressed into service. This brings about an upward price movement. Such increases often trigger a general rise in prices. As explained previously, prices increase faster than do costs. During an upswing, this relationship results in higher profits since, in addition to greater sales, large profit margins will exist. This brings about further incentives for investment. This investment is augmented by the multiplier-and-accelerator effect, and it can further activate the upswing.

### Inventory Accumulation

The build-up of inventories also plays an important role in this phase of the business cycle. Most producers or merchants keep inventories at a certain ratio to sales. Therefore, when sales increase, the size of inventories increases. This means that production must increase not only to satisfy the greater demand by consumers but also must increase to build up inventories.

In addition to the normal build-up to keep the inventory in proper ratio to sales, a second force, namely the price factor, accelerates inventory accumulation. Many businesspeople are very astute. They know how to make profits and that, if they build up inventories at low costs, profits will be magnified as prices increase. Therefore, whenever price increases are anticipated, there is a normal reaction that induces the average merchant to build up inventories to the extent of increasing the ratio of inventory to sales.

When this action is multiplied by the hundreds of thousands of producers, wholesalers, and retailers who keep inventories, it can be seen how production would increase considerably beyond the actual consumer demand. This inventory build-up leads to a further increase in employment, income, and profits.

### Replacement and Interest Rates

In addition to the inventory accumulation that augments the upswing, there is a tendency to replace worn-out assets at an accelerated pace and to add new assets to meet the expected expansion of business, especially as the economy begins to approach the stage of full capacity. This replacement becomes all the more feasible when interest rates are still low. Since the interest rates are "sticky," there is an inclination to borrow before interest rates begin to rise. This increased investment, through the multiplier and the accelerator effects, adds to total income, and the cumulative action of the endogenous factors can push the economy up to a level of full employment.

### Approach to Full Employment

During prosperity the levels of production, employment, and income are high, and high income means a large demand. As demand continues to increase, prices will rise, especially when we reach the stage of full employment where we can no longer increase supply fast enough to satisfy demand. Costs will continue upward because of the competitive bidding for manpower, resources, and capacity. Inventories, investments, and the demand for loans will reach new levels. The decrease in excess reserves and the shortage of loanable funds will force the interest rates upward. Liquidity preference will decrease as prices begin to rise, giving a further impetus to the upswing. As prices rise, the value of money begins to decrease. Thus, many individuals and firms will endeavor to convert their money assets into property and other real goods. This, in turn, increases the total demand for goods and services and adds to the inflationary pressures of the economy.

An increase in the marginal propensity to save (decrease in the marginal propensity to consume) will appear, but it is usually not sufficient to stem the tide of the upswing in the economy. When the general outlook is optimistic, as it usually is during the prosperity period, further encouragement is given to consumption and investment in the economy. The level of economic activity may increase until we reach the stage of full employment. At that time further increases in demand, investment, loans, and such, can only lead to inflation.

## RECESSION

Prosperity does not last forever. Downswings are certain to occur. Exactly when or to what extent is not easy to predict. Nevertheless, individuals and firms can prepare for such emergencies. Once a recession has commenced, it may lead to a mild or serious depression depending on the circumstances existing in the economy at that particular time.

### Cost-Price Relationship

During prosperity periods, the relationships between the endogenous factors eventually change in such a manner that they bring about a downturn in the economy. While production, employment, and income are at their peak, some tapering off in consumer demand may appear. Sometimes the mere fact that demand begins to increase at a decreasing rate can cause difficulty. One element bringing about a slackening of demand is the fact that the marginal propensity to consume declines as incomes increase. Consumer resistance eventually will bring a halt to price increases, and the price level will stabilize at some point. Costs will continue to increase, however, even during prosperity as businesses attempt to increase output by bidding against each other for the relatively scarce manpower, resources, and capacity. The rising costs gradually squeeze out some of the profits, which tends to make businesspeople a bit more cautious about investment.

### Inventory Adjustment

When demand slackens and prices stabilize, producers, wholesalers, and retailers begin to get rid of excess inventory. Just as we have an inventory build-up adding to the recovery, we can have the reverse situation during a recession.

Furthermore, if prices stabilize or begin to fall, the wholesaler will endeavor to deplete any excess inventory being carried. Therefore, goods will be supplied out of inventory rather than being ordered from the producer. In fact, if the price level is dropping, the wholesaler will not only get rid of excess stock but will undoubtedly reduce the ratio of inventory to sales. As merchants fill more and more of the demand out of inventory, an adverse effect on production takes place. This in turn decreases employment and income and can precipitate a downswing in our economy.

According to some economists, inventory accumulation and depletion play a major role in the cause of business cycles. Frequently cycles are characterized by this phenomenon. Inventory depletion, for example, contributed heavily to the slowdown in the economy in early 1967 and to the recession of 1970. It likewise was having some influence on the slowdown in the economy that was taking place in 1974 and 1975.

### Replacement Demand

Reduced employment and income during a recession bring about a further reduction in demand. Profits diminish and investment falls off, especially with high interest rates. Businesses find it unnecessary to replace capital assets that wear out if there is no use for such machinery and equipment. Idle capacity begins to appear as production schedules are cut back. Consumers, likewise, begin postponing the purchase of durable goods. Instead of buying that new car, they will put new tires or retreads on the old one. They will make other durable goods last as long as possible. The more difficult it becomes to repay, the more reluctant individuals will be to extend or renew credit. Prices eventually will begin to fall. This will cause further postponement of purchases as buyers hold off in anticipation of further price cuts. Price declines will bring a further reduction in profits, which means less investment. This, in turn, will further reduce production, employment, and income.

### Liquidity Preference and Saving

Falling prices strengthen the liquidity preference as the value of money increases. The attempt to convert goods into money increases the supply of assets offered at a time when demand is low. This will have a deflationary effect. The propensity to save, however, will decline with the decrease in incomes. Although individuals and families may desire to save even more than they had in the past, they may be unable to do so because of reduced income or unemployment.

### Reverse Multiplier

In general, the declining production, employment, income, profits, demand, and prices become cumulative. This results in a reduction in investment. The reduction in investment and consumer spending will be accompanied by a reverse multipler effect and the accelerator may approach zero. Under such conditions, the general outlook may become pessimistic, which has an adverse psychological effect on both investors and consumers.

### Status of the Endogenous Elements During a Recession

As the recession gets under way, the changing relationships of the endogenous elements are such that they tend to further perpetuate the downswing.

The recession continues until it reaches bottom. Somewhere along the way the stage of depression is reached. Whether the depression is severe or mild, the business cycle will have been completed. The economy will have moved through the four phases of the cycle: depression, recovery, prosperity, and recession. Once in the depression, it will again require a change in the relationships of the endogenous elements to bring about an upswing in business activity. The economy will then move through another cycle, maybe of greater or lesser intensity, maybe of shorter or longer duration. The pattern is similar in each cycle, although the characteristics of each may differ somewhat in regard to cause, amplitude, and duration.

### Modifying Factors

The duration and the intensity of these fluctuations can be modified by the use of monetary, fiscal, and psychological measures, as we shall see later. In fact, it is because we know the pattern so well that action can be taken to avoid the two extremes of the cycle: widespread unemployment and run-away inflation.

External forces also affect the level of economic activity and often generate business fluctuations. For example, a war has a profound effect on the level of economic activity. The requirements for war and defense material necessitate increased production and employment. Additional attempts to increase production may lead to inflation unless definite measures such as material and wage and price controls are utilized to combat rising prices.

Similar impetus may come to the economy from population growth, changes in the money supply, or government deficit spending. On the other hand, the termination of a war can have a depressing effect on the economy as production is cut back unless there is a substantial increase in consumer demand and private investment to offset the decrease in defense spending. Adverse effects can also result from serious catastrophes that force a reduction in production and income.

The typical pattern of the business cycle also is modified to the extent that we do not have perfect competition in the economy. For example, labor unions may be forceful enough to prevent wages from declining during a recessionary period. Oligopolies may push prices up sooner than expected or prevent them from falling in a recession. Government regulations may alter the normal movement of the interest rates.

The fact that all endogenous elements may not move or act in precisely the fashion described heretofore is no indication that the pattern is invalid. In any particular cycle one or more of the elements may act contrary to its usual movement. But generally a sufficient number of them will react in the prescribed manner and with ample strength to overcome any countervailing force of a few maverick elements. Such was the case in the recessions of 1970 and 1974–1975 when, because of institutional factors, the general price level continued to rise instead of declining.

Some economists and government officials suggest that today business cycles are obsolete. They claim that through the use of various monetary, fiscal, and other economic measures we are able to prevent wide oscillations in production, employment, and income. It is true that our measures and power to stabilize the level of economic activity, and keep it growing at a satisfactory rate of expansion, have improved over the years. The underlying need for the use of these stabilizing measures, however, is the fact that in a free economy fluctuations do occur. Stabilization measures do not eliminate the business cycle but merely modify its impact or effects. Furthermore, the occurrence of recessions, nagging unemployment, full employment, inflation, sluggishness, and stagflation in the economy, all in the past 15 years, certainly indicate that business cycles are still with us.


## BUSINESS CYCLE INDICATORS

As business activity changes, these changes are reflected in different areas or sectors of the economy. In many cases we have statistics and indexes indicating the changes that are taking place. Although some of these indexes measure changes in particular activities, they are representative in that what is happening to one particular type of economic activity may be characteristic of the economy as a whole. In other cases we do have some measures of composite types of economic activity that pervade the economy. Therefore, they give a good reflection of the general status of the economy. Some business cycle analysts have combined a number of different indicators in an effort to develop a general indicator for the entire economy. For purposes of analyzing business cycles, statistical indicators are usually divided into three types: representative indicators, composite indicators, and general business indicators.


### Representative Indicators

Although representative indicators are usually indexes that measure changes in a particular area of business activity, those that measure an essential area of business activity will reflect to some degree what is happening to the economy as a whole. The most reliable of these includes the index of iron and steel production, bank clearings or bank debits, railway carloadings, and electric power output.

Other representative indicators include paperboard production; bituminous coal production, and the index of employment want ads. Many others have been used or suggested at various times, such as automobile production, agricultural output, and stock market prices, but these frequently tend to be erratic.

### Composite Indicators

Composite indicators are usually indexes that measure some type of activity that is widespread throughout the economy. Therefore, they are sure to give a good indication of the general level of business activity. Among the most widely used composite indicators are the index of factory employment, the index of payrolls, the Federal Reserve Board Index of Industrial Production, and the gross national product.

### General Business Indicators

Most general business indicators combine a series of different indexes into one general index of business activity. Typical of these indexes are the following.

**Index of American Business Activity**   This index, published by the Cleveland Trust Company, compiles several different indexes and measurements to cover the period from 1790 to the present. The data are expressed in deviations from the norm or trend line.

**Business Week Index**   This index is compiled and published weekly in graphic and tabular form in *Business Week*. It reflects the combined movements of several individual series including raw steel production, automobiles, electric power, crude oil, paperboard, machinery, other transportation equipment, construction, and railroad carloadings. The movements of the *Business Week* Index are shown in Figure 16-4. From earlier data the recession in the economy in 1970 was readily apparent. A slowdown in 1974–1975 is also readily observable from the data shown in Figure 16-4.

**Statistical Indicators of Business-Cycle Changes**   These indicators, published by the Statistical Indicator Associates, North Egremont, Massachusetts, comprise a total of 26 indicators. They include 3 separate groups: the *leading indicators*, which are composed of 12 indexes whose upward and downward turning points generally precede the peaks and troughs of general business activity; the *roughly coincident indicators*, a group of 8 other indexes whose turning points usually correspond with

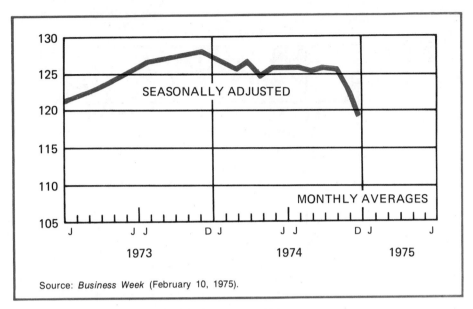

Source: *Business Week* (February 10, 1975).

Figure 16-4    **INDEX OF BUSINESS ACTIVITY**

the peaks and troughs of general business activity; and the *lagging indicators*, made up of 6 indexes whose turning points occur after the turning points for the general level of business activity have been reached.

Data for each of the 26 indicators are shown in tables and graphs released weekly and/or monthly. The relationship of the leaders to the coincident and lagging indicators can be observed in Figure 16-5 on page 332. Note that the leaders turned downward before the coincident and lagging indicators in the recession of 1970. The leading indicators, as well as the coincident indicators, also gave an early warning of the slow-down that occurred in 1974–1975. The current status of these indicators along with their interpretation and forecast of business conditions is maintained and published by the Statistical Indicator Associates.

**Business Conditions Digest**    This set of indicators published by the De-partment of Commerce contains graphs, charts, and tables for more than 100 National Bureau of Economic Research (NBER) business cycle indi-cator series, which are the source of those used by the Statistical Indica-tor Associates. The government publication plots 34 NBER Leading Indi-cators, 25 NBER Roughly Coincident Indicators, 11 NBER Lagging Indicators, numerous other U.S. Series with Business Cycle Significance, and 22 International Comparisons of industrial production. The series are presented in convenient form for analysis and interpretation by spe-cialists in business cycle analysis, but the Department of Commerce makes no attempt to interpret them or to make business forecasts.

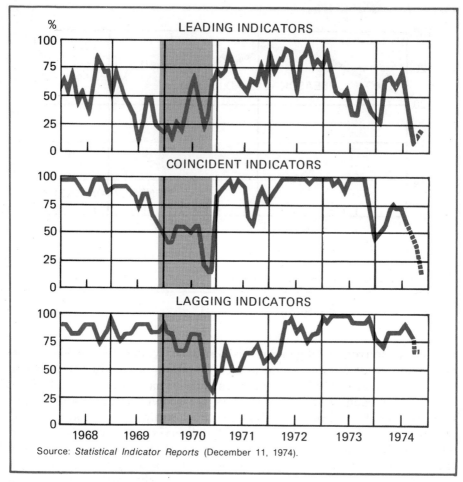

Figure 16-5    **STATISTICAL INDICATORS**

By following the business cycle indicators closely the business cycle analyst or the astute business executive may be able to anticipate pending changes in the level of business activity and try to make proper adjustments in the way of production schedules, employment, inventories, and financing to compensate for expected changes in business activity.

## CAUSES OF THE BUSINESS CYCLE

Business cycles are rather complex phenomena, and a multiplicity of forces are active in the changing level of business activity. During the past 50 years there have been numerous theories offered for the explanation of business fluctuations. To date there is a lack of unanimity regarding the exact cause of the cycle. Moreover, no one theory completely and satisfactorily explains the cause of business cycles. Nevertheless, a study of the various theories permits a better understanding of the possible causes of cycles and a clearer understanding of the complexities involved in their analysis. Although there are disagreements among the theories, these are not always real differences. Frequently they are differences in emphasis. At other times it is obvious that one theory may be more applicable to a particular situation than is some other theory. At times a cycle may reflect some elements of several theories. For this reason it is worthwhile to be acquainted with the major theories. For the sake of simplicity we can classify these theories into four major categories: (1) real or physical causes; (2) psychological causes; (3) monetary causes; and (4) spending and saving causes.

### Real or Physical Causes

A traditional explanation of the cause of the cycle is the *innovation theory*. According to this theory, business cycles are caused by innovations in the form of new products, new methods, new machines, or new techniques.

Innovation leads to increased production, employment, and income in the economy. As businesspeople borrow to finance innovations, they set up new factories, buy raw materials, and hire workers. The increased income resulting from their spending, of course, increases the total demand in the economy. If their ventures are profitable, other investors will seek to imitate them. But as additional firms begin and continue to produce, a point of overexpansion eventually is reached. The reaction to this overexpansion brings about a contraction in the form of declining production, employment, and income. It is contended that the decline will be of a lesser degree than the expansion, and thus there will be a net gain in activity in the economy as a result of the innovation.

The intensity and duration of the cycle depends on the nature of the innovation. A simple innovation will result in a short, mild cycle. A series of innovations may occur in such an integrated manner, however, that the cycle could be more pronounced and continue over a longer period. Major innovations, such as the rise of the corporate form of business enterprise, the development of the steamboat, the perfection and use of electric power, the automobile, the radio, and the development of electrical appliances produced increased business activity on a larger scale.

Fifty years or so ago, *agricultural theories* of the business cycle were very popular. Early theories endeavored to relate the general level of business activity to the weather, which affected the volume of agricultural output, which in turn had a definite effect on the level of business activity. Even though the proportion of agricultural production in the gross national product has declined dramatically, the volume of farm output today can influence to some extent the level of business activity.

In short, a larger volume of agricultural output will require more man-power and equipment to harvest and handle the crop, more transportation facilities, increased storage facilities, and an increased amount of credit to finance these operations. Such activity should give an impetus to the total economy.

A third important real cause of the business cycle is manifest in the *accelerator theory*. According to this theory, an increase in the demand for consumer goods may lead to a greater than proportional increase in the demand for capital goods. On the other hand, as consumer demand stabilizes or slackens, the firm will not require any additional machines. In such case, its demand for machines will decrease in greater proportion than the change in consumer demand. (You will recall that we discussed the accelerator at length in Chapter 13.)

A similar phenomenon exists in the durable consumer goods industries and the handling of business inventories. It is for this reason that fluctuations in the production of capital and durable consumer goods are of greater intensity than are the fluctuations for the economy as a whole.

### Psychological Causes

Although the psychological theory is seldom offered as a complete or independent explanation of the cause of business cycles, it is incorporated in some way in nearly every other theory suggested. In brief, the psychological theory holds that when investors and consumers react according to some belief as to future conditions, their actions tend to cause such a psychological outlook to become a reality. If investors think that conditions in the immediate future are going to be good, for example, they will increase their investment in machinery, equipment, and buildings in an effort to increase their total output and make more profit. Likewise, consumers who foresee good times ahead will spend money more readily and perhaps seek additional credit to increase their spending power. Such actions will tend to give a boost to the level of economic activity. If the investors, on the other hand, expect sales and prices to be lower in the future, they will slacken their investments, and businesspeople will allow their inventories to dwindle and will be cautious about hiring additional workers. Also, if consumers observe that jobs are difficult to obtain, that overtime is no longer available, and that some workers in the plant are being laid off or are on a short workweek, they may be a bit pessimistic about the immediate future. In such a case consumers may limit spending, may be cautious about taking on new debt, and may even try to save for a possible layoff. In such a case the actions of both the investors and the consumers will tend to bring about a slowdown in the economy.

Furthermore, the psychological theory holds that the actions of some business leaders can influence other businesspeople and consumers to feel the same way. If our business leaders exude optimism and back it up with actual investments, this may influence the thinking of smaller businesses about the prospects of the economy. If they follow suit with increased investment, this will add a fillip to the economy. Also, competition exerts a potent force on the economy in a psychological manner. Several firms competing for trade in a given area may misjudge their respective shares of the market. If they are optimistic, they may overestimate their individual shares. For a time there will be a substantial increase in business activity, but as the grim realities of the marketplace unfold, some or all firms may have to retrench on production. This, in turn, means a cutback in the demand for materials, labor, credit, and capital. In such a case a decline in the general level of business activity will set in.

### Monetary Causes

Most monetary theories are based on the premise that the banking system in a typical industrial economy provides an elastic money supply through the use of bank credit. According to the monetary theory, the free and easy expansion of bank credit permits an overexpansion of investment. With the use of bank credit the forces exerting pressure on the interest rates are modified. As a result, interest rates do not rise quickly, and frequently more investment takes place than would take place in the absence of bank credit. Eventually a position is reached in which the economy has excess productive capacity and abundant inventories. Readjustment comes about as businesspeople slacken their investment, prices begin to fall, production schedules are cut back, unemployment increases, and a recession commences. Retraction of credit by the banks during this period further augments the downswing.

Monetary theorists maintain that to eliminate the business cycle it is necessary to eliminate bank credit. The banks, on the other hand, maintain that they do not cause business cycles, since they do not force credit upon anyone, and that they merely service the business community when it needs money. Furthermore, complete elimination of bank credit might eliminate the cycle, but it would also eliminate some of the healthy expansion and growth in the economy brought on by the use of bank credit.

### Spending and Saving Causes

The spending and saving theories are of two broad categories. The first are the *underconsumption theories*. Some underconsumption theories hold that the economy does not distribute a sufficient amount of income among the factors of production to permit the purchase of the total goods and services produced by the economy. The more widely accepted theory, however, is that the economy does distribute a sufficient amount of purchasing power to buy the total goods and services produced but that all the income or purchasing power is not utilized. Hence, some goods will be produced and not sold. As a consequence total production will be reduced which in turn reduces employment and income.

Some of the leading underconsumption theorists maintain that the basic cause of the difficulty is the unequal distribution of income in modern society. The remedy suggested for the elimination or modification of business cycles is the lessening of inequality in the distribution of income. This they say can be accomplished to some degree by the use of steeply progressive income taxes, the strengthening of labor unions, regulation of monopolistic pricing, and an increase of social ownership of certain industries. It is interesting to note that particularly the first three of these suggestions are to some extent present in our economy today.

The other important spending and saving theory is that of underinvestment. The *underinvestment theory* holds that income in the economy is equal to total production and that, to clear all goods off the market, spending equivalent to current income must take place. Since spending on consumption is less than the total income, however, the difference must be made up in the form of investment, or spending on machinery, equipment, and buildings. Whenever investment spending is equal to the gap between income and consumer spending, the economy will be in a stable position. But whenever investment spending is insufficient to fill the gap between consumer spending and total income, total spending will be less than the value of the total output of goods and services and surpluses will exist in the markets. This will initiate a downswing in the economy. If for some reason investment spending is more than sufficient to fill the gap between consumer spending and total income, the total demand for goods and services will be greater than the total output and it will tend to increase the level of business activity. Thus, business cycles are caused by variations in investment. The cycle can be modified or eliminated, therefore, by maintaining an adequate amount of investment. As we have already seen, this is essentially the crux of the modern income-expenditure approach.

### SUMMARY

Unfortunately our economy cannot always be in a position of full employment and prosperity. There are many disturbing forces that cause changes in business activity. These forces include the trend, seasonal variations, irregular fluctuations, and the business cycle. The most dynamic of these is the business cycle.

Business cycles may be classified as either major or minor. The minor cycle occurs every three to four years and the major cycle approximately every 10 years. The average length of the minor cycle is 47.6 months, with 26.2 months spent in expansion and 21.4 months spent in contraction. Business cycles are measured as fluctuations above and below the trend line. The cycle is the result of a complex series of interrelated, cumulative changes in business activity that sometimes lead to prosperity and sometimes to recession and depression. Recessions and depressions can be translated into millions of unemployed and a loss of billions of dollars in the nation's income.

Business cycles have a pattern, but the pattern is not uniform because of various forces within and outside the cycle. This naturally makes forecasting business activity a bit precarious if not sometimes impossible. Certain relationships between or among these forces, such as cost-price relationships and inventory levels, act as upward or downward starters at the turning points of the business cycle.

Numerous indicators of business changes or business cycles are available. These can be categorized as representative indicators, composite indicators, and general business indicators. Among the most widely used are the lead-lag indicators of business cycle changes.

There are several causes or theories of the business cycle. No individual theory explains completely the cause of the cycle. Each theory, however, adds to the total understanding of the business cycle. Business cycles may occur due to real, psychological, monetary, or spending and saving causes, or a combination of these.

Now that we know how the GNP, unemployment, and price level are measured, have a grasp of the fundamentals of the income-expenditure analysis, and have some appreciation of business cycles, we can better evaluate the stabilization, expansionary, and anti-inflationary measures analyzed in the next few chapters.

## DISCUSSION QUESTIONS

1. Distinguish between a cyclical fluctuation and a trend.
2. What are the four phases of the business cycle? How can you determine in which phase of the cycle the economy is at present?
3. What are the internal and external forces that influence the level of business activity?
4. During recovery and prosperity, what forces are building up that eventually will help bring about a downturn in the economy?
5. Differentiate between a representative and a composite business cycle indicator.
6. Why should the index of iron and steel production make a good representative index of U.S. business activity?
7. Distinguish between the leading, roughly coincident, and lagging indicators of the Statistical Indicators of Business-Cycle Changes.
8. What indications of the innovation theory of the business cycle have you observed in recent years?
9. Do you think there is much validity to the underconsumption theory of the business cycle? Why or why not?
10. Which do you think is the most realistic of the business cycle theories? Why?

## SUGGESTED READINGS

Burns, Arthur F. *The Business Cycle in a Changing World*. New York: Columbia University Press, 1969.

Dauten, Carl A., and Lloyd M. Valentine. *Business Cycles and Forecasting*, 4th ed. Cincinnati: South-Western Publishing Co., 1974. Chapters 1 and 2.

Dederick, Robert G. "NABE (National Association of Business Economists) and the Business Forecaster." *Business Economics* (January, 1975).

"The Economy in 1975." *Economic Outlook U.S.A.* University of Michigan, Survey Research Center (Winter, 1975).

"Forecast: U.S. Recession Now — With 9% Inflation." *Wharton Quarterly* (Spring, 1974).

*High Employment Without Inflation: A Positive Program for Economic Stabilization*. Washington: Committee for Economic Development, July, 1972.

Lee, Maurice W. *Macroeconomics: Fluctuations, Growth, and Stability*. Homewood, Ill.: Richard D. Irwin, Inc., 1971.

Moore, Geoffrey H. "New Work on Business Cycles." *53rd Annual Report*, National Bureau of Economic Research (September, 1973).

*Statistical Indicator Reports*. North Egremont, Mass.: Statistical Indicator Associates (January–February, 1975).

"Uphill Road for Business." *U.S. News and World Report* (February 17, 1975).

U.S. Department of Commerce. *Business Conditions Digest* (January–December, 1974).

# Part 5

## Economic Activity and Policies

# 17 EXPANSIONARY POLICIES

## POLICIES FOR DEPRESSION

Since output and effective demand can come into equilibrium at a position of less than full employment, the economy can stabilize at an unemployment level and can remain there for some period of time in the absence of any artificial stimulus to the economy. Fortunately the income-expenditure analysis provides the basis for developing policies and measures, both intrinsic and extrinsic, designed to move the economy into equilibrium at higher levels of employment. In effect, an endeavor is made to put handles on the economy, in the hope that pulling this lever or pushing that button will bring about a favorable expansion in the economy.

## POLICIES TO ALLEVIATE UNEMPLOYMENT

Not only economists but also the general public are concerned with the problems that result from recessions and unemployment. The cost of a severe depression can be measured in billions of dollars. Important also, however, are the hardships that accompany unemployment such as bankruptcies, the waste of productive resources, plant idleness, and the resulting social deterioration.

When financial losses and serious social dislocations occur, economic policies and measures may be developed and implemented in an effort to raise the level of economic activity. Even in the absence of a recession, economic measures may be used to stimulate the rate of growth to provide a higher level of production, employment, and income. These policies and measures should be consistent with the ideals of a democratic society; that is, in helping to create a greater degree of stability or to raise the level of business activity, they should not weaken the spirit of free enterprise.

Three general policies can be developed to promote maximum income with full employment: (1) consumption may be stimulated in such a fashion that the propensity to consume is increased; (2) conditions favorable to a high level of investment may be developed; and (3) government spending may be used in an effort to bolster the level of business activity.

### Built-In Stabilizers

Over the past few decades we have developed a number of economic institutions, or practices, that tend to serve as built-in stabilizers for the economy. An outstanding example is the Social Security System, devised to insure greater continuity of income to the unemployed and to elderly persons. Unemployment compensation and old-age pension payments help to maintain consumption, even when recession occurs; they are shock absorbers that cushion the downward pressure of recession. The supplementary unemployment benefit plans and guaranteed annual income plans developed by businesses or through labor-management negotiations are also helpful in this regard. In addition, economic stabilization features are cited as a major argument for a federally sponsored income maintenance plan.

A stable tax structure can serve as a further built-in stabilizer. When prosperity occurs, higher returns from a given tax rate can result in a budget surplus and thus exert a *fiscal drag* on the economy to help ward off inflation. On the other hand, during a recession the smaller revenue from taxes causes a deficit and leads to the necessity of government borrowing. This creates what economists refer to as a *fiscal stimulus* for the economy.

Although not as noticeable, other government welfare programs have a similar effect. In addition, corporate retained earnings and family savings also can serve as built-in stabilizers.

### Monetary Policy

It can be recalled from Chapter 10 that the Federal Reserve can and does influence the amount of money and credit in the economy and that a liberalization of the money supply can raise the level of economic activity during periods of unemployment.

Whenever a recession occurs, it is important that bank credit be made easier, but only with proper safeguards. The Fed can help in making easier credit available by purchasing government bonds in the open market and paying for them by checks drawn against its own credit, which in turn will put the Federal Reserve member banks in a position to expand their reserves. A reduction of the reserve requirements will give the same result, for in either case the member banks are better able to make loans. A lowering of the discount rate serves as an additional inducement to member banks to borrow from the Federal Reserve Banks. Furthermore, liberalizing the money supply will lower interest rates. This should increase the gap between the marginal efficiency of capital and the rate of interest and encourage private investment. This, of course, raises effective demand and tends to eliminate the production gap.

Whether one or more of these methods will be used by the monetary authorities will depend on their judgment concerning the seriousness of the business recession or the need for expansion and the best way by which more liberal credit measures can be employed to stimulate the economy. Credit can be made more easily obtainable, but there is no certainty that business firms will increase their borrowings. If a recession has become serious and there is little prospect for improvement in business conditions, businesspeople may hesitate to borrow freely, even if credit is readily available at a low interest rate.

Economic stability and growth has become a primary objective of monetary policy. Because of its limitations, however, regulation of the money supply can only serve as a partial corrective to instability. The fiscal powers of the government are probably more effective for the task of raising the level of economic activity, especially during a period of serious unemployment.

### Fiscal Policy

In addition to the efforts of forces in the private sector of the economy, the operation of the built-in stabilizers, the utilization of monetary measures by the Fed and the Treasury, and the use of psychological policies to offset depressions and inflation, the federal government has a powerful tool of stabilization in its fiscal policies and measures. Government revenues and expenditures may be adjusted in a manner that will bolster the economy during a recession, combat inflation when the economy is overheating, and promote economic growth in the long run. To understand the role of fiscal policy in maintaining economic stability, it is helpful to look at the government's sources of revenue and the direction of its spending. Three methods for financing government spending are available: (1) taxation, (2) borrowing, and (3) printing money.

**Taxation**    If taxation is used to finance government spending, caution must be exercised not to tax funds that otherwise would be used for consumption or investment. It would be of very little use to have the government spend more at the expense of consumption and private investment. The total effective demand would remain constant, and no increase of employment would result. On the other hand, if only idle funds were taxed, government taxation and spending would lead to an increase in total effective demand. In fact, if the government could design a tax to absorb all those funds that would not be spent on consumption or investment, government spending would always be sufficient to have total effective demand, including government spending, equal to total output. However, the practicality of designing and enforcing such a tax is rather remote. Furthermore, the equitableness of such a tax is questionable. Any tax structure that is utilized generally will absorb consumer and investment funds to some significant degree.

**Borrowing** Borrowing is a more desirable method of raising funds for government spending when the purpose of spending the funds is to bolster the level of economic activity. The source of borrowing, however, will have a direct bearing on the effect. The government may borrow from individuals, businesses, or banks. In any case, the total effect will depend on whether or not it borrows idle funds. If it borrows funds through the sale of bonds, for example, to individuals and businesses who otherwise would use the funds for consumption and investment, the effect of government spending will be negated because the total effective demand will show no net increase. On the other hand, if the individuals and businesses use idle funds — those they do not intend to spend on consumption and investment — to lend to the government through the purchase of bonds, there will be a net increase in effective demand when the government spends the funds. This will bring about the desired effect by increasing production, employment, and income.

Since some individuals and businesses, especially for patriotic reasons, may give up otherwise spendable funds to buy government bonds, bank borrowing is usually recognized as the most feasible method of financing deficit spending to bring about an increase in the level of economic activity. It is not likely to have an adverse effect on the spending of current income by individuals and firms. It is true that banks may lend money that has been put into the bank by depositors. To this extent there would be merely a transfer of funds from the depositors to the government. However, since bank savings deposits are usually considered idle funds by the depositors, that is, they do not intend to use them for consumption or investment immediately, government borrowing from the banks will have a positive effect toward increasing the level of employment. Furthermore, the government can borrow funds in excess of the actual savings without hampering consumption or investment spending. This is accomplished through the creation of bank credit. Usually when the government borrows by selling large amounts of bonds to the banks, the banks pay for the bonds by creating demand deposits for the government against which the Treasury can write checks. To this extent, there is an increase in the money supply as well as an increase in the total effective demand in the economy.

**Printing Money** Similar results can be accomplished by using printed money to increase government spending. This method has an additional advantage insofar as it eliminates the necessity of having the government go into debt. Increasing government spending by increasing the amount of currency, however, is often difficult unless the government can increase the basis of the money supply, such as gold, government bonds, or bank assets. Even with an inconvertible paper standard there is the possibility of overissue and depreciation of the currency. Printing and engraving presses cannot be run at will without some regard to the valuation of the currency. To print money without regard to its backing can be disastrous. Furthermore, although Americans accept the creation of credit by the commercial banks, we seem to have an aversion to the printing of money by the government without proper backing. As a result, printing money for the purpose of government spending has not been a very acceptable method of bolstering the economy.

Some economists, though, suggest that the government use printed money. They reason that printed money is just as substantial as bank credit. Since the government has the right to coin money and to regulate its value, they think that it would be wise to bypass the banks and print the money directly when needed for federal government expenditures to bolster the economy. These advocates cannot see why banks should be paid an interest rate for providing a service that is primarily a function of the government. If the government prints the money instead of relying on the sale of bonds to the banks, which pay for the bonds by the creation of credit, it can avoid the cost of paying interest. As an alternative, they suggest the use of interest-free financing. With this method, the Treasury would sell non-interest-bearing notes to the Federal Reserve Banks, which in turn would create deposits for the government.

### Methods of Increasing Government Spending

Once it has been decided to use government spending as a means of raising effective demand to increase the level of employment, there remains the question of the exact method of accomplishing the objective. Three methods are suggested: (1) increase spending and hold taxes, (2) hold spending and decrease taxes, and (3) increase both spending and taxes.

**Increase Government Spending and Hold Taxes**    In this method, there is a positive increase in the amount of money spent by the government. For example, if the government has been spending $300 billion annually and taxing the same amount, it has a balanced budget. Now suppose that it is decided to increase government spending to $320 billion annually. If taxes are held constant, the government will be forced to borrow $20 billion for its additional expenditures. If the government borrows from the banks, individuals and business firms will not be forced to give up spendable funds through higher taxation. As a result, the total spending should increase for the economy as a whole. Not only will incomes increase by $20 billion but by some multiple thereof, depending on the size of the multiplier. This method is beneficial insofar as the government can easily maintain close control over the direction of the additional government spending.

**Hold Government Spending and Decrease Taxes**   This is often referred to as the "tax remission" plan. It also results in a deficit budget. For example, assume that the government was running a balanced budget of $300 billion annually, as stated in our first case. If the government decides to decrease taxes $20 billion annually, it will be $20 billion short of needed revenue. As a result, the government will be forced to borrow $20 billion. If it borrows from the banks or borrows otherwise idle funds, it will increase the total spending in the economy by $20 billion plus the multiplier effect. Although the government will not be spending any more, it is assumed that the recipients of the tax remission will spend the money either for consumption or investment. To the extent that they may not, the effect of using this method to increase employment would be lessened. The direction of their spending may also be less effective. This method is politically popular because both individuals and firms are usually happy about reduced taxes.

It is also possible to use a combination of the two methods mentioned above by increasing government spending and decreasing taxes.

**Increase Government Spending and Increase Taxes Proportionately**
In this method a balanced budget is maintained. The effectiveness of the method is limited by the fact that while raising taxes, the government may absorb funds that otherwise would be spent for consumption and investment. Therefore, the whole success of the program depends on the ability of tax measures to take in idle funds and therefore increase the total effective demand in the economy. Since most tax measures force consumers and investors to give up their spendable funds to some degree, it usually requires a larger amount of government spending to raise the level of employment a given amount by this method than it does by the first two methods mentioned. By the previous methods, the government can raise total effective demand by $20 billion, exclusive of the multiplier effect, through borrowing. If it desires to raise effective demand by $20 billion through government spending financed strictly by taxation, however, more than $20 billion will have to be spent.

For example, if the marginal propensity to save were $1/2$, the government would have to tax and spend approximately $40 billion to raise effective demand $20 billion, exclusive of the multiplier. The first $20 billion of government expenditure would merely offset the decrease in consumption and private investment resulting from the tax. The second $20 billion would add to the total effective demand, since it in effect would come from savings that otherwise would not be spent. If the marginal propensity to save were $1/3$ for the economy as a whole, government taxation and spending would have to be $60 billion to effectuate a $20 billion net increase in effective demand, exclusive of the multiplier and accelerator effect. Thus, it is easy to recognize the limitations of this method as a means of raising effective demand to increase the level of employment. It would be practicable only for spending of small amounts or if the tax could be designed to tap primarily idle funds.

## Direction of Emergency Government Spending

If a decision is made to utilize deficit spending as a means of raising the level of employment, a question naturally arises regarding the direction of such emergency government spending. Should the government increase its everyday services? Should it provide extra-governmental services? Should the spending be for consumption or investment purposes? Should spending be concentrated or diversified? How much should it be and how long should it last? It is easy to see that once a decision is made to use deficit financing, it is only the beginning of the issue.

It is possible, for example, to alleviate the effects of unemployment by the use of direct monetary payments to the unemployed and the poor, or by spending for public works.

**Direct Payments**    While this method makes certain that those suffering most from the evils of unemployment will receive direct aid, its total effect may be less than public spending in the form of public works. If the individual is given a direct payment, the bulk of the payment will be spent for consumption. This will increase the level of economic activity to some degree, provided the funds received did not come at the expense of consumption and investment elsewhere in the economy. Even if the individual is employed on a simple project such as leaf raking for the sake of respectability, the total effect will not be much greater. The capital needed to put a group of individuals on such a job is limited to rakes, shovels, wheelbarrows, and perhaps a few trucks. Furthermore, the spending of a direct income payment primarily for consumer goods may have no greater effect than drawing down excess inventories of consumer goods.

**Public Works**    On the other hand, a large public work, such as a bridge, a dam, a highway, or a building, will necessitate the use of a large number of capital goods and the production of a large amount of supplies, such as iron, cement, lumber, electric wiring, and glass plate. Furthermore, transportation will be stimulated to some extent by the movement of goods. Not only are payments made to contractors, but contractors must pay subcontractors, suppliers, and transportation companies in addition to the workers directly on the job. These workers, in turn, spend on consumption. Consequently, workers will be employed in the production of consumer goods that are purchased by these workers. All this tends to build up the multiplier effect and may even stimulate the accelerator principle. Thus, more secondary and tertiary employment is generated through public works than by a leaf-raking project or by direct payments.

Since an endeavor is being made to alleviate unemployment, public works would appear to serve the purpose better than other means. Not only is there a greater multiplier effect, but also there is always something to show for the spending and production efforts involved. In addition workers will have jobs and will be able to purchase the consumer items they require.

The income-expenditure approach makes use of the employment multiplier, in addition to the investment multiplier, to show the net result of an increase in employment. The *employment multiplier, k'*, is the ratio of the total increase in employment, $N$, to the original increase of employment, $N_2$. Therefore, $k' = \dfrac{N}{N_2}$, or $N = k' \times N_2$. This formula is used to measure the change in total employment compared to a primary increase of employment in the investment industries. The employment multiplier may or may not be equal to the investment multiplier.

Once the employment multiplier is known, it can be determined rather easily what amount of employment on public works will be necessary to raise the total level of employment a desired amount. For example, assume an employment multiplier of 3 and a current level of 85 million employed. If it is desired to raise the level of employment to 91 million, it will require the hiring of only 2 million workers in the investment industries or in public works to increase total employment by 6 million (3 × 2 million). If the employment multiplier were 4, it would require the hiring of only 1.5 million workers to raise employment by a total of 6 million (4 × 1.5 million). Thus, the higher the employment multiplier, the easier it is to bring about a desired level of employment through public works.

It is true that emergency spending can be used to fill the gap between output and effective demand whenever consumption and private investment are insufficient to bring about a high level of employment. But it may require sizable amounts of money or extended periods of time. In the United States we did attempt to alleviate the serious unemployment of the 1930s through deficit spending on public works. In spite of the fact that government deficit spending during that period seemed very high to most Americans and we engaged in public investment for nearly a decade, we were still a considerable distance away from full employment at the end of the decade. After World War II broke out, however, and we began to spend billions for defense and war purposes, we moved from a position of nearly 9 million unemployed in 1939 to full employment by 1942.

## ANTIDEPRESSIONARY POLICIES OF THE 1930s

The economic, social, and political evils of unemployment emphasize the need for problem solving. In serious depressions unemployment not only imposes a hardship on individual employees and their families but also on the economy as a whole. Widespread and prolonged unemployment results in a loss of individual income and frequently brings about a deterioration of working skills. Furthermore, the loss of goods and services can be tremendous. Labor is perishable. Labor time lost today through idleness is gone forever. It is true that workers can work double time tomorrow to make up lost time today, but they could work the double time without having lost the original time.

## Setting in the 1930s

Under the laissez-faire policy and the self-adjusting mechanisms of classical economic doctrine, there is nothing to do during a depression except to wait for full employment to return. However, with millions of workers unemployed, people going hungry, mortgages being foreclosed, values dropping, factories closing down, and members of Congress being plagued with complaints, it is difficult to stand by and wait for the economy to adjust to a high level of employment. Furthermore, many people, especially voters, have a tendency to blame adverse economic conditions on the political party in power. Therefore, in addition to the humanitarian motive (the promotion of public welfare) and economic justifications, political considerations usually enter the picture when a decision is being made about the use of antidepressionary measures.

The GNP in the 1930s fell from a high of $103 billion in 1929 to a low of $56 billion in 1933 and averaged about $80 billion per year for the 11-year period. Since the GNP potential during the 1930s was over $100 billion per year, a further comparison reveals that the loss of production due to layoffs during this period was equivalent to a shutdown of the entire economy for a period of more than three years. Thus, it is easy to see that the loss through unemployment during a serious depression can be staggering. Such a situation certainly lends support to the adoption of at least certain income-expenditure policies for raising the level of employment. Therefore, it should come as no surprise to learn that our economic policies of the 1930s and subsequently have paralleled, if not followed, the income-expenditure analysis in a great many respects.

## New Deal Policies and Programs

Although the Administration of President Herbert Hoover moved away from its laissez-faire banner to a certain extent in an effort to improve economic conditions, at the time of the Presidential elections in 1932, according to the Bureau of Labor Statistics, nearly 12 million persons were unemployed in the United States, not including millions more who were only partially employed or workers on short workweeks. In short, one out of every four workers was idle, and many of the others were working only part time. There seemed to be little doubt that the landslide vote for Franklin D. Roosevelt, who promised a New Deal for the people, manifested a minor political revolt brought on by adverse economic conditions and in particular by the excessive amount of unemployment in the economy.

Upon taking office, President Roosevelt pinpointed the primary objective of the Administration to halt the downward spiral of production, employment, income, and prices by bringing about an upward expansion of the economy through the use of monetary and fiscal policies. Like Keynes, he thought that it was the government's responsibility to take action which would help bolster the economy. The money supply was liberalized, even to the extent of devaluing the dollar, and fiscal policy became a tool to bolster the level of employment. Public works and deficit spending became the order of the day. In addition, many programs were established to improve the purchasing power of the consumer.

Roosevelt's objective was to improve the purchasing power of the masses, which would bring about increased demand and with it increased profits, production, and employment. Unlike the previous Administration, which tried to work from the top down, that is, by extending aid to businesses to keep them operational, Roosevelt concentrated on working from the bottom up. Not only does this approach take advantage of the large propensity to consume among the lower income groups, but it usually is wise politically to take this approach since people vote and business firms do not. Measures that provided financial aid to farmers, refinanced home mortgages, set up unemployment compensation and old-age insurance, and established minimum wage laws were all very popular with the people.

In addition, several billion dollars were expended on public works to provide employment for millions of workers. The Civilian Conservation Corps was established to give work and educational opportunities to millions of young men, and the National Youth Administration provided needed work to those in college.

### Rate of Deficit Spending

While these various public works and other public-investment programs were being tried, the federal budget was running a deficit. After 11 years of surplus financing and of reducing the large debt incurred in World War I, the government went into debt each year from 1931 to 1940. Although tax revenues increased after the early Depression years, expenditures moved up at a faster rate and the federal government went deeper into debt. During this period, when government revenues ranged from $2–$5 billion annually, federal deficits averaged over $3 billion annually. The national debt increased from $16 billion to $48 billion. In addition, state and local government debts were increased.

### Lesson of the 1930s

Prior to the Depression, governmental units did their spending and building when everyone else did, that is, during prosperity. In the 1930s, however, public officials and others began to realize the value of public spending during depressions as a means of alleviating unemployment.

They also became aware of the fact that much more could be accomplished through public works than through mere payments for relief. Although the Administration and Congress may not have been influenced by Keynes, certainly they had adopted policies that paralleled those of the income-expenditure analysis. Our experience in the United States between 1933–1945 with the public-spending program indicated the following: (1) our early attempts to alleviate unemployment repudiated the pump-priming theory; (2) it verified the multiplier theory; (3) although large, our spending during the 1930s was insufficient and indicated the need for a very large outlay of government spending during depression periods; (4) the war proved that a sufficiently large outlay of government spending could return an economy from a position of a considerable degree of unemployment to a full-employment stage within a relatively short period; and (5) better results are obtained through spending on public works than could be obtained through direct relief payments.

### Appraisal of Antidepressionary Measures

The actual success of our experiments to raise the level of employment with public investment is difficult to measure. Certainly we did not come even near reaching the full-employment stage, and the expansion that set in after the winter of 1933–34, usually considered as the depth of the Depression, was stopped far short of full employment with the downturn of 1937–38. From a high of more than 12 million unemployed in 1933, conditions improved and unemployment dropped to 7.7 million in 1937. With the so-called "recession" of late 1937 and 1938, however, unemployment jumped over the 11 million mark again. At the time we began producing defense materials for the Allies in 1939, unemployment was still approximately 9 million and as high as 10 million early in 1940. With the expansion of defense and war production it dropped to 2.7 million in 1942 and was less than 1 million at the height of the war in 1944.

It is evident from the available data that there was some improvement in the level of employment as a result of the New Deal efforts. On the other hand, the results left much to be desired. Critics of government deficit spending, especially the advocates of laissez-faire and the balanced budget, point to the figures to demonstrate the lack of success of the spending program. How can a program be called successful when after eight years of spending we still had over 9 million unemployed? Although unemployment was still 9 million, we do not know what it might have been if the government programs had not been in effect. It might have been much higher. On the other hand, it may have been much lower, according to the critics, if the government had stayed out of the picture and let ordinary economic forces return us to full employment. As a result of not knowing or of not being able to determine what might have happened in the absence of our grand experiment, it is impossible to determine the success of the public-spending program.

Our experience of the 1930s leaves little doubt that our New Deal policies were similar to those advocated by the income-expenditure analysis, especially the idea of deficit spending and public works. Further evidence that we have accepted much of the income-expenditure theory can be found by analyzing the Employment Act of 1946.

## RECENT EXPANSIONARY MEASURES

Although the Eisenhower Administration, in addition to its strong reliance on monetary policies, did engage in some direct measures, much more positive, direct action was undertaken by the Kennedy and Johnson Administrations in the 1960s. On the basis that unemployment exceeded 5 percent or more of the labor force in every month except one during the five-year period 1957–1962, and the fact that the economy was operating at less than 90 percent of its capacity, President Kennedy in his 1962 *Economic Report* suggested several depression-proof measures as a means of bolstering the economy and stimulating economic expansion.

### Area Redevelopment Act, 1961

During his first year in office, President Kennedy was instrumental in bringing about passage of the Area Redevelopment Act of 1961, which endeavored to bring industry to depressed areas and jobs to displaced workers. The main features of this Act were the financial aids provided for distressed areas and areas with labor surpluses. These aids took the form of loans and grants for the construction of community projects and loans for private industrial undertakings of various types that would help lessen unemployment in the areas. Included in the program was training to prepare workers for jobs in new and expanded local industries. Between 1961 and 1966, over 1,000 projects involving 65,000 trainees in 250 redevelopment areas had been approved under the ARA.

### Tax Credits to Stimulate New Investment, 1962

As a result of the request in the 1962 *Economic Report*, Congress subsequently enacted a bill providing a 7 percent tax credit allowance for new investment. It also permitted acceleration of depreciation cost as a means of encouraging new investment. The provisions of the Act were widely used by businesses and contributed to record levels of investment in the economy that followed, especially during the mid-1960s. At one time it was estimated that the government's loss of revenue resulting from the tax credits was approximately $2 billion annually.

### Manpower Development and Training Act, 1962

In 1962 Congress also enacted the Manpower Development and Training Act. The primary purpose of this Act was to provide training for the unemployed and the underemployed to qualify them for re-employment or full employment. For this purpose the Act initially provided $435 million to be spent in three years. Unlike the ARA, the MDTA did not seek to allocate funds or benefits particularly to distressed areas of chronic unemployment or substandard levels of income. The Act allocated funds among states on the basis of each state's proportion of the total labor force, its total unemployment, and its average weekly unemployment payment.

The Act established training courses in those skills or occupations where there was a demand for workers and the trainees had a reasonable chance of securing employment upon completion of the training program. Such programs were set up through the local state employment service utilizing state and local vocational education institutions, although private schools and other training institutions could be used. On-the-job training offered by an employer and jointly by employer and local school authorities was also eligible for federal support under the Act.

Although the MDTA program did get off to a slow start because of difficulties and complications involved in such a huge program, it began to pick up momentum toward the end of fiscal 1963. By 1965 the idea of having the states absorb one third of the cost of MDTA programs was abandoned, and the whole program was renewed with the federal government continuing to carry 90 percent of the total cost of the program. President Johnson stated that the Act need no longer be considered temporary, and asked that it be put on a continuing basis. By 1974 over 2 million enrollees had received training under MDTA programs.

### Public Works, 1962

Although President Kennedy was not given standby authority either to reduce taxes or to increase federal spending on public works as requested in his 1962 *Economic Report*, Congress did in 1962 pass the Emergency Public Works Act, and subsequently appropriated $900 million to be spent on various projects to help reduce unemployment and stimulate economic growth.

### The Historic Income Tax Cuts, 1964

In his 1963 *Economic Report*, President Kennedy pointed with pride to the economic accomplishments under his Administration. But he stressed that in spite of the gains we still did not have maximum production, maximum employment, and maximum income as called for under the Employment Act of 1946. He indicated further that the economy was growing at only 3 percent annually compared to a potential growth of 4.5 percent. Consequently, as a means of bolstering the economy and accelerating economic growth, he presented a record level budget and simultaneously requested a net tax reduction on personal and corporate incomes, which would result in an $11.8 billion deficit in the fiscal 1964 budget. After 13 months of intermittent hearings and debate on the merits of the tax cuts, Congress finally, after President Kennedy's death, enacted a two-stage $11.5 billion personal and corporate income tax reduction bill in February, 1964. President Johnson immediately signed the bill into law with a word of encouragement to the general public to go out and spend the increase in their monthly incomes that would result from the tax reduction.

### Excise Tax Cuts, 1965

In addition to the historic income tax reductions spread over a two-year period in 1964 and 1965, Congress added to this stimulant by providing for excise tax reductions of $5–$6 billion on a broad array of goods and services from automobiles to entertainment. These tax cuts were to serve as a means of raising the demand for goods and services and contributing to the improvement of production, employment, and income.

### Appalachian Regional Development Act, 1965

As a result of the findings of President Kennedy's Appalachia Commission, Congress in 1965 enacted the Appalachia Bill which provided for various types of aid for a 13-state area extending along the Appalachian Mountains from New York state to eastern Mississippi. The program for this depressed area was aimed at developing an economic base to encourage subsequent private investment as a means of improving its economy. In the early stages, major emphasis was to be placed on road construction, health facilities, land improvement and erosion control, timber development, mining restoration, and water resource surveys. The Act provided nearly $1 billion to improve the economic condition of the area in the hope of raising production, employment, and the income of the inhabitants of the area.

### The Economic Opportunity Act, 1964

Additional aid in bolstering the economy has come through various poverty programs. After President Johnson delivered a special message to Congress early in 1964 on the state of poverty in the economy and following considerable debate, the Economic Opportunity Act, frequently known as the antipoverty bill, was passed in August, 1964. Initially the Act provided $962 million to launch the *war on poverty*. It continued with annual appropriations of $1.5 to $2.0 billion until the early 1970s. A look at some of the provisions of the Act, carried out through the Office of Economic Opportunity (OEO), will provide an insight into various aspects of the war on poverty.

**Poverty Programs**    The Act provided a number of programs for the youth of the nation, including a Job Corps, work-training programs, and work-study programs. In addition, the Economic Opportunity Act sought to provide stimulation and incentive for urban and rural communities to mobilize their resources to combat poverty through community action programs. Typical programs that fall within this part of the Act include those which provide employment, job training and counseling, health, vocational rehabilitation, housing, home management, welfare, and special remedial and other noncurricular educational assistance for the benefit of low-income families. Particular programs may include dental care for children, legal aid for the poor, rehabilitation houses for prison parolees, and social and recreation services by nonprofit agencies. The Act was also designed to meet some of the special problems related to rural areas in an effort to raise and maintain the income and living standards of low-income families and migrant workers in rural areas.

In an effort to bring about the establishment, preservation, and strengthening of small business enterprises and to improve the managerial skills of business operators, the Act provided for loans to such businesses. Guaranteed loans up to $25,000 are available for the establishment and strengthening of small business enterprises that will have the effect of preserving or raising employment in a given community.

Among other programs, the Act also provided for the recruitment and training of Volunteers in Service to America (VISTA). The VISTA program is very much like the Peace Corps but on a domestic basis. Subsequently the two programs were combined under one director.

**Progress of War on Poverty**    After a relatively slow start, activity on the poverty front picked up in 1965. One of the first programs developed was the Job Corps. By 1974 over 200,000 young men and women had learned basic educational skills at the Corps' 120 centers. The Job Corps had an enrollment of 43,000 in 1973.

Nearly 5 million young people have enrolled in working-training programs as members of the Neighborhood Youth Corps in more than 400 community-operated projects throughout the nation. In 1973 approximately 622,000 students were receiving aid under the work-study programs established in 1,100 colleges and universities.

In 1973 more than 3,500 VISTA members were busy working with the disadvantaged in the city and rural slum areas, on Indian reservations, in mental hospitals, in migrant worker camps, and at Job Corps centers.

By 1973 more than 2 million persons had received special literacy instruction in various programs provided under the Adult Basic Education Programs, and more than 250,000 unemployed parents had received vocational and literacy instruction under the Work Experience Programs.

In regard to Community Action Programs, which have provided a major thrust in the war on poverty, by the spring of 1973 several hundred grants totaling more than $4.0 billion had been made to 700 communities in all 50 states of the nation.

Although in the beginning there were some delays, duplications, and even abuses in the war on poverty, by and large it has made some progress in its effort to reduce poverty. Through 1973 more than $9 billion had been spent directly for war-on-poverty programs. In the early 1970s, however, the Nixon Administration began shifting some of the programs away from the OEO and into other federal agencies, such as the Departments of Labor, HEW, and Agriculture. Still, in 1972 Congress approved funding for the OEO through 1976. President Nixon, however, in early 1973, through the appointment of a new OEO Director, began dismantling that office by eliminating some of the poverty programs, reducing others, and transferring still more programs to other federal agencies. In April, 1973, a federal court issued an injunction against the dismantling of OEO and its programs, declaring that the President had no constitutional authority to undo what Congress had voted. In 1974, however, most of the remaining poverty programs, along with many others, such as those of MDTA, were placed under the direction of the Comprehensive Employment and Training Act implemented that year.

### JOBS Program, 1968

In 1968 a Job Opportunities in the Business Sector (JOBS) program was launched by the Department of Labor and the National Alliance of Businessmen. The program was built on a commitment by groups of businesspeople in 50 metropolitan areas to hire thousands of seriously disadvantaged people and give them on-the-job training, counseling, health care, and other supportive services needed to make these individuals productive workers. The program was built on the premise that immediate placement on a job at regular wages, followed by training and supportive services, rather than training first in an effort to qualify for the job, would provide superior motivation for these disadvantaged workers. Although the program experienced many start-up problems, the most serious of which was worker turnover, or quits, by 1974 more than 425,000 disadvantaged workers had been given jobs by individual company efforts and through Department of Labor contracts. Six of every eight workers hired on federally financed programs were blacks and one in eight was Spanish American. The average JOBS worker had 10.3 years of schooling, had been unemployed more than 20 weeks during the year prior to enrollment in JOBS, and had an annual income of $2,400. About half of the hires were under 22 years old.

### Deficit Spending in the 1960s

All these recent measures were accompanied by continuous deficit spending throughout the 1960s. In fact, President Kennedy knowingly used deficit spending as a means of bolstering the level of economic activity. To his critics who claimed that the deficits resulting from increased spending and decreased taxes would be inflationary, he pointed out on a nationally televised program that his proposal would not be inflationary but would result in an increase in production, employment, and income because at that time the economy was operating at less than full employment of manpower, resources, and capacity. To President Kennedy and his Council of Economic Advisers, the deficits were to be down payments on future surpluses. A proposed deficit was labeled a "fiscal stimulus." In short, the stimulus (deficit) would lead to a higher level of employment and income. At full employment the greater tax revenues would result in a surplus. Supposedly, when we reached the stage of full employment and budget surpluses, we could then declare a "fiscal dividend" in the form of increased government services or a further reduction in taxes. The payment of this fiscal dividend would then help avoid a "fiscal drag" on the economy that results from a surplus budget. Although we had a number of fiscal stimulants in the economy during the first half of the 1960s and eventually reached full employment by 1966, we never quite reached the surplus-budget stage. One part of the problem may have been that we were declaring fiscal dividends before reaching the full-employment and budget-surplus stage. Another major difficulty of determining how well this policy of fiscal stimulants, fiscal dividends, and the avoidance of fiscal drags would work stemmed from the unforeseeable acceleration of spending that resulted from the escalation of the war in Vietnam. The deficits for the period involved are shown in Table 17-1.

It was also suggested by a number of government agencies and private studies that some form of guaranteed annual income be established via a negative income tax or otherwise. President Johnson in December, 1966, established a national committee to examine the merits and disadvantages of such proposals. The committee in 1968 recommended that some form of income maintenance be adopted. Such a proposal was contained in the Nixon Welfare Reform Bill introduced into Congress in the early 1970s.

### Return to Full Employment

During the early 1960s other socioeconomic measures, such as the introduction of the Medicare provisions of the Social Security Act, the increase in Social Security payments, and the hike in the minimum wage rate, were invoked in part with the idea that they would help reduce "nagging unemployment" and help stimulate economic growth. During this period, 1961–1965, the economy was continually establishing new records of production, employment, and income; and our real economic growth rate was exceeding 5 percent annually. In spite of all this, however, the economy did not reach full employment until early 1966. Unemployment, which had been near 7 percent of the labor force when the Kennedy Administration took office, still totaled 4.3 million, or 5.5 percent of the labor force as late as June, 1965. During this time moreover,

Table 17-1   **REVENUES, EXPENDITURES, AND DEBT OF THE FEDERAL
              GOVERNMENT, 1960–1976**
              (Billions)

| Fiscal Year | Revenue | Expenditure | Surplus or Deficit | Total Debt[1] |
|---|---|---|---|---|
| 1960 | 92.5 | 92.2 | + .3 | 290.8 |
| 1961 | 94.4 | 97.8 | − 3.4 | 292.9 |
| 1962 | 99.7 | 106.8 | − 7.1 | 303.3 |
| 1963 | 106.6 | 111.3 | − 4.8 | 310.8 |
| 1964 | 112.7 | 118.6 | − 5.9 | 316.8 |
| 1965 | 116.8 | 118.4 | − 1.6 | 323.2 |
| 1966 | 130.9 | 134.7 | − 3.8 | 329.5 |
| 1967 | 149.6 | 158.3 | − 8.7 | 341.3 |
| 1968 | 153.7 | 178.8 | −25.2 | 369.8 |
| 1969 | 187.8 | 184.5 | + 3.2 | 367.1 |
| 1970 | 193.7 | 196.6 | − 2.9 | 382.6 |
| 1971 | 188.4 | 211.4 | −23.0 | 409.5 |
| 1972 | 208.6 | 231.9 | −23.2 | 437.3 |
| 1973 | 232.2 | 246.5 | −14.3 | 468.4 |
| 1974 | 264.9 | 268.4 | − 3.5 | 486.2 |
| 1975 (est.) | 278.8 | 313.4 | −34.7 | 509.1 |
| 1976 (est.) | 297.5 | 349.4 | −51.9 | 627.9 |

Source: *Economic Report of the President, 1975, and Economic Indicators* (April, 1975).

[1]The change in public debt from year to year reflects not only the budget surplus or deficit, but also reflects changes in the government's cash on hand and the use of corporate debt and investment transactions by certain government enterprises.

the labor force was experiencing its most rapid growth in the history of the economy.

There was some discussion in the executive and legislative branches of the government about declaring another fiscal dividend in the form of a further income tax or excise tax reduction. By late 1965, however, the economy was approaching the stage of full employment. With record investment, high level consumption, large outlays for Great Society programs, and especially accelerated spending resulting from the escalation of the war in Vietnam, we were at full employment by 1966 and beginning to experience noticeable upward pressures on the price level. Discussions then shifted to enactment of anti-inflationary measures, such as tighter money, reductions in government spending, and tax hikes.

### The Recession of 1970

During the period 1966–1969, the economy was at full employment, and we were concerned primarily with measures to combat inflation. As late as 1969 unemployment averaged 3.5 percent. With the recession of 1970, in which the real GNP actually declined (but less than one percent), the rate of unemployment rose to 4.9 percent for the year and in some months reached 5.5 and 6 percent. Although there were still some inflationary pressures in the economy, primarily of a cost-push nature, the Nixon Administration by late 1970 had shifted its emphasis from anti-inflationary policies to expansionary policies to reduce unemployment and generate an increase in production. Included among the measures to bolster the level of economic activity were accelerated depreciation to encourage business investment, the enactment of a public employment program (PEP) which provided federal financing of 150,000 to 200,000 jobs in the state and local governments for unemployed workers, Federal Reserve action to liberalize the money supply and bring about reductions in discount rates, the toleration of a $23 billion federal deficit for fiscal 1971 instead of the originally planned $1.3 billion surplus, the presentation of a federal budget for fiscal 1972 containing a planned $11.6 billion deficit (which finalized with a $23.2 billion deficit), a recommendation for a national health insurance plan, and adoption of a program for federal-state revenue sharing.

While stressing the need for expansionary measures, President Nixon and his Council of Economic Advisers did not abandon anti-inflationary measures. The administration did engage in more "jawboning" in an effort to hold the price line, and much more discussion arose regarding the reinstitution of wage-price guideposts or an incomes policy. President Nixon hoped that the rate of inflation would be reduced to 3.5 percent by the end of 1971 and that the unemployment rate would be down to 4.5 percent by that time. His economic game plan called for a return to full employment and stable prices by mid-1972.

It was evident by mid-1971, however, that progress toward his economic goals was minimal. Unemployment proved to be more stubborn and prices more sticky than anticipated. Sizable wage and price increases were prevalent in spite of an unemployment rate of 5 to 6 percent in the summer of 1971. Consequently, in August, 1971, President Nixon made sweeping and drastic changes in the game plan. Among other domestic and international measures, he imposed a 90-day freeze on all wages and prices, requested reinstitution of the tax credit to stimulate new investment, and asked Congress to reduce personal and corporate income taxes as a means of combating inflation, reducing unemployment, and expanding the economy.

During 1972, strict wage and price controls were enforced as a means of suppressing inflation. Although they were abandoned in favor of voluntary controls early in 1973, by the middle of the year a new, but weaker, version of price controls was reinstituted. But even this attempt to regulate prices went by the boards before the year was out. With continued expansion the economy reached the peak of the business boom by the fall of 1973. By that time the unemployment rate had declined to 4.6 percent. Most of the economic measures up to that time were designed to contain, or eliminate, inflationary pressures in the economy.

### The Recession of 1974

With the advent of the 1974 recession, unemployment rose over 5 percent by midyear. Inflation, however, was running at an annual rate of 12 to 13 percent. This put the economy back in a position of stagflation; that is, stagnation or sluggishness in the production sector of the economy and inflation in the price sector. By November, 1974, unemployment had risen to 6.5 percent. By April, 1975, it was 8.9 percent and rising. With widespread layoffs, a decrease in real income, and a decline in the real GNP for 5 consecutive quarters, even a reluctant Administration had to admit that the economy was in a state of recession and that conditions would likely get worse before they got better.

Toward the end of 1974 the prime rate on borrowed funds declined from 12 to 10 percent, the Fed eased the money supply, and the discount rate was finally lowered. Suggestions were made from many quarters that called for tax reductions, acceleration of the public employment program, an increase and extension of unemployment compensation, the establishment of a public works program, and the organization of a government agency to refinance financially troubled businesses. Faced with simultaneous recession and inflation, President Ford, in December, 1974, met with his various economic advisers to determine the feasibility of shifting the emphasis of economic policy from fighting inflation to economic expansion and fighting unemployment. In January, 1975, the President submitted a comprehensive economic program to Congress. This included a tax reduction of $16 billion and a proposed federal budget deficit of $51 billion. Congress, however, rejected this program for easing the recession. In the spring and early summer income tax rebates of $23 billion were distributed to taxpayers. In addition, several other measures, such as expanded public employment programs and financial aid for home purchases, were being discussed in Congress. On the monetary side, the Fed agreed to expand the money supply at a faster pace and the prime rate fell to 7 percent by midyear.

### SUMMARY

According to the income-expenditure approach, expansionary measures can be used to alleviate widespread unemployment. In addition to the internal forces in the private sector of the economy, the operation of built-in stabilizers, the utilization of monetary measures by the Fed and the Treasury, and the use of psychological policies to offset recessions and inflation, fiscal measures can be used to stabilize the level of economic activity and the price level.

There are three sources of funds available for the government when it desires to increase total spending: taxation, borrowing, and printing money. Each has its advantages and disadvantages. If the government is going to use fiscal policy to bolster the level of business activity, however, more efficient results will be obtained if it is accompanied by a deficit budget.

The government can increase its spending and hold taxes constant, or it can hold spending constant and decrease taxes. In either case, the government will be forced to borrow the difference between what it spends and what it taxes. Some good may be accomplished by increasing both spending and taxes and thus maintaining a balanced budget. However, it will take more total government spending to obtain the same results by this method.

The direction of government spending is also important. For example, spending on public works can be more beneficial than using money for direct payments to the unemployed. Any increase in primary employment will bring about an increase in secondary employment through the employment multiplier effect.

Antidepressionary measures were tried during the serious depression of the 1930s. The grand experiment was that of the New Deal with its various projects, programs, and agencies which attempted to put unemployed people to work.

To what extent these antidepressionary measures of the New Deal were successful is a debatable question. The various programs, however, definitely did increase the level of employment since they put millions of people to work directly on various projects. In a like manner, the measures invoked during the Eisenhower, Kennedy, Johnson, Nixon, and Ford Administrations probably stimulated employment to some degree. Whether unemployment was serious enough, especially since in those years new employment records were being established, to warrant the adoption of such measures is still being argued. Nevertheless, high consumption, record levels of investment, continued spending on Great Society programs, escalation of the war in Vietnam, and continuous deficits led us back to full employment by 1966. After 3 years of full employment and inflation, the economy entered a mild recession in 1970 and unemployment rose to 5 to 6 percent. At that time President Nixon faced the difficult task of simultaneously combating unemployment and inflation. In the summer of 1971 he imposed a surprising 90-day freeze on wages and prices, requested a tax credit as a means of stimulating investment, and asked Congress to reduce personal and corporate income taxes as a means of expanding the economy.

With the expansion of business activity during the next 24 months the economy was subjected to an off-again, on-again, off-again program of wage and price controls. By the fall of 1973 unemployment had dropped to 4.6 percent. With the advent of the 1974 recession and the return of stagflation, however, unemployment rose to 6.5 percent by November, 1974, and rose to 8.9 percent by April, 1975. By that time a host of economic measures were recommended for expanding the economy in the hope of reducing unemployment without aggravating the current double-digit inflation.

The income-expenditure analysis not only provides the basis for the development and implementation of expansionary measures but also for the development and use of anti-inflationary measures. Since inflation at times during the past several decades has been a major problem in the economy, it will be analyzed in the following chapter.

## DISCUSSION QUESTIONS

1. How does unemployment compensation act as a built-in stabilizer for the economy? What do you think of the proposal made in 1974 to extend unemployment compensation from 26 weeks to 52 weeks?
2. If the government decides to utilize deficit spending as a means of bolstering the economy, is it better to borrow from the banks or from the general public? Why?
3. What are the merits of increased government spending versus a tax reduction, provided either is financed through borrowing?
4. What do you think of the idea of "interest-free financing" for government borrowing?
5. Is it true that government spending in any direction during a depression will have the same effect? Why or why not?
6. What are the advantages of government spending on public works compared to direct payments as a means of alleviating a depression? Are there any disadvantages?
7. On emergency public works, do you think that employment should be limited only to those who are currently unemployed? Why?
8. Point out some of the difficulties or problems involved in endeavoring to stabilize the economy during a period of stagflation.
9. What do you think of a federally guaranteed annual income as an expansionary measure?
10. How deep did the recession of 1974–1975 become? What were some of the additional measures, besides those mentioned in your text, that were taken to alleviate unemployment?

## SUGGESTED READINGS

Ackley, Gardner. "Myths About Unemployment." *Dun's* (April, 1973).

Bechter, Daniel M., and J. A. Cacy. "The Economy in 1975 — Uncertainties Cloud the Outlook." *Monthly Review*, Federal Reserve Bank of Kansas City (December, 1974).

Brown, George H. "Stagflation Is the Word." *The Conference Board Record* (January, 1975).

Chandler, Lester V. *America's Greatest Depression, Nineteen Twenty Nine–Nineteen Forty One*. New York: Harper & Row, Publishers, 1970.

Cox, Eli P. "What Is Poverty? Who Are the Poor?" *Business Topics*. Graduate School of Business Administration, Michigan State University (Summer, 1971).

"The Debate over Gauging the GNP Gap," *Business Week* (June 9, 1973).

*Economic Report of the President*, 1962–1975. Washington: U.S. Government Printing Office.

Fellner, William. "Aiming for a Sustainable Second Best During the Recovery from the 1970 Recession." *Special Analysis*. Washington: American Enterprise Institute.

"The Food Stamp Program." *Monthly Review*, Federal Reserve Bank of Kansas City (June, 1969).

Francis, Darryl R. "Inflation, Recession — What's a Policymaker to Do?" *Review*, Federal Reserve Bank of St. Louis (November, 1974).

Freund, James L. "Income Maintenance Programs: Spending the Benefits." *Business Review*, Federal Reserve Bank of Philadelphia (April, 1971).

Galbraith, John Kenneth. *Economics and the Public Purpose*. Boston: Houghton Mifflin Company, 1973.

Goldfinger, Nathaniel. "Full Employment, The Neglected Policy." AFL-CIO *American Federationist* (November, 1972).

Jones, Sidney L. "Are Economists Answering the Right Questions?" *Business Economics* (January, 1975).

*Manpower Report of the President*. Washington: U.S. Government Printing Office, 1967–1975.

Mayer, Lawrence A. "First Aid for Recession's Victims." *Fortune* (February, 1975).

Miller, Glenn H., Jr. *The Federal Budget and Economic Activity*, Federal Reserve Bank of Kansas City (June, 1969).

Miller, Roger Leroy, and Raburn M. Williams. *The New Economics of Richard Nixon*. Scranton, Pa.: Canfield Press, 1972.

"The Modern Paradox: Fighting Inflation and Recession." *Business Week* (December 7, 1974).

Okun, Arthur. "Three Pitfalls for Presidential Advisers." *Monthly Labor Review* (March, 1974).

Paul, Robert. "Training the 'Hard Core' Unemployed." *Marquette Business Review* (Winter, 1974).

Shiskin, Julius. "When You Look Behind the Figures on U.S. Jobless. . . ." *U.S. News and World Report* (February 3, 1975).

Stein, Herbert. "Internal and External Functions of the CEA (Council of Economic Advisers)." *Monthly Labor Review* (March, 1974).

_____. *The Fiscal Revolution in America*. Chicago: University of Chicago Press, 1969.

"Unemployment and Income Maintenance Programs." *Economic Report of the President*, 1975. Chapter 3.

"Unemployment Rate Gives Only Part of the Picture." *Business Review*, Federal Reserve Bank of Dallas (January, 1975).

"Unusual Factors Contributing to Economic Turmoil." *Review*, Federal Reserve Bank of St. Louis (January, 1975).

# 18 ANTI-INFLATIONARY POLICIES

## PROBLEM OF INFLATION

The income-expenditure analysis is often referred to as "depression economics." This stems from the fact that it originated, or at least crystallized, during the 1930s and consequently placed primary emphasis on the problem of unemployment. Concentrated efforts of the early advocates to determine the causes of and the remedies for equilibrium at unemployment levels caused people to think of the theory only in terms of depression policies. As a result, many people are inclined to lose sight of the fact that the income-expenditure approach can also be used to analyze inflation and formulate anti-inflationary policies. Although originally it did not stress the problem of inflation so much as the problem of depression, today much emphasis is placed on the analysis of inflation.

During periods of changing prices, some income recipients gain and others lose. The main hardships of inflation are the redistribution of income caused by rising prices and the deterioration of past savings. On the other hand, during depression there is not only a redistribution of income but also considerable unemployment. Probably due to the circumstances of the times in which the income-expenditure analysis was introduced, the inflationary problem did not appear as urgent as the problem of unemployment.

According to the income-expenditure approach, inflation will occur at the full-employment level if the effective demand exceeds total output. This will result when private investment and government spending are more than sufficient to fill the gap between consumption and total output. In short, investment will exceed savings. In such a case, current demand will exceed the value of the goods and services currently produced. Competitive bidding by spenders will pull prices upward. This is known as demand-pull inflation. In addition, there may exist separately or simultaneously cost-push inflation, structural inflation, and/or social inflation.[1]

Demand-pull inflation may occur due to an easy money situation, high levels of investment and consumption, and large government

_____

[1]It is recommended that the reader review pages 67–69 of Chapter 4 for a refresher regarding the various types of inflation.

outlays and/or deficit spending. Since the effective demand is greater than the output of goods and services, two alternatives exist to combat the inflationary situation. The first and best is to increase the total output of goods and services to satisfy the excess demand. But since this is not feasible in a full-employment economy in the short run, at least not on a scale large enough to alleviate a serious inflationary situation, we must rely on the second alternative — reduce the total spending.

## MEASURES TO REDUCE TOTAL SPENDING

There are a number of methods available for reducing total spending in the economy. The reduction can be made in government spending, in private investment, and/or in consumption. In any case both the economic and the political effect of such action must be considered. The method selected frequently depends on circumstances in the economy. Wartime inflation, for example, will require special measures.

### Built-In Stabilizers

Our built-in or automatic stabilizers may not be sufficiently forceful during the upswing of the economy. Nevertheless, they are still there. With employment at a high level and unemployment at a low ebb, for example, payroll taxes will be maximized and disbursements from the Social Security System minimized. This will help rake off excess spendable funds from the economy. Similarly, the flow into and out of private supplementary unemployment funds will have an anti-inflationary effect. Insofar as our personal and corporate income tax structure is concerned, the given tax rates may yield a full employment surplus, which by its presence will be anti-inflationary if not cause a fiscal drag on the economy. With rising incomes there will be a decrease in the marginal propensity to consume, and the rising rate of personal and corporate savings will act as a deterrent to inflation.

### Monetary Policy

The government may also use monetary policy to combat inflation. Measures designed to tighten the money supply and/or increase the rate of interest tend to discourage investment. This, of course, lowers the total effective demand and tends to bring investment into line with savings. Investment could be reduced to a point where it just fills the gap between the combined effective demand of consumption plus government and total production at full employment. Here there is an advantage in having a central monetary authority that easily can raise, as well as lower, the interest rates for the purpose of raising or lowering the effective demand. The anti-inflationary effects of a rise in the interest rate, however, can be offset by a rise in marginal efficiency of capital. Businesspeople will not hesitate to borrow and invest even at a higher rate if profits are rising. This frequently occurs when prices and, consequently, profits rise quickly during an inflationary period. According to the income-expenditure analysis there is little that can be done directly under our existing economic structure about controlling the marginal efficiency of capital. For this reason the government must rely heavily on the manipulation of the interest rates in combating inflation through its monetary policy.

### Other Measures

The government may discourage investment and consumption by other means. It may impose credit restraint on both commercial and consumer loans. For example, it may limit borrowing for stock market purchases, it may tighten up restrictions on housing credit, and it may restrain consumer credit. The government may also rely on psychological measures to encourage individuals and firms to save instead of spend; and if absolutely necessary, it may impose price and wage controls.

### Government Surplus

Total spending may be reduced in the economy during an inflationary period by using policies opposite to those for increasing spending during a depression. First of all, the government can limit its spending to essentials. Furthermore, it can operate with a surplus budget to reduce consumption and investment. If the government taxes more than it spends, it will tend to reduce the total effective demand in the economy. In this case, unlike the depressionary policies, the government should endeavor to tax spendable funds, those that are going to be spent on consumption and investment, rather than idle funds.

The government can combat inflation by building up a surplus in two ways: hold taxes and decrease spending, or increase taxes and hold or decrease spending. It may also combat inflation to some extent by decreasing taxes and spending simultaneously.

**Hold Taxes and Decrease Spending**   If taxes are held constant and government spending is decreased for the purpose of combating inflation, it is more effective to decrease spending in those areas that tend to have the greatest multiplier effect. This method also has an advantage in that it is more palatable to the public than an increase in taxes. On the other hand, a reduction in government services necessitated by the decrease in spending may meet with some public resistance.

**Increase Taxes and Hold or Decrease Spending**   If higher taxes are to be used to combat inflation, taxes should be increased in such a manner that they absorb funds that otherwise would be spent on consumption or investment. Here again public sentiment may have to be weighed. If taxes are already high, as they are likely to be during an inflationary period, consumers and investors may not be receptive to the idea of higher taxes. If this method is used to combat inflation, however, it is easy to see that a decrease in spending along with higher taxes gives a double effect.

**Decrease Taxes and Decrease Government Spending**    The combination of lower taxes and lower government spending can be deflationary if taxes are decreased in those areas where the money would otherwise be held idle. This will reduce total spending by the amount of the government spending, provided those who receive the tax reduction save more as a result. A major problem with this last procedure is the difficulty involved in designing a tax remission that will not release spendable funds. Furthermore, even if such a plan could be designed, it would be difficult politically to rationalize a tax remission that is beneficial primarily to the higher income groups.

Regardless of the method used, the essential thing is to reduce effective demand. Thus, it is beneficial for government to build up a surplus. In this way, it can absorb the excessive spendable funds in the economy. Through taxation the government can reduce the total effective demand to a point where it will equal total output, and thus remove or lessen the inflationary pressure. A reduction in government spending can be used to bring total investment plus government spending into equality with savings. It can reduce government spending to a point where the combination of government spending and investment will just equal the gap between consumption and output at full employment. On the other hand, an increase in taxes can be used to reduce the amount of consumption and investment to such a degree that government spending will fit into the gap between total private effective demand and total output, thus eliminating the inflationary gap.

If the government does use a surplus budget for the purpose of combating inflation, it is essential that the government maintain rather than spend the surplus. If it chooses to spend the surplus during the inflationary period, the desired antiflationary effects will be obliterated. In such an event government spending merely replaces the decreased spending on consumption and private investment and thus inflationary pressures remain. The desired anti-inflationary effect of a surplus could be negated also if the government were to use the surplus to reduce the national debt. In such a case the recipients of debt repayment may use the funds for other purposes.

### Borrowing

Another method suggested to reduce the excessive spendable funds in the economy is government bond drives. This can be an effective method of reducing total effective demand, provided firms and individuals buy bonds with money they would otherwise spend on investment and consumption. Unlike bond drives during a depression when an attempt should be made to tap idle funds, the greatest anti-inflationary effect in this case will come from tapping spendable funds. A bond drive can be used in conjunction with or in lieu of an increase in taxes. Frequently it is easier to induce firms and individuals to give up spendable funds through bond drives than it is to force them to give up funds through taxation.

## WARTIME INFLATION

Some of our strongest inflationary pressures occur during wartime periods. These are also times, however, when care must be exercised in utilizing anti-inflationary measures that will not hamper the war effort. Some of the methods suitable in peacetime would not be prudent in a war period.

### Causes of Wartime Inflation

The causes of wartime inflation are basically the same as the causes of inflation in peacetime. In either case the inflation is caused primarily by an effective demand in excess of the productive capacity of a full-employment economy. This demand-pull inflation may or may not be augmented by cost-push or structural inflation. In a peacetime economy the high effective demand usually results from high consumption and high investment. In a wartime economy the effective demand exceeds the total output primarily because of the high demand of the government for war materials. Since it is difficult to increase total output and since it would be folly to combat the inflation in wartime by reducing government spending, it is essential to tackle the problem differently than in a peacetime economy.

### Need for Reducing Consumption and Investment

In effect, it is necessary to reduce the effective demand for consumption and investment by an amount sufficient to permit government expenditure to fit into the gap between total output and the effective demand for consumption plus investment. Since much of the private investment will be converted into wartime production, the primary task is to reduce the demand for consumption. It becomes necessary to reduce not only the marginal propensity to consume but also the absolute amount of consumption. This is difficult to do because incomes rise substantially during a wartime economy. Thus, strong governmental measures may be required to adjust consumption to a proper level in a wartime economy.

**Taxation**   The ideal measure to combat wartime inflation is heavy taxation. Through taxation, purchasing power can be transferred from individuals and firms to the government. This reduces the effective demand of the private sector of the economy and makes room for the necessary government spending on military goods and services. At the same time, it gives the government the means to make its purchases without going into debt. The most effective taxes are those that reduce consumption primarily, since a considerable amount of the private investment will still be essential. This means that taxes should hit hard at the middle and lower income groups whose marginal propensity to consume is large. For example, very stiff income and sales taxes are beneficial. However, there may be considerable political and social opposition to such taxes.

Although heavier taxes on higher income groups may have a limited anti-inflationary effect through consumption reduction, they do provide much needed funds for the government. Furthermore, they tend to have a more popular social and political appeal.

**Voluntary Savings**   A second method of combating wartime inflation is a program of voluntary savings, especially on the part of the consumer. Naturally the best method of accomplishing this is to encourage consumers to buy government bonds. In this way they will not only give up the purchase of consumer goods but also will transfer purchasing power to the government, which it can utilize to buy war materials.

Even though an appeal is made to the patriotism of consumers, however, the success of such a measure in reducing consumption on a large scale is questionable. Frequently lower income groups will not readily reduce their consumption, especially since their incomes are increasing and they desire to buy goods and services that they were unable to purchase previously. Available evidence does not indicate that voluntary savings ever have been sufficient to arrest wartime inflation.

**Compulsory Savings**   Since taxation plus voluntary savings are generally inadequate to finance a war, it is sometimes advocated that more positive measures be exercised by the government. One of these is a program of compulsory savings. Compulsory savings may be justified on the basis of need and the common good. The government needs the money to finance the war, and it is in conformity with the common good to prevent inflation. No one individual or group of individuals can restrain the upward movement of prices. If all individuals are forced to save, however, the result can be a very serious restraining effect on inflationary pressures. A compulsory saving plan would require a deduction, in addition to income taxes, to be made from each individual's paycheck. This money would be credited to a special savings account which would remain blocked, except for emergencies, for the duration of the war or longer. Interest would be paid on these savings by the government at an appropriate rate.

Most proponents of compulsory savings suggest a progressive savings rate. Since incomes would be increasing generally, this would permit those in the lowest income groups to maintain and perhaps to increase their normal consumption spending. Others with higher incomes would be required to save to such an extent that they would actually be forced to reduce consumption. Although the idea of permitting lower income groups to increase their consumption may not be anti-inflationary, it is thought to be consistent with the concept of social justice in our economy. Savings would be unblocked at, or sometime after, the end of the war, depending on the extent of inflationary pressures in the economy. In total, such a plan could prove beneficial to consumers in the long run.

If compulsory savings are to be used, it is only equitable to hold the price level constant. It would be unfair to force individuals to save to reduce consumer demand and then let the value of their savings deteriorate by permitting prices to rise. Thus, if necessary, price and wage controls may be used to hold the price level.

In the absence of compulsory savings or some other method of holding the price line, a steeply progressive income tax and a stiff excess profits tax will limit the opportunity of the profiteers to gain at the expense of the consumers in a wartime economy. There is the possibility that the profiteers may lend their newly acquired income to the government through the purchase of bonds if it is not taxed. It may be more justifiable, however, to tax away any unearned increment rather than to permit the profiteers to hold claims against future resources by lending excess profits to the government.

A variation of compulsory savings in the form of a reimbursable income tax surcharge was recommended to combat inflation in late 1973 by certain government officials.

## INFLATIONARY EXPERIENCE IN THE UNITED STATES

The past few decades provide a suitable period for a study, analysis, and evaluation of our attempts to use anti-inflationary measures since they include peacetime, wartime, and postwar conditions. The strong and weak points of our various measures are to some extent evident during this period. During this span of time we experienced varying degrees of price stability, moderately rising prices, and strong inflationary pressures. Higher taxes, voluntary savings, budget surpluses, material restrictions, wage and price controls, credit controls, and rationing were used to combat inflation.

### World War II

Prior to World War II we were still in a condition of unemployment. As indicated previously, in 1939 unemployment was in excess of 9 million. As we began to produce war materials for the Allies, employment picked up. When government spending on military production increased with our entry into the war, we soon reached full employment.

As we began to approach the bottleneck and full-employment stage in late 1941 and early 1942, it became evident that continued increases in government expenditures would result in higher prices. Government expenditures would have to be increased to execute the war properly, and total effective demand would exceed total output and inflation would occur unless steps were taken to prevent it.

We increased taxes substantially, both at the personal and corporate levels, levied a heavy excess profits tax on businesses, and conducted large-scale bond drives in an effort to borrow funds, especially from individuals and businesses. In addition to these monetary and fiscal measures, we imposed many other controls. Included were a *controlled materials plan*, wage and price controls, a system of consumer rationing, the regulation of consumer credit controls, and the use of manpower restrictions.

The total endeavor to reduce effective demand through these measures during World War II proved to be rather successful. The consumer price index (1967 = 100), which had increased from 42 in 1939 to 49 by 1942, increased only moderately during the war. Since some price increases must be permitted due to the exigencies of war production and since not all items are controlled, the price level should be expected to increase somewhat during a control period. Thus, to a certain extent our effort to suppress inflation and hold prices was successful.

### Postwar Period

At the end of World War II, firms and individuals had the largest holdings of liquid assets — cash savings, bonds, and other assets easily convertible into cash — in the history of our nation up to that time. Since demand continued to rise, we still had a potentially inflationary situation. As a result, controls were not removed upon the termination of the war in August, 1945. In the early part of 1946, shortages still prevailed, some rationing existed, and people were still standing in queues to buy certain consumer goods.

Finally, in June, 1946, Congress decontrolled prices. This unleashed a flood of spending that pushed total effective demand beyond our ability to produce. Not only were incomes at a record level, but individuals and firms had large holdings of liquid assets that they were eager to spend. In addition to the removal of price and wage controls, total tax revenues were decreased and the sale of government bonds decreased while bond redemptions increased. Fortunately we did keep the excess profits tax and rent controls, tightened up on the money supply, and reinstituted credit controls, and the government operated at a surplus in 1947 and 1948. Otherwise the inflationary effects would have been greater.

By 1949 total effective demand leveled off and our productive capacity caught up with it. Output remained stable, and unemployment reached a postwar high of nearly 4 million. We had an ample supply of most types of consumer goods, the demand for business expansion had tapered off, and there was a sizable decrease in foreign demand, all of which mollified inflationary pressures and reduced the CPI for the first time in a decade.

### Korean Conflict

In June, 1950, we were enjoying peace and economic prosperity. We were producing at nearly full capacity, and long-awaited consumer goods were readily available. Incomes were at a high level and consumers were spending generously. In addition, many were taking advantage of available credit to increase their purchases of commodities. The price level, which reached a peak in 1948, had stabilized and was beginning to decline slightly — a break for consumers.

With the outbreak of hostilities in Korea on June 25, 1950, the price situation changed rapidly. Prices increased more rapidly after the beginning of the Korean conflict than they did at the beginning of World War II because the former came at a time when we were near the full-employment level. Furthermore, purchases were accelerated as memories of shortages in World War II caused many people to buy and hoard non-perishable goods. It was well known that inflationary pressures would increase as our defense program expanded. As the total effective demand increased and consumer production gave way to military production, there was a growing gap between the demand for consumer goods and the available supply.

To combat the pending inflation, we eventually increased taxes, encouraged savings through bond drives, and used excess profits taxes to raise funds for the military effort and to combat inflation. We also used bank credit controls, reinstituted consumer credit controls, and established controls limiting the purchase of new homes. A controlled materials plan was set up almost immediately.

Although we reinstituted price and wage controls, we were a bit tardy in doing so. Instead, in the early months of the Korean conflict indirect and voluntary measures were suggested to keep prices down. In an attempt to reduce the level of effective demand, businesspeople, laborers, farmers, and consumers were admonished to exericse restraint. It was hoped that with increased production we could eventually strike a balance which would give adequate support to our military program and still fulfill consumer needs.

**Price and Wage Controls**    Recognizing the dangers that lay ahead, Congress approved on September 8, 1950, the Defense Production Act, which among other things authorized price and wage controls. The Act authorized the President to issue regulations and orders establishing ceilings on the prices of various materials and services.

However, in the months immediately following the passage of the Act, the government sought to stabilize prices by general measures and voluntary action. It increased taxes, imposed selective credit restrictions, and established control over the flow of scarce materials. Prices continued to increase, however, especially following the Chinese intervention in Korea in the fall of 1950.

As a result, on December 19, 1950, the Economic Stabilization Agency (ESA) published a set of Voluntary Pricing Standards as a guide to aid sellers who desired to cooperate in a program of voluntary price stabilization. In addition, hundreds of large firms were requested to give advance notice of any intended price increases, and discussions were held among producers of basic commodities to analyze methods of stabilizing prices. By the end of January, 1951, however, the CPI had increased over 7 percent. It became imperative that forceful action be taken since voluntary, partial, and indirect measures had failed to meet the challenge of inflation.

The first major step in the direct fight against inflation was the issuance of the General Ceiling Price Regulation (GCPR) on January 26, 1951. This emergency measure froze prices for all covered commodities and services at the highest level at which they were sold, or offered for sale, during the base period, December 19, 1950, to January 25, 1951.

Shortly after GCPR was issued, other ceiling price regulations began to appear. In general, these regulations superseded GCPR. Their purpose was to remove certain commodities and services from pricing under GCPR and bring them under regulations specifically tailored to the market structure of the respective commodity. This proved to be a satisfactory and equitable approach to control.

During a relatively short period, the Office of Price Stabilization (OPS), which had been established upon the creation of the Economic Stabilization Agency on September 9, 1950, grew from a skeleton crew to a force of more than 12,000 employees. Within six months after a Director of Price Stabilization was appointed, 13 regional and 84 district offices were established. Once started, the OPS did a commendable job of holding prices. During 1951 there was a general leveling off of prices due in large part to price regulations.

**Removal of Controls**    In the latter part of 1951 and the first half of 1952, there was considerable softening in our economy. Price declines were in evidence in certain sectors. The defense program, which was running behind schedule, was extended over a longer period. However, the heavy inflationary pressures expected in late 1951 and 1952 did not materialize. Shortages predicted did not occur. Strengthening of consumer resistance to high prices, obliteration of scare buying, and accelerated debt repayment mitigated consumer demand. Businesses that had scheduled production of consumer goods at high levels in anticipation of increased demand accumulated large, high-priced inventories. As a consequence, widespread sales and curtailment of production pervaded the economy in an attempt to improve inventory positions.

In 1952 government monetary measures were mollified or eliminated as the need for them disappeared. When the private demand for bank credit lessened in the early part of the year, the regulations governing consumer installment credit and the Voluntary Credit Restraint Program were suspended. Lower down payments were also allowed for the purchase of homes.

Subsequently it became possible for OPS to begin suspending controls where they were no longer required. For emergency purposes, however, each suspension order included a specific "recontrol point." Fortunately the inflationary pressures were not too great thereafter, and OPS followed an orderly process of decontrol. Stronger indirect controls, through monetary and fiscal policies, were substituted in many cases for the direct controls. Complete decontrol was accomplished prior to the Korean truce in June, 1953.

Decontrol was more successful after Korea than it was after World War II. This may have been due in part to the fact that a more orderly decontrol process on a gradual basis was utilized, but the big factor was the state of the economy at the end of the Korean conflict compared to what it was after World War II. After Korea there was no large pent-up demand for consumer goods since we did not have to resort to rationing under OPS. Secondly, there was an absence of the large foreign demand since production in other countries of the world had not been interrupted during the Korean conflict as it had been during World War II. Thirdly, businesses generally were not in need of expansion as they were after World War II, since they were able to obtain materials for private investment during the Korean episode. As a result, the price level did not take a jump at the time OPS decontrolled.

## Wage and Price Guideposts

After several years of relative price stability during the 1950s, some price unrest was becoming apparent in the economy in the latter half of 1961. In seeking the continuation of price stability, President Kennedy in his 1962 *Economic Report* established a set of voluntary wage and price guideposts. If accepted by the major firms in the economy and in the collective bargaining power centers, it would do much, according to the President, to restrain upward pressures on the price level. As a guide for noninflationary wage behavior, the rate of increase in wage rates (including fringe benefits) in each industry was to be equated with the national trend in overall productivity increase. Although general acceptance of the guideposts would maintain the stability of labor cost per unit of output for the economy as a whole, it would not stabilize labor cost per unit for individual firms or industries. Based upon the fact that the average productivity per worker in our economy increased about 3 percent annually, the guideposts initially recommended that wage increases be held to 3 percent each year. This would allow the increase in wage cost to be absorbed out of rising productivity without necessitating a price increase. The guideposts did have some flexibility insofar as they suggested that any firm whose gain in productivity per man-hour was more than the guidepost figure should hold its wage increase to 3 percent and give consumers some benefit by reducing prices. On the other hand, it recommended that any firm whose increase in productivity was less than the guidepost figure could grant a 3 percent wage increase but offset this with an increase in prices. Subsequently, using a 5-year average, the guidepost figure was raised to 3.2 percent.

The guideposts, of course, stirred up considerable controversy in both wage and price circles. In many firms and industries where the rate of productivity was less than the national average, the guideposts were used by labor unions as a basis for a wage increase higher than the productivity rate increase within the firm or industry. In other firms or industries where the productivity rate exceeded the national average productivity increase, the firms often used the guidepost in an effort to limit the amount of a wage increase to 3 percent, even though they might have been able to afford higher wage increases. Another complaint was the fact that the guideposts tended to freeze labor's share of the national income.

Although the concept of price and wage guideposts seemed to be pushed out of the limelight by the emphasis on the tax cut in the 1963 *Economic Report* and by the poverty package in the 1964 *Report*, the guideposts were emphasized again by President Johnson and his Economic Advisers in the spring and summer of 1964. The President's personal representative discussed with industry members the importance of noninflationary wage agreements between labor and management, especially in the automobile and other basic industries. Subsequently, however, the AFL-CIO stated officially and publicly that it did not intend to be limited by the wage guidepost in seeking wage increases during that year, and the President of the United Auto Workers stated that since the productivity increase in the automobile industry was much above the national average, the union was not going to limit its wage demands to the average of 3.2 percent. About the same time, steel companies were talking about the need for a price increase to offset some of their increasing costs. At that time President Johnson publicly warned that any increase in steel prices "would strongly conflict with our national interest in price stability."

With the return of stronger inflationary pressures in 1966, some delicate situations and open confrontations regarding the voluntary acceptance of the guideposts developed between the White House and/or the President's Council of Economic Advisers on the one hand and large industries and powerful unions on the other. Consequently, in 1967 the use of a specific guidepost figure was deemphasized, although the guidepost concept was still retained. By 1968, however, the guideposts were pretty well shattered as both labor unions and business firms posted wage and price increases substantially beyond the guidepost figures.

### The War in Vietnam

After 7 years of *nagging unemployment* and relatively stable prices following the 1958 depression, the economy in mid-1965 began approaching full employment. For seven years, 1958–1965, we had been dealing with the problem of a "production gap," with the economy operating at 8–10 percent under its potential capacity. During this time unemployment averaged 5.7 percent. We used several measures to bolster the economy and to accelerate our rate of economic growth during this period, as we saw in the previous chapter.

**Economy in Transition**   In the winter of 1965–1966, the economy entered a transition phase. By the middle of 1965, unemployment had fallen below 5 percent and by the end of the year it had dropped to 4.1 percent, approaching the full employment level for the first time in seven years. With the record rate of private investment, exuberant consumer spending, continued expenses for "Great Society" programs, large federal deficits, and heavy outlays for the escalation of the war in Vietnam, it was obvious that there were likely to be considerable upward pressures on the price level. It appeared that we were moving from an economy of nagging unemployment and undercapacity with emphasis on poverty, to an economy of full employment, full capacity, shortages of skilled labor, scarcities of certain materials, and inflationary pressures.

Early in December, 1965, the Federal Reserve took what it considered an appropriate step to combat the clouds of inflation it foresaw on the horizon by raising the discount rate. Its action was both praised and criticized. Among its most vociferous critics were key officials of the Administration who considered the Federal Reserve's action unwarranted, untimely, and a detriment to the Administration's economic program for continued economic growth and higher employment. Nevertheless, during 1966 the Federal Reserve was successful to some extent in its attempt to apply some brake against inflation by tightening the money supply through the discount rate and open-market operations. This action contributed to the "money crunch" of 1966, which had a substantial impact on the construction industry.

By January, 1966, unemployment fell to 4.0 percent and in February it was down to 3.9 percent, the first time the full employment level had been reached in more than seven years. The Administration, which only a few months earlier had been studying the possibility of declaring a fiscal dividend in the form of an additional tax cut to prevent a fiscal drag on the economy, faced a serious problem of deciding whether it should continue its expansionary fiscal measures or whether it should shift to anti-inflationary measures.

It was concerned, of course, that anti-inflationary devices could slow down the economy. Some contended that the proposed measures might cause the economy to reverse its upward trend of five years and even precipitate a recession. The Administration, and for that matter Congress also, clearly had the following choices of what to do about the inflationary pressures building up in the economy:

1. Do nothing and hope that prices would not increase by any more than the 2 percent predicted earlier.
2. Reduce government spending for domestic programs to offset the increased spending for defense in Vietnam.
3. Raise taxes to cover the cost of increased government spending.
4. Encourage the Federal Reserve to further tighten the money supply.
5. Impose wage and price controls.
6. Rely on *jawbone* tactics and implementation of the voluntary wage-price guideposts.

**Inflation — 1966**    After much discussion and analysis the Johnson Administration took only limited precautionary measures against inflation. In large part it rejected the idea of increasing taxes or reducing federal spending. Wage and price controls appeared to be an extreme. It did little to encourage or supplement the Federal Reserve's tighter money policy. On the other hand, the Administration did not sit by idly and do nothing. Early in 1966 it rescinded the excise tax cuts on automobile sales and telephone service. It also provided for an accelerated method of corporate tax collection and other minor measures to help avert inflation. But the Administration put its primary emphasis on jawbone tactics through its "get tough" policy in regard to implementation of the voluntary wage-price guideposts. Sometimes successful, and at other times not, it endeavored to hold wage increases to the 3.2 percent guidepost figure, and it used persuasion of various types to influence major industries and labor unions to hold the price and wage line. Not until it became apparent that the price level was increasing at a 4 percent annual rate did the Administration take further action by suspending in September, 1966, the 7 percent tax credit on new investment and the accelerated depreciation measures.

Although the price increases slowed down a bit toward the end of the year, the CPI showed an annual increase of 3.3 percent. In December, 1966, unemployment measured 3.8 percent of the civilian labor force compared to 4.0 percent 12 months earlier. Employment increased during the year by approximately 1.5 million workers on a seasonally adjusted basis and 3.4 million on a nonseasonally adjusted basis.

**Mini-Recession — Early 1967**    The price level (CPI) did stabilize in the latter part of 1966 and the first quarter of 1967, increasing by no more than .2 percentage points in any one month. It was evident that the economy was slowing down since GNP during the first quarter of 1967 showed only a $4.8 billion increase compared to quarterly increases of $12 and $14 billion respectively in each of the two previous quarters. In terms of constant dollars, figures for the GNP in the first quarter of 1967 actually declined by $400 million. This mini-recession of 1967, as it has frequently been labeled, was caused primarily by a decline in the rate of private investment of $15.5 billion. No doubt the suspension of tax credits on new investment had a pronounced effect on the rate of decline in new investment.

Although the President in his 1967 *Economic Report* mentioned the need for a 6 percent surcharge on personal and corporate income taxes to combat the inflationary tendency in the economy, the measure was not pushed to any degree in Congress in the early part of 1967. Many government officials, economists, and others naturally felt that inflation had been beaten and cited the fact that it was accomplished without any sizable tax increase, without any drastic cut in government spending, or without the imposition of wage and price controls. In fact, by the end of 1966 the Federal Reserve had ceased its tight money policy and in the first quarter of 1967 it was again displaying a more liberal attitude toward the creation of credit. The discount rate, for example, was decreased from 4.5 percent to 4 percent in April, 1967. As a stimulant to the sluggish economy, the 7 percent tax credit on new investment was restored in June, 1967, six months ahead of schedule.

**Inflation Resumes — Mid-1967**   The joys of the stable-price advocates, however, were short-lived, because by the second quarter of 1967 the consumer price index resumed its upward movement. By the end of 1967 the CPI had risen 3 percent for the year. Although unemployment again averaged 3.8 percent of the civilian labor force for 1967, by the end of the year it was down to 3.5 percent. As a result, members of the Administration and others were again talking about the need for restraint. Some government officials were even suggesting that direct controls of various kinds might be needed to cool the economy if management and labor did not hold wages and prices in check. By the end of 1967 and early 1968, the Federal Reserve moved toward a tighter money position by raising reserve requirements and moving the discount rate back to 4.5 percent.

**The Income Tax Surcharge — 1968**   In his *Economic Report* of 1968 President Johnson called for the imposition of a 10 percent surcharge on personal and corporate income taxes as a means of combating inflation. The size of the proposed surcharge was increased from 6 percent to 10 percent because signs of an overheated economy were more in evidence, including the pending size of the federal deficit in excess of $25 billion for fiscal 1968. The proposed bill to effectuate the tax became embroiled in a Congressional hassle as to whether it was better to increase taxes or reduce federal spending. As a result of prolonged hearings and debate in Congress, final action on the tax bill was delayed until June, 1968. At that time Congress imposed a 10 percent surcharge on personal and corporate income taxes, making the surcharge retroactive to April 1 for individual income and January 1, 1968, on corporate income, effective until June, 1969.

The impact of the surtax fell more heavily on savings than expected, however, as consumers continued their outlays for goods and services, especially for new cars, and the rate of savings fell sharply. Fixed investment for plant equipment, which increased moderately in the first half of 1968, accelerated in the second half. Capital spending was no doubt spurred by the prognostication of investors that the 7 percent investment credit might again be suspended as an anti-inflationary measure. In spite of limited funds available for mortgages, there was no reduction in residential construction during the last half of 1968. There was some dampening in federal expenditures during this time and the federal deficit was reduced from a rate of $9 billion in the first half of the year to $3 billion in the second half.

By mid-1968 a number of hefty national wage increases had taken place within the economy adding to the cost-push inflationary element. The shortage of skilled labor and even unskilled labor was evident in the economy. Average hourly wage gains of 7 percent in manufacturing industries during the year plus a reduction in savings, however, offset the impact of the income surcharge. Thus, labor unit costs rose sharply.

All this, of course, caused prices to continue their upward movement through 1968. The cost of services, such as personal care, medical care, home ownership, and auto repair and maintenance increased rapidly. By the end of 1968, the Consumer Price Index had risen 4.7 percent. Thus, in spite of the addition of a strong fiscal measure to accompany somewhat restrictive monetary measures, little success was achieved in arresting the upward movement of prices in 1968.

### Nixonomics

With prices and wages continuing to rise in 1969, the Federal Reserve, which had reduced the discount rate in August, 1968, in anticipation of strong anti-inflationary reaction to the tax increase, adopted a more restrictive policy. As a result of various monetary measures, the rates of growth of the money stock declined to about 2.5 percent in the first quarter of 1969, compared to an annual increase of 6 percent in 1967 and 7 percent in 1968. The Federal Reserve, through a series of changes, moved the discount rate from 5.5 percent in December, 1968, to 6 percent in April, 1969. By the summer of 1969 the prime rate for commercial loans offered by banks had reached 8.5 percent. Government bonds were yielding between 7 and 8 percent, high grade commercial bonds over 7 percent, and the interest rate on federal funds had approached the 10 percent level.

By the middle of 1969 prices were still rising. The CPI jumped 0.8 percentage points in June. This meant that the CPI in the first half of

1969 rose at an annual rate of 6.3 percent. In 1969 price increases were especially noticeable in food costs, up at the rate of 9 percent annually, and services, which rose at a 7.5 percent annual rate in the first 6 months of the year.

**Gradualism**    With the inauguration of the Nixon Administration, inflation was cited as the nation's number one domestic issue. President Nixon adopted a policy of *gradualism* to bring inflation under control. In this regard, he wanted to return the economy to stable prices without seriously disrupting the growth in economic activity. Among other measures, he asked Congress to retain the 10 percent tax surcharge that was due to expire in June, 1969. The budget was balanced and, in fact, ran a slight surplus in fiscal 1970. Defense and other government spending was cut and the Fed tightened the money supply. Although there was some discussion about the need for wage and price restrictions of some type, the President shied away from either formal or informal wage and price measures. By the end of 1969 it was apparent that the measures employed to "cool off" the economy were effective in slowing down production. But they were not effective in slowing down the rate of inflation. Although the real GNP declined in the fourth quarter of 1969, the price level was increasing at a rate of 6 percent.

With certain reservations, the forecasts for the year 1970 were favorable. Most analysts suggested that there would be some slack in the first half of the year, followed by a rebound in economic activity in the second half. It was the hope of the President's Council of Economic Advisers that the inflationary rate, which had been in the vicinity of 6 percent, would recede to 3.5 percent by the end of the year. Economic measures designed to cool the economy and bring about a reduction in inflation were expected to result in a slightly higher level of unemployment, up from 3.5 percent to, perhaps, 4.5 percent of the civilian labor force.

The economy did cool off in the first half of the year for a number of reasons, including a decline in business investment, a cutback in defense spending, a tightness of money, and a slowdown in housing starts. The two-quarter decline in the real GNP (fourth quarter, 1969, and first quarter, 1970) was followed by a sidewise movement in the second quarter of 1970. The price level, however, continued to rise at an undesirable rate of more than 5 percent annually. Measures designed primarily to arrest demand-pull inflation failed to contain cost-push price pressures. Unemployment increased more than anticipated and reached a rate of 5.5 percent by midyear. This left the Administration in the delicate position of deciding whether to continue anti-inflationary measures and risk the possibility of higher unemployment, or shift to expansionary measures and risk the resurgence of inflationary pressures, an especially delicate decision in an election year.

Unfortunately the economy did not rebound in the second half of the year. Unemployment for the year averaged 4.9 percent and by the end of the year it had reached 6 percent. Although 1970 was officially labeled a recession year, the CPI still managed to increase by 5.9 percent.

In the late months of 1970 the Administration shifted its emphasis to expansionary measures. A number of steps were taken to increase effective demand. Earlier in the year, the personal and corporate income tax surcharge was allowed to lapse. The Federal Reserve liberalized the money supply and adopted an accelerated depreciation schedule to spur business investment. Discount rates were lowered several times, moving down to 4.75 percent within three months, and the Administration announced that the federal deficit for fiscal 1971 would be in excess of $18 billion and that the projected federal budget for fiscal 1972 showed an $11.6 billion deficit. The Administration was trusting that any resulting increase in effective demand would not evoke demand-pull inflationary pressures, since the economy was in a state of less than full employment. The Administration, however, was concerned about cost-push price pressures. Consequently, in early 1971 it began jawboning as a means of holding the price line and more was heard about the possibility of wage and price guideposts and an incomes policy.

**The Game Plan**    Economic forecasts for 1971 were good, but nothing spectacular. Most forecasts expected the GNP to be in the range of $1,045 billion to $1,055 billion for the year. It was anticipated that about half of the projected 6 to 7 percent increase would be in real production and the other half in higher prices. The President's Council of Economic Advisers set year-end goals of 4.5 percent unemployment and a 3.5 percent rate of inflation. The Nixon economic *game plan* was to restore full employment and stable prices by mid-1972. Measures designed to attain that growth rate, remove the production gap, and eliminate nagging unemployment, however, could very well add to price pressures and cause the rate of inflation to accelerate. The task of reaching stable prices was aggravated, too, by the fact that wage increases of 30 percent or more spread over a three-year period had been negotiated in the construction, auto, railroad, and tin can industries. Similar wage concessions in the steel industry in the summer of 1971 led to an immediate 8 percent average increase in steel prices. Some members of Congress, who in early 1971 recommended that President Nixon utilize the authority given to him in 1970 to impose wage and price restrictions on the economy, renewed their efforts after the steel settlement.

At the midyear Congressional hearings on the state of the economy, an Administrative official indicated that the Administration was not going to reach its year-end goals of disinflation and reduction of unemployment. It was stated that price increases and unemployment were much more stubborn than anticipated. A month later, in response to an inquiry of what the Administration was going to do about inflation and unemployment, the Secretary of the Treasury stated that the Administration was not going to impose wage and price controls, adopt wage-price guideposts, increase government spending, or reduce taxes.

### The New Economic Policy

Economic pressures regarding prices, wages, and the balance of payments brought about a change of attitude on the part of the White House by mid-1971.

**Phase I: The 90-Day Freeze** With the knowledge that progress on his economic game plan was being stifled by substantial wage and price increases, President Nixon in August, 1971, made drastic and sweeping changes of domestic and international economic policies. Among other measures he declared a 90-day freeze on all prices, wages, and rents, temporarily suspended convertibility of dollars into gold, imposed a 10 percent surcharge on imports, froze a scheduled pay increase for government employees, sought to reinstitute tax credits as a means of stimulating investment and jobs, asked Congress to reduce personal income taxes, and requested Congress to repeal the 7 percent excise tax on automobiles.

The President established a Cost of Living Council to work out details for restoring free markets without inflation during a transition period following the freeze. Congress did oblige the President by repealing the excise tax on automobiles and reducing personal income taxes by advancing the scheduled date for an increase in personal income tax exemptions.

**Phase II** The 90-day freeze was followed by a Phase II control period. For the implementation of this phase the President established a Pay Board and a Price Commission. Each was to work out what it considered permissible noninflationary wage and price increases, respectively. The Commissions were composed of representatives of labor, management, and the general public. The Pay Board subsequently established a 5.5 percent annual wage increase as a maximum. It did allow for certain exceptions to the 5.5 percent figure. It also allowed scheduled raises that were to have taken effect during the freeze period to take effect during Phase II.

The Price Commission, on the other hand, attempted to hold overall price increases in the CPI to 2.5 percent annually. Since the President did not desire to set up an elaborate formal structure of wage and price controls, such as existed during World War II and during the Korean Conflict, much of the stabilization program had to depend on voluntary compliance. The Cost of Living Council exempted most of the smaller business firms and their workers from any reporting requirements. Intermediate and larger size firms were required to report changes in prices and wages. Larger firms, moreover, had to give prenotification of changes to the Price Commission and/or the Pay Board.

The immediate effectiveness of the New Economic Policy in combating inflation can be gauged somewhat by the fact that during the six months prior to the freeze, prices increased at an annual rate of 4.5

percent; but in the five months subsequent to the freeze, they increased at an annual rate of 2.2 percent. The price level for 1972, during which price controls existed for the entire year, increased 3.3 percent, as shown in Table 18-1.

The stability of prices in the first half of the 1960s compared to the inflationary period starting in 1966 can be seen in Table 18-1. From 1960 to 1965, for example, prices rose at an average annual rate of 1.3 percent. From 1965 to August, 1971, prices rose at an average annual rate of more than 4.5 percent.

Although employment increased substantially during this period, the amount and rate of unemployment, after dwindling early in the decade, rose in the next few years. Note in Table 18-1 the net increase of over 2 million in unemployment between 1969 and 1971.

**Phase III**   In January, 1973, after commenting favorably on the results of Phase II in stabilizing prices and wages, President Nixon announced Phase III of his New Economic Policy, which in effect reestablished voluntary guideposts for price and wage increases. The guidepost figures used at that time were 2.5 percent and 5.5 percent annually for prices and wages, respectively.

**Phase IV**   The removal of compulsory Phase II controls proved to be premature, however. During the first five months after decontrol, the CPI rose at an annual rate of nearly 9 percent. Consequently, on June 13, 1973, President Nixon declared a 60-day freeze on prices. Wages were not affected at this time. Instead of ending the freeze on all goods at the end of the 60-day period, prices were unfrozen selectively, and Phase IV controls were imposed on various categories of goods and services at different times before and after the 60-day period.

Again large firms were required to give a 30-day prenotification of price increases. Unlike Phase II, however, firms did not have to wait for approval by the Cost of Living Council before putting such increases into effect. But the Council had authority to delay any price increases indefinitely, and it reserved the right to reexamine prices at any time. The new base period established was the fiscal quarter prior to January 12, 1973, the date of decontrol of Phase II. Price increases equal to dollar cost increases subsequent to the base period were to be permitted by Phase IV. No allowance was to be made for a profit markup on these cost increases. Controls were imposed on an industry-by-industry basis, thus providing more flexibility than was available under Phase II. At the time of the imposition of Phase IV, several high Administration officials indicated that they hoped controls could be removed by the end of 1973. Most of the controls were removed by early 1974. Unfortunately, the CPI rose 6.2 percent in 1973. (If the CPI were measured from December, 1972, to December, 1973, instead of by yearly averages, the price increase would be 8.8 percent for 1973.)

Table 18-1    **EMPLOYMENT, UNEMPLOYMENT, AND PRICES, 1960–1974**

| Year | Total Employment | Unemployment | Rate of Unemployment | CPI (1967 = 100) | Rate of Inflation |
|------|------|------|------|------|------|
| 1960 | 65,778 | 3,852 | 5.5 | 88.7 | — |
| 1961 | 65,746 | 4,714 | 6.7 | 89.6 | 1.0 |
| 1962 | 66,702 | 3,911 | 5.5 | 90.6 | 1.1 |
| 1963 | 67,762 | 4,070 | 5.7 | 91.7 | 1.0 |
| 1964 | 69,305 | 3,786 | 5.2 | 92.9 | 1.3 |
| 1965 | 71,088 | 3,366 | 4.5 | 94.5 | 1.7 |
| 1966 | 72,895 | 2,875 | 3.8 | 97.2 | 2.9 |
| 1967 | 74,372 | 2,775 | 3.8 | 100.0 | 2.9 |
| 1968 | 75,920 | 2,817 | 3.6 | 104.2 | 4.2 |
| 1969 | 77,902 | 2,813 | 3.5 | 109.8 | 5.4 |
| 1970 | 78,627 | 4,088 | 4.9 | 116.3 | 5.9 |
| 1971 | 79,120 | 4,993 | 5.9 | 121.3 | 4.2 |
| 1972 | 81,702 | 4,840 | 5.6 | 125.3 | 3.3 |
| 1973 | 84,409 | 4,304 | 4.9 | 133.1 | 6.2 |
| 1974 | 85,936 | 5,076 | 5.6 | 147.7 | 11.0 |

Source: *Economic Report of the President*, 1975.

## The Trade-Off Between Unemployment and Inflation

Once the economy is at full employment it is difficult to ride the crest of the economy at the point where unemployment is minimized and the price level stabilized. The debate in recent years about the trade-off between increased unemployment and an increase in prices has renewed interest in the concept known as the *Phillips curve*. This curve was developed by a British economist, A. W. Phillips, who studied the relationship between the level of unemployment and wage increases for the United Kingdom for the years 1861 to 1913. From his studies he found that when unemployment was high money wage increases were smaller and when a low level of unemployment existed wage increases were larger. Phillips concluded that the money wage level would stabilize with a 5 percent unemployment rate.

In the 1960s American economists began to apply the Phillips curve to changes in prices in relation to unemployment. This became feasible especially when the level of unemployment began to fall consistently below the 4 percent level. Subsequently a number of Phillips curves have been developed showing the relationship between price changes and the level of unemployment. Any interpretation of these curves must be made cautiously, since they are constructed with various assumptions. There is absolutely no certainty, for example, that because a given relationship occurred in the past it will hold precisely in the future. Many conditions may change in the interim. Furthermore, several curves have been constructed from the same data, each showing a slightly different relationship depending on the time lag used. Figure 18-1 depicts a Phillips curve developed by Paul Samuelson. It shows price stability at about 5.5 percent unemployment, a 2 percent price rise associated with 4 percent unemployment, and a 4.5 percent price rise associated with 3 percent unemployment.

Several other Phillips curves have been developed over the years. One shows a price rise of about 2.5 percent associated with unemployment of 4 percent. Another shows a price increase of around 4 percent associated with a 4 percent unemployment rate. Still others, developed more recently, depict a rightward shifting of the Phillips curve, indicating a higher

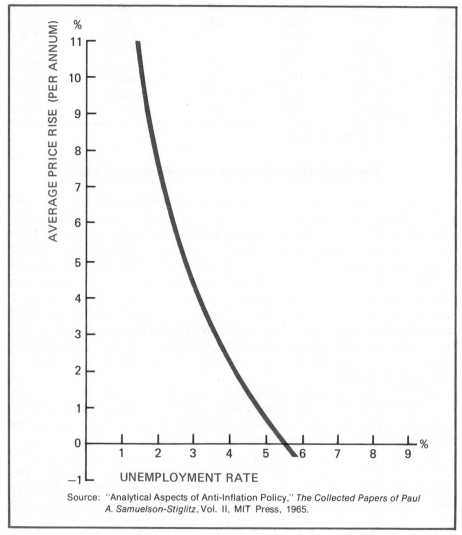

Source: "Analytical Aspects of Anti-Inflation Policy," *The Collected Papers of Paul A. Samuelson-Stiglitz*, Vol. II, MIT Press, 1965.

Figure 18-1   **MODIFIED PHILLIPS CURVE FOR THE UNITED STATES**

price level-unemployment relationship in which both the price level and unemployment rates are higher as one is traded off against the other.

The Phillips curve has some validity when inflation is demand-pull in nature. But the relationship between unemployment and price changes does not hold as well when inflation is cost-push or structural. A Phillips curve for the years 1970 to 1975, excluding the months of price control, for example, would definitely move the price-unemployment line of best fit far to the right. Particularly out of focus would be the years 1974 and 1975 when double-digit inflation prevailed with unemployment ranging between 6 and 9.2 percent. This has led some analysts to challenge the Phillips curve and its relationship between unemployment and price-level changes. It should be remembered, however, that the Phillips curve was originally designed to measure the relationship between demand-pull inflation and unemployment, not cost-push, structural, or other varieties of inflation.

### Slumpflation — A New Ball Game

In spite of an economic slowdown, prices soared in 1974. Unemployment moved back above 5 percent and reached 6.5 percent by the end of the year, its highest level in more than a decade. Upon taking office in mid-1974, President Ford declared that the economy was not in a recession and that it was not moving in that direction. He subsequently called for a series of economic summit meetings among leading economists, businesspeople, labor leaders, and government officials to discuss suggestions for combating inflation. Recommendations were many and diverse. President Ford then presented his anti-inflationary program which advocated a tax surcharge, a decrease in federal spending, a balanced budget, several energy-saving measures, a fuel conservation recommendation, tougher antitrust enforcement, a number of measures to encourage savings, exhortations to consumers to shop for bargains, establishment of a consumer committee, and an organization of inflation fighters, whose slogan was to be WIN (Whip Inflation Now). His proposed program did include some measures to alleviate unemployment. These included an expanded public employment program, the injection of funds into the housing market, and tax credits for new investment. The major emphasis of President Ford's program at that time was very definitely one of anti-inflation.

As the state of the economy deteriorated over the next few months and it became evident to President Ford and his economic advisers that the economy actually was in a recession, the emphasis of economic policy began to shift toward expansionary measures. The real GNP had dropped for a third consecutive quarter, unemployment had reached 6.5 percent and was predicted to reach as high as 8 percent or more, the housing industry was still in the doldrums, inventories of such items as automobiles and appliances were piling up, investment plans were being trimmed, and economic conditions in Europe and Japan were likewise depressed. However, demand-pull price pressure had abated. But with a number of sizable wage settlements and administered prices being set, double-digit inflation still prevailed due to cost-push, structural, and social inflationary pressures in the economy.

It was apparent to all that the state of the economy had slipped downward from stagflation to *slumpflation*. Some analysts were talking in terms of a mini-depression. Consequently, President Ford abandoned his plans to reduce federal spending and balance the budget. Early in 1975 he accelerated a public employment program and recommended an extension of unemployment compensation. He presented a $349.4 billion federal budget, including a huge $52 billion deficit. Included in the budget was a $16 billion tax reduction and other measures to offset growing unemployment, which grew to 9.2 percent in May, 1975. Numerous other expansionary measures were being suggested by economists, businesspeople, labor leaders, and members of Congress.

This slumpflation, of course, threw economists into a new ball game. Previously they had figured they knew what measures to use to expand the economy during a recession and what measures to recommend to combat inflationary pressures. However, when recession and inflation occur simultaneously, a condition with which we have had very little experience, a real dilemma is presented. Should the Administration, for example, emphasize anti-inflationary measures and risk aggravating unemployment or should it emphasize expansionary measures and risk higher prices? Not only is there an absence of foolproof economic measures to deal with slumpflation, but prudent decisions have to be made regarding which is a more serious problem — unemployment or inflation.

## SUMMARY

Demand-pull inflation occurs when the total monetary demand for goods and services exceeds the value of the current goods and services available. When such a situation arises, it can be alleviated either by increasing the output of goods and services or by reducing the demand. In a fully employed economy it is difficult to increase output; therefore, it is necessary to use the latter alternative. In this case, the effective demand of the government, consumers, and investors should be reduced.

In a wartime economy it is difficult to reduce government expenditures without impairing the war effort. Therefore, measures must be used that tend to reduce consumption and private investment. Heavy taxation, voluntary savings, compulsory savings, rationing, and wage, price, and other controls can be used. It should also be remembered that inflation can be of a cost-push, structural, or social type.

In the United States we have had considerable experience combating inflation in the past few decades. Strong demand-pull inflationary pressures occurred just prior to and during World War II. During this period taxes were increased in an effort to transfer purchasing power to the government for military goods and in an effort to reduce consumption and private investment. Widespread savings plans were encouraged through the sale of war bonds. An excess profits tax was instituted, and a controlled materials plan was established to preserve the flow of goods. Consumer credit was tightened considerably. Since total effective demand was still not reduced sufficiently to prevent inflation, wage and price controls were established to suppress the pending inflation in the economy.

With the outbreak of hostilities in Korea, the United States was near a full-employment position. Therefore, prices rose more rapidly than they did after the outbreak of World War II. Delays in imposing proper economic controls permitted the price level to reach a new high. During this time an attempt at voluntary pricing standards proved to be a failure. The first widespread compulsory pricing regulations appeared six months after the outbreak of hostilities. The imposition of heavy taxes, the encouragement of savings through the purchase of government bonds, the establishment of a controlled materials plan, along with price and wage controls, helped to hold prices in check during the latter part of the Korean Conflict. Removal of controls after the Conflict did not result in an increase in the price level, as it did after World War II, since inflationary conditions had been pretty well eliminated by that time.

Even with all our knowledge and experience about combating inflation, a lukewarm approach to the problem during the early years of the war in Vietnam caused the price level to increase noticeably in 1966 and 1967 after a period of substantial price stability. More serious measures, such as an income tax surcharge, tight money, and a balanced budget were somewhat effective in moderating demand-pull inflation. But they were ineffective against cost-push inflationary pressures. In spite of the efforts made to contain inflation, the price level rose 25 percent during the five-year period, 1966–1971. In August, 1971, President Nixon imposed a 90-day freeze on all prices and wages. This was followed by Phase II compulsory controls which were instrumental in holding prices to an annual increase of 3.3 percent during 1972. With the removal of controls in January, 1973, prices rose substantially and Phase IV controls were instituted by midyear. The effect of Phase IV was limited, however, and controls were subsequently removed. During 1974 the price level rose at an annual rate of 11 percent. By that time the economy was in a recession and the emphasis was shifted from anti-inflationary to expansionary measures.

Unfortunately government spending as a means of stabilizing the economy, if not handled properly or because of uncontrollable circumstances, may result in the creation of debt. Problems connected with such debt are discussed in the next chapter.

## DISCUSSION QUESTIONS

1. How does a progressive income tax rate serve as a built-in stabilizer to offset inflation?

2. To combat inflation do you think it is better to decrease government spending and hold taxes constant,

or hold government spending constant and increase taxes?

3. Should we tax sufficiently to pay the full cost of a war, instead of borrowing, as a means of avoiding inflation? Why or why not?

4. Do you agree with the idea of compulsory savings during an inflationary period? Discuss.

5. Do you think that voluntary pricing regulations such as those suggested in the President's wage and price guideposts will ever work in our economy? Why?

6. Explain why measures that may diminish or eliminate demand-pull inflation may not work successfully against cost-push inflation.

7. Do you think that the President was wise in imposing a 90-day freeze on wages and prices in August, 1971?

8. Do you think that Phase II controls should have been terminated in January, 1973?

9. Why is inflation difficult to combat if it occurs during a recession as it did in 1974 and 1975?

10. When did the economy recover from the 1974–1975 recession? What is the current state of the economy?

## SUGGESTED READINGS

Ackley, Gardner. "Two-Stage Recession and Inflation, 1973–1975." *Economic Outlook U.S.A.* University of Michigan (Winter, 1975).

"A Primer on Inflation: Its Conception, Its Cost, Its Consequences." *Review*, Federal Reserve Bank of St. Louis (January, 1975).

*Economic Report of the President.* Washington: U.S. Government Printing Office, 1966–1975.

Ferge, Edgar L., and Douglas D. Pearce. "The Wage-Price Control Experiment — Did It Work?" *Challenge* (July/August, 1973).

Francis, Darryl R. "Inflation, Recession — What's a Policymaker to Do?" *Review*, Federal Reserve Bank of St. Louis (November, 1974).

Haberler, G. "Thoughts on Inflation: The Basic Forces." *Business Economics* (January, 1975).

Heller, Walter W. *New Dimensions of Political Economy.* Cambridge, Mass.: Harvard University Press, 1966. Chapters 1–5.

"Indexation as a Response to Inflation." *Economic Review*, Federal Reserve Bank of Richmond (November/December, 1974).

McCracken, Paul W. "The Economy of 1975." *Economic Outlook U.S.A.* University of Michigan (1975).

——————. "Two Years and Four Phases Later." *The Wall Street Journal*, August 13, 1973.

McKenna, Joseph P. *Aggregate Economic Analysis.* Hinsdale, Ill.: The Dryden Press, 1972.

Miller, Roger L., and Raburn Williams. *The New Economics of Richard Nixon.* New York: Canfield Press, 1972.

——————. *Unemployment and Inflation.* St. Paul, Minn.: West Publishing Co., 1974.

"The Modern Paradox: Fighting Inflation and Recession." *Business Week* (December 7, 1974).

Wachter, Michael L. "Did Wage-Price Controls Reduce Inflation?" *Wharton Quarterly* (Summer/Fall, 1974).

Wallich, Henry. "Why Does This Inflation Hurt So Much?" *Wharton Quarterly* (Summer/Fall, 1974).

# 19 BUDGETARY POLICY AND THE NATIONAL DEBT

## PATTERN OF ANTICYCLICAL MEASURES

Over the past forty years or so, we have accepted and established a policy of economic stabilization and developed a set of anticyclical measures that can be utilized to combat recessions and inflation and accelerate the rate of economic growth. We seek to bring about a more stable economy with the use of monetary, fiscal, and psychological policies. It is easy to observe those monetary measures that change the amount and flow of money. Changes in taxation and spending also are readily noticeable. It is sometimes difficult, however, to determine whether such measures are for stabilization purposes or otherwise. Although we do not have a crystallized psychological policy, there has been a strong tendency in recent years to encourage consumption and investment spending during some periods and to encourage thrift and savings at other times. Moreover, attempts have been made to ward off undesirable movements in economic activity by creating a proper frame of mind among individuals and businesspeople.

In an endeavor to modify sluggish as well as inflationary tendencies in the economy, mild indirect measures are usually employed at first. If the adverse movement persists, however, stronger indirect and then direct anticyclical measures are generally utilized. We can summarize the anticyclical measures available by referring to hypothetical, yet practical, situations. For example, when the economy is in a state of unemployment, we will generally use monetary measures to encourage consumption and private investment. There will be a general liberalization of the money supply. The first efforts in this direction are usually made through the use of open-market operations and by decreasing discount rates. Existing selective controls, especially credit restrictions, are modified or eliminated. Moral suasion is also employed to encourage bank lending, and the Federal Reserve Banks are less restrictive on loans to member banks. Although it is not always noticeable, the Open Market Committee usually begins to buy bonds in early stages of a recessionary period. From past indications, the reserve requirements are the last monetary measure to be put into play.

Fiscal measures may be invoked simultaneously with the stronger monetary measures or may follow shortly after them. Reducing taxes with constant or rising government expenditures is a popular method of increasing the proportion of government spending. However, increased government expenditures with constant or reduced taxes also may be used. Higher government spending coupled with higher taxes is the least likely measure to be used to bolster the economy during a recessionary period. Specific measures such as public employment programs, extension of unemployment compensation, injection of funds into the housing market, and tax measures designed to stimulate investment may also be invoked.

During the time when monetary and fiscal measures are being used, the Administration and various other government agencies, including the Department of Commerce, the Council of Economic Advisers, the Treasury Department, the Federal Reserve Board, and others will be issuing persuasive statements in an endeavor to encourage consumption and private investment. The exact bundle of stabilization measures to be used and the pattern of their implementation will, of course, vary with different political administrations.

## BUDGETARY POLICY

The use of fiscal measures involves the federal budget. The size, growth, and nature of the budget, whether it is balanced or unbalanced, affects our national debt. Interrelated are monetary measures that may be involved in financing any deficit. Monetary measures likewise can have an influence on the structure and maturity of the national debt. In turn the actual management of the national debt can have a stabilizing or destabilizing effect on the level of economic activity and the price level. Consequently, we now turn to an analysis of budgetary policy and the many problems associated with the national debt.

### Types of Budgets

The type of budget we have will affect the level of economic activity to some degree. There are three types: (1) a balanced budget, (2) a deficit budget, and (3) a surplus budget.

**Balanced Budget**    In general, a balanced budget has a neutral effect on the economy. Since government expenditures equal taxation with a balanced budget, total spending in the economy remains unchanged. What individuals and business firms give up in spendable funds to pay their taxes is counterbalanced by the government spending of the tax receipts. At times, however, it is possible for a balanced budget to bring about an expansionary effect in the economy. This occurs if the government taxes to some extent idle funds that will not otherwise be spent by individuals and businesses. Effective demand would then increase in relation to the taxation of otherwise idle funds.

**Deficit Budget**   A deficit budget will generally increase the level of economic activity or be inflationary, depending upon the status of employment in the economy. Remember that with a deficit budget the government spends more than it taxes. To take care of this excess of spending over taxation, the government will be required to borrow funds. If it borrows idle funds or funds from the banks, which create money, the total effective demand of the economy will be increased. This occurs because the total spending by the government is greater than the amount of spendable funds given up by firms and individuals through taxation. Therefore, the level of economic activity will increase if the economy is at less than full employment, and inflation will occur if the economy is at full employment. It is for this reason that a deficit budget is frequently referred to as a fiscal stimulus by economic advisers in Washington. The tendency for a deficit to bring about expansion or inflation in the economy, however, will be offset to some extent if in borrowing the government obtains funds from individuals and firms that they might otherwise spend on consumption and investment.

**Surplus Budget**   A surplus budget tends to have a dampening effect on the economy. To have such a budget, government taxation must exceed government spending. This means that government spending is insufficient to offset the decline in spendable funds given up by individuals and businesses in the form of taxes. As a result, there is a net decrease in effective demand. Consequently, a surplus budget is often considered by some economic policy makers as a fiscal drag on the economy. This drag effect, of course, would be modified to the extent that the government might tax idle funds that would not be spent otherwise. It could also be offset if the government were to use the surplus to retire the debt.

### Budget as a Stabilizer

If used properly, fiscal policy can help to stabilize the economy and modify business cycles. A surplus budget can help prevent inflation during a prosperity period, and a deficit budget helps to offset the tendency of widespread unemployment during a depressionary period. Such use of budgetary policy is shown in Figure 19-1 on page 392.

When the budget is used as a tool for economic stabilization, it is desirable to balance the budget over the period of the cycle instead of trying to do it on an annual basis. To accomplish this, it would be necessary for the surplus of prosperity to equal the deficit of the recession. However, this would be difficult to accomplish. A question might arise as

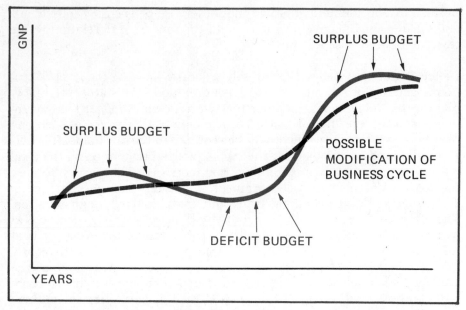

Figure 19-1   **BUDGET USED AS AN ANTICYCLICAL DEVICE**

to whether we should start such a stabilizing practice by building up a surplus during prosperity and then spending it during the next recession, or whether we should incur the deficit during the recession and then repay the debt with the surplus obtained during the subsequent period of prosperity.

Assuming that the first method were utilized, a second problem would arise. How much surplus would need to be accumulated during the prosperity period? This would depend not only upon the inflationary pressures of prosperity but also upon the estimated need, or deficit, during the subsequent recession in the economy. It is practically impossible, however, to determine what the duration and the intensity of the prosperity will be, let alone the duration and the intensity of the subsequent recession. Therefore, it is usually suggested that it is more feasible to run the deficit first. This also has its weaknesses. How can we be assured that the subsequent prosperity will be long enough or strong enough to permit an accumulation of a surplus sufficient to pay off the deficit incurred in the previous recessionary period?

Another weakness of this method is that most administrators and legislators are willing to use deficit spending during a recessionary period to help alleviate unemployment, but many of them are reluctant to build up the necessary surplus during prosperity years. This was very evident from their actions in the recession of 1970 and again in 1974–1975. In short, deficit spending insofar as it can be used to bolster the level of economic activity can be very popular with the public during a recession, but increased taxes to combat inflation during a prosperity period are seldom popular.

It should be remembered also that a surplus acquired during a prosperity period should be held in cash reserve for best results. It can be used to subsequently pay off the debt but not until the level of economic activity begins to decline. If the surplus obtained during prosperity is used immediately to pay off the debt incurred by the deficit spending of the recession, it will merely result in putting back into the economy an amount of money equivalent to the surplus. Thus, the reduction of spendable incomes through taxation will be offset by government expenditures plus debt repayment. This means that the total spending of the economy will remain the same, provided the recipients of debt repayment spend or invest the money received from the government. In such a case, the surplus budget will have a neutral effect instead of being anti-inflationary. The better practice would be to hold the surplus funds until economic activity begins to decline. Repayment of the debt at such time could give a boost to the economy if the recipients of debt repayment were to spend or invest these funds.

## The Full-Employment Budget

In recent years there has been a tendency to look at the so-called *full-employment budget* instead of the actual budget for the purpose of analyzing the fiscal effects of the budget. Regardless of the state of the actual budget, the full-employment budget is a measure of the potential revenue and expenditure that would result if full employment existed. It is said by some that the actual budget may be misleading. Let us say, for example, that the existing budget showed a deficit (or fiscal stimulus) of $12 billion and that the rate of unemployment was 6 percent. Projection may indicate that if the economy were at full employment (4 percent unemployment or less), the budget would show a surplus of $5 billion. Thus, if the economy expands toward the full-employment level, it will encounter a fiscal drag, which would impede the attainment of a full-employment objective.

Proponents of "functional finance," who look at the budget as a tool of stabilization and growth rather than as something to be balanced annually or even periodically, would contend that the inherent drag of the full-employment surplus should be eliminated if the economy is to attain its goal of full employment. This, of course, could be accomplished by increasing the size of the current fiscal stimulus (deficit) through reducing taxes or by increasing government spending.

Carrying the analysis one step further, proponents of this theory claim that once full employment and a balanced budget have been reached, care must be taken to prevent the development of a subsequent drag on the economy. It is pointed out that with a given tax rate, total revenues will increase by $12–$15 billion annually as a result of the normal forces of growth in our economy. To prevent this from occurring, it is suggested that a fiscal dividend be declared either in the form of a tax reduction or an increase in federal spending. They place little emphasis on the notion that surpluses should be accumulated during prosperity to offset the deficits of previous periods.

## PROBLEMS OF THE DEBT

Our experience with budgetary policy as a means of stabilizing business activity is rather limited. It is difficult, therefore, to determine whether we can time our deficits and surpluses accurately and have them of proper size to act as stabilizers of the economy. Furthermore, we have not had sufficient experience in the past 40 years to determine whether, in the absence of emergencies, the deficits and the surpluses can offset each other sufficiently to prevent a growing debt. We incurred a sizable debt during the Depression of the 1930s as a result of our deficit-spending program. Without having had a chance to diminish this debt, we entered World War II, which pushed the debt up to about $285 billion. Our opportunity to reduce the debt was further hampered by the outbreak of the Korean Conflict in 1950. The escalation of the war in Vietnam in the mid-1960s interfered with our experiments to use fiscal stimuli, fiscal dividends, and avoid fiscal drags on the economy. In the interim years, however, we made very little headway in reducing the debt. In fact, the federal debt, now over $500 billion and rapidly moving toward $600 billion, has grown to such proportions that it presents several problems. A few of these problems, such as bankruptcy, redistribution of income, debt burden, size, refunding, and productivity are treated in the following paragraphs.

### Bankruptcy

Many people think that the debt may become so large that it will bankrupt the nation. It is commonly believed that the government may get into a situation where it will be unable to pay off the debt. This misunderstanding arises from the failure to distinguish clearly the true nature of government financing compared to the normal method of business financing. When the government borrows and repays funds, it is more like the financial transactions taking place within a family than the type of financing practiced by private enterprises.

**Comparison to Business Debt**    In accounting we learn that whenever a business has total current liabilities in excess of current assets, it lacks solvency. In short, it does not have sufficient cash to pay its current debts in the immediate future. When debtors press for payment, the company may voluntarily and legally have itself declared bankrupt, or the debtors may force the company into bankruptcy. In either case, the court will decide whether the business should continue under receivership, that is, under a court-appointed manager, or whether the assets of the company should be liquidated to pay off the creditors.

This basic difficulty arises in connection with a business debt because, whenever the firm pays off its debt, it decreases the total assets of the company. Money paid out actually leaves the firm, thereby reducing the assets. If debt payments are so large that the company is forced to suspend payment, the creditors may force liquidation of the firm through bankruptcy proceedings to recover payment on the debt.

**Comparison to Family Debt**   The national debt is more like an internal family debt than a business debt. Consider the family as a spending unit and suppose that a son borrows $200 from his parents for such things as dates, ball games, and school supplies over the period of the school year and that he intends to repay it from the money he earns from summer employment. When he borrows, he does so within the family unit. Likewise, when he repays the $200 in the summer, the money remains within the family.

When the son pays his debt, his individual assets are decreased by $200 but his parent's assets are increased by $200. Therefore, the net assets of the family remain the same. Unlike the debt repayment of the firm, in the family situation no money leaves the family as a result of the debt repayment. There is merely a transfer of cash from one member of the family to another, or a transfer of assets from one member of the family to another. Therefore, there is no net reduction of assets nor is there any money leaving the family.

**The Federal Debt**   When the government borrows money, it borrows primarily from individuals, businesses, and banks within the economy. When it makes repayment on the debt, the money stays within the economy. There is no reduction in total assets when the government makes repayment on the debt. Furthermore, the government's ability to repay is governed only by the total assets of the economy or, more immediately, by the total income of the economy and the government's ability to tax. For example, the national debt in 1974 was $486 billion. Considering that the GNP was $1,397 billion and that the total personal income was $1,150 billion, it is easy to see that the total income of the nation was sufficient to take care of debt repayment if the government decided to raise taxes sufficiently to obtain funds required to pay it off. Theoretically, but unrealistically, the government could tax a sufficient amount to pay the debt off in the course of one year. If the government were to do this, it would not in any way reduce the total income or assets of the nation as a whole. The taxation and repayment of the debt would merely cause a redistribution of income, or cash assets, inside the economy. The income given up by individuals and firms in the form of taxes would be offset by payment to those holding the debt. Thus, the total income or assets of the economy would be the same after payment of the debt as before. The major difference is that income and cash assets held by various individuals and firms would be changed. It must be pointed out, however, that foreigners now hold about 12 percent of the national debt, compared to less than 5 percent as late as 1970.

It is possible, but not probable, that some individuals and firms would have exactly the same holdings of assets after repayment of the debt as they did before. This would occur if an individual or a firm were taxed an amount equal to the amount of debt held. For example, a firm holding $10,000 in government bonds might be taxed $10,000 to help pay off the debt. But since it would receive a payment of $10,000 on its bonds when the debt was repaid, its total assets would remain the same.

Although a tax rate sufficient to pay off the debt in one year would be prohibitive, certainly over a relatively short period, say thirty or fifty years, the government could operate at a surplus sufficient to pay off the debt. Surpluses obtained during prosperous periods could be used to pay the debt during periods of contraction in the economy.

### Effect of Redistribution of Income

The question naturally arises: Why does the government not take more positive steps to pay off the debt? Reluctance to reduce the debt by sizable amounts stems not only from the fact that the large tax burden necessary to do so would be politically unpopular, but also from the fact that it would cause disruptive economic repercussions. One important problem involved would be the redistribution of income brought about by repayment of the debt.

If the debt were to be paid off on a large-scale basis, heavy taxes would reduce total effective demand, especially among the lower income groups. Whether such a reduction in effective demand would be offset when the government used tax money to pay off the debt would depend on what the recipients of debt repayments would do with the money they received. Since it is quite possible that the total propensity to consume or to invest of the debt holders who receive repayment would be less than that of the taxpayers in total, the net effective demand of the economy could easily be reduced by repayment of the debt. The possibility of this occurring becomes evident when we look at the ownership of the debt. It is generally agreed that the lower income groups do not hold much of the federal debt. It is held primarily by banks, businesses, government agencies, and individuals in the higher income groups. This is shown in Table 19-1.

Of course, if the debt holders would spend the income they received at the time the debts were repaid, it would not have an adverse effect on

**Table 19-1  OWNERSHIP OF UNITED STATES GOVERNMENT DEBT, OCTOBER, 1974**
(Percentage)

| | |
|---|---:|
| Commercial banks | 11.1 |
| Federal reserve banks | 16.5 |
| U.S. government agencies and trust funds | 28.8 |
| Individuals | 17.5 |
| Insurance companies | 1.2 |
| Mutual savings banks | 0.5 |
| Other corporations | 2.3 |
| State and local governments | 6.0 |
| Foreign and international | 11.8 |
| Miscellaneous | 4.2 |
| Total | 100.0 |

Source: *Federal Reserve Bulletin* (January, 1975).

the economy. This would tend to be the case if the debt were repaid during a full-employment period. It would be best, however, to pay off the debt during periods of less than full employment with money obtained through taxation during a prosperous or inflationary period. In this way the debt could be used as a tool for economic stabilization.

### Burden of the Debt

It is often thought that when the debt is not paid during the period in which it is incurred, the burden of paying the debt is passed on to future generations. The extent to which this may be true depends upon whether we are considering the effect on the total economy or on individuals and firms.

**Effect on Total Economy**    If we are considering the total economy, it is impossible to pass the real cost of the debt on to future generations. The real cost of the debt to the total economy can only be measured by the cost of goods and services that individuals and firms must forego when they give up their purchasing power to buy government bonds. When consumers and investors purchase such bonds, they not only buy fewer goods and services but they also give the government revenue to make its purchases. For example, during World War II citizens and firms gave up the purchase of automobiles, homes, food, clothing, machinery, raw materials, and the like when they purchased bonds. In the meantime, the government, with its borrowed purchasing power, bought tanks, planes, ships, ammunition, and other necessary war materials. The decrease in consumer production was in effect the real cost of the debt. The people in the economy at the time the debt was incurred shouldered the real burden of the debt through the loss of goods and services.

For the economy as a whole the debt repayment, whether repaid immediately or postponed until future generations, will not cost anything in terms of goods and services. As a result of the redistribution of income that takes place at the time the debt is repaid, some individuals and firms may suffer a loss of purchasing power; but this will be offset by gains to others, and no net decrease in purchasing power in the economy will take place. For example, if the debt were to be paid even in a period of one year, the total tax necessary to pay off the current (1975) debt would be over $500 billion. This would have a tendency to decrease the total purchasing power of the economy. It would reduce effective demand and result in decreased production. When the government paid out the $500 billion to debt holders, however, it would tend to offset the adverse effect of the tax. Total purchasing power in the economy would remain the same. The effective demand, and therefore production, would remain the same, provided the propensity to consume and to invest of the debt holders was the same as that of the general taxpayers. There would be no loss of total goods and services at the time the debt was repaid. Thus, since there is no cost for the economy as a whole when the debt is repaid, it is impossible to pass the cost of the debt on to future generations.

**Effect on Individuals**    Although the cost of the debt cannot be passed on to future generations from the viewpoint of the total economy, the burden for individuals and firms can be passed on to future generations. If the government were to pay off the debt in a relatively short period, say within the generation in which the debt occurred, the particular individuals taxed to pay the debt would have to give up purchasing power. Thus, they would be burdened with individual cost of the debt to the extent that each is taxed. If payment on the debt is postponed for a generation or two, however, the tax will fall to a large extent on the descendants of those individuals and businesses in the economy at the time the debt was incurred. Thus, even though the net cost or burden of the debt cannot be passed on to future generations, the individual burden can be passed on to them.

For example, during the war in Vietnam we incurred a sizable debt. If the debt were to be paid off within the generation in which it was incurred, Mr. Sanchez, a taxpayer of the period, might have to pay $2,000 in taxes to give the government the money to pay Ms. Jones, who, we will assume, is a holder of bonds and therefore an owner of the debt. This payment would decrease the purchasing power of Mr. Sanchez and it would increase the purchasing power of Ms. Jones. If debt payment were postponed until 1990, however, Mr. Sanchez's grandson or someone else in the economy would have to pay the taxes, especially if Mr. Sanchez had died in the meantime. Therefore, the individual burden of the debt would have been passed on from Mr. Sanchez to someone in a subsequent generation. Ms. Jones, who made a personal sacrifice to loan the government money for the purchase of bonds, would be deprived of repayment until a later date. In fact, if she passed away, her descendants would receive the individual gain at the time repayment was made instead of Ms. Jones. In actual practice, however, Ms. Jones could eliminate this difficulty by transferring her ownership of the debt to someone else through the sale of her bonds.

**Effect on the Money Supply**   Another problem involved in the repayment of the debt, which tends to strengthen our reluctance to pay it off, is the effect of the repayment on the money supply. We know that when an individual or a business loans the government money, there is no increase in the money supply. For example, if Mr. Sanchez buys a bond for $1,000, he generally will pay cash for it. Therefore, there is merely a transfer of cash from the individual to the government with no change in the total money supply. If a bank loans the government money, however, it can pay for the bonds in cash or through the creation of a demand deposit against which the government writes checks. In Chapter 9 we learned that the demand deposits brought about by the creation of credit increased the money supply. Therefore, if a bank were to buy $100,000 worth of bonds and pay for them with a demand deposit, it would increase the money supply accordingly. This process is referred to as *monetizing the debt*.

In Chapter 8 we learned that changes in the money supply could affect the level of economic activity and/or the price level. Therefore, when the government goes into debt by borrowing from the banks, it increases the money supply and thus increases the level of economic activity, as it did from 1958 to 1965, or it adds inflationary pressures to the economy, as it did at times from 1966 through 1975.

Today the money supply is approximately $283 billion. Of this amount, $216 billion is in the form of demand deposits. Of the $216 billion, approximately $123 billion came into existence as a result of the sale of government bonds to Federal Reserve and commercial banks. Therefore, the national debt today is supporting a sizable part of the total money supply.

We know that a decrease in the money supply will have a tendency to decrease our level of economic activity and/or decrease the price level, unless offset by some other force such as an increase in the velocity of money. Just as the debt was monetized when the government borrowed from the banks, the money supply will be decreased when the debt is paid off. This is known as *demonetizing the debt*. For example, if the government redeemed the $100,000 in bonds held by the bank, demand deposits would be reduced by that amount and the money supply reduced accordingly. Thus, if the government were to reduce the federal debt by sizable amounts over a relatively short period of time, it could reduce the money supply to such an extent as to have an adverse effect on the level of economic activity. Payment of the debt supported by bank credit would be beneficial during a period of full employment insofar as it could reduce inflationary pressures. During periods of less than full employment, however, such debt repayment could be harmful to the economy as a whole.

### Size of the Debt

The mammoth size of the current debt, well over $500 billion, is in itself sufficient to discourage many people regarding its repayment. It might be pointed out that although we have not reduced the debt absolutely, increased productivity and higher income have reduced the size of the debt relative to our annual income. For example, in 1946 the national debt was $285 billion. Our total income (GNP) for that year was $209 billion. Since the debt was considerably larger than our total income, it could not have been paid out of current income within a period of one year even if we chose to do so. In fact, to pay off at the rate of $10 billion per year would have exerted quite a hardship.

Although the federal debt was a considerably larger amount in 1974, the total production of the nation had increased to $1,397 billion. Since the annual income of the nation exceeded the national debt, it would have been possible to pay off the debt within a period of one year. Although possible, of course, it would not have been feasible to do so. With a total national income exceeding $1,140 billion, however, if we were to decide to pay the debt off at the rate of $10 billion annually, not so much of a hardship would be created on the economy today as it would have been when the GNP was a substantially lesser amount.

In effect, through our increased productivity and higher price level, the monetary income of the nation increased more than fivefold in the period 1946–1974. Since the absolute amount of the debt increased about 75 percent during this period, the burden of the debt relative to national income was reduced by well over two thirds. The debt in 1974 was about 35 percent of our GNP compared to about 135 percent in 1946. For this reason, those who were worried about the size of the debt 25 or 30 years ago have less cause to worry about it today. It should be remembered, however, that decreasing income resulting from either a falling price level or a drop in production or employment would increase the size of the debt relative to income and make repayment more burdensome.

The suggestion has occasionally been made that we should postpone payment on the debt, since it becomes less burdensome as the years go on. To the extent that we increase income as a result of increased productivity, this suggestion has some merit. But if the higher GNP and therefore the greater income is brought about primarily by higher prices, the suggestion is a poor one, since greater problems than that of debt retirement will result from rising prices. Furthermore, if due to continuous inflation the purchasing power of a $100 bond at the maturity date is of less value than the $75 price of the bond at the purchase date, the purchase of bonds by individuals and firms could be discouraged at a time when the government needed money in the future.

## Refunding the Debt

Since government debt obligations may reach maturity at a time when the United States Treasury does not have the money to pay them, the problem of refunding the debt arises. At such a time, the federal government generally will issue and sell new bonds to raise money to pay off the matured obligations. This, however, may not be accomplished easily, especially when billions of dollars worth of bonds may be maturing within a short period of time. Furthermore, the government may be forced to pay a higher interest rate when it borrows funds for this purpose.

In the late 1960s and early to mid-1970s the Treasury was paying interest rates of 7 to 9 percent for money it borrowed in the short-term market. With a 4.25 percent ceiling, it was almost impossible to compete for funds in the long-term market against high-grade corporate securities yielding 8 to 10 percent or more interest. For example, in 1971 billions of dollars worth of bonds paying 4.25 percent interest became due. At that time there was a 4.25 percent ceiling on the interest rate that the Treasury could pay on long-term government securities (those maturing in five years or more) that had been imposed by Congress. There was, however, no interest rate ceiling on short-term government obligations. In 1971 it was possible for an investor to buy many existing long-term government bonds at discounts that were yielding over 6 percent. In addition, many high-grade corporate bonds were yielding more than 7 to 8 percent.

Under these circumstances it would have been difficult for the United States Treasury to sell new long-term bonds at 4.25 percent when existing government bonds yielding more than 6 percent could be purchased in the open market. On a number of previous occasions the Treasury Department requested that the interest rate ceiling on long-term government bonds be removed to permit them to sell bonds at a higher interest rate. Since these requests had been denied the Treasury was forced to sell short-term government obligations on which there was no interest rate ceiling. Consequently, the United States Treasury offered several billion dollars of short-term bonds (those maturing in 5 years or less) at 7 percent interest. Although the Treasury did raise funds to pay off the matured obligations, the total cost of the debt increased because the interest rate on the new obligations (7 percent) was higher than that on the refunded portion of the debt (4.25 percent). Furthermore, it put itself in a position where it would have to pay off or refund again this portion of the debt in another five years. Had the Treasury Department been able to issue long-term securities at a competitive interest rate, it could have prolonged the payment or refunding date for 15, 20, or even 30 years. On a few occasions Congress has permitted the Treasury to extend to more than 5 years the maturity dates of certain short-term notes paying interest rates of more than 4.25 percent. This in effect was a foot in the door in the campaign to raise or eliminate the interest-rate ceiling on the national debt. More relief came in March, 1971, when Congress authorized the

Treasury to issue bonds in amounts up to $10 billion at rates of interest exceeding 4.25 percent per annum. Refunding the debt is quite a problem when one stops to consider that over $90 billion of the national debt, primarily short-term securities, becomes due and payable annually. A similar problem of refunding the federal debt arose in 1973 and 1974 when the yields on corporate bonds and existing government securities reached the level of 8 to 10 percent.

## Burden of Interest Payments

Included each year in our national budget is over $28 billion for payment of interest on the debt. Although taxation for the payment of this interest does not impose a net burden or cost on the economy as a whole, it does cause an annual redistribution of income and, therefore, a burden to individuals and firms in the economy. If the government had originally increased taxes instead of going into debt, or if the government had paid off the debt shortly after it had been incurred, it would have imposed a smaller total burden on the individuals than it does when the debt repayment is postponed. With postponement of the debt the redistribution of income necessary to retire the debt is not only in excess of $500 billion, the principal amount, but also over $28 billion annually for interest on the debt. This interest continues only as a result of postponement of debt repayment. Furthermore, as interest rates rise the cost of carrying the debt rises. Whereas the federal debt increased by 40 percent between 1970 and 1975, the cost of carrying the debt rose 70 percent. It is a matter of judgment whether individuals and firms would prefer the hardship of paying off the debt in a relatively short period of time or of giving up more of total income but spreading the hardship or inconvenience in smaller doses over a longer period of time. In spite of the higher amount of interest paid relative to income, interest payments were equal to 2.5 percent of national income in 1974 compared to 2.6 percent in 1946.

## Productivity of the Debt

If a business firm borrows money to erect a new building, to buy machinery and material, or to hire additional labor to produce goods, it can increase its total productivity. The loan it receives is said to be productive since it can increase the total output of the company and since it may enhance its profits. In fact, firms borrow billions of dollars annually for this very purpose.

Individuals may also borrow to enhance their purchasing power. They may be prompted to do this especially if the purchase of certain commodities has greater utility to them at the time of borrowing than the purchase of these commodities would have in the future. The major decision before borrowing is whether the utility resulting from the current use of the goods purchased with the borrowed funds will be greater than the disutility involved in repaying the loan plus the interest at a later date. Evidently we do prefer present utility in many cases since consumers borrow billions each year to buy automobiles, appliances, homes, consumer goods, and the like.

Government borrowing and the consequent debt may be productive or it may increase the total utility of the economy, in much the same manner as do business and consumer loans. By going into debt, the government is able to obtain the military goods necessary to win a war. Financing government dams, reforestation projects, highways and roads, aircraft developments, educational facilities, labor retraining, the elimination of poverty, medical research, space explorations, agricultural experiments, pollution control, and urban renewal through debt can be very productive. In some cases consumers' satisfaction may be increased as a result of the improvement of roads, the production of electricity, the development of recreation facilities, and the like. Similar to the individual or the firm, the nation or its administrators must decide whether increased productivity and the utilization of current consumption is of greater value than the disutility of paying off the debt.

## DEBT CEILING

The statutory limit or ceiling on the national debt was first established in 1917 when Congress passed the Second Liberty Bond Act. Prior to World War II, Congress set individual ceilings on the various types of government debt. But in 1941 it abolished the individual debt ceilings and created one ceiling on the total debt outstanding. Since the debt ceiling has been raised a dozen or more times in the past 20 years, increasing from $275 billion in 1954 to $531 billion in 1975, the statutory limit on the national debt has been a topic of controversy in recent years.

A federal deficit accompanied by a rise in the debt ceiling will generally provoke more opposition than a deficit that does not involve a hike in the debt ceiling. Furthermore, the cause of the debt plays an important role in its acceptance. Large debt ceiling increases brought about as a result of emergency government spending have traditionally incurred less Congressional opposition than smaller increases related to nonemergency spending.

Many arguments can be marshalled for and against the debt ceiling. Opponents of the ceiling maintain that it may at times limit needed expenditures on important government programs, such as defense or recession spending, whenever tax revenues are not up to expectations or the government has failed to increase taxes sufficiently to take care of its spending obligations. It is claimed also that a debt ceiling results in fiscal subterfuge by the Treasury. The statutory limit is on a defined portion of the total federal debt that is usually associated with the annual federal budget. The federal government, however, has many nonbudgetary financial obligations. Many federal agencies, who normally borrow funds from the Treasury, may be empowered to sell their own securities to private financial institutions and investors if they desire. Frequently when the Treasury is pinched for funds and is approaching the debt limit, it will request a particular agency to sell its own securities in the market rather than to borrow from the Treasury. Critics of the debt ceiling contend further that it restricts the freedom of the Treasury to manage the debt efficiently, especially when the debt is close to the ceiling. In such a circumstance, the Treasury may have to wait until old securities mature before issuing new ones for fear of going over the debt ceiling. Critics of the ceiling argue that it would be better for the Treasury to experiment with new issues sometime before the expiration of the old to try out the interest rate and to have time to make any necessary adjustments to obtain the best price. Otherwise the Treasury will be at the mercy of the market if it must wait until the time various issues expire before issuing new securities to replace them. President Nixon in 1969 endeavored to get around the debt ceiling by proposing a restructuring of the federal debt in such a manner that it would have excluded $100 billion of the current debt from the statutory limit. This would have permitted the Administration to add debt without requesting an increase in the ceiling. His proposal, however, did not receive favorable treatment by Congress.

Proponents of the statutory limit, of course, stress the fact that the debt ceiling is needed to restrain government spending and that it prevents the national debt from getting dangerously high. Congress passes legislation and appropriates money for various bills. Once these are turned over to the Administration, Congress may review the spending bills individually and make adjustments in them. During this time, however, it does not have the opportunity to see the budget in total again. As a result of individual adjustments, total spending might be higher than the original approval. In such cases the debt ceiling would prevent the Treasury from borrowing amounts over the ceiling limit to finance such federal bills. Although the debt ceiling seems to have been raised liberally by Congress in the past several years, the presence of the debt ceiling does tend to make Congress look a bit closer at the budget and decide whether they really want to approve any appropriations that will necessitate borrowing and raising the debt ceiling. It might also be argued that insofar as the ceiling limits deficits in the annual budget, it makes the taxpayers more conscious of the total cost of government services. Many taxpayers may not balk at expenditures of $385 billion with a tax bill scheduled to be only $360 billion. But if they were taxed $385 billion to cover the total cost of the federal spending, they may very well decide to do without some of the government services. In short, deficits and a rising national debt can deceive the taxpayers about the true cost of government services.

In mid-1974 Congress, at the request of the Administration and Treasury, pushed the debt ceiling up to $495 billion to accommodate a possible $15 to $20 billion debt increase associated with rising federal spending. It was raised to $531 billion early in 1975. Also, early in 1975 the Administration requested Congress to push the ceiling to over $600 billion to accommodate the pending $51.9 billion deficit for fiscal 1976 and the projected $40.0 billion deficit incorporated into the fiscal 1977 federal budget.

### SUMMARY

Budgetary policy can be used to stabilize the level of business activity. Deficits incurred during recessionary periods can be offset by surpluses built up during prosperity periods. Instead of endeavoring to balance the budget annually, it could be balanced over the period of the business cycle. Certain difficulties, however, would be involved if this were attempted. The most pronounced, of course, would be the problem of making sure that the surpluses were sufficient to offset the deficits.

As a result of our inability to balance the budget, either annually or over the period of the cycle, we have incurred considerable debt in the past few decades. The present national debt is well over $500 billion.

Contrary to common belief, it would be exceedingly difficult to bankrupt the nation as a result of the large debt, since most of the debt is held domestically. The problem of redistribution of income that accompanies debt repayment is more realistic than the bankruptcy problem. Although we have the ability to pay off the debt, redistribution of income could occur in such a manner as to decrease the total effective demand in the economy.

Although the burden of the debt for the total economy cannot be passed on to future generations, it is possible to pass the burden of the debt on to particular individuals and business firms in those future generations.

Payment of that portion of the debt supported by bank credit could result in a decrease in the money supply. Such demonetization of the debt could have an adverse effect on the level of economic activities just as the monetization of the debt can have an expansionary or an inflationary effect on the economy.

Although our continuous federal debt has caused a burden of over $28 billion annually in the form of interest payments, the total burden of the debt is diminishing as the years pass. Even though the debt is increasing absolutely, it is decreasing relative to the increase in total income, as measured in either current or constant dollars. As a result, the longer we hold onto the debt the easier it will be to repay it.

Just as private consumer or business debt can be productive, likewise the federal debt may be productive and may even create consumer satisfaction.

Now that we are familiar with the economic policies designed to achieve our current national economic goals, some of the more recent goals and emerging problems of the U.S. economy will be presented.

## DISCUSSION QUESTIONS

1. Distinguish between monetary policy and fiscal policy. Which do you think has the greater impact for stabilizing the economy?
2. Do you think it is feasible to balance the budget over the period of a cycle? Give reasons.
3. Discuss the merits and weaknesses of a full employment balanced budget.
4. What is the per capita value of the national debt today? What is the per family share of the national debt today?
5. If you owned a $5,000 government bond, would you be willing to relieve the government of its obligation to pay you in the interest of eliminating our national debt? Why or why not?
6. Would the fear of national bankruptcy be more realistic if the federal debt were held primarily by foreigners? Why?
7. Why do U.S. government agencies, such as the Social Security Administration, hold any federal debt? Since the debt is owed to a federal agency, why can it not be cancelled at will?
8. It is said that the national debt is increasing absolutely but decreasing relatively. Explain.
9. How would the concept of interest-free financing for federal borrowing alleviate the interest burden of the federal debt?
10. Do you think the ceiling on the national debt should be removed? Why or why not?

## SUGGESTED READINGS

Blechman, Barry M., Edward M. Gramlich, and Robert W. Hartman. *Setting National Priorities: The 1975 Budget*. Washington: The Brookings Institution, 1974.

Buchanan, James M., and Richard E. Wagner. *Public Debt in a Democratic Society*. Washington: American Enterprise Institute, January, 1967.

Clark, John J. *The New Economics of National Defense*. New York: Random House, 1966.

Enke, Stephen. *Defense Management*. Englewood Cliffs, N.J.: Prentice-Hall, Inc., 1967.

*The Federal Budget in Brief, Fiscal Year 1976*. Washington: U.S. Government Printing Office, 1975.

Hailstones, Thomas J., and Frank V. Mastrianna. *Contemporary Economic Problems and Issues*, 4th ed. Cincinnati: South-Western Publishing Company, 1976.

Miller, Glenn H., Jr. *The Federal Budget and Economic Activity*. The Federal Reserve Bank of Kansas City (June, 1969).

*The National Debt Ceiling Proposal*, Legislative Analysis No. 4. Washington: American Enterprise Institute, 1969.

# 20 CHANGING ECONOMIC GOALS AND EMERGING PROBLEMS

## RECENT UNITED STATES ECONOMIC POLICY

To anyone closely studying the economic role of our government over the past few decades, it becomes very evident that our overall economic policies and many of the measures used to implement these policies are based on the principles and conclusions of the income-expenditure analysis. A close reading of the Employment Act of 1946 will reveal that we have taken definite steps in the direction of income-expenditure policies. Furthermore, a study of the findings and recommendations of the President's Council of Economic Advisers and of the Congressional Committee on the *Economic Report* will reveal that these groups have been setting goals and suggesting anticyclical measures that are based on the income-expenditure analysis.

The objectives of full employment, stable prices, a healthy rate of economic growth, and the use of monetary, fiscal, and psychological policies to attain these goals are bipartisan. Although early acceptance of government intervention as a means of alleviating unemployment is to be found in New Deal policies, the Republican Administration made some attempt in this direction in 1932. The idea of using monetary and fiscal policies as a means of combating depression was rather new in the 1930s. Therefore, both the attempts of the Republicans and the early New Deal programs meant a struggle for Congressional, business, and public acceptance of the principle of government intervention as a means of stabilizing the level of economic activity.

### Middle Course of Government Intervention

In the past few decades this principle has become much more widely accepted, not only by economists but also by members of Congress, public administrators, businesspeople, and the general public. The President and his Administration made their position clear in the 1954 *Economic Report* by stating that the government would use its "vast powers to help maintain employment and purchasing power." The possibility of and the desire for blending free enterprise and government cooperation for the purpose of stabilizing the economy was further elaborated upon in the 1956 *Economic Report*.

Thus, it would appear that by the mid-1950s the greater role of government in the economy was here to stay. The principle had been accepted by both political parties, by labor unions, by many businesspeople, and in large part by the general public. It was not a question of whether or not the government should play a positive role in helping to maintain a high level of economic activity, but a question of the extent and the nature of government action.

The so-called "new economics" of the Kennedy and Johnson Administrations, with its emphasis on higher employment and faster economic growth, for example, was the basis for measures such as tax credits, public spending, manpower training programs, deficit budgets, and large tax reductions designed to stimulate the economy. But even here a caution was contained in the 1962 *Economic Report:*

> These goals, as the Act recognizes, must be sought within the broad framework of U.S. political and economic institutions — free competitive enterprise and the Federal System of government. And they must be sought by means consistent with other national needs, obligations, and objectives.

More recently the Nixon and Ford Administrations in the past few years have espoused the income-expenditure analysis. Certainly the policies and measures implemented in 1969, and the subsequent shift to stronger expansionary measures when the recessions of 1970 and 1974 occurred, followed what had become standard stabilization measures based on the income-expenditure analysis.

Most economists and political leaders agree that we have followed a middle course. We have not had undue government intervention but, on the other hand, we have taken positive action. We have not gone so far as Keynes suggested in socializing investment, and we have not yet utilized compulsory saving on a national scale to combat inflation. However, in the early 1970s the Administration did reluctantly impose wage and price controls as a last resort. Perhaps we have found a happy medium in the application of the policies and measures based upon the income-expenditure analysis. The extent of government intervention in the economy, however, is destined to continue to be a major economic and political issue in the next few decades.

### Depression and Prosperity Economics

In spite of the evidence to the contrary, some individuals and businesspeople today still think of the income-expenditure analysis as depression economics and therefore out of fashion in a period of relative prosperity. On this score, however, it cannot be denied that the high amount of government spending during war and peace in the last 40 years has been a big factor in helping to maintain a high level of employment.

Even in the nonwar years government spending has been responsible for 11 to 23 percent of the GNP, as shown in Table 20-1.

Table 20-1    **GOVERNMENT SPENDING AND THE GNP, 1946–1974**

| Year | GNP (Billions) | Government Spending (Billions) | Government Spending as Percentage of GNP |
|------|------|------|------|
| 1946 | $209 | $ 27 | 13 |
| 1947 | 231 | 25 | 11 |
| 1948 | 258 | 32 | 12 |
| 1949 | 257 | 38 | 15 |
| 1950 | 285 | 38 | 13 |
| 1951 | 328 | 59 | 18 |
| 1952 | 346 | 75 | 22 |
| 1953 | 365 | 82 | 22 |
| 1955 | 398 | 74 | 19 |
| 1958 | 441 | 94 | 21 |
| 1960 | 504 | 100 | 20 |
| 1964 | 632 | 129 | 20 |
| 1966 | 750 | 157 | 21 |
| 1968 | 865 | 200 | 23 |
| 1970 | 977 | 221 | 23 |
| 1972 | 1,158 | 256 | 22 |
| 1974 | 1,397 | 309 | 22 |

Source: *Economic Report of the President*, 1975.

Whether we would have maintained our high levels of employment during the nonwar years in the absence of a high rate of government spending for defense and other purposes is something about which we can only speculate. It can always be argued that reduced spending would have permitted reduced taxes, and that, therefore, increased consumption and investment would have made up for any decrease in government spending. Although this was true in the immediate post-World War II period, it may not have been true for the post-Korean period. There would have been a good possibility that, in the absence of any pent-up demand for consumer goods, businesses and individuals may have been inclined to save a certain portion of any substantial tax cuts they might have received. A similar impact occurred at the end of the Vietnam war.

What would happen in our economy today with its $85 billion or more military defense spending program if suddenly we were to enter into a disarmament agreement with other nations throughout the world? Certainly in the short run there would be considerable disruption, displacement, and unemployment in the economy. It may even be doubted whether in a longer-run period of three or five years private spending would increase sufficiently to offset such a drop in government spending.

Usually the suggestion is made that if peace and disarmament were negotiated, it would be wise to make the reductions in military spending
gradually. It also is suggested that it would be beneficial to increase government spending in other areas, such as pollution control, urban redevelopment, mass transportation, highway construction, education, medical care, and other public sectors to offset the adverse economic effects of
sizable reductions in military spending. All this, of course, could make
one wonder if military spending is not serving as a built-in crutch for the
economy and camouflaging the fact that we might be more susceptible to
Keynes' prognostication of chronic unemployment than we like to believe. On the other hand, there is no assurance that the economy could
not have done as well as it has in the past 30 years or more had a cold-
war atmosphere not necessitated huge outlays for defense purposes.

It should be remembered that the income-expenditure approach can
be used to analyze an inflationary economy just as well as a depressionary economy. As has been pointed out in Chapter 18, anti-inflationary
policies can be developed as readily as expansionary policies.

One difficulty with the application of policies based on the income-
expenditure approach is that it is easier to obtain public acceptance for
expansionary than it is for anti-inflationary measures. Most members of
Congress will support the idea of government spending, decreased taxes,
public works, easy money, higher wages, and the like to raise the level of
economic activity during slowdowns and recessions. But during prosperity it takes a bold political leader to advocate higher taxes (especially for
the lower and middle income groups), a surplus budget, credit restrictions, tight money, and other controls distasteful to the general voting
public. The reluctance of federal administrators and legislators to adopt
anti-inflationary policies, for example, was very evident in the mid and
late 1960s. Of course, the opposition to these measures is strongest in
election years. As a result, wise economic policy is often sacrificed for
political expediency.

Whether we like it or not, the income-expenditure analysis has become an integral part of our economic education and serves as a guide
for governmental economic policy. A person is free to accept or reject
policies based on this analysis. A dislike for such policies, however, or
disagreement with some of the principles, should not blind one to the
fact that they are excellent tools of analysis for the study of economics.

## CHANGING GOALS AND RECENT PROBLEMS

During the past few decades considerable emphasis has been placed
on the achievement of our primary domestic economic goals of full employment, stable prices, and a healthy rate of economic growth. Coming
out of the prolonged depression of the 1930s with its chronic unemployment, followed by World War II, which caused severe shortages of

consumer goods and services, it was appropriate to stress economic goals such as maximum production, maximum employment, and maximum purchasing power. The desire for steady jobs, good wages, economic security, stable prices, and an abundance of goods and services was quite natural. By and large, during the 1950s and 1960s the economy proved capable of attaining these goals. Indeed, continuing efforts were made to achieve these goals and we even raised our sights in an effort to bring unemployment below the 4 percent level and to accelerate the potential rate of economic growth. In addition, consideration was given to adopting some form of an "incomes policy" as a means of assuring stable prices. In fact, for a while these primary goals in large part were taken for granted. Consequently, citizens of our society, although not ignoring these goals, began placing more emphasis on new or supplementary goals for the economy. With the higher rates of unemployment, double-digit inflation, and negative economic growth which characterized the recession-inflation periods of 1970 and 1974–1975, however, renewed emphasis was once again placed on the primary goals. Even so, people have still become embroiled in a general movement to seek fresh solutions to existing economic and social problems, while learning how to handle new problems that are arising and adopting policies to prevent the occurrence of others that may be destined for the future.

### Elimination of Poverty

Although we have an annual per capita GNP of more than $6,000 and a per capita personal income exceeding $5,400, which are much higher than those of most other major nations, there is great concern on the part of many citizens that a large number of workers and families are still living at poverty levels. From earlier chapters we learned that in the early 1960s, one fifth of our families were living in poverty. Even though the percentage of poor had been reduced to twelve percent by 1974, there is still much concern about the degree of poverty in America. With continued economic growth plus help through poverty and manpower development and training programs, it is hoped that we can bring most of the poor families into the mainstream of economic life by raising their income above the poverty level by the mid-1980s.

### Guaranteed Annual Income (GAI)

Another proposal designed to reduce poverty quickly is the guaranteed annual income. This would provide a minimum income for every family regardless of whether the breadwinner worked or not. An early proposal of this nature was made by the Office of Economic Opportunity in the mid-1960s. Since then, the concept has been proposed by a number of other governmental agencies, labor unions, Presidential commissions, and business leaders. There have been in the last several years a dozen or more definite proposals, including a negative income tax plan, a family allowance plan, and a work bonus plan.

One variation of the negative income tax plan is based on a current poverty level income of $5,000 per annum for a family of four. Families receiving more than $5,000 annually would pay their income tax as usual. But four-person families with less than a $5,000 income would not only pay no income tax, they actually would receive a refund in the form of a negative income tax. It is estimated that the cost of this plan would be about $15 billion annually. This cost could be offset in large part, however, by the elimination of other welfare plans. The cost of other plans range from $20 billion to $60 billion annually. The beginnings of a guaranteed annual income plan were contained in the Nixon Welfare Reform Bill which was stalled in the Senate after it passed the House of Representatives in 1971. The bill provided for a basic income maintenance of $2,400 annually for all families in America. Another variation of the GAI, called a Work Bonus Plan, was passed by a Congressional committee in late 1974. It provides for a payment to those working but receiving a low total income.

A related recommendation for eliminating poverty and providing income for families has been recommended by a number of study groups, both private and governmental. It would establish the federal government as an "employer of last resort." Under this concept, whenever a worker is unable to find a job, the federal government would provide employment. Some semblance of this concept was contained in the Congressional action of 1971 with the passage of the Emergency Employment Act, which provided for federal funding of 150,000 to 200,000 jobs to be created at state and local government levels. Again, in early 1975 various Congressional committees, along with the Administration, were supporting various public employment programs of this nature that would provide up to $5.5 billion to create 375,000 federally-financed jobs.

There are some sociologists and others, however, who believe that we will not conquer poverty until we accept the notion that income should be divorced from work or employment. One such recommendation is that a maintenance income from the government be given to each family or individual as an absolute constitutional right.

## National Health Insurance

With the success of the Medicare programs for the aged and the rising cost of medical care in general, attention is now being turned to the feasibility of medical care coverage for persons of all ages. Here again a number of bills have been formulated for introduction into Congress. Senators Kennedy and Javits, among others, have introduced national health insurance bills into Congress. U.S. Representatives Griffith and Burleson drafted national health insurance bills. A proposal has been drafted by the American Hospital Association, and the American Medical Association is supporting "Medicredit," the Health Insurance Assistance Act, introduced by Senator Hansen. Objectives and coverage of the bills vary. Costs vary, ranging anywhere from $8 billion to $75 billion annually. President Nixon, in an attempt to stem the tide of suggested federally financed plans, recommended a national health plan that would be financed in large part by the private sector of the economy. President Ford likewise in 1975 urged Congress to take action on the matter of national health insurance.

## Preserving Our Natural Environment

People today not only want more goods and services, but they also want clean air, pure water, and noise abatement along with the goods and services. There is a growing awareness that as production of more goods and services increases at an accelerated pace, it is taking its toll on our natural environment through air, water, and noise pollution. Consequently, in the past few years there has been more and more emphasis placed on ecology measures. Federal and state laws along with city ordinances have been passed in an effort to slow down, if not prevent, the deterioration of our environment. In many cases fines have been levied and court orders issued against violators. But much remains to be done. One big issue, of course, is who should pay the cost involved? The polluter, who deteriorates the atmosphere or water with unclean discharge? The depolluter, who must clean the air or water before it can be used in the production process or for consumption purposes? The government, by paying directly to clean up the environment or by paying indirectly, through tax credits, for example, to encourage businesses to install antipollution and depollution devices? Or should it be the consumers who use the products that contribute to pollution? Should the cost be borne out of profits? Or should payment come through higher prices for products to provide the means for the manufacturers and fabricators to install antipollution or depollution devices? In almost any case the consumer is going to have to bear the largest share of the cost, directly or indirectly, in the form of higher prices, fewer products, or higher taxes.

As a nation we can either take more goods and services and not worry about the deterioration of the environment, or take fewer goods and services than we are capable of producing and channel some of our money, labor, and resources into preserving the environment. Once we have made an economic commitment to do the latter, technology can go a long way toward solving the pollution problems of our economy. It is estimated that for the ten-year period from 1971 to 1981 we will spend $300 billion for pollution-related programs.

Enforcement of antipollution measures is another problem. Should it be at the local, state, or federal level? It would do New York little good to pass stringent antipollution laws if New Jersey did not. How fair would it be competitively for the city of Cincinnati to pass stringent antipollution laws that might require a soap producer, such as Procter & Gamble, to raise prices or reduce profits, if Lever Brothers were not subject to the same or similar antipollution costs in operating its plant in Illinois? Some antipollution measures may be effective at the local level, but others have to be carried out on a regional or national scale.

Several federal acts, including the Air Quality Control Act of 1967, the Clean Air Act of 1970, and the Clean Water Act of 1972 represent a systematic effort to deal with pollution problems on a regional basis. Additional local and state programs place a greater emphasis on control and abatement activities. In the early 1970s Ralph Nader's Task Force on Water Pollution accused the federal government of contributing to the declining purity of water by failing to act vigorously against polluters.

Many city, state, and federally operated facilities are as guilty as private enterprise of contributing to air and water pollution. With a national awareness of the adverse effects of pollution, however, new efforts are being made to reverse the trend of environmental deterioration. Private industry, for example, is spending billions of dollars annually on ecological measures and pollution controls. New laws are being passed and government agencies are becoming more active in the enforcement of current controls.

## Consumerism

For decades we have demonstrated our ability to annually produce the world's greatest quantity of goods and services. Today, however, consumers are becoming more and more concerned about the quality of our goods and services. Our governmental agencies are becoming more active in the enforcement of pure food and drug laws, auto safety regulations, medical standards, and environmental protection. The Office of the Special Assistant for Consumer Affairs is taking a more active role in promoting the welfare of consumers in America. The National Commission on Product Safety has made numerous suggestions for new laws to protect consumers in various ways. Businesses now are more liberal in their return sales allowances and in exchanging or repairing faulty merchandise. The enactment of the Truth in Lending Act along with the concern for "truth in packaging" have added emphasis to the growing role of consumers. The crackdown on misrepresentative advertising, the ban on cigarette TV commercials, the withdrawal of polluting soaps and detergents from the market, the recall of millions of faulty automobiles by manufacturers, and the spread of information about mercury poisoning in fish are all part of the new consumer movement. To be sure, the days of *caveat emptor* (let the buyer beware) have long passed. Today in many respects it appears that we are shifting toward the concept of *caveat venditor* (let the seller beware).

### Urban Economics

Since World War II there has been a mass movement of city dwellers and businesses to the suburbs. With the abandonment of the central city by many higher income families and prosperous businesses, this has in large part left the inner city to lower income groups and marginal businesses. Due to inadequate maintenance and repair, many buildings have depreciated and property values have declined. All this, too, has played havoc with city finances by reducing its tax base. The problems of the urban economies have been magnified by the continuous migration of families from rural into urban areas. In many respects the rural poor become a part of the urban poor and end up in slum areas. Although some efforts have been made in the past few decades toward urban renewal, much more needs to be done to prevent urban blight and the evolution of slums. At issue here is the cost of rebuilding the cities. Who shall bear this cost? The private sector of the economy or the government sector? If the government sector, shall it be the local government? If local, shall the cost be shared by the suburban cities as well as the central city? Should part of the cost be financed by the federal government?

**Housing**    As this move to the cities continues during the 1970s and into the 1980s, housing needs will be accentuated. Not only will there be a need for new housing, homes, and apartments in the suburban areas, but there will be a pressing need for urban renewal in the inner cities. This is necessary to provide housing for lower income groups and as a means of attracting some of the suburbanites back into the cities. Housing starts were in the vicinity of 1.5 million annually during the 1960s. But national goals of 2 million or more annually have been set by a national commission. With the rapidly rising cost of construction in recent years, many families are going to find it difficult to finance adequate housing. Private industry will certainly do its share by providing housing to meet economic demand. But more and more pressure will be put on the government to help provide housing for low income families.

An alternative to government housing projects experimented with in the late 1960s and early 1970s was the rent subsidy. As practiced today, a poor family is permitted to live in a higher level economic neighborhood by receiving a rent subsidy from the government to make up the difference between the actual rent and what the family can afford to pay. Proponents of rent subsidies suggested that they were preferable to government-sponsored housing projects. In 1974 the Department of Housing and Urban Development (HUD) officially announced that it would follow a policy of granting rent subsidies and would discontinue its efforts with government-built housing.

**Mass Transportation**    The move into the cities from rural areas and the movement from the inner city to the suburb have accentuated the

transportation problems of the cities. The suburbanite must get into th
city and once there, along with the city dweller, must move around with
in the city. On occasion it is necessary to travel to other cities. With th
decline in the use of buses and the demise of passenger rail traffic, mor
reliability has been placed on the automobile. Along with widesprea
auto ownership, including millions of two and three-car families livin
near the cities, jammed expressways and clogged thoroughfares are th
order of the day. Commuter trains and rapid transit systems are bein
used beyond their optimum capacities, and even some airports ar
crowded. Travel between cities within a megalopolis is becoming mor
burdensome.

To alleviate crowded conditions some cities have installed subway
constructed overhead monorails, banned autos from downtown area
and even experimented with walking-malls and moving sidewalks i
downtown areas. As the movement into the cities increases in the nex
few decades, the problems of traffic control and the mass movement c
people will become more acute. In many cases cities will not be able t
solve their mass transportation problems without help. They will requir
intercity cooperation and planning, state assistance, and aid from th
federal government. A substantial amount of aid came from the federa
government in 1974 when Congress approved a bill providing the Urba
Mass Transportation Administration with $11.8 billion to be allocated t
mass transit projects over a five-year period.

**Ghetto Economics**   In the past decade and a half more light than eve
before has been focused on the economic problems of minority groups
especially blacks. Because of past inequities and injustices, such as inade
quate educational facilities, lack of job opportunities, discrimination i
housing, and racial prejudice, blacks as a group are in the lower incom
brackets. Consequently, measures were started in the 1960s to alleviat
their plight. Improved educational facilities, aid through many federa
and local employment programs, and more opportunities for job
through the private sector of the economy have all contributed towar
this improvement. Although there are more poor whites than there ar
poor blacks, there is still a much higher percentage of blacks living i
poverty.

Currently unemployment among the nonwhites, including blacks
Puerto Ricans, Mexicans, and American Indians, is nearly double the un
employment rate of the labor force as a whole. Unemployment amon
nonwhite teenagers usually runs 20 to 25 percent, double that for al
teenagers in the labor force. With the census and BLS projections tha
the nonwhite population will grow about 75 percent faster than the whit
population in the decade of the seventies, the problem will not mel
away. In fact, it may become more acute.

Industry is faced with the issue of whether it ought to recruit worker
from the ghetto, train them for employment in its suburban plants, an

orient them to suburban living, or whether it should locate its plants in a ghetto area to provide jobs for the labor force there and, in so doing, give economic aid to the ghetto area.

**Black Capitalism**   Another goal of minority groups, particularly the blacks, is to have more of their members become business entrepreneurs. They want a piece of the economic action which they help create by their labor and their spending. Often, however, the blacks lack the professional training, experience, and financial support necessary for success in business. Recently increased emphasis has been placed on the development of black capitalism through programs that will provide the training, skills, knowledge, experience, and money for blacks to become successful entrepreneurs. Again an economic cost is involved. The question arises, what should be the source of this capital? Should the capital originate from savings, equity capital, loans from the private sector of the economy, or grants from the government? In many respects just like the underdeveloped nations, the black community needs an infusion of capital from outside sources if it is going to meet its objectives.

**The Cost of Crime**   Related to our urban problems is the rising cost of crime. Poverty, slums, lack of educational and recreational facilities, and unemployment often breed delinquency and crime. The suburbs, however, are not without their problems in this respect. Drug addiction aggravates the crime problem. Not only is growing crime a terrible social problem, but it is a serious economic problem. The economic loss to individuals and businesses resulting from theft and property damage is enormous, the cost of insurance is rising at a quickening pace, and the financial outlays of individuals, institutions, and businesses for security and protection have skyrocketed. Governmental units have substantially increased their outlays for the prevention and detection of crime and the protection of their citizens. The cost of this crime, now exceeding $90 billion annually, naturally diverts money, resources, and manpower away from legitimate economic activity which could enhance our level of living.

## New Sources of Government Revenue

At the federal, state, and local levels the need for additional revenues has led in the past few years to some new developments in the fields of taxation and revenue funding. Among the concepts being discussed, explored, and implemented are federal-state revenue sharing, the lottery, and the value added tax.

**Federal-State Revenue Sharing**   Not many people realize that state and local government expenditures for goods and services exceed federal expenditures, including federal outlays for defense. In 1974, for example, the federal government's share of the GNP was $116 billion, while state and local expenditures amounted to $192 billion. Furthermore, in the late 1970s federal spending is scheduled to increase rather moderately, while there will be a very substantial increase in the size of state and local expenditures. We are putting more and more demands on state and local governments for services of all kinds. But many municipal and state governments are hard pressed for funds to carry out their current programs. Their sources of tax revenues are limited. Property is already overtaxed, taxes on businesses often drive them to out-of-state locations, consumers resist higher sales taxes, and city and state income taxes add to the already heavy burden of the taxpayer.

After months of debate and hearings, Congress inaugurated federal-state revenue sharing with the enactment of the State and Local Fiscal Assistance Act of 1972. The Act allocated over $30 billion to be shared by the 50 states and about 38,000 state and local government units during a five-year period. During the first few years a little over $5 billion annually was distributed to the various governments, with one third going to the states and two thirds to local governments (cities, counties, villages, and townships). These revenue-sharing funds were in addition to existing federal funds, since no reductions were made in regular federal grant programs. With the projections of higher expenditures and limited tax sources, more and more interest is being generated for the continuation and extension of federal-state revenue sharing.

**Lotteries**   In the past decade the pressures for additional state funds and the growth of taxpayer resistance to new or higher taxes has led to something new in the way of raising revenue — the *lottery*. This has been supplemented in the past few years by the outright sanctioning of other forms of gambling as a means of raising state funds.

In 1964 New Hampshire became the first state to use a lottery as a method of raising revenue for the state. Lottery tickets were sold to the general public, prizes were awarded, and after subtracting the prize and administrative costs the state retained the net proceeds for its treasury. Although a small operation, the success of the New Hampshire lottery encouraged other states to adopt this device. New York entered the business in 1967 and became the largest producer of lottery revenue by a state. A number of states inaugurated lotteries in the early 1970s, including New Jersey, Connecticut, Pennsylvania, Massachusetts, Michigan, Maryland, and Ohio. Similar fund-raising lotteries are under consideration in California, Illinois, Iowa, Maine, Louisiana, Vermont, and the District of Columbia. Although all revenues help when money is needed, lottery revenues have produced less than two percent of the total revenues of the states in which they are used.

**Value Added Tax**   The *value added tax* (VAT), which is widespread in Europe, has been proposed frequently for adoption in the United States.

In fact, enough consideration has been given to a VAT in the United States that the Nixon Administration drafted a Congressional bill for its adoption in 1972, although it subsequently abandoned the plan to introduce the bill into Congress until a more appropriate time. Although in many respects the VAT is similar to a sales tax, VAT is not a sales tax. Neither is it an excise tax. It is, however, a tax on the production of all goods and services imposed at each stage of production. Each producer pays a tax at a specific rate on the value added by his productive process. Consequently, in actuality it is a tax on the GNP, which as we know is the current market value of the total goods and services produced by the nation's economy in a given year. The producer (taxpayer) receives a credit or refund for any VAT tax included in the price of the goods he purchases, or he pays taxes only on the value added by his productive process. In this manner VAT is different from a *cascade tax*, in which the producer pays a tax on the full value or price, including taxes, of the goods purchased. As we shall see, VAT avoids the practice of paying a tax on a tax.

There are several versions or methods of computing VAT. The simplest is the subtraction method. Take Commodity $X$, for example, which retails at $3,500 but has various intermediate transactions totaling $8,500. Assume that the processor of the raw material required to produce Commodity $X$ started from scratch but sold the raw materials to the manufacturer for $800. If the VAT rate were 5 percent, the processor of the raw material would pay a tax of $40. The manufacturer who purchases the raw materials then fabricates them into finished goods and sells them for $1,800. Through this fabrication a value of $1,000 has been added to the product. Consequently, the manufacturer would be required to pay a tax of $50 ($1,000 × .05 = $50). Notice that if the tax were on the sale value of the product instead of the value added, the manufacturer would pay a tax of $90 ($1,800 × .05 = $90). In similar fashion the wholesaler who adds value of $600 would be taxed $30, and the retailer would pay a tax of $55 on value added of $1,100. This, of course, can be passed on to the consumer, as can the taxes of the earlier processors, by incorporating the tax into the sale price of the product.

Notice, too, that the total VAT paid is $175 on a total value added of $3,500 ($3,500 × .05 = $175). On the other hand, a 5 percent sales tax on the total transactions would yield $425 ($8,500 × .05 = $425).

VAT rates in most foreign nations are high, since VAT is generally a major source of government revenue. In most cases VAT was adopted as a replacement for the sales tax. Furthermore, many of the European nations have multirate structures, with lower rates on foodstuffs and necessities and the highest rates on luxuries. In France there are four different VAT rates. The general rate is 23 percent; farm and food products are taxed at 7.5 percent; fuel and electricity at 17.6 percent; and luxuries at 33.3 percent. In Germany the general rate is 12 percent. In European countries VAT usually applies to both goods and services. There are certain exceptions where it does not apply, however, such as doctor or lawyer fees, and in some places, rent.

It has been estimated that a 10 percent VAT rate applied to the United States economy would generate about $70 billion annually in tax revenues. If adopted in the United States, however, in all probability it would be at a lower rate until taxpayers became accustomed to the tax and until the Internal Revenue Service worked any bugs out of the system.

VAT has been proposed as a means of raising additional revenue, as an alternative to other new forms of taxation, such as a national sales tax, and as a substitute in whole or in part for existing forms of taxation, such as the corporate income tax and the property tax. In particular VAT has been suggested as an alternative to a national retail sales tax. Although it is similar in many respects to a sales tax, there are a number of differences between the two. One such difference is the fact that the retail sales tax makes little or no attempt to differentiate between the sale of goods and services for final consumption and the sale of goods and services to be used as intermediary products in the production of other commodities. Thus, much more tax revenue would be collected through a retail sales tax, unless several types of exemptions were provided.

## Growth and Disarmament Dividends

One way of looking at where we are going and the resources and manpower we have to devote to additional output is through the *growth dividend*. Assuming that we obtain a projected real economic growth rate of 4 percent or more annually during the remainder of the 1970s, this means an approximate annual gain of $60 billion in the next few years, rising to a real gain of approximately $80 billion annually by the end of the decade. Some analysts refer to this in a broad sense as the growth dividend. Thus, a major question arises. How will we use this additional output of goods and services? Traditionally the decisions of what and how much to produce have been decided primarily in the marketplace. We no doubt will continue to use this mechanism in the future for deciding the kinds of goods and services to produce. Consequently, a sizable portion of our future increases in productivity will be in the form of consumer goods and services and private investment.

There is a specific amount of our productivity gain, however, that can be readily shifted in one direction or another by forces other than those of the marketplace. The initial influence or control of this segment of goods and services comes in the form of higher taxes. If existing federal tax rates are maintained in a growing economy, they will tend to produce increasing tax revenues. It is estimated that at current tax rates, for example, a $60 billion increase in the GNP will produce an additional $22 billion in federal revenue. Approximately one half of this increment is absorbed in providing existing services, which are called baseline expenditures, for the additional population. This leaves a residual of $10 to $12 billion which, in a narrow sense, is more often referred to as the growth dividend.

Somewhere along the line a decision will have to be made in regard to the use or uses of the potential growth dividend. Basically, it can be allocated in several directions — in the form of lower taxes, for the accumulation of a budget surplus, or for increased government spending.

More specifically, the benefits of the growth dividend can be used to:

1. Expand existing federal services and programs, especially those not now fully funded;
2. Inaugurate new federally sponsored socioeconomic programs, such as a guaranteed annual income plan, national health insurance, or mass transit;
3. Share revenue with states to alleviate their pressing financial needs;
4. Reduce taxes and let the private sector decide what use should be made of the growth dividend;
5. Accumulate a surplus for the purpose of retiring the federal debt.

During the past decade or more we have been spending $60 to $80 billion annually for defense purposes. If world political and military conditions were such that defense spending could be greatly reduced or eliminated, the manpower, resources, and capacity now utilized in defense industries could be channeled to other, more economically useful purposes that could enhance our level of living. Currently the major powers of the world are engaged in Strategic Arms Limitation Talks (SALT). As these serious, albeit sporadic, meetings bear fruit, they hopefully will result in substantial disarmament in the future that should produce a sizable *disarmament dividend* for the United States and others.

### Energy, Food, and Fuel Shortages

A number of studies and reports in the past decade, including those sponsored by the Club of Rome and conducted by Dennis Meadows of M.I.T., which resulted in the publication of their *Limits to Growth* in 1972, warned of pending scarcities of natural resources vis-à-vis the growth of world population. A second study, *Mankind at the Turning Point*, reinforced the phenomenon of scarcities and shortages. Limited attention was given to pending shortages, however, until just a few years ago.

A first real indication that shortages could occur in the United States economy was the electrical power blackout in New York City and the subsequent brownout periods that resulted from an insufficiency of electrical power. In the early 1970s poor harvests, inclement weather, and a rise in the price of feed grains and chemicals, along with a growing demand for meat, caused a scarcity of beef in 1972 and 1973. Consequently, the price of beef rose substantially, and in some markets there was a shortage of beef. The large-scale purchase of grains from the United States by the Soviet Union in 1972 highlighted a scarcity of wheat that sent the price of wheat skyrocketing from $1.50 per bushel to more than $5.00 per bushel within a year.

The presence of shortages was further dramatized in 1973 when the oil embargo by the OPEC countries reduced petroleum supplies for the United States. Although imports account for only 6 percent of the United States oil supply, the loss of imports was sufficient to cause a shortage of fuel oil for homes and factories and gasoline for motor vehicles. As a result, fuel oil was rationed in several Eastern states, and gasoline for autos and trucks was supplied in limited quantities. A number of states rationed gasoline by various methods, many service stations went out of business because of lack of supplies, and truckers demonstrated and struck in protest of limited supplies and high prices. In response, the Administration appointed a Federal Energy Director to coordinate the production, allocation, and pricing of scarce petroleum products. As a result of the shortages, however, the price of gasoline rose from an average of 35¢ per gallon to more than 50¢ per gallon, and in some places sold for $1.00 per gallon. The Federal Energy Office also had rationing coupons preprinted in the event that it became necessary to resort to coupon rationing to allocate scarce gasoline supplies.

The fuel and energy shortages, of course, were instrumental in hastening Congressional approval of the Alaskan pipeline to eventually bring oil from the North Slope into the United States mainland markets. The bill had been stalled in Congress for environmental considerations. The shortages also accelerated the experimentation and processing of shale oil, a process that had been considered too costly beforehand.

The energy, fuel, and gasoline shortages were in part responsible for the GNP slipping from a limited growth outlook to a no-growth, or recession, period in 1974. Hundreds of thousands of layoffs in 1973, 1974, and 1975 were directly attributable to these shortages. In the auto industry the gasoline shortages led to such a dramatic shift in demand away from larger size cars to smaller cars that the industry was forced to make a mass conversion of its facilities to small car production. By late 1974 and early 1975, demand for all sizes of cars had fallen so badly that the auto makers were forced to offer rebates on new car purchases to trim their inventories.

Much of the consternation in the economy in the form of scarcities, shortages, layoffs, shifting of resources and manpower, and higher prices was a normal market reaction. There were, however, certain charges of monopolistic restrictions and oligopolistic pricing. Nevertheless, the shortages did confirm previous suggestions that resources could be pinching against an increasing demand, which could affect the growth pattern and even the standard of living of American consumers. Although the shortages may be somewhat short-lived as new sources of energy, food, and fuels are produced or developed, no longer can the American producer or consumer take for granted that supplies will readily be forthcoming even though the money to pay for them may be readily available. More and more the American producer and consumer will have to engage more consciously in the process of economizing — how best to apply scarce means to satisfy unlimited wants.

### Quality of Life

Although still interested in having an abundance of goods and services, it is apparent that Americans have been shifting to an emphasis on the quality of goods and services and to a stress on the quality of life. They are interested in eliminating injustices and inequities, and they seek to improve the economic and social conditions of their fellow citizens. Some of them are more interested in making a contribution to society than they are in promoting their own economic well-being. Leading corporations have moved away from a prime emphasis on profit maximization toward a desire to provide quality goods and services and better working conditions for their employees. Consumers, businesses, and government are working together to improve economic and social conditions. New goals, such as the elimination of poverty, income maintenance (GAI), and a system of national health insurance are indicative of this change. Our interest in preserving our national environment indicates a willingness to sacrifice goods and services to prevent a deterioration of the gifts of nature. The problems of urban economics are in large part social in nature and the many proposals to improve the economic and social welfare of minority groups indicates a strong willingness to cooperate in working out solutions to these problems.

### International Issues

In addition to domestic goals and priorities, as a nation we are interested also in cooperating with other nations in seeking solutions to multinational issues and problems. Stabilizing our international balance of payments and arresting the gold problem, promoting trade among nations, providing foodstuffs to help alleviate world hunger, and contributing toward the support of international organizations all require time, resources, and financing. Should the United States, for example, follow the recommendation of the World Bank that each developed nation contribute an amount of aid equivalent to seven tenths of one percent (0.7%) of its GNP in the form of aid to underdeveloped nations? This would increase our foreign aid bill from $3 billion annually to more than $10 billion. If we did so, we obviously would be able to do less in other directions. Consequently, in the order of national priorities, this and other multinational demands have to be balanced with our domestic goals.

### SUMMARY

The major economic policies of our nation for the past 40 years or more have been an outgrowth of the income-expenditure analysis. Fundamentals of this analysis are evident in our monetary, fiscal, and psychological policies, and they are spelled out in the President's *Economic Reports*. The objectives of full employment, stable prices, a healthy rate of economic growth, and the use of government intervention to stabilize the level of economic activity are stated clearly in these *Reports*.

We have taken a middle course regarding the use of government intervention as a means of stabilizing the level of business activity. In most instances we use indirect measures before resorting to direct government action.

Although we will in the future continue to pursue our primary goals of full employment, stable prices, and a healthy rate of economic growth, more emphasis will be placed on supplementary and/or new goals and problems. Finding the means to hasten the elimination of poverty in America through a guaranteed annual income, by using the government as an employer of last resort, or through expanding manpower training programs will involve major decisions. The proposed adoption of a national health insurance plan is sure to promote much discussion in private and public forums. Cost allocation for ecology measures to preserve our natural environment will be subject to much analysis. It appears, too, that we are beginning the "age of the consumer," as new efforts by private and government agencies are made to protect and promote the welfare of consumers. Urban economics will involve a major area of analysis with problems of housing, mass transportation, crime, and black capitalism. The need for increased local and state tax revenues will throw new light on such issues as federal-state revenue sharing plans, state lotteries, and the VAT. Tied into the improvement in the quality of life will be the decisions during the next decade of what to do with the growth and possible disarmament dividends and the establishment of economic priorities. Our problems related to shortages and allocations of resources will continue to be major economic issues in the future.

In the first 20 chapters we dealt primarily with the operations and issues of our domestic economy. But we do not live in isolation from the rest of the world. Our economic actions frequently have an international flavor, and many events occurring abroad have an impact on our domestic economy. Consequently, to round out the understanding of our economic system, it is imperative that we gain some insight into the area of international economics, the subject matter of the next two chapters.

### DISCUSSION QUESTIONS

1. Should the President of the United States be given standby authority to adjust taxes and change the rate of government spending as a means of stabilizing the economy? Why or why not?

2. Why does it seem easier to get expansionary measures passed by Congress than it does to have anti-inflationary bills enacted?

3. Do you think we should have some definite guides for the institution of anticyclical measures, such as lowering the discount rate at one level of employment or prices, engaging in deficit spending at another level, and so forth? Explain.

4. Should we have a guaranteed annual income for every American family? Why or why not?

5. Do you think that the adoption of a national health insurance plan is a violation of the principle of subsidiarity as explained in Chapter 3? Why or why not?

6. Do you think that the government or private enterprise ought to bear the cost of antipollution devices? Explain.

7. Do you think the federal government was wise in shifting its emphasis on housing to the practice of rent subsidies as opposed to building low-cost housing for the poor? Why or why not?

8. If the growth dividend were to be used primarily for social and economic programs, would it be better to put all resources into a few major programs or divide the resources (or funds) among several programs? Explain.

9. During periods of shortages, do you think it best to ration goods like gasoline through the pricing mechanism by allowing the price to rise, or to use coupon rationing of some type? Explain.

10. Would you personally prefer to have more economic gains or an improvement in the quality of your life? Explain.

## SUGGESTED READINGS

"After $160 Billion to Rescue Cities —" *U.S. News and World Report* (April 10, 1972).

Brown, George H. "Stagflation is the Word." *The Conference Board Record* (January, 1975).

*Building a National Health Care System*. New York: Committee for Economic Development, 1973.

Campbell, Rex R., and Jerry L. Wade. *Society and Environment*. Boston: Allyn & Bacon, Inc., 1972.

"Can Capitalism Survive?" *Business Week* (July 14, 1975).

"Can We Prevent Material Shortages?" *Business in Brief*, Chase Manhattan Bank (April, 1974).

*Economic Report of the President*. Washington: U.S. Government Printing Office, 1974 and 1975.

*Energy Outlook 1975–1990*. Houston, Texas: Exxon Company, U.S.A., 1975.

Falk, Richard A. *This Endangered Planet*. New York: Random House, Inc., 1971.

Galbraith, John Kenneth. *Economics and the Public Purpose*. Boston: Houghton Mifflin, 1973.

"Into a New Era — How Your Life Will Change." *U.S. News and World Report* (March 3, 1975).

Jones, Sidney L. "Are Economists Answering the Right Questions?" *Business Economics* (January, 1975).

LuBove, Roy. *Poverty and Social Welfare in the United States*. Chase Manhattan Bank (April, 1974).

McLure, Charles E., and Norman B. True. *Value Added Tax: Two Views*. Domestic Affairs Study No. 7. Washington: American Enterprise Institute for Public Policy Research, November, 1972.

Meadows, Donella H., et al. *The Limits to Growth*. New York: Universe Books, 1972.

Moynihan, Daniel P. *The Politics of a Guaranteed Annual Income*. New York: Random House, Inc., 1972.

*National Health Insurance Proposals*. Washington: American Enterprise Institute for Public Policy Research, November, 1974.

Nickson, Jack W. *Economics and Social Choice*, 2d ed. New York: Mc Graw-Hill Book Company, Inc., 1974.

"Now an Epidemic of Legalized Gambling." *U.S. News & World Report* (July 23, 1973).

Nutter, G. Warren. *Where Are We Headed?* Washington: American Enterprise Institute for Public Policy Research, Reprint No. 34, August, 1975.

*State-Local Finances in the Last Half of the 1970's*. Washington: American Enterprise Institute for Public Policy Research, April, 1975.

"Unemployment and Income Maintenance Programs." *Economic Report of the President*, 1975. Chapter 3.

U.S. Department of Housing and Urban Development. *Experimental Housing Allowance Program*. Interim Report. Washington: U.S. Government Printing Office, April, 1975.

Weiss, Leonard W. *Economics and Society*. New York: John Wiley & Sons, Inc., 1975.

# Part 6

# International Economics

# 21 INTERNATIONAL TRADE AND AID

## UNITED STATES INTERNATIONAL TRADE

Just as trade between various sections of a nation can improve the welfare of all people involved, so too can trade between nations benefit both the exporter and the importer. The fact that a river, mountain, or an ocean separates two nations or that people have different languages, habits, or customs is no more a justifiable economic reason for not carrying on trade than is the presence of an imaginary boundary line between states or regions a valid reason for stifling trade within a nation.

In some nations the amount of international trade is minimal, but in others it comprises a substantial portion of the nation's total production and trade. In many countries, such as Australia, Belgium, Canada, Denmark, Great Britain, Norway, and Switzerland, the values of either exports or imports amount to more than 20 percent of their respective national incomes. Although the United States has a much larger total value of foreign trade than any other nation in the world — indeed the value of its exports alone exceeds the total production of many nations — the value of its exports or imports is only 8 to 10 percent of its large gross national product. In 1974, for example, United States total exports were about $139 billion and imports $137 billion, or 9.9 percent and 9.8 percent, respectively, of our GNP of $1,397 billion.

International trade, nevertheless, is important to our economy. In 1973 we engaged in trade with nearly 150 nations, possessions, or territories throughout the world. Our biggest customer was Canada, to which we exported over $15 billion in merchandise. During the same year we sent $8.9 billion worth of goods to Latin America, with Venezuela, Brazil, and Mexico all being sizable buyers. A total of $21.4 billion was shipped to various countries in Western Europe, where Great Britain and West Germany each accounted for more than $3.5 billion worth of our exports. Another $18.4 billion went to Asia. Our big customers in Asia were Japan with $8.3 billion and Taiwan and Korea, each with over $1 billion. Over $2.3 billion of our exports found their way into Africa and nearly $2 billion into Australia and Oceania islands. In broad categories some of our leading imports and exports of merchandise are shown in Table 21-1.

Table 21-1  **SELECTED EXPORTS AND IMPORTS OF THE UNITED STATES, 1973**
(In Millions)

| COMMODITY | |
| --- | --- |
| Exports | |
| 1. Machinery | $17,587 |
| 2. Grain and preparations | 8,495 |
| 3. Chemicals | 5,748 |
| 4. Automobiles and parts | 5,541 |
| 5. Electrical machinery and apparatus | 5,031 |
| 6. Aircraft and parts | 4,124 |
| 7. Iron and steel mill products | 1,258 |
| 8. Coal | 1,014 |
| 9. Tobacco and manufactures | 970 |
| 10. Oils and fats | 684 |
| 11. Petroleum and products | 518 |
| 12. Cotton, unmanufactured | 263 |
| Imports | |
| 1. Machinery | $10,093 |
| 2. Automobiles and parts | 9,216 |
| 3. Petroleum and products | 7,548 |
| 4. Iron and steel mill products | 2,769 |
| 5. Nonferrous base metals | 1,994 |
| 6. Cocoa, coffee, and tea | 1,847 |
| 7. Meat products | 1,668 |
| 8. Paper and manufactures | 1,457 |
| 9. Fish | 1,387 |
| 10. Sugar | 918 |

Source: *Statistical Abstract of the United States, 1974.*

Further insight into our international trade shows that we depended 100 percent on imports for such commodities as coffee, tea, crude rubber, silk, cocoa, bananas, carpet wool, and certain field and crop fibers. In addition, we imported 80 percent or more of such commodities as manganese ore, bauxite, natural abrasives (mainly industrial diamonds), and cordage and twine. On the other hand, exports absorbed more than 30 percent of our total production of cotton, farm products, leaf tobacco, aluminum ore, molybdenum, sulfur, rice, grease and tallow, medicinals and botanicals, construction equipment, and stone work.

All this trade, of course, takes place as nations seek to improve their economic standards and to take advantage of the laws of absolute and comparative advantage, explained earlier in Chapter 2. The law of absolute advantage is manifest readily in the exchange of cocoa or rubber from abroad in return for United States machinery. The law of comparative advantage may help explain why the United States exports large-sized automobiles while at the same time it is importing sport-type and

smaller cars. At any rate much is gained by all the countries involved in
the international flow of goods and services. Unfortunately, however,
most of the trade is carried on among developed nations since most other
nations have very little to trade.

Nevertheless, most nations of the world are reluctant to adopt a free-
trade policy, and numerous restrictions are still invoked in the area of
international trade. Although economic arguments strongly favor free
trade, most decisions affecting international trade are made in the political arena. Unfortunately, the pressures of apparent short-run economic
advantages and political expediency usually overshadow the less obvious
and long-run advantages of free trade. Consequently, a myriad of restrictions still prevail in trade markets throughout the world today. One of
the most common forms of restriction is the tariff.

### THE TARIFF

A *tariff* is a duty or tax levied on foreign imports. It may be a *specific
tariff* in absolute terms, such as 25 cents per pound or per unit of a commodity. It may be an *ad valorem tariff* in relative or percentage terms,
such as 15 percent of the value of the imported commodity.

#### Purpose of a Tariff

A tariff may be levied either for revenue or for protective purposes. In
the early days of the United States, the primary purpose of import duties
was to raise revenue to help defray the expenses of operating the new
federal government. After 25 or 30 years, however, we shifted in large
part to a protectionist tariff policy to protect our new industries.

To be effective, a tariff must serve one purpose or the other, since the
two objectives are to a large extent incompatible. If it is designed to obtain revenue, the tariff must be high enough to yield a revenue. But if it is
too high, it will discourage the importation of goods and services, and
consequently there will be very little revenue flow from the tariff. On the
other hand, if protection is desired, the tariff must be high enough to
keep out foreign products. If it keeps out foreign products, however, there
will be very little tariff yield for revenue purposes. Although there may
be an optimal tariff, which will serve both purposes, it cannot serve either purpose as well as a tariff designed with only one objective in mind.

#### Argument for Free Trade

Since there are many other sources of national revenue and at present a relatively small amount of income is derived from import duties, it
is difficult to support any argument that a tariff is essential to raise
revenue.

The fundamental argument for free trade, and against a protective
tariff, lies in the fact that a tariff disturbs and restricts free movement of

goods and services, aborts the advantages of specialization and exchange, prevents the optimum use of scarce factors of production, and denies individuals and nations the benefits of greater productivity and the higher standard of living possible from the exercise of the laws of absolute and comparative advantage. The gain or advantage of trade between regions or nations is obvious. Insofar as a tariff reduces or restricts this trade, it lessens these advantages. In fact, tariffs could be high enough to shut off trade altogether between two nations, in which case all benefits would be lost. From an economic point of view the argument for free trade is so basic that it is easy to refute most arguments against free trade and for tariffs. As a result, the trade restrictionists must apply many arguments or use several offensives to make a dent in the free-trade defense. Even at that, restrictionists must move outside the area of economics to find their most reasonable arguments against free trade.

Regardless of what type of argument is put forth, it should be remembered that ultimately the consumer pays the tariff. Although the actual customs duty is levied on the importer, it generally is passed on to the consumer in the form of higher prices. The main beneficiary of the tariff is the relatively inefficient producer and perhaps in the short run his employees, whose jobs are more secure because of the tariff.

## Arguments for Tariffs

Numerous arguments in favor of tariffs have been offered over the past centuries. They touch upon the military, social, and political as well as upon the economic aspects of international trade. Although a few of the arguments have some validity and merit, by and large tariffs are difficult to justify from a long-run economic point of view.

**Protect Infant Industries**   This is one of the oldest and most valid of the tariff arguments. It was instrumental in promoting the shift in our tariff policy from one of revenue to one of protectionism in the early part of the 19th century. In its simplest form it states that new or infant industries, especially in developing nations, are frequently at a cost disadvantage compared with mature firms in the same industry in the more developed nations. It follows then that if this cost disadvantage is removed by applying a tariff to industry imports from the foreign countries, the domestic firms will be given an opportunity to compete at least on an equal footing with foreign producers. This supposedly gives the infant industry an opportunity to grow and develop. The true infant-industry protectionist maintains that the tariff should be continued until the firms in the domestic industry have reached a state of maturity. At that point, however, the tariff should be removed and the domestic industry forced to compete with the foreign imports or go out of business.

**Equalize Costs**   A similar argument is made for the so-called scientific tariff that is designed to equalize the cost of production between domestic and foreign producers. Advocates of this tariff argue that it would remove any advantage to foreign producers arising from availability of raw materials, differences in efficiency, low wage cost, and the like. The imposition of such a tariff, however, would defeat in part the purpose of international trade. It would make the cost (including tariff) or the price of both the foreign and domestic products equal. Consequently, this would remove the fundamental benefit and reasons — increased productivity, lower costs, and a higher standard of living — for international trade.

**Protect American Jobs**     It is often suggested that the use of tariffs creates or protects domestic jobs. Arguments of this type tend to be short-sighted and take into account only one side of international trade. They propose that if tariffs are imposed, foreign products will be kept out of America. As a result, consumers will shift to the purchase of domestically produced goods and services, which in turn will necessitate an increase in domestic production and employment. These protectionists forget, however, that international trade is a two-way street. We not only import goods and services, but we also export them. Foreigners cannot continue to buy from us unless they have American dollars, and the primary way they obtain these dollars is by selling goods to America. If we impose tariffs and cut down imports, foreigners will have fewer American dollars to buy our goods. The net result will be that any immediate increase in employment generated by tariffs will be offset by a decrease in production and employment in our export-producing industries.

**Protect High American Wages**     It is frequently argued that tariffs are necessary to protect our high American wage rates. It is pointed out that most foreigners have lower wage rates than do Americans, and therefore foreign exporters have an unfair advantage over domestic producers. It is contended further that, if lower priced foreign goods are admitted into our nation, competition will force American producers to cut cost, particularly wages, in an effort to stay in business. There would be some element of truth in this agrument were it not for the fact that the wage cost per unit of a commodity is more important in determining cost than is the aggregate wage rate. Since productivity per worker varies among different countries, it is possible that nations with high wage rates may have lower labor costs per unit because of their higher level of productivity per man-hour. This is not only possible but also probable, since many studies show a high correlation between wage rates and productivity throughout the world. Consequently, a nation with a high wage rate may very well have a lower unit cost of production, in which case there should be no need for tariffs to protect the high wage rates.

Even if it is granted that the wage cost per unit may be lower in some foreign industries, it is still a disservice to the American consumer in the long run to subsidize the less efficient domestic producer with a tariff. It would be far better to force the domestic producer to improve efficiency and to lower costs or go out of business. In that way, as mentioned previously, our manpower, resources, and capital would be channeled into more productive uses.

**Retain Money at Home**   One of the weakest arguments for the tariff is the proposal that it keeps our money at home instead of sending it abroad. It is often stated that if we buy a car from West Germany, we have the car but West Germany has the money; whereas if we buy domestically produced automobiles, we have both the cars and the money in the United States. This argument, of course, completely loses sight of the fact that West Germany probably would use the dollars received from the sale of their automobiles to purchase American goods and services, and the dollars would return to the United States. It also neglects the basic fact that most imports are paid for, or canceled, by exports and that very little money actually leaves the nation.

**Develop and Protect Defense Industries**   One of the strongest and most valid of the protectionist arguments for tariffs is the fact that tariffs will help develop and protect defense industries. This is an especially poignant argument when one remembers that we were shut off from very important imports of German chemicals during World War I and that the Japanese invasion of Southeast Asia cut us off from our rubber supply in Malaya in the early stages of World War II. Thus, a strong argument can be made from a military point of view that we should establish and maintain tariffs for industries producing strategic defense materials. It can be reasoned that without tariff protection some of these industries may have to close down as a result of foreign competition. In such a case our manpower, resources, and capital formerly used in these industries will be dispersed elsewhere. Consequently, if a war breaks out we will be at a distinct disadvantage in the production of military goods and armaments if we are unable to secure needed imports. At the present time many producers of strategic military goods and services are protected by tariffs, subsidies, or other measures.

**Diversify Industry**   A similar argument is put forth regarding the use of tariffs to diversify the industrial structure of a nation. When a country specializes in the production of one or a few commodities, its economy is very vulnerable to wide fluctuations of prosperity and depression resulting from variations in foreign demand for its product(s). Many times a softening of world demand and prices can bring economic disaster to such a nation. Therefore, it is contended that tariffs can be used to keep out imports and to encourage the development of other industries in the domestic economy. With a more heterogenous industrial structure the economy will become more stable and be less affected by world fluctuations in the demand for certain products. Although this argument has a certain amount of validity, it has relatively little application to countries like the United States, Canada, Great Britian, and West Germany, which are known for their widely diversified industries.

## QUOTAS, SUBSIDIES, AND EXCHANGE CONTROLS

In addition to tariffs several other devices are used to grant an advantage to domestic producers. Each has an effect similar to the tariff insofar as it restricts imports, grants aid to domestic producers to compete with foreign imports, or encourages the export of commodities. The most frequently used of these measures are import quotas, export subsidies, and exchange controls.

### Import Quotas

An *import quota* is simply the setting of a maximum absolute amount of a particular commodity that may be imported. Setting definite limits to the amount that may be imported serves to protect the domestic producer and industry against the full effect of foreign competition. Consequently, it is similar in effect to, but more restrictive than, a tariff. Sometimes both a tariff and a quota are used, in which case the limited amount that is imported is subject to a customs duty.

Another form of the quota is the *tariff quota*, which does not set absolute limits to imports but places a restriction against excessive imports. The tariff quota permits a certain amount of an imported commodity to come in at one tariff rate, but charges a higher tariff rate for imports over and above the so-called optimum amount.

### Export Subsidies

Another common practice in international trade has been the use of the export subsidy. This is designed to encourage exportation of certain commodities or to prevent discrimination against exporters who may have to sell at a world price that is below the domestic price for a commodity. Not only have direct cash payments been made for the exportation of some commodities, but also the large-scale sale of a number of surplus farm products has been promoted through the use of subsidies. In the United States, for example, the government has purchased surplus crops, such as wheat and cotton, from American farmers at government-supported prices, which have often been above the domestic price. These crops have subsequently been sold to foreign nations at world prices below the United States domestic price. In this way the government, or we should say the American consumer, has paid a subsidy to have goods exported.

### Exchange Controls

The flow of international trade can be affected greatly by the use of exchange controls. Controls may take the form of rationing a nation's scarce foreign exchange, which would limit the overall imports into the nation. More specific regulation of imports is possible through the use of multiple exchange rates. In this case different exchange rates are set for various commodities. In this manner the importation of some commodities can be encouraged while others are discouraged. Since exchange rates can be set arbitrarily by the government, they can be applied readily to restrict the free flow of goods and services that might put a nation in a disadvantageous position.

## UNITED STATES TARIFF POLICY

In its early history the United States endeavored to be a leader in the promotion of world trade, but its attitude has changed from time to time. In its first few decades the new nation used the tariff primarily for revenue purposes. Tariffs were necessarily low to encourage the importation of goods so that customs duties could be collected. In fact, in the first few decades 90 percent or more of the revenue obtained by the federal government came from tariffs. About 1815, as a result of the effects of British and other import competition on our infant American industries, which had been given a fillip during the War of 1812 and the prewar embargo acts, the federal government began to shift from a revenue to a protectionist tariff policy.

### High-Tariff Era

Although protection became more important in United States tariff policy thereafter, the tariff continued to be a major source of federal revenue until the Civil War. Since then it has declined in relative importance as a source of federal funds. As protection became more predominant with the growth of American industry, tariff rates continued to climb, at least intermittently. After World War I, tariff rates were at their highest level in history, but they were pushed still higher by the Hawley-Smoot Tariff Act of 1930. Shortly thereafter there was hardly an import commodity that did not have a customs duty, and some rates exceeded 100 percent of the original value of the commodity. The average tariff as a percentage of the value of all imports was about 33 percent.

### Reciprocal Trade Agreements

The Great Depression of the thirties and the inauguration of the New Deal political program by the newly elected Democratic Administration ushered in a new policy of lower tariffs. Under the Reciprocal Trade Agreements Act of 1934, the President of the United States was given authority to lower tariffs by as much as 50 percent, without further Congressional approval, provided other nations would make reciprocal concessions. As a result of this Act more than 30 separate agreements were made with foreign nations. Tariff rates were reduced on nearly 2,000 commodities, and the average level of American tariffs was cut by more than 50 percent under the Act. Included in the Act was the famous "most-favored nation clause" by which concessions made in bilateral agreements were generalized to all nations. When we lowered our tariff on wool imports from Australia, for example, it was required that this lower rate must apply also to the importation of wool from any other nation that did not discriminate against the United States. In short, we had to extend to all nations the same tariff benefits we gave to most-favored nations. On the other hand, we did not enter into any trade agreement with a foreign nation unless it extended to us the same tariff concessions on various commodities that it gave to its most-favored nation(s).

Although tariffs were reduced substantially under the Reciprocal Trade Agreements Act in the next two decades, the reductions and coverage permitted by the Act were weakened by various amendments and revisions. In 1948, for example, the "peril-point provision" gave the Federal Tariff Commission the authority to specify the rates below which tariffs could not be reduced in certain industries without injuring domestic producers. In 1951 the "escape clause" became a part of the Act. This clause permitted the raising of tariff rates if the Tariff Commission found that existing tariffs were causing harm or seriously threatening domestic producers. A 1954 amendment prohibited any tariff reduction that might threaten national security.

### The Export-Import Bank

In the past few decades not only has the United States endeavored to promote freer trade by direct internal legislation and by cooperation through international organizations and agreements, but it has also given substantial financial assistance in an effort to promote world trade. In addition to membership in the World Bank, the International Monetary Fund, and other financial organizations, which we shall examine in greater detail later, the United States has its own Bank for financing world trade. As a financial aid to the development of world trade, in 1934 the federal government established a government instrumentality known as the Export-Import Bank. The Bank was inaugurated during the Depression for a number of purposes, primarily for financing exports from the United States. It was anticipated that the Bank would aid in the financing of expected increases in trade with the Soviet Union, officially recognized by the United States in 1933, and with various Latin American countries. The Bank has been a source of aid in trade with numerous nations. The Bank under certain conditions guarantees American exporters that they will be paid for the sale of their goods to foreign nations. Sometimes the Bank makes loans to foreign importers to buy American goods. The Bank mainly finances private exports and imports between the United States and other nations that cannot be financed at reasonable rates through regular international financial channels. In recent years, however, the Bank, as a result of growing financial resources, has been making loans for private and government development projects in underdeveloped nations. In this regard it does not attempt to compete with national and international fianancial agencies, such as the World Bank and the International Finance Corporation. Since World War II, the Ex-Im Bank, as it is often called, has made loans and grants in excess of $20 billion and had $7.0 billion in credit outstanding in 1974.

## General Agreement on Tariffs and Trade

After World War II several of the Allied nations, exclusive of the Soviet Union, met for the purpose of promoting free trade among nations of the world. The outcome was the formulation of the General Agreement on Tariffs and Trade (GATT), which was drawn up at Geneva in 1947 and accepted by 23 signatory nations, including the United States. The General Agreement called for equal and nondiscriminatory treatment for all nations in international trade, the reduction of tariffs by negotiations similar to the method used in reciprocal trade agreements, and the easing or elimination of import quotas. One of the main provisions of the Act was that of extending the most-favored-nation principle to all signers. At the present time 80 nations have adopted the General Agreement on Tariffs and Trade.

Although some progress toward liberalizing trade had taken place under GATT, it was rather limited until the so-called Kennedy Round of negotiations from 1964 to 1967. Since GATT is not a formal agreement, but rather an informal one, there is nothing compelling a nation to eliminate or reduce any of its trade restrictions.

## Trade Expansion Act of 1962

The policy toward lower tariffs was reinforced in the United States by the passage of the Trade Expansion Act of 1962. This Act was designed for three purposes: (1) to stimulate the economic growth of the United States and to enlarge foreign markets for its products; (2) to strengthen economic relations with foreign countries through the development of open and nondiscriminatory trading in the free world; and (3) to prevent Communist economic penetration. The Act authorized the President to enter into international trade agreements between 1962 and 1967 with foreign nations and to decrease tariff rates on particular commodities by as much as 50 percent below the rate existing on July 1, 1962. The Act contained special provisions for dealings and agreements with the European Economic Community (Common Market).

To ease any hardship that may have resulted from liberalizing trade restrictions, the Act provided relief for import-injured industries. Individual firms could under certain conditions be eligible for adjustment assistance. Workers who were laid off or displaced because of increased foreign imports resulting from implementation of the Act were also eligible for assistance.

On the basis of the authority given to the President under the Trade Expansion Act of 1962, the United States entered negotiations with other nations in an effort to bring about substantial reductions in world tariffs. After three years of difficult negotiations in the Kennedy Round, one of the most massive assaults on tariffs in history was agreed upon by the 53 nations participating in the talks under the auspices of the General Agreement on Tariffs and Trade. The United States, for example, granted tariff concessions on thousands of items ranging from automobiles, steel, and chemicals to nuts, cameras, and toupees. These items accounted for one third of the United States total import trade value at that time. Before the agreement United States tariffs averaged about 11 percent of the foreign value of its imported goods. According to the Kennedy Round agreement the United States agreed to reduce its tariffs almost 35 percent, with a few items dropping by a full 50 percent. According to the agreement the United States and other nations reduced duties by one fifth of the agreed amount on January 1, 1968, and the remainder took place in four equal annual installments. These tariff reductions have been a great inducement to world trade and have helped bring many of the nations closer together economically as well as politically.

## U.S. Trade with Communist Countries

Until the late 1960s U.S. trade with communist nations was severely limited. Not only did a cold war atmosphere prevail between the East and the West during much of the 1950s and the 1960s, but restrictive trade policies were also imposed by both the United States and the Soviet Union. In the late 1960s and early 1970s political antagonisms abated somewhat and relations between the United States and the communist nations began to mellow. As the communist economies grew, the advantages of trade with the United States and other free nations became more and more apparent to both sides. The United States Department of Commerce in the late 1960s began to encourage American businesspeople to carry on trade with the Soviet satellite nations of Eastern Europe.

This trade, as well as direct trade with the Soviet Union and Mainland China, was given a boost in the early 1970s when American trade delegations visited both nations. This was followed by personal visits to Peking and Moscow by the President. During these visits, designed to improve detente between the nations, increased trade was emphasized.

In spite of ideological and political differences and dissimilarities in economic structures, trade between the U.S. and communist countries grew rapidly in the early 1970s. Large commercial transactions developed in certain specialized areas, such as equipment and technology for the automobile, chemical, petroleum, and agricultural industries. U.S. trade with the communist countries (U.S.S.R., People's Republic of China, and the Eastern European countries of Bulgaria, Czechoslovakia, East Germany, Hungary, Poland, and Rumania) increased dramatically from $600 million in 1971 to $3.1 billion in 1973.

Both the United States and the communist nations are making adjustments to remove trade barriers and pave the way for smoother exchanges of goods and services. In addition, many American manufacturers, banks, and other types of businesses have established contacts or offices in communist countries. Since the population, area, and resources of the communist nations are substantial and these nations are in need of many goods and services which the United States and other western nations can supply, there is a strong indication that East-West trade will grow during the forthcoming years. Such trade will be economically beneficial to all nations involved. Whether it is a wise move on the part of the United States from a political or military viewpoint may be another question.

### Trade Reform Act of 1974

After nearly a year of discussion and debate Congress in December, 1974, passed the Trade Reform Act of 1974 as a successor to the Trade Expansion Act of 1962. Provisions of the Act cleared the way for the United States to play a major role in the spring of 1975 when 105 nations were scheduled to meet in Geneva to draw up new rules of international trade and commerce. The Act provides the President with a wide range of measures designed to open trade doors around the world. According to the Act the President may (1) reduce or raise U.S. tariffs during negotiations; (2) impose an import surcharge up to 15 percent; (3) reduce or eliminate nontariff barriers, such as export subsidies, import quotas, investment restrictions, health and safety codes, and pollution standards, subject to Congressional approval; and (4) retaliate against unreasonable foreign restrictions on U.S. trade. The Act also permits the President to extend most-favored-nation treatment to communist nations. Like its predecessor Act, the Trade Reform Act provides various types of assistance to import-injured firms and workers.

### EUROPEAN ECONOMIC INTEGRATION

Since the end of World War II, many outstanding developments have taken place in the sphere of international economics. One development has been the voluntary efforts on the part of a number of nations to integrate certain of their economic activities for mutual benefit. Another development has been the effort of some of the more affluent nations to extend economic and technical assistance to the emerging or developing nations. Both of these movements are having a pronounced influence on the economic, social, political, and military relations of the family of nations throughout the world.

The significant economic integration effort has been that made in Europe. This has come in a series of steps involving coordination, cooperation, and eventually economic integration.

### Organization for Economic Cooperation and Development

In 1948 eighteen European nations joined together to form the Organization for European Economic Cooperation (OEEC). One important function of the organization was to administer aid under the Marshall Plan. But its general purpose was the joining together of European nations to use their individual capacities and potentialities to increase their production, to develop and modernize their industries, and to expand trade among themselves by reducing tariff barriers.

The OEEC was replaced in 1960 when the United States and Canada joined the 18 European nations of the OEEC to sign a pact setting up a new agency known as the Organization for Economic Cooperation and Development (OECD). The stated objectives of this new organization were to promote prosperity, to maximize economic growth, to establish financial stability in the nations of the industrial West, and to help underdeveloped nations to obtain sound economic growth and contribute toward the expansion of world trade.

### European Coal and Steel Community

In 1952 a more definite step was taken with the formation of the European Coal and Steel Community for the purpose of pooling coal and steel resources of six nations and eliminating trade barriers on coal, iron ore, iron, and steel. The six nations that joined in the agreement were France, West Germany, Italy, Belgium, The Netherlands, and Luxembourg. The last three nations had previously formed Benelux, a customs union, which had reduced and eliminated tariffs and import quotas among the three nations.

### European Common Market

The success of the European Coal and Steel Community led to the formation of the European Economic Community (EEC), promoted in part by the United States, by the same six nations in 1958. The goals established by the Common Market, as it is usually called, were: (1) to abolish tariff and import quotas among the six nations over a period of 10 to 12 years; (2) to establish within a similar period a common tariff applicable to all imports from outside the Common Market area; (3) to attain eventually the free movement of capital and labor within the Common Market nations; and (4) to adopt a common policy regarding monopolies and agriculture.

By July, 1968, all tariff barriers among the six nations were removed, two years ahead of schedule. The common external tariff was achieved a few years later. Some progress has been made toward common internal policies regarding monopoly control, transportation, and social security systems. Furthermore, labor-force training and mobility have received increased coordination. The existence of the Common Market has contributed greatly toward economic growth and prosperity in Western Europe.

Since the early 1970s a considerable amount of discussion has taken place among the Common Market nations about the establishment of a common currency. It has been suggested that European Monetary Units (EMUs) be created for the member nations. It is the belief of some that not only could EMUs serve as a domestic currency for each of the member nations, but the EMUs, symbolized £, would serve as an international currency and rival in prestige the U.S. dollar, other hard currencies, and gold as a means of settling international financial transactions.

Although many of the economic concessions made within the Common Market have been extended to outside countries, some nations consider the Common Market to be a threat to their trade. This could be true if the promotion of trade within the member nations resulting from reduction of the internal tariff comes at the expense of imports from outside the Common Market. In fact, the common external tariff could be used, if desired, to form a strong trading bloc. In this regard, with the enactment of the Trade Expansion Act of 1962, the Congress of the United States gave the President special powers of negotiation in dealing with the Common Market nations.

Great Britain did not join the Common Market when it was formed because of its reluctance to abandon its preferential treatment of other members of the British Commonwealth. But discrimination and the threat of competition from the Common Market led Britain to take the initiative in the formation of another economic organization in 1959 known as the European Free Trade Association (EFTA). In addition to Great Britain, other members were Austria, Denmark, Norway, Portugal, Sweden, and Switzerland. The EFTA differed from the Common Market insofar as it called for the reduction and elimination of internal tariffs and quotas among member nations, but it did not propose the establishment of a common external tariff. Nations were left to establish their own external tariffs and to conduct outside trade negotiations.

Twice during the 1960s Great Britain made an attempt to join the Common Market. These requests for admission were denied, however, on the basis of conditions Britain established for entry into the Common Market. By 1973, however, these differences were reconciled and, along with Denmark and Ireland, Britain became a member of the Common Market.

The importance of carrying on trade with the Common Market is reflected in the fact that outside of the United States it is the largest free-trade area in the world. It has more than 255 million people with relatively high incomes. In 1973, for example, it had a gross national product of $695 billion in comparable United States dollars. At that time the Common Market was the world's largest producer of steel and the leading external trade area. Indicators show that its annual real economic growth rate was higher than that of the United States as well as many other nations throughout the world.

## OTHER REGIONAL TRADE AGREEMENTS

The success of the Common Market encouraged similar organizations thoughout the world. One such organization, the Council for Mutual Economic Assistance (CMEA or Comecon), entered the planning stage at about the time the Common Market was established. Founded in 1960, Comecon had an initial membership of seven: the Soviet Union and the six communist countries of Eastern Europe. Membership was extended to Mongolia in 1962 and to Cuba in 1972. By 1973 the Comecon countries represented 32 percent of the world's total production. Their combined exports exceeded $86 billion, or about 10 percent of the world total. Approximately 65 percent of their exports and imports arise from trade with each other.

The Montevideo Treaty signed in 1960 created the Latin American Free Trade Association (LAFTA). Comprised of Argentina, Brazil, Chile, Mexico, Paraguay, Peru, and Uruguay, this Association is patterned after the EFTA with the exclusion of an external tariff. Five Central American nations — Costa Rica, El Salvador, Guatemala, Honduras, and Nicaragua — have entered into two treaties calling for integration of industries, removal of internal trade barriers, and the eventual establishment of a common external tariff. Now known as the Central American Common Market, this group has recently encountered many political obstacles to economic integration. Nevertheless, internal tariff reductions have been accelerated.

European influence has been felt in other areas as well. The Association of Southeast Asian Nations aspires to trade liberalization among its members and a common policy with respect to all nonmembers. So too does the Organization of African Unity and the Common Organization of Africa. Members and associates of the Caribbean Free Trade Area are now referred to as the East Caribbean Common Market. Indeed, this organization and the Association of Southeast Asian Nations sought associate member status in the Common Market in 1973. As a response, the Common Market initiated negotiations early in 1974 for a trade agreement between its members and 42 African, Caribbean, and Asiatic nations.

## UNITED STATES FOREIGN AID

In addition to its endeavor to promote world trade through its direct efforts and through international organizations and agencies, the United States has extended a considerable amount of direct economic aid to other countries. In early post-World War II years funds were utilized especially for reconstruction purposes, but in more recent years much aid has been given to developing nations. Here again aid has been both direct and indirect through international financial institutions.

### Bilateral Aid

During World War II we exported nearly $40 billion in military and nonmilitary goods under the Lend-Lease program. Nearly two thirds of this amount went to Great Britain. The Soviet Union received nearly $10 billion and France received about $2.5 billion. Smaller amounts were shipped to other nations. Since that time other forms of aid have been granted to many foreign nations.

When World War II ended, the principal source of foreign aid was the United Nations Relief and Rehabilitation Administration, which dispensed several billion dollars in aid to war-injured nations, especially in Western Europe. In addition, the British government in 1946 negotiated a $3.5 billion long-term loan from the United States for purposes of reconstruction. The United States also increased the lending powers of the Export-Import Bank as an additional assistance measure to foreign nations.

**Economic Cooperation Administration**   In 1948 the United States Economic Cooperation Administration (ECA) program, otherwise known as the famous Marshall Plan, went into effect to aid the nations of Western Europe. In total, sixteen nations became members of ECA, including Great Britain, France, Denmark, Italy, Belgium, and Sweden. In addition to receiving financial aid from the United States, the various nations agreed to take domestic steps necessary to improve their respective economies and to participate and cooperate with one another in seeking solutions to their common economic problems. Subsequently the name of the Economic Cooperation Administration was changed a number of times. But the objective remained the same, and aid continued to pour into Western Europe during the 1950s.

**Technical Assistance**  In his inaugural address in 1949, President Truman laid the foundation for a new type of foreign-aid program designed to encourage the advancement of underdeveloped nations through the extension of technical assistance from the United States. The establishment of the "Point Four Program" of technical assistance was initiated in the fourth point of his speech when the President stated:

> Fourth, we must embark on a bold new program for making the benefits of our scientific advances and industrial progress available for the improvement and growth of underdeveloped nations.
>
> Our aim should be to help the free people of the world, through their own efforts, to produce more food, more clothing, more materials for housing, and more mechanical power to lighten their burdens.

Thus, Point Four was stressing the need for a new concept in foreign aid — that to underdeveloped nations. Most previous aid had gone to developed nations in need of reconstruction. Although the aid to underdeveloped nations concept was implied in the formation of the International Bank for Reconstruction and Development in 1946, little had been accomplished in that area by 1949. Point Four was put into effect in 1950 when Congress approved the Act for International Development. Millions of dollars have since been appropriated for technical assistance, and today there are more than 5,000 American technical experts throughout the world giving advice and assistance to foreign nations endeavoring to improve their agricultural and industrial production.

**Development Loan Funds**  As a further indication of the increased emphasis on economic development as the principal goal of our foreign aid program, in 1957 Congress established the Development Loan Fund and appropriated nearly $1.5 billion for its operation. The Fund was empowered to guarantee or make loans to persons, businesses, governments, or other entities in foreign nations for various industrial, financial, and commercial development projects. All projects and loans must have the approval of the foreign government. The Development Loan Fund was combined with the International Cooperation Administration as part of the Agency for International Development in 1961.

In the 26-year period 1947–1973, the United States distributed $163.7 billion in foreign assistance to more than 120 nations. Of this total, $62.2 billion was in the form of military grants, $4.9 billion was contributed to four separate international financial institutions (exclusive of the International Monetary Fund), and the remaining $96.6 billion was used primarily for economic and technical aid.

### Aid Through International Organizations

Since World War II the United States has been the largest contributor to foreign aid through various international financial institutions, both on a worldwide and a regional scale. At present there are at least four such major organizations to which the United States contributes.

**The International Bank for Reconstruction and Development (World Bank)**   This institution, now usually referred to as the World Bank, is intended "to supplement private investments in foreign countries by nations and individuals having capital to lend." The present subscription of member nations amounts to over $25 billion. The United States has subscribed almost $8 billion, slightly less than one third of the total.

This bank can issue and sell bonds and use the proceeds for loans to "any business, industrial, or agricultural enterprise in the territory of a member," and it can guarantee loans by private investors. The overall purpose is to develop world production and trade by stimulating investment in enterprises that may be considered "good risks." Obviously the objectives of the bank are predicated on the assumption of a policy by nations of lowering most of their tariff restrictions and other impediments to trade between nations. Over 110 countries had become members by 1974, and loans totaled more than $12 billion.

**The International Finance Corporation (IFC)**   The IFC, which was formed in 1956, is an international financial institution and an affiliate of the International Bank for Reconstruction and Development. By 1974 it had over 94 members and a subscribed capital of over $105 million. Again, the largest subscriber has been the United States. The general objective of the IFC is to stimulate economic development by encouraging the growth of private productive enterprise in its member countries, and especially in the less developed areas. To accomplish its objective, the IFC proposes (1) to invest in productive private enterprises along with private investors but without government guarantees of repayment; (2) to serve as a clearinghouse for bringing together foreign and domestic private capital and management; and (3) to help stimulate the growth of domestic and foreign capital.

**The International Development Administration (IDA)**   This institution is an affiliate of the World Bank. The purpose in establishing IDA was to enable a growing number of the underdeveloped nations to borrow funds. According to the terms of IDA, development credits and loans are intended to impose less burden on the balance of payments of borrowing countries than do the usual or conventional types of loans. IDA came into existence in 1960 and began operations the same year. Membership in the organization is open to members of the World Bank. By 1974, 107 countries had joined and total subscriptions amounted to more than a billion dollars. Again, the United States was the largest contributor, exceeding $320 million.

**The Inter-American Development Bank (I-ADB)**   The Inter-American Development Bank came into existence in 1960. The general purpose of the Bank is to stimulate the economic development and the cohesion of the Latin American nations. It originally had capital resources amounting to $1 billion, which could be increased by the sale of the Bank's own resources. Of its total capital subscriptions, $850 million was available for usual lending purposes, while $150 million could be used for special or unusual lending purposes.

The Bank's Board of Governors in 1964 increased the authorized capital of the Bank to $2.15 billion. By 1974 its capital subscription equaled $3 billion, which had been contributed by 25 nations. With its own resources it furnishes funds for business capital with charges for interest and special reserve of less than 6 percent. From the fund itself, long-term loans with low interest rates are available for hydroelectric power, agricultural, and reclamation projects. Every member nation, exclusive of the United States, has benefited directly by loans from the Bank.

The I-ADB resembles the World Bank as to structure, organization, and general purposes, and both operate in the American regions. But certain differences as to the requirements for loans enables I-ADB to supplement the loans of the World Bank in this part of the world.

### SUMMARY

Although international trade can enhance the welfare of all nations concerned, there are still many restrictions to the free flow of goods and services among nations. Probably the most widespread restriction is the tariff, which may be levied for either revenue or protectionist purposes.

Supporters of the tariff have many arguments, including the fact that tariffs are needed for the protection of infant industries, to equalize costs of production, to protect American jobs, to protect high American wages, to help retain money at home, to help develop and protect defense industries, and to diversify industry. Most of the arguments in favor of the tariff are based on short-run disadvantages that would arise in the move toward freer trade. They tend to neglect, however, the long-run economic advantages that would accrue to American consumers if tariffs were reduced or eliminated. Other devices used to restrict trade are import quotas, export subsidies, and exchange controls.

During the 19th century and the early 20th century tariff rates rose intermittently. Record rates after World War I were pushed still higher by the Hawley-Smoot Tariff Act of 1930. But in the mid-1930s a new policy of lower tariffs was inaugurated in the United States. Under the Reciprocal Trade Agreements Act of 1934 the President was given authority to lower tariffs by as much as 50 percent. The Export-Import Bank, established in 1934, helps promote international trade by rendering financial assistance for American exporters and foreign importers. In 1947 we entered the General Agreement on Tariffs and Trade with several other nations of the world. In 1962 the Trade Expansion Act gave the President further powers to reduce tariffs. This Act also provided relief for import-injured firms and workers. Substantial progress in tariff reductions was made under this Act as a result of the "Kennedy-Round" negotiations with other GATT nations. U.S. trade with communist countries has greatly expanded in the 1970s, and the Trade Reform Act of 1974 has paved the way for the U.S. to play an even greater role in international trade and commerce.

One of the most significant economic developments since the end of World War II has been the trend toward European economic integration. This has been promoted through a series of organizations, such as the Organization for European Economic Cooperation in 1948 (which subsequently became the Organization for Economic Cooperation and Development in 1960), the European Coal and Steel Community in 1952, the European Economic Community in 1958, and the European Free Trade Association in 1959. The success of these organizations, especially the Common Market with its goal to eliminate international trade barriers among the member nations and the establishment of a common external tariff, has stimulated the formation of similar organizations in other parts of the world.

In addition to promoting international trade, the United States has given more than $163 billion in foreign aid since 1947. Much of this aid has been given directly under such programs as the Marshall Plan, the Economic Cooperation Administration, and the Development Loan Fund. Technical assistance, as well as direct loans and grants, is a part of American foreign aid policy.

Another sizable portion of our foreign aid has been given through international organizations. The United States, for example, is the largest single contributor to the World Bank. In fact, our capital subcription amounts to about one third of the total World Bank subscription. We are also heavy contributors to the International Finance Corporation, the International Development Administration, and the Inter-American Development Bank.

Now that the role of international trade and aid in the world today has been evaluated, the next chapter takes a closer look at the problem of balancing international payments.

## DISCUSSION QUESTIONS

1. Explain how the law of comparative advantage, demonstrated in Chapter 2, can promote world trade.
2. What is the relative importance of international trade for the United States as compared with foreign nations?
3. It is frequently said that a revenue tariff and a protective tariff are incompatible. Explain.
4. Explain how international trade can raise the standard of living of any two countries involved.
5. Is the argument that a tariff protects infant industries valid? Why or why not?
6. Should we subsidize certain industries with a tariff for defense purposes? Why or why not?

7. Under what conditions is technical assistance more valuable to a developing nation than a loan? Justify your answer.
8. Do you believe the growth of major trading organizations promotes free trade? Explain.
9. In 1970 the Pearson Report of the World Bank suggested that developed nations should grant aid to developing nations in amounts equivalent to seven tenths of one percent of the total GNP of the developed nations. Comment on what this would mean for the United States.
10. Do you think United States aid to developing nations should be given directly or through international organizations? Why?

## SUGGESTED READINGS

*Annual Report*. Washington: International Monetary Fund, 1974.

Cohen, Stephen D. *International Monetary Reform, 1964–69*. New York: Praeger Publishers, 1970.

"EMU: Precursor of a Common Currency?" *European Community* (January, 1971).

"The European Common Market: The Next Phase." *Monthly Economic Letter*, First National City Bank of New York (August, 1970).

Haberler, Gottfried, and Thomas D. Willet. *A Strategy for U.S. Balance of Payments, Special Analysis*. Washington: American Enterprise Institute, February, 1971.

*International Economic Report of the President*. Washington: U.S. Government Printing Office, 1974 and 1975.

*International Monetary Statistics*. Washington: International Monetary Fund, August, 1974.

Kindleberger, Charles P. *International Economics*, 5th ed. Homewood, Ill.: Richard D. Irwin, Inc., 1973.

──────────. *Power and Money: The Politics of International Economics and the Economics of International Politics*. New York: Harper and Row, Publishers, 1971.

"Landmark Trade Act — Meaning for Detente." *U.S. News & World Report* (December 30, 1974).

Morowetz, David. *The Andean Group: Case Study in Economic Integration Among Developing Countries*. Boston: MIT Press, 1974.

Root, Franklin R. *International Trade and Investment*, 3d ed. Cincinnati: South-Western Publishing Co., 1973.

"SDR's — A New Asset Supplementing Reserves for Growth in Free World Trade." *Business Review*, Federal Reserve Bank of Dallas (December, 1970).

Snider, Delbert A. *Introduction to International Economics*, 6th ed. Homewood, Ill.: Richard D. Irwin, Inc., 1975.

U.S. Department of Commerce. "DISC (Domestic International Sales Corporation) Tax Deferral Benefits for Exporters Are Outlined." *Commerce Today* (January 10, 1972).

U.S. Department of Commerce. "Exploring Trade Prospects in the Soviet Union." *Commerce Today* (January 10, 1972).

# 22 THE BALANCE OF INTERNATIONAL PAYMENTS

## BALANCE OF TRADE

As mentioned in the previous chapter, the United States does not live in isolation from the rest of the world. The economic actions of the U.S. and many other nations frequently have international repercussions. There are nearly four billion people in the world spread throughout more than 135 countries. These people and countries produce more than $4 trillion worth of goods and services annually. The disparity between the productivity, natural resources, population, and types of goods produced in different countries helps encourage trade between them. Businesspeople in various countries are aggressive and seek to expand trade beyond domestic boundaries. All this, plus a general lack of domestic self-sufficiency, naturally promotes world trade among various nations. This in turn means that payment must be made for goods and services exchanged and that we must deal in the complexities of providing payment.

As nations engage in world trade, some tend to export more than they import from other specific nations, and vice versa. In many cases of multilateral trade, however, an export surplus against one nation will be offset by an import deficit from another nation. Country A, for example, may export $100 million in commodities to Country B, but import $100 million from Countries C and D combined. At the same time Country B may be exporting $100 million in goods to Countries C and D. In such a case, not only would world exports be equal to world imports, as they necessarily must be, but all nations would have an even balance of exports and imports.

This will not happen often, however, and some nations end up with a so-called *favorable balance of trade*, in which exports exceed imports, or an *unfavorable balance*, in which imports exceed exports. The term "favorable balance" is a misnomer, however. It is a holdover from the 18th and 19th centuries, when it was stressed that a nation with an excess of exports over imports was in a favorable position because it could force its debtor nations to pay the differences in gold and silver. We shall see later, however, that a nation with a continuous "favorable balance" eventually will find itself at a disadvantage when foreigners experience a shortage of the favored nation's currency and are unable to continue to purchase from it. It is common knowledge today that a nation which sells abroad must also buy from foreign nations to give them its currency with which they can purchase its goods.

History also reveals a correlation between the economic development of a nation and the status of the balance of trade. Emerging or developing nations are generally heavy importers, especially of machinery, equipment, and various types of finished goods. Exports in the early stages of economic growth will generally consist largely of raw materials from the nation's natural resources. A developing nation, lacking aid and investment capital, must finance imports by diverting natural resources and agricultural commodities in sufficient quantities from domestic to foreign (export) uses. As a country develops and is able to produce more of its own capital and finished goods, there will be less need for imports and an even balance of trade may come about. Finally, its debts liquidated, a fully developed industrial nation tends to be a large exporter of capital. Consequently, a nation may shift from a longtime debtor position to a creditor position as its balance of trade shifts from one side to another. For nearly a century prior to 1971 the United States usually had an annual excess of exports over imports of merchandise, as reflected in Table 22-1.

Table 22-1    **EXPORTS AND IMPORTS OF MERCHANDISE FOR THE UNITED STATES, 1940–1974**
(Millions of Dollars)

| Time Period or Year | Exports | Imports | Excess of Exports (+) or Imports (−) |
|---|---|---|---|
| 1940 | 4,124 | 2,698 | + 1,426 |
| 1945 | 12,473 | 5,245 | + 7,228 |
| 1950 | 10,203 | 9,081 | + 1,122 |
| 1955 | 14,424 | 11,527 | + 2,897 |
| 1960 | 19,650 | 14,758 | + 4,892 |
| 1965 | 26,461 | 21,510 | + 4,951 |
| 1970 | 41,947 | 39,788 | + 2,159 |
| 1971 | 42,754 | 45,476 | − 2,722 |
| 1972 | 48,768 | 55,754 | − 6,986 |
| 1973 | 70,277 | 69,806 | + 471 |
| 1974 | 94,696 | 100,379 | − 5,683 |

Source: *Economic Report of the President*, 1975.

## United States Trade Items

In 1974 the United States had a merchandise import balance of $5.7 billion. In addition to the export and import of merchandise, income from services performed by one country for another enters into the balance of trade. These services may include such items as shipping charges, insurance, banking services, and tourist transportation services. On this latter point not only travel charges enter the balance of trade, but likewise tourist spending on commodities and services in foreign nations is tantamount to an import to the tourist's homeland. When an American, for example, buys a bottle of wine in Paris, it has about the same effect on the balance of trade as the importation of French wine for table consumption in an American home. Tourist spending is an item of notable magnitude in our balance of trade. Americans in 1974 had a net debit balance (outflow) of $2.4 billion as a result of spending on travel abroad compared with foreign spending in the United States.

The balance of trade is also affected by the receipt of income from foreign investments. The receipt of interest payments and dividends by Americans for their investments in Germany, Canada, France, and other countries constitutes a flow of funds into the United States. On the other hand, the payment of interest and dividends to foreigners on their investments in the United States constitutes an outflow of funds. In 1974 Americans had a net private balance of $12.6 billion from foreign investment. However, the U.S. government lost over $3.1 billion from its foreign investments.

Another item that must be considered in the balance of trade is expenditures for military purposes. The sale of military goods by the United States to foreigners is a part of the total exports of our nation. Conversely, overseas military expenditures for various purposes constitute an outflow of income and has the same effect as tourist spending abroad or the importation of foreign goods. Expenditures by the United States government to maintain American troops and installations in West Germany, Japan, South Korea, Indochina, and elsewhere have been sizable. In addition to military expenditures for our own armed forces abroad, billions more are spent in the form of grants of military supplies and equipment for the armed services of noncommunist nations. Sometimes in analyzing the balance of trade, such military payments and grants are excluded from the balance of trade, but not from the balance of payments. Payment in this regard is made by the United States government. In most cases, however, a grant involving agricultural commodities and certain military items is recorded as a debit in our foreign aid account.

When these various items mentioned above were added to the export and import of merchandise, the *balance of trade on goods and services* for 1974 showed an excess of exports over imports of nearly $3.2 billion, as indicated in Table 22-2 on page 452.

## Debits and Credits

International trade items are recorded as debits or credits on the international balance of accounts. A debit entry is made for transactions that give rise to a claim for payment by foreigners against any American resident, business, or the government. The largest debit category arises from the importation of goods and services. In addition to commodities, this debit includes charges for shipping and freight services for commodities carried on foreign vessels, insurance, banking and brokerage charges, and the like. It also includes expenditures overseas by American tourists and government personnel.

Table 22-2 **UNITED STATES BALANCE OF PAYMENTS, 1974**
(Millions of Dollars)

| | | | | | | | |
|---|---|---|---|---|---|---|---|
| Merchandise trade balance | | | − | 5,683 | | | |
| Exports | + | 94,696 | | | | | |
| Imports | − | 100,379 | | | | | |
| Military transactions, net | | | − | 2,150 | | | |
| Direct expenditures | − | 4,989 | | | | | |
| Sales | + | 2,839 | | | | | |
| Net investment income | | | + | 9,516 | | | |
| Private | + | 12,649 | | | | | |
| U.S. government | − | 3,133 | | | | | |
| Net travel and transportation expenditures | | | − | 2,355 | | | |
| Other services | | | + | 3,837 | | | |
| Balance of trade on goods and services | | | | | + | 3,165 | |
| Remittances, pensions, and other unilateral transfers | | | − | 8,136 | | | |
| Balance on current account | | | | | − | 4,971 | |
| Long-term capital flows | | | − | 716 | | | |
| U.S. government | + | 2,571 | | | | | |
| Private | − | 3,287 | | | | | |
| Balance on current account and long-term capital flows | | | | | − | 5,687 | |
| Non-liquid short-term private capital flows, net | − | 14,751 | | | | | |
| Errors and omissions | + | 4,783 | | | | | |
| Net liquidity balance | | | | | − | 15,655 | |
| Liquid private capital flows | + | 10,573 | | | | | |
| Official reserve transactions balance | | | | | − | 5,082 | |
| Changes in liabilities to foreign official agencies, net | + | 7,176 | | | | | |
| Changes in U.S. official reserve assets, net | − | 2,095 | | | | | |

Source: *Economic Report of the President*, 1975, pp. 350–351.

In addition to the import of goods and services, another important debit category is our capital outflow. Any time American residents purchase foreign bonds, stocks, and other securities, a debit entry is registered in our balance of payments. Evidences of debt in the form of currency or bank deposits, which are obligations of the issuing institution, are also debit items. When an American resident purchases a foreign bond, for example, or builds up a bank account in a foreign nation, a debit arises in the United States balance of payments. Direct investment abroad arising from the acquisition or construction of a building or factory is treated as a debit item, even though there is no claim by foreigners to payment from the American owner.

Debit entries are also made for unilateral transfers abroad, which arise as a result of gifts and grants, personal remittances, contributions, and other similar one-way transactions, whether made by individuals, institutions, or the government. Large expenditures for foreign aid by our government are included in this debit category.

Movements of gold in settlement of international balances of payment are also entered as debits or credits. An inflow of gold from abroad, like an import of goods or services, is a debit transaction in the balance of payments.

Credit transactions are the opposite of debit transactions and give rise to American claims against persons, firms, institutions, and governments of foreign nations. Major credit items in the United States balance of payments include exports of goods and services, inflow of capital into America, increases in foreign-held American bank deposits or decreases in American bank balances held abroad, increases in foreign investment in United States securities and physical assets, unilateral transfers from abroad, and gold exports from the United States.

In total, debits must equal credits, and they do. To make them balance, however, changes in the ownership of securities, buildup or depletion of bank deposits, or an inflow or outflow of gold may take place. In Table 22-2 on page 452 credits are designated with a (+) and debits with a (−) sign.

## BALANCE OF PAYMENTS

More important than the balance of trade on goods and services in international economics is the balance of payments. It is the latter which designates whether or not a nation is going to have an inflow or outflow of currency or gold, or the purchase or sale of short-term securities.

Although the flow of goods and services is the largest category of international transactions, it is by no means the only segment that must be considered. Whether or not a particular nation will have a positive or deficit balance of payments will depend on many other transactions. Even though a nation may have an excess of exports over imports, it does not assure a favorable balance of payments. In spite of its very favorable export balances over a number of decades, the United States, for example, has had sizable deficits in its balance of payments in the past fifteen or twenty years.

In looking at the balance of payments, one must not only consider the dollar claims of the rest of the world against the United States that result from sending imports into the United States, but one must also look at the dollar claims of foreigners arising from other sources. These claims arise in large part from the flow of funds and capital among nations.

A typical balance of payments for 1974 is shown in Table 22-2. This balance of payments shows a deficit. This deficit may be measured in several ways, however.

First, it is obvious that our imports of merchandise exceeded our exports by a sizable amount, and on this basis we owed foreigners $5.7 billion. We must add to this deficit an additional $2,150 million, since our military expenditures abroad exceeded our sales of military goods to foreigners by this amount, plus another net deficit balance of $2,355 million for U.S. travel and transportation expenditures abroad.

On the income side, our investment income exceeded that of foreigners by $9,516 million and they owed us $3,837 million for other services. This left a positive or credit balance on goods and services of $3,165 million. From this, however, we must subtract $8,136 million for remittances, pension payments to Americans living abroad, and unilateral transfers. This changes the balance in the so-called current account to a deficit of $4,971 million. After taking into account long-term and short-term capital flows and making an adjustment for errors and omissions, the U.S. had a deficit liquidity balance of $15,655 million. This was finally adjusted for the $10,573 million in private capital flows, leaving a deficit of $5,082 million in the official reserve transactions balance of payments. This balance was taken care of primarily by U.S. payments to foreign official agencies through the U.S. government, American banks, and the International Monetary Fund.

Prior to August, 1971, the U.S. settled its deficit balance of payments in part through the payment of gold in exchange for dollars held by foreign central banks and governments. Since August, 1971, however, payments by the U.S. to foreigners have not been made in gold.

Since apparent deficits, such as that for 1974, are usually settled or eliminated by changes in United States and foreign liquid assets and at times by the flow of gold, some international trade analysts object to the use of the term *deficit balance of payments*. They contend that both sides of the balance of payments account must balance, just as does any balance sheet based on the double-entry method of accounting. Although this is technically correct, the terms *deficit* and *surplus* are commonly used today by most economists, financiers, and government officials in reference to the balance of payments; and the balance of payments is considered to be more nearly equivalent to a statement of income, showing income or loss, rather than a balance sheet that shows changes in assets, liabilities, and stockholders' equity.

It should be remembered that the surplus or deficit is not nearly so important as is the means of settlement. Whether the means is a temporary stopgap measure, whether it is remedial or preventive, and how permanent or enduring it is in its nature will all have an important effect in determining whether an imbalance in trade will be corrected.

## FOREIGN EXCHANGE RATES

As trade takes place among different countries, goods and services are exchanged, international investments are made, and money and gold flows settle differences between debtor and creditor nations. Since most of the international exchange of goods and services is carried on by individual persons and business firms, the question naturally arises regarding the manner in which payment is made for the purchase of foreign goods and services.

To start with, it should be mentioned that international sales are similar to domestic sales except that the international sellers usually desire to be paid in their domestic currency for the commodities they sell, rather than in the domestic currency of the buyers. Consequently, a conversion must be made from the buyer's currency to the seller's currency to complete the transaction. The method of settlement for the purchase of a foreign good or service can be hypothetically demonstrated by assuming that an American sports-car dealer desires to purchase a British MG at a cost of £1,000. Assuming the rate of exchange between British pounds and American dollars is approximately £1 = $2.40, the American auto dealer will go to a bank such as the Chase Manhattan and purchase a bank draft for £1,000 by paying $2,400, plus a small service charge. He will then mail this draft on a British bank to the British automobile manufacturer, who will present it to his bank in London, let us say Barclay's Bank, for payment of the £1,000 or for deposit to his account. Since the Chase Manhattan and other American banks dealing in foreign exchange maintain deposits in foreign banks such as Barclay's Bank of London, Barclay's Bank will honor the draft and reduce by £1,000 the deposit account of the Chase Manhattan Bank in Barclay's Bank.

On the other hand, if a British manufacturer purchased $2,400 worth of tools and equipment from an American machine tool shop, the British manufacturer would go to his bank, again let us say to Barclay's Bank in London, and purchase a bank draft for $2,400, paying £1,000 for it plus the service charge. In this case, when he sent the draft to the American tool company, it would present the draft for payment at the Chase Manhattan Bank, which, in turn, after paying the American exporter $2,400, would debit the London bank's dollar deposit account on its records.

In that way the $2,400 paid to the Chase Manhattan Bank by the American importer for his £1,000 foreign exchange draft can be used to pay the American export company who presents the $2,400 draft sent to it by the British importer. In London the £1,000 paid by the British importer for the $2,400 bank draft can be used to pay the £1,000 draft presented by the British exporter. In this simplified case, as depicted in Figure 22-1 on page 456, the foreign deposits of the respective banks would remain the same. It is easy to see that much of our foreign trade transactions can be paid by offsetting charges without necessarily involving a large currency flow among nations. But as simple as it is, the example demonstrates how funds are converted from one currency into another. It should be remembered, however, that imbalances often exist between nations that must be settled in one way or another.

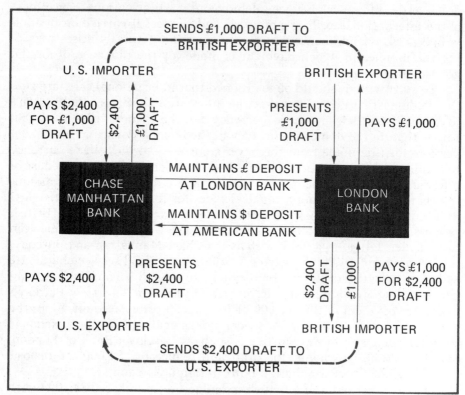

Figure 22-1   **PURCHASE AND REDEMPTION
OF FOREIGN EXCHANGE DRAFTS**

Currency exchange rates between countries play an important role in international economics. A particular exchange rate may make it more or less expensive to buy foreign goods and services. If an American importer, for example, can purchase a British pound for $2.40, she may find it profitable to purchase a £10 British camera that would cost her $24. But if the exchange rate were $2.80, she might not find the £10 camera such a bargain. Since a change in the exchange rate may actually reverse the flow of goods and currencies between different countries, it is essential to understand how exchange rates are determined if one is to understand the international movement of goods. Exchange rates may be flexible, they may be fixed, or they may be controlled, depending on what system is in force.

## Flexible Exchange Rates

Exchange rates, which are the prices of foreign moneys or claims thereto, may be determined by the free forces of supply and demand. In such a case the exchange rate will, in the absence of restrictions, fluctuate with changes in exports and imports and the consequent changes in all factors affecting the supply of and the demand for foreign exchange. In international exchange, the term *floating rate* is commonly used to refer to an exchange rate that is not fixed.

If we assume that the exchange rate between Canadian and United States currencies, for example, is one Canadian dollar for one American dollar and that a certain balance of trade exists, it can be demonstrated how exchange rates fluctuate in the absence of controls. If Canadians increase their purchases of American goods and services and spend more on tourist trade while visiting the United States, there could be a sharp increase in the demand for American dollars to pay for the imports from the United States and for vacation spending in this country. This could make American dollars scarce relative to Canadian dollars in the Canadian foreign exchange markets, and the price of the American dollar in Canada may rise to $1.05 Canadian, or the Canadian dollar would be discounted at 95 cents American when used to purchase American goods and services. For example, an item in the United States that formerly cost the Canadian importer 10 Canadian dollars will now cost 10.5 Canadian dollars.

As the cost of the American dollar in terms of Canadian dollars rises, however, corrective forces come into play. The relatively higher prices on American goods and services, now selling at 5 percent more as far as Canadians are concerned, may reduce Canadian purchases of American goods or enjoyment of vacations in the United States. Many of them will find it more attractive to increase their purchases of domestically produced goods and services. On the other hand, Americans, finding that Canadian goods and services can be purchased for 5 percent less than before, because one American dollar will exchange for 1.05 Canadian dollars, or one Canadian dollar can be purchased for 95 cents in American currency, will find it advantageous to purchase Canadian goods and services rather than those produced in the United States. Furthermore, many tourists may be induced to vacation in Canada because of the Canadian exchange advantage. The corresponding increase in demand for Canadian dollars, of course, would raise the price of Canadian dollars, while the lessening of demand for United States dollars by Canadians would decrease the price of American dollars until the two currencies came into balance again or moved in the opposite direction. In the mid-1950s, for example, the price of the Canadian dollar was $1.04 American. In the early 1960s, however, Americans could obtain a Canadian dollar for 93 cents American. Then in May, 1962, the exchange rate between the two currencies was fixed at one Canadian dollar for 92.5 American cents by international agreement. Subsequently the exchange rate was permitted to *float*, that is, to seek its own level. In 1973 it took $1.02 in U.S. currency to purchase a Canadian dollar, and in 1974, $1.04.

Flexible exchange rates serve as a means of correcting a disequilibrium in the balance of payments. As such, they keep international commercial relations from becoming one-sided and keep alive comparative advantage as the principle of world trade.

### Fixed Exchange Rates

A common method of establishing fixed exchange rates used in the earlier part of this century was through the use of the gold standard. Under the gold standard, nations defined their currencies in terms of gold and permitted the unrestricted purchase and sale of gold as well as the freedom to import and export gold as a means of settling international balances of payment. The American dollar at one time was defined as 23.22 grains of pure gold and the British pound as 113 grains of gold. At these values the British pound contained 4.87 times as much gold as the American dollar. Consequently, the exchange rate between pounds and dollars was set at £1 = $4.87.

During the days of the gold standard the cost of shipping (insurance plus freight) 113 grains of gold between New York and London was 3 cents. Therefore, anytime an American importer had to pay more than $4.90 for a British pound in New York, he would find it less costly to purchase the gold with dollars and to ship gold in payment of his purchase rather than to buy an exchange draft. On the other hand, a British importer would find it less costly to convert his pounds into gold and ship gold in payment of American imports when the exchange rate fell below £1 = $4.84. As a result, the exchange rates remained fixed at $4.87 plus or minus 3 cents. The two extremes, $4.90 and $4.84, were often referred to as the *gold points* because as the price moved out of this range, gold would flow from one nation to another.

Under this system, adjustments in the balance of trade or in the flow of gold came through changes in the price levels of various countries. If the demand for British pounds, for example, was so great that the exchange rate moved beyond the gold outflow point, £1 = $4.90, United States importers would buy gold from the government at a price of $4.87 for 113 grains and ship the gold to Great Britain in payment of their imports, rather than buy an exchange draft for $4.91 or $4.92. This flow of gold out of the United States and into Great Britain would set in motion forces to lower the exchange rate and eventually reverse the outflow of gold. The loss of gold from the United States and the reduction of bank deposits would result in a tightening of credit in the United States and a reduction in the money supply. This, of course, would cause a decrease in the price level and/or a decline in the level of business activity.

At the same time the inflow of gold into Great Britain, assuming a full-employment economy, would cause prices to rise in Great Britain. The high price in Britain, accompanied by lower prices in America, would deter American imports from Great Britain and stimulate domestic purchases by Americans. Conversely, the exchange rate and the price situation between the two nations would discourage domestic purchases in Great Britain in favor of imports of lower-priced American commodities. The corresponding decrease in demand for British pounds and the increase in demand for American dollars would drive the exchange rate back to normal or down toward the lower extreme. If the exchange rate fell below the gold import point, £1 = $4.84, the flow of gold into the United States would force prices upward and British prices would decrease until adjustments were brought about again by the flow of gold.

Since most nations are no longer on the gold standard and restrict the purchase and outflow of gold, this method is no longer useful as a means of fixing exchange rates. Exchange rates today, however, may resemble those of this bygone era.

### Controlled or Managed Exchange Rates

With the widespread abandonment of the gold standard in the 1930s by most major nations throughout the world, including Great Britain and the United States, many nations adopted exchange controls or restricted convertibility immediately. Although some nations did allow their exchange rates to fluctuate freely, most of these nations imposed controls when World War II erupted. As a result, today most nations have adopted some type of a managed or controlled exchange rate, rather than rely on a freely fluctuating or a fixed exchange rate. By controlling the exchange rate, a nation hopes to avoid the severe effects on domestic employment, income, and prices sometimes brought about by exchange-rate corrections in a freely fluctuating market.

Exchange control usually involves a government agreement to maintain a particular exchange rate between its currency and that of other nations. As previously mentioned, the Canadian government in 1962, for example, agreed to establish an official exchange rate of $1 Canadian equal to 92.5 American cents. To maintain that rate of exchange, the Canadian government agreed to buy and sell foreign exchange as the market price deviated up or down. Thus, if there were a strong demand for American dollars that might send the market rate of exchange down to $1 Canadian equals 90 cents American, the Canadian government would buy American dollars for $1.10 in Canadian money and sell the dollars to Canadian importers for $1.075 Canadian ($1 Canadian = $.925 American). In short, the Canadian government would simply make more American dollars available in Canadian exchange markets.

If for some reason there were a strong demand for the Canadian dollar and the market rate of exchange moved up to $1 Canadian equals 94

American cents, the Canadian government would purchase American dollars for $1.06 or more in sufficient quantity to drive the price up to $1.075 ($1 Canadian = $.925), the official exchange rate. Nations with such managed currencies usually established an "exchange stabilization fund" composed of its own currency, foreign currencies, and gold that was used for buying and selling foreign exchange.

On June 1, 1970, the Canadian government announced that, for the time being, Canada would not maintain the exchange rate of the Canadian dollar within the margins required by International Monetary Fund rules. Canada decided to let the exchange rate float to seek its own level. By the end of the year, 98.3 Canadian cents were exchanging for $1.00 American; and by 1974, 96.1 Canadian cents were exchanging for $1.00 American.

Exchange controls may be unilateral in nature insofar as one nation may determine the rate at which it desires to stabilize the exchange rate between itself and other nations. Such a rate, however, may work to the detriment of other nations, in which case exchange-rate competition or retaliation may ensue and give rise to a "currency rate war." To avert this possibility, exchange controls have been established in which two or more nations agree on the exchange rates to be established and all make an effort to maintain such agreed-upon rates.

Exchange rates may be managed to an even greater degree by any nation through rationing the supply of exchange that is available for particular uses. This, in turn, limits the total demand for foreign exchange and influences the market rate. In recent years international exchange rates have been established in large part through the International Monetary Fund.

## INTERNATIONAL MONETARY FUND

With the demise of the gold standard in the 1930s and the outbreak of World War II, an unstable exchange situation developed as more and more nations moved to exchange controls.

It became evident to major nations throughout the world that more stability in exchange rates was desirable, but by some method less rigid than the gold standard. As a result of international deliberations at a conference in Bretton Woods, New Hampshire, in 1944, an international organization known as the International Monetary Fund (IMF) was established in an attempt to stabilize exchange rates and to provide temporary assistance to nations with deficit balances of payments.

### Establishing Exchange Rates

To fulfill the objectives of the Fund, each of the thirty original signatory members was asked to establish a par value for its currency in terms of gold or United States dollars. Once these values were established with the aid of the Fund, the Fund then established international exchange rates. Members are charged with an obligation to maintain their respective exchange rates within certain limitations. In the case of Great Britain, for example, the exchange rate of the pound was set at a par value of $2.40 with permissible fluctuation from $2.424 to $2.376. If the rate exceeded either limit, however, Great Britain was expected to use its stabilization fund to buy or sell pounds in an effort to bring the rate within the limits.

### Assistance to Members

Each member nation was assigned a quota or subscription of funds, which it had to contribute to the Fund in the form of gold or its own currency. Member nation quotas were established on the basis of a number of factors, but primarily on the basis of national income, population, and the flow of foreign exchange transactions. The current quota for the United States, for example, is $6.7 billion, an amount equal to about one third of the total size of the Fund. At least 25 percent of the subscription had to be paid in gold (or 10% of the nation's gold holdings, whichever was less) and the remainder in domestic currency. In 1975 there were 126 member nations, and the Fund held gold equivalent in value to 6.6 billion American dollars.

With the existence of the International Monetary Fund any particular nation that has a deficit balance of payments or a shortage of foreign exchange should not be required to alter its domestic prices, as was the case under the gold standard, or to change its exchange rates, as experienced under the individually controlled exchange rate system, to obtain relief. Furthermore, the mechanism of the Fund has tended also to prevent wide fluctuations that could come about under a system of freely fluctuating exchange rates. Any member nation that has had a shortage of a particular type of foreign exchange can obtain temporary relief by borrowing exchange, gold, or SDRs (Special Drawing Rights) from the Fund.

One of the main functions of the IMF is the administration of Special Drawing Rights introduced in 1970. SDRs are a collectively managed asset of the Fund, sometimes referred to as "paper gold." They are now a principal source of international reserves. A country with a balance-of-payments deficit can draw upon these reserves to settle its indebtedness to others rather than transferring ownership of gold. In effect, what a nation does is buy the needed exchange with its own currency. It is intended that ordinary transactions between nations will continue to involve private agencies. Only when a nation has a shortage of foreign exchange is it expected to resort to this form of borrowing from the Fund. Similarly, nations with balance-of-payments surpluses may accumulate these drawing rights much as they would accumulate gold reserves. In 1974, for example, the United States was holding $1.8 billion in SDRs of other nations.

To date, approximately 75 member nations have purchased (borrowed) currencies from the Fund. Since its beginning the Fund has made loans totaling over $30 billion, and about one half has been repaid. In 1974 alone, 24 nations borrowed an amount equivalent to $1,058 million in exchange and SDRs from the Fund. The Fund's biggest borrower over the years has been Great Britain, and the currency most often purchased by it and other nations has been the American dollar.

Nations that continually experience a deficit balance of payments or shortage of exchange and whose difficulty cannot be corrected by temporary borrowings from the Fund may have to seek other remedies. All member nations have agreed that they will consult through the Fund on all such major international problems. Any nation may, however, change its exchange rate by 10 percent merely by notifying the Fund; but any further devaluation must have the Fund's prior approval.

### Experience of the Fund

Although the establishment of the Fund was heralded with great expectations, it has met with only modest success in its 30 years of operations. Since its primary function is to offer relief from temporary disequilibrium in the balance of payments rather than the solution to fundamental and long-run balance of payments problems, it will necessarily function better in a more stable international situation than in one replete with serious monetary crises.

Although international exchange rates have been established in large part through the International Monetary Fund, many changes have come about in the 1970s. Due to widespread international financial changes in recent years, several major nations such as West Germany, France, Japan, and Canada have at times broken away from established or managed exchange rates and gone to floating (flexible) exchange rates. They have done this for the purpose of letting the market seek a newer, or more natural, exchange rate. Due to these and other causes, in reality today's exchange rates can best be described as being in a state of flux.

## UNITED STATES BALANCE OF PAYMENTS

The United States balance of international payments reflects events of the world, such as the Depression of the 1930s, the flight of capital from Europe prior to World War II, our entry into the war, the postwar dollar shortage, the rebuilding of foreign economies, the gold outflow, and the worldwide energy and resource crisis.

### Dollar Shortage

The United States was the only major nation in the world whose industrial structure was unscathed by World War II; consequently, many of the war-torn countries, especially in Europe, turned to the United States for the purchase of essential goods and services. Since they had little in the way of imports to offer in exchange for our exports, the United States during World War II developed large surpluses in its balance of payments. Foreign nations, however, had limited holdings of United States dollars or gold with which to pay their deficits. In fact, as a result of their war spending, at the end of World War II the entire dollar and gold holdings of the rest of the world amounted to less than $15 billion. At the same time the United States held approximately 75 percent of the world's gold supply, outside of the U.S.S.R. Therefore, there was an extreme "dollar shortage" in international exchange markets throughout the world in the early postwar days, which continued until the mid-1950s, as foreigners clamored for United States dollars.

The United States did endeavor to ease the dollar shortage to some extent by the Marshall Plan, through which we extended billions of dollars in aid to our allies for reconstruction purposes, and by other grants and loans to foreign nations, as well as dollar contributions to various international financial institutions. But the dollar shortage was further aggravated in the 1950s by the cost of military preparations in connection with the cold war and by the fact that many of the emerging and underdeveloped nations were looking toward the United States for both economic and military assistance.

In the late 1950s there occurred a dramatic shift in the dollar shortage and the demand for United States dollars. By that time many of the war-torn countries had rebuilt their economies, most of them with new and modern industrial structures which increased their productive capacity considerably. As a result they were no longer as dependent on the United States for goods and services. In fact, many of them by that time were competing successfully with America in world markets. Furthermore, inflation in the United States had made the purchase of our goods and services less appealing to foreigners and the purchase of foreign goods more appealing to Americans. Although we retained a favorable balance of trade, the size of our export-import gap did dwindle in some years. Furthermore, we continued to increase our outlays for military operations overseas, to extend large grants and loans to foreign nations, to increase our direct investments abroad, and to purchase short- and long-term foreign securities. As a result we experienced a notable shift in the dollar demand beginning in 1958. Since that time we have had deficits in our balance of payments ranging from $1 billion to $30 billion annually. And since foreign nations were becoming less inclined to hold dollars, the situation was reversed and instead of a "dollar shortage," foreign nations began to build up claims against United States dollars.

### Gold Outflow

Since these dollar claims were not needed to buy additional American goods and services, some nations used them to purchase short-term United States government obligations on which they received an interest income. Many nations, however, requested gold payment in exchange for their dollar claims. As a result there was a continuous drain or outflow of gold from the United States commencing in 1957, when our gold supply was $22.9 billion, nearly 60 percent of the world's known monetary gold stock. By March, 1967, our gold stock had dwindled to $13.2 billion, or about 30 percent of the world supply. Increased production of gold and shifts of gold holdings resulted in sizable amounts of gold flowing into such nations as Belgium, France, West Germany, Italy, The Netherlands, Switzerland, and the United Kingdom.

Some authorities viewed the gold drain with alarm and, as a means of arresting the gold outflow from the United States, suggested numerous measures, such as the reduction of overseas military spending, decreases in foreign aid, the adoption of more tying clauses to our aid, accelerated export promotion, and taxes on American investments abroad. In fact, a number of such measures were invoked in an effort to ease the outflow of gold.

Some monetary authorities suggested a devaluation of the dollar as a means of correcting our deficit balance of payments position and reversing the drain of gold. Early in 1965 our 25 percent gold reserve requirement behind Federal Reserve Bank deposits was eliminated to free more gold for use, if necessary, for the international support of the dollar and the settlement of deficit balances of payments. In March, 1968, a bill eliminating the 25 percent gold cover (reserve) behind Federal Reserve notes was passed in Congress. At that time the bulk of our $10.7 billion gold supply was serving as a reserve behind our money supply. This left very little gold as free reserve that could be used for the settlement of dollar claims. Although it was not felt that we would need much, if any, of our reserve supply to make gold payments in exchange for dollars, it was suggested that there would be a great psychological advantage in letting the rest of the world know that we stood ready to use all our gold to support the dollar. Furthermore, it was becoming evident that with continued increases in our money supply over the next few years the current gold holding would be inadequate to maintain the 25 percent reserve ratio.

On the other hand, some monetary authorities looked upon the gold drain from the United States simply as a normal reaction in international economics. They suggested that any nation would inevitably gain and lose gold at various times and under certain conditions, and that the better distribution of gold and the improved convertibility of several of the foreign currencies resulting from our gold drain would promote and facilitate world trade.

Since many other nations were having difficulties with deficit balances of payments and gold flows, it was frequently suggested that our gold outflow problem in the United States was merely symptomatic of a more basic widespread problem — a shortage of international liquidity. At that time the primary means of settling international balances was through the flow of American dollars, British pounds, and gold. Since world trade had increased at a much faster pace than the increase in dollars, pounds, and gold, it had become more difficult for nations and banks to obtain the current forms of international liquidity.

To ease the gold drain from the United States, the Gold Pool nations of the world in 1968 agreed to the adoption of a two-tier gold price, one price for monetary purposes and one price for the free gold market. In short, instead of trying to keep both prices at $35 per ounce, it was decided to let the market price of gold fluctuate. At the same time, these ten nations agreed not to supply the free market with gold. Prior to this the central banks of some of these nations had supplied gold to the free markets, and in turn used dollars to buy gold from the United States to replenish their gold reserves. The Gold Pool nations also agreed to stop buying gold for monetary purposes in an effort to divert gold into the free market. By increasing the supply relative to demand, they hoped to keep the free price of gold in line with the monetary price of $35 per ounce.

In 1969 the shortage of international liquidity was eased when the major financial nations of the world, through the International Monetary Fund, agreed to the creation of $9.5 billion in Special Drawing Rights, which were formally introduced in 1970. Since SDRs can be used for the settlement of international payments, this move took some of the pressure off the demand for dollars and gold. This, along with the two-tier gold price and other measures, helped to reduce the speculation in gold and bring the free market price of gold, which had reached $42.50 per ounce, down to the monetary price of $35 per ounce by December, 1969.

The stable price of gold was temporary, however, as further disquieting forces sounded. A near crisis of the French franc resulted in a devaluation of the franc and a revaluation of the German deutsche mark. In 1971 the United States experienced a substantial deterioration in its trade position and faced a deficit balance of trade for the first time in nearly a century. Speculation emerged that the dollar and some other currencies might be devalued. Consequently, the price of gold began to rise substantially. By the middle of 1971 it was estimated that foreign official institutions held $50 to $60 billion in liquid claims against the United States. That was double the amount of a year earlier. On the other hand, the total U.S. gold stock was only $10.4 billion.

In the spring of 1971 many dollars were being sold in exchange for other currencies, particularly German deutsche marks. On speculation that the deutsche mark would be revalued again and thus worth more dollars, the sale of dollars became so heavy that foreign exchange markets in Germany, Switzerland, Belgium, Austria, and The Netherlands were temporarily closed. When the markets reopened, changes were made. The Austrian schilling was revalued. The German deutsche mark was allowed to "float" (that is, the rate of exchange was unpegged) to permit the market to seek and establish new exchange rates between the deutsche mark and other currencies. At the same time The Netherlands guilder also was floated and the Swiss franc was revalued. Within a short time the average appreciation of the major world currencies vis-à-vis the dollar was 10 to 12 percent.

It was under these circumstances that President Nixon, on August 15, 1971, among other sweeping changes in domestic and foreign economic measures, established a 10 percent surcharge on imports and suspended the convertibility of dollars for gold.

### Devaluation of the Dollar

It was evident that the U.S. dollar was overvalued in world markets and that currencies of several other nations, especially those with substantial balances of payments, such as Japan and West Germany, were undervalued. It was also evident that the United States could not continue forever as a major supplier of international liquidity for the entire world. In spite of this, the action of President Nixon on August 15, 1971, startled the international financial world and brought about serious repercussions.

The United States subsequently used the 10 percent surcharge as a club to encourage various nations to adjust their currencies and to take other steps for the improvement of world trade. In December, 1971, after numerous meetings the Group of Ten in cooperation with the IMF, agreed to the so-called Smithsonian Accord, by which they pledged to work for an "effective" realignment of important world currencies. Some nations suggested that the United States devalue the dollar by 15 percent, but the U.S. continued to push for revaluation of other reserve currencies as well. Subsequently, in early 1972 the U.S. import surcharge was modified and the U.S. dollar was devalued by 8.57 percent when Congress officially raised the price of gold to $38 per ounce. As a part of the international accord, the Japanese agreed to revalue the yen, and the deutsche mark and the guilder would continue to float before new exchange values were set for them. In addition, to provide greater flexibility in official exchange rates the official "band" within which exchange rates were permitted to fluctuate was widened from one percent to 2.25 percent.

While world traders, financiers, and nations were adjusting to these changes, the United States, the Group of Ten, and the IMF were analyzing their effects and studying a more elaborate agenda dealing with other issues related to the development of a new international monetary structure. Still to be considered were the future convertibility of the dollar for gold, the expanded use of Special Drawing Rights, the volume and control of international liquidity, and the possibility of moving from fixed to flexible exchange rates, with a "wider band" or "crawling peg." Action on any of these issues would affect the role of the dollar, the U.S. flow of gold, and the United States balance of payments position. Thus, it appeared that the gold outflow and related problems would be with us for some time. Furthermore, since the free market price of gold was driven up to more than $60 per ounce by the fall of 1972, it was evident that speculators were unconvinced that the gold problem had been settled.

The United States balance of payments failed to improve substantially in 1972. Moreover, the international monetary authorities failed to come up with any further solutions to the world monetary problems, and the relationship of the American dollar vis-à-vis foreign currency, especially the deutsche mark and the yen, continued to deteriorate. Consequently, in February, 1973, the United States again devalued the dollar. This time the value of the dollar was decreased by 10 percent and the price of gold raised to $42.22 per ounce.

A prolonged meeting of the Committee of Twenty (an enlargement of the original Group of Ten) in Kenya, Africa, in the summer of 1973 developed an outline of reforms and set a target date of July 31, 1974, to implement the reforms. The meeting, however, failed to produce any positive remedies for the world monetary situation. In addition, the Arab oil embargo in late 1973 and early 1974 and the subsequent heavy increases in the price of oil had an adverse effect on the economies and the balances of payments of the United States, Japan, West Germany, France, the United Kingdom, and other industrial nations. World financial conditions became more unsettled, and the OPEC (Organization of Petroleum Exporting Countries) nations began having more influence on world financial matters as a result of their accumulation of dollars and other currencies from the sale of oil at the new, higher prices. It was estimated that at the start of 1975 these nations had nearly $100 billion in so-called "petrodollars" (currency claims against the U.S. and others). This brought a new monetary problem to the international scene as the question now became how to invest or recycle this currency back into the world money markets.

As world financial conditions became more uncertain, speculators bid the price of gold to more than $175 per ounce by the summer of 1974. With the announcement that the United States would permit its citizens to purchase and hold gold beginning December 31, 1974, the price of gold in the free market reached $200 per ounce by Christmas. When gold sales in America proved to be less vigorous than anticipated, however, the market price of gold dropped back below $200 per ounce in early 1975.

## SUMMARY

Nations of the world are not completely independent. Consequently, they engage in trade with one another and numerous commodities are transferred among them. Some nations at certain times export more goods and services than they import, and as a result they have a favorable balance of trade. Prior to 1971, the United States, for example, had a favorable trade balance for the previous 30 years or more. More important than the balance of trade, however, is a nation's balance of payments, which takes into account the spending of money abroad and foreign spending in the domestic nation. When a nation has a surplus or deficit balance of payments, settlement is made by paying the difference in foreign currencies, gold, SDRs, or by the sale of securities.

The United States' deficit balance of payments in 1973 was $5.3 billion and $5.1 billion in 1974. These deficits were settled primarily by changes in our liquid liabilities to foreigners. In previous years deficits were settled in part by the sale of gold to the creditor nations.

Since payment for imports is made by the purchase of foreign exchange, international exchange rates play an important role in the trade between nations. A decrease or increase in exchange rates can make the purchase of foreign goods more or less attractive and affect the balance of payments. Exchange rates can be established in various ways. They may be fixed as they were under the gold standard, they may be flexible and be determined at any time by the supply and demand for different currencies, or they may be managed or controlled by the government or by an international organization. Many of the present exchange rates have been established through the International Monetary Fund.

The United States, after having sizable surplus balances of payments during World War II, has been in a deficit balance position during the past 20 years or more. Although there was a dollar shortage during the early postwar days and during the mid-1950s, the situation has reversed considerably since then. In the 1950s and the 1960s foreign claims against American dollars resulted in a heavy outflow of gold, causing our gold supply to dwindle from nearly $23 billion in 1957 to $10.7 billion by 1968. Then a number of corrective measures, including the creation of SDRs and the adoption of a two-tier gold price, were instrumental in arresting the U.S. gold outflow, at least temporarily. U.S. gold reserves rose to nearly $12 billion early in 1970. But continued deficits of payment caused the gold drain to resume and our gold reserves were down to nearly $10 billion by mid-1971. Dramatic action by President Nixon in August, 1971, which stopped the redemption of dollars for gold by the U.S. Treasury and imposed a 10 percent surcharge on most American imports, had a worldwide impact.

In the past few years a number of adjustments have been made in various exchange rates as a result of devaluations and revaluations of currencies. The United States, for example, devalued the dollar in 1972 and again in early 1973. The monetary price of gold on January 1, 1975, was $42.22 per ounce. Due to unsettled world financial conditions, however, the market price of gold at that time was nearly $200 per ounce.

## DISCUSSION QUESTIONS

1. How is it possible for a nation to have a favorable balance of trade but still have a deficit balance of payments?
2. How does United States direct private investment abroad affect the balance of payments?
3. If interest rates in foreign nations rise substantially compared to interest rates for borrowed or invested funds in the United States, what effect do you think this has on our balance of payments?
4. If an American merchant were to purchase a dozen Necchi sewing machines from Italy, explain the process involved in making payment for the machines.
5. Explain the difference between a flexible exchange rate and a managed exchange rate.
6. When exchange rates were pegged to the gold standard, how did the flow of gold from a debtor nation to a creditor nation tend eventually to reverse the balance of payments?
7. Explain what impact higher prices have had on the U.S. international balance of payments.
8. Do you think that the United States should have devalued the dollar as a means of arresting the outflow of gold? Why or why not?
9. Assume a speculator purchased a million dollars worth of West German deutsche marks and the U.S. subsequently devalued the dollar by 20 percent. How much in dollars would the speculator gain or lose by converting the deutsche marks back to dollars after the devaluation?
10. Has the United States as yet resumed the gold convertibility of the dollar?

## SUGGESTED READINGS

"The Deadlock Over the Dollar." *Business Week* (September 25, 1971).

Drozdiak, Bill. "Europe Invests in the United States." *European Community* (August–September, 1974).

"Economic Consequences of the OPEC Cartel." *Business Review*, Federal Reserve Bank of Dallas (May, 1975).

"Euro-Dollar Crisis." *Business Economics*, Vol. VI, No. 4 (September, 1971).

Friedman, Milton. "The Euro-Dollar Market: Some First Principles." *Review*, Federal Reserve Bank of St. Louis (July, 1971).

"The Future of the Dollar." *Monthly Economic Letter*, First National City Bank of New York (November, 1970).

Gilbert, Milton. "The International Monetary System: Status and Prospects." *The Morgan Guaranty Survey* (December, 1971).

"Gold." *Monthly Review*, Federal Reserve Bank of San Francisco, Special Issue (Winter, 1974–1975).

Heller, H. Robert. *International Trade Theory and Empirical Evidence*. Englewood Cliffs, New Jersey: Prentice-Hall, Inc., 1968.

*International Economic Report of the President*. Washington: U.S. Government Printing Office, 1974 and 1975.

Kindleberger, Charles P. *International Economics*, 5th ed. Homewood, Ill.: Richard D. Irwin, Inc., 1973.

*Multinational Enterprise*. New York: Exxon Corporation, 1974.

Peterson, Peter G. *U.S.-Soviet Commercial Relationships in a New Era*. Washington: U.S. Department of Commerce, August, 1972.

"Recurrant Crises Plague World Monetary System." *Business Review*, Federal Reserve Bank of Dallas (August, 1971).

Safer, Arnold E., and Anne Parker Mills. "Oil: Prices and Petrodollars." *Business Economics* (September, 1975).

"SDR's — A New Asset Supplementing Reserves for Growth in Free World Trade." *Business Review*, Federal Reserve Bank of Dallas (December, 1970).

Throop, Adrian W. "Economic Consequence of the OPEC Cartel." *Business Review*, Federal Reserve Bank of Dallas (May, 1975).

U.S. Department of Commerce. *Survey of Current Business*. Washington: U.S. Government Printing Office, January, 1975.

Von Hayek, Friedrich A. "World Inflationary Recession." *First Chicago Report*, First National Bank of Chicago (May, 1975).

"The World Bank at Quarter Century." *The Brookings Bulletin* (Fall, 1973).

"The World's Money on the Eve of the IMF Meetings." *Monthly Economic Letter*, First National City Bank of New York (September, 1970).

# INDEX